THE SEARCH FOR
MODERN
CHINA

THIRD EDITION

A
DOCUMENTARY
COLLECTION

Edited by JANET CHEN,

PEI-KAI CHENG, and

MICHAEL LESTZ *with*

JONATHAN D. SPENCE

W·W·NORTON & COMPANY | New York · London

THE SEARCH FOR MODERN CHINA

THIRD EDITION

A DOCUMENTARY COLLECTION

W. W. Norton & Company has been independent since its founding in 1923, when William Warder Norton and Mary D. Herter Norton first published lectures delivered at the People's Institute, the adult education division of New York City's Cooper Union. The firm soon expanded its program beyond the Institute, publishing books by celebrated academics from America and abroad. By midcentury, the two major pillars of Norton's publishing program— trade books and college texts—were firmly established. In the 1950s, the Norton family trans- ferred control of the company to its employees, and today—with a staff of four hundred and a comparable number of trade, college, and professional titles published each year— W. W. Norton & Company stands as the largest and oldest publishing house owned wholly by its employees.

Editor: Steve Forman
Assistant Editor: Justin Cahill
Project Editor: Diane Cipollone
Production Manager: Andrew Ensor
Photo Editor: Nelson Colón
Permissions Manager: Megan Jackson
Text Design: Jack Meserole
Composition: Westchester Book Group
Manufacturing: Quad — Taunton

The text of this book is composed in Granjon.

Library of Congress Cataloging-in-Publication Data has been applied for.

ISBN: 978-0-393-92085-7 (pbk.)

W. W. Norton & Company, Inc., 500 Fifth Avenue, New York, NY 10110-0017
wwnorton.com

W. W. Norton & Company Ltd., 15 Carlisle Street, London W1D 3BS
3 4 5 6 7 8 9 0

For Our Parents

Hsu-tung Cheng and Shu-chen Yin Cheng
Gerald Lestz, Edith Allport Lestz, and Margaret Gordon Lestz
Paul and Susie Chen

Contents

Preface to the Third Edition

In the fourteen years since the original edition of this volume appeared, the study of modern Chinese history has expanded significantly. The rise of China on the international stage and its dramatic economic growth have stimulated student interest and sustained academic research. Likewise, the breadth and variety of available primary source materials have increased considerably. This revised edition of *The Search for Modern China: A Documentary Collection* draws on the wealth of recent scholarship and new translations, reflecting burgeoning topics of research and new areas of historical inquiry.

In revising this collection, I have preserved the organization and structure of the original edition, which was conceived as a companion volume to Jonathan D. Spence's *The Search for Modern China*. In particular, I have matched the documents to the Third Edition of that magisterial work, which updates the history through the first decade of the twenty-first century. Chapter 28 of the anthology consists of new documents on popular nationalism, the 2008 earthquake in Sichuan, the Beijing Olympics, and the Charter 08 human rights manifesto. In the rest of the volume, new selections highlight the themes of women's history, urban culture, and social reform. Among the additions, excerpts on barefoot doctors, the one-child policy, the Three Gorges dam, the posthumous resurrection of Mao Zedong in popular culture, as well as writings from late Qing feminist Qiu Jin and May Fourth iconoclast Lu Xun, provide different opportunities for students to explore the social and cultural aspects of Chinese history. Overall the revised edition incorporates thirty-seven new documents. To make room for these additions, some selections have been cut and others edited for brevity. Following the format of the previous edition, a short editorial note precedes each document or set of documents, briefly providing historical background and context.

I would like to express my thanks to the colleagues who responded to a questionnaire about the use of this anthology in the classroom. Many took the time to contribute detailed comments and suggestions, none more so than Roger DeForges at the University at Buffalo. I regret that I have not been able to follow all of their advice, but their collective wisdom and invaluable feedback guided many of the decisions I made in the revision process.

Kristin Bayer, Marist College

Roger Des Forges, University at Buffalo (SUNY)

Robert Croskey, Muhlenberg College

Ryan Dunch, University of Alberta, Edmonton

Timothy George, University of Rhode Island, Kingston

Thomas Radice, Southern Connecticut State University

N. Harry Rothschild, University of North Florida

John Sagers, Linfield College

Timothy Sedo, Concordia University, Loyola

Roland Spickermann, University of Texas, Permian Basin

Steve Forman, Justin Cahill, and the capable team at W. W. Norton shepherded this work through the production process. I thank them all for their patience and assistance. Daniel Barish deserves a special note of thanks. His expert translation of excerpts from *China Can Say No* appears in Chapter 28. In addition, Dan checked the bibliography and wrestled with many of the details. I am grateful for his careful attention to the minutiae of page numbers and dates.

Finally, I would like to thank Pei-kai Cheng and Michael Lestz, who compiled the original edition of this anthology. Most of all, our teacher Jonathan Spence has been a formative intellectual and personal influence. We owe him an eternal debt of gratitude.

Janet Y. Chen
Princeton, New Jersey
April 2013

Preface to the First Edition

It is a daunting task to represent four hundred years of Chinese history through documents. The process of sifting through mountains of paper to discover characteristic and illuminating pages is a challenge that repeatedly tests one's sense of historical evidence and notions of relevance. To build this anthology a great wall of paper needed to be reduced to a manageable stack of documents illustrating concerns of central importance in the complex story told through this book.

One complication for us as anthologizers was that many of the documents we thought were vital for illustrating aspects of social life, political and military problems, ethical conceptions and practice, and the inner dynamics of everyday life were not available in English. To give satisfactory breadth to the documents volume, we were obliged to unearth and translate many documents that had become available only in recent years. Accordingly, more than one-third of the documents in this volume are new translations.

Another cardinal concern for this anthology was to match the documents to the chapters of Jonathan Spence's *The Search for Modern China,* Second Edition. When we started collecting documents, both of us had recently finished our graduate work at Yale. We had been teaching assistants in Jonathan Spence's huge undergraduate course on modern China and wrote dissertations under his direction. These experiences gave us a sense of the Spence approach to the history of Qing, Republican, and post-1949 China that was invaluable as we weighed the use of documents to reinforce his text.

Since our anthology was conceived as a companion work to Spence's survey, any reader of both works will notice intentional parallelism and cross-references that unite the two books. But like the matching calligraphic panels of a hanging couplet (*duilian*), the two works are original and independent in an understood framework of relatedness. Although the chapters in both books have identical titles, the anthology does not simply repeat the historical narrative in notes and documents; rather, it comments on the text and develops themes of its own in a way designed to extend the scope of historical inquiry.

One theme followed throughout this volume in many separate documents is the question of how the state defined ideal or model political behavior in its subjects or citizens. Throughout China's political history since ancient times, ruling elites have attempted to place the stamp of state orthodoxy on the ruled. Ruling groups have sought to channel and control the conduct of the ruled in both public and private settings and devised explicit standards of behavior. To do this, they borrowed from Confucian and Legalist statecraft but, as can be seen in many documents included here, a focus on right thinking and conduct was incorporated into the political practice of many different groups in ways that reflected their ideological and social credos and the tumultuous changes produced by dynastic decline, the founding of new states, imperialism, and revolution.

The Sacred Edict of the Kangxi emperor, the Ten Commandments of Hong Xiuquan who led the Taiping rebellion, the rules proposed by the New Life Promotion Society in 1934, Liu Shaoqi's speech "How To Be a Good Communist" during the war with Japan, and propaganda to encourage emulation of Lei Feng in the early 1960s all distinguished good, orderly, valuable, and healthy behavior from harmful or even hateful behavior. While this process of splitting orthodox and heterodox as a means of control was hardly unique to China's rulers, the documents compiled around this theme permit readers to glimpse a recurrent feature of China's traditional political culture. Such documents help a student of China's past to understand how the line between approved and seditious has been laid down at many moments and in an eerily similar way during the centuries since the founding of the Qing dynasty.

A related theme that we have traced with a number of documents is that of commitment to transcendent values and the willingness to endure martyrdom for a higher cause. In a society in which right and wrong were rigidly defined in a variety of contexts, identification with high ideals that defied moral or behavioral orthodoxies often resulted in acts of self-destructive courage that proved an individual's devotion to a belief system. The account of the death of Ge Xian, leader of the Suzhou silk weavers' riot in the late Ming; the description of the desperate defense of Jiangyin by the Ming loyalist Yen; descriptions of the death of "chaste women" in village society of the nineteenth century; Zou Rong's explosive attack on the Manchu rulers of China; the last speech of Wen Yiduo in Kunming; and the declaration of the student hunger-strikers in Tiananmen Square in the spring of 1989 capture the moralistic bravado that so often animated key actors in the history of modern China.

Women's history is another focal theme in this text. The struggle for women's rights and equality with men continues today throughout all of "greater China." A number of the documents assembled here provide a sense of the hardship suffered by women in their private lives and as subjects and citizens in various sociopolitical settings in the modern era. To do full justice to this theme would require another document anthology of similar length, but we have tried, nonetheless, to sketch some facets of the picture.

Each document is preceded by a short headnote that creates a sense of the historical context that produced it. In preparing these notes we avoided the temptation of writing an extensive *explication de texte* and tried, instead, simply to provide some guideposts that teachers and students might use if more work was to be done outside of class or as part of a project related to a particular document. The documents that are translated here for the first time or in new translations were translated as literally as possible. We did not attempt to embellish the style of the original documents or improve upon their internal system of logic and organizations. Instead, our intent as translators was to permit the reader to encounter each document in a form that would be immediately intelligible and yet so close to the first text that no reader of Chinese would be puzzled by the relationship of our English to the original language of the document.

Readers of this anthology will note that *pinyin* is the dominant system of transliteration in the book as it is in *The Search for Modern China*. Documents containing names according to the Wade-Giles system were left unaltered; however, when we encountered idiosyncratic systems of romanization in nineteenth-and early-twentieth-century documents we converted them, insofar as it was possible to do so, into *pinyin* for the convenience of those who will use the book.

Finally, readers of this book will notice that we have often used selections from novels, short story collections, or poetry anthologies. In deciding to select pieces of fiction to illuminate historical concerns—which are usually described in the headnote—we were guided by the Chinese adage that "history and literature cannot be divided" (*wenshi bufen*).

Pei-Kai Cheng
Michael Lestz

Acknowledgments

Our deepest debt of gratitude goes to our teacher, Jonathan Spence, who drew us into this project and worked with us in a profoundly satisfying partnership to create a collection of documents to complement *The Search for Modern China*. Both in suggesting documents we might use and assisting in the shaping of the text, Jonathan played a critical role in the making of this book. Whatever elegance of line it may display is owing in no small way to his contribution.

As the book evolved, no one could have been more supportive than our editor Steven Forman and we are also deeply thankful to him for his assistance. He, too, provided us with sound advice as we formed the architecture of the book and suggested ways of tailoring the manuscript to match it to the needs of our readers. In the final stages of the book's composition his work as an editor helped give this collection of documents an inner consistency we were striving for all along. We would also like to thank our manuscript editor at W. W. Norton, Katharine Nicholson Ings, for a thorough and attentive reading of the drafts of the manuscript and Kristin Sheerin for steering us through copyright law and obtaining the permissions for documents published elsewhere.

We were put on course toward finding individual documents by Shen Jin (formerly of the Shanghai Municipal Library and now rare book librarian in the Yenching Library at Harvard) and Trinity College librarians Jeff Kaimowitz (director of Trinity's Watkinson Library) and Pat Bunker (of the Trinity Library reference department). We thank them warmly for their support. We also acknowledge with gratitude the help of many other librarians at Yale's Sterling Library and elsewhere who helped us obtain materials now fitted into this text.

In addition, we are grateful to colleagues and friends, including Andrew Hsieh (Grinnell College), Parks Coble (University of Nebraska), Sherman Cochran (Cornell University), Lai Tse-han (Academia Sinica), Vera Schwarcz (Wesleyan University), William Alford (Harvard Law School), and others who suggested documents or read and commented on parts of the text. Early in the project, Madeleine Zelin (Columbia University) and Michael Gasster (Rutgers University) provided a valuable critique of selected chapters of the book. Their comments, together with those of several anonymous readers who provided tough and searching judgments of our selections and the structure of the document collection as it was emerging, helped us immensely as we went forward. We also acknowledge faculty colleagues at Trinity College and Pace University who were enthusiastic about this project and helped us in large and small ways during the time we worked on it.

Finally, we would like to thank Michelle Iacino and Martha O'Rourke, who helped with the typing and preparation of the manuscript, and Gigi St. Peter, who facilitated the passage of successive drafts and versions of the galleys from Trinity and Pace to W. W. Norton.

ML
Trinity College
Hartford

PKC
Pace University
Manhattan

THE SEARCH FOR
MODERN
CHINA

THIRD EDITION

A
DOCUMENTARY
COLLECTION

CHAPTER 1

The Late Ming

1.1 AND 1.2 TWO ACCOUNTS OF THE SUZHOU RIOT, 1601

In the final decades of the Ming dynasty, the imperial court relied heavily on eunuch advisors who won their prestige through their presence in the Forbidden City and imperial patronage. The eunuchs were despised by the scholar officials of Peking who saw their growing power as illegitimate. The result of this opposition was a series of factional battles in which eunuchs sought to consolidate their position at the expense of their literati opponents while the officials aimed at purging the court of eunuch influence. Ultimately, the eunuchs were largely successful in obtaining their ends and continued to play a powerful role until the collapse of the Ming dynasty in 1644.

The two documents translated below trace the consequences of eunuch encroachment within the ranks of officialdom in the context of a set of riots and disturbances that occurred in Suzhou in 1601. The Wanli emperor (1563–1620) used eunuch commissioners to fulfill a variety of official tasks and their corruption and venality reached scandalous proportions in a number of celebrated cases.

When the powerful eunuch Sun Long (d. 1601) was appointed to oversee the imperial silk works in Suzhou, one of the three factories that provided silk for the imperial household and the state, he abused his powers in ways found intolerable by local silk workers.[1] The result was the set of popular disturbances in Suzhou that are described here by the Ming scholars and

---

1. L. Carrington Goodrich and Chaoying Fang, *Dictionary of Ming Biography, 1368–1644* (New York: Columbia University Press, 1976), pp. 405, 868.

chroniclers Shen Zan (1558–1612) and Wen Bing (1609–1669). The two sources are in contradiction about the date of the Suzhou riot. Shen Zan's *Jinshi congchan* records the riot as having occurred in July 1601 while Wen Bing's *Dingling zhulue* suggests that it happened in July 1600. According to the *Ming Veritable Records*, 1601 is the correct date.

1.1 Shen Zan's Account

Ge Xian was from Kunshan. He was hired to work as a silk weaver in the prefectural seat [Suzhou]. In the sixth moon of 1601, some treacherous people presented a plan to Tax Commissioner Sun which said: "We would like to propose a new tax law. A tax of three silver cents for every bolt of silk should be paid before it is marketed. We are willing to make efforts to take charge of this matter." They gathered substantial funds from several wealthy households to bribe the Tax Commissioner [to allow the tax]. The plan succeeded and the Commissioner made the announcement [of the tax] and let it be practiced.

All the artisans and silk dealers suffered from this and could find no method to stop it. Ge Xian then came forward and said: "I will be the leader and will eliminate this disorder for the people of Suzhou." He led dozens of people to the Xuanmiao Temple. He made an arrangement with his followers, saying: "Let the palm-leaf fan in my hand be the signal for your actions." The crowd said: "We agree!" Thereupon, they first went to the homes of a certain Tang and a certain Xu who had first proposed the tax plan and beat them to death. Then they went to the house of an officer named Ding Yuanfu and the home of a certain rich family named Gui and burned their residences. Both Ding and Gui had helped in arranging loans to the local bullies for bribing the Tax Commissioner. The rioters forbade looting and nothing was taken. They split into two groups and went to the tax collection stations outside of the Lu and Xu Gates. They stopped at each station and beat all of the collectors to death. They then went in person to see the prefect and said: "We want Tax Commissioner Sun or we won't be satisfied." The prefect tried to mollify them but dared not investigate. On the second day, the crowd still would not disperse. They said: "We won't stop until we get the Tax Commissioner!" Thereupon, Sun summoned garrison troops and local militia to make a display of force before his headquarters. Ge Xian and others also gathered a mob and approached the gate of the Tax Commission office.

Fortunately, Ge Xian's followers and the troops did not confront each other. At sunset, the mob dispersed. The Tax Commissioner took this opportunity to flee away with his escort and went to Hangzhou. Ge Xian then volunteered to go to prison. The prefect asked what he wanted. He replied: "There are many mosquitoes at night. I just need a mosquito net." People in the jail and outsiders who were not afraid of the consequences often praised him and brought wine and dried meat for him every day. Ge Xian expected that he must die but a memorial was presented and an order pardoning him was sent down. He is still in prison and is well. This is a strange matter!

1.2 Wen Bing's Account

When the local uprising took place in Suzhou in the sixth moon of 1600, Sun Long, the Imperial Eunuch Commissioner for Silk Weaving in Suzhou and Hangzhou, was concurrently in charge of tax collection. Many local hoodlums joined his entourage and were given official duties as tax collectors. At all of the gates of the city, they set up tax collection stations and not even a single chicken or bunch of vegetables was exempted. The people could not stand living this way and were so stirred up that they considered rioting.

On the sixth day of the sixth moon, twenty-seven people suddenly appeared [in Suzhou]; their hair was loose, they were barefoot, and all of them wore short, white shirts. Each of them held a palm-leaf fan in his hand and they went to the residences of every tax collector and set fire to their homes and property. They seized the collectors and beat them to death in the streets. Although there were only twenty-seven people, they struck like a torrential storm; nobody dared resist them. When they came to high walls or tall buildings, their leader would merely wave his fan and all of them would immediately jump up on top.

The second day, they mistakenly entered a common household. This family made its living through business but was guilty of no crime. The family knelt down and welcomed them and begged to know their offense. The leader pulled a list from his belt, looked at it and said: "We have made an error!" Both this home and that of a tax collector were located beside a bean curd shop. The leader then led his men in apologizing to the family. The group then ran over to the tax collector's house. The tax collector was frightened and jumped into a canal. The men pulled him out of the canal and began beating him. The tax collector's eyes were protruding but they still continued beating him with their fists and finally killed him.

A certain person named Tong was a local judge and possessed property worth tens of thousands of taels.[2] He also served as the tax collector in charge of the Liuhe tax station. When the riot took place, he leaped into a canal to flee but died of the cold. The rioters also burned an official household. All of the members of the household hid or eluded the rioters. The son of the family, who was a local scholar, secreted himself in a chest which was left in a neighbor's house, and thereby escaped. Tax Commissioner Sun fled by night to Hangzhou to escape.

---

2. The unit of exchange in imperial China, equivalent to one Chinese ounce of silver (with fluctuating value against copper cash).

The riot continued for three days and all of the tax collectors were eliminated. On the fourth day, a large announcement was posted alongside each of the six city gates. It read: "The tax collectors wantonly committed abuses. The people could not bear it. We started this uprising to eliminate this harm for the people. Now things are settled. All residents should return to their professions and not use this as a pretext to make more trouble. . . ."

For days the whole city was quiet. There were no people in the streets. On the fifth day, the circuit intendant issued an order to arrest all those responsible for starting the riot. A certain Ge Xian came forward and appeared before the officials. He said: "I started the riot. It would be enough to execute me. You should not involve other people because if you do it will start further rioting." The officials then stopped their investigation and simply tried Ge Xian. He was sentenced to be executed but later was pardoned and paroled. Thirty years later, Ge Xian was still living. When he was asked about the happenings of that time, he dodged the questions. Some said that the true instigator of the uprising was not Ge Xian. But the fact that he voluntarily submitted himself for trial to save the people was, itself, praiseworthy.

1.3 AND 1.4 A MING OFFICIAL ON THE DECLINE AND FALL OF THE DYNASTY

Song Yingxing (1600?–1646?) was a minor official of the late Ming. He is known to history for his *Tiangong kaiwu,* a survey of science and technology that was later in part incorporated into the *Gujin tushu jicheng*, a massive encyclopedia compiled during the Kangxi reign. The text translated here is a part of Song's 1636 work *Yeyi* (Unofficial opinions), a long lost treatise that was rediscovered in Jiangxi province during the Cultural Revolution. The two selections include Song's reflections on the troubled years that preceded the collapse of the Ming and his observations on the crisis of financial mismanagement.

1.3 *The Trend of the World*

It is said: "When order is at its peak, chaos results; when chaos is at its peak, order results." This cycle of change follows the Heavenly mathematics of division and multiplication. After characters were invented and writing and cart axles were standardized, from the time of the Shang dynasty forward,[3] no dynasty other than

---

3. Traditional Chinese historians believed that the standardization of written characters and cart axles occurred during the Shang instead of during the Qin dynasty.

our own has successfully created continuous order and stability for three hundred years. Presently, some people fear that winter cold is striking in midsummer. They are unaware that when chaos is at its peak, order is coming.

The disaster caused by the bandits in the northwest has already spread to the central plain.[4] Only the walled cities remain; no one knows how many villages, towns, and markets have been burned to the ground. Today, people are killed by bandit mobs; tomorrow, they may die at the hands of government troops. No one can tell how many fields have been left fallow by farmers fleeing disaster or in how many fields already-planted crops now wither under the sun. No one can count how many families have been broken apart or number the dead lying piled in ditches. Nobody can know how many walled cities have been invaded and then recovered or how many towns have been put to the torch and then rebuilt.

Those fortunate enough to live in the southeast continue to prosper, but the eyebrows of officials are knotted with concern and the foreheads of the people creased with worry. They are distressed by the bandits who are everywhere and by the scourge of flood and drought.[5] Nothing remains of the spirit of the times of Emperors Longqing [1567–1572] and Wanli [1573–1620]! But this instant, precisely when chaos is at its peak, foretells that order is coming. The affairs of the world can still be managed; do not be perplexed at the working of cosmic mathematics.

1.4 *On the Management of the Salt Gabelle*[6]

Everyone needs to eat salt and there is great profit for the state in its administration. Management fails when corruption appears and merchants are impoverished when management is disorderly. It is human nature to seek profit and even risk death rushing after it. Since there is profit in trading in salt, who will not exhaust himself in pursuit of it? Why is it that the same merchants who once amassed jade and gold, have today emptied their purses and piled up debts? This is because the merchants are poor and the management of salt [production, transport, and sale] is not functioning.

Half of the state's salt levy comes from the Huai region. The other half comes from Changlu, Xiechi, Liangzhe, the Sichuan wells, the Guangdong salt ponds, and the Fujian coast.[7] Although the tax levy for Changlu and other places has

---

4. The rebellions of Li Zicheng and Zhang Xianzhong.

5. Here Song refers to the troubles that afflicted the north of China but which at the time he wrote had yet to affect the territories below the Yangzi River.

6. From Han times onward, a government monopoly over the production and sale of salt was an important source of revenue for the imperial state.

7. The major sources of salt were salt fields along the coast, particularly the Huai River region in today's northern Jiangsu province (the Subei area) and inland salt mines in Sichuan.

been increased, the merchants there can still manage to pay. But for the Huai region, an increase is unbearable. The Huai tax quota was originally 930,000 taels. Now it has been increased to one million five hundred. If salt management was as effective as it was in the times of the Chenghua [1465–1487] and Hongzhi [1488–1505] emperors and if the merchants were still as rich as they were during the reigns of Longqing and Wanli, then such an increase could be comfortably met.

The merchants with capital are primarily from Shaanxi, Shanxi, and Huizhou. During the most prosperous years of Wanli's reign, they controlled no less than thirty million taels in the Yangzhou region. Each year this capital could produce interest of nine million taels. One million taels were paid to the government and three million were used to cover the innumerable expenses related to salt production. There was enough money for both the public and private sectors. Monks, Daoist priests, beggars, and servants were benefited and bridge building projects and Buddhist monasteries also drew from the remaining five million taels. All merchants could fatten their families and themselves; their funds were inexhaustible. Presently we can only imagine how prosperous they must have been.

The decline of the merchants started at the beginning of the Tianqi era [1621–1627]. For the state, the conflagration set by the eunuchs blazed out of control; for merchants, misfortunes were brought by spendthrift sons; in various localities, profit-seeking bullies assembled; officials became increasingly corrupt; and clerks and runners devised new, wicked techniques [to extort funds]. All of these problems grew worse each day. Just as the merchants were about to maneuver their way out of their straits, the new tax levy order fell down upon them and they were afflicted by the bandit invasions. When they could not pay the tax, the merchant's family members were arrested to force them to pay. Presently, half of them are poor and in debt. Their entire assembled capital is no more than five million taels; how could such a sum produce enough interest to pay the state's quota? . . . [The remaining portion of this essay provides a detailed description of the vast array of miscellaneous taxes and duties on salt that had driven salt merchants to the brink of bankruptcy.]

1.5 BROADSHEET FROM LI ZICHENG

This rare broadsheet announced the advance of Li Zicheng's troops into Huangzhou. Its polemical analysis of the troubles of the late Ming era is an interesting match for the more measured description furnished by Song Yingxing. It is notable for its effort to reassure local officials and win them to the side of the rebels and its reassurance that the framework of professional life would remain the same. Its penultimate line, however, makes it clear resistors will pay a heavy price.

For the calming and pacification of the people:

The fatuous and self-indulgent Emperor of the Ming dynasty was not humane. He spoiled his eunuchs, relied heavily on exam graduates, was greedy for taxes and levies, used harsh punishments, and could not save the people from calamities. Every day the army robbed the people of their wealth, raped their wives and daughters, and exploited everyone most harshly. Our army is made up of good peasants who have worked the fields for ten generations; we formed this humane and righteous army to rescue the people from destruction. We have pacified Chengtian and De'an [prefectures in Hubei] and now are personally approaching Huangzhou. Orders have been dispatched to notify scholars and commoners not to be alarmed. Each should quietly practice his profession. Any battalion that kills good people without permission will be executed to the last man. Those of you people who happily welcome our kingly divisions with horns and bugles will establish your merit and be rewarded with weighty positions. Others should not wear arms because it is hard to distinguish jade from stones. This is our announcement.

1.6 AND 1.7 TWO ACCOUNTS OF ZHANG XIANZHONG

Zhang Xianzhong (1605–1647) was a peasant rebel who, unlike his contemporary Li Zicheng, made no pretense of having a social program. Like some of the worst warlords of the twentieth century, he ravaged the areas of north and northwestern China through which his armies passed. After holding off the Ming armies that were sent to suppress him, Zhang's rebellion was quelled by Qing forces after the foundation of the Manchu state in 1644.

The two documents included here are colorful biographies by literati chroniclers who detested Zhang Xianzhong and were eager to gather folk recollections of his rebellion into damning accounts of his activities.

1.6 *The Career of Zhang Xianzhong*

Zhang Xianzhong came from Fushi county in Shaanxi province.[8] He was wicked and shrewd. Both his father, Zhang Kuai, who practiced a debased profession, and his mother, née Shen, died at an early age. Zhang Xianzhong became the ward of a beggar named Big Xu. Once he stole a neighbor's chicken. By chance he was seen and was scolded. Zhang Xianzhong replied: "If I have my way, all here will be

---

8. This is the region where the Chinese Communist Party built its headquarters after the Long March in 1935.

killed like chickens!" His cruel nature had already sprouted in childhood. When he grew up, he became a hoodlum. When the roving bandit Wang Jiayin rebelled, Zhang Xianzhong joined him and called himself "the Eighth Great King" or "the Yellow Tiger."

In 1631, he was given amnesty and was enlisted into the Ming army by Governor General Hong Chengchou.[9] The next year he mutinied and plundered territories from Henan to Jiangbei. He then moved into the Chu region [present day Hunan and Hubei]. There, he was given amnesty again by Superintendent Xiong Wencan.[10] Soon he rebelled again and joined with other bandits like Luo Rucai. The Bandit Pacifying General Zuo Liangyu defeated him and so Zhang fled into Sichuan. Then he moved to Xiangyuang and burned the prefectural capital. He captured a [Ming] Prince [Zhu Yiming] there and seated him in his reception hall; Zhang Xianzhong urged the Prince to drink a cup of wine and then had him bound and killed.[11] Not long after this, Luo Rucai clashed with Zhang Xianzhong and went to join Li Zicheng. Zhang Xianzhong himself left for Yunxi and gained much plunder there. His ant-like mob of adherents now numbered several hundred thousand. Zuo Liang-yu again brought troops to attack him and Zhang Xianzhong was defeated and fled. Owing to Luo Rucai's intercession on his behalf, Zhang was able to flee to Li Zicheng. Li was very powerful and wanted to subdue Zhang Xianzhong but Zhang refused to be Li's subordinate. Li Zicheng was angered and wanted to kill him but Luo Rucai secretly provided Zhang with five hundred cavalrymen and provisions and told him to go. Because of this, Zhang Xianzhong was able to dash to the east and join another group of bandits. They sacked Bozhou, Luzhou, Liuhe, and other localities. In all of these places, they cut off the left arms of the men and the right arms of the women. He [Zhang] then entered southern Zhili and [Ming] Commanders Huang Degong and Liu Liang-zuo repeatedly defeated him. Zhang Xianzhong then went westward into the Chu region and Huang and Liu turned back. Zhang then followed the Yangtze River upstream and sacked Hanyang and approached Wuchang. On the fifth day of the first moon of 1642, he captured Prince Chu [in Wuchang] and stole a palace

9. Hong Chengchou (1593–1665) was later charged with the defense of north and northeast-ern China. He surrendered to the Manchus in 1642 and became a general under the Qing.

10. Xiong Wencan (d. 1640) was a high military commander later executed for military failures by the last Ming emperor.

11. Another source, Zha Jizuo's *Zuiweilu*, contains a more detailed version of this story: "Xianzhong sat proudly in the palace of Prince Xiang and had the Prince prostrate himself before him. He presented him with a cup of wine and said: 'I want to borrow your head to kill Yang Sichang. Please drink up.' His intention was that the Army Commander-in-Chief [Yang] would be executed for losing an Imperial Prince. The Prince was tied up and killed and his body was thrown into a well. It happened that Henan had also fallen into the hands of Li Zicheng at this time and Prince Fu was killed there. For losing these two imperial relatives, Yang Sichang felt that a grim fate was inescapable, and hanged himself. These events occurred exactly as Zhang Xianzhong had calculated."

treasure worth several million taels. The bandit army's carts and horses were insufficient to carry it all away. Previously, when the Prince had been asked by the Provincial Secretary of Revenue for a loan to support the [Ming] army, he had refused. Now the people of Chu hated the Prince for his stupidity. The bandit put the Prince in a bamboo cage and sank it in West Lake. He slaughtered several million people [*sic*] and floating corpses covered the river.

Zhang Xianzhong occupied the Prince's palace [in Wuchang] and took the title "King of the West." He set up a spurious system of Six Boards and Five Prefectural Offices and initiated an examination system to select officials for the appointment to prefectural and county offices. Later he occupied the entire Chu region and tore down the palace of Prince Gui and moved it to Changsha and built an illegitimate imperial palace for himself. He also dispatched troops to capture part of Jiangxi but these territories were later captured back by Zuo Liangyu. Zhang Xianzhong then abandoned Changsha and retreated into Sichuan.

He captured the Fotu Pass and sacked Chongqing. The whole family of Prince Rui was killed. He arrested more than ten thousand able-bodied men and sliced off their ears and noses and cut off one hand. They were then driven to various surrounding counties to announce this policy. If the local people did not surrender when Zhang Xianzhong's troops arrived, this same order would be applied. This threw the people and officials of all of these counties into disarray.

By the tenth moon of 1644, Zhang Xianzhong had completed his plundering and slaughter in Hunan and so he advanced and sacked Chengdu. Prince Shu and all of his retainers committed suicide by throwing themselves into wells. Governor Long Wenguang resisted but his troops were defeated and he was killed. When Zhang Xianzhong entered Sichuan he wanted to kill all of its people. Sun Kewang admonished him not to do so and so he was restrained but, even so, only one or two out of every ten Sichuanese survived. . . .

On the sixteenth day of the eleventh moon of 1644, Zhang illegitimately enthroned himself and renamed Chengdu the Western Capital [Xijing]. He took the name Daxi [The Great West] as the name of his state and his reign title was Dashun. He honored the deity Wenchang as his great ancestral progenitor.[12] He set up government offices and posts and a certain Fan was the valedictorian of the examination class. Zhang Xianzhong himself wrote an essay critically evaluating all previous emperors and kings and praised Xiang Yu as the greatest of them.[13] This essay was called: "The Emperor-Authored Ten Thousand Word Essay." He launched a great search to find all of the gentry scholars of Sichuan and brought them all to Chengdu and had them killed by slicing. He then again made an announcement

12. Wenchanggong was the guardian of literature honored within the pantheon of Chinese folk religion.

13. Xiang Yu was the military commander of the forces that overthrew the Qin state in the third century B.C. He called himself the "hegemon king of Western Chu" and this possibly inspired Zhang to imitate him.

of a new scholarly examination and scholars from far and near flocked to take it. When they arrived, Zhang Xianzhong attacked them with his army and some 22,300 would-be examination candidates died. Afterwards, a huge heap of brushes and inkstones were left behind. Zhang Xianzhong hated the people of Sichuan; he first slaughtered the people and then slaughtered the scholars. He even wanted to kill the Sichuanese who were soldiers in his army. Among his generals were many Sichuanese. One such commander was Liu Jinzhong; Zhang Xianzhong wanted to arrest him and kill his troops. The plan did not succeed because word leaked to a gate guard and when the army heard of it they all ran away. Thereupon, Zhang Xianzhong's generals were gone and his army was scattered. When the great [Qing] army came to Hanzhong, Liu Jinzhong joined them. When asked where Zhang Xianzhong was, Liu Jinzhong replied: "He is in Jinchuanpu of Shunqing." He guided them to Zhang Xianzhong's camp. Zhang fled and hid under some firewood. He was hit by a stray arrow and cried out. He was then dragged from his hiding place and beheaded. Some said that Zhang Xianzhong heard of Li Zicheng's fall and hid away and died of illness. This is a false tale.

1.7 *A Colorful Early Qing Biography of the Bandit Leader Zhang Xianzhong*

Zhang Xianzhong was from Fushi county, in Shaanxi province. When he was a boy, he followed his father, who was a dealer in dates, to Neijiang in Sichuan. Their donkey was tied up to the pillar of a *paifang* [an ornamental archway erected to commemorate some exceptional deed] belonging to a gentry family. The donkey defecated on the stone pillar of the archway and a servant of the family cursed them and whipped Zhang Xianzhong's father. The servant then forced the father to remove the donkey shit with his own hands. Zhang Xianzhong was close by and, although he was enraged, dared not fight back. He vowed: "I will return and kill you all. Only then will my anger be appeased." Later, when he entered Sichuan, the whole population of Neijiang was wiped out.

On the tenth day of the first moon in 1644, the Bandit Xianzhong was slaughtering the population of Chengdu at the Hongshun Bridge outside of the East Gate. Just as his men's blades were poised and ready to strike, there were three claps of thunder. The Bandit pointed to Heaven and said in a fuming rage: "You allowed me to come into the world to kill people and now you dare to use thunder to scare me?!" He returned the attack of Heaven by firing three cannon shots into the sky. That day, there were so many bodies in the water of the river that they broke the supports of the Hongshun Bridge.

Previously, when Xianzhong entered the Huguang region to escape arrest, he led a group of five or six followers. At night he tried to steal a golden ornament on the top of the roof of the main temple of Wudangshan [a Daoist retreat]. As he was climbing up, he saw the Daoist god Wang Lingguan holding a cudgel. He shouted at Zhang Xianzhong saying: "Go away! It is only because Heaven has sent you to collect lives that I do not kill you!" Because of this Zhang Xianzhong believed that he was "appointed by Heaven to kill" and put this motto on his banners and flags.

A certain Wang who was the unlawful magistrate of Jiajiang [serving under Zhang Xianzhong] presented to the Bandit a tribute of fresh lichee nuts that were cut open and marinated with salt. Zhang Xianzhong was furious about this and ordered his personal bodyguard Wang Ke to go to that county yamen to cut off the magistrate's head. After Wang Ke was dispatched, members of Zhang's entourage said: "That person [the magistrate] was just a hick. He doesn't know what he's doing. This crime is not a capital offense." Zhang Xianzhong said: "You're right!" He immediately sent an edict that read: "The Emperor who has been entrusted by Heaven with the care of the Empire orders: Wang Ke, come back. Let's spare the life of that turtle magistrate." This unlawful edict has been preserved and still exists.

In the twelfth moon of 1646, Prince Su [Haoge] of our [Qing] dynasty entered Sichuan to suppress Zhang Xianzhong. In a dense fog, Prince Su directly attacked Zhang's army. A Banner adjutant named Yabulan shot an arrow at Zhang Xianzhong and hit him in the throat. The Bandit rode off on his horse and the Adjutant Oboi came forward and captured him. As Prince Su enumerated his crimes, he was executed by slicing. His corpse was exposed before the gate of the garrison headquarters and men and women came to hack at it. It was soon reduced to ground-up meat. He was forty-one years old.

Some said that after Zhang Xianzhong was shot he pulled out the arrow and shouted: "I was born on Swallow Peak and I'm dying on Phoenix Mountain." He then fell over his arrow quiver and died. Poisonous shrubs and thornbushes grew up over the place he was buried. People who touched these plants got skin ulcers or sores. Sometimes a black tiger came out of these bushes to devour people. When the sky was dark or cloudy, nobody dared to go by this burial ground. Alas, can someone be so venomous and as harmful as this even after death? Some others said: "When the people cut up Xianzhong's body they discovered that his heart was as black as ink." Yet others said his heart was twisted to one side and he had no liver.

Zhang Xianzhong also took the name Jingxuan when he was given amnesty at Fang'gu. He loved to have friends. When he met someone he liked, he would drink with this person for a whole night. When his new friend left, Zhang Xianzhong would load him down with gifts but then send men after him to ambush him on his way home. He would have his new friend's head cut off and brought back and would keep it in a case. When he was drinking alone and felt unhappy, he would send for the case, saying: "Ask my good friend to come!" Then he would put the head on the table, raise his cup and drink as happily as though he was drinking with a living person. He called this: "Gathering heads for a party."

There was a person named Zhang from Emei who was nearly killed by the Bandit. His neck was cut but his head was not severed. He hid himself among a pile of bodies. When night fell and all was calm, he saw someone coming with people calling to clear the way before him. This person was very imposing and solemn; he looked like a prince or king. When he arrived, he ordered his clerks to bring the registers and called out the names of the dead. Each dead person who was called would stand up holding his own head. When all the names had been called they all left. Zhang was surprised that his name was not included. He rose and was told by the imposing figure's followers: "This is the Prefectural City God!" Subsequently, Zhang came to his senses and escaped at dawn. He was still living in 1721. A long scar was still clearly visible on his neck. People called him "Cut-neck Zhang." He had many children and grandchildren. Some of them even became scholars.

Zhang Xianzhong had a certain nephew who secreted himself among the Thirty-Six Peaks of Kuan county. He was nicknamed "The Scarred Monk." When the world was again at peace he came out and traveled and described the past activities of the Bandit Zhang Xianzhong in great detail.

1.8 SONG MAOCHENG: *THE TALE OF THE UNGRATEFUL LOVER*

This famous tale of love, treachery, and sacrificial vindication was first written in a literary Chinese version, heavily adorned with classical allusions and poetic devices, during the Wanli reign (1573–1620). The author, Song Maocheng, notes in the text that he first heard the tragic tale of the courtesan Du Shiniang from a friend in 1600. Subsequent retellings, including a more embroidered vernacular version by the celebrated writer Feng Menglong (1574–1646), spread the legend of Du Shiniang and gave her story an enduring fame in popular culture.

At the heart of the story are the themes of unwavering love and sincerity. Song Maocheng focuses on these qualities to highlight the contrast between Scholar Li, the feckless man who spends years studying moralizing neo-Confucian texts, and the loyal courtesan Du Shiniang, who radiates a natural understanding of morality and human relations. While Li is weak to the core, Du Shiniang devotes herself entirely to him and protects his interests—even when he betrays her. Each of her actions, including her suicide, embodies Confucian ideals of morality.

For students of the late Ming, this story provides a trove of historical information. It speaks suggestively about gender roles, gives a fascinating view of the quasi-official work of Peking and the city's pleasure quarters, and offers insights into contemporary ideals of love. In the starkest way, the tale also illustrates the helplessness of women, trapped in amoral social frameworks, who yet sought to adhere to the standards of Confucian society. The translation below is of the earliest version of the story.

During the Wanli era, a scholar named Li from eastern Zhejiang, who was the son of a provincial judicial chief, made a donation of funds and traveled to Beijing to study in the national academy.[14] He and the courtesan Du Shiniang fell deeply in love. They had a relationship for several years. Although Li's funds were depleted and the girl's 'mother' detested the frequent visits of the scholar, the friendship between the two grew even closer.[15] The girl was the most beautiful woman of her generation in the gay quarter. She also excelled as a musician, singer, and dancer. The young men of the capital all sought her out to pass their leisure moments. Du Shiniang's 'mother' was disturbed by Li's constant presence and tried to provoke him with her scolding. When Li was as humble and prudent as before, the 'mother' treated him even more harshly. The young courtesan could not endure this humili- ation and vowed to marry Scholar Li.

The 'mother' considered that since the girl was not her own daughter she could go. But the convention of the gay quarter was that when a courtesan sought to leave a payment of several hundred silver taels was necessary. The 'mother' was clearly aware that Li had no money and so she conceived of a way to corner him. She sought to shame him and leave him with no means to protest so that he would gradually forget about taking Du away. And so she gestured with her hand at her 'daughter' and scolded her, saying: 'If you can urge the young gentleman to gather three hundred taels and give them to me, I will let you go wherever you please.' The young girl readily consented and replied: 'Although Scholar Li is impover- ished because of his travels, it should not be difficult for him to get three hundred taels. But the money cannot be easily assembled. What will happen if the money is prepared and you break the agreement?' The mother knew that Scholar Li was poor and so she baited him by pointing laughingly at a flickering candle flame and said: 'If Scholar Li can get the money, you can go with him. The flickering candle is an omen that he will succeed in winning you.' And so, after making their agreement, they parted company.

In the middle of the night the girl cried piteously and said to Scholar Li: 'I know that you are so far away from your home that your funds are insufficient to buy my freedom. Would it be possible to receive some aid from your relatives or friends in this emergency?' Li was surprised by the suggestion and replied: 'Oh yes, yes. I have always had this intention but did not dare to say so.' The next day, he pretended to pack his belongings to start for home and, in the meantime, begged for loans from all of his friends and relatives [in the capital]. His intimates all knew that he had been deeply involved in the life of the gay quarter for years and doubted the sincerity of his intention to travel southward. Furthermore, Scholar Li's father

14. During the Ming and Qing periods, young scholars could purchase titles through "dona- tions" and qualify for study in the national academy, a preparatory school for higher examina- tion degrees or government offices, located in Peking.

15. The 'mother' referred to here is the madam who controlled the group of courtesans to which Du Shiniang belonged.

was angry about his son's floating life style and wrote letters to halt his return home. If loans were supplied to him they would purchase no virtue and there would be no way for them to be repaid. All those in his circle found excuses to refuse him. This went on for over one month and finally he returned with empty hands.

During the night, the courtesan sighed and said: 'And so you were finally unable to obtain any funds? There are one hundred and fifty silver taels hidden in my mattress. I hid them in the cotton ticking along the seam. Tomorrow ask a servant to take the money and secretly bring it to you. Then pay it to "mother." Besides this, there is nothing I can do.' The scholar was surprised and happy. He carefully arranged for the mattress to be removed. Next he took the money out of the mattress and told his friends and relatives. They sympathized with Du Shiniang's sincere intentions and all of them generously provided the scholar with funds. But the total was only one hundred taels. The scholar wept as he told the girl: 'I have exhausted my resources. Where can I get another fifty taels?' The girl jumped up gleefully and said: 'Do not worry. Tomorrow I will make arrangements with my "sisters."' The next day she obtained the fifty taels. They assembled the money and presented it to the 'mother.' The 'mother' wanted to break the agreement, but the girl cried piteously before her and said: 'In the past you demanded three hundred taels from the young gentleman. Now the money is ready but you are breaking your word. He can take the money back but I am going to die.' The 'mother' was afraid that she would lose the money and the girl and so she said: 'I will do as I agreed. You may go, but you must leave every stitch of your clothing and your jewelry behind. None of this is yours.' The girl happily agreed.

The next day, wearing cotton clothing and with no ornaments in her hair, Du Shiniang left following the young scholar. When she went to bid farewell to all of her 'sisters' in the house, they were moved to tears and said: 'Shiniang was the leading talent of the time. Now she is following her man and leaving this place in rags. Does this not shame us "sisters"?' Thereupon, they made a present to her of what they had and in a short time she was wearing entirely new hairpins, rings, clothing, and jewelry. The sisters said: 'The young gentleman and our sister are going on a long journey of one thousand *li* [one *li* = ⅓ mile] and you have no luggage tied up for your travels. All of us would like to give you a box as a gift.' The young scholar did not know what was in the box and the girl also seemed not to know. At dusk that evening the 'sisters' tearfully bid adieu to Du Shiniang and the girl went to the scholar's lodging place. The four walls were utterly bare and the scholar was merely able to stare before him at his desk. The girl unraveled her long left silk sleeve and threw down twenty silver taels and said: 'Use this for our travel expenses.' The next day, the scholar made arrangements to obtain a carriage and horse and they left through the Chongwen Gate. When they arrived at Luhe, they boarded a postal boat, but by now their money was already exhausted. Du Shiniang then unraveled her right silk sleeve and produced thirty silver taels. She said: 'We can buy our food with this.'

The scholar felt happy and fortunate about his frequent and unforeseen good fortune. As they traveled, autumn changed to winter. They laughed at the lone wild goose in the sky and the fish who did not swim in pairs. They vowed to live together until their hair turned as white as the autumn frost. Their ardent hearts were as red as the blazing foliage of the maple. We can guess how happy they were!

When they reached Guazhou, they left the postal boat and rented a small junk with the intention of crossing the [Yangzi] river the next day. That night the moon was like a jade *bi* [a flat, round, ceremonial jade object with a hole in its center] flashing in the water of the river. It was like flying silk or writing on a mirror. The scholar said to the girl: 'Since departing the capital, we have not wanted others to notice us. Tonight we have our own boat, what is there to fear? Moreover, the water and moon of Jiangnan is different from the wind and the dust of the north. How can we be silent?' The girl, too, had hid herself and her traces for a long time. She felt the sadness of the long passage through passes and mountains and was moved by the mingling of the river and moon. She and the young scholar linked their hands in the moonlight and sat in the bow of the boat. The scholar was in high spirits and he raised his wine cup; the comely girl sang a pure song to recompense somewhat the beauty of the river and moon. The girl's song swirled and lingered in the night air; even the cry of birds or the call of monkeys could not evoke so melancholy a feeling.

On a nearby boat was a young man who was a salt merchant in Yangzhou. He was returning at the end of the year to his native place in Xin'an [Huizhou]. He was about twenty years old and was a champion heartbreaker in the gay quarter. As he was drinking he heard this song and his emotions soared. But then the melody ceased and he was unable to rest that night. At dawn, a snowstorm suspended all crossing of the river. The Xin'an man searched for the scholar's boat and knew that there must be a great beauty aboard it. He put on a cap with mink tassels and a fur coat and paid great attention to his appearance. He glimpsed something and began to sing to attract attention. The scholar pushed open the window of his boat. The snow was still and cold. The Xin'an man called to the young scholar in a friendly way and arranged to meet with him on the bank.

The two went to a wine house and talked. After they were a bit tipsy, the Xin'an man asked who sang the pure song he had heard the night before. The scholar told him the truth. The Xin'an man then asked: 'Are you crossing the river to return to your native place?' The scholar sadly told him the reason he could not return home. The beauty would travel with him among the mountains and rivers of the Wu and Yue regions. They drank cup after cup of wine and the scholar disclosed his whole history. The Xin'an man sadly said to the young scholar: 'You are traveling with a gorgeous orchid. Haven't you heard it said that when a beautiful pearl is cast down on the road all the mighty and powerful come to contend for it? Moreover, the people in Jiangnan are most skilled in flirtation. When they feel affection for someone they will do anything for love. Even I, your humble friend, have the sprouts of such feeling in my heart. Is it not possible that someone so talented as your beautiful lady, who has behaved so unexpectedly in the past, might not in the future use you as a gangplank? Might she not secretly make some other agreement in the future? If this were to happen, the misty waves of Zhenzhe, the billows of Qiantang, the bellies of fish and the teeth of whales would be your tomb. I, your foolish friend, have also heard it asked: "Is a father or a woman more important?" and "Is present pleasure or future harm to yourself a more serious concern?" I hope you can give all of this some deep thought.'

The scholar then frowned and said: 'What can I do?' The Xin'an man replied: 'Your stupid friend has an excellent plan that will benefit you but I am afraid you cannot carry it out.' The young scholar said: 'What is the plan?' The Xin'an man answered: 'If you really cut off the remaining love you feel, I, your humble servant, although I am not quick, am willing to give you one thousand taels for your health and long life. You can take this one thousand taels and return home to present it to your esteemed father. If you desert the beauty, you will have nothing to fear on your journey home. I sincerely hope you will give this careful thought.' The scholar had led a solitary and floating existence for years. Although he and the girl had sworn to live forever, like a pair of mandarin ducks or the entwined roots of a tree, a leisurely and comfortable existence was impossible. There was no way to achieve it. He began to feel doubt and to think about the destructive and notorious beauties of history. He became more depressed and felt as though he was crying in a dream. The young scholar lowered his head and seemed lost in thought. Then, he excused himself and said that he wanted to return to discuss all of this with his woman. He and the Xin'an man returned hand in hand to the riverfront and boarded their own boats.

The girl had lit the lamp and was waiting for the scholar to return so that they could drink wine together. The scholar's eyes moved back and forth but his mouth was dry. He was unable to say what was on his mind. Finally they went to bed and held each other tightly through the night. In the middle of the night, the scholar began sobbing. The girl quickly sat up and embraced him and said: 'We have been in love for almost three years and have traveled several thousand *li* together but I have never seen you so sad. Now we are about to cross the river; we should feel happy that we will soon be tied together forever. Why are you suddenly so sad? I don't understand it. There seems to be a tone of parting in your voice. What is it?' The scholar spoke through his tears. Although his sadness was overwhelming, he finally told her the whole story and wept as before. Du Shiniang released him from her embrace and said: 'Who made this plan for you? This person is a great hero! You will receive one thousand taels which you can present to your parents. I will have another man to follow and we will be unencumbered. This plan is inspired by feeling and will lead to propriety and righteousness. How brilliant! We both obtain something from it! Where is the money?' The scholar replied that because he did not know the lady's intention, the money was still in the other man's traveling chest. The girl said: 'Go over early tomorrow morning and make the agreement with him. But one thousand silver taels is a large sum. I will not go to that man's boat until the money is safely in your luggage.'

It was already past midnight. The girl asked leave to rise and put on her most lavish make-up. She said: 'I should expend great efforts on my attire and make-up today since I shall say good-bye to an old love and meet my new gentleman.' By the time she finished with her make-up, it was already dawn. The Xin'an man had previously brought his boat to the side of the Scholar Li to give it to him. Then the Xin'an man was asked to pass the wedding price to the other boat. The sum was counted and it was correct.

Thereupon, the girl stepped out of the cabin and her boat and, holding onto the gunnels, said to the Xin'an man: 'Scholar Li's travel pass is inside the makeup case we have just passed over. Please return it to us so that we can find it.' The Xin'an man hastily did as he was told. The girl then asked Scholar Li to remove one drawer. Inside it were lovely clothes made of emerald colored feathers; she took them and threw them into the water. Their value was several hundred silver taels. Scholar Li, the champion heartbreaker, and all of the boatmen of both boats were greatly surprised. She then asked the scholar to pull out another drawer. It was full with ornaments, jewelry and jade, and golden musical instruments. It was worth several thousand taels. She again threw everything into the river. She then asked the scholar to remove a leather purse from the case. In it were antique jade pieces and ancient gold objects. There were articles rarely to be seen in the whole world. Their value was immeasurable. The objects, too, she threw into the river. Finally, she asked the scholar to pull out another box. It was full of the finest 'night-glowing' pearls. Everyone on the boat was alarmed and the hubbub caused a crowd of people to gather on the bank. The girl again began emptying everything into the river.

Scholar Li began to feel greatly regretful. He embraced the girl and, crying loudly, tried to restrain her. Even the Xin'an man came over to try to persuade her to stop. The girl pushed the scholar to the side. She spat on the Xin'an man and cursed him: 'You heard a song that moved you and then started flicking your tongue like a parrot. You did not care about destroying our love.[16] You will cause my bones to be stained with my pure blood. I regret that I am not stronger so that I could use a knife to kill so vulgar a person as you. With your greed for money, you tried to force me into your embrace. How are you different from a mad dog? A moment ago you came running up like the wind and wanted to seize me. When I die, my spirit will accuse you before the gods of hell and they will take your life

16. There is a reference here to an obscure story mentioned in a folk song of the Period of Disunion and a poem by Bai Juyi. The story tells of a young girl who could not marry the man of her choice because of his parents' opposition. They finally agreed that if she could draw water from a well with a silver bottle attached to a silk thread she could marry their son. The thread broke, hence the figure of speech *jiangeng loping* [breaking the thread and dropping the bottle], and the marriage plan failed.

and your human form. I used every device to hide my property and entrusted it to my "sisters." They secretly stored all of those precious objects for me. I was going to use these things to help Scholar Li return home to see his parents. The reason I am now no longer keeping them and have thrown them away is to let people know that Scholar Li has no eyes in his sockets! I have cried so many tears for Scholar Li that my eyes are nearly dry. I have been driven to distraction for him. Our marriage was almost completed when he forgot our relationship. He was afraid that his shoes would be stained by the morning dew. In a single moment, I am abandoned: I am less significant than scraps and leftover gravy! But now he is greedy for the leftovers and wants to collect the spilt water. How can I have face if I let him lead me by the nose again? This life is over. The sands of the Eastern Sea glisten, the millet of Western China grows over the ruins. My sorrow twists and coils around me and is unending!'

Everyone on the bank and on the boats was crying. They cursed Scholar Li as an ungrateful lover. But holding the last pearls, the girl threw herself into the river and was drowned. At that moment, all of the bystanders wanted to beat the Xin'an man and Scholar Li. Scholar Li and the Xin'an man hurriedly departed in their boats and no one knows where they went.

Alas, such a woman would not be shamed to appear before the model women described by Liu Xiang![17] Even the chastity of those women living deep in women's quarters cannot exceed hers.

---

17. This is a reference to a Han classic by Liu Xiang, the *Lienuzhuan* (Biographies of model women), which contains descriptions of the lives of paragons of Confucian virtue.

CHAPTER 2

The Manchu Conquest

2.1 NURHACI'S SEVEN GRIEVANCES

Nurhaci (1559–1626), the founder of the banner system and unifier of the Manchu people, issued these grievances against the Ming state in 1618. The grievances constituted a declaration of war and shortly after they were delivered to Peking, the first skirmishes began. One year later, in a pitched battle with Ming border garrisons specially raised to defeat them, Nurhaci's troops crushed General Yang Hao's army at Sarhu. The invasion of China was now clearly under way.

The text of the Seven Grievances translated here comes from a 1630 edict by Nurhaci's son Hong Taiji (Abahai, 1592–1643) that recalled the circumstances behind his father's decision to revolt against his Ming overlords. According to Meng Sen, one of twentieth-century China's major specialists on the history of the early Qing period, this version of the Grievances contains the most reliable version of its text. Later transcriptions, including a version that appeared in the *Veritable Records* of the Qing dynasty, were doctored by court archivists intent on stressing Nurhaci's loyalty to the Ming throne and to temper the blunt language of the original.

By order of the Khan of the Jin kingdom, let it be known to all officials, soldiers, and commoners:

Since the time of our ancestors, we have overseen the border region for the great Ming dynasty and for many years have shown our loyalty and obedience. Because the emperor of the southern dynasty [the Ming] inhabits the deep recesses of his palace, he is cheated and deceived by civil and military officials of the border regions and has created no policy to comfort the people. He uses power in devious ways; his strength is exerted to the ultimate degree and all possible profit is scraped off. The insults, invasions, damage, and suffering that have resulted are indescribable! Among these abuses of power, seven are most atrocious.

Our ancestors always guarded the border region and paid tribute to the southern dynasty. They were for a long period loyal and obedient to the court. Suddenly, during the Wanli reign, two of our ancestors were arrested and executed without being convicted of any crime. This is the first grievance.

In the Guisi year [1593], nine tribes, including the Nanguan, Beiguan [the Yehe], Huipa, Wula, the Mongols, and others, gathered troops to attack us. The southern dynasty did not stand with us and paid no attention. They sat watching with their hands in their sleeves. It was only owing to Heaven that we defeated all of these tribes. Later our state sought revenge and attacked and defeated the Nanguan. We moved into their inner territory and took Wuerhuda of the Nanguan as our son-in-law. The southern dynasty blamed us for this invasion and ordered us to send him back. We immediately followed this order and restored him to his domain. Later when the Beiguan attacked the Nanguan, the southern dynasty did not blame them for their destruction and looting. Although our state and Beiguan are equal tribal states we were treated differently when we acted in the same way. How can we take comfort from this? This is the second grievance.

Our Khan's [Nurhaci] loyalty to the great Ming was as firm as metal or stone. Because of the slaughter of his two esteemed relatives, he feared that the Ming doubted him. The late Khan joined with Wu Xihan, Deputy Commander of Liaoyang, in the slaughter of horses and oxen and offered sacrifices to Heaven and earth. They erected a tablet on the border with this inscription: "Han people who go beyond this border without permission will be killed." Later, Han people living in the border region crossed this line without permission to dig for and gather ginseng. Since our livelihood comes from such natural wealth, we reported this repeatedly to superior officials but our reports were unheeded. Although we had a grievance, there was no channel for expressing our accusation. We were then forced to follow the rules established by the inscription and began to kill and harm violators. We sought to confirm our sworn oath and stop future [violations]; we did not want to betray our original agreement. When the new [Chinese] governor took office, we followed precedent and sought to express our humble greeting. Ganguli, Fangjinna, and others were sent to show our homage. At this time the [Han] superior officials did not attempt to determine [character missing] the responsibility for the border incidents. To the contrary, they arrested those who had come to the ceremony and demanded ten barbarian [Manchu] lives in revenge. How could anyone bear such an insult? This is the third grievance.

Beiguan and Jianzhou [Manchu tribes] are both subordinate barbarian groups; when our two houses clash, the southern dynasty should seek to resolve the issue fairly. Why should it send troops and firearms to Beiguan to help them resist us? This partiality is surely hurtful! This is the fourth grievance.

An old crone of the Beiguan tribe was betrothed to our late Khan and we sent our bridal presents to them. Later the engagement was broken by the Beiguan and the marriage did not take place. Because of this, they would not have dared to permit her to marry for some time. With the support of the southern dynasty, however, she was married to a Mongol. Who could stand such a humiliation? This is the fifth grievance.

The people of our tribe who have guarded the border for over two hundred years have always lived in the border region. Later the Ming listened to the slanders of the Beiguan and sent troops to force our tribe to retreat ten miles from the border. They erected a tablet, occupied this land, burned down our peoples' houses and left the crops to rot [character missing] in the fields. Our people had no food nor lodging and were left there to die. This is the sixth grievance.

Our state was always obedient and never acted out of turn. Suddenly, the Censor Xiao Bozhi was sent [to the Manchu court] wearing court garb and jade belt. He showed his authority overbearingly; his language was crude and filthy and he insulted us in hundreds of ways. Our [character missing] officials could not endure this poisonous behavior! This is the seventh grievance.

There was no means of reporting these seven grievances. The superior officials of Liaodong were like gods and addressing the Wanli emperor was like trying to reach Heaven. He [Nurhaci] hesitated and could think of no other method than report it to Heaven. He revolted and captured Fushun in the hope that the Wanli emperor would seek to know the details of this matter and redress his [Nurhaci's] feelings of being wronged. Subsequently, he drew up a detailed list of seven grievances and circulated them among merchants of various provinces. He waited expectantly but received no reply.

... Now we are again letting this be known. We do not fear repeating in order to clearly tell the reason for our uprising and to show clearly the meaning of our acceptance of Heaven's Mandate. We fear that the people of the world are unaware of our reasons and blame us for being wild and presumptuous. Therefore, we make this announcement and let it be known to all.

2.2 AND 2.3 EXCHANGE OF LETTERS BETWEEN WU SANGUI AND DORGON

The following letters were reprinted in the *Qing Veritable Records*, a historical account compiled at the beginning of the new Manchu dynasty. The exchange, between Prince Dorgon (1612–1650) and Ming general Wu Sangui (1612–1678), marked a critical turning point in the Qing conquest. As the commander of the Ming garrison at the Shanhai Pass, Wu blocked the Manchus' southern advance. In Peking, the forces of Li Zicheng had deposed the Ming emperor and held Wu's father hostage. When Wu decided to accept the Manchu offer, he combined forces with Dorgon to defeat Li Zicheng's army in May 1644. By

Zhong as a chief advisor to win hegemony. If your excellence is willing to lead your troops to us, we will enfeoff you with a domain and ennoble you as a prince. Your state will then be avenged and you and your family will be protected. Your posterity will enjoy wealth and nobility as eternal as the mountains and rivers.

2.4 A LETTER FROM DORGON TO THE MING LOYALIST SHI KEFA, SIXTH MOON, 1644

Shi Kefa (1602–1645) was a leading official during the Ming-Qing transition period. After the fall of Peking to Li Zicheng, many imperial relatives and former Ming officials fled to Nanjing, which became the first center of southern Ming resistance. After an abortive attempt to help in the defense of Peking, Shi Kefa participated in the selection of a new Ming emperor in the south. As the commander of the Yangzhou garrison, he led the defense of the city against Manchu troops. As this letter shows, Dorgon was eager to use the example of Wu Sangui and promises of similar rewards to win over Shi Kefa. Shi refused these offers, however, and the Ming garrison under his command mounted a spirited defense. Following the siege, he was taken prisoner and executed.

When I was formerly in Shenyang, I was aware that your excellency was one of the most esteemed officials of Peking. Later, when I crossed the Great Wall to destroy the bandits and had contact with people in the capital, I came to know your younger brother. I asked him to send you a letter of greeting and affection and am unsure whether the letter reached you. Presently it is rumored that someone has been enthroned in Nanjing. Hatred for the murderer of one monarch dictates that one must not share the same sky with the murderer. This is the meaning of the *Spring and Autumn Annals* in which it is written that before the murderer has been punished, the dead monarch cannot be described in history as having been formally buried, nor can a new ruler rightfully take the throne. In order to guard against rebellious statesmen and unfilial sons, this rule is very strict. The "Dashing Bandit," Li Zicheng, led troops in an invasion of the capital; he harmed the Emperor and no Chinese subject came to his defense. Only the Pacifying King of the West, Wu Sangui, who was then stationed on the eastern border, emulated the ancient example of Shen Baoxu.[1] Our court was moved by his loyalty and righteousness. We remembered the generations of friendly relations between our two states and overlooked the minor quarrels of recent times. We sent our most ferocious troops to his aid to drive out these vicious animals.[2] When we entered the capital, we first paid our

---

1. Shen Baoxu was an official of the state of Chu who, after the invasion of his state by Wu, journeyed to the Qin court and tearfully implored its aid to restore his state.

2. The term used in the original text is *xiaojing*, or owls and cat-like monsters, two creatures deemed particularly evil. According to legend, the owl ate its young and the mythical *jing* devoured its mother after birth.

homage to your deceased Emperor; we gave him posthumous titles of honor and buried him in the imperial tomb. All of this was done in proper ritual fashion. Imperial princes, generals, and others were permitted to retain their original titles. Meritorious relatives and all civil and military officials were allowed to stay in the court and continue to enjoy imperial grace. Tillers of the soil and merchants were unalarmed and not a single straw was disturbed. In the fall we plan to dispatch our troops on a western expedition; we will send a declaration of war to the Jiangnan region [south of the Yangzi River] and hope to form an alliance with you to fight in the west. We can then deploy our divisions together and single-mindedly exert all of our strength to take revenge for your Emperor and state and to manifest our dynasty's virtue. I am exceedingly puzzled that you gentlemen in the southern provinces are shamefully clinging to the illusion of peace and to empty fame. You refuse to grasp the moment and forget about the actual perils.

Our state, in its pacification of Peking, seized it from the "Dashing Bandit" Li Zicheng and not from the Ming state. The bandits destroyed the ancestral temples of the Ming dynasty and humiliated the Ming ancestors; our state felt no qualms about the toil of dispatching expeditions or the expense of using tax revenues to wipe clean the shame that befell you. Any filial son or humane person should feel indebted and repay our generosity. But you are taking advantage of our liquidation of the treasonous bandits and the temporary halt of our imperial army's advance. You seek to occupy Jiangnan and enjoy benefits obtained for you by others. If reason is applied to judge this behavior, can it be called fair? Do you think that the Yangzi cannot be crossed or that by throwing down our whips we could not halt the rivers?[3] The "Dashing Bandit" was a peril only to your Ming dynasty and never offended our state. However, our sympathy for your plight and common hatred of the enemy has caused us to manifest great righteousness. But if you now claim you hold the exalted title, then there will be two suns in heaven and we will become enemies. China with its whole strength was unable to overcome the troubles caused by the rebels; you now control merely a corner of the south and yet seek, simultaneously, to face our great country and the remaining bandits. Neither straws nor turtle shells are needed to divine what the outcome will be. I have heard that a gentleman uses virtue to manifest his love for the people; a mean man is complacent. If you gentlemen truly understand the times and the will of heaven, if you sincerely consider your late Emperor and deeply love your capable king, it is appropriate that you advise him to relinquish his title and pledge his allegiance to us. Thus, he can maintain his eternal happiness and good fortune. Our court will treat your king as an honored guest and permit him to carry on the rituals of the Ming court and possess the rivers and mountains of his own domain. His rank will be

---

3. This figure of speech, *toubian duanliu* (throwing down whips to stop the river's flow), is an allusion to the Period of Disunity and the invasion of the north by Fu Jian of the former Qin state. He claimed to have so many troops that the mass of their whips tossed into the river together could halt the Yangzi. Since Fu Jian was, in fact, defeated, the use of this allusion in this context was less than ideal.

superior to that of other princes and nobles. This will not defy the original intention of our court to manifest righteousness by pacifying the rebels and to restore what has been severed and ruined. As for you talented gentlemen in the southern provinces, should you present yourselves to us then you shall enjoy titles of nobility and will be rewarded with lands. There exists the model of the Pacifying King of the West and I can only hope that you who are in command will make plans for the benefit of all.

Recently, your scholars have been fond of establishing unreachable standards of virtue and have ignored the crisis of the state. In each moment of emergency they natter about how to set up the defenses of the house. In former times, while the people of the Song debated the course they might take, the invaders had already crossed the river. This should be a clear example for you. Your excellency is the leader of a famed circle and is charged with making state policy. You certainly understand all the implications of this moment; how could you bear to follow the vulgar trend and float listlessly at such a time? You should decide soon whether to follow us or to resist. Our army is ready; it can advance east or west. Peace or peril for your southern state depends on the course you select. I hope you gentlemen will be unified in your intention to pay the bandits and will not be greedy for a transient glory that will surely prolong the interminable calamity suffered by your state. I deeply hope that you will not give rebellious statesmen and unfilial sons reason to laugh at you. It is said in the classics: "Only good men can appreciate straightforward advice." I respectfully open my mind to you and, standing on tiptoe, watch the horizon, as I anxiously await words of enlightenment from you. This letter cannot fully express my meaning.

2.5 AND 2.6 TWO EDICTS CONCERNING HAIR

Qing leaders decided, even before taking Peking, that Chinese subjects should wear their hair dressed in the Manchu tribal style. The hair was to be shaved to the middle of the skull, with the remaining hair pulled back around a "cash-shaped" circle of the scalp and braided as it grew. Former Ming subjects who resisted this order symbolizing submission to the new regime did so at the risk of their lives. The colloquial saying "Lose your hair or lose your head" (*Liutou bu liufa, liufa bu liutou*) succinctly described the dangers for those still sentimentally attached to the long style of hair-dress popular during the Ming period. Later in the dynasty, cutting off the queue was a symbol of resistance to the Manchus adopted by the Taiping rebels, who were sometimes called "the long-haired rebels," and early twentieth-century revolutionaries often cut off their *bianzi* as a sign of defiance. When the Qing collapsed in 1911, groups of anti-Qing activists cornered wearers of the queue in Shanghai and other cities to cut off their pigtails. The piles of queues lying in the street symbolized the fallen fortunes of the dynasty.

2.5 Regent Dorgon's Edict to the Board of War

Now that our dynasty has established its authority in Peking, the soldiers and common people who endured recent calamities are all our children. We will save them from disasters and give them security. Send messengers to cities and forts of all regions requesting their surrender. If, on the day this message arrives, their inhabitants shave their heads and submit, all local officials shall be promoted one rank. Soldiers and common people will be exempt from deportation. Leading civil and military officials should personally collect tax registers and army rosters and immediately bring them to the capital for imperial audience. Those who claim to submit but do not shave their heads are hesitant and watchful. They should be given a deadline for compliance based on their distance from the capital and rewarded accordingly when they arrive in Peking. If they do not meet the deadline, it is clear that they are resisting and definitely should be punished; troops are to be sent to supress them. Princes with the surname Zhu [members of the Ming imperial family] who conform to this order shall not be deprived of their titles and will continue to enjoy imperial grace.

2.6 Imperial Edict to the Board of Rites

In the past the system of dressing the hair in a queue was not uniformly enforced. People were allowed to do as they pleased because we wanted to wait until the whole country was pacified before putting into force this system. Now, within and without, we are one family. The Emperor is like the father and the people are like his sons. The father and sons are of the same body; how can they be different from one another? If they are not as one then it will be as if they had two hearts and would they then not be like the people of different countries? We do not need to mention this because we believe all subjects under Heaven must be aware of it themselves. All residents of the capital and its vicinity will fulfill the order to shave their heads within ten days of this proclamation. For Zhili and other provinces compliance must take place within ten days of receipt of the order from the Board of Rites. Those who follow this order belong to our country; those who hesitate will be considered treasonous bandits and will be heavily penalized. Anyone who attempts to evade this order to protect his hair or who uses cunning language to argue against it will not be lightly dealt with. All officials in regions that we have already pacified who insultingly advance a memorial related to this matter arguing for the continuation of the Ming system and not following the system of our dynasty will be executed without possibility of pardon. As for other apparel, unhurried change is permitted, but it cannot differ from the system of our dynasty. The aforementioned Board will immediately dispatch this message to the capital and its vicinity and to the provincial, prefectural, sub-prefectural, and county yamen and garrisons of Zhili and other provinces. Civil and military yamen officials, clerks, scholars, students, and all members of military and civilian households shall carry this out without exception.

2.7 THE SIEGE OF JIANGYIN, 1645

The hair-cutting decrees were a dramatic sign of the changing political order and prompted strong resistance in many parts of the south. In the city of Jiangyin in Jiangsu province, just south of the Yangzi River, local elites used this issue to muster resistance to the advancing Qing forces. In August 1645, a fierce battle ensued.

This account of the eight-day siege of Jiangyin was written by Xu Chongxi, a controversial scholar and historian of the late Ming. Xu was praised by some of his contemporaries for his scholarly diligence, but criticized by others for his frank commentary on the events of his time. (During the Qianlong era, Xu's history of the final years of the Ming dynasty was banned.) This translation is drawn from Xu Chongxin's *Postscript on the Defense of Jiangyin City*. The excerpt provides a vivid sense of the violence of the conquest period and describes how local elites struggled to build forces of resistance to the Qing invaders. After the defeat of Jiangyin, the Manchu army burned the city and massacred many of its inhabitants.

In the sixth moon of 1645, Magistrate Fang of Jiangyin arrived in the city and conveyed the [Qing] edict to dress the hair in the queue. On the first day of the intercalary sixth moon,[4] a local scholar, Xu Yongde, hung a portrait of the Ming founder in the Minglun Lecture Hall [the official local academy for instruction in the classics] and led a crowd who prostrated themselves before it and cried out: "Cut off our heads, we refuse to shave our hair!" That afternoon, the local militia in the North Gate area were the first to rise up; they arrested the magistrate and jailed him in the local guest house. Tens of thousands of people within and outside the city supported them. Those in revolt requested the release of stores of weapons and ammunition and the local judge Chen Mingxuan agreed. The chief of the local reserve unit was then arrested and a search began for spies within the city. The Huizhou merchant Shao Kanggong who was a master of the martial arts was appointed as commander and enlisted soldiers for the defense of the city. Former *Dusi*[5] Zhou Ruilong stationed ships at the mouth of the river and asked Shao Kanggong to bring his troops out through the east gate so that they could combine

---

4. Intercalary months were added to the lunar calendar to keep it in harmony with the solar year.
5. Ming military rank equivalent to commander or captain.

forces at the north gate to fight the [Qing] invaders. When the battle was joined, they were successful. The enemy's force grew larger day by day and the militia men did their best to attack it and kill Manchu soldiers. Whenever they presented one head, the city rewarded them with four taels of silver. At this time, slaves and servants were in revolt against their masters and the great local families were occupied in saving themselves from death.

The Qing army first attacked the western quarter of the city and then moved to the south gate. Shao Kanggong went forward to command the defense but could not prevail. The enemy burned the eastern quarter and looted the homes of rich families living outside the city wall. The militia fought ferociously and a certain pair of brothers killed a cavalry general. . . . Zhou Ruilong boarded his boat and fled.

The former judge, Yan Yingyuan, had been promoted to Deputy Magistrate of Yingde county in Guangdong but had not yet left to fill the position because his mother was ill. When the national calamity occurred, he and his family moved to Shashan, located east of the city. Chen Mingxuan said: "My wisdom and courage are no match for Mister Yan's; he should come to take charge of this great matter." That night riders were sent to meet with Yan Yingyuan. Yingyuan accepted and led more than forty of this family's retainers to rush to defend the city. Scattered groups of enemy soldiers were burning and looting outside the city walls. The militia had fled and no reinforcements were coming.

Now the enemy concentrated on attacking the walled city. Within the city walls there were less than a thousand soldiers and about ten thousand households. No source of pay or rations existed for the troops. Yan Yingyuan gathered up household registers and set in order defense towers. He ordered each household to present X [character missing] men to mount the city wall and commanded all others remaining to assist in preparing meals. He then released munitions and firearms made by Zeng Hualong, the former military circuit intendant, and stored them in battle towers. He sent an order to the great families of the city encouraging contributions: "Contributions will not necessarily consist of money. Clothing, grain, and other materials are all acceptable." The national academy scholar Cheng Bi came forward first with a donation of twenty-five thousand silver taels and then many other donors came forward. Within the besieged city there were three hundred charges of gunpowder, one thousand *dan* [one *dan* = 133⅓ pounds] of lead and iron blunderbuss ammunition, one hundred cannons, one thousand fowling pieces, ten million copper cash and ten thousand *dan* of millet, wheat, and beans. Wine, salt, iron, and hay were also available. The city was divided up into sectors for its defense. The military *juren*[6] Huang Lue guarded the east gate. A certain sub-lieutenant commanded the south gate. Chen Mingxuan guarded the west gate and Yan Yingyuan himself guarded the north gate. Patrols circulated among the four gates.

---

6. The *juren* degree is the second level of attainment in the imperial civil service examination system, awarded to those who passed the provincial exam.

By now there were already one hundred thousand men in the Qing army that surrounded the city. They set up more than one hundred camps and dozens of rings of soldiers surrounded the city. They fired their arrows into the air and wounded some of the men on the city wall. But on the wall the defenders used catapults and crossbows and used the advantage of the wall's height to wound many of the enemy. The Qing then used large cannons to attack the city and the wall began to crack. Yan Yingyuan ordered his men to wrap wooden doors with iron sheet tied on with iron bands. These doors were then lowered to cover the cracks. Empty coffins were stuffed with soil and used to fill in collapsed areas. The Qing next attacked the northern city and one man climbed up a scaling ladder placed against the city wall. The defenders resisted him with a long spear but this officer grasped the spear with his teeth and projected himself onto the wall. A boy grabbed him and another defender cut off the enemy's head. It was said that: "This was the seventh prince." Another Qing officer wore dozens of sharp knives and climbed up by driving long, thick nails into the wall. The defenders used an iron hammer to kill him. . . .

Among the residents of Jiangyin was one Huang Yunjiang; he was a skilled maker of arrowheads. When someone was hit in the face by one of Huang's arrows fired from an incendiary crossbow, he would howl with pain and die. Chen Riu's son made wooden grenades in the prison which looked like ones made of steel. When they were dropped from the city wall they would explode in a fiery mass showering scraps of iron in all directions. People hit by this shrapnel would immediately die. Yan Yingyuan made an iron grappling hook to which was attached a long cotton rope. When it caught the enemy soldiers they were dragged up the wall into the city. They also made fire rugs and fire arrows. The enemy so feared these weapons that they camped three *li* from the city wall.

The enemy commander Liu Langzuo was originally one of the four division commanders of the Hongguang court and was ennobled as the Earl of Guangchang. However, he surrendered to the Qing and was made a senior general. Liu devised an ox-hide canopy and attacked the eastern corner of the city. The crowd of defending troops threw down huge rocks and hundreds of enemy soldiers died. Then Liu Langzuo moved his camp to the Sifang Temple and ordered its monks to kneel and tearfully implore the defenders to surrender. But the defenders did not listen. Liu Langzuo then approached the city wall on horseback and shouted: "Mister Yan and I are old friends. Tell him I want to see him." Yan Yingyuan then appeared and planted himself on the city wall. Liu told him: "The Hongguang emperor has already fled. There is no master in all of Jiangnan. If you surrender early you will keep your wealth and nobility." Yingyuan said: "I am just a local judge of the Ming dynasty. My death is of no importance! But you who were enfeoffed and ennobled by the court and appointed to serve as its chief officer in the central command could not defend the Yangtze-Huai river zone. Instead, today you come to invade and oppress us. Do you have the face to confront the righteous scholars and commoners of our country?" Langzuo felt ashamed and departed.

Yan Yingyuan was tall and powerful; his complexion was dark and he had a light beard. His character was stern and persistent. When he gave orders he pardoned no failures in carrying them out. But he cared little for money and was generous in giving rewards. He personally bandaged the wounded and provided excellent funerals for the men who were killed. He drank libations and wept for the dead. When he spoke with his officers and troops, he called them "good brothers" instead of using their names. Chen Mingxuan was warm and generous; each time he circled the city wall he shared the labor and hardship of the soldiers and sometimes even wept with them. Therefore, these two men were able to win the hearts of their troops and the troops were happy to die for them.

One night there was a howling rainstorm and there was no light in the entire city. Suddenly a divine light illuminated the city. The enemy saw three red-clothed figures giving commands inside the walls. In fact, there was no such thing. They also saw a woman officer waving a flag and giving commands but this too was an illusion. . . .

Beneath the city walls, day by day, the number of large cannons increased. One was located every five or six feet from the next and soon flying cannon balls fell like hail. A man stood on the city wall and was decapitated by cannon shot but his body still stood there erect. Another man was struck in the chest by a ball that passed through him but he still stood as before.

On the fifteenth day of the eighth moon, Yan Yingyuan donated money to the soldiers and people to allow them to have a good time enjoying the beauty of the moon. His subordinates brought drinking vessels onto the city wall and hearty drinking took place. Xu Yongde composed a folk song with five variations and ordered a good singer to sing it slowly and gracefully. The sound of the song and alarm bells and bugles made a lovely harmony. This lasted for three nights.

The *beile*,[7] when he realized that the city had no intention of surrendering, ordered his troops to attack more urgently. Risking their lives, they threw up ladders against the city walls. Their armor and helmets were all made of iron; when they were hit by a knife or ax, there was a clanging sound and the blades were broken. The sound of cannon echoed day and night and places within one hundred *li* of the battleground were shaken by the sound. Each day there were more wounded and dead within the city and the sounds of weeping and mourning were heard along its streets. But Yingyuan courageously mounted the city and was undaunted.

One morning there was a huge downpour; at midday, a thread-like red light rose from the Mud Bridge and shot toward the western quarter and soon thereafter the city fell.

Qing troops swarmed up like bees through the smoke, mist, and rain and entered the city. Yan Yingyuan, leading one hundred fearless men, fought in eight street battles and killed or wounded thousands of the enemy. Yan and his men rushed to the gate but it was closed and they could not escape. Yingyuan determined that

7. A title for Manchu princes; here, the degree is indeterminable.

death was unavoidable and threw himself into the water of the Qian Lake but was not drowned. Liu Langzuo ordered his troops to take Yan Yingyuan alive and so he was captured. Langzuo sat proudly in the Qianming Temple hall; when he saw Yingyuan, he jumped up and tearfully embraced him. Yingyuan laughed and said: "What are you crying for? Since things have reached this stage, all that is left for me is death!" When he saw the *beile*, Yingyuan stood upright and refused to bow. A soldier pierced his shin with a spear, which broke the bone and made him topple to the ground. Toward dusk, he was carried to the Xixia Monastery and that night the monks heard him crying: "Kill me quickly!" Without ceasing his imprecations, Yingyuan died.

Chen Mingxuan dismounted and engaged in the melee. He was killed in the fighting before the Military Circuit Intendant's office. He was already mortally wounded but stood erect against a wall holding a sword and would not fall to the ground. (Some said that his entire family committed suicide by leaping into a fire.) Someone named Han, after killing three Qing soldiers, slashed his own throat. A certain local instructor Feng from Jintan, hung himself in the Minglun Lecture Hall. The Junior Imperial Secretary Qi Xun, also known as Boping, whose family was from Qingyang, entered the city to aid in its defense. He exhausted his strength fighting and wrote in large characters on the wall of his residence: "Qi Xun died here. His wife, children, and daughter-in-law all died here." Then the entire family immolated themselves. The entire family of Xu Yongde also burned themselves. Huang Yunjiang had been good at playing the *huqin*;[8] after the city fell he disguised himself as a musician and escaped. No one recognized him as the master designer of the arrows used to defend the city. The defense lasted eighty-one days.

Two hundred and forty thousand Qing troops took part and sixty-seven thousand of them died during the siege. Another seven thousand died in street fighting. In all, more than seventy-five thousand soldiers were lost. The dead in the city filled every well. Sunlangzhong Pond and Chong Pond were packed with layers of corpses. Not one person surrendered.

This official historian of Jiangyin says: During the Ming dynasty officials had no sense of shame. Those who were high officials enjoyed great renown but they were willing to hide their faces and beg to surrender. And all of the great commanders guarding the frontiers turned their spears and advanced into China: Only Chen and Yan, these two local judges, showed righteousness in this one city. If the defense of the Jingkou fortifications had been so strong, then Jiangnan would not have been handed over to the enemy! Contemporaries remarked: "For eighty days they kept hair to show loyalty and they were outstanding among the historical figures of the seventeen reigns since the founding of the Ming by Taizu. Sixty thousand people were of one mind and died for righteousness to preserve this three hundred *li* of territory."

---

8. A two-stringed musical instrument originally brought to China from central Asia and used in the Peking opera.

CHAPTER 3 | # Kangxi's Consolidation

3.1 WU SANGUI ON THE EXECUTION OF THE PRINCE OF GUI

After the Manchu conquest, resistance to Qing rule continued only on the periphery of China, with the remnant armies of Li Zicheng and Zhang Xianzhong and the navy of Koxinga holding out against the new regime. In the south and southwest, Ming forces loyal to the prince of Gui entered unlikely coalitions to continue the fight. The prince of Gui was the most prominent of several Ming pretenders, enthroned as Emperor Yongli in November 1646 in Wuzhou, Guangxi. In the years that followed, he was in constant flight from Qing forces. In 1652, Yongli's fortunes briefly changed as he joined with Zhang Xianzhong's lieutenants to form a new base on the Guangxi-Yunnan border. Until its final downfall, the southern Ming was defended by some of the same rebels who had helped bring down the dynasty.

In 1659, with the Qing army in pursuit, Yongli crossed the border into Burma, where he was placed under virtual house arrest but was not mistreated. Two years later, following a coup that brought to power a new Burmese king eager to mollify the Qing state, the last Ming pretender was turned over to Wu Sangui, the celebrated turncoat. As the following document suggests, Wu had no compunction about putting Yongli to death. This 1662 memorial, sent to the court by Wu Sangui and Aixing, includes a copy of a letter from Yongli imploring Wu for mercy.

We were ordered to send an expedition into Burma and advanced our troops along two fronts. In the eleventh moon of 1661, the two forces met in Mubang. The false Prince Jin, Li Dingguo, fled to Jingxian and the false Prince Gong-change, Bai

| 3 3

Wenxuan, fled and took up a new position along the Xibo River. His troops built
rafts to cross the river and Bai Wenxuan then fled to Chashan. General Ma Ning
and others were sent in pursuit to Mengmao where they obtained Bai Wenxuan's
surrender. As Wu Sangui and Aixing approached Miancheng they received a letter from the false Prince Yongli to Sangui which read:

> Your excellency is a meritorious official of the new dynasty and was also an impor-
> tant general of the previous dynasty. For generations your family has been rewarded
> with noble ranks and you were enfeoffed as a garrison commander in the border regions.
> It can be said that the late Emperor was extremely generous to you. Who could know
> that our country would experience the unexpected disaster brought about by Li Zicheng's
> bandits who rushed into our capital, ruined our country, and forced our late Emperor
> to meet an early death. They unleashed great evil and slaughtered many of our people.
> Your excellency, like Shen Baoxu who tearfully implored aid from the Qin court to
> restore Chu, wore mourning garb and made a vow to lead your troops to punish the
> criminals. Your original intention at that time cannot be condemned.
>
> But how, later, could you side with a powerful state and, like a fox walking beside a
> tiger, assume an overbearing demeanor? You appeared to seek revenge but secretly you
> sought to be an officer of the new dynasty. After the traitor [Li Zicheng] was killed and
> the southern territories were no longer under the control of the previous dynasty, offi-
> cials of the south could not bear to see the dynasty fail and so they invited me to be
> enthroned in Nanyang. Who could expect that there would be no peace and that war
> would come again? Prince Hongguang met a tragic end and Prince Longwu was exe-
> cuted. At this time, your humble servant almost did not want to go on living. How could
> I bear to make plans for the state? After repeated urging from my officials, I undeserv-
> ingly agreed to carry on the previous imperial line. Since then, the territory of Chu was
> lost in one battle and the territory of eastern Guangdong was lost in another. It is hard
> to calculate how many times I have fled in terror.
>
> Fortunately, Li Dingguo invited your servant to Guizhou and received me at Nan'an.
> I believed this would harm no one and sought no conflict with anyone in the world!
> However, your excellency forgot the great righteousness shown to you by your late
> Emperor and sought to win merit by opening new territories and by leading troops into
> Yunnan to overturn my little nest. Your servant, owing to this, was forced to cross the
> desert and strengthen his domain by seeking the support of the Burmese. In such a
> distant land, who could feel happy? How miserable it is! Although I have lost the rivers
> and mountains that generations of my family guarded, I am now shamefully resigned
> to preserving my humble life among a barbarian people. And yet, I feel fortunate for
> this! However, your excellency accepts hardships and requests this mission to come from
> afar with hundreds of thousands of soldiers to doggedly pursue my transient body; is
> this not too narrow a view of the world? Is there no space between heaven and earth
> where your servant can be accommodated? After being ennobled and bestowed with
> titles, do you still seek merit by killing your humble servant?
>
> I have come to think that in this empire built through struggle by our founding
> Emperor, there no longer remains even a single parcel of land where your excellency
> can win more merit. Your excellency has already ruined my family and you now seek
> to take away my posterity. This is like reading the poem in the *Shijing* about the owl

that devours its own young. Can you not feel moved? Your excellency is the descendant of a family long honored with appointments; even if you cannot pity your servant, can you not think of the late Emperor? If you have no consideration for the late Emperor, can you not recall the Ming ancestors? If you do not recall the Ming ancestors, can you not remember your own father and grandfather? I cannot understand what sort of grace the great Qing has bestowed you or what sort of grievance your servant has given to your excellency. Your excellency considers himself clever but is actually foolish. You believe yourself to be generous but you are mean. After some time has passed, there will be biographies and historical accounts; what sort of person will future generations consider your excellency to have been?

Your servant's armies have crumbled and his strength is depleted. He stands alone and desolate and his humble life rests in your excellency's hands. If you really want your servant's head, I dare not refuse it even though it may mean my bones will be ground into fragments and my blood smeared on the grass and weeds. I do not dare to hope that disaster can be turned into good fortune or that in some remote region there is still a piece of land to maintain the state rituals. If your servant could be like the grass or trees in peaceful times which obtain rain and dew from a sage dynasty, then, even if he had millions of troops he would turn them over to your excellency and let them merely follow your excellency's commands. Your excellency now serves the great Qing as an official but [to spare me] would show that you do not forget sacrifices due your former lords nor ignore the great grace of your former Emperor. I hope you can consider this.

On the first day of the twelfth moon, the grand army arrived at Miancheng. The chieftain of Burma, Mangyingshi, captured Zhu Yulang [Yongli] and presented him to the army. The false Marquis Huating, Wang Weigong, and a hundred others were killed. The region south of Yunnan is pacified.

3.2 SHI LANG'S MEMORIAL ON THE CAPTURE OF TAIWAN

Zheng Chenggong (1624–1662) was a formidable supporter of the Ming cause after 1644 and received the imperial surname Zhu as an honorific in 1645. He was then widely known as *Guoxingye,* "Lord of the Imperial Surname." The Dutch who occupied Taiwan called him Koxinga, mistaking the unofficial title for his name. From 1647 to 1661, Zheng waged an active campaign of resistance on behalf of the southern Ming on the southeastern coast. When pressured to withdraw from the mainland, he retreated to Taiwan, where he besieged and captured the Dutch fortress of Zeelandia (Tainan) in 1662. Shortly thereafter Zheng Chenggong died, and command of his army and fleet passed to his son. The Zheng family controlled Taiwan for the next twenty years.

To eliminate this last base of resistance, the Kangxi emperor dispatched Admiral Shi Lang (1621–1696) with a large fleet from Fujian. Shi Lang had begun his career as a subordinate officer in the naval forces of Zheng Zhilong and Zheng Chenggong. The Shi family genealogy records that after a dispute between Shi Lang and Zheng Chenggong, Shi's father and other family members were arrested and executed. Shi Lang escaped this fate and followed Zheng Zhilong into service with the Manchus. His skill as a naval tactician and enmity against Zheng Chenggong made him a reliable choice as the leader of the Qing expeditionary force. The following document vividly describes the final battle in the Taiwan Straits in 1683.

EXPRESS MEMORIAL DESCRIBING THE GREAT VICTORY, 1683

The Junior Guardian of the Heir Apparent, Admiral of the Fujian Fleet, and Right Chief Military Commissioner, the Earl Shi Lang most carefully, via express memorial, hereby describes the great victory of our fleet which crossed the sea to conquer and capture Penghu.

From the time of the sixth moon one year ago, your humble subject and Governor [of Fujian] Yao Qisheng, began stationing a fleet at Tongshan. When Liu Guoxuan [an admiral of the Ming loyalist group on Taiwan] was apprised of this, he returned to Taiwan but left behind an unlawful garrison of ships and soldiers to hold Penghu. Since then, he has frequently journeyed back and forth to deploy his defenses. In the fourth and fifth moon of this year, when Liu Guoxuan learned that I planned to use the south wind to carry out my campaign of suppression, he selected a group of sturdy and daring fighters from the Taiwan bandit gang, enlisted tenant farmers and militia men, and refitted foreign vessels as warships. All private vessels belonging to the civil and military officials of the unlawful regime were set in order and gathered together off Penghu. There were more than two hundred large and small gunboats, "birdboats" [?], silk trading junks, foreign vessels, two-masted junks, and a bandit mob of over twenty thousand men [in this area]. To strengthen their navy's resolve to fight to the death, the family members of all unlawful garrison commanders and troops were detained in the Hongmao Fort [the Red-haired City] and the Chikan Fort on Taiwan. Liu Guoxuan personally took command and left his lair with all of his followers to come to Penghu.

The bandits built two new gun batteries on Niangmagong Island, constructed one at Fengguiwei on Penghu, another on Sijiaoshan, one on Jilongshan, set up a stronghold of four in the Dongxishi area, four more on the west face of Neiwaiqian and Xiyutou, and put up another on the hilltop of Niuxinwan. All along the coast, wherever it was possible for a small boat to land, they threw up short mud walls and installed musket emplacements. These fortifications stretched for more than twenty *li* and a throng of bandits was dispatched to defend them to the death. Their defenseworks were scattered everywhere like stars in the sky or chessmen and were as sturdy as an iron bucket.

Your subject took command of the fleet and had the names of all of his captains written in large characters on the sails of their ships, to permit convenient observation of their movements and distinguish who should be rewarded or punished. Between seven and nine a.m. on the 14th day of the sixth moon, we departed Tongshan and began our advance. On the 15th day, between three and five p.m., we reached Cat Island and Flower Island. Several dozen bandit picket ships saw our fleet coming and fled back to Penghu. Since nightfall was imminent, we moored our fleet in Shuian Bay of Bazhao Island and sent our picket boats to Jiangjun Island and Nanda Island to pacify the people.

We attacked Penghu on the morning of the 16th day and the bandits deployed their ships to face us. . . . [Here Shi includes a list of Qing fleet commanders who led the advance.] Our ships charged forward and hurled themselves into the mass of enemy vessels. They attacked two bandit gunboats, six silk trading junks and almost entirely wiped out the bandit crews. These vessels were then set on fire and destroyed. Our warships then turned their guns on one "birdboat" and two silk junks and promptly sank them. . . . [Here Shi inserts a second list of Qing commanders who distinguished themselves in a successive episode of this battle.] [The second group of commanders] used cannons to sink one bandit "birdboat" and two more silk junks. Almost all of the bandits aboard these vessels drowned.

At this time, the southward tide was surging and the ships leading our fleet were pushed toward the shore batteries. The bandit ships regrouped and rushed out together to encircle the [imperiled Qing] ships. Your servant feared that these ships would be trapped and dashed directly into the group of enemy ships to kill the enemy and withdraw. The Xinghua Garrison Commander, Wu Ying, followed me into the fray and we killed the false admiral Shen Cheng . . . and more than seventy other bandit commanders whose names we do not know and cannot present here. The false naval commander-in-chief Lin Sheng was hit by three arrows and two blunderbuss projectiles, and his left leg was broken by a cannon ball. He was immediately taken back to Taiwan but his wounds were surely fatal. The bandits who were killed, burned to death, or drowned totaled more than two thousand and because of this action our ships were rescued. Your subject's right eye was wounded by a piece of shot but his eyesight was not destroyed. Dusk was falling and, hence, we moored our fleet in the sea off Xiyutou.

On the morning of the 17th day, all of the ships of the fleet were gathered in the bay of Shuian of Bazhao and stern orders were made clear to all. Merit and failings were evaluated and rewards and punishments doled out to the officers and men. On the 18th day, the fleet advanced and took Hujing and Tongpan Island. On the 19th day, your subject boarded a small silk trading junk and personally went to Neiwaiqian and Shinei to carefully examine their situation. On the 20th and 21st days, using the strategy of "feigning old age and weakness to make the enemy feel arrogant," we dispatched silk junks and two-masted junks in two groups to pretend to attack Shinei and Neiwaiqian and thus divide the enemy's forces.

On the 22nd day, your subject repeated his orders and launched a broad attack with various battle groups. . . . [Here, Shi Lang describes the groups and their commanders in detail.] Your subject led this powerful fleet forward to Niangma-gong and then attacked all of the batteries and confronted the various enemy gunboats, "birdboats," and silk junks which ventured out from all points to attack us. A huge brass, barbarian, cannon weighing three to four thousand catties [one catty = 1⅓ pounds] was mounted on each bandit gunboat; on each side of the prow of their ships, were arrayed some twenty smaller guns and one to two hundred blunderbusses.

Cannon shot and arrows fell like rain; smoke and flame covered the sky. It was impossible to see even a foot beyond the ships. . . . [Another list of the attackers and the ships they served on follows.] The fighting went on from the early morning until the late afternoon. Our sailors fought without regard for their own lives and used all of their energy to attack and kill the bandits. Eighteen of the bandits' big gunboats were set aflame and destroyed by our navy's incendiary buckets and grenades. Eight other heavy gunboats were sunk by cannon fire. Thirty-six large "birdboats," sixty-seven silk junks, and five refitted foreign ships were also burned and destroyed. Moreover, our navy used the wind to propel incendiary boats into other bandit ships; one "birdboat" and two silk junks were destroyed in this way. The rebellious bandits fought feverishly and when their forces were exhausted packed gunpowder in holds of their own ships and blew themselves up. In this way, they burned nine gunboats and thirteen "birdboats." Some bandits panicked and jumped into the sea and, in this way, we captured two "birdboats," eight silk junks, and twenty-five two-masted junks. What was to be burnt was burnt; those to be killed were killed. . . . [A list of enemy commanders captured by Qing forces follows.] Members of the bandit mob who were burned to death in the fighting, killed in combat, or who blew themselves up or who jumped into the sea and were drowned totaled roughly twelve thousand. Bodies covered the surface of the sea. . . .

The surviving bandits fled north toward Houmen in three small gunboats, two little "birdboats," eleven silk junks, and fifteen two-masted junks. It was discovered that Liu Guoxuan boarded a small, swift vessel and also ran for Houmen. . . . [Shi Lang next lists the names of 165 surrendered enemy commanders and captains and states that 4,853 sailors followed their leaders into captivity.] Your subject, knowing of your majesty's love of human life, pardoned the bandit prisoners and permitted them to reform themselves. They have already been ordered to shave their heads. As a manifestation of our dynasty's dislike of killing and to set an example for others to follow, false commanders and captains of the surrendered forces were presented with robes and honorary caps and the bandit followers were given silver and food. . . . If there are some among the surrendered officers and soldiers who are willing to return to farming, your subject will investigate their original place of registry and contact that prefecture or county in order to have them accepted. The old and the weak will also be discharged. Those who seek to be enlisted in our forces must be supplied with food and wages and I beg for an imperial decree to the Board [of War?] and consultation between the Board and the local governor so that this can be provided. This will enable all who have defected to obtain what they sought and have a place to reside. This will cause the rebels on Taiwan to see the direction of the wind and surrender. After the pacification is completed we will follow this example to deal with our captives. . . .

3.3 FANG BAO'S "RANDOM NOTES FROM PRISON," 1711

During the reign of the Kangxi emperor any sign of affection for the defunct Ming dynasty was regarded as treason. In their writings, scholars or officials who mentioned either the Ming or the southern Ming in sympathetic terms faced harsh penalties. One of the most infamous literary inquisitions of the Kangxi era involved Dai Mingshi (1653–1713), who printed a set of nostalgic essays in 1701 titled *Nanshan ji* (The southern hills collection). Ten years later, when Dai had become a compiler in the Hanlin Academy, he was arrested for having used southern-Ming-reign titles in this work. In the roundups that followed, many of Dai's relatives and friends were taken into custody. Dai himself was decapitated.

One of the scholars implicated by the circles of recrimination was Fang Bao, a close friend of Dai Mingshi and one of the most outstanding prose stylists of his time. Gali, a high Manchu official, accused Fang of writing a preface for Dai's treasonous volume. Fang was cast into prison, where he languished for two years before receiving a pardon. The document translated below is Fang Bao's description of his experience in prison. Its stark portrayal of prison conditions illustrates the perils faced by those who ran afoul of the law in the early Qing era. Only an unceasing flow of silver proferred to the guards and wardens could save one from the worst abuses.

In the third moon of the fifty-first year of the Kangxi emperor [1712], while I was jailed in the prison of the Board of Punishments, I saw three or four dead prisoners dumped out through a hole each day. Mr. Du, the magistrate of Hongdong [a county of Shanxi province], stood up and said: "This comes from an epidemic. Presently things are normal and so there aren't many people who die. In the past, dozens died every day." I asked him why this was so. Mr. Du said: "This kind of illness spreads easily. Even the relatives of those who get it dare not sleep in the same room with them."

In the prison there were four old cells. Each cell had five rooms. The jail guards lived in the center with a window in the front of their quarters for light. At the end of this room there was another opening for ventilation. There were no such windows for the other four rooms and yet more than two hundred prisoners were always confined there. Each day toward dusk, the cells were locked and the odor of the urine and excrement would mingle with that of the food and drink. Moreover, in the coldest months of the winter, the poor prisoners had to sleep on the ground and when the spring breezes came everyone got sick. The established rule in the prison was that the door would be unlocked only at dawn. During the night, the living and the dead slept side by side with no room to turn their bodies and this is why so many people became infected. Even more terrible was that robbers, veteran criminals, and murderers had strong constitutions. Only one or two out of ten would be infected and even so they would recover immediately. Those who died from the malady were all light offenders or sequestered witnesses who would not normally be subjected to legal penalties.

I said: "In the capital there are the metropolitan prefectural prison and the censorial prisons of the five wards. How is it then that the Board of Punishments' prison has so many prisoners?" Mr. Du answered: "In the recent times, the metropolitan prefectural prison and the censorial prisons of the five wards have not dared to take jurisdiction for the more serious cases. Furthermore, in the cases when the city garrison commander orders arrest and interrogation, the prisoners are sent to the Board of Punishments. The chiefs and deputy heads of the Fourteen Bureaus like to get new prisoners; the clerks, prison officials, and guards all benefit from having so many prisoners. If there is the slightest pretext or connection they use every method to trap new prisoners. Once someone is put into the prison his guilt or innocence does not matter. The prisoner's hands and feet are shackled and he is put in one of the old cells until he can bear the suffering no more. Then he is led to obtain bail and permitted to live outside the jail. His family's property is measured to decide the payment and the officials and clerks all split it. Middling households and those just above exhaust their wealth to get bail. Those families somewhat less wealthy seek to have the shackles removed and to obtain lodging [for the prisoner-relative] in the custody sheds outside the jail. This also costs tens of silver taels. As for the poorest prisoners or those with no one to rely on, their shackles are not loosened at all and they are used as examples to warn the others. Sometimes cellmates guilty of serious crimes are bailed out but those guilty of small crimes and the innocent suffer the most poisonous abuse. They store up their anger and indignation, fail to eat or sleep normally, are not treated with medicine, and when they get sick they often die."

"I have humbly witnessed our Emperor's virtuous love for all beings which is as great as that of the sages of the past ages. Whenever he examines the documents related to a case, he tries to find life for those who should die. But now it has come to this [state of affairs] for the innocent. A virtuous gentleman might save many lives if he was to speak to the Emperor saying: 'Leaving aside those prisoners sentenced to death or exiled to the border region for great crimes, should not small offenders and those involved in a case but not convicted be placed in a separate place without chaining their hands and feet?' Some say: 'The jail used to have five rooms called temporary cells. Those who were charged but not convicted lived in them. If this old practice could be restored it would be of some help.'"

Mr. Du said: "The Emperor extends his grace by permitting [convicted] government officials to live in the custody sheds. But now the poor are imprisoned in the old cells and some important criminals live in the sheds. How is it possible to ask the details? It would be better to set up a separate ward to halt this immoral practice." My cellmate Old Zhu, Young Yu, and a certain government official named Seng who all died of illness in prison should not have been heavily punished. There was also a certain person who accused his own son of unfiliality. The [father's] neighbors [involved in the case only as witnesses] were all chained and imprisoned in the old cells. They cried all night long. I was moved by this and so I made inquiries. Everyone corroborated this account and so I am writing this document.

Whenever the death sentence is being carried out, the executioner waits outside the door and lets his confederates enter the cell to ask for money or property. This is called *siluo*. For the rich, they ask the relatives, for the poor they simply ask the condemned man himself. If slicing is the penalty, they say: "If you satisfy me, I will stab you in the heart. Otherwise, even after your four limbs have been sliced to bits, your heart will still be beating." If strangulation is imposed, they say: "If you satisfy me, you will die after the first pull of the garotte. Otherwise, three ropes and other instruments will be used and then you will die." For decapitation there is nothing they can threaten but they can hold the head hostage afterwards. Because of these threats, the rich are obliged to bribe them [the prison personnel] with many dozens of ounces of silver and the poor are forced to sell their clothes. Dealing with those who have nothing, they do as they have said they would. Those who tie up the prisoners for execution also ask for money. If their desires are not satisfied, they break the bones or sinews with the ropes. Every year at the peak time for executions [after the Autumn Assizes], 30 or 40 percent of the condemned are really checked off for execution but 60 to 70 percent are spared for the year. All of the prisoners are bound and taken to the Western Market to await their destiny. If those who are spared are injured by being bound, it will take them months to recover and some have to live with the damage for life. Once I asked an old clerk, "Since there is no animosity between the prisoners and those who tie them up and since the jailers simply want to gain something, would it not be humane, if a person really has nothing, to let the bonds be looser?" He replied, "This is done to set a model for the rest and as a warning to future violators. Were this not so they would take their chances." The beaters are also the same. Among three of my cellmates who were beaten with clubs, one paid thirty taels and his bones were only slightly damaged and he was sick for two months; another paid double and his skin was hurt but he recovered in twenty days; the third paid five times more and was able to walk as usual that very night. Someone asked a beater, "Since some of the prisoners are rich and others poor but all give something, why draw a distinction in punishing them simply because of their payments?" The answer was, "If there were no difference, who would pay more?" . . .

3.4 KANGXI'S VALEDICTORY EDICT, 1717

The imperial edict below was issued by the Kangxi emperor (1654–1722) on December 23, 1717. By this time, Kangxi had ruled China for over fifty years and placed the stamp of his thoughtful and inquiring mind on the workings of the imperial state. The ambitious rivals who threatened the throne at the outset of Kangxi's reign were long since under control. Oboi, Galdan, Wu Sangui, and Koxinga were all dead and the forces they had commanded followed them into oblivion. In the final years of his life, Kangxi was the master of a powerful and unified state.

While one glimpses through this edict the emperor's sense of his own accomplishments, there are also ruminations on mortality and the concerns of ruling a vast and complex state. One of the agonizing difficulties of the final years of Kangxi's reign was the problem of finding an appropriate successor. Until 1712, Kangxi favored his second son, Yinreng, but the erratic and conspiratorial behavior of the heir-apparent made him an impossible choice. By the time of the 1717 edict, Kangxi appeared to favor Yinti, his fourteenth son, for the throne, but the document merely suggests how burdensome this problem had become and makes no explicit reference to how Kangxi intended to resolve it.[1]

When I was young, Heaven gave me great strength, and I didn't know what sickness was. This spring I started to get serious attacks of dizziness and grew increasingly emaciated. Then I went hunting in the autumn beyond the borders, and the fine climate of the Mongolian regions made my spirits stronger day by day, and my face filled out again. Although I was riding and shooting every day, I didn't feel fatigued. After I returned to Peking the Empress Dowager fell ill, and I was dejected in mind; the dizziness grew almost incessant. Since there are some things that I have wanted to say to you on a normal day, I have specially summoned you today to hear my edict, face to face with me.

The rulers of the past all took reverence for Heaven and observance of ancestral precepts as the fundamental way in ruling the country. To be sincere in reverence for Heaven and ancestors entails the following: Be kind to men from afar and keep the able ones near, nourish the people, think of the profit of all as being the real profit and the mind of the whole country as being the real mind, be considerate to officials and act as a father to the people, protect the state before danger comes and govern well before there is any disturbance, be always diligent and always careful, and maintain the balance between leniency and strictness, between

---

1. "Unofficial histories" (*yeshi*) of the Qing era have suggested that Yinzhen (later Emperor Yongzheng), son number four (*si*), erased the character for ten (*shi*), in Kangxi's decree appointing the fourteenth son (*shisi*) as his heir.

principle and expediency, so that long-range plans can be made for the country. That's all there is to it.

No dynasty in history has been as just as ours in gaining the right to rule. The Emperors Taizu and Taizong initially had no intention of taking over the country; and when Taizong's armies were near Peking and his ministers advised him to take it, he replied: "The Ming have not been on good terms with our people, and it would be very easy to conquer them now. But I am aware of what an unbearable act it is to overthrow the ruler of China." Later the roving bandit Li Zicheng stormed the city of Peking, the Ming emperor Chongzhen hanged himself, and the officials and people all came out to welcome us. Then we exterminated the violent bandits and inherited the empire. In olden times, it was Xiang Yu who raised an army and defeated the Qin yet the country then passed to the Han, even though initially Emperor Han Gaozu was only a local constable on the Si River. At the end of the Yuan, it was Chen Yuliang and others who rebelled, yet the country then passed to the Ming, even though initially Emperor Ming Taizu was only a monk in the Huangjue Temple. The forebears of our dynasty were men who obeyed Heaven and lived in harmony with other men; and the empire was pacified. From this we can tell that all the rebellious officials and bandits are finally pushed aside by truly legitimate rulers.

I am now close to seventy, and have been over fifty years on the throne—this is all due to the quiet protection of Heaven and earth and the ancestral spirits; it was not my meager virtue that did it. Since I began reading in my childhood, I have managed to get a rough understanding of the constant historical principles. Every emperor and ruler has been subject to the Mandate of Heaven. Those fated to enjoy old age cannot prevent themselves from enjoying that old age; those fated to enjoy a time of Great Peace cannot prevent themselves from enjoying that Great Peace.

Over 4,350 years have passed from the first year of the Yellow Emperor to the present, and over three hundred emperors are listed as having reigned, though the data from the Three Dynasties—that is, for the period before the Qin burning of the books—are not wholly credible. In the 1,960 years from the first year of Qin Shihuang to the present, there have been 211 people who have been named emperor and have taken era names. What man am I, that among all those who have reigned long since the Qin and Han dynasties, it should be I who have reigned the longest?

Among the Ancients, only those who were not boastful and knew not to go too far could attain a good end. Since the Three Dynasties, those who ruled long did not leave a good name to posterity, while those who did not live long did not know the world's grief. I am already old, and have reigned long, and I cannot foretell what posterity will think of me. Besides which, because of what is going on now, I cannot hold back my tears of bitterness; and so I have prepared these notes to make my own record, for I still fear that the country may not know the depth of my sorrow.

Many emperors and rulers in the past made a taboo of the subject of death, and as we look at their valedictory decrees we find that they are not at all written in imperial tones, and do not record what the emperor really wanted to say. It was always when the emperors were weak and dying that they found some scholar-official to write out something as he chose.

With me it is different. I am letting you know what my sincerest feelings are in advance.

When I had been twenty years on the throne I didn't dare conjecture that I might reign thirty. After thirty years I didn't dare conjecture that I might reign forty. Now I have reigned fifty-seven years. The "Great Plan" section of the *Book of History* says of the five joys:

> The first is long life;
> The second is riches;
> The third is soundness of body and serenity of mind;
> The fourth is the love of virtue;
> The fifth is an end crowning the life.

The "end crowning the life" is placed last because it is so hard to attain. I am now approaching seventy, and my sons, grandsons, and great-grandsons number over 150. The country is more or less at peace and the world is at peace. Even if we haven't improved all manners and customs, and made all the people prosperous and contented, yet I have worked with unceasing diligence and intense watchfulness, never resting, never idle. So for decades I have exhausted all my strength, day after day. How can all this just be summed up in a two-word phrase like "hard work"?

Those among the rulers of earlier dynasties who did not live long have all been judged in the Histories as having caused this themselves through their own wild excesses, by overaddiction to drink and sex. Such remarks are just the sneers of pedants who have to find some blemishes in even the purest and most perfect of rulers. I exonerate these earlier rulers, because the affairs of the country are so troublesome that one can't help getting exhausted. Zhuge Liang said: "I shall bow down in service and wear myself out until death comes," but among all the officials only Zhuge Liang acted in this way. Whereas the emperor's responsibilities are terribly heavy, there is no way he can evade them. How can this be compared with being an official? If an official wants to serve, then he serves; if he wants to stop, then he stops. When he grows old he resigns and returns home, to look after his sons and play with his grandsons; he still has the chance to relax and enjoy himself. Whereas the ruler in all his hardworking life finds no place to rest. Thus, though the Emperor Shun said, "Through non-action one governs," he died in Cangwu [while on tour of inspection]; and after four years on the throne Emperor Yu had blistered hands and feet and found death in Kuaiqi. To work as hard at government as these men, to travel on inspection, to have never a leisure moment—how can this be called the valuing of "non-action" or tranquilly looking after oneself? In the *I Ching* hexagram "Retreat" not one of the six lines deals with a ruler's concerns—from this we can see that there is no place for rulers to rest, and no resting place to which they can retreat. "Bowing down in service and wearing oneself out" indeed applied to this situation.

All the Ancients used to say that the emperor should concern himself with general principles, but need not deal with the smaller details. I find that I cannot agree with this. Careless handling of one item might bring harm to the whole world; a moment's carelessness could damage all future generations. Failure to attend to details will end up endangering your greater virtues. So I always attend carefully to the details. For example: if I neglect a couple of matters today and leave them unsettled, there will be a couple more matters for tomorrow. And if tomorrow I again don't want to be bothered, that will pile up even more obstructions for the future. The emperor's work is of great importance, and there should not be delays, so I attend to all matters, whether they are great or small. Even if it is just one character wrong in a memorial, I always correct it before forwarding it. Not to neglect anything, that is my nature. For over fifty years I have usually prepared in advance for things—and the world's millions all honor my virtuous intentions. How can one still hold to "there being no need to deal with the smaller details"?

I was strong from my childhood onward, with fine muscles; I could bend a bow with a pull of 15 *li*, and fire a fifty-two inch arrow. I was good at using troops and confronting the enemy, but I have never recklessly killed a single person. In pacifying the Three Feudatories and clearing out the northern deserts, I made all the plans myself. Unless it was for military matters or famine relief, I didn't take funds from the Board of Revenue treasury, and spent nothing recklessly, for the reason that this was the people's wealth. On my inspection tours, I didn't set out colored embroideries, and the expenses at each place were only 10,000 or 20,000 taels. In comparison, the annual expense on the river conservancy system is over 3,000,000—so the cost was not even one percent of that.

When I studied as a child, I already knew that one should be careful with drink and sex, and guard against mean people. So I grew old without illness. But after my serious illness in the forty-seventh year of my reign, my spirits had been too much wounded, and gradually I failed to regain my former state. Moreover, every day there was my work, all requiring decisions; frequently I felt that my vitality was slipping away and my internal energy diminishing. I fear that in the future if some accident happened to me I would not be able to say a word, and so my real feelings would not be disclosed. Wouldn't that be regretful? Therefore I am using this occasion when I feel clear-headed and lively to complete my life by telling you all that can be revealed, item by item. Isn't that wonderful?

All men who live must die. As Zhu Xi said, "The principle of the cyclical cosmic forces is like dawn and night." And Confucius said, "Live contentedly and await Heaven's will." These sayings express the great Way of the Sages, so why should we be afraid? I have been seriously ill recently: my mind was blurred and my body exhausted. As I moved around, if no one held me up by the arms it was hard for me to walk. In the past I fixed my mind on my responsibilities to the country; to work "until death comes" was my goal. Now that I am ill I am querulous and forgetful, and terrified of muddling right with wrong, and leaving my work in chaos. I exhaust my mind for the country's sake, and fragment my spirits for the world. When your wits aren't guarding your body, your heart has no nourishment, your eyes can't tell far from near nor ears distinguish true from false, and you eat little and have a lot to do—how can you last long? Moreover, since the country has long been at peace and people have grown lazy, joy goes and sorrows mount, "peace" departs and "stagnation" comes. When the head is crammed with trifles, the limbs are indolent—until everything is in ruins and you inevitably bring down at random and together calamities from Heaven and destruction for men. Even if you want to do something, your vitality is insufficient, and by then it's too late to admit your mistakes. No more can you be roused up, and moaning in your bed you'll die with eyes open—won't you feel anguish just before you die?

Emperor Wudi of the Liang was a martial dynastic founder, but when he reached old age he was forced by Hou-ching into the tragedy at Taicheng. Emperor Wendi of the Sui also was a founding emperor, but he could not anticipate the evil ways of his son Yangdi and was finally unable to die in peace. There are other examples, like killing oneself by taking cinnabar, or being poisoned and eating the cakes, or the case of Song Taizu, when people saw the candlelight from afar. There are records of all kinds of suspicious cases—are these not tracks of the past that we can see? All these happened because [the emperors] didn't understand in time. And all brought harm to country and people. Han Gaozu told Empress Lu about the mandate; Tang Taizong decided on the heir apparent with Zhangsun Wuji. When I read such things I feel deeply ashamed. Perhaps there are mean persons who hope to use the confusion, and will act on their own authority to alter the succession, pushing someone forward in expectation of future rewards. As long as I still have one breath left, how could I tolerate that sort of thing?

My birth was nothing miraculous—nor did anything extraordinary happen when I grew up. I came to the throne at eight, fifty-seven years ago. I've never let people talk on about supernatural influences of the kind that have been recorded in the Histories: lucky stars, auspicious clouds, unicorns and phoenixes, *chih* grass and such like blessings, or burning pearls and jade in the front of the palace, or heavenly books sent down to manifest Heaven's will. Those are all empty words, and I don't presume so far. I just go on each day in an ordinary way, and concentrate on ruling properly.

Now, officials have memorialized, requesting that I set up an heir-apparent to share duties with me—that's because they feared my life might end abruptly. Death and life are ordinary phenomena—I've never avoided talking about them. It's just that all the power of the country has to be united in one person. For the last ten years, I've been writing out (and keeping sealed) what I intend to do and what my feelings are, though I haven't finished yet. Appointing the heir-apparent is a great matter; how could I neglect it? The throne of this country is one of the utmost importance. If I were to relieve myself of this burden and relax in comfort, disentangling my mind from every problem, then I could certainly expect to live longer. You officials have all received great mercies from me—how can I attain the day when I will have no more burdens?

My energies have shrunk, I have to force myself to endure, and if everything finally goes awry, won't the hard work of the last fifty-seven years indeed be wasted? It is my intense sincerity that leads me to say this. Whenever I read an old official's memorial requesting retirement, I can't stop the tears from flowing. You all have a time for retiring, but where can I find rest? But if I could have a few weeks to restore myself and a chance to conclude my life with a natural death, then my happiness would be indescribable. There is time ahead of me; maybe I will live as long as Song Gaozong. We cannot tell.

Not until I was fifty-seven did I begin to have a few white hairs in my beard, and I was offered some lotion to make it black again. But I laughed and refused, saying: "How many white-haired emperors have there been in the past? If my hair and whiskers whiten, won't that be a splendid tale for later generations?" Not one man is now left from those who worked with me in my early years. Those who came later to their new appointments are harmonious and respectful with their colleagues, they are just and law-abiding, and their white heads fill the Court. This has been the case for a long time, and for this I am grateful.

I have enjoyed the veneration of my country and the riches of the world; there is no object I do not have, nothing I have not experienced. But now that I have reached old age I cannot rest easy for a moment. Therefore, I regard the whole country as a worn-out sandal, and all riches as mud and sand. If I can die without there being an outbreak of trouble, my desires will be fulfilled. I wish all of you officials to remember that I have been the peace-bearing Son of Heaven for over fifty years, and that what I have said to you over and over again is really sincere. Then that will complete this fitting end to my life.

I've been preparing this edict for ten years. If a "valedictory edict" is issued, let it contain nothing but these same words.

I've revealed my entrails and shown my guts, there's nothing left within me to reveal.

I will say no more.

CHAPTER 4 | # Yongzheng's Authority

4.1 AND 4.2 KANGXI'S SACRED EDICT AND WANG YUPU AND YONGZHENG'S AMPLIFICATION

The purpose of Kangxi's sixteen hortatory maxims, each expressed in seven characters, was to articulate an ethical and moral framework for subjects of the Qing state. In 1724, the Yongzheng emperor issued an amplified version of his father's maxims in literary Chinese. Soon thereafter, Wang Yupu, a Shaanxi salt commissioner, wrote an expanded third version in a colloquial style. This last version was read aloud at yamens throughout the empire twice a month.

A full translation is provided below of the original Sacred Edict, followed by portions of Wang Yupu's vernacular exposition of the Yongzheng text. For the Confucian ruler, well-managed families and harmonious personal relations were the foundation of an orderly state, and both the Kangxi and Yongzheng versions of the Sacred Edict stressed this basic principle.

4.1 *The Sacred Edict of the Kangxi Emperor, 1670*

THE SIXTEEN MAXIMS (SHENGYU)

1. Strengthen filial piety and brotherly affection to emphasize human relations.
2. Strengthen clan relations to illustrate harmony.
3. Pacify relations between local groups to put an end to quarrels and litigation.

4. Stress agriculture and sericulture so that there may be sufficient food and clothing.
5. Prize frugality so as to make careful use of wealth.
6. Promote education to improve the habits of scholars.
7. Extirpate heresy to exalt orthodoxy.
8. Speak of the law to give warning to the stupid and stubborn.
9. Clarify rites and manners to improve customs.
10. Let each work at his own occupation so that the people's minds will be settled.
11. Instruct young people to prevent them from doing wrong.
12. Prevent false accusations to shield the law-abiding.
13. Prohibit sheltering of runaways to avoid being implicated in their crime.
14. Pay taxes to avoid being pressed for payment.
15. Unite the *baojia*[1] system to eliminate theft and armed robbery.
16. Resolve hatred and quarrels to respect life.

4.2 Wang Yupu and Yongzheng's Amplification of Kangxi's Sacred Edict, 1724

1. AMPLIFICATION OF MAXIM TWO: STRENGTHEN CLAN RELATIONS TO ILLUSTRATE HARMONY.

... The clan is like the water of a spring which branches into several streams and then dozens of streams as it emerges. But all of these branches originated from the same spring. It is also like a tree which grows a thousand branches and ten thousand leaves that all emerge from the same root. A clan, whether it is divided into a branch of several dozens of able bodied men or hundreds of men, comes from the same body of the same ancestor. The clan members are like the hands, feet, ears, eyes, mouth, nose, and other parts of the ancestor's body; when you put them together they are one body. Just think, if there is a sore on my body or if I sprain my ankle or break my leg, doesn't my whole body feel uncomfortable? If you try to entrap or harm a clan member or insult or cheat him and make him feel uncomfortable, can you imagine that you will feel happy? You should treat them as you would yourself. You should look at clan members as part of one body; if one place hurts then all other places will hurt. If one spot itches, all spots will itch. Only when the blood flows throughout the body will things be as they should be. Therefore,

---

1. Mutual surveillance organizations in the countryside used to preserve order and monitor taxation.

the ancients said: 'To educate the people, filial piety, brotherly affection, harmony, love, willingness to endure for others, and charity are necessary.' When it [the section of the ancient classic the *Zhouli* quoted by Yongzheng] says filial piety, next it says brotherly affection and then it says harmony and that's because clan members are descended from the same ancestor. If someone does not want harmony in his own clan he is unfilial and goes against brotherly affection. . . .

2. AMPLIFICATION OF MAXIM SEVEN: EXTIRPATE HERESY TO EXALT ORTHODOXY.

. . . What is heterodoxy? From ancient times there have been three teachings. Besides Confucian scholars there are Buddhist monks and Taoist priests. These latter sects are heretical. All the Buddhist priests talk about is meditation, enlightenment, and becoming a Buddha. They also say: 'If one son becomes a monk, the whole clan will ascend to heaven.' Just think about it, who has ever seen a Buddha? What is a Buddha? Buddha is in the heart. What is the meaning of chanting the name of the Buddha? It is for the mind to be constantly concerned about the heart. If the heart is good this is Buddha.

Just look at their sutras. The first sutra is the Heart Sutra. All the Heart Sutra says is that the heart should be straight; it should not be twisted or devious. It should be honest and not false and lying. It should be frank and not unclean. If one can cut oneself off from greed, anger, and stupid attachments and be, in all things, like a flower in a looking glass or the moon in water, then all doubts and fears will cease and the heart will be perfect. Therefore, Master Zhu Xi of the Song dynasty said: 'Buddhism does not concern itself with anything in the four corners of the universe but is concerned simply with the heart.' This sentence goes to the bottom of Buddhism and expresses it entirely.

. . . All this talk about fasts, processions, building temples, and making idols is invented by idle and lazy Buddhists monks and Taoist priests as a plan for swindling you. But you want to believe them and not only go yourselves to burn incense and worship in their temples but also ask your wives and daughters to go to the temples to burn incense. With oiled hair and powdered faces, dressed in bright colors, they crowd and jostle shoulder to shoulder with these Taoist and Buddhist priests and riffraff. Where the 'practicing goodness' comes in nobody knows, but many vile things are done that provoke anger, vexation, and ridicule. . . .

. . . As for reciting prayers to Buddha: You say it does good and that by burning paper, offering presents, and performing services for the release of souls, calamity may be averted, sin destroyed, happiness increased, and life prolonged. Now just consider, it has always been said: 'The wise and upright are divine.' If someone is a divine Buddha, how can he be greedy for your contributions of silver in order to protect you? And if you don't burn paper money and make sacrifices, and the 'divine Buddha' then gets angry and sends a calamity down upon you, is he not a mean person? Take the example of your local official. If you attend to your own business and are a good person, even if you don't go to flatter him, he will still naturally regard you with respect. If you do evil and behave in a bullying and presumptuous way, even if you think of a hundred ways to flatter him, he will still be angry with you and get rid of you to spare the people harm. You say: 'If we repeat the Buddha's name we can be rid of our sins.' If you do something evil and break the law and then cry out, 'Your honor,' a thousand times in a loud voice when you reach the yamen, will he pardon you? Every time you do something, you ask several monks and Taoists to chant the sutras and carry out rituals. It is said that chanting the sutras secures peace, averts disaster, and prolongs happiness and life. Suppose you don't follow the teachings in the Sacred Edict, but instead merely recite it several thousand times or tens of thousands of times. It is unlikely that the Emperor will be so pleased with you that you will be given an official post or rewarded with silver.

. . . To be perfectly loyal to the Ruler and to fulfill filial duty to the utmost is the whole duty of man and the means of obtaining the blessing of heaven. If you do not seek happiness which is not your lot in life and do not meddle in matters that do not concern you but simply mind your own business, you will enjoy the protection of the gods. Farmers should look after farming. Soldiers should go about their patrols and garrison duties. Each should attend to his own occupation and duties and then the realm will be naturally at peace and the people will be naturally happy. If none of you believe in heretical sects, they will not have to wait to be driven out but will become extinct naturally.

3. AMPLIFICATION OF MAXIM EIGHT: SPEAK OF THE LAW TO GIVE WARNING TO THE STUPID AND STUBBORN.

. . . Is it possible that the State could enjoy beating and decapitating people? It is only because the people do not learn to be good and do not obey instructions that there is no other alternative than to use the penal law to control them. Since in many cases, the people break the law because they do not know it, this book has been compiled to instruct them to be good people and not bad people. For those who do bad, punishment is proportional to the offense, but even should you merely curse someone or take a blade of grass or stick of wood you will not escape the law.

. . . The law contains a profound meaning and was originally drawn up in accordance with human nature. If everyone knew the meaning of the law, they would not break it. There would be nobody in the prisons and few litigations. It follows that it is best to warn people before they break the law and to frequently warn them rather than waiting for them to break the law and then punishing them.

But you are also aware that breaking the law is not good and yet you incessantly disobey it. What is the reason for this? It is entirely because you do not understand

CHAPTER 5

Chinese Society and the Reign of Qianlong

5.1 *THE SCHOLARS*: "FAN JIN PASSES THE *JUREN* EXAMINATION"

The Scholars (Rulin waishi) was probably written between 1740 and 1750. An example of the mode of satirical realism in Chinese literature, the novel captures the moods and tensions of everyday life in Qing China. Like the contemporaneous works of Henry Fielding, *The Scholars* provides a witty portrait of the pretensions and hypocrisies of society.

The author, Wu Jingzi (1701–1754), was the son of a noted family from Anhui. Despite repeated attempts for higher achievements, he succeeded only in obtaining the *xiucai,* the lowest examination title. In his own village Wu was apparently denigrated as a ne'er-do-well. In 1733 he left for Nanjing, where in his middle and later years he lived in somewhat straitened circumstances, in the company of other "failed" scholars.

Frustrated and disillusioned, Wu Jingzi drew up on his own experiences and those of his friends to attack the suffocating formalism and false social hierarchies produced by the examination system. In "Fan Jin Passes the *Juren* Examination," he shows how a scorned middle-aged scholar is drastically elevated in the esteem of his neighbors when he passes the provincial-level exam. This chapter of the novel is frequently anthologized because of the clarity of its style and the powerful swipes it takes at the myths and false ideals of the examination system.

Soon it was time to go to the examination in the capital. Zhou Jin's traveling expenses and clothes were provided by Jin. He passed the metropolitan examination too; and after the palace examination he was given an official post. In three years he rose to the rank of censor and was appointed commissioner of education for Guangdong Province.

Now though Zhou Jin engaged several secretaries, he thought, "I had bad luck myself so long; now that I'm in office I mean to read all the papers carefully. I must not leave everything to my secretaries, and suppress real talent." Having come to this decision, he went to Canton to take up his post. The day after his arrival he burnt incense, posted up placards, and held two examinations.

The third examination was for candidates from Nanhai and Panyu counties. Commissioner Zhou sat in the hall and watched the candidates crowding in. There were young and old, handsome and homely, smart and shabby men among them. The last candidate to enter was thin and sallow, had a grizzled beard and was wearing an old felt hat. Guangdong has a warm climate; still, this was the twelfth month, and yet this candidate had on a linen gown only, so he was shivering with cold as he took his paper and went to his cell. Zhou Jin made a mental note of this before sealing up their doors. During the first interval, from his seat at the head of the hall he watched this candidate in the linen gown come up to hand in his paper. The man's clothes were so threadbare that a few more holes had appeared since he went into the cell. Commissioner Zhou looked at his own garments—his magnificent crimson robe and gilt belt—then he referred to the register of names, and asked, "You are Fan Jin, aren't you?"

Kneeling, Fan Jin answered, "Yes, Your Excellency."

"How old are you this year?"

"I gave my age as thirty. Actually, I am fifty-four."

"How many times have you taken the examination?"

"I first went in for it when I was twenty, and I have taken it over twenty times since then."

"How is it you have never passed?"

"My essays are too poor," replied Fan Jin, "so none of the honorable examiners will pass me."

"That may not be the only reason," said Commissioner Zhou. "Leave your paper here, and I will read it through carefully."

Fan Jin kowtowed and left.

It was still early, and no other candidates were coming to hand in their papers, so Commissioner Zhou picked up Fan Jin's essay and read it through. But he was disappointed. "Whatever is the fellow driving at in this essay?" he wondered. "I see now why he never passed." He put it aside. However, when no other candidates appeared, he thought, "I might as well have another look at Fan Jin's paper. If he shows the least talent, I'll pass him to reward his perseverance." He read it through again, and this time felt there was something in it. He was just going to read it through once more, when another candidate came up to hand in his paper.

This man knelt down, and said, "Sir, I beg for an oral test."

"I have your paper here," said Commissioner Zhou kindly. "What need is there for an oral test?"

"I can compose poems in all the ancient styles. I beg you to set a subject to test me."

The commissioner frowned and said, "Since the emperor attaches importance to essays, why should you bring up the poems of the Han and Tang dynasties? A candidate like you should devote all his energy to writing compositions, instead of wasting time on heterodox studies. I have come here at the imperial command to examine essays, not to discuss miscellaneous literary forms with you. This devotion to superficial things means that your real work must be neglected. No doubt your essay is nothing but flashy talk, not worth reading. Attendants! Drive him out!" At the word of command, attendants ran in from both sides to seize the candidate and push him outside the gate.

But although Commissioner Zhou had had this man driven out, he still read his paper. This candidate was called Wei Haogu, and he wrote in a tolerably clear and straightforward style. "I will pass him lowest on the list," Zhou Jin decided. And, taking up his brush, he made a mark at the end of the paper as a reminder.

Then he read Fan Jin's paper again. This time he gave a gasp of amazement. "Even I failed to understand this paper the first two times I read it!" he exclaimed. "But, after reading it for the third time, I realize it is the most wonderful essay in the world—every word a pearl. This shows how often bad examiners must have suppressed real genius." Hastily taking up his brush, he carefully drew three circles on Fan Jin's paper, marking it as first. He then picked up Wei Haogu's paper again, and marked it as twentieth. After this he collected all the other essays and took them away with him.

Soon the results were published, and Fan Jin's name was first on the list. When he went in to see the commissioner, Zhou Jin commended him warmly. And when the last successful candidate—Wei Haogu—went in, Commissioner Zhou gave him some encouragement and advised him to work hard and stop studying miscellaneous works. Then, to the sound of drums and trumpets, the successful candidates left.

The next day, Commissioner Zhou set off for the capital. Fan Jin alone escorted him for ten miles of the way, doing reverence before his chair. Then the commissioner called him to his side. "First-class honors go to the mature," he said. "Your essay showed real maturity, and you are certain to do well in the provincial examination too. After I have made my report to the authorities, I will wait for you in the capital."

Fan Jin kowtowed again in thanks, then stood to one side of the road as the examiner's chair was carried swiftly off. Only when the banners had passed out of sight behind the next hill did he turn back to his lodgings to settle his bill. His home was about fifteen miles from the city, and he had to travel all night to reach it. He bowed to his mother, who lived with him in a thatched cottage with a thatched shed outside, his mother occupying the front room and his wife the back one. His wife was the daughter of Butcher Hu of the market.

Fan Jin's mother and wife were delighted by his success. They were preparing a meal when his father-in-law arrived, bringing pork sausages and a bottle of wine. Fan Jin greeted him, and they sat down together.

"Since I had the bad luck to marry my daughter to a scarecrow like you," said Butcher Hu, "Heaven knows how much you have cost me. Now I must have done some good deed to make you pass the examination. I've brought this wine to celebrate."

Fan Jin assented meekly, and called his wife to cook the sausages and warm the wine. He and his father-in-law sat in the thatched shed, while his mother and wife prepared food in the kitchen.

"Now that you have become a gentleman," went on Butcher Hu, "you must do things in proper style. Of course, men in my profession are decent, high-class people; and I am your elder too—you mustn't put on any airs before me. But these peasants round here, dung-carriers and the like, are low people. If you greet them and treat them as equals, that will be a breach of etiquette and will make me lose face too. You're such an easy-going, good-for-nothing fellow, I'm telling you this for your own good, so that you won't make a laughingstock of yourself."

"Your advice is quite right, father," replied Fan Jin.

"Let your mother eat with us too," went on Butcher Hu. "She has only vegetables usually—it's a shame! Let my daughter join us too. She can't have tasted lard more than two or three times since she married you a dozen years ago, poor thing!"

So Fan Jin's mother and wife sat down to share the meal with them. They ate until sunset, by which time Butcher Hu was tipsy. Mother and son thanked him profusely; then, throwing his jacket over his shoulders, the butcher staggered home bloated. The next day Fan Jin had to call on relatives and friends.

Wei Haogu invited him to meet some other fellow candidates, and since it was the year for the provincial examination they held a number of literary meetings. Soon it was the end of the sixth month. Fan Jin's fellow candidates asked him to go with them to the provincial capital for the examination, but he had no money for the journey. He went to ask his father-in-law to help.

Butcher Hu spat in his face, and poured out a torrent of abuse. "Don't be a fool!" he roared. "Just passing one examination has turned your head completely— you're like a toad trying to swallow a swan! And I hear that you scraped through not because of your essay, but because the examiner pitied you for being so old. Now, like a fool, you want to pass the higher examination and become an official. But do you know who those officials are? They are all stars in heaven! Look at the Chang family in the city. All those officials have pots of money, dignified faces, and big ears. But your mouth sticks out and you've a chin like an ape's. You should piss on the ground and look at your face in the puddle! You look like a monkey, yet you want to become an official. Come off it! Next year I shall find a teaching job for you with one of my friends so that you can make a few taels of silver to support that old, never-dying mother of yours and your wife—and it's high time you did!

Yet you ask me for traveling expenses! I kill just one pig a day, and make only ten cents per pig. If I give you all my silver to play ducks and drakes with, my family will have to live on air." The butcher went on cursing at full blast, till Fan Jin's head spun.

When he got home again, he thought to himself, "Commissioner Zhou said that I showed maturity. And, from ancient times till now, who ever passed the first examination without going in for the second? I shan't rest easy till I've taken it." So he asked his fellow candidates to help him, and went to the city, without telling his father-in-law, to take the examination. When the examination was over he returned home, only to find that his family had had no food for two days. And Butcher Hu cursed him again.

The day the results came out there was nothing to eat in the house, and Fan Jin's mother told him, "Take that hen of mine to the market and sell it; then buy a few measures of rice to make gruel. I'm faint with hunger."

Fan Jin tucked the hen under his arm and hurried out.

He had only been gone an hour or so, when gongs sounded and three horsemen galloped up. They alighted, tethered their horses to the shed, and called out: "Where is the honorable Mr. Fan? We have come to congratulate him on passing the provincial examination."

Not knowing what had happened, Fan Jin's mother had hidden herself in the house for fear. But when she heard that he had passed, she plucked up courage to poke her head out and say, "Please come in and sit down. My son has gone out."

"So this is the old lady," said the heralds. And they pressed forward to demand a tip.

In the midst of this excitement two more batches of horsemen arrived. Some squeezed inside while the others packed themselves into the shed, where they had to sit on the ground. Neighbors gathered round, too, to watch; and the flustered old lady asked one of them to go to look for her son. The neighbor ran to the marketplace, but Fan Jin was nowhere to be seen. Only when he reached the cast end of the market did he discover the scholar, clutching the hen tightly against his chest and holding a sales sign in one hand. Fan Jin was pacing slowly along, looking right and left for a customer.

"Go home quickly, Mr. Fan!" cried the neighbor. "Congratulations! You have passed the provincial examination. Your house is full of heralds."

Thinking this fellow was making fun of him, Fan Jin pretended not to hear, and walked forward with a lowered head. Seeing that he paid no attention, the neighbor went up to him and tried to grab the hen.

"Why are you taking my hen?" protested Fan Jin. "You don't want to buy it."

"You have passed," insisted the neighbor. "They want you to go home and to send off the heralds."

"Good neighbor," said Fan Jin, "we have no rice left at home, so I have to sell this hen. It's a matter of life and death. This is no time for jokes! Do go away, so as not to spoil my chance of a sale."

When the neighbor saw that Fan Jin did not believe him, he seized the hen, threw it to the ground and dragged his scholar back by main force to his home.

The heralds cried, "Good! The newly honored one is back." They pressed forward to congratulate him. But Fan Jin brushed past them into the house to look at the official announcement, already hung up, which read: "This is to announce that the master of your honorable mansion, Fan Jin, has passed the provincial examination in Guangdong, coming seventh in the list. May better news follow in rapid succession!"

Fan Jin feasted his eyes on the announcement, and, after reading it through once to himself, read it once more aloud. Clapping his hands, he laughed and exclaimed, "Ha! Good! I have passed." Then, stepping back, he fell down in a dead faint. His mother hastily poured some boiled water between his lips, whereupon he recovered consciousness and struggled to his feet. Clapping his hands again, he let out a peal of laughter and shouted, "Aha! I've passed! I've passed!" Laughing wildly he ran outside, giving the heralds and the neighbors the fright of their lives. Not far from the front door he slipped and fell into a pond. When he clambered out, his hair was disheveled, his hands muddied and his whole body dripping with slime. But nobody could stop him. Still clapping his hands and laughing, he headed straight for the market.

They all looked at each other in consternation, and said, "The new honor has sent him off his head!"

His mother wailed, "Aren't we out of luck! Why should passing an examination do this to him? Now he's mad, goodness knows when he'll get better."

"He was all right this morning when he went out," said his wife. "What could have brought on this attack? What *shall* we do?"

The neighbors consoled them. "Don't be upset," they said. "We will send a couple of men to keep an eye on Mr. Fan. And we'll all bring wine and eggs and rice for these heralds. Then we can discuss what's to be done."

The neighbors brought eggs or wine, lugged along sacks of rice or carried over chickens. Fan Jin's wife wailed as she prepared the food in the kitchen. Then she took it to the shed, neighbors brought tables and stools, and they asked the heralds to sit down to a meal while they discussed what to do.

"I have an idea," said one of the heralds. "But I don't know whether it will work or not."

"What idea?" they asked.

"There must be someone the honorable Mr. Fan usually stands in awe of," said the herald. "He's only been thrown off his balance because sudden joy made him choke on his phlegm. If you can get someone he's afraid of to slap him in the face and say, 'It's all a joke. You haven't passed any examination!'—then the fright will make him cough up his phlegm, and he'll come to his senses again."

They all clapped their hands and said, "That's a fine idea. Mr. Fan is more afraid of Butcher Hu than of anyone else. Let's hurry up and fetch him. He's probably still in the market, and hasn't yet heard the news."

"If he were selling meat in the market, he would have heard the news by now," said a neighbor. "He went out at dawn to the cast market to fetch pigs, and he can't have come back yet. Someone had better go quickly to find him."

One of the neighbors hurried off in search of the butcher, and presently met him on the road, followed by an assistant who was carrying seven or eight catties of meat and four or five strings of cash.[1] Butcher Hu was coming to offer his congratulations. Fan Jin's mother, crying bitterly, told him what had happened.

"How could he be so unlucky!" exclaimed the butcher. They were calling for him outside, so he gave the meat and the money to his daughter, and went out. The heralds put their plan before him, but Butcher Hu demurred.

"He may be my son-in-law," he said, "but he's an official[2] now—one of the stars in heaven. How can you hit one of the stars in heaven? I've heard that whoever hits the stars in heaven will be carried away by the King of Hell, given a hundred strokes with an iron rod, and shut up in the eighteenth hell, never to become a human being again. I daren't do a thing like that."

"Mr. Hu!" cried a sarcastic neighbor. "You make your living by killing pigs. Every day the blade goes in white and comes out red. After all the blood you've shed, the King of Hell must have marked you down for several thousand strokes by iron rods, so what does it matter if he adds a hundred more? Quite likely he will have used up all his iron rods before getting round to beating you for this, anyway. Or maybe, if you cure your son-in-law, the King of Hell may consider that as a good deed, and promote you from the eighteenth hell to the seventeenth."

"This is not time for joking," protested one of the heralds. "This is the only way to handle it, Mr. Hu. There's nothing else for it, so please don't make difficulties."

Butcher Hu had to give in. Two bowls of wine bolstered up his courage, making him lose his scruples and start his usual rampaging. Rolling up his greasy sleeves, he strode off toward the market, followed by small groups of neighbors.

Fan Jin's mother ran out and called after him, "Just frighten him a little! Mind you don't hurt him!"

"Of course," the neighbors reassured her. "That goes without saying."

When they reached the market, they found Fan Jin standing in the doorway of a temple. His hair was tousled, his face streaked with mud, and one of his shoes had come off. But he was still clapping his hands and crowing, "Aha! I've passed! I've passed!"

Butcher Hu bore down on him like an avenging fury, roaring, "You blasted idiot! What have you passed?" and fetched him a blow. The bystanders and neighbors could hardly suppress their laughter. But although Butcher Hu had screwed up his courage to strike once, he was still afraid at heart, and his hand was trembling too much to strike a second time. The one blow, however, had been enough to knock Fan Jin out.

1. Round coins with a square hole that were threaded through with string for convenience.

2. A scholar who passed the provincial examination was sometimes eligible for such posts as that of a county magistrate.

The neighbors pressed round to rub Fan Jin's chest and massage his back, until presently he gave a sigh and came to. His eyes were clear and his madness had passed! They helped him up and borrowed a bench from Apothecary Chen, a hunchback who lived by the temple, so that Fan Jin might sit down.

Butcher Hu, who was standing a little way off, felt his hand begin to ache; when he raised his palm, he found to his dismay that he could not bend it. "It's true, then, that you mustn't strike the stars in heaven," he thought. "Now Buddha is punishing me!" The more he thought about it, the worse his hand hurt, and he asked the apothecary to give him some ointment for it.

Meanwhile Fan Jin was looking round and asking, "How do I come to be sitting here? My mind has been in a whirl, as if in a dream."

The neighbors said, "Congratulations, sir, on having passed the examination! A short time ago, in your happiness, you brought up some phlegm; but just now you spat out several mouthfuls and recovered. Please go home quickly to send away the heralds."

"That's right," said Fan Jin. "And I seem to remember coming seventh in the list." As he was speaking, he fastened up his hair and asked the apothecary for a basin of water to wash his face, while one of the neighbors found his shoe and helped him put it on.

The sight of his father-in-law made Fan Jin afraid that he was in for another cursing. But Butcher Hu stepped forward and said, "Worthy son-in-law, I would never have presumed to slap you just now if not for your mother. She sent me to help you."

"That was what I call a friendly slap," said one of the neighbors. "Wait till Mr. Fan finishes washing his face. I bet he can easily wash off half a basin of lard!"

"Mr. Hu!" said another. "This hand of yours will be too good to kill pigs any more."

"No, indeed," replied the butcher. "Why should I go on killing pigs? My worthy son-in-law will be able to support me in style for the rest of my life. I always said that this worthy son-in-law of mine was very learned and handsome, and that not one of those Zhang and Zhou family officials in the city looked so much the fine gentleman. I have always been a good judge of character, I don't mind telling you. My daughter stayed at home till she was more than thirty, although many rich families wanted to marry her to their sons; but I saw signs of good fortune in her face, and knew that she would end up marrying an official. You see today how right I was." He gave a great guffaw, and they all started to laugh.

When Fan Jin had washed and drunk the tea brought him by the apothecary, they all started back, Fan Jin in front, Butcher Hu and the neighbors behind. The butcher, noticing that the seat of his son-in-law's gown was crumpled, kept bending forward all the way home to tug out the creases for him.

When they reached Fan Jin's house, Butcher Hu shouted: "The master is back!" The old lady came out to greet them, and was overjoyed to find her son no longer mad. The heralds, she told them, had already been sent off with the money that Butcher Hu had brought. Fan Jin bowed to his mother and thanked his father-in-law, making Butcher Hu so embarrassed that he muttered, "That bit of money was nothing."

After thanking the neighbors too, Fan Jin was just going to sit down when a smart-looking retainer hurried in, holding a big red card, and announced, "Mr. Zhang has come to pay his respects to the newly successful Mr. Fan."

By this time the sedan-chair was already at the door. Butcher Hu dived into his daughter's room and dared not come out, while the neighbors scattered in all directions. Fan Jin went out to welcome the visitor, who was one of the local gentry, and Mr. Zhang alighted from the chair and came in. He was wearing an official's gauze cap, sunflower-colored gown, gilt belt and black shoes. He was a provincial graduate, and had served as a magistrate in his time. His name was Zhang Jinzhai. He and Fan Jin made way for each other ceremoniously, and once inside the house bowed to each other as equals and sat down in the places of guest and host. Mr. Zhang began the conversation.

"Sir," he said, "although we live in the same district, I have never been able to call on you."

"I have long respected you," replied Fan Jin, "but have never had the chance to pay you a visit."

"Just now I saw the list of successful candidates. Your patron, Mr. Tang, was a pupil of my grandfather; so I feel very close to you."

"I did not deserve to pass, I am afraid," said Fan Jin. "But I am delighted to be the pupil of one of your family."

After a glance round the room, Mr. Zhang remarked, "Sir, you are certainly frugal." He took from his servant a packet of silver, and stated, "I have brought nothing to show my respect except these fifty taels of silver, which I beg you to accept. Your honorable home is not good enough for you, and it will not be very convenient when you have many callers. I have an empty house on the main street by the cast gate, which has three courtyards and three rooms in each. Although it is not big, it is quite clean. Allow me to present it to you. When you move there, I can profit by your instruction more easily."

Fan Jin declined many times, but Mr. Zhang pressed him. "With all we have in common, we should be like brothers," he said. "But if you refuse, you are treating me like a stranger." Then Fan Jin accepted the silver and expressed his thanks. After some more conversation they bowed and parted. Not until the visitor was in his chair did Butcher Hu dare to emerge.

Fan Jin gave the silver to his wife. When she opened it, and they saw the white ingots with their fine markings, he asked Butcher Hu to come in and gave him two ingots, saying, "Just now I troubled you for five thousand coppers. Please accept these six taels of silver."

Butcher Hu gripped the silver tight, but thrust out his clenched fist, saying, "You keep this. I gave you that money to congratulate you, so how can I take it back?"

"I have some more silver here," said Fan Jin. "When it is spent, I will ask you for more."

Butcher Hu immediately drew back his fist, stuffed the silver into his pocket and said, "All right. Now that you are on good terms with that Mr. Zhang, you needn't be afraid of going short. His family has more silver than the emperor, and they are my best customers. Every year, even if they have no particular occasions to celebrate, they still buy four or five thousand catties of meat. Silver is nothing to him."

Then he turned to his daughter and said, "Your rascally brother didn't want me to bring that money this morning. I told him, 'Now my honorable son-in-law is not the man he was. There will be lots of people sending him presents of money. I am only afraid he may refuse my gift.' Wasn't I right? Now I shall take this silver home and curse that dirty scoundrel." After a thousand thanks he made off, his head thrust forward and a broad grin on his face.

True enough, many people came to Fan Jin after that and made him presents of land and shops; while some poor couples came to serve him in return for his protection. In two or three months he had manservants and maidservants, to say nothing of money and rice. When Mr. Zhang came again to urge him, he moved into the new house; and for three days he entertained guests with feasts and operas. On the morning of the fourth day, after Fan Jin's mother had got up and had breakfast, she went to the rooms in the back courtyard. There she found Fan Jin's wife with a silver pin in her hair. Although this was the middle of the tenth month, it was still warm and she was wearing a sky-blue silk tunic and a green silk skirt. She was supervising the maids as they washed bowls, cups, plates and chopsticks.

"You must be very careful," the old lady warned them. "These things don't belong to us, so don't break them."

"How can you say they don't belong to you, madam?" they asked. "They are all yours."

"No, no, these aren't ours," she protested with a smile.

"Oh yes, they are," the maids cried. "Not only are these things, but all of us servants and this house belong to you."

When the old lady heard this, she picked up the fine porcelain and the cups and chopsticks inlaid with silver, and examined them carefully one by one. Then she went into a fit of laughter. "All mine!" she crowed. Screaming with laughter she fell backwards, choked and lost consciousness.

5.2 A MURDER CASE FROM THE RECORDS OF THE OFFICE FOR THE SCRUTINY OF PUNISHMENTS, 1747–1748

Many Qing murder cases grew out of minor disputes involving land or other property. When a local official recommended capital punishment, he was required to submit the case through the Board of Punishments to the emperor for a final decision. Because of this regulation, the Qing archives contain an abundance of documents dealing with local violence.

In solving crimes, local officials often interviewed a wide range of witnesses. The magistrate was tacitly permitted to use torture to elicit confessions from uncooperative witnesses or suspects. In the case translated below, the official in charge of investigating the murder of a monk provides a summary of his findings. The confession of Li Jinru, recorded in vernacular Chinese, is appended. In retelling the story of the murder, Li's vivid and detailed narrative recounts long-standing resentments that incited the violence.

A MURDER CASE INVOLVING A RENT DISPUTE IN HUBEI

The report of Liu Fang'ai, Surveillance Commissioner of Hubei stationed with the Surveillance Commission in Wuchang, concerning the interrogation of Li Jinru, age 55, from Xiaogan county, Hanyang prefecture, states the following: Li Jinru was a person of vicious and brutal character. He ignored law and principled behavior. He and the murdered monk Chengyuan lived in the same neighborhood. Li Jinru normally rented two *dou* of land[3] from Chengyuan and they divided the produce of the property equally. The rent was never overdue. In the tenth year of Qianlong [1745], Monk Chengyuan took the land back and used it himself and although Li Jinru wanted to rent it he was not permitted to do so. The next year, Li Jinru again asked to rent the land but Chengyuan stubbornly refused his request and strongly rebuked him. This led to a quarrel and afterwards Li Jinru harbored hatred for the monk. In the spring of the twelfth year of Qianlong [1747], Chengyuan dug out some soil from Jinru's land to build up a raised pathway adjacent to his field and the two men again quarreled. Later, Li Jinru asked Chengyuan to give him some wine. Chengyuan refused his request and so Li Jinru's hatred deepened.

On the night of the twenty-sixth day of the eighth month of 1747, Jinru, following some drinking, encountered Chengyuan who was himself returning home after a late night of drinking. Li Jinru's hatred was touched off and it suddenly occurred to him to murder Chengyuan. Between nine and eleven p.m., Li Jinru took some bark ropes and set out for the temple with the intention of strangling Chengyuan to vent his hatred. The gate of the temple was already closed and so Li Jinru used a board to help him to climb over the wall to gain entrance. He then saw a wooden club in the courtyard and took it to beat Chengyuan to death. The temple hall and the door to Chengyuan's room happened to be unlocked and so Jinru pushed open the door and crept in. The light from the lamp in the temple hall illuminated the bed and Li Jinru found Chengyuan was sleeping soundly. Jinru raised the club to strike Chengyuan but mistakenly hit the bed. He turned

---

3. A *dou* = one decaliter, a Chinese peck. The grain production of this small plot in dispute was two *dou* per year.

to strike again but this caused Chengyuan to cry out in alarm and struggle. In this struggle, Jinru bruised the back of Chengyuan's right hand and the rear part of his head. Jinru also scratched the left side of Chengyuan's face, his right arm, and the back of his left hand. Chengyuan held the club tightly and refused to release it and so Li Jinru then took an iron ax lying on a trunk and struck and wounded the left side of Chengyuan's head. Li also hacked at the top of Chengyuan's head and killed him. Jinru threw the ax under the bed and used the rope to tie up Chengyuan by the neck in an endeavor to make the death seem like suicide. However, because the rope was not previously tied to the beam it was impossible to raise the corpse. Li Jinru next left the corpse on the ground, took some money, a wool blanket, and fled from the scene.

The investigation is based on testimonies of Monk Xujiao and Li Jinru.

According to Monk Xujiao: "The dead monk Chengyuan was my own brother. He was 73 *sui* [years old] this year. My surname before I became a monk was Zheng. Because we were very poor, my brother joined the Cheng Family Temple. He had one disciple but he died and afterwards, brother did not find a new disciple. I became a monk in the Cheng Family Temple in Guangyangpu. This temple of my brother had two *dan* of land to support it. He himself planted part of it and part of it was rented to Li Nanzheng and Wei Zhouzhen. Every year they split up the produce. . . ."

According to Li Jinru: "I'm from Lijiayuan of Xiaogan county and am fifty-five *sui*. My parents and my wife died a long time ago. I have only one son named Li Yifei and he left home to be a laborer in the seventh month of last year. The house I rented was returned to the original owner and since I had no place to live, I lived by myself in my brother Li Mingzhi's place. I made a living on my own. My brother is a trader and doesn't live at home. In his family, there's only my sister-in-law and nobody else.

"Originally I rented two *dou* of land from Chengyuan. We split the grain equally and I never owed him anything. In 1745, he suddenly refused to let me rent the land. I asked him several times but he wouldn't give in and I began to hate him. In the fall of 1746, I again begged him to be able to rent but he would not agree and said I was no good. I was really angry and had a quarrel with him but still never expressed my anger. In the spring of 1747, he dug soil from my land to build up his paddy dike. We had another quarrel then. And so I hated him for a long time. Later he bought a few catties of wine to sell to others. I asked him if I could buy wine but he deliberately said he was sold out. Even though he had it, he refused to sell it to me. He was a monk! But he was an old, cunning, wicked man. He had no sense of compassion. He always insulted and bullied me. I really hated him and wanted to teach him a lesson. But because I never had a chance, I couldn't do anything until the evening of the twenty-sixth day of the eighth month of 1747. I had had some drinks and ran into Chengyuan who was coming home from drinking. I saw he was a little drunk and then remembered all the mean things he'd done to me in the past. I got furious and under the influence of the wine wanted to hurt him. I figured that since he was an old man, was drunk, and slept by himself, he would go to bed early that night and would not have any protection. I tied a rope made of bark around my waist and intended to strangle him in his sleep. I went there late at night and the gate of the temple was closed. So I took a plank from a bridge behind the temple and propped it against the wall to climb in. I saw a wooden club next to the steps going into the temple hall and thought that this could kill him with one stroke. I picked it up and went on. I knew the door of the temple hall and the bedroom door well from the time I had rented land and I knew how to open them. I did not expect that Chengyuan would leave the door unlocked after he was drunk but he did and so I just lightly pushed the door and entered his room. The room was on the east and it was connected to the temple hall. There was no wall in between, just some eaves. In the temple hall there were three lamps that threw their light into the bedroom. I got close to the bed and saw that he hadn't even pulled down his mosquito netting. His head was inclined toward the east and he was sleeping soundly. I struck out with the club but had raised it too high and it caught on the canopy frame of the bed. When I got the club free, he was already awake and had sat up and started crying out. I hit out again with the club but he grabbed it tightly. I twisted it left and right and banged his hand against the bedframe and cut the skin on the back of his hand. Then I pulled it forward and pushed him back and the back of his head hit the bedboard and again scratched him but he still held on to the club. I grabbed the club and pushed him in the face and caused cuts on the left side of his face. Because I couldn't push him down, I scratched the back of his left hand and his right arm. But he would still not let go of the club. I looked around and saw that on the trunk by the west end of his bed there was an ax. Holding the club with my right hand, I grabbed the ax with my left and hit his head. He tried to turn his head away but I cut him on the left side. He yelled even more and so I hit him again on the left crown of his head. He stopped making noise and fell back on the bed. I threw the ax under the bed and tied the bark rope around his neck to make it seem like suicide. I dragged his body out from the bed but found out that since I hadn't looped the rope over the beam, I couldn't raise him up. I was confused and scared and so I just left him where he lay. When I left the room, I saw two hundred cash on the trunk and a wool blanket on a hanging rack. I grabbed them and opened the door on the west side. I closed the door behind me when I went out. I went back to the side of my brother's house and hid the wool blanket under some hay and slept by the haystack. The next morning, I found that my shirt and jacket were stained with blood and so I secretly went into my room and took out some pieces of cloth and sewing equipment I kept there and covered the blood stained jacket with patches. I took off the shirt and washed out the bloodstains. On the twenty-eighth day, I took the money and wrapped up the wool blanket and my old shirt with a rope and went to the shop of Tailor Shu in Zhujiajing. I found that a short blue shirt was for sale and so I spent 160 cash to buy it and spent fifteen cash to buy a pair of white cloth stockings. I also left the package I'd tied with the rope in his shop. I said that I would pick everything up together when he finished making the stockings. But now all the money was gone and I couldn't get more and so I haven't gone there to pick them up. And then I was caught by the runners and taken away. Tailor Shu had no idea what was happening. All of this happened because of my old grudge with Chengyuan and not because of money. No one helped me. I dare not make any false confession. . . ."

The aforementioned official [Liu Fang'ai], after investigating the case of Li Jinru of Xiaogan county's murder of Monk Chengyuan arrived at the following sentence: Li Jinru is guilty under the statute concerning premeditated murder. He should be sentenced to death by decapitation after the Autumn Assizes and tattooed in accordance with precedent. The younger brother of the deceased should receive the stolen money and the value of the blanket and the blanket already retrieved. . . .

13th day of the 10th month, 1748

5.3 GLORIFYING THE ORIGINS OF THE MANCHUS, FROM AN ACCOUNT IN THE STATE ARCHIVE

Jiang Liangqi (1723–1789) was a 1751 *jinshi*[4] degree holder from Guangxi who served as compiler in the state archive (*Guoshiguan*). Jiang's *Donghualu* (East Flower Gate records) was a historical chronicle, based largely on the *Qing Veritable Records*, that examined the history of China from the beginning of the Qing period to the end of Yongzheng's reign in 1735. Jiang Liangqi made a broad and scrupulous selection of documents in compiling this work and even today it is a major source for the history of the early Qing reign periods.

The mythical account of the origins of the Manchus recounted here was taken most seriously by later generations and became a staple part of the education of Manchu nobles. Its wooden quality suggests the cultural divide which still separated Manchu society from the refined literary world of sixteenth- and seventeenth-century China. The Manchus' view of their own genesis, as captured in this short piece, is hardly so elaborate a declaration of the "divine light" of the Aisin-Gioro ruling clan as a contemporary Chinese scholar might have composed if given the same assignment. However, using language and images from the myth cycles of the Manchus, the piece communicates a sense that the Manchu ruling clan was divinely blessed in its enterprise to rule China.

4. Highest degree in the imperial civil service exam system.

The ancestors of our dynasty originated in the region of the Changbai Mountains. The mountains are more than two hundred *li* high and stretch for more than a thousand *li*. Set on the mountain range is a lake called Damen which is about eighty *li* around. The three rivers, the Yalu, the Huntong, and the Aihu, all start here. Geomancers said that this place would give birth to a sage who would unify the world. East of these mountains is Bukuli Mountain and beneath it is a lake called Buerhuli. Legends tell that three heavenly maidens, Engulun and her two younger sisters Zheng'gulun and Fogulun, were bathing in this lake and that after their bath a divine bird placed a red fruit on the clothing of Fogulun. She swallowed it and then became pregnant. Later she gave birth to a boy. When he was born he was already able to speak and his physique was extraordinary. When he grew up, his mother told him the story of his birth and said: "Heaven gave birth to you to pacify unsettled countries. You are to use Aisin-Gioro as your surname and Bukuliyongshun as your name." His mother then ascended to heaven and the son boarded a boat and rode downstream to Hebu.

When he stepped upon the bank, he broke willow branches and reeds to make a mat and sat cross-legged upon it. In this region there were three families contending for control. They formed armed bands and killed each other in their vendettas. Someone came to the river to get water and was surprised by Bukuliyongshun's appearance and returned home and told others. A crowd came to question Bukuliyongshun and he told them his name and said: "I am the son of the Heavenly Maiden Fogulun and heaven has ordered me to quell the unrest among you." The crowd was surprised and said: "You are a divine sage!" They carried him to their village and worshipped him as their lord. They lived east of the Changbai Mountains in Ye'edoli City in the Emohui region; they called their state Manzhou. After a few generations, they were betrayed by fellow-countrymen and their people were slaughtered. Only a young boy named Fancha escaped and hid in the wilderness. When his enemies pursued him, a small bird settled on his head and his pursuers mistook him for a withered tree. He was thus able to escape. After several more generations, the imperial ancestor who founded our dynasty was born. His surname was Aisin-Gioro and his given name was Dudumengtemu. He lived in the Hetuala region below Mount Hulanhada. He was very intelligent and a careful planner. He captured more than forty descendants of his ancestor's foes; he killed some and released others and completely recovered the lost lands.

5.4 AND 5.5 HESHEN: ACCUSATION AND INVENTORY

Within days of the death of Emperor Qianlong in 1799, his favorite Heshen (1750–1799) was arrested and charged with twenty "great crimes" by Qianlong's successor, Jiaqing. In a gesture of deference to Qianlong, the bannerman was not executed but was granted the favor of taking his own life. During the more than twenty years that Heshen had enjoyed imperial favor, he exercised great power in the Qing court. As an intimate of the emperor, he was immune from impeachment or criticism and was able to amass a huge fortune that made him an object of envy and hostility. Alone among Qianlong's retainers, Heshen rode his horse in the precincts of the Forbidden City and was able to appoint or cashier high officials in the state bureaucracy. But once deprived of the protection of his imperial patron, Heshen's fall was predictably precipitous.

The Heshen scandal is often cited as a symptom of the decline of the Qing state system and a symbol of the abuse of power that had become possible by the end of the eighteenth century. Relying solely on his tie to the emperor, Heshen was able to manipulate affairs of state, place his cronies in important positions, and build a lavishly furnished estate for himself, his family, and his retainers. The following edict and the accompanying list of confiscated household goods reveal Heshen's offenses against the state and suggest the magnitude of his raids on the government treasury.

5.4 *The Twenty Crimes of Heshen*

Here we list the twenty crimes of Heshen and issue this special Edict to make this known to all.

1. I was specially selected as the Crown Prince by my father, the late Emperor, on the third day of the ninth month of 1795. On the day before the Imperial Edict was promulgated, Heshen presented me with a *ruyi* [an S-shaped ornamental object symbolizing good luck]. He thus revealed this great secret [the secret of the succession] and attempted to gain merit from his support of me. This was his first great crime.
2. In the first month of last year [1798], when my departed father the Emperor summoned Heshen to the Yuanmingyuan Palace, he dared to ride a horse past the Hall of Justice and Honor [a main reception hall near the entrance of the Summer Palace] and made his way to the entrance of Longevity Hill. He had no respect for his master and no crime is greater than this one. This was his second great crime.[5]
3. Owing to a sickness affecting his leg, Heshen was carried in a sedan chair directly into the Forbidden City. He entered and departed through the Shenwu Gate [the north gate] and this was witnessed by all. He never dreaded the prohibition of such behavior. This was his third great crime.

---

5. Only the emperor was permitted to ride horseback or to be carried in a sedan chair on the grounds of the imperial palaces.

4. He took a former palace concubine as his own concubine. This was utterly shameless. This was his fourth great crime.[6]

5. From the time of the campaign against the White Lotus bandits in the Sichuan and Hubei region, my late father the Emperor was so over-burdened with military dispatches that he was unable even to sleep. But Heshen deliberately delayed consideration of military memorials from the various army commands and prolonged the campaign a great deal. This was his fifth great crime.

6. At the time when the holy, sagely body of my late father the Emperor was ailing, Heshen showed no sorrow. When he entered or departed from his visits with the Emperor, he talked and joked as in normal times with other court officials. This was heartless and deranged behavior! This was his sixth great crime.

7. Last winter, my late father the Emperor struggled against his illness to write comments on memorials and on the drafts of edicts. His brush sometimes wavered and Heshen dared to suggest that these documents should be torn up. His intention was to draw up different edicts. This was his seventh great crime.

8. My late father the Emperor originally appointed Heshen to take charge of the affairs of both the Board of Personnel and the Board of Punishments. Later because there were immediate needs for expenditures in military affairs and because Heshen was experienced in this regard he was further charged with responsibility for submitting receipts to the Board of Revenue. He then usurped all the functions of the Board, changed its set rules and regulations, and refused to allow other officials of the Board to interfere. This was his eighth great crime.

9. In the twelfth month of 1798, Kuei Shu reported in a memorial that an army of more than a thousand bandits had joined together in Xunhua and Guide [two areas in Qinghai]. They were robbing lamas and merchants of their oxen and had murdered two people. Heshen burned the memorial and hid these events. He did not take border affairs seriously. This was his ninth great crime.

10. After my late father the Emperor passed away, I ordered that those Mongol princes who had not suffered from smallpox might be exempted from coming to the capital. But Heshen disobeyed my Edict and ordered all Mongol princes to come and thereby disregard our country's special consideration for border feudatories [waifan]. His real intentions were unknown. This was his tenth crime.

11. Grand Secretary Su-ling-a had serious hearing problems with both ears and was utterly weak and feeble. He should have been retired but simply

6. Imperial concubines were occasionally permitted to leave the Forbidden City but were forbidden from remarrying after their departure from the emperor's service.

because he was Heshen's brother He Lin's relative through marriage, the facts were hidden and not reported. Because Vice-Ministers Wu Xinglan and Li Huang and Li Guangyun, Chief of the Court of the Imperial Study, had all tutored Heshen's family members, they were all recommended for the rank of Minister and to head educational commissions. This was his eleventh great crime.

12. Heshen dismissed at will those who worked in the Grand Council. His abuses of power were innumerable. This was his twelfth great crime.

13. Just yesterday we confiscated and took inventory of Heshen's family property. The buildings were all built of *nanmu* [a precious wood] and were extravagant and illegally mimicked the imperial style. The patterns and designs of the buildings followed those of the Ningshou Palace [in the Forbidden City] and the pattern of the gardens and kiosks did not differ from those of the Summer Palace. It is impossible to know what was in his heart. This was his thirteenth great crime.

14. Heshen's ancestral tombs at Jinzhou [in Hebei] were equipped with a sacrificial hall and underground tunnels. The local residents called them the He imperial tombs. This was his fourteenth great crime.

15. In his home, Heshen amassed more than two hundred pearl bracelets. This was several times more than the number of such bracelets in the palace collection. He also had giant pearls that were larger than those used in the Emperor's crown. This was his fifteenth great crime.

16. Although he was not permitted to wear a precious stone on the peak of his cap, dozens of such jewels were found hidden in his home. Moreover, he had an incalculable number of gigantic jewels unlike any found in the imperial treasury. This was his sixteenth great crime.

17. The quantities of silver, clothing, and other objects found in his home were uncountable. This was his seventeenth great crime.

18. In false double walls in his home, tens of thousands of ounces of gold were hidden. Buried in his cellars were millions of ounces of silver. In the rear chambers were huge pearls, giant gold and silver ingots, gold pagodas, and other objects. This was his eighteenth great crime.

19. In the vicinity of the capital, in Tongzhou and Jinzhou, he set up pawnshops and banks. A chief minister was competing with mean people for profit. This was his nineteenth great crime.

20. The Liu and Ma families were low-ranking slaves of the He family but after their family properties were confiscated and inventoried it was found that the property of each family was worth more than two million ounces of silver. They also had huge pearls and pearl bracelets. If this was not permitted, how could they grasp so much? This was his twentieth great crime.

5.5 *An Inventory of the Household Property Confiscated from the Home of Heshen*

[1. HOUSES AND LAND]
One garden bestowed by the Emperor
Twenty original pavilions and kiosks
Sixteen newly added pavilions
One main residence with thirteen sections and 730 rooms
One eastern residential wing with seven sections and 360 rooms
One western residential wing with seven sections and 350 rooms
One Huizhou style new residence with seven sections and 620 rooms
One counting house with 730 rooms
One garden with sixty-four pavilions and kiosks
Eight hundred thousand *mou* [6.6 *mou* = one acre] of farmland
Ten banks with capital of six hundred thousand ounces of silver
Ten pawnshops with capital of eight hundred thousand ounces of silver . . .

[2. GOLD, SILVER, AND COPPER CASH]
Fifty-eight thousand ounces of pure gold
Fifty-five thousand six hundred silver ingots
Five million eight hundred and thirty thousand capital-type silver ingots
Three million one hundred and fifty thousand Suzhou ingots
Fifty-eight thousand foreign silver dollars
One million five hundred thousand strings of copper cash
The value of the above was more than fifty-four million ounces of silver.

[3. GINSENG AND JADE]
Ginseng storehouse:
Individual pieces of ginseng were not counted but the total weight was six
    hundred catties
Jade storehouse:
Thirteen jade tripods two and a half feet high
Twenty sets of jade chimes
One hundred and thirty jade *ruyi*
One thousand one hundred and six *ruyi* decorated with jade
Forty-eight jade snuff bottles
One hundred and thirty jade buckles
Two jade screens with twenty-four panels
Thirteen settings of jade bowls
Thirty jade vases
Eighteen jade basins
Ninety-three cases of jade utensils; individual pieces not counted

Converted to silver the value of the above would be seven million ounces of silver.

In addition there were three other jade pieces not evaluated: a jade longevity Buddha three feet six inches tall, one jade Guanyin statue three feet eight inches tall, both incised with characters reading: "Presented by Governor General of Yunnan and Guizhou," and one jade horse four feet three inches long and two feet eight inches high.

[4. JEWELRY]

Pearl storehouse:
Ten giant longan shaped Eastern pearls
Two hundred and thirty pearl bracelets
Ten huge rubies weighing 280 catties
Eighty small rubies (not weighed)
Forty blue precious stones (not weighed)
Ninety ruby cap top decorations
Eighty coral cap top decorations
Ten screens with precious stones and gold
Silver jewelry storehouse:
Seventy-two settings of silver bowls
Two hundred pairs of gold-incised chopsticks
Five hundred pairs of silver-incised chopsticks
Sixty gold teaspoons
Three hundred and eighty silver teaspoons
One hundred and eight silver mouthwashing bowls
Forty gold cloisonné mouthwashing bowls
Eighty silver cloisonné mouthwashing bowls
Antiques:
Twenty antique bronze vessels
Twenty-one antique tripods
Thirty-three bronze flat vessels
Two antique swords
Ten Song inkstones
Seven hundred and six *duan* inkstones

The total value of the above converted to silver is eight million ounces of silver.

In addition, there were three kinds of objects not evaluated in silver: Seven coral trees, three feet six inches high; four coral trees, three feet four inches high; and one gold-incised jade-decorated clock. . . . [The inventory next lists the furs, furniture, household furnishings, and miscellaneous other items taken from Heshen. It ends with a count of his serving men and women. The document also mentions the twenty-six thousand ounces of gold hidden behind false walls in Heshen's residence and the millions of ounces of silver buried in his cellars.]

5.6 LAN DINGYUAN ON THE EDUCATION OF WOMEN, 1712

Lan Dingyuan (1680–1733), a native of Fujian, served as the magistrate in two counties in neighboring Guangdong province. He also spent time in Taiwan, as secretary to his cousin, a military commander, where he became known for writings advocating aggressive settlement of the island. Lan is the author of an influential text on female learning. In his preface to that volume, translated below, Lan explains his rationale for advocating education for women, and outlines the appropriate parameters for female learning.

The basis of the government of the empire lies in the habits of the people, and the surety that their usages will be correct is in the orderly management of families, which last depends chiefly upon the females. In the good old times of Zhou, the virtuous women set such an excellent example, that it influenced the customs of the empire—an influence that descended even to the times of the Zheng and Wei states. If the curtain of the inner apartment gets thin, or is hung awry (i.e. if the sexes are not kept apart), disorder will enter the family, and ultimately pervade the empire. Females are doubtless the sources of good manners; from ancient times to the present this has been the case. The inclination to virtue and vice in women differs exceedingly; their dispositions incline contrary ways, and if it is wished to form them alike, there is nothing like education. In ancient times, youth of both sexes were instructed. According to the Ritual of Zhou, the imperial wives regulated the law for educating females, in order to educate the ladies of the palace in morals, conversation, manners, and work; and each led out their respective classes, at proper times, and arranged them for examination in the imperial presence. But these treatises have not reached us, and it cannot be distinctly ascertained what was their plan of arrangement. . . .

The education of a woman and that of a man are very dissimilar. Thus, a man can study during his whole life; whether he is abroad or at home, he can always look in to the classics and histories, and become thoroughly acquainted with the whole range of authors. But a woman does not study more than ten years, when she takes upon her the management of a family, where a multiplicity of cares distract her attention, and having no leisure for undisturbed study, she cannot easily understand learned authors; not having obtained a thorough acquaintance with letters, she does not fully comprehend their principles; and, like water that has flowed from its fountain, she cannot regulate her conduct by their guidance. How can it be said that a standard work on female education is not wanted! Every profession and trade has its appropriate master; and ought not those also who possess such an influence over manners (as females) to be taught their duties and their proper limits? It is a matter of regret, that in these books no extracts have been made from the works of Confucius in order to make them introductory to the writings on polite literature; and it is also to be regretted that selections have not been made from the commentaries of Cheng, Zhu, and other scholars, who have explained his writings clearly, as also from the whole range of writers, gathering from them all that which was appropriate, and omitting the rest. These are circulated among mankind together with such books as the Juvenile Instructor; yet if they are put into the hands of females, they cause them to become like a blind man without a guide, wandering hither and thither without knowing where he is going. There has been this great deficiency from very remote times until now.

When I was left in my childhood an orphan, and I had not yet been taught to read my father's books, I was exceedingly grieved and disheartened; I was like a geometrical worm curled up in a tussoc of grass. Whenever I reflected upon the manners of society, which was very frequently, I thought that if I was capable, I would select from the classics, the histories, and the various other standard authorities, from the Narratives of Distinguished Women, the Female Precepts, and other works of that kind, and following the rules given for female education in the Ritual of Zhou, commence a treatise with all that was to be found most important in them; then, under the four heads of morals, conversation, manners, and work, I would arrange the other various subdivisions, so that the reader could see the whole subject at a glance and each topic be in its appropriate place.

Woman's influence is according to her moral character, therefore that point is largely explained. First, concerning their obedience to their husband and to his parents; then in regard to their complaisance to his brothers and sisters, and kindness to their sisters-in-law. If unmarried, they have duties towards their parents, and to the wives of their elder brothers; if a principal wife, a woman must have no jealous feelings; if in straitened circumstances, she must be contented with her lot; if rich and honorable she must avoid extravagance and haughtiness. Then teach her, in times of trouble and in days of ease, how to maintain her purity, how to give importance to fight principles, how to observe widowhood, and how to avenge the murder of a relative. Is she a mother, let her teach her children; is she a stepmother, let her love and cherish her husband's children; is her rank in life high, let her not be condescending to her inferiors; let her wholly discard all sorcerers, superstitious nuns, and witches; in a word, let her adhere to propriety, and avoid vice. If there are any other points they shall be fully discoursed upon; but the above is a general sketch of the first chapter on female morals.

In conversation, females should not be froward and garrulous, but observe strictly what is correct, whether in suggesting advice to her husband, in remonstrating with him, or teaching her children; in maintaining etiquette, humbly imparting her experience, or in averting misfortune. The deportment of females should be strictly grave and sober, and yet adapted to the occasion; whether in waiting on her parents, receiving or reverencing her husband, rising up or sitting down, when pregnant, in times of mourning, or when fleeing in war, she should be perfectly decorous. Rearing the silkworm, and working cloth are the most important of the employments of a female; preparing and serving up the food for the household, and setting in order the sacrifices follow next, each of which must be attended to; after them, study and learning can fill up the time. This is a general outline of the three books treating on female conversation, manners, and employments, though if there are other points they shall be fully discussed.

The education of females is limited and superficial; they see but little of the world, and hear much that is bad. Therefore, it will be well to take the most distinguished and well-known examples [of celebrated women], and insert them orderly in a book intended to aid in their education. Within the last century, there have been so many notable instances of virtuous, chaste, and upright women, that the pencil would weary, and the time fail, to write them all, and I fear they would be wearisome. There have been, besides these, accomplished ladies distinguished for their talents as poetesses, extemporaneous bards, and writers on the passions; but, although these productions are exceedingly clever, they do not appertain to female education, and none of them have been introduced. . . . To guard against introducing the least error and vicious example has demanded my utmost caution. If, however, the principles here laid down do not accord with just propriety, or the examples adduced are erroneous, my overpassing offense will find no place to hide itself. But if these rules for females are found in the main correct, and if they conduce, though partially, to amend the manners of the age, the common sense of men will not look upon the work as one of no importance. Ching footsze observes, 'If every family in the empire is correct, then will the empire be peaceful.' I wish that every man in the nation should regulate his own family, by which he would silently laud the dignified peacefulness of the emperor's influence. And when the manners of the people are elegant and courteous, and families are harmonious, then I, Lu Zhao, will sing the odes. . . . I bow my head in salutation, wishing these happinesses may abound.

CHAPTER 6

China and the Eighteenth-Century World

6.1 LORD MACARTNEY'S COMMISSION FROM HENRY DUNDAS, 1792

By the end of the eighteenth century, the expansion of foreign trade, and especially trade in Asia, was a central preoccupation of the British government. The British East India Company (BEIC), organized in 1600 to compete with the Dutch in Asia, was a trading monopoly that dominated English trade with China until the dissolution of its monopoly rights in 1834. In India, the company was a mercantile combine, evolving into the agency of British rule in colonial Asia. By the time of the Macartney mission, the BEIC was amassing huge profits from its traffic in Indian and Chinese tea and had already begun, on a small scale, to smuggle contraband opium from Bengal to Canton, where it was exchanged for silver.

From the British perspective, the framework for Indian-Chinese trading activities was far from satisfactory. The Canton system limited British ships to a single port and imposed numerous conditions on trading activities. To seek remedies for these problems, Sir Henry Dundas (1742–1811), a member of William Pitt's inner circle, president of the board of the BEIC, and, in 1792, Great Britain's home minister, urged the dispatch of a mission to Peking. Subsequently, Lord Macartney, who was a personal friend of Dundas, was appointed "Ambassador Extraordinary and Plenipotentiary from the King of Great Britain to the Emperor of China." In September 1792 Macartney set out with an eighty-four-man mission from London to make contact with the Chinese.

The document that follows was the official charge of the Home Ministry to Macartney. While it outlines the Crown's hopes for the mission, it also shows a certain befuddlement about the nature of the Qing government. It is important to note that Dundas's charge shows that Great Britain was willing to negotiate a reduction in opium imports if more important conditions were met.

Whitehall 8th September 1792

My Lord.

Having to signify to your Excellency His Majesty's Commands and Instructions on the subject of the Embassy to which he has been pleased to appoint you, I shall introduce them by recalling to your attention the occasion and object of this measure.

A greater number of His Majesty's subjects than of any other Europeans, have been trading for a considerable time past in China. The commercial intercourse between several nations and that great empire, has been preceded, accompanied or followed, by special communications with its Sovereign. Others had the support of Missionaries, who from their eminence in Science or ingenuity in the arts, were frequently admitted to the familiarity of a curious and polished Court, and which Missionaries in the midst of their care for the propagation of their faith are not supposed to have been unmindful of the view and interests of their Country; while the English traders remained unaided, and as it were, unavowed, at a distance so remote, as to admit of a misrepresentation of the national character and importance, and where too, their occupation was not held in that esteem which ought to procure their safety and respect.

Under the circumstances it would become the dignity and character of his Majesty, to extend his paternal regard to these his distant subjects, even if the commerce and prosperity of the Nation were not concerned in their success; and to claim the Emperor of China's particular protection for them, with the weight which is due to the requisition of one great Sovereign from another.

A free communication with a people, perhaps the most singular on the Globe, among whom civilization has existed, and the arts have been cultivated thro' a long series of ages, with fewer interruptions than elsewhere, is well worthy, also, of this Nation, which saw with pleasure, and applauded with gratitude, the several voyages undertaken already by his Majesty's command, and at the public expense, in the pursuit of knowledge, and for the discovery and observation of distant Countries and manners.

The extent and value of the British dominions in India, which connect us in some degree with every part of that Country, point out also the propriety of establishing sufficient means of representation and transaction of business with our principal Neighbours there.

The measures lately taken by Government respecting the Tea trade, having more than trebled the former legal importation of this article into Great Britain, it is become particularly desirable to cultivate a friendship, and increase the communication with China, which may lead to such a vent throughout that extensive Empire, of the manufactures of the mother Country, and of our Indian Territories, as beside contributing to their prosperity will out of the sales of such produce, furnish resources for the investment to Europe, now requiring no less an annual sum than one-million, four hundred thousand pounds.

Hitherto, however, Great Britain has been obliged to pursue the Trade with that Country under circumstances the most discouraging, hazardous to its agents employed in conducting it, and precarious to the various interests involved in it. The only place where His Majesty's subjects have the privilege of a factory is Canton. The fair competition of the Market is there destroyed by associations of the Chinese; our Supercargoes are denied open access to the tribunals of the Country, and to the equal execution of its laws, and are kept altogether in a most arbitrary state of depression, ill suited to the importance of the concerns which are entrusted to their care, and scarcely compatible with the regulations of civilized society. . . .

His Majesty from his earnest desire to promote the present undertaking and in order to give the greater dignity to the Embassy, has been graciously pleased to order one of His Ships of War to convey you and your Suite to the Coast of China. With the same view he has ordered a Military Guard to attend your Person, to be composed of chosen Men from the light Dragoons, Infantry and Artillery, with proper Officers, under the command of Major Benson, whom he has determined to raise to the rank of Lieutenant Colonel upon this occasion. This guard will add splendour and procure respect to the Embassy; the order, appearance and evolutions of the Men may convey no useless idea of our military Character and discipline, and if it should excite in the Emperor a desire of adopting any of the exercise or maneuvers, among the Troops, an opportunity thus offers to him, for which a return of good offices on his part is natural to be expected. It will be at your option to detach one of the Lieutenants of the Ship, or of your Guard, in His Majesty's uniform to accompany the Messenger whom you will send to announce at Pekin [Peking] your arrival on the coast, if you should approach that Capital by Sea.

Besides the Chinese Interpreters whom you have already procured you will perhaps meet in your progress some Portuguese, Spanish, or Italian Missionary, or other intelligent Person free from national attachments or prejudices, who may be useful to be employed in your Service.

Should your answer be satisfactory, and I will not suppose the contrary, you will then assume the Character and public appearance of His Majesty's Ambassador Extraordinary, and proceed with as much ceremony as can be admitted without causing a material delay, or incurring an unreasonable expense. You will procure an audience as early as possible after your arrival, conforming to all ceremonials of that Court, which may not commit the honour of your Sovereign, or lessen your own dignity, so as to endanger the success of your negotiation.

Whilst I make this reserve, I am satisfied you will be too prudent and considerate, to let any trifling punctilio stand in the way of the important benefits which may be obtained by engaging the favourable disposition of the Emperor and his Ministers. You will take the earliest opportunity of representing to His Imperial Majesty, that your Royal Master, already so justly celebrated in Foreign Countries on account of the voyages projected under his immediate auspices, for the acquisition and diffusion of knowledge, was from the same disposition desirous of sending an embassy to the most civilized as well as most ancient and populous Nation in the World in order to observe its celebrated institutions, and to communicate and receive the benefits which must result from an unreserved and friendly intercourse between that Country and his own. You will take care to express the high esteem which His Majesty has conceived for the Emperor, from the wisdom and virtue with which his character has been distinguished. A like compliment may be made in the event of the death of Hien-long [Qianlong], to the Prince who will be his Successor, as he has been in the management of the Public affairs for some time.

It is not unlikely that the Emperor's curiosity may lead to a degree of familiarity with you, in conversing upon the manners or circumstances of Europe and other Countries; and as despotic Princes are frequently more easy of access than their Ministers and dependents, you will not fail to turn such contingency to proper advantage. I do not mean to prescribe to you the particular mode of your negotiation; much must be left to your circumspection, and the judgement to be formed upon occurrences as they arise; but upon the present view of the matter, I am inclined to believe that instead of attempting to gain upon the Chinese Administration by representations founded upon the intricacies of either European or Indian Politicks, you should fairly state, after repeating the general assurances of His Majesty's friendly and pacific inclinations towards the Emperor, and his respect for the reputed mildness of his Administration, first the mutual benefit to be derived from a trade between the two Nations, in the course of which we receive beside other articles to the amount of twenty millions of Pounds weight of a Chinese herb, which would find very little vent, as not being in general use in other Countries, European or Asiatic, and for which we return woolens, cottons, and other articles useful to the Chinese, but a considerable part is actually paid to China in bullion.

Secondly, that the great extent of our commercial concerns in China, requires a place of security as a depot for such of our Goods as cannot be sold off or shipped during the short season that is allowed for our shipping to arrive and depart, and that for this purpose we wish to obtain a grant of a small tract of ground or detached Island, but in a more convenient situation than Canton, where our present warehouses are at a great distance from our Ships, and where we are not able to restrain the irregularities which are occasionally committed by the seamen of the Company's Ships, and those of private traders.

Thirdly, that our views are purely commercial, having not even a wish for territory; that we desire neither fortification nor defense but only the protection of the Chinese Government for our Merchants or their agents in trading or travelling thro the Country and a security to us against the encroachments of other powers, who might ever aim to disturb our trade; and you must here be prepared to obviate any prejudice which may arise from the argument of our present dominions in India by stating our situation in this respect to have arisen without our intending it, from the necessity of our defending ourselves against the oppressions of the revolted Nabobs, who entered into Cabals to our prejudice with other Nations of Europe, and disregarded the privileges granted to us by different Emperors, or by such other arguments as your own reflections upon the subject will suggest.

This topic I have reason to believe will be very necessary to enforce by every means in your power, as it is the great object of other European Nations to injure not only the Indian powers, but likewise the Emperor and Ministers of China with an idea of danger in countenancing the Subjects of Great Britain, as if it were the intention of this Country to aim at extending its territory in every quarter. As nothing can be more untrue than these representations it will not be difficult for you to find arguments which may counteract the effect of them.

If any favorable opportunity should be afforded to your Excellency it will be advisable that the difficulties with which our trade has long laboured at Canton should be represented; but in making such a representation you will endeavour to convince the Emperor that it is from His Majesty's design to attribute any act of misconduct to persons employed under the Chinese Government but with a view only to appease [apprise] his Imperial Majesty that such difficulties do exist, in full confidence that from his wisdom and justice they will not hereafter be experienced.

Should a new establishment be conceded you will take it in the name of the King of Great Britain. You will endeavour to obtain it on the most beneficial terms, with a power of regulating the police, and exercising jurisdiction over our own dependents, for which competent powers would be given so as effectually to prevent or punish the disorders of our people, which the Company's Supercargos in their limited sphere of action must see committed with impunity. Should it be required that no native Chinese be subject to be punished by our jurisdiction, or should any particular modification of this power be exacted it is not material ultimately to reject either of these propositions provided British subjects can be exempted from the Chinese jurisdiction for crimes, and that the British Chief or those under him be not held responsible if any Culprit should escape the pursuit of Justice, after search has been made by British and Chinese Officers acting in conjunction. . . .

It is necessary you should be on your Guard against one stipulation which, perhaps, will be demanded from you: which is that of the exclusion of the trade of opium from the Chinese dominions as being prohibited by the Laws of the Empire; if this subject should come into discussion, it must be handled with the greatest circumspection. It is beyond a doubt that no inconsiderable portion of the opium raised within our Indian territories actually finds its way to China: but if it should be made a positive requisition or any article of any proposed commercial treaty, that none of that drug should be sent by us to China, you must accede to it, rather than risk any essential benefit by contending for a liberty in this respect in which case the sale of our opium in Bengal must be left to take its chance in an open market, or to find a consumption in the dispersed and circuitous traffic of the eastern Seas.

A due sense of wisdom and justice of the King of Great Britain, which it will be your business to impress, as well as of the wealth and power of this Country, and of the genius and knowledge of its People, may naturally lead to a preferable acceptance of a treaty of friendship and alliance with us, as most worthy of themselves; and in a political light, as most likely to be useful to them, from our naval force, being the only assistance of which they may foresee the occasional importance to them.

In case the embassy should have an amicable and prosperous termination, it may be proposed to his Imperial Majesty to receive an occasional or perpetual Minister from the King of Great Britain, and to send one on his own part to the Court of London, in the assurance that all proper honours will be paid to any person who may be deputed in that sacred character. . . .

During the continuance of the Embassy you will take every possible opportunity that may arise, of transmitting to me for His Majesty's information, an account of your proceedings, and also of communicating with Earl Cornwallis, or the Governor General of Bengal for the time being, with whose views and efforts for promoting the trade of India to the East, it is particularly desirable you should co-operate, as far as they may be consistent with the present instructions.

Sincerely wishing your Excellency a prosperous voyage and complete success in the very important objects of it, I have the honour to be with great regard, My Lord,

> Your Excellency's most obedient
> and most humble Servant
> Henry Dundas.

6.2 AND 6.3 MACARTNEY'S AUDIENCE WITH QIANLONG AND MACARTNEY'S DESCRIPTION OF CHINA'S GOVERNMENT

After his arrival in China in June 1793, Lord Macartney met twice with the Qianlong emperor at the Rehe summer palace. Although Macartney was treated with great courtesy, he was ultimately frustrated in achieving any of the concrete objects of his mission.

Despite failures in negotiating trade or diplomatic accords, Macartney was remarkably successful in piercing the veils of mystery and misconception that had hitherto prevented Europeans from grasping the nature of Qing China. The following document represents Macartney's assessment of the Qing state and is notable for its acute portrayal of many of the problems that would frustrate Manchu rulers until the abdication of Puyi in 1911. Especially prescient in this regard are Macartney's remarks on the frictions inherent in the system of Manchu/Han dyarchy[1] and his accurate comprehension of the dangers of peasant revolt.

---

1. The system of double-rule practices throughout the Qing as Han Chinese and Manchu officials served together within many organs of the state bureaucracy.

6.2 *Audience with Qianlong*

Saturday, September 14. This morning at four o'clock a.m. we set out for the Court under the convoy of Wang and Chou, and reached it in little more than an hour, the distance being about three miles from our hotel. I proceeded in great state with all my train music, guards, etc. Sir George Staunton and I went in palanquins and the officers and gentlemen of the Embassy on horseback. Over a rich embroidered velvet I wore the mantle of the Order of the Bath, with the collar, a diamond badge and a diamond star.

Sir George Staunton was dressed in a rich embroidered velvet also, and, being a Doctor of Laws in the University of Oxford, wore the habit of his degree, which is of scarlet silk, full and flowing. I mention these little particulars to show the attention I always paid, where a proper opportunity offered, to oriental customs and ideas. We alighted at the park gate, from whence we walked to the Imperial encampment, and were conducted to a large, handsome tent prepared for us on one side of the Emperor's. After waiting there about an hour his approach was announced by drums and music, on which we quitted our tent and came forward upon the green carpet.

He was seated in an open palanquin, carried by sixteen bearers, attended by numbers of officers bearing flags, standards, and umbrellas, and as he passed we paid him our compliments by kneeling on one knee, whilst all the Chinese made their usual prostrations. As soon as he had ascended his throne I came to the entrance of the tent, and, holding in both my hands a large gold box enriched with diamonds in which was enclosed the King's letter, I walked deliberately up, and ascending the side-steps of the throne, delivered it into the Emperor's own hands, who, having received it, passed it to the Minister, by whom it was placed on the cushion. He then gave me as the first present from him to His Majesty the *ju-eu-jou* or *giou-giou*, as the symbol of peace and prosperity, and expressed his hopes that my Sovereign and he should always live in good correspondence and amity. It is a whitish, agate-looking stone about a foot and a half long, curiously carved, and highly prized by the Chinese, but to me it does not appear in itself to be of any great value.

The Emperor then presented me with a *ju-eu-jou* of a greenish-coloured stone of the same emblematic character; at the same time he very graciously received from me a pair of beautiful enamelled watches set with diamonds, which I had prepared in consequence of the information given me, and which, having looked at, he passed to the Minister. Sir George Staunton, whom, as he had been appointed Minister Plenipotentiary to act in case of my death or departure, I introduced to him as such, now came forward, and after kneeling upon one knee in the same manner which I had done, presented to him two elegant air-guns, and received from him a *ju-eu-jou* of greenish stone nearly similar to mine. Other presents were sent at the same time to all the gentlemen of my train. We then descended from the steps of the throne, and sat down upon cushions at one of the tables on the

Emperor's left hand; and at other tables, according to their different ranks, the chief Tartar Princes and the Mandarins of the Court at the same time took their places, all dressed in the proper robes of their respective ranks. These tables were then uncovered and exhibited a sumptuous banquet. The Emperor sent us several dishes from his own table, together with some liquors, which the Chinese call wine, not, however, expressed from the grape, but distilled or extracted from rice, herbs, and honey. In about half an hour he sent for Sir George Staunton and me to come to him, and gave to each of us, with his own hands, a cup of warm wine, which we immediately drank in his presence, and found it very pleasant and comfortable, the morning being cold and raw.

Amongst other things, he asked me the age of my King, and being informed of it, said he hoped he might live as many years as himself, which are eighty-three. His manner is dignified, but affable, and condescending, and his reception of us has been very gracious and satisfactory. He is a very fine old gentleman, still healthy and vigorous, not having the appearance of a man of more than sixty.

The order and regularity in serving and removing the dinner was wonderfully exact, and every function of the ceremony performed with such silence and solemnity as in some measure to resemble the celebration of a religious mystery. The Emperor's tent or pavilion, which is circular, I should calculate to be about twenty-four or twenty-five yards in diameter, and is supported by a number of pillars, either gilded, painted, or varnished, according to their distance and position. In the front was an opening of six yards, and from this opening a yellow fly-tent projected so as to lengthen considerably the space between the entrance and the throne.

The materials and distribution of the furniture within at once displayed grandeur and elegance. The tapestry, the curtains, the carpets, the lanterns, the fringes, the tassels were disposed with such harmony, the colours so artfully varied, and the light and shades so judiciously managed, that the whole assemblage filled the eye with delight, and diffused over the mind a pleasing serenity and repose undisturbed by glitter or affected embellishments. The commanding feature of the ceremony was that calm dignity, that sober pomp of Asiatic greatness, which European refinements have not yet attained.

I forgot to mention that there were present on this occasion three ambassadors from Tatze or Pegu and six Mohammedan ambassadors from the Kalmucks of the south-west, but their appearance was not very splendid. Neither must I omit that, during the ceremony, which lasted five hours, various entertainments of wrestling, tumbling, wire-dancing, together with dramatic representations, were exhibited opposite to the tent, but at a considerable distance from it.

Thus, then, have I seen 'King Solomon in all his glory.' I use this expression, as the scene recalled perfectly to my memory a puppet show of that name which I recollect to have seen in my childhood, and which made so strong an impression on my mind that I then thought it a true representation of the highest pitch of human greatness and felicity.

6.3 Description of China's Government

The ancient constitution of China differed essentially from the present. Although the Emperor was styled despotic, and decorated with all the titles and epithets of oriental hyperbole, the power and administration of the state resided in the great councils or tribunals, whose functions were not to be violated or disturbed by court intrigue or ministerial caprice. It was government by law, and when attempts were made by their princes to render it otherwise, as often happened, rebellion was the consequence and expulsion the penalty. Hence according to history the regular succession of the crown was broken through, new sovereigns elected, and the former constitution restored. The present family on the throne is the twenty-second distinct dynasty whose hands have swayed the sceptre of China. The government as it now stands is properly the tyranny of a handful of Tartars over more than three hundred millions of Chinese.

An uninterrupted succession of four Emperors, all endowed with excellent understandings, uncommon vigor of mind and decision of character, has hitherto obviated the danger of such an enormous disproportion, and not only maintained itself on the throne, but enlarged its dominions to a prodigious extent.

Various causes have contributed to this wonderful phenomenon in the political world. When the Tartars entered China a century and a half ago, the country had long languished under a weak administration, had been desolated by civil wars and rebellions, and was then disputed by several unworthy competitors. The Tartars availing themselves of these circumstances, at first took part as auxiliaries in favour of one of the candidates but they soon became principals, and at last by valour and perseverance surmounted every obstacle to their own establishment. The spirit of the Chinese was now effectually subdued by the weight of calamity; they were wearied with contending for the mere choice of tyrants among themselves, and they less reluctantly submitted to a foreign usurpation. The conquerors, however terrible in arms and ferocious in their manners, were conducted by a leader of a calm judgement as well as of a resolute mind, who tempered the despotism he introduced with so much prudence and policy that it seemed preferable to the other evils which they had so recently groaned under. A state of tranquil subjection succeeded for some time to the turbulence and horrors of a doubtful hostility; the government, though absolute, was at least methodical and regular. It menaced but did not injure; the blow might be dreaded, but it seldom was felt. . . .

The government of China, as now instituted, may not inaptly be compared to Astley's amphitheatre, where a single jockey rides a number of horses at once, who are so nicely bitted and dressed that he can impel them with a whisper, or stop them with a hair. But at the same time he knows the consequence of mismanagement or neglect, and that if they are not properly matched, curried and fed, patted and stoked, some of them will be liable to run out of the circle, to kick at their keepers and refuse to be mounted any longer. Considering then all circumstances, the

original defect of title to the inheritance, the incessant anxiety of forcible possession, the odium of a foreign yoke, the inevitable combats of passion in a sovereign's
breast, when deceived by artifice, betrayed by perfidy, or provoked by rebellion,
the doubtful and intricate boundaries of reward and punishment, where vigor and
indulgence may be equally misapplied, the almost incalculable population, the
immense extent of dominion, the personal exertions requisite in war, and the no
less difficult talents of administration in peace—considering, I say, all these circumstances, the government of such an empire must be a task that has hitherto been
performed with wonderful ability and unparalleled success. That such singular
skill in the art of reigning should have been uninterruptedly transmitted through
a succession of four princes for upwards of a century and a half would be very difficult to account for, if we did not constantly bear in mind a fundamental principle
of the state. All power and authority in China derive solely from the sovereign, and
they are not only distributed by him in his life time, but attest their origin after his
decease. The appointment of his successor is exclusively vested in him. Without
regard to primogeniture, without the fondness of a parent, without the partiality
of a friend, he acts on this occasion as the father of the state, and selects the person of
his family, whom he judges the most worthy to replace him. Every choice of this
kind as yet made has been unexceptionably fortunate. K'ang-hsi proved as great a
prince as his father; Yung-cheng was inferior to neither, and Ch'ien-lung sur-
passes the glory of all his predecessors. Who is the Atlas destined by him to bear
this load of empire when he dies is yet unknown, but on whatever shoulders it
may fall, another transmigration of Fo-hi into the next emperor will be necessary
to enable him to sustain it on its present balance; for though within the serene
atmosphere of the Court everything wears the face of happiness and applause, yet
it cannot be concealed that the nation in general is far from being easy or contented. The frequent insurrections in the distant provinces are unambiguous ora-
cles of the real sentiments and temper of the people. The predominance of the
Tartars and the Emperor's partiality to them are the common subject of conversation among the Chinese whenever they meet together in private, and the constant
theme of their discourse. There are certain mysterious societies in every province
who are known to be dis-affected, and although narrowly watched by the government, they find means to elude its vigilance and often to hold secret assemblies,
where they revive the memory of ancient glory and independence, brood over
recent injuries, and mediate revenge.

Though much circumscribed in the course of our travels we had opportunities
of observation seldom afforded to others, and not neglected by us. The genuine
character of the inhabitants, and the effects resulting from the refined polity and
principles of the government, which are meant to restrain and direct them, naturally claimed my particular attention and inquiry. In my researches I often perceived the ground to be hollow under a vast superstructure, and in trees of the
most stately and flourishing appearance I discovered symptoms of speedy decay,
whilst humbler plants were held by vigorous roots, and mean edifices rested on

steady foundations. The Chinese are now recovering from the blows that had stunned them; they are awaking from the political stupor they had been thrown into by the Tartar impression, and begin to feel their native energies revive. A slight collision might elicit fire from the flint, and spread flames of revolt from one extremity of China to the other. In fact the volume of the empire is now grown too ponderous and disproportionate to be easily grasped by a single hand, be it ever so capacious and strong. It is possible, notwithstanding, that the momentum impressed on the machine by the vigor and wisdom of the present Emperor may keep it steady and entire in its orbit for a considerable time longer; but I should not be surprised if its dislocation or dismemberment were to take place before my own dissolution. Whenever such an event happens, it will probably be attended with all the horrors and atrocities from which they were delivered by the Tartar domination; but men are apt to lose the memory of former evils under the pressure of immediate suffering; and what can be expected from those who are corrupted by servitude, exasperated by despotism and maddened by despair? Their condition, however, might then become still worse than it can be at present. Like the slave who fled into the desert from his chains and was devoured by the lion, they may draw down upon themselves oppression and destruction by their very effort to avoid them, may be poisoned by their own remedies and be buried themselves in the graves which they dug for others. A sudden transition from slavery to freedom, from dependence to authority, can seldom be borne with moderation or discretion. Every change in the state of man ought to be gentle and gradual, otherwise it is commonly dangerous to himself and intolerable to others. A due preparation may be as necessary for liberty as for inoculation of the smallpox which, like liberty, is future health but without due preparation is almost certain destruction. Thus then the Chinese, if not led to emancipation by degrees, but let loose on a burst of enthusiasm would probably fall into all the excesses of folly, suffer all the paroxysms of madness, and be found as unfit for the enjoyment of freedom as the French and the negroes.

6.4 AND 6.5 QIANLONG'S REJECTION OF MACARTNEY'S DEMANDS: TWO EDICTS

Qianlong's famous edicts to George III were the Qing government's response to the proposals carried to Peking by Lord George Macartney. In 1793, Qianlong ruled the largest unified empire in the world. Each year, in adherence to a schedule established by the Board of Rites, tribute emissaries from Burma, Korea, Vietnam, and other territories trekked to Peking to pay their respects to the throne. It is thus little wonder that the Qianlong emperor regarded Lord Macartney as nothing more than a self-important tributary emissary and rejected all of his requests. In the edicts that follow, Macartney's charge from Henry Dundas was refused point by point. On his own turf, the emperor was used to defining things in a peremptory way but also with regard to the precedents built into the Qing scheme of foreign affairs. The logic in these edicts was solidly founded on history, power, and a belief that a tiny maritime state thousands of *li* from China was not a force to be reckoned with.

6.4 *The First Edict, September 1793*

You, O King, live beyond the confines of many seas, nevertheless, impelled by your humble desire to partake of the benefits of our civilization, you have dispatched a mission respectfully bearing your memorial. Your Envoy has crossed the seas and paid his respects at my Court on the anniversary of my birthday. To show your devotion, you have also sent offerings of your country's produce.

I have perused your memorial: the earnest terms in which it is couched reveal a respectful humility on your part, which is highly praiseworthy. In consideration of the fact that your Ambassador and his deputy have come a long way with your memorial and tribute, I have shown them high favour and have allowed them to be introduced into my presence. To manifest my indulgence, I have entertained them at a banquet and made them numerous gifts. I have also caused presents to be forwarded to the Naval Commander and six hundred of his officers and men, although they did not come to Peking, so that they too may share in my all-embracing kindness.

As to your entreaty to send one of your nationals to be accredited to my Celestial Court and to be in control of your country's trade with China, this request is contrary to all usage of my dynasty and cannot possibly be entertained. It is true that Europeans, in the service of the dynasty, have been permitted to live at Peking, but they are compelled to adopt Chinese dress, they are strictly confined to their own precincts and are never permitted to return home. You are presumably familiar with our dynastic regulations. Your proposed Envoy to my Court could not be placed in a position similar to that of European officials in Peking who are forbidden to leave China, nor could he, on the other hand, be allowed liberty of movement and the privilege of corresponding with his own country; so that you would gain nothing by his residence in our midst.

Moreover, Our Celestial dynasty possesses vast territories, and tribute missions from the dependencies are provided for by the Department for Tributary States, which ministers to their wants and exercises strict control over their movements. It would be quite impossible to leave them to their own devices. Supposing that your Envoy should come to our Court, his language and national dress differ from that of our people, and there would be no place in which he might reside. It may be suggested that he might imitate the Europeans permanently resident in Peking and adopt the dress and customs of China, but, it has never been our dynasty's wish to force people to do things unseemly and inconvenient. Besides, supposing I sent an Ambassador to reside in your country, how could you possibly make for him the requisite arrangements? Europe consists of many other nations besides your own: if each and all demanded to be represented at our Court, how could we possibly consent? The thing is utterly impracticable. How can our dynasty alter its whole procedure and regulations, established for more than a century, in order to meet your individual views? If it be said that your object is to exercise control over your country's trade, your nationals have had full liberty to trade at Canton for many a year, and have received the greatest consideration at our hands. Missions have been sent by Portugal and Italy, preferring similar requests. The Throne appreciated their sincerity and loaded them with favours, besides authorizing measures to facilitate their trade with China. You are no doubt aware that, when my Canton merchant, Wu Chao-p'ing, was in debt to the foreign ships, I made the Viceroy advance the monies due, out of the provincial treasury, and ordered him to punish the culprit severely. Why then should foreign nations advance this utterly unreasonable request to be represented at my Court? Peking is nearly 10,000 *li* from Canton, and at such a distance what possible control could any British representative exercise?

If you assert that your reverence for Our Celestial dynasty fills you with a desire to acquire our civilization, our ceremonies and code laws differ so completely from your own that, even if your Envoy were able to acquire the rudiments of our civilization, you could not possibly transplant our manners and customs to your alien soil. Therefore, however adept the Envoy might become, nothing would be gained thereby.

Swaying the wide world, I have but one aim in view, namely, to maintain a perfect governance and to fulfil the duties of the State; strange and costly objects do not interest me. If I have commanded that the tribute offerings sent by you, O King, are to be accepted, this was solely in consideration for the spirit which prompted you to dispatch them from afar. Our dynasty's majestic virtue has penetrated unto every country under Heaven, and Kings of nations have offered their costly tribute by land and sea. As your Ambassador can see for himself, we possess all things. I set no value on objects strange or ingenious, and have no use for your country's manufactures. This then is my answer to your request to appoint a representative at my Court, a request contrary to our dynastic usage, which would only result in inconvenience to yourself. I have expounded my wishes in detail and have commanded your tribute Envoys to leave in peace on their homeward journey. It behooves you, O King, to respect my sentiments and to display even greater devotion and loyalty in future, so that, by perpetual submission to our Throne, you may secure peace and prosperity for your country hereafter. Besides making gifts (of which I enclose a list) to each member of your Mission, I confer upon you, O King, valuable presents in excess of the number usually bestowed on such occasions, including silks and curios—a list of which is likewise enclosed. Do you reverently receive them and take note of my tender goodwill towards you! A special mandate.

6.5 *The Second Edict, September 1793*

You, O King from afar, have yearned after the blessings of our civilization, and in your eagerness to come into touch with our converting influence have sent an Embassy across the sea bearing a memorial. I have already taken note of your respectful spirit of submission, have treated your mission with extreme favour and loaded it with gifts, besides issuing a mandate to you, O King, and honouring you with the bestowal of valuable presents. Thus has my indulgence been manifested.

Yesterday your Ambassador petitioned my Ministers to memorialize me regarding your trade with China, but his proposal is not consistent with our dynastic usage and cannot be entertained. Hitherto, all European nations, including your own country's barbarian merchants, have carried on their trade with Our Celestial Empire at Canton. Such has been the procedure for many years, although Our Celestial Empire possesses all things in prolific abundance and lacks no product within its own borders. There was therefore no need to import the manufactures of outside barbarians in exchange for our own produce. But as the tea, silk, and porcelain which the Celestial Empire produces are absolute necessities to European nations and to yourselves, we have permitted, as a signal mark of favour, that foreign *hongs* [merchant guilds] should be established at Canton, so that your wants might be supplied and your country thus participate in our beneficence. But your Ambassador has now put forward new requests which completely fail to recognize the Throne's principle to "treat strangers from afar with indulgence," and to exercise a pacifying control over barbarian tribes, the world over. Moreover, our dynasty, swaying the myriad races of the globe, extends the same benevolence towards all. Your England is not the only nation trading at Canton. If other nations, following your bad example, wrongfully importune my ear with further impossible requests, how will it be possible for me to treat them with easy indulgence? Nevertheless, I do not forget the lonely remoteness of your island, cut off from the world by intervening wastes of sea, nor do I overlook your excusable ignorance of the usages of Our Celestial Empire. I have consequently commanded my Ministers to enlighten your Ambassador on the subject, and have ordered the departure of the mission. But I have doubts that, after your Envoy's return he may fail to acquaint you with my view in detail or that he may be lacking in lucidity, so that I shall now proceed to take your requests *seriatim* and to issue my mandate on each question separately. In this way you will, I trust, comprehend my meaning.

1. Your Ambassador requests facilities for ships of your nation to call at Ningpo, Chusan, Tientsin and other places for purposes of trade. Until now trade with European nations has always been conducted at Macao, where the foreign *hongs* are established to store and sell foreign merchandise. Your nation has obediently complied with this regulation for years past without raising any objection. In none of the other ports named have *hongs* been established,

so that even if your vessels were to proceed thither, they would have no means of disposing of their cargoes. Furthermore, no interpreters are available, so you would have no means of explaining your wants, and nothing but general inconvenience would result. For the future, as in the past, I decree that your request is refused and that the trade shall be limited to Macao.

2. The request that your merchants may establish a repository in the capital of my Empire for the storing and sale of your produce, in accordance with the precedent granted to Russia, is even more impracticable than the last. My capital is the hub and centre about which all quarters of the globe revolve. Its ordinances are most august and its laws are strict in the extreme. The subjects of our dependencies have never been allowed to open places of business in Peking. Foreign trade has hitherto been conducted at Macao, because it is conveniently near to the sea, and therefore an important gathering place for the ships of all nations sailing to and fro. If warehouses were established in Peking, the remoteness of your country lying far to the northwest of any capital, would render transport extremely difficult. Before Kiakhta was opened, the Russians were permitted to trade at Peking, but the accommodation furnished them was only temporary. As soon as Kiakhta was available, they were compelled to withdraw from Peking, which has been closed to their trade these many years. Their frontier trade at Kiakhta is equivalent to your trade at Macao. Possessing facilities at the latter place, you now ask for further privileges at Peking, although our dynasty observes the severest restrictions respecting the admission of foreigners within its boundaries, and has never permitted the subjects of dependencies to cross the Empire's barriers and settle at will amongst the Chinese people. This request is also refused.

3. Your request for a small island near Chusan, where your merchants may reside and goods be warehoused, arises from your desire to develop trade. As there are neither foreign *hongs* nor interpreters in or near Chusan, where none of your ships have ever called, such an island would be utterly useless for your purposes. Every inch of the territory of our Empire is marked on the map and the strictest vigilance is exercised over it all: even tiny islets and far-lying sandbanks are clearly defined as part of the provinces to which they belong. Consider, moreover, that England is not the only barbarian land which wishes to establish relations with our civilization and trade with our Empire: supposing that other nations were all to imitate your evil example and beseech me to present them each and all with a site for trading purposes, how could I possibly comply. This also is a flagrant infringement of the usage of my Empire and cannot possibly be entertained.

4. The next request, for a small site in the vicinity of Canton city, where your barbarian merchants may lodge or, alternatively, that there be no longer any restrictions over their movements at Macao, has arisen from the following causes. Hitherto, the barbarian merchants of Europe have had a definite locality assigned to them at Macao for residence and trade, and have been

forbidden to encroach an inch beyond the limits assigned to that locality. Barbarian merchants having business with the *hongs* have never been allowed to enter the city of Canton; by these measures, disputes between Chinese and barbarians are prevented, and a firm barrier is raised between my subjects and those of other nations. The present request is quite contrary to precedent; furthermore, European nations have been trading with Canton for a number of years and, as they make large profits, the number of traders is constantly increasing. How could it be possible to grant such a site to each country? The merchants of the foreign *hongs* are responsible to the local officials for the proceedings of barbarian merchants and they carry out periodical inspections. If these restrictions were withdrawn, friction would inevitably occur between the Chinese and your barbarian subjects, and the results would militate against the benevolent regard that I feel towards you. From every point of view, therefore, it is best that the regulations now in force should continue unchanged.

5. Regarding your request for remission or reduction of duties on merchandise discharged by your British barbarian merchants at Macao and distributed throughout the interior, there is a regular tariff in force for barbarian merchants' goods, which applies equally to all European nations. It would be as wrong to increase the duty imposed on your nation's merchandise on the ground that the bulk of foreign trade is in your hands, as to make an exception in your case in the shape of specially reduced duties. In the future, duties shall be levied equitably without discrimination between your nation and any other, and, in order to manifest my regard, your barbarian merchants shall continue to be shown every consideration at Macao.

6. As to your request that your ships shall pay the duties leviable by tariff, there are regular rules in force at the Canton Custom house respecting the amounts payable, and since I have refused your request to be allowed to trade at other ports, this duty will naturally continue to be paid at Canton as heretofore.

7. Regarding your nation's worship of the Lord of Heaven, it is the same religion as that of other European nations. Ever since the beginning of history, sage Emperors and wise rulers have bestowed on China a moral system and inculcated a code, which from time immemorial has been religiously observed by the myriads of my subjects. There has been no hankering after heterodox doctrines. Even the European [missionary] officials in my capital are forbidden to hold intercourse with Chinese subjects; they are restricted within the limits of their appointed residences, and may not go about propagating their religion. The distinction between Chinese and barbarian is most strict, and your Ambassador's request that barbarians shall be given full liberty to disseminate their religion is utterly unreasonable.

It may be, O King, that the above proposals have been wantonly made by your Ambassador on his own responsibility or peradventure you yourself are ignorant of our dynastic regulations and had no intention of transgressing them when you expressed these wild ideas and hopes. I have ever shown the greatest condescension to the tribute missions of all States which sincerely yearn after the blessings of civilization, so as to manifest my kindly indulgence. I have even gone out of my way to grant any requests which were in any way consistent with Chinese usage. Above all, upon you, who live in a remote and inaccessible region, far across the spaces of ocean, but who have shown your submissive loyalty by sending this tribute mission, I have heaped benefits far in excess of those accorded to other nations. But the demands presented by your Embassy are not only a contravention of dynastic tradition, but would be utterly unproductive of good result to yourself, besides being quite impracticable. I have accordingly stated the facts to you in detail, and it is your bounden duty reverently to appreciate my feelings and to obey these instructions henceforward for all time, so that you may enjoy the blessings of perpetual peace. If, after the receipt of this explicit decree, you lightly give ear to the representation of your subordinates and allow your barbarian merchants to proceed to Chekiang and Tientsin, with the object of landing and trading there, the ordinances of my Celestial Empire are strict in the extreme, and the local officials, both civil and military, are bound reverently to obey the law of the land. Should your vessels touch shore, your merchants will assuredly never be permitted to land or to reside there, but will be subject to instant expulsion. In that event your barbarian merchants will have had a long journey for nothing. Do not say that you were not warned in due time! Tremblingly obey and show no negligence! A special mandate!

7.2 Memorial on Banning Opium, October 1836

Zhu Zun, member of the council and of the Board of Rites, kneeling, presents the following memorial, wherein he suggests the propriety of increasing the severity of certain prohibitory enactments, with a view to maintain the dignity of the laws, and to remove a great evil from among the people: to this end he respectfully states his views on the subject, and earnestly entreats his sacred majesty to cast a glance thereon.

I would humbly point out, that wherever an evil exists it should be at once removed; and that the laws should never be suffered to fall into desuetude. Our government, having received from heaven, the gift of peace, has transmitted it for two centuries: this has afforded opportunity for the removal of evils from among the people. For governing the central nation, and for holding in submission all the surrounding barbarians, rules exist perfect in their nature, and well-fitted to attain their end. And in regard to opium, special enactments were passed for the prohibitions of its use in the first year of Jiaqing [1796]; and since then, memorials presented at various successive periods, have given rise to additional prohibitions, all which have been inserted in the code and the several tariffs. The laws, then, relating thereto are not wanting in severity; but there are those in office who, for want of energy, fail to carry them into execution. Hence the people's minds gradually become callous; and base desires, springing up among them, increase day by day and month by month, till their rank luxuriance has spread over the whole empire. These noisome weeds, having been long neglected, it has become impossible to eradicate. And those to whom this duty is entrusted are, as if handbound, wholly at a loss what to do.

When the foreign ships convey opium to the coast, it is impossible for them to sell it by retail. Hence there are at Canton, in the provincial city, brokers, named 'melters.' These engage money-changers to arrange the price with the foreigners, and to obtain orders for them; with which orders they proceed to the receiving ships, and there the vile drug is delivered to them. This part of the transaction is notorious, and the actors in it are easily discoverable. The boats which carry the drug and which are called 'fast-crabs' and 'scrambling-dragons,' are all well furnished with guns and other weapons, and ply their oars as swiftly as though they were wings. Their crews have all the over-bearing assumption and audacity of pirates. Shall such men be suffered to navigate the surrounding seas according to their own will? And shall such conduct be passed over without investigation? . . .

It is said that the opium should be admitted, subject to a duty, the importers being required to give it into the hands of the *hong* merchants, in barter only for merchandise, without being allowed to sell it for money. And this is proposed as a means of preventing money from secretly oozing out of the country. But the English, by whom opium is sold, have been driven out to Lintin [a small island in the Pearl River estuary] so long since as the first year of Daoguang [1821], when the then governor of Guangdong and Guangxi discovered and punished the ware-housers of opium: so long have they been expelled, nor have they ever since imported it into Macao. Having once suppressed the trade and driven them away, shall we now again call upon them and invite them to return? This would be, indeed, a derogation from the true dignity of government. As to the proposition to give tea in exchange, and entirely to prohibit the exportation of even *foreign* silver I appre-hend that, if the tea should not be found sufficient, money will still be given in exchange for the drug. Besides, if it is in our power to prevent the extortion of dol-lars, why not also to prevent the importation of opium? And if we can but prevent the importation of opium, the exportation of dollars will then cease of itself, and the two offenses will both at once be stopped. Moreover, is it not better, by con-tinuing the old enactments, to find even a partial remedy for the evil, than by a change of the laws to increase the importation still further? As to levying a duty of opium, the thing sounds so awkwardly, and reads so unbeseemingly, that such a duty ought sorely not to be levied.

Again, it is said that the prohibitions against the planting of the poppy by natives should be relaxed; and that the direct consequences will be, daily diminu-tion of the profits of foreigners, and in course of time the entire cessation of the trade without the aid of prohibitions. Is it, then, forgotten that it is natural to the common people to prize things heard of only by the ear and to undervalue those which are before their eyes,—to pass by those things which are near at hand, and to seek after those which are afar off—and, though they have a thing in their own land, yet to esteem more highly such as comes to them from beyond the seas? Thus, in Jiangsu, Zhejiang, Fujian, and Guangdong, they will not quietly be guided by the laws of the empire, but must needs make use of foreign money: and this foreign money, though of an inferior standard, is nevertheless exchanged by them at a higher rate than the native sycee silver, which is pure. And although money is cast in China after exactly the same pattern, under the names of Jiangsu pieces, Fujian pieces, and native or Canton pieces, yet this money has not been able to gain currency among the people. Thus, also, the silk and cotton goods of China are not insufficient in quantity; and yet the broadcloths, and comlets, and cotton goods of the barbarians from beyond the place of the empire are in constant request. Taking men generally the minds of all are equally unenlightened in this respect, so that all men prize what is strange, and undervalue whatever is in ordi-nary use.

From Fujian, Guangdong, Zhejiang, Shandong, Yunnan, and Guizhou, memo-rials have been presented by the censors and other officers, requesting that prohi-bitions should be enacted against the cultivation of the poppy, and against the preparation of opium; but while nominally prohibited, the cultivation of it has not been really stopped in those places. Of any of those provinces, except Yunnan, I do not presume to speak; but of that portion of the country I have it in any power to say, that the poppy is cultivated all over the hills and the open campaign, and that the quantity of opium annually produced there cannot be less than several thousand chests. And yet we do not see any diminution in the quantity of silver exported as compared with any previous period; while, on the other hand, the lack of the metal in Yunnan is double in degree to what it formerly was. To what cause is this to be ascribed? To what but that the consumers of the drug are very many, and that those who are choice and dainty, with regard to its quality prefer always the foreign article?

Those of your majesty's advisers who compare the drug to the dried leaf of the tobacco plant are in error. The tobacco leaf does not destroy the human constitution. The profit too arising from the sale of tobacco is small, while that arising from opium is large. Besides, tobacco may be cultivated on bare and barren ground, while the poppy needs a rich and fertile soil. If all the rich and fertile ground be used for planting the poppy; and if the people, hoping for a large profit therefrom, madly engage in its cultivation; where will flax and the mulberry tree be culti-vated, or wheat and rye be planted? To draw off in this way the waters of the great fountain, requisite for the production of goods and raiment, and to lavish them upon the root whence calamity and disaster spring forth, is an error which may be compared to that of a physician, who, when treating a mere external disease, should drive it inwards to the heart and centre of the body. It may in such a case be found impossible even to preserve *life*. And shall the fine fields of Guangdong, that produce their three crops every year, be given up for the cultivation of this nox-ious weed—those fields in comparison with which the unequal soil of all other parts of the empire is not even to be mentioned?

To sum up the matter—the wide-spreading and baneful influence of opium, when regarded simply as injurious to property, is of inferior importance; but when regarded as hurtful to the people, it demands most anxious consideration: for in the *people* lies the very foundation of the empire. Property, it is true, is that on which the subsistence of the people depends. Yet a deficiency of it may be supplied, and an impoverished people improved; whereas it is beyond the power of any artificial means to save a people enervated by luxury. In the history of Formosa we find the following passage: 'Opium was first produced in Kaoutsinne [?], which by some is said to be the same as Kalapa [or Batavia]. The natives of this place were at the first sprightly and active, and being good soldiers, were always successful in battle. But the people called Hongmao [Red-hairs, a term originally applied to the Dutch] came thither, and having manufactured opium, seduced some of the natives into the habit of smoking it; from this the mania for it rapidly spread throughout the whole nation, so that in process of time, the natives became feeble and enervated, submitted to the foreign rule, and ultimately were completely subjugated.' Now the English are of the race of foreigners called Hongmao. In introducing opium into this country, their purpose has been to weaken and enfeeble the central empire. If not early aroused to a sense of our danger, we shall find ourselves, ere long, on the last step towards ruin. . . .

Since your majesty's accession to the throne, the maxim of your illustrious house that horsemanship and archery are the foundations of its existence, has ever been

carefully remembered. And hence the governors, the lt. governors, the commanders of the forces, and their subordinates have again and again been directed to pay
the strictest attention to the discipline and exercise of the troops, and of the naval
forces; and have been urged and required to create by their exertions strong and
powerful legions. With admiration I contemplate my sacred sovereign's anxious
care for imparting a military as well as a civil education, prompted as this anxiety
is by desire to establish on a firm basis the foundations of the empire, and to hold
in awe the barbarians on every side. But while the stream of importation of opium is
not turned aside, it is impossible to attain any certainty that none within the camp
do ever secretly inhale the drug. And if the camp be once contaminated by it, the
baneful influence will work its way, and the habit will be contracted beyond the
power of reform. When the periodical times of desire for it come round, how can
the victims—their legs tottering, their hands trembling, their eyes flowing with
child-like tears—be able in any way to attend to their proper exercises? Or how
can such men form strong and powerful legions? Under these circumstances, the
military will become alike unfit to advance to the fight, or in a retreat to defend
their posts. Of this there is clear proof in the instance of the campaign against the
Yao rebels in the 12th year of our sovereign's reign [1832]. In the army sent to Yong-
zhou [Hunan], on that occasion, great numbers of the soldiers were opium-smokers;
so that although their numerical force was large, there was hardly any strength to
be found among them. . . .

At the present moment, throughout the empire, the minds of men are in imminent danger; the more foolish, being seduced by teachers of false doctrines, are
sunk in vain superstitions and cannot be aroused; and the more intelligent, being
intoxicated by opium, are carried away as by a whirlpool, and are beyond recovery.
Most thoughtfully have I sought for some plan by which to arouse and awaken all
but in vain. While, however, the empire preserves and maintains its laws, the plain
and honest rustic will see what he has to fear, and will be deterred from evil; and
the man of intelligence and cultivated habits will learn what is wrong in himself,
and will refrain from it. And thus, though the laws be declared by some to be but
waste paper, yet these their unseen effects will be of no trifling nature. If, on the
other hand, the prohibitions be suddenly repealed, and the action which was a crime
be no longer counted such by the government, how shall the dull clown and the
mean among the people know that the action is still in itself wrong? In open day
and with unblushing front, they will continue to use opium till they shall become
so accustomed to it, that eventually they will find it as indispensable as their daily
meat and drink, and will inhale the noxious drug with perfect indifference.
When shame shall thus be entirely destroyed, and fear removed wholly out of the
way, the evil consequences that will result to morality and to the minds of men will
assuredly be neither few nor unimportant. As your majesty's minister, I know that
the laws of the empire, being in their existing state well fitted to effect their end, will
not for any slight cause be changed. But the proposal to alter the law on this subject having been made and discussed in the provinces, the instant effect has been,
that crafty thieves and villains have on all hands begun to raise their heads and

open their eyes, gazing about, and pointing their finger, under the nation that, when once these prohibitions are repealed thenceforth and for ever they may regard themselves free from every restraint and from every cause of fear.

Though possessing very poor abilities I have nevertheless had the happiness to enjoy the favor of your sacred majesty, and have, within a space of but few years, been raised though the several grades of the censorate, and the presidency of various courts in the metropolis, to the high elevation of a seat in the Inner Council. I have been copiously embued with the rich dew of favors; yet have been unable to offer the feeblest token of gratitude; but if there is aught within the compass of my knowledge, I dare not to pass it by unnoticed. I feel it my duty to request that your majesty's commands may be proclaimed to the governors and lieut-governors of all the provinces, requiring them to direct the local officers to redouble their efforts for the enforcement of the existing prohibitions against opium; and to impress on everyone, in the plainest and strictest manner, that all who are already contaminated by the vile habit must return and become new men,—that if any continue to walk in their former courses, strangers to repentance and to reformation, they shall assuredly be subjected to the full penalty of the law, and shall not meet with the least indulgence—and that any found guilty of storing up or selling opium to the amount of 1000 catties or upwards, the most severe punishment shall be inflicted. Thus happily the minds of men may be impressed with fear, and the report thereof, spreading over the seas (among foreigners) may even there produce reformation. Submitting to my sovereign my feeble and obscure views, I prostrate implore your sacred majesty to cast a glance on this my respectful memorial.

7.3 Imperial Edict, September 1836

The councillor Zhu Zun has presented a memorial, requesting that the severity of the prohibitory enactments against opium may be increased. The sub-censor Xu Qiu also has laid before us a respectful representation of his views; and, in a supplementary statement, a recommendation to punish severely Chinese traitors.

Opium, coming from the distant regions of barbarians, has pervaded the country with its baneful influence, and has been made a subject of very severe prohibitory enactments. But, of late, there has been a diversity of opinion in regard to it, some requesting a change in the policy hitherto adopted, and others recommending the continuance of the severe prohibitions. It is highly important to consider the subject carefully in all its bearings, surveying at once the whole field of action, so that such measures may be adopted as shall continue for ever in force, free from all failures.

Let Deng [Deng Tingzhen, the Qing governor-general of Guangdong and Guangxi] and his colleagues anxiously and carefully consult together upon the recommendation to search for, and with utmost strictness apprehend, all those traitorous natives who sell the drug, the *hong* merchants who arrange the transactions in it, the brokers who purchase it by wholesale, the boat-men who are engaged in transporting it, and the naval militia who receive bribes; and having determined on the steps to be taken in order to stop up the source of the evil, let them present a true and faithful report. Let them also carefully ascertain and report whether the circumstances stated by Xu Qiu in his supplementary document, in reference to the foreigners from beyond the seas, be true or not, whether such things as are mentioned therein have or have not taken place. Copies of the several documents are to be herewith sent to those officers for perusal; and this edict is to be made known to Deng and Ke, who are to enjoin it also on Wan, the superintendent of maritime customs. Respect this.

7.4 Annexed Laws on Banning Opium, July 1839

FURNACE KEEPERS OR WHOLESALE DEALERS

Whoever shall hereafter open a "furnace," and connive with and secretly buy opium of the outside barbarians, storing it up for sale, shall, if he be the principal, be decapitated immediately on conviction.

The royal authority shall be respectfully produced and the law executed, ere a report is sent to the crown. The head of the offender shall then be stuck upon a pole, and exposed upon the seacoast as a warning to all. The accomplices, advisers, participators, receivers, givers (those who deliver the drug), and boatmen who knowingly receive opium on board their boats for transport, shall be sentenced to strangulation and thrown into dungeons to wait the royal warrant for their execution. The houses and boats of these parties shall be sequestrated.

1. Any officer or soldier on the coast station who shall receive bribes to connive at opium being brought in, whether the quantity be large or small, shall immediately upon conviction be strangled. He who, knowing it to be such, allows opium to be brought in, but without receiving a bribe, shall be transported to Xinjiang [Chinese Turkestan].
2. If any persons join together and open a furnace for the purpose of selling opium, he who originates the plan shall be considered as the principal.
3. He who stores opium brought by the foreign ships shall be dealt with in the same manner as accomplices in a "furnace." He who, knowing it to be such, consents to conceal opium for any notorious dealers who may have fallen into the hands of government, shall be punished one degree less severely than the principal.

4. He who receives a bribe to release any opium seller or smoker from his custody, shall be punished in the same manner as if he were an opium seller or smoker himself. Should the amount received be considerable, he shall be held punishable under the law against "False and malicious information."

5. Any jailor who shall buy opium and supply it to the prisoners under his charge, shall be transported to the most distant and unhealthy settlements. Any guard or overseer, guilty of a similar offence, shall be transported to a nearer settlement; should the amount received for purchases be considerable, it shall be computed and the offender held punishable under the act against "False and malicious information."

6. Any soldier or policeman, or any of those idle blackguards who infest every place, who shall, without a warrant, enter a house and under pretence of searching for opium forcibly carry of other articles, or who shall, through malice or a desire to extort money, themselves secrete opium in the house, that an accusation may be supported [against their victim], shall, whether principal or accomplice, be held punishable under the law against "False and malicious information," and transported to the most distant settlements. If the amount stolen shall exceed in value 120 taels, the principal shall be sentenced to strangulation, and kept in prison till the warrant for his execution shall arrive.

7. All persons sentenced to transportation for crimes connected with opium shall be excluded from the benefit of the law respecting "indulgence to offenders for the sake of their parents."

SECTION 2ND. KEEPERS OF RETAIL AND SMOKING SHOPS.

Any person who shall keep a shop for selling opium to be smoked on the premises, shall, if the principal, be sentenced, on conviction, to immediate strangulation, and his house shall be sequestrated. Accomplices, accessories, or those who knowing for what purpose, still consent to let their houses to such characters, shall, on conviction, be transported to Xinjiang to be slaves to the military, and their houses sequestrated. Any soldier or policeman who shall receive a bribe for conniving at and "securing" these dens, shall receive the same punishment as a principal. "Ground-sureties" and neighbors, who know of the existence of such places and do not report the same to government, shall be punished with 100 blows, and transported for 3 years. If they shall receive hush money, the amount shall be computed, and the law respecting "False and malicious information" put in force against them.

1. Any native traitor who shall cultivate the poppy for the purpose of expressing its juice to make opium, for preparations and sale, or who shall sell either the "paste" or "mud" to the extent of 500 taels, or if, altho' the amount does not equal that sum, he shall sell at a great number of different places and

times, he shall, if apprehended within the next 18 months, be sentenced to strangulation [if a principal], and thrown into prison to wait the arrival of the warrant for his execution. Accomplices shall be transported to the most distant and unhealthy places. If any are convicted of selling only once or twice, the whole amount of such sales not being taels 500—they shall be transported, if principals to Xinjiang to be slaves to the military, if accomplices they shall be transported to a distance of *li* 4000. After the expiration of the 18 months, both principals and accomplices shall be sentenced to be strangled. If any soldier or policeman receives a bribe to connive at and screen them, he shall be punished in the same manner as the principal. If the amount received be considerable, it shall be computed, and the offender punished under the law against "false and malicious information." Any landlord, who, knowing for what purpose, lets a field or house to opium dealers, or any boatman who shall knowingly hire his boat for transporting the drug, shall, if the offence take place before the expiration of one year from this time, receive a hundred blows, and be transported 2000 *li*—if after one year, he shall be transported to the most distant settlement, if within half a year he shall be sentenced to receive a hundred blows and three years transportation. The fields, grounds, houses, and boats, shall in all cases be sequestrated. If any dealer shall voluntarily confess his crime and cause by his information the apprehension of other dealers, he shall be pardoned, and his house, ground, or boat shall not be sequestrated. If the parties implicated by the said person's confession shall escape and elude the vigilance of government, although his crime shall be pardoned, his house, ground, field, or boat shall not be confiscated. Any "ground surety" or neighbor, who knows of the existence of such dealers and does not forthwith inform against them, shall be punished with 100 blows. If he receives hush money, the amount shall be computed and the law respecting "false and malicious information" put in force against him.

2. The law against the crime of opium smoking, shall take effect in Peking from the day the sacred commands were received; in the provinces from the day that the commands of the board were made known. These were received in the city of Canton on the 26th day of the 5th moon from which time they will date in all the cities, and towns, throughout the province. One year from that date will be allowed for all to renounce the habit. At the expiration of that period all who have *not* renounced the habit, whether they be of the nobles, the military, or vulgar, shall on conviction be sentenced to strangulation and thrown into prison to wait the arrival of the warrant for their execution. If any are apprehended *within* the year of probation, if of the vulgar, they shall be punished with 100 blows and transported to a distance of 2000 *li* &c. If they are unable to say from whom they got the opium, their punishment shall be one degree more severe; they shall receive 100 blows and transported to a distance of 2500 *li*; if of the Tartar soldiery, the offender

shall first be expelled from his banner, (or regiment) and then dealt with as one of the common people; if a government underling, a relation of an officer, a secretary or follower, the offender shall be punished one degree more severely than a common man; if an officer of government, the offender shall be sent to Xinjiang on some degrading and laborious mission; if of the provincials or general army, the offender shall be transported to a shorter distance. . . .

7.5 LORD PALMERSTON'S DECLARATION OF WAR, FEBRUARY 20, 1840

After the seizure of British opium in Canton, Charles Elliot and the British community rejected Lin Zexu's demand for a bond pledging that they would no longer engage in the opium trade. The fled to Macao, where Elliot and the merchants separately petitioned the Tory foreign minister, Lord Palmerston, to take measures against the Qing government. Palmerston was initially reluctant to intervene. However, the minister changed his mind as domestic pressure intensified, in the form of energetic lobbying by William Jardine (a leading opium trader) and Manchester textile firms that feared being cut out of the Chinese and Indian markets.

On October 18, 1839, Palmerston informed Charles Elliot that a British expeditionary force would reach China in the spring of 1840. Since the structure of the British constitution provided Parliament with little control over foreign policy, the decision for war was made without parliamentary consultation. Indeed, until Palmerston's departure from the government in 1841, he single-handedly shaped the China policy.

The following dispatch from Lord Palmerston informs the Qing government of Britain's intention to use force to "protect" the interests of its subjects.

DESPATCH FROM LORD PALMERSTON TO THE MINISTER OF THE EMPEROR OF CHINA

F.O. London, *February* 20, 1840.

THE UNDERSIGNED, Her Britannick Majesty's Principal Secretary of State for Foreign Affairs, has the honour to inform the Minister of the Emperor of China, that Her Majesty The Queen of Great Britain has sent a Naval and Military Force to the Coast of China, to demand from the Emperor satisfaction and redress for injuries inflicted by Chinese Authorities upon British Subjects resident in China, and for insults offered by those same Authorities to the British Crown.

For more than a hundred years, commercial intercourse has existed between China and Great Britain; and during that long period of time, British Subjects have been allowed by the Chinese Government to reside within the territory of China for the purpose of carrying on trade therein. Hence it has happened that British Subjects, trusting in the good faith of the Chinese Government, have fixed themselves in Canton as Merchants, and have brought into that city from time to time property to a large amount; while other British Subjects who wished to trade with China, but who could not for various reasons go thither themselves, have sent commodities to Canton, placing those commodities in the care of some of their fellow Countrymen resident in China, with directions that such commodities should be sold in China, and that the produce of the sale thereof should be sent to the Owners in the British Dominions.

Thus there has always been within the territory of The Emperor of China a certain number of British Subjects, and a large amount of British Property; and though no Treaty has existed between the Sovereign of England and the Emperor of China, yet British Subjects have continued to resort to China for purposes of trade, placing full confidence in the justice and good faith of the Emperor.

Moreover, of late years the Sovereign of Great Britain has stationed at Canton an officer of the British Crown, no wise connected with trade, and specially forbidden to trade, but ordered to place himself in direct communication with the local Authorities at Canton in order to afford protection to British Subjects, and to be the organ of communication between the British and the Chinese Governments.

But the British Government has learnt with much regret, and with extreme surprise, that during the last year certain officers, acting under the Authority of The Emperor of China, have committed violent outrages against the British Residents at Canton, who were living peaceably in that City, trusting to the good faith of the Chinese Government; and that those same Chinese officers, forgetting the respect which was due to the British Superintendent in his Character of Agent of the British Crown, have treated that Superintendent also with violence and indignity.

It seems that the course [cause] assigned for these proceedings was the contraband trade in Opium, carried on by some British Subjects.

It appeared that the Laws of the Chinese Empire forbid the importation of Opium into China, and declare that all opium which may be brought into the Country is liable to confiscation.

The Queen of England desires that Her Subjects who may go into Foreign Countries should obey the Laws of those Countries; and Her Majesty does not wish to protect them from the just consequences of any offenses which they may commit in foreign parts. But, on the other hand, Her Majesty cannot permit that Her Subjects residing abroad should be treated with violence, and be exposed to insult and injustice; and when wrong is done to them, Her Majesty will see that they obtain redress.

Now if a Government makes a Law which applies both to its own Subjects and to Foreigners, such Government ought to enforce that Law impartially or not at all. If it enforces that Law on Foreigners, it is bound to enforce it also upon its own

Subjects; and it has no right to permit its own Subjects to violate the Law with impunity, and then to punish Foreigners for doing the very same thing.

Neither is it just that such a Law should for a great length of time be allowed to sleep as a dead letter, and that both Natives and Foreigners should be taught to consider it as of no effect, and that then suddenly, and without sufficient warning, it should be put in force with the utmost rigor and severity.

Now, although the Law of China declared that the importation of Opium should be forbidden, yet it is notorious that for many years past, that importation has been connived at and permitted by the Chinese Authorities at Canton; nay, more, that those Authorities, from the Governor downwards, have made an annual and considerable profit by taking money from Foreigners for the permission to import Opium: and of late the Chinese Authorities have gone so far in setting this Law at defiance, that Mandarin Boats were employed to bring opium to Canton from the Foreign Ships lying at Lintin.

Did the Imperial Government at Peking know these things?

If it did know these things, it virtually abolished its own Law, by permitting its own officers to act as if no such Law existed. If the Chinese Government says it did not know of these things, if it says that it knew indeed that the Law was violated by Foreigners who brought in opium, but did not know that the Law was violated by its own Officers who assisted in the importation, and received fixed sums of money for permitting it, then may Foreign Governments ask, how it happened that a Government so watchful as that of China should have one eye open to see the transgressions of Foreigners, but should have the other eye shut, and unable to see the transgressions of its own officers. . . .

Now as the distance is great which separated England from China, and as the matter in question is of urgent importance, the British Government cannot wait to know the answer which the Chinese Government may give to these demands, and thus postpone till that answer shall have been received in England, the measures which may be necessary in order to vindicate the honour and dignity of the British Crown, in the event of that answer not being satisfactory.

The British Government therefore has determined at once to send out a Naval and Military Force to the Coast of China to act in support of these demands, and in order to convince the Imperial Government that the British Government attaches the utmost importance to this matter, and that the affair is one which will not admit of delay.

And further, for the purpose of impressing still more strongly upon the Government of Peking the importance which the British Government attaches to this matter, and the urgent necessity which exists for an immediate as well as a satisfactory settlement thereof, the Commander of the Expedition has received orders that, immediately upon his arrival upon the Chinese Coast, he shall proceed to blockade the principal Chinese ports, that he shall intercept and detain and hold in deposit all Chinese Vessels which he may meet with, and that he shall take possession of some convenient part of the Chinese territory, to be held and occupied by the British Forces until everything shall be concluded and executed to the satisfaction of the British Government.

These measures of hostility on the part of Great Britain against China are not only justified, but even rendered absolutely necessary, by the outrages which have been committed by the Chinese Authorities against British officers and Subjects, and these hostilities will not cease, until a satisfactory arrangement shall have been made by the Chinese Government.

The British Government in order to save time, and to afford to the Government of China every facility for coming to an early arrangement, have given to the Admiral and to the Superintendent, Full Powers and Instructions to treat upon these matters with the Imperial Government, and have ordered the said Admiral and Superintendent to go up to the Mouth of the Peiho River, in the Gulph of Pechelee, that they may be within a short distance of the Imperial Cabinet. But after the indignity which was offered to Her Majesty's Superintendent at Canton, in the course of last year, it is impossible for Her Majesty's Government to permit any of Her Majesty's Officers to place themselves in the power of the Chinese Authorities until some formal Treaty shall have been duly signed, securing to British Subjects safety and respect in China; and therefore the Undersigned must request that the Chinese Government will have the goodness to send on board the Admiral's Ship the Plenipotentiaries whom the Emperor may appoint to treat upon these matters with the Plenipotentiaries of The Queen of England. Those Chinese Plenipotentiaries shall be received on board the Admiral's Ship, with every honour which is due to the Envoys of the Emperor, and shall be treated with all possible courtesy and respect.

The Undersigned has further to state, that the necessity for sending this Expedition to the Coast of China having been occasioned by the violent and unjustifiable acts of the Chinese Authorities, the British Government expects and demands that the expenses incurred thereby shall be repaid to Great Britain by the Government of China.

The Undersigned has now stated and explained to the Chinese Minister, without reserve, the causes of complaint on the part of Great Britain; the reparation which Great Britain demands, and the nature of the measures which the British officer commanding the Expedition has been instructed in the first instance to take. The British Government fervently hopes that the wisdom and spirit of Justice for which The Emperor is famed in all parts of the World, will lead the Chinese Government to see the equity of the foregoing demands; and it is the sincere wish of Her Majesty's Government that a prompt and full compliance with those demands may lead to a speedy re-establishment of that friendly intercourse which has for so great a period of time subsisted between the British and Chinese Nations, to the manifest advantage of both.

The Undersigned, in conclusion, has the honour to state to the Minister of The Emperor of China that he has directed Her Majesty's Plenipotentiaries to forward to His Excellency the present Note, of which he has transmitted to the

Plenipotentiaries a copy, with instructions to cause a Translation of it to be made into the Chinese language, and to forward to the Chinese Minister the Translation at the same time with the original Note.

The Undersigned avails himself of this opportunity to offer to His Excellency the Minister of The Emperor of China the assurances of his most distinguished consideration.

PALMERSTON.

CHAPTER 8

The Crisis Within

8.1 QIAN YONG ON POPULAR RELIGION, 1838

The scholar Qian Yong (1759–1844) was a specialist in etymology and bronze and stone inscriptions. He traveled throughout China serving in various yamens but never occupied a powerful position. His famous *Luyuan conghua* is a collection of miscellaneous jottings on many subjects.

In an appendix to this work, Qian included the following injunction against "evil customs" in south China. It was apparently written by one of his acquaintances and was introduced in the volume with an approving note. The essay exhibits the scorn felt by the literati for folk religion and "heterodox" festivals in the years immediately preceding the Opium War, and illustrates the impulse felt by the elite to rein in the unrestrained behavior of untutored peasants, villagers, and city dwellers.

GOING OUT FOR A GATHERING

There have always been religious festivals and parades in China but presently these practices are really flourishing. In the cities, the so-called "heads" of these assemblies are the scribes, clerks, and runners of the prefectural and county yamens. In the countryside, they are the chiefs of *baojia* units and local idlers. Generally, those who understand to some degree the rites and codes of the society and who have family responsibilities will not take part.

Every year in the spring when there is no farm work to tend to, people feel superstitious doubts about ghosts and spirits. What happens then is called "going out for a gathering." Everyone says that this [religious processions and gatherings] can "exorcise evil and bring good fortune" or "get rid of hardship and eliminate locusts." There is a great commotion when these gatherings occur and the whole area goes wild. Tens of thousands of men and women appear to watch these parades and although local magistrates occasionally ban such activities, they grow and prosper from year to year.

Leading the processions are banners to clear the way and people banging gongs and drums. Others hold wooden placards, just like those carried by local officials, reading "silence" and "avoidance." Some of them paint their faces and carry spears or staves. Some dress up as government soldiers and carry swords and bows and arrows or fowling pieces and rattan shields. Some others pretend to be scribes and clerks of the six departments of the local yamen and carry mock documents, case files, and registration books. Still others wear chains and shackles and pretend to be prisoners guilty of serious offenses. Two false executioners, dressed in red, lead a prisoner stripped to the waist on whose back is a tablet saying that he is to be decapitated. They [the people] are accustomed to these wicked spectacles and treat them as natural. They have no sense of shame and think that this is fun. This is really ludicrous!

Recently, Scholar Li Jiantian of Jiangyin urgently commented on this and wrote "The Ten Evils of Religious Gatherings." He considered that people should only make sacrifices to ghosts and spirits of their own clans and that only community temples were appropriate to mediate between heaven and earth. Since ancient times, whenever harvest sacrifices were presented at community temples, the people merely burned paper money and beat ceremonial drums. Beneath the altar, the libations of wine were as fragrant as the spring wind and people frolicked in nearby groves of mulberry trees. It was the very image of happiness and peace! Rites and rituals were followed without error and none went astray. There was no insult to the spirits or raucous shouting in the community. There was no violation of the rites and ceremonies or injury to social customs to this great degree. Since Li Jiantian's account of the "ten evils" is clear and precisely appropriate to the problem, I have recorded it here:

1. Blaspheming the ghosts and spirits. In the *Analects* it says: "If you are unable to attend to human affairs, how can you serve the spirits?" Paying reverence to the spirits by trying to get close to them is unheard of! This is merely a means of taking other people's money so that the "heads" of the societies can eat their fill and get drunk. The stupid commoners do not know what they are doing and so they follow them. After time, all of this becomes social custom and hundreds of problems arise. This is the first reason for imposing a ban.
2. Confusing the ritual code. In every prefecture and county there are altars for the spirits of the mountains, the rivers, and the land. There are also temples for the civil and military city gods and shrines dedicated to local sages and worthies and famous officials of former times. All of these temples

are enumerated in the local ritual handbook and it is right and appropriate for officials and the people to present sacrifices at these temples in the spring and autumn. If a certain village earth god comes to be identified as having been a certain prince, marquis, general, or prime minister, this is not listed in the ritual handbook. The names and ranks are different, there is no distinction between high and low, the past and present are all topsy turvy, and the symbols and rituals are all wrong. This is a debasement of ritual practice. But the monks and Daoist priests rely on such practices to make money and women use them to disport themselves. This is the second reason for imposing a ban.

3. Squandering money. A religious festival in any area relies on the support of tens of thousands of households. Some people stretch their finances to the utmost to participate and think of hundreds of ways to borrow funds to join in the gathering. Some even pawn their clothes or sell their stores of food and, in so doing, wreck their family finances to participate. They use their limited funds for this useless expense and are unable to pay back the debts they incur or to fulfill their rent obligations. Impoverished and disconsolate, they freeze and starve without understanding how this came to be. Although these people bring this suffering on themselves it also comes about because of evil local customs. This is the third reason for imposing a ban.

4. Disrupting normal occupations. People living in a city all have their own occupations. People living in the countryside all have their own work to do. All of them should accept frugality and diligence as the root of their lives. How is it possible for them to find the leisure time for these [heterodox, religious] activities? Moreover, all of the festivals are held in the spring time and this disrupts natural timing and their professional schedules. I surely cannot understand what is in their minds! Ask yourself, are these activities designed to win fame or profit or to obtain food or clothing? That the stupidity of small people has reached such a degree is the fourth reason for imposing a ban.

5. Mixing of men and women. Whenever a village or city has such a festival, there are multitudes of spectators. How can women be prevented from coming out? Since there are many women, how can the roving flirts who follow the parades be prevented from watching these women? These flirts take the opportunities provided by this boiling mass of people to seize the fragrance so near at hand. When a smiling head is turned toward them, they mistakenly consider that this is affection. When they hear the chattering of a sweet voice, they lose their senses. They overturn ferry boats and die in their excitement; they jostle and knock over sedan chairs and loosen the hair and hair ornaments of their female occupants. There is no worse injury to customs than this! This is the fifth reason for imposing a ban.

6. Causing fires. Whether a religious festival occurs in the city or countryside, candles and lamps are lit up in a splendid display. Incense and smoke fill

the air. The fires of teahouses and wineships are constantly burning. Sometimes colorful lanterns are made for night parades and the people are asked for contributions to pay for fireworks. If something unexpected happens, it is difficult to come to the rescue. If vicious people were to take this opportunity to loot and rob, the situation would be uncontrollable. This is the sixth reason for imposing a ban.

7. Promoting gambling. During festivals where there are so many different types of people mixed together, it is easy for them to form groups to gamble. They play dice and make wagers on shell games. Some lose all of their money but still hope to get it back. Some find it impossible to borrow money and are trapped in a terrible situation. Some leave stripped of their clothes and some come back waving their arms to fight. This causes endless harm to an area and this is the seventh reason for imposing a ban.

8. Causing fighting. Normally, small numbers of wild hoodlums and bandits in villages and market towns do get together to drink and, on occasion, they beat and attack each other. But during festivals there are thousands of people who gather; drinking occurs in all of the shops and gambling takes place everywhere. If someone becomes angry, he is likely to behave violently and murderously. Without intervention to mediate the problem such disputes can lead to homicide. Because of this, the calamity would extend to the *baojia* and the lawsuit might burden the village community. This is the eighth reason for imposing a ban.

9. Attracting robbers and thieves. If bandits from various places mix with the masses, it is difficult to find them out but easy for them to steal. During the day, the excitement is so great that everyone becomes exhausted and in the calm of the night they sleep so deeply that they can be robbed. In an instant, the rich lose their gold and silk and the stores of grain of the poor are swept away. It is already too late to catch the thieves or to seek the return of the stolen goods. This is the ninth reason for imposing a ban.

10. Damaging social customs. The people's original nature is simple. But because of these gatherings they make all kinds of clothes. The families are mostly poor but because of these festivals they have all sorts of expenses and in both the city and countryside they come to adore luxury. In the little streets and alleys, friends and relatives are constantly coming and going and this makes the people fall into a pattern of extravagance. This damages social customs and this is the tenth reason for imposing a ban.

8.2 THE CONVERSION OF LIANG FA: *GOOD WORDS TO EXHORT THE AGE*, 1832

One of the first converts of the London Missionary Society was Liang Fa (1789–1855), a young Cantonese printer and employee of the Society's press in Malacca. In the first years of missionary work in south China, Liang Fa (also known as Liang Afa) played a vital role in the Society's efforts to spread the faith to potential converts. He helped translate the New Testament into Chinese and wrote religious tracts, personally distributing them in market-places. These pamphlets, printed on fragile paper and bound with string, featured Bible stories, cautionary tales warning against opium use, or question-and-answer discussions (similar to the format of the conversation between Liang Fa and "Mr. Mi" below).

Good Words to Exhort the Age, written by Liang Fa in 1832, became the most famous work of this genre due to its formative influence on Hong Xiuquan (1813–1864), the future leader of the Taiping Rebellion. Hong received a copy of this nine-volume set in 1836, outside the provincial exami-nation hall in Canton. Initially ignored, *Good Words* played an important role as a theoretical source book and guide to Christianity as Hong elaborated his own eclectic and eccentric doctrines. In the following excerpt, Liang Fa describes his own conversion and discusses the reasons he was drawn to Christianity.

Before I received the Lord's grace, my mind was full of evil and folly and had yet to be enlightened. I still did not piously believe the Savior's true scripture and holy way and although I slightly understood that my daily behavior and words were those of a sinful person, I did not know how to seek redemption for my sins. On the first and the fifteenth of the month, early in the morning, in an airy place, I would burn incense and pay my respects to the passing immortals. I wanted to beg the passing gods for grace and mercy and to seek protection and good fortune. I also recited the "Guanyin Sutra" and the "Duoxin Sutra" one time and implored the Boddhisattva Guanyin and Buddha to pity me, protect my health, and give me spiritual peace. I also begged for wealth and fortune. I practiced this method of paying my respect to the various gods and deities for many years. Although I was physically worshipping various gods and buddhas, I still held evil and obscene notions in the heart and spoke false and deceitful words. I was filled with vicious desires that never left my heart or were far from my mouth.

At that time, every day, I listened to a certain Mr. Mi [William Milne of the London Missionary Society] preach the true and holy message of how the Savior had sacrificed himself to save mankind from its sins. Although I was physically present listening to him preach the truth, my mind was not there but racing about in contemplation of worldly things. At times I skimmed through the pages of the Holy Bible but could not understand its meaning. Even when I lis-tened to Mr. Mi as he spoke of the truth, my mind could still not fathom the significance of what he was saying. After listening to his sermons I ignored them and despised them; I did not want to hear them. Often I talked to my friends and said: "How can this be right? Asking people not to worship various gods and buddhas? This has to be an evil and heretical teaching. Who will believe this? If we follow this kind of reasoning, then all of those people who sell gold paper,

their bodies tainted by sin and their souls besmirched by sin, the baptismal water is to clean their bodies as they implore the Lord on high and send down the divine wind to cleanse their souls."

After hearing Mr. Mi explain all of this, I asked, "Now that I know that I am a sinner, how can my sins be pardoned?"

Mr. Mi said: "If you truly believe in Jesus and are baptized, then it will be as if Jesus suffered and died for your sins. When the Lord our God considers Jesus' great accomplishment in dying for the sins of others, he can pardon your sins and accept you as good subject of the Lord. When it is time for you to die and go on to the next life, Jesus' merit [*gonglau*] also becomes your merit and you will be granted eternal happiness in heaven."

Mr. Mi's explanation was so wonderful that after I heard it I took my leave and returned to my small room to meditate [on these lessons]. I thought: "I am a sinner. If I do not rely on Jesus' merit in taking the sins of man upon himself, how can my sin simply be pardoned by the Lord our God? In believing in the way of Jesus one could be considered one of the Lord's good subjects and also enjoy the fortune of living in heaven after death. But the most fortunate thing of all was that one would not fall into hell after death and suffer eternal pain." I had now made up my mind: The following Sunday, I would accept Jesus' way, receive baptism, and enter through the gate of truth and holy reason. I went to ask Mr. Mi whether he was willing to baptize me.

Mr. Mi said: "If you will sincerely confess your sins and change your evil ways and follow the way Jesus the Savior and not worship graven images of God and Buddha but piously worship only the Lord and master of heaven, earth, and all beings and eradicate all traces of the obscene and evil behavior of your past and rid yourself of deceitful and false words, then, next Sunday, on the sabbath, you may receive baptism. If you cannot do this, you may not receive baptism."

I said: "I will obey all that you have taught me." And on the following Sunday, at noontime, I went to implore Mr. Mi to baptize me. Mr. Mi asked me again whether I would confess and renounce all my evil deeds and then read with me several passages from the Holy Scriptures. He then knelt down with me to pray to the Lord our God to bestow his grace upon me and used his hand to sprinkle a bit of pure water on my head.

After I received baptism and expressed my thanks in prayer to the Lord, I then asked Mr. Mi: "What is the sign of people who believe in Jesus?"

Mr. Mi said: "To fully concentrate one's heart on doing good is the sign of people who believe in Jesus."

I thanked Mr. Mi and returned to my small room and sitting alone there felt happy in the belief that I had obtained pardon from the Lord for my great sins. I then gave myself a new name: "Xueshanzhe" [the one who studies good]. This meant that in the future I would concentrate on changing my evil ways and studying the good and would not dare to do evil.

8.3 Executions of Taiping Rebels at Canton, 1851

Under the Qing legal code, no crime (with the possible exception of patricide) was more serious than insurrection. Joining a rebellion was the ultimate political risk one could take under the imperial system, and rebels could expect no mercy from government forces sent to crush them.

The following document, describing an execution of rebels in Canton, is drawn from a volume of foreign eyewitness accounts of the Taiping Rebellion collected by a missionary-interpreter and a physician attached to the French embassy in China. It was written originally in French and translated and published for an English-reading audience in 1853.

In the course of the year 1851, more than 700 unfortunate persons were executed at Canton. The severity of the mandarins seemed to increase in the same proportion as the extension of the insurrection; and every day some arrest took place, and some unhappy wretch, shut up in a bamboo cage, or shackled like a wild beast, was brought from the province of Guangxi or the revolted districts of the Guangdong. Generally they had not to wait for their sentence; since, in case of insurrection, the superior authority of the province has a right to inflict capital punishment, and makes abundant use of this sanguinary privilege. An execution is a horrible thing in any country, but in China its horror is doubled by its attendant circumstances. We give here the letter of one of our friends, who had the melancholy curiosity to be present at the execution of fifty-three rebels of the Guangxi.

"On the 1st of May," he writes, "I attended an execution with three of my friends. The street in which these frightful scenes occur, is situated as you are aware, without the walled city of Canton, towards that part of the suburbs which lies to the south along the river. This narrow, dirty street, which is about 100 *meters* long and 15 wide, is called by the Europeans, the 'Potter's Field.' All the houses on each side are in fact inhabited by workmen who make common services of porcelain, and those portable furnaces which you have often seen in the poorest houses, and in the floating residences on the river. For fear that a Chinese Scholar like you may dispute names with me, I must tell you at once that this dismal place is called by the natives, Tsien-Tse-Ma-Teou [*Qianzi matou*], or the 'Quay of the Thousand Characters,' in allusion to the numerous signs which are seen there from the river.

"We arrived there at ten o'clock in the morning, and took our station in front of a shop belonging to a mender of old stockings. This was an excellent position to take a survey of the whole ceremony, and we remained there quietly till noon; at which time some soldiers and officers attached to the service of the mandarins, arrived to clear the street and thrust back the curious. As in Europe, the persons who came to see the spectacle were the vilest dregs of the populace,—dirty, ragged people, with sinister countenances, who wandered about the ensanguined soil; where most likely they had already seen the execution of a number of their companions, and perhaps of their accomplices.

"In a short time the roll of the tam tam announced to us the arrival of the whole procession. Mandarins of every degree, with the red, white, blue, or yellow ball, riding on horseback, or carried in palanquins, and followed by an escort of musicians, sbirri [police officers], and standard-bearers, alighted at a short distance from the place of execution. Contrary to their ceremonious habits, they arranged themselves in the dismal enclosure.

"Then arrived the criminals. They were fifty-three in number, each shut up in a basket, with his hands tied behind his back, his legs chained, and a board inscribed with his sentence hanging from his neck. You have often met in the Chinese streets a pair of coolies carrying a pig stretched out at its full length in a bamboo case. Well, just imagine a human being put in the place of the unclean animal, and you can form an idea of the fifty-three unfortunate creatures in their cages. When the cages were set down, they were opened and emptied, just as when a pig is turned out at a butcher's shop. I examined these unfortunate wretches with attention: they were worn out with hunger, and looked more like skeletons than living beings. It was evident that they had suffered the most dreadful privations. They were clothed in loathsome tatters, wore long hair, and the dishevelled tail attached to the crown of the head, had been reduced to a third of its usual length. They had evidently belonged to the insurgent bands, who had adopted the fashion of the Mings, and allowed all their hair to grow.

"Many of these unfortunate persons were very young: some were not sixteen years of age; while others had gray hair. Scarcely were they thrown on the ground pell-mell, when they were compelled to kneel; but the greater part of them was so debilitated from suffering, that they could not keep in this position, and rolled in the mud. An executioner's assistant then picked them up, and arranged them all in a row; while three executioners placed themselves behind them and waited the fatal moment. You doubtless recollect those horrible figures whom we have often seen together in the *cortege* [procession] of the criminal judge of Canton—those figures dressed in a red blouse, and wearing a copper crown, adorned above the ears with two long pheasant's feathers. Well! These were the executioners who now waited the signal with a rude and heavy cutlass in their hands. These enormous weapons are about two feet long, and the back of the blade is two inches thick: altogether it is a cumbrous instrument, shaped like a Chinese razor, with a rude handle of wood.

"A mandarin who closed the *cortege*, then entered the enclosure. He was adorned with the white ball, and held in his hand a board, inscribed with the order for execution. As soon as this man appeared the frightful work began. The executioner's assistants, each clothed in a long black robe, and wearing a sort of head-dress of iron wickerwork, seized the criminals from behind, and passing their arms under the shoulders of their victims, gave them a swinging movement, which made them stretch out their necks. The executioner who was now in front, holding his sword in both hands, threw all his strength into the weapon, and divided the cervical vertebra with incredible rapidity, severing the head from the body at a single blow. The executioner never had to strike twice; for even if the flesh was not completely cut through, the weight was sufficient to tear it, and the head rolled on the ground. An assistant then levelled the victim with a kick, for the corpse would otherwise have remained in a kneeling position. After three or four decapitations, the executioner changed his weapon; the edge of the blade seeming completely turned. The execution of these fifty-three wretches only lasted some minutes.

"When the last head had fallen, the mandarins retired from the scene as silent as they had come. Seeing the highest provincial officers present at the execution of these unfortunate men, I was struck with the reflection that in all countries— horrible to say—the political scaffold has been elevated instead of degraded. After the departure of the mandarins, the executioner picked up all the heads, and threw them into a chest brought for the purpose. At the same time the assistants took the chains off the victims as they lay in a pool of blood. The heads were carried away, but the bodies were left on the place of execution.

"A lamentable scene then commenced. A troop of women with dishevelled hair approached the fatal spot, shrieking aloud in wild disorder. These unhappy beings were endeavoring to distinguish their fathers, their husbands, and their children, among the headless corpses. It was a frightful scene to see them hurrying about, pondering, and constantly mistaken among these headless remains. This search continued all day, accompanied by a mournful noise; funeral dirges being mingled with cries and sobs. The women never ceased repeating that kind of chant common to all funeral ceremonies and which was composed, it is said, in the time of the Mings. It is a sort of rhythmical plaint, in which the same words constantly recur: 'Oh, misery! Oh, despair! My happiness is gone forever! Your kindness will no longer soften the bitterness of life! Alone and bereaved of all, I can only weep and die over your ashes!' and so on.

"To these details, which I saw with my own eyes, I should add some others which have been communicated to me by the Chinese. When the criminals left their prison, each was provided with a cake. This was one of those pies cooked by steam, and filled with sweetmeats, that you have often seen on the table of mandarins.

"I asked the reason of this practice, and was informed that the criminal stomach was filled for two reasons. First, that the illusion of blood should not be too copious; and, secondly, that the soul, famished by too long an abstinence, might not torment those who separated it from its mortal tenement. I give you this explanation, that nothing may be omitted. The following particular statement is curious. It was given me by a man of letters, who stood by my side during the horrid spectacle. The execution did not take place quite according to rule. Generally the culprit is brought before a kind of altar, formed of stones brought from the eighteen provinces. This expiatory altar is raised on the day previous to the execution, and when all is over it is taken down. This custom—so thought my informant—is excellent. It inspires the criminal with feelings of contrition, because he seems to pay the penalty of his crime before the inhabitants of the empire."

8.4 AND 8.5 "THE TEN COMMANDMENTS" AND THE "ODE FOR YOUTH": THE TAIPING IDEOLOGY OF HONG XIUQUAN, 1852 AND 1853

Hong Xiuquan's idiosyncratic Taiping ideology drew on three major sources: Christian tracts and translations of the Scripture published by foreign missionaries; the Confucian classics he had studied as an aspiring examination candidate; and the Buddhist and Daoist folk religions of south China. The documents below are translations of the earliest extant versions of two important declarations of Taiping ideology. "The Ten Commandments" was printed in the early years of the rebellion. Each commandment is followed by a commentary and a poem. The "Ode for Youth," a hymn of religious verses, describes the roles and duties of Taiping followers.

8.4 "The Ten Commandments"

Decalogue

THE TEN CELESTIAL COMMANDMENTS WHICH ARE TO BE CONSTANTLY OBSERVED

THE FIRST COMMANDMENT
THOU SHALT HONOUR AND WORSHIP THE GREAT GOD.

Remark. The great God is the universal Father of all men, in every nation under Heaven. Every man is produced and nourished by him: every man ought, therefore, morning and evening, to honour and worship him, with acknowledgements of his goodness. It is a common saying, that Heaven produces, nourishes, and protects men. Also, that being provided with food we must not deceive Heaven. Therefore, whoever does not worship the great God breaks the commands of Heaven.

The Hymn says:
Imperial Heaven, the Supreme God is the true Spirit (God):
Worship him every morning and evening, and you will be taken up;

You ought deeply to consider the ten celestial commands,
And not by your foolishness obscure the right principles of nature.

THE SECOND COMMANDMENT
THOU SHALT NOT WORSHIP CORRUPT SPIRITS (GODS).

Remark.   The great God says, Thou shalt have no other spirits (gods) besides me. Therefore all besides the great God are corrupt spirits (gods), deceiving and destroying mankind; they must on no account be worshipped: whoever worships the whole class of corrupt spirits (gods) offends against the commands of Heaven.

The Hymn says:
Corrupt devils very easily delude the souls of men.
If you perversely believe in them, you will at last go down to hell.
We exhort you all, brave people, to awake from your lethargy,
And early make your peace with your exalted Heavenly Father.

THE THIRD COMMANDMENT
THOU SHALT NOT TAKE THE NAME OF THE
GREAT GOD IN VAIN.

Remark.   The name of the great God is Jehovah, which men must not take in vain. Whoever takes God's name in vain, and rails against Heaven, offends against this command.

The Hymn says:
Our exalted Heavenly Father is infinitely honorable;
Those who disobey and profane his name, seldom come to a good end.
If unacquainted with the true doctrine, you should be on your guard,
For those who wantonly blaspheme involve themselves in endless crime.

THE FOURTH COMMANDMENT
ON THE SEVENTH DAY, THE DAY OF WORSHIP,
YOU SHOULD PRAISE THE GREAT GOD FOR HIS GOODNESS.

Remark.   In the beginning the great God made heaven and earth, land and sea, men and things, in six days; and having finished his works on the seventh day, he called it the day of rest (or Sabbath): therefore all the men of the world, who enjoy the blessing of the great God, should on every seventh day especially reverence and worship the great God, and praise him for his goodness.

The Hymn says:
All the happiness enjoyed in the world comes from Heaven;
It is therefore reasonable that men should give thanks and sing;
At the daily morning and evening meal there should be thanksgiving,
But on the seventh day, the worship should be more intense.

THE FIFTH COMMANDMENT
THOU SHALT HONOUR THY FATHER AND THY
MOTHER, THAT THY DAYS MAY BE PROLONGED.

Remark. Whoever disobeys his parents breaks this command.

The Hymn says:

> History records that Shun honoured his parents to the end of his days,
> Causing them to experience the interest pleasure and delight:
> August Heaven will abundantly reward all who act thus,
> And do not disappoint the expectation of the authors of their being.

THE SIXTH COMMANDMENT
THOU SHALT NOT KILL OR INJURE MEN.

Remark. He who kills another kills himself, and he who injures another injures himself. Whoever does either of these breaks the above command.

The Hymn says:

> The whole world is one family, and all men are brethren,
> How can they be permitted to kill and destroy one another?
> The outward form and the inward principle are both conferred by Heaven:
> Allow every one, then, to enjoy the ease and comfort which he desires.

THE SEVENTH COMMANDMENT
THOU SHALT NOT COMMIT ADULTERY OR ANY
THING UNCLEAN.

Remark. All the men in the world are brethren, and all the women in the world are sisters. Among the sons and daughters of the celestial hall the males are on one side and the females on the other, and are not allowed to intermix. Should either men or women practice lewdness they are considered outcasts, as having offended against one of the chief commands of Heaven. The casting of amorous glances, the forbearing of boastful imaginations, the smoking of foreign tobacco (opium), or the singing of blasphemous songs must all be considered as breaches of this command.

The Hymn says:

> Lust and lewdness constitute the chief transgression,
> Those who practice it become outcasts, and are the objects of pity.
> If you wish to enjoy the substantial happiness of heaven,
> It is necessary to deny yourself and earnestly cultivate virtue.

THE EIGHTH COMMANDMENT
THOU SHALT NOT ROB OR STEAL.

Remark. Riches and poverty are determined by the great God; but whosoever robs or plunders the property of others transgresses this command.

The Hymn says:

> Rest contented with your station, however poor, and do not steal.
> Robbery and violence are low and abandoned practices.
> Those who injure others really injure themselves.
> Let the noble-minded among you immediately reform.

THE NINTH COMMANDMENT
THOU SHALT NOT UTTER FALSEHOOD.

Remark. All those who tell lies, and indulge in devilish deceits, with every kind of coarse and abandoned talk, offend against this command.

The Hymn says:

> Lying discourse and unfounded stories must all be abandoned.
> Deceitful and wicked words are offences against Heaven.
> Much talk will, in the end, bring evil on the speakers.
> It is then much better to be cautious, and regulate one's own mind.

THE TENTH COMMANDMENT
THOU SHALT NOT CONCEIVE A COVETOUS DESIRE.

Remark. When a man looks upon the beauty of another's wife and daughters with covetous desires, or when he regards the elegance of another man's possessions with covetous desires, or when he engages in gambling, he offends against this command.

The Hymn says:

> In your daily conduct do not harbour covetous desires.
> When involved in the sea of lust the consequences are very serious.
> The above injunction was handed down on Mount Sinai;
> And to this day the celestial command retains all its force.

8.5 Taiping Religious Verses (from the "Ode for Youth")

ON THE WORSHIP OF GOD.

> Let the true Spirit, the great God,
> Be honoured and adorned by all nations;
> Let all the inhabitants of the world
> Unite in the worship, morning and evening.
>
> Above and below, look where you may,
> All thing are imbued with the Divine favour.
> At the beginning, in six days,
> All things were created, perfect and complete.

Whether circumcised or uncircumcised,
Who is not produced by God?
Reverently praise the Divine favour
And you will obtain eternal glory.

ON REVERENCE FOR JESUS.

Jesus, his first-born Son,
Was in former times sent by God:
He willingly gave his life to redeem us from sin;
Of a truth his merits are pre-eminent.

His cross was hard to bear;
The sorrowing clouds obscured the sun.
The adorable Son, the honoured of Heaven,
Died for you, the children of men.

After his resurrection he ascended to heaven;
Resplendent in glory, he wields authority supreme.
In him we know what we may trust
To secure salvation and ascend to Heaven.

ON THE HONOUR DUE TO PARENTS.

As grain is stored against a day of need,
So men bring up children to tend their old age:
A filial son begets filial children,
The recompense here is truly wonderful.

Do you ask how this our body
Is to attain to length of years?
Keep the fifth command, we say,
And honour and emolument will descend upon you.

ON THE COURT.

The imperial court is an awe-inspiring spot,
Let those about it dread celestial majesty;
Life and death emanate from Heaven's son,
Let every officer avoid disobedience.

ON THE DUTIES OF THE SOVEREIGN.

When one man presides over the government
All nations become settled and tranquilized:
When the sovereign grasps the sceptre of power
Calumny and corruption sink and disappear.

ON THE DUTIES OF MINISTERS.

When the prince is upright, ministers are true;
When the sovereign is intelligent, ministers will be honest.

E and Chow are models worthy of imitation:
They acted uprightly and aided the government. . . .

ON THE DUTIES OF A FATHER.

When the main beam is straight the joists will be regular;
When a father is strict his duty will be fulfilled;
Let him not provoke his children to wrath,
And delightful harmony will pervade the dwelling.

ON THE DUTIES OF A MOTHER.

Ye mothers, beware of partiality,
But tenderly instruct your children in virtue;
When you are a fit example to your daughters,
The happy feeling will reach to the clouds.

ON THE DUTIES OF SONS.

Sons, be patterns to your wives;
Consider obedience to parents the chief duty;
Do not listen to the tattle of women
And you will not be estranged from your own flesh.

ON THE DUTIES OF DAUGHTERS-IN-LAW.

Ye that are espoused into other families,
Be gentle and yielding, and your duty is fulfilled;
Do not quarrel with your sisters-in-law,
And thereby vex the old father and mother. . . .

OF THE DUTIES OF HUSBANDS.

Unbending firmness is natural to the man,
Love for a wife should be qualified by prudence;
And should the lions roar
Let not terror fill the mind.

ON THE DUTIES OF WIVES.

Women, be obedient to your three male relatives,
And do not disobey your lords:
When hens crow in the morning
Sorrow may be expected in the family.

ON THE DUTIES OF THE MALE SEX.

Let every man have his own partner
And maintain the duties of the human relations
Firm and unbending; his duties lie from home,
But he should avoid such things as cause suspicion.

ON THE DUTIES OF THE FEMALE SEX.

The duty of women is to maintain chastity,
She should shun proximity to the other sex;
Sober and decorous she should keep at home:
Thus she can secure happiness and felicity.

ON THE CONTRACTING MARRIAGES.

Marriages are the result of some relation in a former state
The disposal of which rests with Heaven.
When contracted, affection should flow in a continued stream,
And the association should be uninterrupted.

ON MANAGING THE HEART.

For the purpose of controlling the whole body
God has given to man an intelligent mind;
When the heart is correct it becomes the true regulator
To which the senses and members are all obedient.

ON MANAGING THE EYES.

The various corruptions first delude the eye,
But if the eye is correct all evil will be avoided;
Let the pupil of the eye be sternly fixed,
And the light of the body will shine up to heaven.

ON MANAGING THE FEET.

Let the feet walk in the path of rectitude,
And ever follow it, without treading awry;
For the countless by-paths of life
Lead only to mischief in the end.

THE WAY TO GET TO HEAVEN.

Honour and disgrace come from a man's self;
But men should exert themselves
To keep the Ten Commandments,
And they will enjoy bliss in Heaven.

8.6 AND 8.7 ZENG GUOFAN: CONFUCIAN OFFICIAL AND GENERAL

Zeng Guofan (1811–1872), born in Hunan, rose from a humble background to become one of the most influential officials of the mid-nineteenth century. He gained renown as the commander of the Hunan Army, which defeated the Taipings in 1864. In his later career, he promoted a series of forward-looking reforms on behalf of the Qing court.

In Document 8.6, Zeng Guofan, denouncing the Taiping rebels, compares them to Li Zicheng and Zhang Xianzhong, the notorious "bandits" who played instrumental roles in the fall of the Ming dynasty. In Document 8.7, a letter Zeng wrote to his two brothers just a year before his death, the family patriarch reminds the younger generations of their duties and emphasizes the importance of propriety and diligence. In both government service and private life, Confucian teachings and morality were central to Zeng Guofan's view of the world.

8.6 A Proclamation Against the Bandits of Guangdong and Guangxi, 1884

It has been five years since the rebels Hong Xiuquan and Yang Xiuqing started their rebellion. They have inflicted bitter sorrow upon millions of people and devastated more than 5000 *li* of *chou* [regions] and *xian* [counties] Wherever they pass, boats of all sizes, and people rich and poor alike, have all been plundered and stripped bare; not once inch of grass has been left standing. The clothing has been stripped from the bodies of those captured by these bandits, and their money has been seized. Anyone with five taels or more of silver who does not contribute it to the bandits is forthwith decapitated. Men are given one *he* [1/10th pint] of rice per day, and forced to march in the forefront in battle, to construct city walls, and dredge moats. Women are also given one *he* of rice per day, and forced to stand guard on the parapets at night, and to haul rice and carry coal. The feet of women who refuse to unbind them are cut off and shown to other women as a warning. The corpses of boatmen who secretly conspired to flee were hung upside down to show other boatmen as a warning. The Yue [Guangdong and Guangxi] bandits indulge themselves in luxury and high position, while the people in our own Yangtze provinces living under their coercion are treated worse than animals. This cruelty and brutality appalls anyone with blood in his veins.

Ever since the times of Yao, Shun, and the Three Dynasties, sages, generation after generation, have upheld the Confucian teachings, stressing proper human relationships, between ruler and minister, father and son, superiors and subordinates, the high and the low, all in their proper place, just as hats and shoes are not interchangeable. The Yue bandits have stolen a few scraps from the foreign barbarians and worship the Christian religion. From their bogus ruler and bogus chief ministers down to their soldiers and menial underlings, all are called brothers. They say that only heaven can be called father; aside from him, all fathers among the people are called brothers, and all mothers are called sisters. Peasants are not allowed to till the land for themselves and pay taxes, for they say that the fields all belong to the Tian Wang [Heavenly King]. Merchants are not allowed to trade for profit, for they say that all goods belong to the Tian Wang. Scholars may not read the Confucian classics, for they have their so-called teachings of Jesus and the New Testament. In a single day several thousand years of Chinese ethical principles and proper human relationships, classical books, social institutions and statutes have all been completely swept away. This is not just a crisis for our Qing dynasty, but the most extraordinary crisis of all time for the Confucian teachings, which is why our Confucius and Mencius are weeping bitterly in the nether world. How can any educated person sit idly by without thinking of doing something?

Since ancient times, those with meritorious accomplishments during their lifetimes have become spirits after death; the Kingly Way governs the living and the Way of the Spirits governs among the dead. Even rebellious ministers and wicked sons of the most vicious and vile sort show respect and awe toward the spirits. When Li Zicheng reached Qufu [Confucius' birthplace in Shandong province], he did not molest the Temple of the Sage.[1] When Zhang Xianzhong reached Zitong, he sacrificed to Wen Chang [the patron spirit of literature].[2] But the Yue bandits burned the school at Shen-chou, destroyed the wooden tablet of Confucius, and wildly scattered the tablets of the Ten Paragons in the two corridors all over the ground.[3] Afterwards, wherever they have passed, in every district, the first thing they have done is to burn down the temples, defiling the shrines and maiming the statues even of loyal ministers and righteous heroes such as the awesome Kuan Yü and Yüe Fei.[4] Even Buddhist and Taoist temples, shrines of guardian deities and altars to local gods have all been burned, and every statue destroyed. The ghosts and spirits in the world of darkness are enraged at this, and want to avenge their resentment.

I, the Governor-General, having received His Imperial Majesty's command leading 20,000 men advancing together on land and water, vow that I shall sleep on nettles and ship gall [to strengthen my determination] to exterminate these vicious traitors, to rescue our captured boats, and to deliver the persecuted people, not only in order to relieve the Emperor of his strenuous and conscientious labors from dawn to dusk, but also to comfort Confucius and Mencius for their

1. Li Zicheng was a major rebel leader at the end of the Ming dynasty.

2. Zhang Xianzhong was another important rebel leader at the end of the Ming period. Wen Chang was the God of Literature, closely associated with the literati, and with the civil service examination system.

3. The Ten Paragons were ten famous Confucians, whose tablets were arranged along corridors, east and west, in Confucian temples.

4. Two famous generals and loyal officials. Kuan Yü was deified as the God of War.

silent sufferings over the proper human relationships; and only to avenge the millions who have died unjust deaths, but also to avenge the insults to all the spirits.

Therefore, let this proclamation be disseminated far and near so that all may know the following: Any red-blooded hero who assembles a company of righteous troops to assist in our extermination campaign will be taken in as my personal friend, and the troops given rations. Any Confucian gentleman who cherishes the Way, is pained at Christianity running rampant over the land, and who, in a towering rage, wants to defend our Way, will be made a member of the Governor-General's personal staff and treated as a guest teacher. Any benevolent person, stirred by moral indignation, who contributes silver or assists with provisions, will be given a treasury receipt and a commission from the Board of Civil Appointments for a donation of 1000 *jin* [one *jin* = 1⅓ pounds] or less, and a special memorial will be composed requesting a liberal reward for a donation of over 1000 *jin*. If anyone voluntarily returns after a long stay among the bandits, and kills one of their leaders or leads a city to surrender, he will be taken into the army of the Governor-General and upon the request of the Governor-General to the Emperor, will be given an official title. Anyone who has lived under the bandits' coercion for some years, whose hair has grown several inches long, but who discards his weapon when the fighting is about to commence and returns to the fold barehanded, will receive an amnesty from the death sentence, and will be given travel expenses to return home.

In the past, at the end of the Han, Tang, Yuan, and Ming, bands of rebels were innumerable, all because of foolish rulers and misgovernment, so that none of these rebellions could be stamped out. But today the Son of Heaven is deeply concerned and examines his character in order to reform himself, worships Heaven, and is sympathetic to the people. He has not increased the land tax, nor has he conscripted soldiers from households. With the profound benevolence of the sages, he is suppressing the cruel and worthless bandits. It does not require any great wisdom to see that sooner or later they will all be destroyed.

Those of you who have been coerced into joining the rebels, or who willingly follow the traitors, and oppose the Imperial Crusade [are warned that] when the Imperial forces sweep down it will no longer be possible to discriminate between the good and evil—every person will be crushed.

I, the Governor-General, am scant in virtue and of meager ability. I rely solely on two words, trust and loyalty, as the foundation for running the army. Above are the sun and the moon, below the ghosts and spirits; in this world, the vast waters of the Yangtze, and in the other world, the souls of loyal ministers and stalwart heroes who gave their lives in battle against previous rebellions. Let all peer into my heart and listen to my words.

Upon arrival, this proclamation immediately has the force of law. Do not disregard it!

8.7 Zeng Guofan's Letter to His Younger Brothers

Dear Cheng and Yuan,

I have received your frequent letters as well as that which you sent to Jize and his brother, so I am apprised of everything. I left Jinling on the thirteenth day of the eighth month, returning to the ministry there on the fifteenth of the tenth month. I was kept so busy during the trip that I have not been able to write regularly to my brothers, for which I am deeply sorry. So Cheng has a baby son and Yuesong has embarked upon his studies—these are recent causes for family celebration. It is also good to hear that Yuan and his wife have made a speedy recovery from their illness and we can take comfort in the fact that their daughter married to Zhu was not too depressed over the loss of her baby.

I feel that the younger generation of our household are all physically rather weak; neither have they progressed very well in their studies. I have exhorted the younger generation to follow six rules on strengthening their constitution: (1) take a walk of a thousand steps after meals; (2) wash the feet before retiring; (3) harbour no anger; (4) meditate regularly; (5) practise archery regularly (archery is good for deportment and toning the muscles; our youngsters should practise more often); and (6) eat nothing but plain rice for breakfast. These things I learned from our elders and my experience has shown that no harm comes of such practices. I hope that all of our younger generation will try to follow them.

I have also exhorted them to follow four rules concerning studies: (1) in reading new books, one should strive for speed. If one does not read a great deal, one will be ill-informed; (2) in revising old books, one should strive to master them thoroughly; if one does not intone them to oneself they will be easily forgotten; (3) in learning calligraphy, it is necessary to have perseverance; if one does not write a good hand, one will be like a body without clothes or a mountain without trees; (4) in writing essays one should ponder deeply; if one is not good at composition, one will be like a man without a voice or a horse without legs. Of these four rules, not one can be lacking. From my lifelong experience, I know this well and deeply regret not having tried hard enough.

The maintenance of good health and diligence in study must progress together. A strong will and a strong body will result. This may well be a good sign that the family will be prosperous. If the two of you agree with this, I hope you will frequently instruct your sons accordingly.

I have been travelling on official business for over two months and have been busy with social engagements, but luckily have had no recurrence of vertigo or hernia and because I've been wearing foreign stockings the swelling in my feet has disappeared. However, my eyesight is failing day by day, and I urinate too frequently: feebleness is pressing nearer. This is the natural course of things, nothing out of the ordinary. Nie Yifeng wrote to say that his son will come next spring and he also raised the matter of sending our daughter to Guangdong to be married. I replied that I still held to the decision that the couple should live with us, but that I would allow things to be delayed until spring.

Mount Dongtai is part of the public land of the district. It is in the public eye and too close to the city. Though the soil is good, I am not willing to pursue the matter. I have already written to Shutang about it.

I am in receipt of the tea, razor clams, Sichuan bamboo shoots and soya sauce, thank you! I have not yet sent you a single delicacy, my brothers, yet you have repeatedly sent me various fresh and rare things. How ashamed I feel. The bamboo shoots do not seem as tasty as those we had as children (certainly not as good as the ones Yuan sent me in the sixth year of Tongzhi). I wonder why? As for the *Mingyuantang wen*, I cannot remember which essays I selected for this; please copy out the table of contents and send it to me. I should select a hundred pieces and keep the promise I made.

About the inscription for grandfather's tomb, I will send it at once. I want Yuan to do the calligraphy. If it is as good as the set of scrolls hanging on Zhang Shiqing's wall (I believe Yuan did those in the seventh year of Tongzhi), it will be fine. Yuan, there's no need for you to decline out of modesty.

CHAPTER 9

Restoration through Reform

9.1 YUNG WING: INTERVIEW WITH ZENG GUOFAN, 1863

By the late nineteenth century it was clear to Qing reformers that the preservation of civil order might well depend on how successfully Peking could deploy naval and ground forces built on Western models. Yung Wing (Rong Hong) (1828–1912) was one such advocate for reform. Born in Guangdong, Yung was a student of the Morrison Educational Society, founded by Protestant missionaries in honor of Robert Morrison (1782–1834). With the financial support of missionary sponsors, Yung Wing went to the United States to study. When he graduated from Yale in 1854, he became the first Chinese to earn a degree from an American university. Yung returned to China shortly thereafter and worked as an interpreter and assistant to foreign missionaries.

In 1863, Yung Wing, now the head of a flourishing tea business, was invited to meet with Zeng Guofan to discuss the purchase of Western machinery and weapons for the Jiangnan Arsenal in Shanghai. In later years, the arsenal produced warships and munitions for the Qing navy, a major reform project undertaken by Li Hongzhang. As the following selection from Yung Wing's autobiography shows, in the 1860s there were few experts who could address the technical questions of procuring the equipment and weapons needed to modernize the Qing military. With a commission from Zeng Guofan to purchase armaments abroad, Yung returned to the United States, ten years after his graduation from Yale. While he waited for the Putnam Machine Company to complete the procurement order, Yung tried (unsuccessfully) to enlist as a volunteer in the Union Army, to fight in the American Civil War for his adopted country.

After winding up my business in New Keang, I took passage in a native boat and landed at Ngan Khing in September. There, in the military headquarters of Viceroy Tsang Kwoh Fan [Zeng Guofan], I was met by my friends, Chang Si Kwei, Li Sien Lan, Wha Yuh Ting and Chu Siuh Chune, all old friends from Shanghai. They were glad to see me, and told me that the viceroy for the past six months, after hearing them tell that as a boy I had gone to America to get a Western education, had manifested the utmost curiosity and interest to see me, which accounted for the three letters which Chang and Li had written urging me to come. Now, since I had arrived, their efforts to get me there had not been fruitless, and they certainly claimed some credit for praising me up to the viceroy. I asked them if they knew what His Excellency wanted me for, aside from the curiosity of seeing a native of China made into a veritable Occidental. They all smiled significantly and told me that I would find out after one or two interviews. From this, I judged that they knew the object for which I was wanted by the Viceroy, and perhaps, they were at the bottom of the whole secret.

The next day I was to make my debut, and called. My card was sent in, and without a moment's delay or waiting in the ante-room, I was ushered into the presence of the great man of China. After the usual ceremonies of greeting, I was pointed to a seat right in front of him. For a few minutes he sat in silence, smiling all the while as though he were much pleased to see me, but at the same time his keen eyes scanned me over from head to foot to see if he could discover anything strange in my outward appearance. Finally, he took a steady look into my eyes which seemed to attract his special attention. I must confess I felt quite uneasy all the while, though I was not abashed. Then came his first question.

"How long were you abroad?"

"I was absent from China eight years in pursuit of a Western education."

"Would you like to be a soldier in charge of a company?"

"I should be pleased to head one if I had been fitted for it. I have never studied military science."

"I should judge from your looks, you would make a fine soldier, for I can see from your eyes that you are brave and can command."

"I thank Your Excellency for the compliment. I may have the courage of a soldier, but I certainly lack military training and experience, and on that account I may not be able to meet Your Excellency's expectations."

When the question of being a soldier was suggested, I thought he really meant to have me enrolled as an officer in his army against the rebels; but in this I was mistaken, as my Shanghai friends told me afterwards. He simply put it forward to find out whether my mind was at all martially inclined. But when he found by my response that the bent of my thought was something else, he dropped the military subject and asked me my age and whether or not I was married. The last question closed my first introductory interview, which had lasted only about half an hour. He began to sip his tea and I did likewise, which according to Chinese official etiquette means that the interview is ended and the guest is at liberty to take his departure.

I returned to my room, and my Shanghai friends soon flocked around me to know what had passed between the Viceroy and myself. I told them everything, and they were highly delighted. . . .

To resume the thread of my story, I was nearly two weeks in the Viceroy's headquarters, occupying a suite of rooms in the same building assigned to my Shanghai friends—Li, Chang, Wha and Chu. There were living in his military headquarters at least two hundred officials, gathered there from all parts of the Empire, for various objects and purposes. Besides his secretaries, who numbered no less than a hundred, there were expectant officials, learned scholars, lawyers, mathematicians, astronomers and machinists; in short, the picked and noted men of China were all drawn there by the magnetic force of his character and great name. He always had a great admiration for men of distinguished learning and talents, and loved to associate and mingle with them. During the two weeks of my sojourn there, I had ample opportunity to call upon my Shanghai friends, and in that way incidentally found out what the object of the Viceroy was in urging me to be enrolled in the government service. It seemed that my friends had had frequent interviews with the Viceroy in regard to having a foreign machine shop established in China, but it had not been determined what kind of machine shop should be established. One evening they gave me a dinner, at which time the subject of the machine shop was brought up and it became the chief topic. After each man had expressed his views on the subject excepting myself, they wanted to know what my views were, intimating that in all likelihood in my next interview with the Viceroy he would bring up the subject. I said that as I was not an expert in the matter, my opinions or suggestions might not be worth much, but nevertheless from my personal observation in the United States and from a common-sense point of view, I would say that a machine shop in the present state of China should be of a general and fundamental character and not one for specific purposes. In other words, I told them they ought to have a machine shop that would be able to create or reproduce other machine shops of the same character as itself; each and all of these should be able to turn out specific machinery for the manufacture of specific things. In plain words, they would have to have general and fundamental machinery in order to turn out specific machinery. A machine shop consisting of lathes of different kinds and sizes, planers and drills, would be able to turn out machinery for making guns, engines, agricultural implements, clocks, etc. In a large country like China, I told them, they would need many primary or fundamental machine shops, but that after they had one (and a first-class one at that) they could make it the mother shop for reproducing others—perhaps better and more improved. If they had a number of them, it would enable them to have the shops co-operate with each other in case of need. It would be cheaper to have them reproduced and multiplied in China, I said, where labor and material were cheaper, than in Europe and America. Such was my crude idea of the subject.

After I had finished, they were apparently much pleased and interested, and expressed the hope that I would state the same views to the Viceroy if he should ask me about the subject.

Several days after the dinner and conversation, the Viceroy did send for me. In this interview he asked me what in my opinion was the best thing to do for China at that time. The question came with such a force of meaning, that if I had not been forewarned by my friends a few evenings before, or if their hearts had not been set on the introduction of a machine shop, and they had not practically won the Viceroy over to their pet scheme, I might have been strongly tempted to launch forth upon my educational scheme as a reply to the question as to what was the best thing to do for China. But in such an event, being a stranger to the Viceroy, having been brought to his notice simply through the influence of my friends, I would have run a greater risk of jeopardizing my pet scheme of education than if I were left to act independently. My obligations to them were great, and I therefore decided that my constancy and fidelity to their friendship should be correspondingly great. So, instead of finding myself embarrassed in answering such a large and important question, I had a preconceived answer to give, which seemed to dove-tail into his views already crystallized into definite form, and which was ready to be carried out at once. So my educational scheme was put in the background, and the machine shop was allowed to take precedence. I repeated in substance what I had said to my friends previously in regard to establishing a mother machine shop, capable of reproducing other machine shops of like character, etc. I especially mentioned the manufacture of rifles, which, I said, required for the manufacture of their component parts separate machinery, but that the machine shop I would recommend was not one adapted for making the rifles, but adapted to turn out specific machinery for the making of rifles, cannons, cartridges, or anything else.

"Well," said he, "this is a subject quite beyond my knowledge. It would be well for you to discuss the matter with Wha and Chu, who are more familiar with it than I am and we will then decide what is best to be done."

This ended my interview with the Viceroy. After I left him, I met my friends, who were anxious to know the result of the interview. I told them of the outcome. They were highly elated over it. In our last conference it was decided that the matter of the character of the machine shop was to be left entirely to my discretion and judgment, after consulting a professional mechanical engineer. At the end of another two weeks, Wha was authorized to tell me that the Viceroy, after having seen all the four men, had decided to empower me to go abroad and make purchases of such machinery as in the opinion of a professional engineer would be the best and the right machinery for China to adopt. It was also left entirely to me to decide where the machinery should be purchased,—either in England, France or the United States of America.

The location of the machine shop was to be at a place called Kow Chang Meu, about four miles northwest of the city of Shanghai. The Kow Chang Meu machine shop was afterwards known as the Kiang Nan Arsenal, an establishment that covers several acres of ground and embraces under its roof all the leading branches of mechanical work. Millions have been invested in it since I brought the first machinery from Fitchburg, Mass., in order to make it one of the greatest arsenals east of the Cape of Good Hope. It may properly be regarded as a lasting monument to commemorate Tsang Kwoh Fan's broadmindedness as well as far-sightedness in establishing Western machinery in China.

9.2 PRINCE GONG ON THE TONGWEN COLLEGE: THREE MEMORIALS, 1861, 1865, 1866

Founded in 1862, the original goal of the *Tongwenguan* was to teach foreign languages and train linguists who could serve as interpreters in the conduct of international affairs. When Prince Gong, the moving force behind the project, proposed that the school's curriculum be expanded to include subjects such as mathematics, chemistry, and international law, he encountered fierce opposition from conservative officials who objected to foreign learning. Grand Secretary Woren, the most important neo-Confucian scholar of his time, particularly despised "foreign studies" and argued that these subjects should never replace the classical curriculum. The following excerpts from three memorials address the difficulties reformers faced and illustrate the clashes provoked in the imperial court by new forms of learning.

OCTOBER 1861 MEMORIAL

In the tenth year of Xianfeng (1860) we had the honor to lay before the throne a statement of new measures, rendered necessary by the events of the late war. Among other things, we stated that a knowledge of the character and institutions of foreign nations is indispensable to the conduct of intercourse. We accordingly requested your Majesty to command the viceroy and governor at Canton and Shanghai to find natives well acquainted with foreign letters, and to send them, with a good supply of foreign books, to the capital, with a view to the instruction of youth to be chosen from the Eight Banners.

The viceroy of Canton reported that there was no man whom he could recommend, and the governor of Jiangsu reported that though *one* candidate had presented himself, he was by no means deeply versed in the subject.

This explains the long delay in carrying our plan into execution. Your Majesty's servants are penetrated with the conviction that to know the state of several nations it is necessary first to understand their language and letters. This is the sole means to protect ourselves from becoming the victims of crafty imposition.

Now these nations at large expense employ natives of China to teach them our literature, and yet China has not a man who possesses a ripe knowledge of foreign languages and letters—a state of things quite incompatible with a thorough knowledge of those countries.

As therefore no native candidates were sent up from Canton and Shanghai, we have no resource but to seek among foreigners for suitable men.

1865 MEMORIAL

The school has now been in operation nearly five years, and the students have made fair progress in the languages and letters of the West. Being, however, very young, and imperfectly acquainted with the letters of their own country, their time is unavoidably divided between Chinese and foreign studies. Should we, in addition, require them to take up astronomy and mathematics, we fear they would not succeed in acquiring more than a smattering of anything.

The machinery of the West, its steamers, its firearms, and its military tactics, all have their source in mathematical science. Now at Shanghai and elsewhere the building of steamers has been commenced; but we fear that if we are content with a superficial knowledge, and do not go to the root of the matter, such efforts will not issue in solid success.

Your Majesty's servants have accordingly to propose, after mature deliberation, that an additional department shall be established, into which none shall be admitted but those who are over twenty years of age, having previously gained a degree in Chinese learning. For we are convinced that if we are able to master the mysteries of mathematical calculation, physical investigation, astronomical observation, the construction of engines, the engineering of watercourses, this, and only this, will assure the steady growth of the power of the empire.

No sooner were these proposals laid before the throne than they were made a target for bitter attack by mandarins of the old school. A second memorial replies to these objectors. In both the provision and breadth of view are truly admirable: but how lamentable that men of such intelligence should be forced by national bigotry to repudiate all sympathy with the civilization of the West!

1866 MEMORIAL

We have now to explain that in proposing these measures we have neither been influenced by a love of novelty nor fascinated by the arts of the West, but actuated solely by the consideration that to attempt to introduce the arts without the sciences would be likely to prove an abortive and useless expenditure of public funds. Those who criticize this proceeding object that it is at present not an affair of urgent necessity; that we are wrong in renouncing our own methods to follow those of the West; or, finally, that it would be a deep disgrace for China to become the pupil of the West.

Now not only do the nations of the West learn from each other the new things that are daily produced, but Japan in the Eastern seas has recently sent men to England to learn the language and science of that country. When a small nation like Japan knows how to enter on a career of progress, what could be a greater disgrace than for China to adhere to her old traditions and never think of waking up?

9.3 AND 9.4 THE BURLINGAME TREATY AND THE UNITED STATES EXCLUSION ACT

In the decades after the start of the California gold rush in 1849, tens of thousands of Chinese immigrants arrived in the United States. By the time of the U.S. census of 1870, there were Chinese living in every state, with the largest concentration settling in California.

The new immigrants were initially welcomed to California's gold fields and pioneer settlements. Even when the gold rush ended work was plentiful for the Chinese laborers, although they were often exploited by unscrupulous contractors who sold their labor for a fraction of its value. The word for these contract laborers, "coolie," is sometimes claimed to be a Chinese loan word meaning "bitter toil." Certainly the demeaning and ill-paid labor they found after coming to the "Golden Mountain" merited this appellation.

The documents below trace the changing attitude of the American government toward Chinese labor. The first document consists of two parts of an agreement, signed by Anson Burlingame in 1868, that permitted free immigration between China and the United States: Chinese were treated like other immigrants to America. By the mid-1870s, however, this tolerance had waned and a movement was under way in Washington to restrict and even halt Chinese immigration to the United States. The second document in this section is the Exclusion Act of 1882, the first American law restricting immigration on the basis of race and national origin.

9.3 The Burlingame Treaty, 1868

ARTICLE V. The United States of America and the Emperor of China cordially recognize the inherent and inalienable right of man to change his home and allegiance, and also the mutual advantage of the free immigration and emigration of their citizens and subjects, respectively, from the one country to the other, for purposes of curiosity, of trade, or as permanent residents. The High Contracting Parties, therefore, join in reprobating any other than an entirely voluntary emigration for these purposes. They consequently agree to pass laws making it a penal offense for a citizen of the United States or Chinese subject to take Chinese subjects either to the United States or to any other foreign country, or for a Chinese subject or citizen of the United States to take citizens of the United States to China or to any other foreign country, without their free and voluntary consent, respectively.

ARTICLE VI.   Citizens of the United States visiting or residing in China shall enjoy the same privileges, or exemptions in respect to travel or residence as may there be enjoyed by the citizens or subjects of the most favored nation. And, reciprocally, Chinese subjects visiting or residing in the United States shall enjoy the same privileges, immunities, and exemptions in respect to travel or residences as may there be enjoyed by the citizens or subjects of the most favored nation. But nothing herein contained shall be held to confer naturalization upon citizens of the United States in China, nor upon the subjects of China in the United States.

9.4 *The Exclusion Act, May 6, 1882*

An Act to execute certain treaty stipulations relating to Chinese.

Whereas, in the opinion of the Government of the United States, the coming of Chinese laborers to this country endangers the good order of certain localities within the territory thereof: Therefore,

Be it enacted by the Senate and House of Representatives of the United States of America in Congress assembled, That from and after the expiration of ninety days next after the passage of this act, and until the expiration of ten years next after the passage of this act, the coming of Chinese laborers to the United States be, and the same is hereby, suspended; and during such suspension it shall not be lawful for any Chinese laborer to come, or, having so come after the expiration of said ninety days, to remain within the United States. . . .

SEC. 2.   That the master of any vessel who shall knowingly bring within the United States on such vessel, and land or permit to be landed, any Chinese laborer, from any foreign port or place, shall be deemed guilty of a misdemeanor and on conviction thereof shall be punished by a fine of not more than five hundred dollars for each and every such Chinese laborer so brought, and may be also imprisoned for a term not exceeding one year. . . .

SEC. 8.   That the master of any vessel arriving in the United States from any foreign port or place shall, at the same time he delivers a manifest of the cargo and if there be no cargo, then at the time of making a report of the entry of the vessel pursuant to law, in addition to the other matter required to be reported, and before landing, or permitting to land, any Chinese passengers, deliver and report to the collector of customs of the district in which such vessel shall have arrived a separate list of all Chinese passengers taken on board his vessel at any foreign port or place, and all such passengers on board the vessel at that time.

Such lists shall show the names of such passengers (and if accredited officers of the Chinese Government traveling on the business of that Government or their servants, with a note of such facts), and the names and other particulars, as shown by their respective certificates; and such list shall be sworn to by the master in the manner required by law in relation to the manifest of the cargo.

Any willful refusal or neglect of any such master to comply with the provisions of this section shall incur the same penalties and forfeiture as are provided for a refusal or neglect to report and deliver a manifest of the cargo.

SEC. 9.   That before any Chinese passengers are landed from any such vessel, the collector or his deputy shall proceed to examine such passengers, comparing the certificates with the list and with the passengers, and no passenger shall be allowed to land in the United States from such vessel in violation of law.

SEC. 10.   That every vessel whose master shall knowingly violate any of the provisions of this act shall be deemed forfeited to the United States, and shall be liable to seizure and condemnation in any district of the United States into which such vessel may enter or in which she may be found.

SEC. 11.   That any person who shall knowingly bring into or cause to be brought into the United States by land or who shall knowingly aid or abet the same, or aid or abet the landing in the United States from any vessel of any Chinese person not lawfully entitled to enter the United States, shall be deemed guilty of a misdemeanor, and shall, on conviction thereof, be fined in a sum [not] exceeding one thousand dollars, and imprisoned for a term not exceeding one year.

SEC. 12.   That no Chinese person shall be permitted to enter the United States by land without producing to the proper officer of customs the certificate in this act required of Chinese persons seeking to land from a vessel.

And any Chinese person found unlawfully within the United States shall be caused to be removed therefrom to the country from whence he came, by direction of the President of the United States, and at the cost of the United States, after being brought before some justice, judge, or commissioner or a court of the United States and found to be one not lawfully entitled to be or remain in the United States.

SEC. 13.   That this act shall not apply to diplomatic and other officers of the Chinese Government traveling upon the business of that Government, whose credentials shall be taken as equivalent to the certificate in this act mentioned, and shall exempt them and their body and household servants from the provisions of this act as to other Chinese persons.

SEC. 14.   That hereafter no State court or court of the United States shall admit Chinese to citizenship; and all laws in conflict with this act are hereby repealed.

SEC. 15.   That the words "Chinese laborers," wherever used in this act, shall be construed to mean both skilled and unskilled laborers and Chinese employed in mining.

Approved, May 6, 1882

9.5 A PROPOSAL TO BUILD RAILROADS, 1879

Born in Jiangsu to a Catholic family, Ma Jianzhong (1845–1900) attended a French missionary school in Shanghai, where he studied several foreign languages. From 1877 to 1879, he served as a diplomatic attaché, accompanying a group of students from the Fuzhou Naval Dockyard sent to France for training. While in Paris, Ma took the opportunity to study, earning a baccalaureate and a law diploma. When he returned to China in 1880, Ma became a member of Li Hongzhang's staff and later a manager in the China Merchant Steam Navigation Company. His ideas, advocating technology and commerce, later influenced reform-minded officials.

In this essay, written in France in 1879, Ma argues that railroads played a crucial role in the modernization of Western countries, and could similarly advance China's aspirations for wealth and power. He addresses the arguments of critics and outlines the strategic and economic imperative for railroad construction.

There are some who say that the railroad originated in England while others say Germany, but for the time being I will not pursue this question further. What *can* be said is that the construction of roughly made iron tracks to accommodate wheels, thereby facilitating transportation and dispensing with animal power, first occurred in 1825 in the vicinity of coal mines in England. Thereafter, during the next twenty-four years, America, Austria, France, Belgium, Germany, Russia, Italy and Spain, fearing they would fall behind, all rushed to build railroad tracks of their own. By 1875, the first year of the Emperor Guangxu, there were 136,298 miles of railroad track in Europe. Of this total, England possessed 26,472 miles, France 26,298 miles, Germany 25,772 miles, Austria 16,238 miles and Russia 17,733 miles. Other countries such as Italy, Spain, Belgium, Sweden, Holland, Turkey and Switzerland all have at least 1,000 miles of railroad track. North and South America possess a total of 136,085 miles of railroad track, of which 116,874 have been laid in the United States. Today British India has over 10,000 miles of railroad track; in the north the railway extends beyond Nepal to Ngari in Tibet. Railroads in Russia also wind their way more than one thousand *li* east of the Urals and in the southeast have penetrated the grasslands of the Kazakhs.

During the last fifty years, in all countries of the world which have forged communications by land and water there is not one in which railways have not played a crucial role. The railroad has facilitated the convenient and rapid movement of military personnel, the transportation of grain supplies, the despatch of famine relief and the transfer of supplies from wealthier regions to less well-off ones. The sheer convenience of railroad transportation has dispelled worries about the effects of floods, drought and banditry, as well as preventing fluctuations in the price of grain. Consequently, countries that estimated their revenues to be either in the thousands or millions before they built railroads all could reckon on an income totalling either millions or billions once railroads had been built. This is because trains travel as fast as lightning or a whirlwind. They can transport huge amounts of material to distant places and cover thousands of *li* as if it were next door. In the past long-distance mail took several weeks to reach its destination; now the time can be calculated in hours. In the past journeys by water or land might take several months; now one arrives before the journey has hardly begun. Also, whereas previously several decades of tax administration did not guarantee constant revenues, now in less than a few months the state coffers often enjoy a surplus. Thus there is no other way to establish the basis for wealth and strength than to build railways. There are innumerable measures to be undertaken with regard to this endeavour, but all can be subsumed under three general headings: fundraising, construction, and management. Let me outline each in turn.

An enormous amount of capital has to be mobilized in order to begin building railroads, so obviously the most important priority is to raise the funds. Such funds can be sought from merchants, the government, or from government and merchants working in partnership. If merchants invest the capital themselves then they sell the shares and set up the railway companies without any government interference. The problem with this system is that merchant-run companies all compete for the market by lowering their freight charges, the result being that they become unprofitable and have to close down. England and America both carry out this method and if we look at the period from 1875 to 1877 (the first three years of Emperor Guangxu's reign), we see that 196 railway companies went bankrupt. If the government assumes responsibility then officials supervise the enterprise, ensuring that work is not begun on useless lines; furthermore the railroads that are built tend to be for the purpose of transporting troops rather than carrying out domestic trade. Germany and Russia have, to some extent, adopted this approach. Perhaps also officials might first be responsible for building railroads and then hand them over to private management, or the reverse might happen with private capital initiating railroad construction and then officials taking over the management. Germany is experimenting with this approach, which serves both military and commercial purposes.

However, if profits are unlikely to compensate for construction and management costs there is the method of officials and merchants assuming joint responsibility. France carries out this method, with Germany and Austria seeking to emulate it. The method consists in government leasing land to private entrepreneurs, using potential profits rather than the land's value to determine the duration of the lease. When the lease expires the land is returned to government ownership. Construction and management of the railroad is in private hands, although the government may provide subsidies. If merchant share capital is not sufficiently forthcoming the government may offer to pay the interest on share dividends itself in order to encourage investment. On the other hand, if the required capital to start the enterprise is so enormous that it is difficult to raise loans because of a lack of public confidence, the government may act as official guarantor; officials and merchants working closely together draw up the loan agreements and regulations. In sum, all these strategies are nothing more than simply adopting appropriate measures to suit particular situations and to ensure as much as possible that income exceeds expenditure.

Some will say: 'Official assistance to merchants will result in the expenditure of hundreds of millions of *taels* and we worry that this will represent a serious drain on government reserves.' They do not know that although in 1875 (the first year of Emperor Guangxu's reign) the French government's annual subsidy to railway companies totalled 40 million francs, the taxes on railway transport for that year amounted to 127 million francs and that, moreover, savings made in despatching mail and transporting troops amounted to 56 million francs. Thus in a year the government gained 183 million francs. Other countries might well learn from France's example.

Once the question of funds is settled the next matter to consider is the actual building of the railroad. This involves surveying the terrain, laying the tracks, manufacturing the trains and erecting stations. Since the terrain has to be even and the route convenient for travel, it is best to locate the track near well populated villages and towns and alongside rivers, where the ground is flat and moist. If this cannot be done and the track has to cross mountainous terrain then valleys should be sought in which to lay the track and the gradient should not exceed one in twenty. The steepness of those railways in America that exceed this gradient make travelling difficult and we should not follow that example. If a mountain proves to be an obstacle then it can be tunnelled from above to a depth of no more than twenty metres; otherwise it is better to tunnel from the side. Mont Blanc tunnel, which joins France and Italy, is 12,000 metres in length. Depending on whether the rock was hard or soft, every three feet tunnelled at Mont Blanc involved costs ranging from 700 to 2,600 francs on top of expenditures for machinery. Gorges can be filled, again as long as they do not exceed twenty metres in length; otherwise it is better to build bridges across them. Bridges that cross large rivers should be raised so as to enable river traffic to pass under. The costs in building such bridges are difficult to estimate. Where the track intersects with the public thoroughfare barriers should be set up and attendants posted. The attendant should close the barriers when a train is about to pass so as to prevent road traffic from crossing the line.

Railtracks are generally made from steel or iron. Steel can withstand wear and tear and is much superior to iron. The only problem is that steel tends to be more expensive, although it is nevertheless widely used today; the two most common methods for producing steel are those associated with Bessemers and Siemens. Railroad tracks are shaped like the character for *gong* (I), with some raised at the top and bottom to facilitate convenient use and others protruding at the top to allow wooden beams to be nailed across them. These are the easiest and most appropriate types to use since railroad tracks tend to alter shape slightly with time and it is not possible to change them. The wooden beams that span the track must be sturdy. The most durable type of wood is either fir or pine coated with creosote. The coating of each beam costs about one franc. Beams should not be more than five *chi*[1] in length, seven or eight *cun*[2] in width, and five or six *cun* thick. When laying the beams across the track they should be covered with small stones. The stones should be strong enough to bear heavy loads as well as arranged to allow air to pass through, thereby preventing the wood from decaying. Railroads can be either dual or single track. Double-line tracks are 1.3 *zhang*[3] in width, while single-line tracks are seven *chi* in width. The gauge width is determined by the distance between wheels on either side of the engine. Train wheels in England are two French *chi* apart. In other countries wheels are generally 1.5 *chi* apart, although in Russia it is sometimes 1.8 *chi*. The distance between wooden beams is determined by the length of each section of the track. Thus if it is six French *chi*, seven beams are laid down. Germany in the past has used cast-iron tracks with built-in beams but they have deteriorated and are difficult to change, so they are gradually being abandoned today. There are many other aspects to railroad construction which cannot be discussed here. What should be noted is that for every mile of railroad built the land costs 6,000 francs, bridge construction costs about 8,000 francs, the tracks and beams 5,000 francs and miscellaneous expenses 4,000 francs. Altogether the cost of building one mile of railroad comes to 23,000 francs. This represents the most economical estimate for single-track lines in each country. If it is a double-track line the cost is doubled, and if the line traverses high mountains and large rivers the costs are further increased.

There are different kinds of train. Those that have limited horsepower but move quickly just carry passengers; those that have considerable horsepower but move slowly just carry freight. The speed of those trains that carry both passengers and freight varies. Passenger trains can travel between 80 and 160 miles in an hour. The wheels of a passenger train are large but the crankshaft is short, thus driving the wheel faster. One revolution of a large wheel is equivalent to several revolutions of a smaller wheel, and covers a little over two French *chi*. The train thus travels quickly. Since the crankshaft on such trains is short, however, the engine's horsepower is not great and therefore the train cannot pull heavy loads. Depending on its capacity each passenger train costs between 42,000 and 55,000 francs. The wheels of freight trains are small and the crankshaft is long, giving the train more horsepower. With smaller wheels freight trains move slowly, each revolution of the wheel covering just over one French *chi*. In one hour such trains do not travel more than 60 miles, although they can carry loads of up to 28,000 piculs. A freight train can cost 117,000 francs. The wheel revolution of trains that

1. *Chi* is a unit of measurement; its length varied in different periods and regions. In the Qing dynasty the official length was 32 cm.

2. *Cun* is a unit of length, equivalent to one tenth of a *chi*.

3. *Zhang* is a unit of length, equivalent to 3.33 meters.

carry both freight and passengers covers 1.5 French *chi* and such trains cannot travel more than 100 miles in an hour. Such trains cost 50,000 francs. The minimum number of engine wheels is four, although some trains have six, eight or even twelve. In all cases, however, only two wheels actually move. The moving wheels can be in the front of the back, while the funnels can be placed along the side or the middle of the engine. In the world of today changes are occurring all the time, so that the form of train transport never stays the same. Nevertheless, we can say that generally all trains perform the three functions mentioned above.

Passengers travel by first, second or third class. Each train has three kinds of wagon with the first class wagon having twenty-four seats, the second class forty seats and the third class fifty seats. First class wagons cost 10,000 francs, while second and third class wagons do not cost more than 6,000 francs each. Freight wagons cost from 800 to 3,000 francs. The style of passenger train wagons can vary from country to country; some may have additional sleeper carriages for the use of night travellers. These sleeper carriages are the most expensive of all, costing about 13,000 francs each. Passenger trains can draw twenty wagons while freight trains can draw thirty. Wagons are joined together from end to end, winding their way along the track like an awesome dragon circling the skies.

There are certain places where approaching trains stop and stations built for the convenience of embarking and disembarking passengers; waiting rooms are provided for those passengers remaining at the station. In the vicinity of the station there are water tanks to supply the steam furnaces and coal mines to provide plentiful stockpiles of fuel. Stations also have telegraph offices to receive and send information, inspection bureaux to tax goods and prevent smuggling, accountancy offices to receive payment and issue tickets, sheds and warehouses to house trains and store goods. Finally, there are signals to ensure that trains enter the sheds in an orderly way. Train stations can be as elaborate as the planners want, although the difference in cost would be enormous.

Once construction is underway it is then appropriate to deal with the question of management. Train stations can be divided into first, second or third class depending on how busy they are. Such a distinction determines the kind of management structure. Each station should have a general manager in overall charge, an accountant to check receipts and expenditures, a ticketing official, a warehouse official to supervise storage, a communications official to transmit postal news, and an official to ensure proper maintenance of the track. The grade and size of the station will determine the numbers and functions of subordinate officials. A small station can have one official combining several tasks, while in a larger station officials might have two deputies. On a moving train the speed is controlled by the driver, inspection of passengers' tickets is the responsibility of the conductor, the handling of baggage is carried out by the freight official, and the ensurance of safety is the responsibility of the railway guard.

In addition to the individual stations there should be a main station in which would be located a head office responsible for general affairs and the supervision of

the items themselves so that ultimately it is the poorer people everywhere who suffer because of expensive food. This has to do with the problem of inefficient transportation. If, on the other hand, we had railroads there would be yearly savings on the transport costs of purchased grain amounting to millions of *taels*. Hence railroads should be built in the interests of greater economy. It is said that England attained prosperity because its coal and iron was used by countries all over the world. Today there are Western experts who point out that coal and iron ore deposits in Henan and Shanxi provinces are potentially richer than those in England; however, I have not even heard of coal and iron from Henan and Shanxi being transported more than 1,000 *li* away so how could we expect these resources to be exported overseas in order to compete with English coal and iron! This has to do with an absence of transport. A popular saying goes: 'Beyond a hundred *li* one does not trade in firewood; beyond a thousand *li* one does not trade in grain.' This shows that goods cannot be marketed over long distances. Furthermore, in the name of profit, officials tax whatever trade does exist, assuming that one more customs office will mean the tapping of one more source of revenue. They do not realize that the more burdensome taxes become so people become more impoverished. If the people are more impoverished the country becomes poorer. This is because the relationship between wealth and the country's well-being is akin to that of blood and the body. If blood does not circulate freely the body becomes sick; likewise, if wealth does not circulate freely the country declines. On the other hand the use of railroads will dispel worries concerning unexploited natural resources and stagnant markets. Hence railroads should be built in order to open up resources.

I am not simply presenting a leisurely 'take it or leave it' argument in favour of railroad construction, but rather I am urging that it should be carried out without the slightest delay. If we look at the world beyond China today we see that railroads have appeared in every region bordering our country. England is advancing northwards from India and its railroad has gone beyond Nepal to reach Kashmir. The Russian railroad has gone beyond the Urals, with 200 to 300 *li* of track being built yearly; it has now reached Tashkent and is approaching Khokand. France, with its greedy ambitions to take over Annam, has already explored the sources of several rivers there and is planning to build a railroad directly into Yunnan province. The English again have built a railroad to Burma. The Japanese 'dwarf pirates' are striving to emulate Western ways and, having already joined Tokyo and Kyoto by rail, are now casting their eyes disdainfully across the East China Sea. The Russians have occupied the area around the mouth of the Tumen river and have set up a telegraph office there linking Kyakhta with Moscow. They are also building a railroad to the Amur river in order to facilitate the transport of supplies. If we do not take advantage of the current lull in the international situation and immediately begin the urgent task of building railroads, I fear that within the next few years all the countries surrounding us will have completed construction of their rail networks; then, as soon as relations became less harmonious the foreign powers would be able to profit from the situation and surreptitiously stir up trouble for us. At that point we would be caught unawares, unable to mobilize troops and to set into motion the means of defence. The foreign powers would encroach on our frontier regions in order to control the very heart of China, fragmenting the country and cutting off our grain supplies. Such a scenario is indeed fraught with danger.

Moreover, we should take into account the fact that steamships are now in constant use, enabling Western countries to transport troops to our country in less than forty days; even Russia would be able to transport troops from the Baltic Sea to China in less than fifty days. Could we, on the other hand, move troops from the central provinces to Yunnan or to frontier regions beyond the Great Wall with similar extraordinary speed? When one considers that steamships, although slower than trains, can still bring people from tens of thousands of *li* away to our doorstep at such a speed, one can imagine how much quicker it would take in the future when foreign countries have surrounded us with railroads! How would the troops of a relatively well-off province be placed at the disposal of several other provinces, or its wealth be used to finance the armies of other provinces, so that a coordinated system of mutual support might emerge? Only railroads can thwart the foreigners' ambitions to encroach on our border regions and provide adequate defence. This is why I say they should be built without the slightest delay.

Nevertheless, pessimists will still say: 'Even if it is understood that railways can and should be built without the slightest delay, at the end of the day such approval does not tackle the problem of amassing funds. What you have said before on this subject simply pertained to devising regulations for official-merchant joint management, and did not fundamentally broach the question of where the required funds were to come from. Moreover, an imperial edict has already been issued calling for a reorganization of finances and it is clear that each province can hardly save more than a million taels while customs revenue does not exceed twenty million taels. Yet defence of the eastern coast requires funds, the Western frontier regions are experiencing difficulties in receiving supplies, and there is no more taxable land to mark out. Furthermore, there are never-ending requests from frontier officials pleading poverty and seeking assistance; Board officials in the capital can only look up to the sky in helpless resignation. At such a time is it at all possible to mobilize a huge sum of money? With the national treasury having no reserves, to imagine that one can temporarily rely on the people for such a task is to be unaware of the fact that nine out of ten households have nothing to spare and are as impoverished as the national treasury. Even if there are two or three wealthy people willing to be involved, ultimately it is impossible to achieve anything without support and most people will hesitate to come forward. Moreover, since the law regards the possession of wealth as a trifling matter officials look down on merchants as unimportant. If merchants suffer a mishap they cannot look to officialdom for redress, neither can they seek a legal solution. Who on earth would be willing to court catastrophe by putting one's family and wealth at risk just for the sake of the minutest profit?'

Alas! This response betrays an unawareness of the need to act adroitly according to circumstances. When railroad construction first began there was indeed much uncertainty over the relative merits of official-run or merchant-run enterprises. Today, however, we are beginning to follow in the footsteps of other countries by promoting merchant-run enterprises and this has produced effective results. The government treasury may be empty for the moment, but how could it fail to make use of credit to create a surplus? Also, although the people might be strapped financially how could they collectively fail to amalgamate shares and accumulate large sums of money? Once officials and merchants are of one mind there is nothing that cannot be accomplished.

Yet others might still say: 'If the government carries out this policy of borrowing the foundations of the state will be harmed. If we thoughtlessly encourage a policy of incurring foreign debts our freedom of manoeuvre will be extremely limited.' These people do not understand that all Western countries owe debts worth billions of *taels*, and yet England, France, Germany and Russia are still as powerful as before. As long as we do not borrow at excessive rates of interest and we meet interest repayments on time, why should we fear becoming tied down? Moreover, borrowing money to build railroads is like drawing from one source to replenish another; it is certainly not comparable to borrowing money continuously to pay for indemnities and repaying inherited interest. Moreover, this policy of borrowing money is flexible in another way. The proposed railroads will be solely under merchant management with officials providing cast-iron guarantees for the loan. Thus on the surface we will simply be borrowing money, but in reality we will obtain long-term benefits. Foreign capital will be used to improve the Chinese people's standard of living; we will obtain a daily increase of profits with which to repay a yearly diminishing amount of interest.

If people are still unwilling to go along with this policy, having been influenced by the views of mediocrities and hoodwinked by groundless rhetoric, they obviously do not realize that in 1842 (the 22nd year of Emperor Daoguang's reign) China had to pay Britain an indemnity of six million dollars for confiscated opium, as well as three million dollars to compensate British merchants and thirteen million dollars to compensate for Britain's military expenses. Also, in 1860 (the 10th year of Emperor Xianfeng's reign) China had to pay Britain and France four million *taels* and two million *taels* respectively for their expenses in occupying Guangzhou; on top of this China also paid out sixteen million *taels* to cover those two countries' military expenses. Are these sums larger than those required for railroad construction? Just as there was no alternative then, so there is no alternative now to building railroads. If we do not consider building railroads immediately as very important then I fear that in the future we will be compelled to pay out indemnities totalling much more than those already paid. Have you ever thought seriously about the consequences of such a negative attitude?

9.6 CHINESE ANTI-FOREIGNISM, 1892

In the last decades of the nineteenth century, as Western missionaries spread throughout China, anti-foreign activity in China became a source of tension between the Qing government and the foreign powers. As this pamphlet circulated in Canton in the early 1890s suggests, the activities of foreign missionaries were often interpreted in a strikingly polemical and unfounded way by activists eager to diminish the influence of foreign churches and remove Westerners from their communities. The clashes that resulted from such agitations resulted in a new cycle of unequal treaties and compensatory agreements forced upon Peking by Western states outraged by the treatment of their nationals.

The Roman Catholic religion had its origin from Jesus, and is practiced by all the Western countries, and taught by them to others; it exhorts men to virtue. The founder was nailed by wicked men on a cross, and cut to death. His disciples then scattered about the world to disseminate the doctrine. The Principal is called the Fa Wang Fu [the Kingly Father of the Doctrine]. Sexual congress without shame is called "a public meeting," or "a benevolent society." When they marry they use no go-between, and make no distinctions between old and young. Any man and woman who like may come together, only must first do obeisance to the bishop, and pray to Shangdi [God]. The bride must invariably first sleep with the spiritual teacher, who takes the first fruits of her virginity. . . . Two wives may not be taken, they say, because Shangdi created one man and one woman at first. In these countries therefore concubinage is not practiced, but no unchastity in other directions is forbidden. When a wife dies another may be had. When a father dies, his son may marry the mother who bore him. When a son dies, his father may marry the son's wife; and even his own daughter. Brothers, uncles, and nieces may intermarry promiscuously. Brothers and sisters of same parents also marry together.

Zhang Shoucai was a boat-tracker on the Hun river. A man named Liu informed him that by kidnapping little children and scooping out their hearts and eyes he could earn fifty taels a set.

A foreign devil at Canton went dropping poison down the wells at night. Every one fell ill of a strange disease, which could only be cured by foreign doctors. Untold numbers died. At last the Prefect found it out, arrested over thirty people, and put them all to death.

When these [foreign] devils open a chapel, they begin with their female converts by administering a pill. When they have swallowed it, they are beguiled, and allow themselves to be defiled. Then after the priest has outraged them, he recites an incantation. The *placenta* then is easily drawn out, and is chopped up to make an ingredient for their hocussing drugs.

At Tientsin they used constantly to beguile and entice away young children in order to scoop out their eyes and hearts. When the people discovered it, they tore down their tall foreign houses, and found heaped up inside bodies of kidnapped children, boys and girls.

All these facts should make us careful not to incur similar dangers. We should unite hands and hearts to keep out the evil before it is upon us.

His Excellency the Commander-in-chief for the Canton province.

CHAPTER 10

New Tensions in the Late Qing

10.1 SUN YAT-SEN'S REFORM PROPOSAL TO LI HONGZHANG, 1894

Before Sun Yat-sen (1866–1925) started his career as a revolutionary, he sought an audience with Li Hongzhang, hoping to enlist the senior official's support for a set of reforms for China. Sun had no influential friends in the north to facilitate an introduction, however, and he was unable to meet with Li or to feel certain that his letter had received any serious attention. Unlike his fellow Cantonese Yung Wing (Document 9.1), Sun never found the opportunity to use his knowledge of the West on behalf of the Qing government. He left north China feeling alienated and ready to embark on other political paths.

The reform proposals that Sun drew up in 1894 resembled plans proposed by a number of his contemporaries, who were likewise trained in the West and heavily influenced by foreign educational and political models. It is worth noting that this 1894 plan was more moderate than others proposed by reformers in the state bureaucracy in 1898, a faction led by Kang Youwei and Liang Qichao, who saw the need for large-scale constitutional and institutional change.

Though my family originated in eastern Guangdong, it has lived for generations in Xiangshan.[1] Having been educated as a British physician in Hong Kong and having in fact travelled abroad during my younger days, I am more than familiar with the languages, political institutions, and customs of the Western countries, as well

---

1. Since 1928 the county has been renamed Zhongshan Xian to commemorate Sun Yat-sen.

as the natural and applied sciences. As I have paid particular attention to the way in which these Western countries strengthen themselves economically and militarily and the method whereby they refine their customs, I believe that I understand the causes of the constant shift of current events, as well as the rules and laws that govern international relations. Today people from all parts of China, being more informed than they used to be, have come to the capital to present proposals on national affairs. Meanwhile the government is doing its utmost to bring about a most efficient administration and tirelessly pursues such policies as those that will bring maximum benefit to the nation. As the future of our nation brightens, I myself have often thought of presenting my views to the attention of the authorities, hoping that some of these views may be judged good enough to be adopted. Until now I have not ventured to make such a presentation, knowing in advance that from a man of unknown reputation or prestige, my voice would be too feeble to be heard.

Now that the nation is sparing no effort to make itself wealthy and strong, it will not be long before we can march side by side with Europe in terms of achievement. We have in our possession all modern inventions, such as steamships, locomotives, telegraph, and firearms, which the Westerners have used so effectively in the past to advance their interest at our expense. As new programs continue to be introduced, the authorities of our government will acquire the means of not only bringing about peace at home and resisting aggression from abroad but also putting into practice the long-range plan of enriching our nation and strengthening its armed forces. Besides, we know in advance each move foreign countries might choose to make, since we have envoys stationed abroad. How fortunate it is for an insignificant person like me to live in such a great age as this! How impudent I would appear to be if I venture to present some of my own ideas! However, there are things about which I have thought a great deal and wish to speak. Taking advantage of this opportune moment when China enjoys the brightest prospect for the future, I shall present my thoughts, however insignificant for Your Excellency's kind consideration.

I have always felt that the real reason for Europe's wealth and power lies less in the superiority of its military might than in the fact that in Europe every man can fully develop his talent, land resources are totally utilized, each object functions to its maximum capacity, and every item of merchandise circulates freely. The full development of personal talent, the total utilization of land resources, the functioning of each object to its maximum capacity, and the free circulation of merchandise—these four items are the most basic if our nation is to become wealthy, strong, and well governed. For our nation to ignore these four items while concerning itself exclusively with ships and guns is to seek the insignificant at the expense of the basic. . . .

As man continues to search for laws that govern objects and things, the utility of these laws to his well-being will become greater and greater. Among his new discoveries none is more awe-inspiring than electricity. Electricity has neither form nor substance; it is an object and yet it is not. It exists in every object, circulates freely in the universe, and provides more and wider utility to man than anything else. It can be used for illumination or communication; it can be used for turning motors, preserving food, or opening mines. The use of electricity for illumination or communication has been a wide practice for some time, but its use for turning motors will be found in the mines for the extraction of ores. As scientists continue their research, we shall not be surprised if electricity is also used for the growth of plants, including food crops.

All this shows that the future of man is determined by man, and not by nature. Electricity, until very recently, has been generated exclusively by burning coal. Now some scientists have devised a new method; the generation of electricity by waterfalls. Furthermore, the electricity thus generated can be preserved, to be used whenever and wherever it is needed. This is another way of saying that the supply of electricity is nearly inexhaustible, no matter how much man uses it. As machines gradually replace the physical strength of man, a point will be eventually reached when all that man has to do is to use his brain, leaving all the physical work to the machines. This is not idle speculation; it will soon become a reality.

As machines become more and more intricate and their applications become wider and wider, industries of all kinds will mushroom across each of the industrialized countries. They provide not only what the government, especially its military establishment, needs but also what the people want, especially the daily necessities. Machines can produce more efficiently and at a smaller cost, as compared to a situation without them. Besides, they can do kinds of work not performed by human labor. They can be used to pulverize huge rocks for the extraction of minerals, to drill wells to such a depth as hitherto unimaginable, and to spin and weave at such a lightning speed that they can complete in an hour what a thousand workers cannot do in a day. When machines are used to spin and weave silk dregs or woolen waste, they are performing a miracle by transforming unusable materials to useful products. The kinds of work they can do are too numerous to be cited one by one.

China's territory is large and her natural resources are broad and varied. If we can promote the use of machinery on a nationwide scale, the benefit to the people will be enormous. As long as machinery is not used, our natural resources will remain hidden, and our people will continue to be poor. For all of us who want our nation to become wealthy and strong, the choice is rather obvious. . . .

It has been thirty years since we began to imitate the West. We have language schools, as well as military and naval academies, to train specialists in Western affairs. We have mining and textile enterprises to open up financial resources. We have steamship and railroad companies to facilitate transportation. Yet we still lag behind Europe in overall achievement. Why? The reason is that we have not, really, embarked upon the completion of the four tasks, as described above, on a nationwide basis. When we do, given China's human and natural resources, we should be able to overtake Europe in twenty years.

Look at Japan. She opened her country for Western trade later than we did, and her imitation of the West also came later. Yet only in a short period her success in strengthening herself has been enormously impressive. She succeeds because she has been able to proceed with the four tasks, as described above, on a nationwide basis, with no opposition to speak of. There is no such thing as an impossible task—a so-called impossible task will become possible if there are enough dedicated people to perform it. The difficulty with China is not only the lack of enough dedicated people to perform but also the ignorance of too many people on the importance of performance. Had our difficulty been the former and nothing else, we could certainly hire foreigners to perform for us. Unfortunately, our real difficulty has been the latter, namely, the ignorance of too many people on the importance of performance. Had there been foreigners able and willing to work for us, the ignorant among us would obstruct and sabotage and make sure that these foreigners could not succeed. Here lies the real reason why we have not accomplished much; public opinion and entrenched ideas simply will not allow it.

For four decades Your Excellency has argued vigorously and toiled tirelessly for the building of a modern navy and the construction of railroads. Despite this valiant effort, our naval force remains the Beiyang Fleet and the railroad that has been constructed so far is the Tientsin-Shanhaiguan line. If a man like Your Excellency, who enjoys unqualified support from His Imperial Majesty and enormous popularity among his colleagues, has to encounter so many difficulties in modernizing China, we can easily imagine the kind of obstruction others have to face if they try to achieve the same. Even if Yao and Shun were living today, they would not be able to do much. That is why so many patriots have become dispirited and lost hope; that is why I myself have abandoned my own specialty to seek anonymity in medicine.

Since the Restoration Your Excellency has been most concerned with the cultivation of talent. Schools have been established to enroll young men of promise, and Western specialists have been invited to teach them. Large sums of money have been spent on education; a man of talent or skill, whenever he is found, is cherished like a newly discovered gem. Your Excellency must be highly commended for placing the cultivation of talent as the first priority of the nation. It is my misfortune that so far I have not had the privilege of making Your Excellency's acquaintance.

I was born twenty-seven years ago and have studied uninterruptedly since childhood. Though I have not been able to compose the eight-legged essays[2] to pass the civil service examination or write in such a way as to distinguish myself among the literati, I am more than familiar with the works of our ancient sages, the art of good government, and the principle whereby the livelihood of our people can be improved. Besides, I have studied Western subjects and have been more than proficient in one particular discipline [medicine]. Knowing that Your Excellency is interested in the cultivation of talent and the employment of talent whenever one is found, I would like to enlist myself as one of the candidates, at a time when all men of conscience must rise to meet the urgent challenge of our time. . . .

2. During the Ming-Qing period the eight-legged style (*baguwen*) was the standard form for examination essays.

10.2 LI HONGZHANG NEGOTIATES WITH JAPAN, 1895

After Japan's victory in Korea in 1894, Li Hongzhang was dismissed from office and blamed for the ignominious defeat. When the Japanese rejected the Chinese embassy for peace and insisted on negotiating with higher ranking Qing officials, Li Hongzhang was selected as the plenipotentiary for the negotiations. He arrived in Shimonoseki on March 20, 1895, and after exchanging credentials with Ito Hirobumi and Prince Mutsu, began talks the same day. Four days later, a Japanese assassin shot and slightly wounded Li Hongzhang. The ensuing public outcry caused the Japanese to temper their demands and agree to a temporary armistice. Li Hongzhang returned to the bargaining table and the Treaty of Shimonoseki was signed on April 17, 1895.

This unique transcript of Li and Ito's discussions at Shimonoseki shows clearly that the Japanese were negotiating from a position of towering strength. Although polite, in the clipped exchanges Ito Hirobumi dictated to his Qing counterpart with chilly imperiousness. Japan's enormous demands were subsequently modified by the "Triple Intervention" of France, Germany, and Russia. But the treaty firmly opened the door to Japanese military and economic penetration and set the stage for the Sino-Japanese conflicts of the twentieth century.

VERBAL DISCUSSIONS DURING PEACE NEGOTIATIONS, BETWEEN THE CHINESE PLENIPOTENTIARY VICEROY LI HUNG-CHANG AND THE JAPANESE PLENIPOTENTIARIES COUNT ITO AND VISCOUNT MUTSU, AT SHIMONOSEKI, JAPAN, MARCH–APRIL, 1895

FIRST INTERVIEW
MARCH 20, 1895

H(IS) E(XCELLENCY) LI. Your Excellencies may be assured that if my Government had not been actuated by a sincere desire to restore peace, I would not have been sent here; and if I had not been of like mind I would not have come.

H.E. ITO. Yours is a heavy responsibility and the issue at stake—the termination of the present war and restoring cordial relations between our countries—is of paramount importance. As Your Excellency is wise and experienced we may hope that our negotiations will end happily in a Treaty of lasting peace alike beneficial to both countries.

H.E. LI. On the Asiatic continent China and Japan are close neighbors and the written language of the two nations is the same. Is it well that we should live at enmity? The conclusion of our present differences in a lasting peace should be our great concern, for prolonging hostilities will but injure China without benefitting Japan. The European Powers which maintain vast armaments nevertheless take the greatest care not to provoke war. And we,

H.E. ITO. We should specify that within two months the transfer shall be wholly accomplished.

10.3 ZHANG ZHIDONG ON THE CENTRAL GOVERNMENT, 1898

Zhang Zhidong (1837–1909), the leading *qingyi* scholar,[3] sought to combine Chinese and Western learning in a way that would enable China to launch reforms without losing the essential qualities of the Confucian political and cultural way. In 1898 he published *Quanxuepian* (Exhortation to study), a highly influential work designed to boost the reform cause, which was issued by the Guangxu emperor for distribution to all officials and students. It was Zhang Zhidong who coined the expression "Chinese learning as the foundation, Western learning for application" (*zhongxue wei ti, xixue wei yong*), suggesting that the material aspects of foreign culture were valuable to China only when fitted to a philosophical and ethical matrix that remained Chinese. After chapters devoted to national unity, travel, study of foreign technologies, and the need to learn from Japan, Zhang turned his attention to government.

CHAPTER VI, CENTRALIZATION OF POWER

There is a class of Chinese in the country just now who have become impatient and vexed with the present order of things. They chafe at the insults offered to us by foreigners, the impotency of the mandarins in war, and the unwillingness of the high officials to reform our mercantile and educational methods: and they would lead any movement to assemble the people together for the discussion of a republic. Alas! where did they find this word that savors so much of a rebellion? A republic, indeed! There is not a particle of good to be derived from it. On the contrary, such a system is fraught with a hundred evils. These evils we will now demonstrate. The first thing necessary in a republic is a Parliament, and it is said that China ought to establish a House. Against such a proceeding we say that the Chinese officials and people are obstructive as well as stupid. They understand nothing about the affairs of the world at the present time, are utterly ignorant of the details and intricacies of civil government. They have never heard of the demand for foreign schools, governments, military tactics, and machinery. With such men as members, what a brilliant Parliament it would be! A vast amount of good would come from such a hubbub as this assembly would make, with perhaps one sensible man in the lot, and the rest a set of fools! Then the power of adopting ways and means, etc., is vested in the Lower House. Legislation and matters of that kind are effected by the Upper House. To obtain a seat

---

3. Outspoken scholars of the *qingyi* or "pure-opinion school," who voiced reform sentiments.

in the Parliament the candidate must possess a fairly good income. Chinese merchants do not possess these qualifications. They are not wealthy, and the experience of the people in legislative matters is very limited. Now, if any important measures were to come up for discussion, army supplies for instance, in a Parliament constituted of these unqualified members, a deadlock would ensue at once. Discussion or non-discussion would be all the same, for these M.P.'s would be ignorant of the matter in hand; they would have no knowledge to carry the appropriation bill, and no money to pay the appropriation if the bill were carried. A useless institution, indeed!

Then it is said that under a republic the Chinese can establish mercantile companies and build factories. And what is to hinder them from doing this under the present Government? There is no law to hinder the launching of such enterprises. The truth is that the merchants of China are skilled in trickery, and we have again and again cases where bogus shares have been put on the market to defraud people. If there were no official power to restrain and punish these evil-doers, the company alone would realize any profit; but where would the shareholders be? Or if a manufactory was started, and there were no official power to check the counterfeiting of trade-marks, or to quiet the brawls of the workmen, who would intervene?

The same may be said about the establishment of schools. Our laws have ever encouraged the opening of colleges, schools, and benevolent institutions by wealthy *literati*, and why ask for a republic to bring about this end? But supposing these were established, and there was no official power whatever which would confer rank on the graduates or grant their stipends; with no hope of rank or stipend, who would enter any institution established on this basis?

Again, it is said that we ought to institute a republic in order to drill troops to resist the encroachments of foreigners. But we have no arsenals or dockyards, and if ships and arms were purchased abroad, they could not be brought into a Chinese port if China was a republic, for in that case there would be no officials, and they could not be classed as "official material." An army formed under these conditions would be a noisy, cowardly flock of crows, utterly incapable of fighting a single battle. But taking for granted that this Falstaff regiment could exert itself, who would levy supplies if there were no official power? And who would go security for a foreign loan if there were no government?

We confess that China is not a powerful nation, but the people under the present government get along very well by themselves; if this republic is inaugurated, only the ignorant and foolish will rejoice. For rebellion and anarchy will come down upon us like night, and massacre will seal our eternal grave. Even those who establish the republic will not escape. Murder and rapine will hold sway in city and village. The burning of churches will follow, and under the pretext of protection, the foreigners will send troops and men-of-war to penetrate the far interior of our country and slice off our territory to be foreign dependencies, which we, perforce, submissively grant. This talk about a republic is very agreeable to the adversaries of China.

Years ago the Government of France was changed from a monarchy to a republic. The common people rose against the upper class, because the rulers were vicious

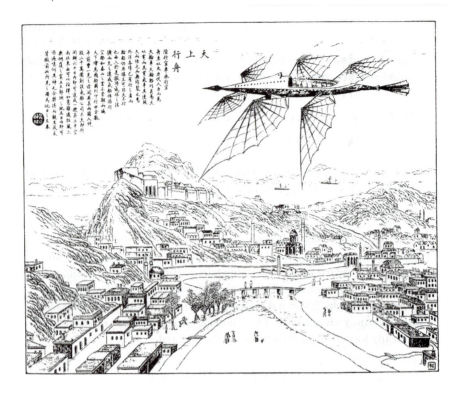

I would be very pleased to be able to view this grand achievement in person. In the meantime, however, I have drawn this picture of the flying ship based on my recollection of the illustration I saw several years ago.

PRESERVING THE WRITTEN WORD FOR THE SAKE OF FILIAL PIETY

There is nothing particularly strange or objectionable about using scraps of paper with printing or writing on them to paste on window frames or to seal up the odd jug or bottle. Yet there are certain people who go out of their way to collect such scraps and burn them out of a deeply felt reverence for the written word.

While those who feel this way carry out their missions with great zeal, those who remain unmoved in this respect go on living with no apparent breach of conscience. Among the latter there are people who will use old books or account ledgers to file away embroidery patterns or cloth shoe uppers.

A Mr. Xu of Yangzhou found this sort of behaviour thoroughly reprehensible. To ameliorate the situation, he hired a professional artist to paint more than fifty pictures, including the famous series "Twenty-four Illustrations of Filial Piety," as well as scenes filled with flowers, birds, pavilions, fountains and human figures so

life-like they appeared ready to jump off the page. He then had them reproduced in great numbers and bound in volumes. When they were ready, Mr. Xu had the books carried through the residential quarters of the city, where he offered to exchange them for old books, account ledgers or any other written or printed materials being used for such purposes as storing embroidery patterns. As it turned out, the local housewives were more than willing to make such exchanges, and in this way the message of filial piety was delivered into people's homes under the guise of reverence for the written word.

Mr. Xu's generosity and ingenuity are to be commended. If other nobly minded souls were to carry out similar missions with the aid of modern lithography, how vast would be the benefits to the common good.

WOULD THAT HE BE FAITHFUL . . .

Love affairs between men and women are based on the subtle workings of fate. For if fate has sealed a marriage, both spouses' hearts will beat as one and their minds reverberate in perfect harmony. Even if the seas dry up, the mountains crumble to dust, or the universe comes to an end, a loving couple's souls are so helplessly entwined that even the mere thought of separation would have to be dismissed as absurd. In such circumstances, a husband abandoning his wife after

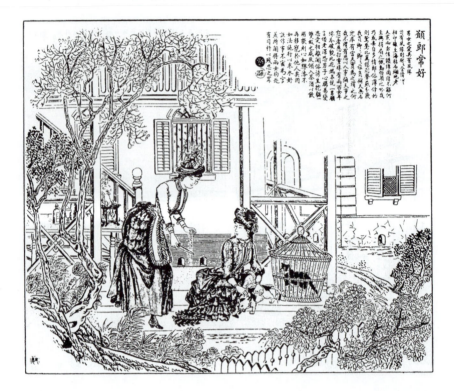

she passes her prime, or a wife writing threatening letters to her husband when he proposes to take a lover are unthinkable. Nor would a marriage between a woman with a passionate disposition and a fickle man, at first a model of ducky together-ness, ever evolve into the sorry situation wherein "the sparrows become weary and fly off their own ways."

Is it true love when a husband betrays his darling beloved, leaving her no one to betray? Man cannot trifle with the workings of Heaven. If there is truly a para-dise in Heaven, it was created by divine design, leaving man little recourse for intervention. It is all too easy for those in love to overlook the fact that it is hopeless to amend by human means the inscrutable Way of Heaven.

In a certain city there lived two European ladies of eminently marriageable age, in the very blossom of their youth. Though both had beaus with whom they were soon to take marital vows, they greatly feared their husbands-to-be would be unfaithful and direct their attentions to other quarters. The women had heard that by disem-bowling a pair of cats, roasting their hearts, and decocting the ashes in wine or tea, they could produce a potion that would ensure their husbands' constancy and cement forever the bonds of affection. Believing what they heard, they carried out the das-tardly deed in the hope of attaining their desired ends. Little did they know that due to carelessness on their part their actions became known to the police, who took the two ladies into custody and charged them with Cruelty to Animals.

THE DUCKS WITH THE GOLDEN INNARDS

There once was a man from Xintangxu in Guangdong Province who, following in the footsteps of General Fan Kuai, earned his living as a butcher. Not long ago, a stranger was seen walking through the streets of the city peddling live ducks. The butcher bought several from the man, whose name was Wang, and proceeded to slaughter one of them. Much to his surprise, when removing the duck's innards, the butcher noticed something bright and shiny like gold sloshing around inside, and a knowledgable person confirmed that indeed it was the precious metal. The butcher then slaughtered the remaining ducks and found gold inside each and every one of them.

When Wang returned to the city several days later, the butcher purchased his entire stock. And once again, he discovered gold inside each of the duck's bellies. At this point, the butcher made an offer to purchase Wang's entire flock and, without revealing the least trace of excitement, asked Wang where he obtained his ducks. Wang replied that he raised them in a ravine in Luoyangdong Mountain. The butcher then told Wang what he had discovered, and suggested that he mine the gold. Wang replied that he knew nothing about this, but went ahead and hired a team of miners who, taking advantage of his ignorance, appropriated nearly all

branch office of his company, and since this office was equipped to send telegrams to other offices of the company three hundred or more miles away, he sent a message to one of them requesting that they cable another message back to the office where he worked. Within minutes, the great gate clanked open and the manager proceeded to his office as originally planned. In order to accomplish this, however, messages had to be sent to and from a place three hundred miles away.

10.5 AND 10.6 ORAL ACCOUNTS OF THE BOXER REBELLION

The Boxer Rebellion was sparked in part by the disruption of life in north China brought about by Western penetration. The influx of missionaries, the building of railroads, seizures of Chinese territory in Shandong, and other aspects of imperialism outraged Chinese peasants and caused them to organize to fight the foreign presence in Shandong and Hebei. Initially, Qing troops suppressed the Boxers, but in January 1900 the court ordered that the Boxers not be considered bandits. In the spring of the same year the court, now controlled by the conservative officials allied with the empress dowager, suggested that it provisionally approved of the Boxers' activities.

These oral historical accounts of the Boxer Rebellion were compiled by the Modern Chinese History Section of the History Department of Shandong University in Jinan. Beginning in 1960, the department had conducted extensive field investigations, interviewing surviving Boxers and others who experienced the rebellion, until the Cultural Revolution brought the project to a close.

10.5 *Several Accounts of "The Shining Red Lantern"*

1. The Shining Red Lantern got started a little later than Spirit Boxing. Around here Spirit Boxing started in 1898. The Shining Red Lantern started either in 1899 or 1900. I just remember that it was about a year or so later. When Spirit Boxing was about finished, the Shining Red Lantern started. The Shining Red Lantern also set up a practice field. Majiafang had one and all the people who went were unmarried girls in their teens and twenties. They also practiced spirit possession. Fenglou had two or three sent there to learn. In 1900, or maybe 1899, the Shining Red Lanterns took their spears and knives and went to the county seat to register. That is to say, they wanted to report their names and villages to the county magistrate and get him to do something. But the county magistrate didn't pay any attention to them. [Reminiscence of Dong Yuyao, age 86, from Houzhang village of the Chengguan commune of Renping county, January 1966.]

2. When I was ten, I went to Fenglou to watch people play with the Shining Red Lantern. Their practice ground was set up in a house and it was really exciting and crazy! Liu Laizhu's old lady was running things. She was all dressed in red and it was really dazzling. She was teaching a dozen or so seventeen- or eighteen-year-old girls. All these big girls were dressed from head to toe in red. Their footbinding cloths were red, their socks were red, their shoes were red, their pants were red, their shirts were all red, and they wore a red hair wrapping. Why even the little string to tie on the head wrapping was red! They carried red lanterns and waved red fans. Sometimes they practiced during the day and sometimes at night. They were all girls from poor families. Some couldn't afford to buy red clothes so they tore off strips of cloth from their bedding and dyed it to make their red costume. [Interview with Liu Shaocheng, age 73, from Wangzhuang village, the Zhuwang brigade of Chengguan commune, Renping county, December 1965.]

3. Fenglou had the Shining Red Lantern. All the Shining Red Lanterns were women who dressed up completely in red. They waved red fans and carried red lanterns and they could get wind or rain or ride the clouds and call in

the mist. Two women facing each other would wave their fans and while waving them they could ascend into the sky. That was the kind of thing they did. The elder sister of Wang San of Wangguang village was a Shining Red Lantern. This sister later got married to someone from Nanguan in the city. Before this woman was married, at the age of eighteen, she was a Shining Red Lantern. I used to go to watch the hustle and bustle. [Interview with Zhang Yuqi, age 82, Ma village, Sanlitun commune, Renping county, January 1966.]

4. The Shining Red Lanterns were all women. All of them were unmarried girls about eighteen or nineteen years old. They dressed all in red and when they waved fans or bowls they could go up to heaven. They could ride clouds in the sky and become magic fairies! [Interview with Feng Jinyu, age 84, Feng village, Wulizhuang commune, Renping county, January 1966.]

5. Girls who joined the Boxers were called "Shining Red Lanterns." They dressed all in red. In one hand they had a little red lantern and in the other a little red fan. They carried a basket in the crook of their arm. When bullets were shot at them they waved their fans and the bullets were caught in the basket. You couldn't hit them! Some were also possessed by spirits and would say that they were Ma Guiying or Hu Jinchan.[5] [Interview with Zhu Yunze, age 82, Zhu village, Yeguantun commune, Renping county, December 1965.]

6. In every village there were girls who studied the Shining Red Lantern. In my village there were eight or ten of them. They all carried a red lantern in their right hand and a red fan in the left hand. They'd wave the fans and go up into the sky. They didn't want people to watch and so they'd practice at night when it was dark. There was a song then that went:

> "Learn to be a Boxer, study the Red Lantern.
> Kill all the foreign devils and make the churches burn."

[Interview with Li Mingde, age 74, Liuli Temple, Liuli Temple commune, Gaotang county, January 1966.]

10.6 Four Accounts of the Fate of Miss Han (Han Guniang)

1. Miss Han was from Hebei. On the twenty-seventh day of the fifth moon [in 1900], at the time of the big hemp marketing day, she rode a horse into the town Longgu with about a dozen followers. They stayed in the town and

---

5. Ma Guiying and Hu Jinchan were famous women warriors who were often portrayed in popular dramas in north China.

she gave out food. There was a big drought then and so within two or three days, over a thousand people joined her Big Knife Society [Dadaohui]. She took food from wealthy households and passed it out to the masses of the Big Knife Society.

After two or three days, there was a big rainstorm. The next day you couldn't find any Big Knife Society members; they'd all gone. To start with they'd all joined to get something to eat. When it rained, they all went home to plant their fields. [Interview with Yu Keyi, age 78, Juye county, February 1960.]

2. Miss Han was from Long'gu in Zhili [Hebei]. Her family had several hundred *mou* of land. She was invited to come from Hebei by Xu Chuanzhong who was from Big Xu village, located southeast of Shatuji which is east of the Hezhe county seat. Miss Han came to Long'gu on the big hemp marketing day, the twenty-seventh day of the fifth moon, in 1900. She was riding a big horse and a dozen or so followers came with her. They entered Long'gu blowing bugles and many people ran to watch her. Her followers came from all over Long'gu; there were several thousand of them. She was short and had a long face. Her face was a yellowish ivory color. She was about twenty-five or twenty-six. It was said that she was a Shining Red Lantern. She was very skillful; she could fight with spears or a sword. When she rode on a bench, it would turn into a horse; if she rode a rope, it would change into a dragon; if she sat on a mat it would become a cloud and she could ride the cloud and fly away.

Miss Han was invited by Xu Chuanzhong of Xu village. She came from the west side. She stayed in Long'gu a half month or a month. After she came she set up a "Righteous Gruel Station." Since there was a big drought that year many people came into the town. But later there wasn't enough rice and so Miss Han asked some families to provide wheat to make steamed buns. Within a few days, four or five thousand people came into town. All of them were Big Knife Society members. In Long'gu, Miss Han sent people to confiscate everything from the Huang village church and the Ma village church. Miss Han was the leader. She stayed in town. She didn't go herself. Then there was a big rainstorm and the next day they were all gone. Some said that when she went to Maliang in Henan, they all dispersed. Some said that after the rainstorm, the whole Big Knife Society in Long'gu dispersed because all of them were farmers and they all went home to plant crops. Others said that the very night of the rainstorm they all went off toward the northwest.

Xu Chuanzhong was the Big Knife Society leader of the villages around Long'gu. He often went to these different villages to teach boxing. You'd find his disciples in all these villages. After Miss Han came to Long'gu, he also came. He stayed a few days and left.

Later Miss Han was caught by her father and elder brother. They beat her to death with a rake. [Interview with Yuan Luanyu, Juye county, 1960.]

3. After Miss Han came to Long'gu, she gathered four or five thousand people. When the converts from Ma village heard that there were so many Big

Knife Society people in Long'gu, they all ran away. Miss Han's Big Knife Society stayed in Long'gu for about a month. All the converts had fled to Huang village and so at the beginning of the sixth moon, the Big Knife Society attacked it. The first time they attacked they didn't send enough people and so they were fought off. Three days later, they sent more than two thousand people but they still couldn't get into the village.

At the time Huang village was surrounded by a wall and they had a dozen or so platform guns on it. Shi Chuangu, the head of the church from Ma village, led the converts in the fight. There was a big drought that year and later there was a big rainstorm and Miss Han's Big Knife Society all went off to the north.

In the fifth and sixth moon of 1900, several hundred Big Knife Society people came to Ma village from Long'gu. Before the Big Knife Society came, the people of Ma village all ran away and so they came into Ma village without a struggle. They took away the cattle, they took things, and knocked down the church. They came just after breakfast time and left around the time people here eat their soup. After two or three days, when the Big Knife Society in Long'gu heard that the converts had all gone to Huang village, they sent about two thousand people to attack it.

Altogether there were only a dozen or so households of converts in Ma village. The church was a little one-story building that the converts built with money they contributed. The Huang village church was built under Shi Chuangu's direction. After the Ma village converts fled to Huang village, the minister Shi Chuangu led the Ma village converts (there were only about a dozen) in the defense of Huang village. They all had guns, there were a dozen or so platform guns. The Big Knife Society attacked from morning to dusk and still couldn't get in. It was because Shi Chuangu had guns and a wall to defend! At that time, the people who defended Huang village were all Ma village converts. The Huang village people helped them because there were no converts in Huang village. The Big Sword Society couldn't get in and so they left. Then there was a big rainstorm and they all went off to the north west. [Interview with Huang Ruixian, Huang village, Juye county, 1960.]

4. When I was twelve they tore down the foreign building. The leader of the Big Knife Society was a woman who people called Miss Han. When she led her troops, she carried a spear with red tassels and a big knife. They first stayed in Long'gu and then went to Caozhou to rip down churches. She carried a big knife that was four feet long and two inches thick. It had an iron hand guard. [Interview with Qiu Xinli, age 75, Qiu village, east of Shatu town in Heze county, 1960.]

CHAPTER 11

The End of
the Dynasty

11.1 ZOU RONG ON REVOLUTION, 1903

Zou Rong (1885–1905) grew up in a well-to-do merchant family in Sichuan.
He resisted pressures to prepare for the imperial examinations, and at an
early age took part in political activities in local schools that twice resulted
in expulsion. In the fall of 1902, Zou registered for classes at Japan's Dobun
Shoin, a preparatory school for Chinese and Korean students hoping to
pursue studies in Japanese universities. During this year abroad, Zou read
widely in Western political philosophy, including Rousseau, Montesquieu,
Carlyle, and Spencer. While in Japan he became acquainted with members
of Sun Yat-sen's Revive China Association and other revolutionary patriots;
he often spoke out against the Manchu regime. In 1903, Zou returned to
China, carrying the manuscript of *The Revolutionary Army* (Geming jun) in
his valise. Published in Shanghai, it quickly became the most widely circulated revolutionary pamphlet of its time, with tens of thousands of copies
reprinted in China and in overseas communities.

The police of Shanghai's International Settlement arrested Zou Rong soon
after the publication of *The Revolutionary Army.* He died in prison in April
1905, at age 21. In later years both the Nationalists and the Communists
regarded him as a revolutionary martyr.

ON REVOLUTION

Revolution is a universal rule of evolution. Revolution is a universal principle of
the world. Revolution is the essence of a transitional period of struggle for survival. Revolution follows nature and corresponds to the nature of man. Revolution
eliminates what is corrupt and holds on to what is good. Revolution is to advance

from savagery to civilization. Revolution is to eradicate slavery and become the master. . . . I have heard that the English Revolution of 1688, the American Revolution of 1775, and the French Revolution of 1870 were all revolutions that followed nature and corresponded to the nature of man. They were all revolutions designed to eliminate what was corrupt and hold on to what is good and to advance from savagery to civilization. They were all revolutions to eradicate slavery and become the master. The individual was sacrificed to save the world; the nobility was sacrificed to benefit the common people and to allow everyone to enjoy the happiness of equality and freedom.

THE YANGZHOU AND JIADING MASSACRES

Before I finished reading the *Yangzhou shiriji* [Diary of ten days at Yangzhou] and the *Jiading tuchengji* [The massacre of the city of Jiading], I began crying spontaneously. Let me say these words to my fellow countrymen: Do the ten days of Yangzhou and the three massacres of Jiading represent the entire picture of how the Manchu bandits slaughtered the Han people in a prefecture and a county? The accounts in these two books merely mention two cases. Just imagine, at that time they unleashed their army to burn and loot and also issued their hair-cutting decree; wherever the horsemen of the Manchu bandits struck, the massacres and looting must have been ten times worse than in these two places. If the infamous cases of Yangzhou and Jiading occurred, there must have been thousands of other Yangzhous and Jiadings. Whenever I think of this, my heart is moved:

> On the second day of the month, it is said that the Qing army established new officials and clerks in the prefectures and counties and then set up signboards to calm the people and prevent them from panicking. They also instructed the monks in all of the temples to burn the piles of corpses. There were also a number of women hiding in the temples and some of them died of fear or hunger. If the register for the corpses burned is consulted, it can be seen that in eight days more than eight hundred bodies were destroyed. No count was made of those who threw themselves into wells or rivers or hung themselves.

Let me inform my countrymen: When the Manchu bandits came through the passes into China, weren't the people they slaughtered our ancestral grandfathers and their uncles and brothers? Were not the women raped by the Manchu bandits the wives, daughters, and sisters of our ancestral grandfathers? The *Book of Rites* says: "One must not share the same heaven with the murderer of one's father and brothers." Even a small child knows this! Therefore, when a son cannot take revenge for his murdered father or brother, he must pass this responsibility to his own son, and his own son should pass it to his son and onward to future generations. Thus, a forebear's feud is, in fact, the feud of one's own father and elder brothers. If one does not avenge the feud of his father and elder brothers but, rather, serves those who are the object of the feud while talking about filial piety and brotherly love day in and day out, I cannot understand where filial piety and brotherly love are to be found. If the spirits of our ancestors exist, they certainly cannot lie still in the underworld.

ON REVOLUTIONARY EDUCATION

If there is to be great construction, there must be destruction. For great destruction, there must first be construction. This has been an immutable and fixed principle through the ages. The revolution we are carrying on today is a revolution to destroy in order to permit construction. However, to implement destruction we should be able to construct. This was put very well by the great hero of Italian nation-building, Mazzini, who said: "Revolution and education must be carried out together." Before all of you, my countrymen, I cry out: Revolutionary education! Moreover, there must be education before the revolution and education after the revolution. . . .

CHINESE TRAITORS

Zeng Guofan, Zuo Zongtang, and Li Hongzhang were posthumously honored as Dukes Wenzheng, Wenxiang, and Wenzhong by the emperor of the great Qing dynasty. They were revered by the worthies of their time as the three heroes of the Restoration. Their ennoblement and appointment as ministers was envied by mediocre and vulgar people. They were endlessly worshipped and held up as models by later examination scholars. But I have heard that the German Prime Minister Bismarck scolded Li Hongzhang saying: "We Europeans see merit in the pacification of alien races. I have never heard of claiming merit for the slaughter of one's own people." Oh! How I wish I could raise Zeng and Zuo from the underworld to hear these words. How I wish I could bring back all the Chinese traitors who lived before Zeng and Zuo to hear this. How I wish I could bring together all future Chinese traitors, from those officials with full authority to the petty officials and clerks, to hear this. Zeng, Zuo, and Li all claimed that they were well-read and could be compared to the sages of the past. And yet, they mercilessly slaughtered their countrymen and served as the most loyal and submissive slaves of the Manchus. . . . There is no one to compare them to. They were even worse than Li Zicheng and Zhang Xianzhong. Li and Zhang were responsible for murdering their own people and helped bring about the Manchus' conquest of China. But Li and Zhang were not learned and they were also forced to do as they did by the corrupt politics of the Ming. I can still forgive them. Zeng, Zuo, and Li were clearly aware that they belonged to the Han race. They slaughtered their own people to win noble titles for their wives and sons and permitted the Manchus to master China for a second time. I can think of no excuse that will allow me to forgive them.

ON REVOLUTIONARY INDEPENDENCE

I am a young person with little learning or refinement. I cannot really discuss the great significance of revolutionary independence but, timidly and with trepidation, I have conscientiously tried to copy the meaning of American revolutionary independence. Prostrating myself before my most respected and beloved four hundred million exalted Han Chinese countrymen, I list the following proposals for your consideration and action:

1. China belongs to the Chinese. Our countrymen should all recognize that this is the China of the Han race.
2. We will not permit any alien race to tamper with the slightest right of our China.
3. All responsibility to obey the Manchus is abolished.
4. Let us overthrow the barbaric government established by the Manchu people in Peking.
5. Drive out Manchus who live in China or kill them to take revenge.
6. Kill the emperor set up by the Manchus in order to assure that in perpetuity there will never be another despotic monarch.
7. Oppose foreigners and Chinese who interfere with our Chinese revolutionary independence.
8. Set up a central government as the central mechanism for the entire country.
9. Divide the country into provinces and cast votes to elect a general provincial representative. From the general provincial representatives of all provinces cast votes to elect a provisional president as representative of the entire nation. Also select a vice-president. Various prefectures and counties will also elect legislators.
10. Everyone in the country, male or female, will be a citizen.
11. All men in the country will have an obligation to perform military service.
12. Everyone will have an obligation to pay national taxes.
13. All people should be loyal to the newly founded nation.
14. All citizens of the nation, male or female, will be equal and there will be no distinction between high and low, noble and base.
15. Everyone will have inalienable natural rights.
16. Life, liberty, and the pursuit of happiness are all heaven-bestowed rights.
17. Such freedoms as the freedom of speech, thought, and publication cannot be violated.
18. Everyone's individual rights should be protected. The establishment of the government should occur through public agreement and the government will fully employ its power to protect the rights of the people.
19. Whenever the government violates the rights of the people, the people should be able to make a revolution to overthrow the old government in order to satisfy their hopes for peace and happiness. When the people have attained peace and happiness, they should be able through public discussion to rear-

range rights and set up a new government. That is also a right that the people should possess.

THE GOVERNMENT TO BE ESTABLISHED AFTER THE REVOLUTION

When revolutionary independence is accomplished, people will not be satisfied if there is still the bitterness of a despotic system. This is the reason we must change the national polity of the past.

1. The government will be named the Republic of China.
2. The Republic of China will be a free and independent nation.
3. This free and independent nation should enjoy equal rights with other great nations in international affairs like the declaration of war, peace negotiations, signing treaties, commercial agreements, and all necessary affairs of state.
4. The constitution will be modeled on the American constitution and will conform to China's situation.
5. Laws for self-governance should all follow American laws for self-governance.
6. Any matter involving the whole populace or an individual, diplomatic negotiations, and the domestic division of government should all follow the American model.

11.2 AND 11.3 QIU JIN: FEMINIST REVOLUTIONARY

Qiu Jin (1875–1907) has been called "China's first feminist" for her participation in the revolutionary movement of the early twentieth century. Born to a scholarly family, she received both a classical education and unconventional lessons (for women) in fencing, archery, and horseback riding. In 1904, disillusioned by her arranged marriage, Qiu Jin left her husband and two children to study in Japan. In Tokyo she met members of Sun Yat-sen's Revolutionary Alliance and became involved in anti-Manchu activities. When Qiu Jin returned to China in 1906, she continued to plot against the Qing government with coconspirators. A failed uprising ended in her capture and execution in 1907.

An accomplished poet and political essayist best known for appearing in public in male attire and brandishing a sword, Qiu Jin cut a dramatic figure. The two pieces below show her poetic ability as well as her political passion. Qiu composed "Song of the Precious Sword" in 1903, while she was living in Peking with her family. "An Address to My Two Hundred Million Women Compatriots in China" was a lecture given in Tokyo in 1904 and subsequently published.

11.2 *Song of the Precious Sword*

The palaces of the house of Han in the light of the setting sun:
After more than five thousand years the old nation has died—
For over hundreds of years it has been sunk in a deep sleep,
No one aware of our shameful state of slavery!

Long ago, I recall, our very first ancestor Xianyuan
Rose to power from his base in the Kunlun Mountains.
He opened up the lands of the Yellow and Yangzi Rivers,
And his flashing great sword pacified the Central Plain.

My bitter weeping over Plum Hill is completely useless:
The imperial city overgrown, the bronze camels buried.[1]
Whenever I am moved to turn and gaze upon the capital,
The sad song of a defeated nation fills my eyes with tears.

When the allied troops of the eight powers marched north,
We again handed our mountains and rivers over to others.
Those white devils coming from the West served as a bell,
That woke us Chinese up from our slaves' dream!

You, my lord, gave me this gold-speckled sword,
Today as I receive it, my mind is virile and brave.
These are the days when red-hot iron rules,
And a million heads are not worth a feather.

Bathed by the sun and moon, shinier than jewels:
Risking my life, I am suddenly filled with elation.
I swear I'll find a way to lead us from death to life:
World peace now depends on military armament.

Don't you recall Jing Ke's visit to the court of Qin?
When the map was unrolled, the dagger appeared!
Although he failed to stab him there in his palace,
He still managed to rob that evil tyrant of his soul!

I personally long to save the land of my ancestors,
But a race of slaves has overrun the land of Yu.
What can one do about those whose hearts have died?
With brush in hand, I write the "Song of the Precious Sword."
May this "Song of the Precious Sword" strengthen their courage,
And bring back many souls from the land of the dead!
A precious sword, heroic bones; who is our equal?
All my life I've known who are my enemies and friends.

---

1. In the late third century Suo Jing predicted the destruction of the capital Luoyang by pointing at the bronze camels in front of the imperial palace and sighing: "I will see you overgrown by weeds."

Don't despise this foot-long iron for not being brave:
The rare merit of saving the nation is yours to garner!
Could I but use heaven and earth as my oven, and yin and yang as my
coal, and gathering all the iron of the six continents,
Produce thousands, ten thousands of precious swords to purify this sacred land,
And continuing the glorious power and fame of our first ancestor, the
    Yellow Emperor,
Cleanse once and for all what, in its thousand-, its hundred-year-long
    history, has been its vilest shame!

11.3 *An Address to My Two Hundred Million Women Compatriots in China*

Alas, the most unfair treatment in the entire world is suffered by us, my two hundred million women compatriots. And this is true from the moment we are born: if you have a good father, things may still be all right, but if your father is a muddleheaded, unreasonable type, he will only keep shouting: "What bad luck! Yet another useless one!" And he will want to snatch you and crush you to death! With the thought constantly in mind of the saying "Later she will belong to another family," they will treat you harshly and with disdain. As soon as you are a few years old, they will, completely ignoring the consequences, take your snow-white and so very tender natural feet and bind them tightly with white linen—even when you are asleep, you will not be allowed to loosen them even the tiniest bit! Eventually all the flesh will rot away and the bones will be broken, just so that relatives, friends, and neighbors may say: "Such-and-such little girl has such tiny feet!"

And that is not the worst of it! When it comes to selecting a marriage partner, they will completely rely on the words of two shameless matchmakers. As long as the family of the groom has money and power, they don't care whether or not he is sound of body, and without knowing whether the groom's character is good or bad or whether his scholarship is wide-ranging, they will agree to the match. When it comes to the day of the wedding, they will force you to sit inside a gaudy red and green sedan chair, and you will hardly be able to breathe. When you arrive [at the home of the groom] if you have good fortune from a former life you will be allowed to enjoy it in this life if the fellow is a decent sort, even if he is nothing special. But if you've been married off to a good-for-nothing, all they'll have to say is: "That is your bad karma from a former life," if not: "That's just your bad luck." If you utter even a few words of complaint or say a few words of reproof to your husband, they'll change their tune, and you'll be beaten and cursed. When outsiders hear about it, they'll just say: "She's stupid and does not understand the Wifely Way." Dear listeners, is this not a case of suffering an injustice and having nowhere to lodge a complaint?

There is also still another unfair matter. When a man dies, a woman is forced to dress in mourning for three years, and she is not allowed to marry again. But

Singapore, Saigon, Vancouver, San Francisco, and Chicago, the alliance probably comprised some one thousand members in its first year of existence.

In the proclamation that follows, the Revolutionary Alliance called for the expulsion of the Manchus and also declared the need to change the fundamental political and economic structure of the country. The proposed program, outlining a three-stage passage from military to constitutional government and the equalization of land rights, was visionary but vague in details.

A PUBLIC DECLARATION

Since the beginning of China as a nation, we Chinese have governed our own country despite occasional interruptions. When China was occasionally occupied by a foreign race, our ancestors could always in the end drive these foreigners out, restore the fatherland, and preserve China for future generations of Chinese. Today when we raise the righteous standard of revolt in order to expel an alien race that has been occupying China, we are doing no more than our ancestors have done or expected us to do. Justice is so much on our side that all Chinese, once familiarizing themselves with our stand, will have no doubt about the righteousness of our cause.

There is a difference, however, between our revolution and the revolutions of our ancestors. The purpose of past revolutions, such as those conducted by the Mings and the Taipings, was to restore China to the Chinese, and nothing else. We, on the other hand, strive not only to expel the ruling aliens and thus restore China to the Chinese but also to change basically the political and economic structure of our country. While we cannot describe in detail this new political and economic structure since so much is involved, the basic principle behind it is liberty, equality, and fraternity. The revolutions of yesterday were revolutions by and for the heroes; our revolution, on the other hand, is a revolution by and for the people. In a people's revolution everyone who believes in the principles of liberty, equality, and fraternity has an obligation to participate in it, and the Military Government is merely the means whereby he can fulfill this revolutionary obligation. In short, the responsibility of the people and the responsibility of the Military Government are one and the same, and the accomplishments of the Military Government are also the accomplishments of the people. Only when they cooperate fully with each other can our revolutionary goal be attained.

At this juncture we wish to express candidly and fully how to make our revolution today and how to govern our country tomorrow.

1. *Expulsion of the Manchus from China.* The Manchus of today were known as the Eastern Barbarians (Donghu) during bygone years. Toward the end of the Ming dynasty they repeatedly invaded our border areas and caused great difficulties. Then, taking advantage of the chaotic situation in China, they marched southward and forcibly occupied our country. They compelled all Chinese to become their slaves, and those who did not wish to subjugate

themselves were slaughtered, numbering millions. In fact, we Chinese have not had a country for the past two hundred and sixty years. Now that the day has finally arrived when the brutal and evil rule by the Manchus must come to an end, we do not expect much resistance when our righteous army begins to move. We shall quickly overthrow the Manchu government so as to restore the sovereignty of China to the Chinese. All the soldiers on the Manchu side, whether they are Manchus or Chinese, will be pardoned despite their past crimes if they express repentance and surrender. If they choose to resist the people's army, they will be killed without mercy. The same can be also said about the Chinese who have collaborated with the Manchu government as traitors.

2. *Restoration of China to the Chinese.* China belongs to the Chinese who have the right to govern themselves. After the Manchus are expelled from China, we will have a national government of our own. Those who choose to follow the example of Shi Jingtang and Wu Sangui will be crushed.

3. *Establishment of a Republic.* Since one of the principles of our revolution is equality, we intend to establish a republic when we succeed in overthrowing the Manchu regime. In a republic all citizens will have the right to participate in the government, the president of the republic will be elected by the people, and the parliament will have deputies elected by and responsible to their respective constituents. A constitution of the Chinese Republic will then be formulated, to be observed by all Chinese. Anyone who entertains the thought of becoming an emperor will be crushed without mercy.

4. *Equalization of landownership.* The social and economic structure of China must be so reconstructed that the fruits of labor will be shared by all Chinese on an equal basis. Every tract of land in China must be assessed to determine its fair value in monetary terms, and this value belongs, of course, to the landowner. Any added value, which results from social progress after the revolution, will, however, belong to the nation as a whole and must be shared by all Chinese. The ultimate goal of a responsible society is the guarantee of a satisfactory livelihood for all of its members and everyone, whomever he happens to be, shall have his own means of support, via gainful employment or some other source. Anyone who attempts to monopolize the livelihood of others will be ostracized.

To attain the four goals as outlined above, we propose a procedure of three stages. The first stage is that of a military rule. During this stage when people all over China are responding to our righteous uprising and when all the territories are only recently freed from the Manchu control, we should strive for harmony and cooperation among all Chinese, so that jointly we can face our common enemy. It is essential that during this period of chaos and disturbance both the people and the army must be subject to military rule. While the revolutionary army is fighting in the front, people in the rear must supply it with what it needs and must not do anything that would affect adversely its security or its capacity to complete successfully its mission. In areas that have been recently taken over by the revolutionary army, local governments will be administered by the military command which shall see to it that all the political and social abuses of the past will be eliminated. By political abuses are meant governmental oppression, bureaucratic corruption, extortion by the police, marshals, and other law-enforcement personnel, cruelty in punishment, excessive taxation, and the wearing of pigtails as a symbol of submission to the Manchu government. By social abuses are meant the ownership of domestic slaves, the cruel custom of foot-binding, the smoking of poisonous opium, and the belief in geomancy and other superstitions that are an impediment to modern progress. All these abuses must be eliminated when the Manchu influence in China is eliminated.

The stage of military rule should not last for more than three years. After a district has succeeded in attaining the goals prescribed for the stage of military rule, military rule will come to an end, and the second stage, the stage of provisional constitution, will then begin. After a district has entered the second stage, a provisional constitution will have been proclaimed and put in force, since by then the military command would have already handed over the power of government to the people of that district. The people then govern themselves by electing as their representatives deputies in the district council as well as all the executive officials. The rights and obligations of the Military Government toward the people and the people's rights and obligations toward the Military Government will be prescribed in the provisional constitution and must be observed by the Military Government, the district council, and the people in the district. The party that violates the provisional constitution shall be held responsible for the redress of its action.

Six years after the nation has been pacified, a constitution will be proclaimed to replace the provisional constitution as described above, and the nation then formally enters the third or final stage, the stage of constitutional rule. The Military Government relinquishes its executive power, including its control over the nation's armed forces and hands this power to the people's representatives. The President of China will be popularly elected; so will all members of the Parliament. All policies to be pursued by the nation must be in conformity with the letter and spirit of the proclaimed constitution.

In short, during the first stage the Military Government, in cooperation with the people, will eradicate all the abuses of the past; with the arrival of the second stage the Military Government will hand over local administration to the people while reserving for itself the right of jurisdiction over all matters that concern the nation as a whole; during the third or final stage the Military Government will cease to exist and all governmental power will be invested in organs as prescribed in a national constitution. This orderly procedure is necessary because our people need time to acquaint themselves with the idea of liberty and equality. Liberty and equality are the basis on which the Republic of China rests.

To the attainment of the four goals and the implementation of the three stages, as outlined above, the Military Government will dedicate itself on behalf of all the people in the nation. It will do so with loyalty, faith, and total determination. We firmly believe that all our brethren will join us in performing the difficult task ahead, so we can accomplish a great deed together. The brilliant achievements of China have been known throughout the world, and only recently has she suffered numerous difficulties. We shall overcome these difficulties and march forward. The harder the task is, the harder we shall work.

On this day of restoring China to her own people, we urge everyone to step forward and to do the best he can. As the descendants of Huangdi, we shall regard one another as brothers and sisters and assist each other regardless of the difficulty of the circumstances. Whatever our station in society is, rich or poor, we are all equal in our determination to safeguard the security of China as a nation and to preserve the Chinese people as a race. We shall do so with one heart and one mind. When our soldiers are willing to sacrifice their lives and when everyone else is sparing no effort for the attainment of our noble goals, the revolution will succeed and the Republic of China will be established. Let each and every one of the 400 million people do his very best.

11.5 Press Coverage of the Wuchang Uprising, 1911

The 1911 Revolution started with an uprising in Wuchang, the provincial capital of Hubei, on October 10, 1911. On the night of October 9, bombs accidentally exploded in one of the revolutionaries' secret branches in the Russian concession in Hankou (now part of Wuhan). Police arrested dozens of revolutionaries, searched their secret meeting places, and discovered weapons, explosives, and name lists of participants in the New Army, which were handed over to the Qing authorities. Upon hearing the news of impending arrests, the revolutionaries hastily launched their uprising. There was no coordinated plan or structured leadership, but their efforts succeeded in scaring the local Qing civilian and military officials into flight. While battles raged on in the Wuchang-Hankou region, provincial governments all over the country proclaimed their independence from the Qing central government and finally forced the regents of the Xuantong emperor to abdicate.

The documents selected here are reprinted from contemporary accounts in *The Hankow Daily News*, a local English newspaper. The dating used in the first proclamation follows a calendar based on the Yellow emperor, the legendary progenitor of the Han Chinese. The use of this date emphasizes the end of Manchu domination and the dawn of a new Chinese historical era.

PROCLAMATION

The eighth moon of the four thousand six hundred and ninth year of the Wu-chang dynasty.

I, the Hubei General of the People's Army, am to overthrow the Manchu Government, and am here to revive the rights of the Han people. Let all remain orderly and not disobey military law.

Those who conceal any Government officials will be beheaded.

Those who inflict injuries on foreigners will be beheaded.

Those who interfere with commerce will be beheaded.

Those who indulge in wanton slaughter, burning, or adultery will be beheaded.

Those who fight against the volunteers will be beheaded.

Those who attempt to close the shops will be beheaded.

Rewards

Those who supply the troops with foodstuffs with be rewarded.

Those who afford protection to the foreign concessions will be highly rewarded.

Those who guard the churches will be highly rewarded.

Those who lead the people to submission will be highly rewarded.

Those who encourage the country people to join the revolution will be rewarded.

Those who give information as to the movements of the enemy will be rewarded.

Those who maintain the prosperity of commerce will be rewarded.

THE VICEROY'S ESCAPE

The above proclamation showed that the worthy General of the People's Army [the identity of the general in question is unclear] had great hopes of success and these were apparently justified by the arrival, in the morning off the Russian Bund, of the Viceroy's launch accompanied by a cruiser. It was soon learned that the Viceroy had made his escape during cover of darkness and had reached his launch without mishap, teaming over to the side of the river later on to be out of the way of an attack. At 2 p.m. the cruiser and the launch again weighed anchor, the former proceeding close to the Wuchang shore while the latter steamed up slowly in midstream. The cruiser was shortly joined by two torpedo boats and firing on the city was commenced, but as far as could be judged only black ammunition was used.

FIGHTING IN WUCHANG

Meanwhile heavy fighting was going on in the city, especially to the southward where the sound of field guns could be heard and an occasional prolonged rattle of small arms, while shots were also being exchanged between the soldiers inside and outside the city, and it was stated that the revolutionary troops were rapidly gaining the upper hand. These petty shop-keepers, even coolies were clamoring in their thousands for tickets to enable them to proceed anywhere away from Hankow. Two extra trains were put on and pulled out from the station crowded to their uttermost capacity, baggage being piled high on the platforms and buffers even, while a seat on the roof of a car was considered quite a luxury.

At 11 a.m. the express left, quite an empty express be it noted, there being but few passengers either native or foreign. A guard of twenty khaki-clad soldiers, revolutionaries though no white badges were visible, were stationed on the platform and these were contentedly consuming an ample morning meal of rice and beans.

OUTSIDE THE TARTAR YAMEN

The Xiao Kao Pavillion and the Tartar [Manchu] General's Yamen in the native city were found to be standing and intact, but outside the latter two heads were displayed on poles, evidently newly severed from their bodies. One of the victims was said to be the leader of a gang of looters and the other the unfortunate secretary of the Tartar General.

More decapitations for incendiarism and looting were made during the day and in all it is said some twenty lost their lives.

PROCLAMATION ISSUED

Outside the Tartar General's Yamen was a proclamation of which we give the following free translation.

"I have the honor of the Military Government to let you, my dear country men, know that ours is a righteous cause. Don't be suspicious of our army as wherever they march there will be a true reason. I raise the National Army against the Manchus not for the good or merit of myself, but for us as a whole. To rescue you out from the hot fires and deep waters. To deliver you from the sufferings of Manchus just as to heal your ulcers and sores. Why have the Manchus put you under such sufferings? Because they are a different tribe, and naturally cast you away just like a bit of straw.

"So far as to-day, you must have known that the Manchus are not the sons of Han. Although you have been so loyal and righteous to them, yet they pay nothing for your service.

"Now I can bear it no longer so that we suddenly gather ourselves together under the righteous flag and the foremost thing we want to do is to demolish what is harmful or injurious to you, and we are perfectly willing to exert as much effort as we can only for the welfare of you. We will not allow those who are treacherous to the sons of Han and those who are the thieves of our countrymen to breathe any longer.

"Formerly they ate our flesh and now we are going to eat them.

"Those who are in favor of this righteous movement are requested to enroll their names. Come and consult with us about the object, how to recover our Kingdom,

'Zhonghua [China].' Now is the time for us to reestablish our country and faithfully work out our due duty as the country men of Zhonghua should do.

"We wish you, my dear brothers not to misunderstand each other.

"You—scholars, farmers, workers and merchants should try with one accord to drive out the savages. Lastly I wish all of you to treat each other as justly as possible.

"I wish you all my dear brethren to listen to my words.

By order.

Huang Dynasty 4609, 8th moon, 19th day."

THE OATH OF ENLISTMENT

The following is a copy of the official document for enlisting in the Revolutionary Army.

I, a native of_____Xian, of Prefecture of_____in the Province of Hubei, through the introduction of_____, enabled to understand that the aim of the People's Army Government is to drive out the Manchus, to recover the loss of the Sons of Han, to establish a government for the people and foster liberty and equality, am now self-willing to be listed as a member of the Central Association of Hubei. Hereafter I will forever obey all its constitutions and by-laws. In case of any violation, I am prepared to receive the due punishment. . . . I hope, this will be made known to the President of the People's Army Government Sun Zhongshan (sometimes known as Sung Wen.)

The name of the Introducer (signed.)

The name of the Admitted member (signed.)

Huang Dynasty 4609, 8th moon.

11.6 THE MANCHU ABDICATION EDICT

Immediately after the Wuchang Uprising, the republican forces swept through central and southern China at a pace that shocked the Manchu rulers in Peking. Incapable of handling the crisis, the imperial government showered new appointments on Yuan Shikai, who had only shortly before been forced into retirement and deprived of his authority as the most powerful leader of the Qing New Army. The Qing court hoped that the appointment of Yuan, a Han Chinese, as the chief executive of a constitutional government would halt the revolutionary tide. Through cunning maneuvers and manipulation of the uncertainties shared by both sides, Yuan finally persuaded the Qing emperor to abdicate and extracted a promise from the revolutionaries that they would elect him the first president of the new republic.

The documents that follow reflect the futile last-ditch effort of the Qing court to assure its survival and win favorable terms from the revolutionary government. The abdication edict shows how Yuan Shikai manipulated the crisis, mollifying both sides during the transition as a means of taking power. The second half of the edict, often called "The Articles of Favorable Treatment of the Qing Imperial Court," stipulates the courtesies, subsidies, and residential rights to be granted to the abdicated emperor by the new government.

THE NINETEEN ARTICLES
(NOVEMBER 3, 1911)

1. The Daqing [Great Qing] Dynasty shall reign for ever.
2. The person of the Emperor shall be inviolable.
3. The power of the Emperor shall be limited by a Constitution.
4. The order of the succession shall be prescribed in the Constitution.
5. The Constitution shall be drawn up and adopted by the National Assembly, and promulgated by the Emperor.
6. The power of amending the Constitution belongs to Parliament.
7. The members of the Upper House shall be elected by the people from among those particularly eligible for the position.
8. Parliament shall select, and the Emperor shall appoint, the Premier, who will recommend the other members of the Cabinet, these also being appointed by the Emperor. The Imperial Princes shall be ineligible as Premier, Cabinet Ministers, or administrative heads of provinces.
9. If the Premier, on being impeached by Parliament, does not dissolve Parliament he must resign but one Cabinet shall not be allowed to dissolve Parliament more than once.
10. The Emperor shall assume direct control of the army and navy, but when that power is used with regard to internal affairs, he must observe special conditions, to be decided upon by Parliament, otherwise he is prohibited from exercising such power.
11. Imperial decrees cannot be made to replace the law except in the event of immediate necessity in which case decrees in the nature of a law may be issued in accordance with special conditions, but only when they are in connection with the execution of a law or what has by law been delegated.
12. International treaties shall not be concluded without the consent of Parliament, but the conclusion of peace or a declaration of war may be made by the Emperor if Parliament is not sitting, the approval of Parliament to be obtained afterwards.
13. Ordinances in connection with the administration shall be settled by Acts of Parliament.
14. In case the Budget fails to receive the approval of Parliament the Government cannot act upon the previous year's Budget, nor may items of expenditure not provided for in the Budget be appended to it. Further, the Government shall not be allowed to adopt extraordinary financial measures outside the Budget.

15. Parliament shall fix the expenses of the Imperial household, and any increase or decrease therein.
16. Regulations in connection with the Imperial family must not conflict with the Constitution.
17. The two Houses shall establish the machinery of an administrative court.
18. The Emperor shall promulgate the decisions of Parliament.
19. The National Assembly shall act upon Articles 8, 9, 10, 12, 13, 14, 15 and 18 until the opening of Parliament.

EDICT OF ABDICATION
(FEBRUARY 12, 1912)

I

We (the Emperor) have respectfully received the following Imperial Edict from Her Imperial Majesty the Empress Dowager Longyu:—

As a consequence of the uprising of the Republican Army, to which the different provinces immediately responded, the Empire seethed like a boiling cauldron and the people were plunged into utter misery. Yuan Shikai was, therefore, especially commanded some time ago to dispatch commissioners to confer with the representatives of the Republican Army on the general situation and to discuss matters pertaining to the convening of a National Assembly for the decision of the suitable mode of settlement has been discovered. Separated as the South and the North are by great distances, the unwillingness of either side to yield to the other can result only in the continued interruption of trade and the prolongation of hostilities, for, so long as the form of government is undecided, the Nation can have no peace. It is now evident that the hearts of the majority of the people are in favor of a republican form of government: the provinces of the South were the first to espouse the cause, and the generals of the North have since pledged their support. From the preference of the people's hearts, the Will of Heaven can be discerned. How could We then bear to oppose the will of the millions for the glory of one Family! Therefore, observing the tendencies of the age on the one hand and studying the opinions of the people on the other, We and His Majesty the Emperor hereby vest the sovereignty in the People and decide in favor of a republican form of constitutional government. Thus we would gratify on the one hand the desires of the whole nation who, tired of anarchy, are desirous of peace, and on the other hand would follow in the footsteps of the Ancient Sages, who regarded the Throne as the sacred trust of the Nation.

Now Yuan Shikai was elected by the provisional parliament [*zizheng yuan*][5] to be the Premier. During this period of transference of government from the old to

5. This refers to the provisional national assembly brought into existence by the 1911 Revolution.

the new, there should be some means of uniting the South and the North. Let Yuan Shikai organize with full powers a provisional republican government and confer with the Republican Army as to the methods of union, thus assuring peace to the people and tranquility to the Empire, and forming to one Great Republic of China by the union as heretofore, of the five peoples, namely, Manchus, Chinese, Mongols, Mohammedans, and Tibetans together with their territory in its integrity. We and His Majesty the Emperor, thus enabled to live in retirement, free from responsibilities, and cares and passing the time in case and comfort, shall enjoy without interruption the courteous treatment of the Nation and see with Our own eyes the consummation of an illustrious government. Is not this highly advisable. . . .

I I

We have respectfully received the following Imperial Edict from Her Imperial Majesty the Empress Dowager Longyu:—

On account of the perilous situation of the State and the intense sufferings of the people, We some time ago commanded the Cabinet to negotiate with the Republican Army the terms for the courteous treatment of the Imperial House, with a view to a peaceful settlement. According to the memorial now submitted to Us by the cabinet embodying the articles of courteous treatment proposed by the Republican Army, they undertake to hold themselves responsible for the perpetual offering of sacrifices before the Imperial Ancestral Temples and the Imperial Mausolea and the completion as planned of the Mausoleum of His Late Majesty the Emperor Guangxu. His Majesty the Emperor is understood to resign only his political power, while the Imperial Title is not abolished. There have also been concluded eight articles for the courteous treatment of the Imperial House, four articles for the favorable treatment of Manchus, Mongols, Mohammedans, and Tibetans. We find the terms of perusal to be fairly comprehensive. We hereby proclaim to the Imperial Kinsman and the Manchus, Mongols, Mohammedans, and Tibetans that they should endeavor in the future to fuse and remove all racial differences and prejudices and maintain law and order with united efforts. It is our sincere hope that peace will once more be seen in the country and all the people will enjoy happiness under a republican government.

11.7 "SELECTING A WIFE" BY ZHU ZIQING

Zhu Ziqing (1898–1948) was an acclaimed writer who played an instrumental role in the new literature and poetry movements of the 1920s. Born in Jiangsu province, Zhu grew up in Yangzhou and graduated from Peking University. He was a secondary school teacher for a number of years, before gaining prominence as a poet and writer. In 1925 Zhu was appointed to the Chinese literature faculty at Qinghua University, where he taught (at its various campuses in wartime exile) until his death in 1948.

> In this memoir, Zhu recalls how his family made arrangements to find a
> wife for him in the years just before the Republican Revolution. Dressmakers
> and family servants facilitated the process of matchmaking, passing along
> information and verifying details such as the size of the prospective bride's
> feet. Zhu's remembrance describes how families with children of marriageable
> age negotiated expectations and desirable traits in future in-laws. Small feet,
> formerly considered an essential prerequisite for making a good match, were
> no longer mandatory, underscoring how cultural norms of footbinding were
> changing in the decade after the turn of the century.

Being the eldest son of the eldest son of the family, I hadn't reached eleven years of
age before they set about making a match for me. At that time I was totally ignorant about what a wife was, but somehow or other they settled on a match. She was
someone from my great-grandmother's side of the family, and lived in the country
in a small county in northern Jiangsu. Members of the family used to pay long
visits there, and probably took me as well with them, but being as stupid as I am,
not the slightest trace remains in my memory. My grandmother often used to lie
on her opium couch talking about things down there, and would speak of some
countryman or other by name. At first it all seemed to be only something that was
wreathed in white smoke, but as the days went by, it imperceptibly became familiar
to me, and even intimate. Besides the house itself, I used to think that the locality,
which they called "Garden Estate," must be really the most interesting place. So
when I heard that I was betrothed to someone down there, it all seemed quite
natural, and there were no objections. Every year someone came up from the farm
down there, in blue workman's outfit, with a pipe between his teeth, and bringing
a large quantity of barley flour, dried yam and such like. Now and then in conversation with the family, he would also mention the young lady, who was about four
years older than me and was said to be tall, and have bound feet. My chief interest
at that time, though, was really in the barley flour and dried yams.

I remember that I was twelve years old when news was brought from down
there that the young lady had died from consumption. No one in the family actually expressed much grief, probably because she was still little when they saw her,
and as the years went by, they could not remember very clearly what kind of a
person she was. At that time father had an official posting in another province, and
mother was quite anxious to have my marriage settled, so she asked a dressmaker
who often came to make clothes for us to act as go-between. The reason was that,
as a dressmaker, she visited many households, and was able to see for herself many
ladies and their daughters. It was not a bad idea: the dressmaker came up with a
certain family, which was wealthy, and had two daughters; one was the daughter
of a concubine, but the one that she was proposing was the elder daughter of the
wife. She said that the family would like to inspect me. Mother agreed and a date
was fixed, when I was taken to a teahouse by the dressmaker. I remember that it
was winter, and on the day mother had me wear a gown of dark red Ningbo silk,

with a jacket of black Ningbo silk, and a black satin skullcap with a red button on top, and she also told me to be circumspect. In the teahouse I met the gentleman who was there to inspect me. He had a plump face and big ears, and was about the same age as I am now. He wore a cotton cloth gown and jacket, as though in mourning for someone. This person was, however, quite kindly-looking. He kept looking me up and down, and also asked me questions like what sort of books I was studying. When we got back, the dressmaker said that he had been very careful in his inspection: said that my face featured a large space between my nose and lips, and this was a sign of a long life. He also watched me walk, and said that he was afraid there was something the matter with my feet. All in all, I was thought acceptable, and it was our family's turn for the inspection. My mother sent a trusty old *amah* [female servant]. This *amah* reported back that the elder daughter was much taller than me, and when she sat down she fully filled a round arm chair, but the second daughter was nice and slim. My mother said that women who are fat don't produce children, such as X, Y, Z among our relatives; and told the dressmaker to propose the second daughter. Apparently the other side took offence, and would not agree, so the matter fell through.

Then my mother met a lady when she was playing mahjong, who had a daughter who was very clever and sprightly. Mother began to have ideas, and when she got home said that the girl was the same age as me, and skipped around the place and was still a child. After a few days she asked someone to find out if they were interested. It seemed their family held an official rank that was even lower than my father's; in those days, actually the year before the Revolution, such things still counted, so they were very happy to make this match. Things were already ninety-nine percent agreed, when something went wrong. There was an elderly widowed *amah* in service with a great-aunt on my father's side, who knew the family well. Somehow or other my mother got to hear of it. She was summoned to be questioned, and her words were evasive. In the end they got it out of her that the little girl had been adopted, though she was much loved by the whole family, just as if she were their own. My mother lost interest. After a couple of years, we heard that she had developed consumption, and had also become addicted to opium. My mother said that it was a good thing that the match was called off. I was beginning to understand the ways of the world, and I thought so too.

In the year of the Revolution, my father got typhoid, and many doctors were summoned to attend to him. In the end they called a Doctor Wu, who later became my father-in-law. One day the servant who had often been sent to fetch the doctor said that there was a young lady in the doctor's house. Since my father was ill, my mother was naturally bound to be even more concerned about my affairs. As soon as she heard this remark, she enquired further. The servant happened to be just making idle talk and could not come up with any details. So when the doctor came, my mother sent someone to ask his sedan bearer whether the young lady belonged to their family or not. The sedan bearer said she did. Mother then consulted father, and asked her brother to find out what the doctor thought. That day I was standing by my father's sickbed and heard them carry on the conversation. My uncle found out that the young lady was not yet betrothed, then he said, "What about a family like Mr X's?" The doctor said that was fine. Having spoken this far, the next thing was the inspection, and it was again carried out by the same trusty old *amah*. This time the report was quite good, the only thing was her feet were a bit big. Things having been as good as settled, mother told the sedan bearer to take back word and ask that the young lady should have her feet bound a bit. After my wife was married to me, she said that at the time of the inspection she had hidden herself away, and the person inspected was someone else. As far as the message brought by the sedan bearer was concerned, it raised a small ripple. Father-in-law said to mother-in-law, "I told you long ago to bind her feet, and you wouldn't believe me. Look what they are saying." Mother-in-law said, "I am jolly well not having her feet bound, and they will have to put up with it." In the end they compromised, right until the time of the marriage, when my wife came to live in our house.

Written in March of the 23rd year of the Republic (1934)

CHAPTER 12 | # The New Republic

12.1 AND 12.2 YUAN SHIKAI: TWO DOCUMENTS

The "Soldier's Song," written by Yuan Shikai shortly after he became president of the Chinese Republic in 1912, is typical of a genre of patriotic writings in the early Republican period that attempted to expand the nationalistic consciousness of military men. Similar motivational songs had been composed for soldiers by Zeng Guofan and other commanders during the Taiping and Nian rebellions, but the stress in Yuan's song on protecting the nation, patriotism, and the soldier as "citizen" was new. The soldier of the modern armies was to be an exemplar of the purest national virtues; unlike the sedentary scholar-official who despised physical exertion and suspected change, he was to be a disciplined, forceful, modern-thinking, and dynamic agent of the state. The document that follows the "song" is Yuan Shikai's declaration of allegiance to the Republic.

12.1 *Poem to the Soldiers*

SOLDIER'S SONG

(1)

Listen to me soldiers—heed what I say!
You have been called to arms to protect the nation.
Your nation and mine.
He who bears arms for his country is a patriot.
He who disturbs it,

Commits a grave crime.
To rob or assail one's own is against human nature and manhood.

(2)

In his own home, the soldier is a citizen,
Once he joins his regiment his heart and his hand belong to all citizens
Soldiers and citizens are as one in the nation's great family:
He has old ones and young ones to support,
He has wealth and property to protect.
Compare your lot with that of others,
And your love for all the people will be reborn.

(3)

The term "soldier" is honorable.
All citizens should respect those who are called to defend the nation.
But he who becomes a soldier must learn first to respect himself.
He must be honorable, obedient, frugal, and brave.
One base act, one man who forgets home and duty,
Disgraces the name of a regiment.
It is a pride and a duty to obey orders.

(4)

After obedience comes respect for your officers,
Civilian officials, too, are enlisted to your respect.
Foreign and Chinese officials have equal claims,
To the respect and the salute of the soldier.
The winning of victory, the defeat of an enemy,
Depends on the skill of the soldier.
Drill, whose hardships patience overcomes
Brings skill to the handling of arms.

(5)

He who hastens to be first in the field is a hero.
His name is forever revered and held in respect.
While he who flees from battle is disgraced,
And dies the death of a coward.
We must all one day die, so
Better is it to die bravely fighting the fight
Your deeds remembered and beloved.

12.2 Yuan Pledges Allegiance to the Republic, February 12, 1912

A republic is the best form of government. The whole world admits this. That in one leap we have passed from autocracy to republicanism is really the outcome of the many years of strenuous efforts exerted by you all, and is the greatest blessing to the people. The Da Qing emperor has proclaimed his abdication by edict countersigned by myself. The day of the promulgation of this edict shall be the end of Imperial rule and the inauguration of the Republic. Henceforth we shall exert our utmost strength to move forward in progress until we reach perfection. Henceforth, forever, we shall not allow a monarchical government in our country. I shall be most happy to come to the South and to listen to your counsels in our conference as to the methods of procedure. Only on account of the difficulty of maintaining order in the North and the existence of a large army requiring control, and the popular mind in the North and South not being united, the slightest disturbance will affect the whole country. All of you who thoroughly understand the situation will realize my difficult position. You have studied the important question of establishing a Republic, and have definite plans in your minds. I beg you to inform me as to the best means of cooperation in the work of consolidation.

[Signed] Yuan Shikai

12.3 JAPAN'S TWENTY-ONE DEMANDS, 1915

After the signing of the Treaty of Shimonoseki in 1895, the Japanese government aggressively pursued a policy of territorial expansion at the expense of Korea and China. In 1910, Korea was formally annexed into the Japanese empire. At the same time, the South Manchurian Railway Company and Japanese investors and migrants extended the Japanese sphere of influence in Manchuria.

When World War I broke out in Europe, the Japanese government moved quickly to oust Germany from Shandong, taking control of the colonial interests that Germany had developed there since 1898. Then, striking just as President Yuan Shikai was plotting to realize his monarchical ambitions, Japan moved to affirm the claim to Shandong and reinforce its dominance in Manchuria and Inner Mongolia through the Twenty-one Demands.

The following is the full text of the Twenty-one Demands, issued on January 18, 1915, which included the incendiary conditions that sought to turn China into a Japanese protectorate. Faced with vehement public indignation, Yuan Shikai's administration tried to negotiate, to which the Japanese government responded with a tough ultimatum. The second document below is Yuan's acquiescence to the Demands, with the request that the fifth group

204 | THE NEW REPUBLIC

of conditions be left for future negotiation. Yuan Shikai's acceptance of the Twenty-one Demands, albeit conditionally, provoked a wave of nationwide protests and prepared the ground for the nationalist movement of subsequent years.

TRANSLATION OF DOCUMENTS HANDED TO THE PRESIDENT YUAN SHIKAI BY MR. HIOKI, THE JAPANESE MINISTER, ON JANUARY 18, 1915.

I

The Japanese Government and the Chinese Government being desirous of maintaining the general peace in Eastern Asia and further strengthening the friendly relations and good neighborhood existing between the two nations agree to the following articles:

ART. 1.   The Chinese Government engages to give full assent to all matters upon which the Japanese Government may hereafter agree with the German Government relating to the disposition of all rights, interests and concessions which Germany, by virtue of treaties or otherwise, possesses in relation to the Province of Shantung.

ART. 2.   The Chinese Government engages that within the Province of Shantung and along its coast, no territory or island will be ceded or leased to a third Power under any pretext.

ART. 3.   The Chinese Government consents to Japan's building a railway from Chefoo or Lungkow to join the Kiaochow-Chinanfu Railway.

ART. 4.   The Chinese Government engages, in interest of trade and for the residence of foreigners, to open by herself as soon as possible certain important cities and towns in the Province of Shantung as Commercial Ports. What places shall be opened are to be jointly decided upon in a separate agreement.

I I

The Japanese Government and the Chinese Government, since the Chinese Government has always acknowledged the special position enjoyed by Japan in South Manchuria and Eastern Inner Mongolia, agree to the following articles:

ART. 1.   The two Contracting Parties mutually agree that the term of lease of Port Arthur and Dalny and the term of lease of the South Manchurian Railway and the Antung-Mukden Railway shall be extended to the period of 99 years.

ART. 2.   Japanese subjects in South Manchuria and Eastern Inner Mongolia shall have the right to lease or own land required either for erecting suitable buildings for trade and manufacture or for farming.

ART. 3.   Japanese subjects shall be free to reside and travel in South Manchuria and Eastern Inner Mongolia and to engage in business and in manufacture of any kind whatsoever.

Art. 4.   The Chinese Government agrees to grant to Japanese subjects the right of opening the mines in South Manchuria and Eastern Inner Mongolia. As regards what mines are to be opened, they shall be decided upon jointly.

Art. 5.   The Chinese Government agrees that in respect of the (two) cases mentioned herein below the Japanese Government's consent shall be first obtained before action is taken:

(a) Whenever permission is granted to the subject of a third Power to build a railway or to make a loan with a third Power for the purpose of building a railway in South Manchuria and Eastern Inner Mongolia.

(b) Whenever a loan is to be made with a third Power pledging the local taxes of South Manchuria and Eastern Inner Mongolia as security.

Art. 6.   The Chinese Government agrees that if the Chinese Government employs political, financial or military advisers or instructors in South Manchuria or Eastern Inner Mongolia, the Japanese Government shall first be consulted.

Art. 7.   The Chinese Government agrees that the control and management of the Kirin-Changchun Railway shall be handed over to the Japanese Government for a term of 99 years dating from the signing of this agreement.

III

The Japanese Government and the Chinese Government, seeing that Japanese financiers and the Hanyehping Co. have close relations with each other at present and desiring that the common interests of the two nations shall be advanced, agree to the following articles:

Art. 1.   The two Contracting Parties mutually agree that when the opportune moment arrives the Hanyehping Company shall be made a joint concern of the two nations and they further agree that without the previous consent of Japan China shall not by her own act dispose of the rights and property of whatsoever nature of the said Company nor cause the said Company to dispose freely of the same.

Art. 2.   The Chinese Government agrees that all mines in the neighborhood of those owned by the Hanyehping Company shall not be permitted, without the consent of the said Company, to be worked by other persons outside of the said Company; and further agrees that if it is desired to carry out any undertaking which, it is apprehended, may directly or indirectly affect the interests of the said Company, the consent of the said Company shall first be obtained.

IV

The Japanese Government and the Chinese Government with the object of effectively preserving the territorial integrity of China agree to the following special article:

The Chinese Government engages not to cede or lease to a third Power any harbor or bay or island along the coast of China.

V

ART. 1.   The Chinese Central Government shall employ influential Japanese as advisers in political, financial and military affairs.

ART. 2.   Japanese hospitals, churches and schools in the interior of China shall be granted the right of owning land.

ART. 3.   Inasmuch as the Japanese Government and the Chinese Government have had many cases of disputes between Japanese and Chinese police which caused no little misunderstanding, it is for this reason necessary that the police departments of important places (in China) shall be jointly administered by Japanese and Chinese or that the police departments of these places shall employ numerous Japanese, so that they may at the same time help to plan for the improvement of the Chinese Police Service.

ART. 4.   China shall purchase from Japan a fixed amount of munitions of war (say 50% or more of what is needed by the Chinese Government) or that there shall be established in China a Sino-Japanese jointly worked arsenal. Japanese technical experts are to be employed and Japanese material to be purchased.

ART. 5.   China agrees to grant to Japan the right of constructing a railway connecting Wuchang with Kiu-kiang and Nanchang, another line between Nanchang and Hangchow, and another between Nanchang and Chao-chow.

ART. 6.   If China needs foreign capital to work mines, build railways and construct harbor-works (including dockyards) in the Province of Fukien, Japan shall be first consulted.

ART. 7.   China agrees that Japanese subjects shall have the right of missionary propaganda in China.

THE REPLY OF THE CHINESE GOVERNMENT TO THE ULTIMATUM OF THE JAPANESE GOVERNMENT, DELIVERED TO THE JAPANESE MINISTER ON THE 8TH OF MAY, 1915.

On the 7th of this month, at three o'clock, the Chinese Government received an Ultimatum from the Japanese Government together with an Explanatory Note of seven articles. The Ultimatum concluded with the hope that the Chinese Government by six o'clock on the 9th of May will give a satisfactory reply, and "it is hereby declared that if no satisfactory reply is received before or at the designated time, the Japanese Government will take steps they may deem necessary."

The Chinese Government with a view to preserving the peace of the Far East hereby accepts, with the exception of those five articles of Group V postponed for later negotiation, all the articles of Groups I, II, III and IV and the exchange of Notes in connection with Fukien Province in Group V, as contained in the revised proposals presented on the 26th of April and in accordance with the Explanatory Note of seven articles accompanying the Ultimatum of the Japanese Government, with the hope that thereby all outstanding questions are settled, so that the cordial relationship between the two countries may be further consolidated. The Japanese Minister is hereby requested to appoint a day to call at the Ministry of Foreign Affairs to make the literary improvement of the text and sign the Agreement as soon as possible.

12.4 FENG YUXIANG: PRAISING THE LORD

After the warlord Feng Yuxiang converted to Methodism in 1914, he energetically proselytized his faith in the ranks of his army. Foreign missionaries welcomed Feng's efforts to build a Christian army and were frequent visitors to his headquarters at Nanyuan in Hebei. They applauded his mass baptisms of soldiers, the army's Spartan training, and supported Feng's efforts to halt opium smoking, gambling, and drinking. For some, Feng Yuxiang was a dream come true: a charismatic native Christian leader who could produce the mass conversions that had eluded several generations of missionaries.

The following description by missionary George T. B. Davis provides a sense of the life of the soldiers in the Feng Yuxiang's army (ca. 1919) and vividly demonstrates how Feng and his subordinate commanders utilized hymns, prayer meetings, fiery sermons, and conversions as motivating tools and as means to attract foreign support.

There is a strict schedule of work and study from the rising bugle in the morning, to "lights out" at night. In the summer the men rise at 4 A.M. The first order of the day after dressing, is a bit of spiritual drill. They assemble by companies in the open air in the quiet of the early dawn. The captain leads in the singing of a gospel hymn. Then all heads are reverently bowed while an officer or corporal or private soldier prays earnestly for God's blessing upon the army and the duties of the day.

Physical drill follows spiritual. The men go out for a twenty minutes run, and clamber up and down curious little mounds with steps, to make them fit for mountain climbing, and for the day's program of study and work. Then comes military drill, followed by various forms of physical training, industrial work, study of Chinese, moral lectures, a noon prayer meeting, and so on. From morning until night there is a varied program of study and work and worship.

The army is up-to-the-minute in physical fitness, as might be expected where there is an absence of immorality, wine drinking, and cigarette smoking. The men are alert, athletic, clear-eyed, strong-muscled. Sir James Startin, a retired Admiral of the British Navy, who recently visited Peking, was much impressed with the fine physique of the men. He was also delighted with the feats they performed on the horizontal bars. The other day I saw a soldier do the full swing nearly a dozen times in succession just in their ordinary practice.

A striking feature of the army-school is its industrial branch. This was started by Gen. Feng in order that many of the men might learn a trade while in the army, and have a means of support on their return home. As you pass through one room after another you see the young men busily engaged in making shoes and clothes, knitting stockings, weaving rugs, boiling soap, and making chairs and other articles of furniture. When one set of men have learned a trade, another lot takes their place.

But the most interesting and striking phase of the army life is its spiritual side. In my early visits to the camp the thing that most impressed me was the sight of a hundred or more men standing outside a mess-room before a meal singing a gospel hymn. Then all heads were bowed while someone led in prayer; not a few formal phrases, but an earnest petition, often of some length. And imagine my surprise when calmly informed that this was the custom throughout the entire army before each of the two meals of the day!

Later I witnessed a still more striking scene that occurs at noon each day. At twelve o'clock a gun is fired. At ten minutes past twelve the men gather by companies outside their various quarters for half an hour of Bible reading and prayer. Sometimes the meeting is conducted by the captain; sometimes the companies are divided into smaller groups in charge of a corporal. First a hymn is sung; then a chapter in the New Testament is read verse about, often with brief explanations, followed by a number of earnest petitions from the men as well as the officers. It is really Family Worship for the day. Just as a father gathers his family about him for Bible reading and prayer; so the captains and corporals of the army conduct the service for those committed to their care.

And it is a singing, as well as a Bible-reading and praying, army. How the men love to sing the old hymns that are favorites at home! They sing the first thing in the morning; they sing at noon; they sing the last thing at night. They sing at meetings, they sing before meals, they sing as they march. The favorite hymn of the army is "Onward Christian Soldiers." Some others that the troops especially enjoy are: "Stand Up, Stand Up for Jesus!" "Ye Soldiers of the Cross"; "Room for Thee"; "All People That on Earth Do Dwell"; and "O Happy Day."

12.5 ZHANG ZONGCHANG: WITH PLEASURE RIFE

Not all warlords shared the pious worldview of Feng Yuxiang. Many were opportunists of the first order, who capitalized on the multiple crises of the post-1911 era to advance their own interests, indulge their vices, and carve out independent kingdoms. Many warlords were indifferent to the welfare of the people they ruled, treating them as an inert mass to be taxed, exploited, and killed at will.

One such warlord was Zhang Zongchang (1881–1932), the "Dog-meat General" of Shandong. The following satirical sketch by Lin Yutang (1895–1976), one of China's most famous twentieth-century humorists, was written shortly after Zhang's death.

So General Zhang Zongchang, the "Dog-meat General," has been killed, according to this morning's report. I am sorry for him, and I am sorry for his mother, and I am sorry for the sixteen concubines he has left behind him and the four times sixteen that had left him before he died. As I intend to specialize in writing "in memoriams" for the bewildering generals of this bewildering generation, I am going to begin with the Dog-meat General first.

So our Dog-meat General is dead! What an event! It is full of mystic significance for me and for China and us poor folk who do not wear boots and carry bayonets! Such a thing could not happen every day, and if it could there would be an end to all China's sorrows. In such an eventuality you could abolish all the five Yuan [government ministries], tear up the will of Dr. Sun Yat-sen, dismiss the hundred odd members of the Central Executive Committee of the Guomindang, close up all the schools and universities of China, and you wouldn't have to bother your head about Communism, Fascism, and Democracy, and universal suffrage, and emancipation of women, and we poor folk would still be able to live in peace and prosperity.

So one more of the colorful, legendary figures of medieval China has passed into eternity. And yet Dog-meat General's death has a special significance for me, because he was the most colorful, legendary, medieval, and unashamed ruler of modern China. He was a born ruler such as modern China wants. He was six feet tall, a towering giant, with a pair of squint eyes and a pair of abnormally massive hands. He was direct, forceful, terribly efficient at times: obstinate and gifted with moderate intelligence. He was patriotic according to his lights, and he was anti-communist, which made up for his being anti-Guomindang. All his critics must allow that he wasn't anti-Guomindang from convictions, but by accident. He didn't want to fight the Guomindang: it was the Guomindang that wanted to fight him and grab his territory, and, being an honest man, he fought rather than turn tail. Given a chance, and if the Guomindang would return him his Shandong he would join the Guomindang, because he said that the Sanmin doctrine can't do any harm.

He could drink, and he was awfully fond of "dog-meat," and he could swear all he wanted to and as much as he wanted to, irrespective of his official superiors and inferiors. He made no pretence to being a gentleman, and didn't affect to send nice-sounding circular telegrams, like the rest of them. He was ruthlessly honest, and this honesty made him much loved by all his close associates. If he loved women he said so, and he could see foreign consuls while he had a Russian girl sitting on his knee. If he made orgies he didn't try to conceal them from his friends and foes. If he coveted his subordinate's wife he told him openly, and wrote no psalm of repentance about it like King David. And he always played square. If he took his subordinate's wife he made her husband the chief of police of Jinan [Shandong].

"whatever may happen to you, you must always forgive me, and always think of my feelings for you. I will always love you. I am willing even to sacrifice my life in this world for you. If you should go to the ends of the earth, I will follow you to the ends of the earth. I would never let you go by yourself, lonely and without a companion." Covering her pretty face with her hands, she knelt there perfectly motionless.

Freeman was most surprised to see her this way. But he still did not understand. He could only imagine it was because of the previous day's talk about returning to England. Feeling depressed at this, he once again held Guifang's face in his hands, smiled, kissed her, and said, "Dear one, all of this is a simple matter. Of course I will bring you along wherever I go. I may lose every one of my possessions, but I will never spend a single day out of sight of my Guifang." Guifang stood several moments in a daze next to the couch, then moved daintily across the room to disappear behind the screen.

Before long she returned with a tea tray. Hesitating a moment, she then held out a cup of coffee for Freeman, her hand trembling. "Dear sir, a cup of coffee for you," she said.

"Thank you, my love," answered Freeman with a smile. Raising the cup to his lips, he drank until it was dry. When he was finished he fell with a thud back onto the couch, as the cup fell to the floor and shattered. Guifang stood staring at her sweetheart with tear-filled eyes. Then she slowly stretched her neck down to give him one final kiss. Kneeling on the floor, her utterly despondent voice cried out in spine-chilling lament, "Dear sir! Till we meet again!"

CHAPTER 13 | "A Road Is Made"

13.1 CHEN DUXIU: "CALL TO YOUTH," 1915

Chen Duxiu (1879–1942), one of the cofounders of the Chinese Communist Party in 1921, was the founding editor of *New Youth* (Xin Qingnian), a leading avant-garde journal of the May Fourth period. Through its pages, Chen promoted science and democracy and led the attack on "Confucianism," casting the weight of "tradition" as one of the major causes of the nation's backwardness.

In this manifesto, published in 1915, Chen called on China's youth to rise up and take responsibility for the country's future, invoking principles drawn from social Darwinism and other Western political philosophies. His prescription for national renewal focused on cultural change: rejecting the strictures of the Confucian past and embracing individualism, progress, and scientific inquiry.

The Chinese compliment others by saying, "He acts like an old man although still young." Englishmen and Americans encourage one another by saying, "Keep young while growing old." Such is one respect in which the different ways of thought of the East and West are manifested. Youth is like early spring, like the rising sun, like trees and grass in bud, like a newly sharpened blade. It is the most valuable period of life. The function of youth in society is the same as that of a fresh and vital cell in a human body. In the processes of metabolism, the old and the rotten are incessantly eliminated to be replaced by the fresh and living . . . If metabolism functions properly in a human body, the person will be healthy; if the old and rotten cells accumulate and fill the body, the person will die. If metabolism functions properly in a society, it will flourish; if old and rotten elements fill the society, then it will cease to exist.

According to this standard, then, is the society of our nation flourishing, or is it about to perish? I cannot bear to answer. As for those old and rotten elements, I shall leave them to the process of natural selection. I do not wish to waste my fleeting time in arguing with them on this and that and hoping for them to be reborn and thoroughly remodeled. I only, with tears, place my plea before the young and vital youth, in the hope that they will achieve self-awareness, and begin to struggle. What is this self-awareness? It is to be conscious of the value and responsibility of one's young life and vitality, to maintain one's self-respect, which should not be lowered. What is the struggle? It is to exert one's intellect, discard resolutely the old and the rotten, regard them as enemies and as the flood or savage beasts, keep away from their neighborhood and refuse to be contaminated by their poisonous germs. Alas! Do these words really fit the youth of our country? I have seen that, out of every ten youths who are young in age, five are old in physique; and out of every ten who are young in both age and physique, nine are old in mentality. Those with shining hair, smooth countenance, a straight back and a wide chest are indeed magnificent youths! Yet if you ask what thoughts and aims are entertained in their heads, then they all turn out to be the same as the old and rotten, like moles from the same hill. In the beginning the youth are not without freshness and vitality. Gradually some are assimilated by the old and rotten elements; then there are others who fear the tremendous influence of those elements, who hesitate, stammer and stall, and dare not openly rebel against them. It is the old and rotten air that fills society everywhere. One cannot even find a bit of fresh and vital air to comfort those of us who are suffocating in despair.

Such a phenomenon, if found in a human body, would kill a man; if found in a society, would destroy it. A heavy sigh or two cannot cure this malady. What is needed is for one or two youths, who are quick in self-consciousness and brave in a struggle, to use to the full the natural intellect of man, and judge and choose all the thoughts of mankind, distinguishing which are fresh and vital and suitable for the present struggle for survival, and which are old and rotten and unworthy to be retained in the mind. Treat this problem as a sharp tool cleaves iron, or a sharp knife cuts hemp. Resolutely make no compromises and entertain no hesitations. Consider yourself and consider others; then perhaps society can hope to become clean and peaceful. O youth, is there anyone who takes upon himself such responsibilities? As for understanding what is right and wrong, in order that you may make your choice, I carefully propose the following six principles, and hope you will give them your calm consideration.

1. BE INDEPENDENT, NOT SERVILE

All men are equal. Each has his right to be independent, but absolutely no right to enslave others nor any obligation to make himself servile. By slavery we mean that in ancient times the ignorant and the weak lost their right of freedom, which was savagely usurped by tyrants. Since the rise of the theories of the rights of man and of equality, no red-blooded person can endure [the name of slave]. The history of modern Europe is commonly referred to as a "history of emancipation": the destruction of monarchical power aimed at political emancipation; the denial of Church authority aimed at religious emancipation; the rise of the theory of equal property aimed at economic emancipation; and the suffragist movement aimed at emancipation from male authority.

Emancipation means freeing oneself from the bondage of slavery and achieving a completely independent and free personality. I have hands and feet, and I can earn my own living. I have a mouth and a tongue, and I can voice my own likes and dislikes. I have a mind, and I can determine my own beliefs. I will absolutely not let others do these things in my behalf, nor should I assume an overlordship and enslave others. For once the independent personality is recognized, all matters of conduct, all rights and privileges, and all belief should be left to the natural ability of each person; there is definitely no reason why one should blindly follow others. On the other hand, loyalty, filial piety, chastity and righteousness are a slavish morality. (Note: The great German philosopher Nietzsche divided morality into two categories—that which is independent and courageous is called "morality of the noble," and that which is humble and submissive is called "morality of the slave.") Light penalties and light taxation constitute the happiness of slaves; panegyrics and eulogies are slavish literature; . . . noble ranks or magnificent mansions are glory only to slaves; resplendent tablets and grand tombs are their memorials. That is because such persons, by submitting to the judgment of others regarding right and wrong, glory and shame, instead of depending on their own standard of judgment, have completely annihilated their independent and equal personalities as individuals. In their conduct, whether good or bad, they cannot appeal to their own will-power, but are confined to receiving merits or demerits (from others). Who can say that it is improper to call such persons slaves? Therefore, before we speak of contributing to mankind in moral example or in deed, we must first make this distinction between the independent and the servile.

2. BE PROGRESSIVE, NOT CONSERVATIVE

"Without progress there will be retrogression" is an old Chinese saying. Considering the fundamental laws of the universe, all things or phenomena are daily progressing in evolution, and the maintenance of the status quo is definitely out of the question; only the limitation of man's ordinary view has rendered possible the differentiation between the two states of things. This is why the theory of creative evolution, "L'Evolution créatrice," of the contemporary French philosopher Henri Bergson, has become immensely popular throughout a whole generation. Considered in the light of the evolution of human affairs, it is plain that those races that cling to antiquated ways are declining, or disappearing, day by day, and the peoples who seek progress and advancement are just beginning to ascend in power and strength. It is possible to predict which of these will survive and which will not.

precepts of ethical convention, the hopes and purposes of the people—there is nothing which does not run counter to the practical life of society today. If we do not restring our bow and renew our effort, there will be no way to revive the strength of our nation, and our society will never see a peaceful day. As for praying to gods to relieve flood and famine, or reciting the *Book of Filial Piety* to ward off the Yellow Turbans [i.e., bandits]—people are not infants or morons, and they see through these absurdities. Though a thing is of gold or of jade, if it is of no practical use, then it is of less value than coarse cloth, grain, manure or dirt. That which brings no benefit to the practical life of an individual or of society is all empty formalism and the stuff of cheats. And even though it were bequeathed to us by our ancestors, taught by the sages, advocated by the government and worshiped by society, the stuff of cheats is still not worth one cent.

6. BE SCIENTIFIC, NOT IMAGINATIVE

What is science? It is our general conception of matter which, being the sum of objective phenomena as analyzed by subjective reason, contains no contradiction within itself. What is imagination? It first oversteps the realm of objective phenomena, and then discards reason itself; it is something constructed out of thin air, consisting of hypotheses without proof, and all the existing wisdom of mankind cannot be made to find reason in it or explain its laws and principles. There was only imagination and no science in the unenlightened days of old, as well as among the uncivilized peoples of today. Religion, art, and literature were the products of the period of imagination. The contribution of the growth of science to the supremacy of modern Europe over other races is not less than that of the theory of the rights of man . . . Our scholars do not know science, therefore they borrow the yin-yang school's notions of auspicious signs and of the five elements to confuse the world and cheat the people, and the ideas of topography and geomancy to beg for miracles from dry skeletons (spirits). Our farmers do not know science; therefore they have no technique for seed selection and insecticide. Our industrialists do not know science; therefore goods lie wasted on the ground, while we depend on foreign countries for everything that we need in warfare and in production. Our merchants know no science; therefore they are only concerned with obtaining short-term profits, and give not a thought to calculating for the future. Our physicians know no science; not only are they not acquainted with human anatomy, but also they do not analyze the properties of medicines; as for bacteria and contagious diseases, they have never heard of them. They can only parrot the talk about the five elements, their mutual promotions and preventions, cold and heat, yin and yang, and prescribe medicine according to ancient formulae. Their technique is practically the same as that of an archer! The height of their marvelous imaginations is the theory of qi (primal force), which even extends to the techniques of professional strong men and Taoist priests. But though you seek high and low in the universe, you will never know what this "primal force" exactly is. All these nonsensical ideas and unreasonable beliefs can be cured at the root only by science. For to explain truth by science means proving everything with fact. Although the process is slower than that of imagination and arbitrary decision, yet every step taken is on firm ground; it is different from those imaginative flights which eventually cannot advance even one inch. The amount of truth in the universe is boundless, and the fertile areas in the realm of science awaiting the pioneer are immense! Youth, take up the task!

13.2 Li Dazhao: "The Victory of Bolshevism," 1918

Li Dazhao (1889–1927), one of the cofounders of the Chinese Communist Party with Chen Duxiu, was a professor of philosophy and chief librarian at Peking University. An active participant in the New Culture movement, he organized a "Marxist Research Society" in September 1918. He was one of the first Chinese intellectuals to grasp the significance of the Bolshevik Revolution.

The article translated here captures the spirit of Li Dazhao's first forays into Marxist theory. When Li wrote it, there was no communist organization in China, and most theoretical works by Marx and his followers had yet to be translated into Chinese. It is also worth noting that this article predates the announcement of the Versailles Treaty in spring 1919. In the fall of 1918, Li Dazhao was already skeptical of the significance of the Allied victory in Europe.

"Victory! Victory! Victory to the Allies! Surrender! Surrender! The Germans have surrendered!" On the doors of homes everywhere hang national flags and people all over are crying out *"wansui"* [Long live!]. Voices and the colors all seem to be expressions of these words. Men and women from the Allied countries run back and forth on the streets celebrating their victory; soldiers of the Allied countries loudly sing their victory songs in the cities. Suddenly there is the sound of breaking glass as the store windows of German merchants are broken and of a crash as the monument to von Ketteler is pulled down.[1] And these sounds mix together with the noise of happy celebration. It goes without saying that foreign nationals of the Allied powers resident in our country are exceedingly happy. Even people in our country who had little to do with the changing situation in the world have felt obliged to engage in obsequious displays of happiness as they take the joy and glory of others as their own. In academic circles there are lantern parades,

1. Clemens von Ketteler was the German minister in Peking at the time of the Boxer Rebellion. He was shot by a soldier on June 20, 1900, when he ventured out to attempt negotiations with the Boxers. After the rebellion, per provision of the Boxer Protocol, a marble memorial arch was built to commemorate his death.

politicians hold celebratory meetings, and generals who never led a single soldier in the year or so that China participated in the war, review parades of troops and are awe-inspiringly martial. Political hacks who once wrote histories of the European war which argued that Germany must inevitably win and who then turned around to declare war on Germany now claim all merit for themselves and print articles in newspapers that advertise their own activities and declaim those of others. Little people like us in the world can only follow along and join in the commotion, celebrating the victory and shouting *wansui*. This is the situation as the Allied victory has been celebrated recently in Peking.

However, let us carefully consider all of this from our standpoint as members of the world's human race: In the final analysis, whose victory is this and who has really surrendered? Who has accomplished this task and for whom are we celebrating? If we consider these questions, our generals who never led troops and yet flaunt their martial prowess and the shameless politicians who claim all merit for themselves, are truly disgraceful. It is also meaningless for the people of Allied countries to say that the war was a victory of Allied arms over the military forces of Germany. Their boasts and celebrations are totally meaningless for it is probable that their political hacks will soon share the same fate as German militarism.

In fact, the victory of Allied military strength over German military strength was not the true cause of the conclusion of this war; the real cause for victory was German socialism's defeat of German militarism. The German people were not obliged to surrender by Allied armed force; in actuality, Germany's emperor, warlords, and militarism were forced to surrender by the tide of world affairs. It was not the Allies who defeated German militarism but rather the spirit of the awakened people of Germany. The failure of German militarism was the failure of Germany's Hohenzollern family (the German imperial family) and not the failure of the German people. As for the victory over German militarism, it was not the victory of the Allies and it certainly was not the victory of either the military men in our country who are scrabbling to claim merit for their participation or the politicians who are opportunistically and cunningly promoting themselves. This was the victory of humanitarianism, pacifism, justice, freedom, democracy, and socialism. This was the victory of Bolshevism, the red flag, the working class of the world, and the victory of the new tide of the twentieth century. This accomplishment belongs not so much to Wilson and others as to Lenin, Kollontai, Leibknecht, Scheidemann, and Marx. This should not be a celebration merely for one country or a group within a certain country; rather, it should be a celebration of a new dawn for world mankind. It should be a celebration not of the victory of one side's military forces over the other but a celebration of democracy and socialism's triumph over monarchy and militarism. . . .

From the facts of what the "Bolsheviki" are doing, it is possible to see that their doctrine is revolutionary socialism and their party is a revolutionary socialist party. They honor the German socialist economist Marx as the founder of their doctrine. Their goal is to break down the national boundaries which today are the obstacle

blocking socialism. They seek to destroy the monopoly capitalist system of production. The true cause of the war was the destruction of national boundaries
because the expanded productive force of capitalism could not be contained by the
national boundaries of today. The territories enclosed by national boundaries are
too constricted to permit the development of productive force. Therefore, the capitalists depend on war to break down these boundaries and they want to create a
global economic organization that will tie together all parts. Socialists agree with
capitalists that international borders should be broken down, but the hope of capitalist governments is to give benefits to the middle classes of their countries. These
governments depend on the global economic development of the capitalist class of
the victorious countries of the world. They do not rely the humanistic and rational
coordination and mutual help of the producers of the world. The victorious countries of this kind will because of this war advance and change in the future from
powerful countries to imperialistic countries. The "Bolsheviki" observed this and
cried out and announced that this war was the Czar's war, the Kaiser's war, a war
of kings, a war of emperors, a war of capitalist governments, but not their war. Their
war is class war. It is a war of the proletariat of the entire world against the capitalists of the world. Although they oppose war, they are not afraid of war. They
believe that everyone, male or female, should work and that all workers should
belong to a union. Every union should have a central governing council and such
a council should be the basic organization for all the governments of the world.
There will be no congresses, no parliaments, no presidents, no premiers, no cabi-
nets, no legislative branches, and no rulers. Only councils of labor unions will exist
and they will decide everything. All industries will belong to the people working
there; there will be no private ownership. The Bolsheviki will unite the proletariat
of the entire world and use to the utmost their power and force of resistance to
create a land of freedom and they will first create a democratic federation in Europe
as the basis of a world federation. These are the new beliefs of the Bolsheviki and
the new doctrine of world revolution in the twentieth century. . . .

　　Up to now, . . . there have been revolutions in Austria-Hungary, Germany,
Bavaria, and there are rumors that revolutionary socialist parties are launching
uprisings in Holland, Sweden, and Spain. The revolutionary situation in these countries is basically similar to that of Russia. Red flags are flying everywhere. Labor
unions are being established one after another. It can be said that this is a Russian-
style revolution or it can be said that this is a twentieth-century-style revolution. The
crashing waves of revolution cannot be halted by today's capitalist governments
because the mass movements of the twentieth century have brought together world
humankind into one great mass. Each person within this great mass unconsciously
follows the motion of the mass and all are pulled together into a great, irresistible
social force. When this global force begins to rumble, the wind roars throughout
the whole world, clouds surge, there is a pounding in the mountains, and valleys
echo with the sound. In the face of this global, mass movement, historical remnants—
such as emperors, noblemen, warlords, bureaucrats, militarism, capitalism—and

all other things that obstruct the advance of this new movement will be crushed by the thunderous force. When confronted by this irresistible tide, these remnants of the past are like withered leaves facing the bitter autumn wind; one by one they will drop to the ground. On all sides one sees the victorious banners of Bolshevism and everywhere one hears the victorious songs of Bolshevism. Everyone says that the bells are ringing! The dawn of freedom is breaking! Just take a look at the world of the future, it is sure to be a world of red flags!

I said once: "History is the general psychological record of people. People's lives are closely connected and linked with one another like parts of a big mechanism. The future of an individual corresponds to the future of all of mankind. The portents revealed by one event are interrelated with portents of the entire world situation. The French Revolution of 1789 was not merely a sign of the changed mentality of the French. It was actually a sign of the general changing mentality of nineteenth-century man. The Russian Revolution of 1917 is not only an obvious omen of the changing mentality of twentieth-century man." The Russian Revolution is the first fallen leaf that warns the world of the coming of autumn. Although the word Bolshevism was coined by Russians, its spirit is a spirit of enlightenment that every member of mankind can share. Therefore, the victory of Bolshevism is the victory of the new spirit of enlightenment that all mankind can share in the twentieth century.

13.3 DENG CHUNLAN: "MY PLAN FOR WOMEN'S EMANCIPATION AND MY PLAN FOR SELF-IMPROVEMENT," 1919

Deng Chunlan (1892–1982), a leading activist of the women's movement, was born and raised in Gansu and attended a teacher training school run by her father. In 1919, she traveled to Peking to advocate for equal educational opportunities for women. As her essay mentions, she arrived too late to participate in the May Fourth protests, but in time to witness the aftermath. In this essay, Deng declares that education was the foundational issue in the cause of women's emancipation. Her analysis of the gendered division of labor, ideas about women's nature, and family obligations addresses many of the key issues confronting the women's movement. In 1920, a year after this essay was published, Peking University became the first institution of higher learning to admit women. Deng Chunlan was accepted into the first coeducational class.

Last month I published in the newspapers of Beijing and Shanghai a letter on behalf of all the advanced female elementary and middle school graduates of the nation, demanding that universities address the question of women's exclusion from higher education. I think those who pay attention to the woman question have seen this letter, but I still have not received a single reply. My family lives in Lanzhou, over four thousand *li* away from Beijing. The distance is just about ten thousand *li* if you go by raft on the Yellow River, which takes you on a roundabout route through Inner Mongolia. I got to Beijing just in time to see our great president, the great commander exuding power and prestige, deploying military troops to suppress a group of men and women at Xinhua Gate. This poured some cold water on my demand that universities address the question of women's exclusion from higher education! This was probably also the reason no one replied to the letter I wrote last month. But can we just let it end like this? In my view, it certainly cannot end. I am very happy we women have worked hard in all the patriotic movements that have followed May Fourth, and have not let anyone get in our way. I only regret that I have come too late to this endeavor, and have not fulfilled my duty to the utmost. But I also think that, while the patriotic movement is certainly urgent, our women's movement to emancipate ourselves is even more urgent. I say this for two reasons. First, passively speaking: because women have not been given the political rights of the day, our complicity cannot even be assessed when it comes to the wrongful deeds that have devastated the nation. Second, actively speaking: if a group is to have the right to lead others in discussions of "democracy," its members must have a "democratic" spirit at home. Thus, when America advocates a "democratic" League of Nations, people believe it, while people would be suspicious if Japan were to do this. Therefore, if we women are to struggle to bring a truly "democratic" spirit to the Chinese people, we must first struggle to bring a truly "democratic" spirit to the women of China. Only then can we win people's trust. As for the sequential order of the issues we address within the project of women's emancipation, I think we should first deal with education, then deal with employment, and then deal with political rights. After we have accomplished our goals in the area of political rights, the abolition of concubinage and the system of prostitution and the reform of the marriage system will be right within our grasp. As for my plan for this emancipation movement, I think we can organize a women's association in Beijing, with branches outside Beijing as well. The aim of the society would be to build a superb emancipation movement. Its work would proceed along two tracks, one focusing on making preparations and the other focusing on advocacy. Its preparatory work would include the creation of a school specifically for the purpose of preparing women to enroll in men's colleges. Its advocacy work would include producing publications and sending out speakers. When I arrived in Beijing I read in the *Weekly Review* an essay written by Bang Shijun arguing that women's emancipation and the transformation of the family must proceed simultaneously. But I beg to differ. The division of labor is one thing, and women's emancipation is another; we cannot mix the two together when we talk. During the period of barbarism, men had to cut firewood as soon as they finished tilling the fields, and fire up the kiln as soon as they finished cutting firewood. Likewise, women of that period had to be nursemaids, tailors, and cooks all at once. It was inefficient for each person to have so many different kinds of work with no specialty to speak of. Things are better now that there is already a division of labor emerging in the big cities. Look at what is happening to what is said to be women's work—cooking, sewing, and washing. There are now professional tailors and cobblers to make clothes and shoes, and we can pay others to make meals for a few yuan a month. Indeed, these kinds of professions have been appropriated by men. Today, the only work that we women do which is not subject to a division of labor is the work of the nursemaid who takes care of children. But that is work that belongs to us women; why should it be an issue implicated in the emancipation of women and the transformation of the family? I think that the obligation to take care of small children is the only physiologically imposed handicap we have. And if pre-natal education and kindergartens are put in place, women will only be held back twenty months to two years when they have a child. Moreover, we women have inherited a relatively kindly nature; we cannot become cutthroat grunts. These two issues aside, I do not think we women have any other handicaps. And there are those who say that the emancipation of women will be as difficult as the emancipation of black slaves in the United States, the emancipation of serfs in Russia, and the recent Chinese revolution against the Manchus. Again I beg to differ. The emancipation of black slaves in the United States naturally encountered resistance from the white masters who were to be dispossessed; the emancipation of serfs in Russia naturally encountered resistance from landlords who were to be dispossessed; the anti-Manchu revolution in our own country naturally encountered resistance from the Manchus who were fighting with everything they had. But the 200 million of us Chinese who are women are in fact the mothers, daughters, sisters, aunts, wives, and daughters-in-law of the 200 million of us Chinese who are men, and those 200 million men are also the fathers, sons, brothers, uncles, husbands, and sons-in-law of those 200 million of us who are women. Of course they cannot say that they have anything to lose by emancipating us women, so what would be the difficulty? And as difficult as our revolution against the Manchus was, we were still able to thoroughly accomplish our goals because people of Sun Yat-sen's caliber emerged to lead us. Sun Yat-sen wrote in *The Teachings of Sun Yat-sen* that he suffered ten failures before he led his revolutionary movement to victory. I myself was born in the frontier area of Gansu. I was able to get some education thanks to my father. But there was a shortage of educators in our area, so I had to end my own education and become an elementary school teacher early on. Thus, I never did manage to get up to a high school graduate's level of education in English, math, etc., and I had even less opportunity to cultivate my social skills and public speaking skills. So now my own plan for self-improvement is, on the one hand, to get my education up to speed by taking classes at the Advanced Normal School for Women, and, on the other hand, to get in touch with like-minded comrades to work for self-improvement. If there is someone in the women's circles comparable to Sun Yat-sen and Cai Jiemin of the men's circles, I beseech her to be my teacher.

13.4 AND 13.5 LU XUN: MAY FOURTH LITERATURE

Widely regarded as the greatest Chinese writer of the twentieth century, Lu Xu (1881–1936) was born in Shaoxing, Zhejiang, to an impoverished gentry family. After a peripatetic academic career, with stints at the Jiangnan Naval Academy and the School of Mines and Railways, Lu went to Japan to study medicine on a Qing government scholarship. He abandoned his medical studies in 1906, but remained in Tokyo to study literature and write. After an unsuccessful stint as a writer and translator, Lu Xun returned to China to take up a series of teaching and administrative posts, before vaulting to fame as the most influential voice of May Fourth literature.

"A Madman's Diary," published in 1918, was Lu Xun's first notable work of fiction and caused a sensation when it appeared in the avant-garde journal *New Youth*. In the lecture "What Happens After Nora Leaves Home?" Lu Xun considered the question of women's emancipation, using the female protagonist of Ibsen's *A Doll's House* as the point of departure.

13.4 *"A Madman's Diary"*

Two brothers, whose names I need not mention here, were both good friends of mine in high school; but after a separation of many years we gradually lost touch. Some time ago I happened to hear that one of them was seriously ill, and since I was going back to my old home I broke my journey to call on them. I saw only one, however, who told me that the invalid was his younger brother.

"I appreciate your coming such a long way to see us," he said, "but my brother recovered some time ago and has gone elsewhere to take up an official post." Then, laughing, he produced two volumes of his brother's diary, saying that from these the nature of his past illness could be seen and there was no harm in showing them to an old friend. I took the diary away, read it through, and found that he had suffered from a form of persecution complex. The writing was most confused and incoherent, and he had made many wild statements; moreover he had omitted to give any dates, so that only by the colour of the ink and the differences in the writing could one tell that it was not all written at one time. Certain sections, however, were not altogether disconnected, and I have copied out a part to serve as a subject for medical research. I have not altered a single illogicality in the diary and have changed only the names, even though the people referred to are all country folk, unknown to the world and of no consequence. As for the title, it was chosen by the diarist himself after his recovery, and I did not change it.

I

Tonight the moon is very bright.

I have not seen it for over thirty years, so today when I saw it I felt in unusually high spirits. I begin to realize that during the past thirty-odd years I have been in the dark; but now I must be extremely careful. Otherwise why should the Zhaos' dog have looked at me twice?

I have reason for my fear.

I I

Tonight there is no moon at all, I know that this is a bad omen. This morning when I went out cautiously, Mr. Zhao had a strange look in his eyes, as if he were afraid of me, as if he wanted to murder me. There were seven or eight others who discussed me in a whisper. And they were afraid of my seeing them. So, indeed, were all the people I passed. The fiercest among them grinned at me; whereupon I shivered from head to foot, knowing that their preparations were complete.

I was not afraid, however, but continued on my way. A group of children in front were also discussing me, and the look in their eyes was just like that in Mr. Zhao's while their faces too were ghastly pale. I wondered what grudge these children could have against me to make them behave like this. I could not help calling out, "Tell me!" But then they ran away.

I wonder what grudge Mr. Zhao has against me, what grudge the people on the road have against me. I can think of nothing except that twenty years ago I trod on Mr. Gu Jiu's[2] old ledgers, and Mr. Gu was most displeased. Although Mr. Zhao does not know him, he must have heard talk of this and decided to avenge him, thus he is conspiring against me with the people on the road. But then what of the children? At that time they were not yet born, so why should they eye me so strangely today, as if they were afraid of me, as if they wanted to murder me? This really frightens me, it is so bewildering and upsetting.

I know. They must have learned this from their parents!

I I I

I can't sleep at night. Everything requires careful consideration if one is to understand it.

Those people, some of whom have been pilloried by the magistrate, slapped in the face by the local gentry, had their wives taken away by bailiffs or their parents driven to suicide by creditors, never looked as frightened and as fierce then as they did yesterday.

The most extraordinary thing was that woman on the street yesterday who was spanking her son. "Little devil!" she cried. "I'm so angry I could eat you!" Yet all

---

2. The characters Gu Jiu mean "old." This refers to the age-old history of feudalism in China.

the time it was me she was looking at. I gave a start, unable to hide my alarm. Then all those long-toothed people with livid faces began to hoot with laughter. Old Chen hurried forward and dragged me home.

He dragged me home. The folk at home all pretended not to know me; they had the same look in their eyes as all the others. When I went into the study, they locked me in as if cooping up a chicken or a duck. This incident left me even more bewildered.

A few days ago a tenant of ours from Wolf Cub Village came to report the failure of the crops and told my elder brother that a notorious character in their village had been beaten to death; then some people had taken out his heart and liver, fried them in oil, and eaten them as a means of increasing their courage. When I interrupted, the tenant and my brother both stared at me. Only today have I realized that they had exactly the same look in their eyes as those people outside.

Just to think of it sets me shivering from the crown of my head to the soles of my feet.

They eat human beings, so they may eat me.

I see that the woman's "eat you," the laughter of those long-toothed people with livid faces, and the tenant's story the other day are obviously secret signs. I realize all the poison in their speech, all the daggers in their laughter. Their teeth are white and glistening: they use these teeth to eat men.

Evidently, although I am not a bad man, ever since I trod on Mr. Gu's ledgers it has been touch-and-go with me. They seem to have secrets which I cannot guess, and once they are angry they will call anyone a bad character. I remember when my elder brother taught me to write compositions, no matter how good a man was, if I produced arguments to the contrary he would mark that passage to show his approval; while if I excused evildoers he would say, "Good for you, that shows originality." How can I possibly guess their secret thoughts—especially when they are ready to eat people?

Everything requires careful consideration if one is to understand it. In ancient times, as I recollect, people often ate human beings, but I am rather hazy about it. I tried to look this up, but my history has no chronology and scrawled all over each page are the words: "Confucian Virtue and Morality." Since I could not sleep anyway, I read intently half the night until I began to see words between the lines. The whole book was filled with the two words—"Eat people."

All these words written in the book, all the words spoken by our tenant, eye me quizzically with an enigmatic smile.

I too am a man, and they want to eat me!

I V

In the morning I sat quietly for some time. Old Chen brought in lunch: one bowl of vegetables, one bowl of steamed fish. The eyes of the fish were white and hard, and its mouth was open just like those people who want to eat human beings.

VIII

Actually such arguments should have convinced them long ago. . . .

Suddenly someone came in. He was only about twenty years old and I did not see his features very clearly. His face was wreathed in smiles, but when he nodded to me his smile didn't seem genuine. I asked him, "Is it right to eat human beings?"

Still smiling, he replied, "When there is no famine how can one eat human beings?"

I realized at once he was one of them; but still I summoned up courage to repeat my question:

"Is it right?"

"What makes you ask such a thing? You really are . . . fond of a joke. . . . It is very fine today."

"It is fine, and the moon is very bright. But I want to ask you: Is it right?"

He looked disconcerted and muttered, "No. . . ."

"No? Then why do they still do it?"

"What are you talking about?"

"What am I talking about? They are eating men now in Wolf Cub Village, and you can see it written all over the books, in fresh red ink."

His expression changed. He grew ghastly pale. "It may be so," he said staring at me. "That's the way it's always been. . . ."

"Does that make it right?"

"I refuse to discuss it with you. Anyway, you shouldn't talk about it. It's wrong for anyone to talk about it."

I leaped up and opened my eyes wide, but the man had vanished. I was soaked with sweat. He was much younger than my elder brother, but even so he was in it. He must have been taught by his parents. And I am afraid he has already taught his son; that is why even the children look at me so fiercely.

IX

Wanting to eat men, at the same time afraid of being eaten themselves, they all eye each other with the deepest suspicion. . . .

How comfortable life would be for them if they could rid themselves of such obsessions and go to work, walk, eat and sleep at ease. They have only this one step to take. Yet fathers and sons, husbands and wives, brothers, friends, teachers and students, sworn enemies and even strangers, have all joined in this conspiracy, discouraging and preventing each other from taking this step.

X

Early this morning I went to find my elder brother. He was standing outside the hall door looking at the sky when I walked up behind him, standing between him and the door, and addressed him with exceptional poise and politeness:

"Brother, I have something to say to you."

"Go ahead then." He turned quickly towards me, nodding.

"It's nothing much, but I find it hard to say. Brother, probably all primitive people ate a little human flesh to begin with. Later, because their views altered some of them stopped and tried so hard to do what was right that they changed into men, into real men. But some are still eating people—just like reptiles. Some have changed into fish, birds, monkeys, and finally men; but those who make no effort to do what's right are still reptiles. When those who eat men compare themselves with those who don't, how ashamed they must be. Probably much more ashamed than the reptiles are before monkeys.

"In ancient times Yi Ya boiled his son for Jie and Zhou[5] to eat; that is the old story. But actually since the creation of heaven and earth by Pan Gu[6] men have been eating each other, from the time of Yi Ya's son to the time of Xu Xilin,[7] and from the time of Xu Xilin down to the man caught in Wolf Cub Village. Last year they executed a criminal in the city, and a consumptive soaked a piece of bread in his blood and sucked it.

"They want to eat me, and of course you can do nothing about it single-handed; but why must you join them? As man-eaters they are capable of anything. If they eat me, they can eat you as well; members of the same group can still eat each other. But if you will just change your ways, change right away, then everyone will have peace. Although this has been going on since time immemorial, today we could make a special effort to do what is right, and say this can't be done! I'm sure you can say that, Brother. The other day when the tenant wanted the rent reduced, you said it couldn't be done."

At first he only smiled cynically, then a murderous gleam came into his eyes, and when I spoke of their secret he turned pale. Outside the gate quite a crowd had gathered, among them Mr. Zhao and his dog, all craning their necks to peer in. I could not see all their faces, some of them seemed to be masked; others were the old lot, long-toothed with livid faces, concealing their laughter. I knew they were one gang, all eaters of human flesh. But I also knew that they did not all think alike by any means. Some of them thought that since it had always been so, men should be eaten. Others knew they shouldn't eat men but still wanted to, and were afraid people might discover their secret; so although what I said made them angry they still smiled their cynical, tight-lipped smiles.

Suddenly my brother's face darkened.

---

5. Yi Ya, a favourite of Duke of Huan of Qi in the seventh century B.C., was a good cook and sycophant. When the duke remarked that he had never tasted the flesh of children, Yi Ya cooked his own son for him to eat. Jie and Zhou were kings of earlier periods. This misstatement is presented as a sign of mental derangement.

6. A mythological figure.

7. A revolutionary executed in 1907 for assassinating a Qing official. His heart and liver were eaten.

"Clear off, the whole lot of you!" he roared. "What's the point of looking at a madman?"

Then I realized part of their cunning. They would never be willing to change their stand, and their plans were all laid: they had labelled me a madman. In future when I was eaten, not only would there be no trouble but people would probably be grateful to them. When our tenant spoke of the villagers eating a bad character, it was exactly the same device. This is their old trick.

Old Chen came in too in a towering temper. But they could not stop my mouth, I had to warn those people:

"You should change, change from the bottom of your hearts. You must realize that there will be no place for man-eaters in the world in future.

"If you don't change, you may all be eaten by each other. However many of you there are, you will be wiped out by the real men, just as wolves are killed by hunters—just like reptiles!"

Old Chen drove everybody away. My brother had disappeared. Old Chen advised me to go back to my room. It was pitch dark in there. The beams and rafters shook above my head. After shaking for a while they grew bigger and bigger. They piled on top of me.

The weight was so great, I couldn't move. They meant that I should die. However, knowing that the weight was false I struggled out, dripping with sweat. But I had to warn them:

"You must change at once, change from the bottom of your hearts! You must know that there'll be no place for man-eaters in future. . . ."

XI

The sun has stopped shining, the door is never opened. Just two meals day after day.

Picking up my chopsticks, I thought of my elder brother. I know now how my little sister died: it was all through him. My sister was only five at the time. I can still remember how sweet she looked, poor thing. Mother wept as if she would never stop, but he begged her not to cry, probably because he had eaten our sister himself and so this weeping made him rather ashamed. If he had any sense of shame. . . .

My sister was eaten by my brother, but I don't know whether Mother realized it or not.

I think Mother must have known, but when she wept she didn't say so outright, probably because she also thought it proper. I remember when I was four or five, sitting in the cool of the hall, my brother told me that if a man's parents were ill he should cut off a piece of his flesh and boil it for them,[8] if he wanted to be considered a good son; and Mother didn't contradict him. If one piece could be eaten, obviously so could the whole. And yet just to think of the weeping then still makes my heart bleed; that is the extraordinary thing about it!

---

8. The doctrine of filial piety used by the feudal ruling class to poison the people preached that a son should, if necessary, cut off his own flesh to feed his parents.

XII

I can't bear to think of it.

It has only just dawned on me that all these years I have been living in a place where for four thousand years human flesh has been eaten. My brother had just taken over the charge of the house when our sister died, and he may well have used her flesh in our food, making us eat it unwittingly.

I may have eaten several pieces of my sister's flesh unwittingly, and now it is my turn. . . .

How can a man like myself, after four thousand years of man-eating history—even though I knew nothing about it at first—ever hope to face real men?

XIII

Perhaps there are still children who haven't eaten men? Save the children. . . .

April 2, 1918

13.5 *What Happens after Nora Leaves Home?*

A TALK GIVEN AT THE BEIJING WOMEN'S NORMAL COLLEGE, DECEMBER 26, 1923

My subject today is: What happens after Nora leaves home?

Ibsen was a Norwegian writer in the second half of the nineteenth century. All his works, apart from a few dozen poems, are dramas. Most of the dramas he wrote during one period deal with social problems and are known as social-problem plays. One of these is the play *Nora*.[9]

Another title for *Nora* is *Ein Puppenheim*, translated in Chinese as *A Puppet's House*. However, "puppe" are not only marionettes but also children's dolls; in a wider sense the term also includes people whose actions are controlled by others. Nora originally lives contentedly in a so-called happy home, but then she wakes up to the fact that she is simply a puppet of her husband's and her children are her puppets. So she leaves home—as the door is heard closing, the curtain falls. Since presumably you all know this play, there is no need to go into details.

What could keep Nora from leaving? Some say that Ibsen himself has supplied the answer in *The Lady from the Sea*. The heroine of this play is married but her former lover, who lives just across the sea, seeks her out suddenly to ask her to elope with him. She tells her husband that she wants to meet this man and finally her husband says, "I give you complete freedom. Choose for yourself (whether to go or not). On your own head be it." This changes everything and she decides not to go.

9. Chinese translation for *A Doll's House*.

It seems from this that if Nora were to be granted similar freedom she might perhaps stay at home.

But Nora still goes away. What becomes of her afterwards Ibsen does not say, and now he is dead. Even if he were still living, he would not be obliged to give an answer. For Ibsen was writing poetry, not raising a problem for society and supplying the answer to it. This is like the golden oriole which sings because it wants to, not to amuse or benefit anyone else. Ibsen was rather lacking in worldly wisdom. It is said that when a number of women gave a banquet in his honour and their representative rose to thank him for writing *Nora*, which gave people a new insight into the social consciousness and emancipation of women, he rejoined, "I didn't write with any such ideas in mind. I was only writing poetry."

What happens after Nora leaves home? Others have also voiced their views on this. An Englishman has written a play about a modern woman who leaves home but finds no road open to her and therefore goes to the bad, ending up in a brothel. There is also a Chinese—how shall I describe him? A Shanghai man of letters, I suppose—who claims to have read a different version of the play, in which Nora returns home in the end. Unfortunately no one else ever saw this edition, unless it was one sent him by Ibsen himself. But by logical deduction, Nora actually has two alternatives only: to go to the bad or to return to her husband. It is like the case of a caged bird: of course there is no freedom in the cage, but if it leaves the cage there are hawks, cats, and other hazards outside; while if imprisonment has atrophied its wings, or if it has forgotten how to fly, there certainly is nowhere it can go. Another alternative is to starve to death, but since that means departing this life it presents no problem and no solution either.

The most painful thing in life is to wake up from a dream and find no way out. Dreamers are fortunate people. If no way out can be seen, the important thing is not to awaken the sleepers. Look at the Tang dynasty poet Li He whose whole life was dogged by misfortune. When he lay dying he said to his mother, "The Emperor of Heaven has built a palace of white jade, Mother, and summoned me there to write something to celebrate its completion." What was this if not a lie, a dream? But this made it possible for the young man who was dying to die happily, and for the old woman who lived on to set her heart at rest. At such times there is something great about lying and dreaming. To my mind, then, if we can find no way out, what we need are dreams.

However, it won't do to dream about the future. In one of his novels Artzybashev[10] challenges those idealists who, in order to build a future golden world, call on many people here and now to suffer. "You promise their descendants a golden world, but what are you giving them themselves?" he demands. Something is given, of course—hope for the future. But the cost is exorbitant. For the sake of this hope, people are made more sensitive to the intensity of their misery, are awakened in spirit to see their own putrid corpses. At such times there is greatness only in lying

10. Russian novelist (1878–1927).

and dreaming. To my mind, then, if we can find no way out, what we need are dreams; but not dreams of the future, just dreams of the present.

However, since Nora has awakened it is hard for her to return to the dream world; hence all she can do is to leave. After leaving, though, she can hardly avoid going to the bad or returning. Otherwise the question arises: What has she taken away with her apart from her awakened heart? If she has nothing but a crimson woollen scarf of the kind you young ladies are wearing, even if two or three feet wide it will prove completely useless. She needs more than that, needs something in her purse. To put it bluntly, what she needs is money.

Dreams are fine; otherwise money is essential.

The word money has an ugly sound. Fine gentlemen may scoff at it, but I believe that men's views often vary, not only from day to day but from before a meal to after it. All who admit that food costs money yet call money filthy lucre will probably be found, on investigation, to have some fish or pork not yet completely digested in their stomachs. You should hear their views again after they have fasted for a day.

Thus the crucial thing for Nora is money or—to give it a more high-sounding name—economic resources. Of course money cannot buy freedom, but freedom can be sold for money. Human beings have one great drawback, which is that they often get hungry. To remedy this drawback and to avoid being puppets, the most important thing in society today seems to be economic rights. First, there must be a fair sharing out between men and women in the family; secondly, men and women must have equal rights in society.

Unfortunately I have no idea how we are to get hold of these rights; all I know is that we have to fight for them. We may even have to fight harder for these than for political rights.

The demand for economic rights is undoubtedly something very commonplace, yet it may involve more difficulties than the demand for noble political rights or for the grand emancipation of women. In this world countless small actions involve more difficulties than big actions do. In a winter like this, for instance, if we have only a single padded jacket we must choose between saving a poor man from freezing to death or sitting like Buddha under a bo-tree to ponder ways of saving all mankind. The difference between saving all mankind and saving one individual is certainly vast. But given the choice I would not hesitate to sit down under the bo-tree, for that would obviate the need to take off my only padded jacket and freeze to death myself. This is why, at home, if you demand political rights you will not meet with much opposition, whereas if you speak about the equal distribution of wealth you will probably find yourself up against enemies, and this of course will lead to bitter fighting.

Fighting is not a good thing and we can't ask everybody to be a fighter. In that case the peaceful method is best, that is using parental authority to liberate one's children in future. Since in China parental authority is absolute, you can share out your property fairly among your children so that they enjoy equal economic rights in peace, free from conflict. They can then go to study, start a business, enjoy themselves, do something for society, or spend the lot just as they please, responsible to no one but themselves. Though this is also a rather distant dream, it is much closer than the dream of a golden age. But the first prerequisite is a good memory. A bad memory is an advantage to its owner but injurious to his descendants. The ability to forget the past enables people to free themselves gradually from the pain they once suffered; but it also often makes them repeat the mistakes of their predecessors. When a cruelly treated daughter-in-law becomes a mother-in-law, she may still treat her daughter-in-law cruelly; officials who detest students were often students who denounced officials; some parents who oppress their children now were probably rebels against their own families ten years ago. This perhaps has something to do with one's age and status; still bad memory is also a big factor here. The remedy for this is for everyone to buy a notebook and record his thoughts and actions from day to day, to serve as reference material in future when his age and status have changed. If you are annoyed with your child for wanting to go to the park, you can look through your notes and find an entry saying, "I want to go to the Central Park." This will at once mollify and calm you down. The same applies to other matters too.

There is a kind of hooliganism today, the essence of which is tenacity. It is said that after the Boxer Uprising some ruffians in Tianjin behaved quite lawlessly. For instance, if one were to carry luggage for you, he would demand two dollars. If you argued that it was a small piece of luggage, he would demand two dollars. If you argued that the distance was short, he would demand two dollars. If you said you didn't need him, he would still demand two dollars. Of course hooligans are not good models, yet that tenacity is most admirable. It is the same in demanding economic rights. If someone says this is old hat, tell him you want your economic rights. If he says this is too low, tell him you want your economic rights. If he says the economic system will soon be changing and there is no need to worry, tell him you want your economic rights.

Actually, today, if just one Nora left home she might not find herself in difficulties; because such a case, being so exceptional, would enlist a good deal of sympathy and certain people would help her out. To live on the sympathy of others already means having no freedom; but if a hundred Noras were to leave home, even that sympathy would diminish; while if a thousand or ten thousand were to leave, they would arouse disgust. So having economic power in your own hands is far more reliable.

Are you not a puppet then when you have economic freedom? No, you are still a puppet. But you will be less at the beck and call of others and able to control more puppets yourself. For in present-day society it is not just women who are often the puppets of men; men often control other men, and women other women, while men are often women's puppets too. This is not something which can be remedied by a few women's possession of economic rights. However, people with empty stomachs cannot wait quietly for the arrival of a golden age; they must at least husband their last breath just as a fish in a dry rut flounders about to find a little water.

So we need this relatively attainable economic power before we can devise other measures.

Of course, if the economic system changes then all this is empty talk.

In speaking as I have, however, I have assumed Nora to be an ordinary woman. If she is someone exceptional who prefers to dash off to sacrifice herself, that is a different matter. We have no right to urge people to sacrifice themselves, no right to stop them either. Besides, there are many people in the world who delight in self-sacrifice and suffering. In Europe there is a legend that when Jesus was on his way to be crucified he rested under the eaves of Ahasuerus' house, and because Ahasuerus turned Jesus away he became accursed, doomed to find no rest until the Day of Judgment. So since then Ahasuerus has been wandering, unable to rest, and he is still wandering now. Wandering is painful while resting is comfortable, so why doesn't he stop to rest? Because even if under a curse he must prefer wandering to resting; that is why he keeps up this frenzied wandering.

But this choice of sacrifice is a personal one which has nothing in common with the social commitment of revolutionaries. The masses, especially in China, are always spectators at a drama. If the victim on the stage acts heroically, they are watching a tragedy; if he shivers and shakes they are watching a comedy. Before the mutton shops in Beijing a few people often gather to gape, with evident enjoyment, at the skinning of the sheep. And this is all they get out of it if a man lays down his life. Moreover, after walking a few steps away from the scene they forget even this modicum of enjoyment.

There is nothing you can do with such people; the only way to save them is to give them no drama to watch. Thus there is no need for spectacular sacrifices; it is better to have persistent, tenacious struggle.

Unfortunately China is very hard to change. Just to move a table or overhaul a stove probably involves shedding blood; and even so, the change may not get made. Unless some great whip lashes her on the back, China will never budge. Such a whip is bound to come, I think. Whether good or bad, this whipping is bound to come. But where it will come from or how it will come I do not know exactly.

And here my talk ends.

might; though this may have been the dream of a few pioneers and some oppressed peoples. When they come into power themselves, though, right and might are always separated again.

Still, there are genuinely civilized men in England. Today we have seen the friendly "Declaration to the Chinese People" sent by the International Workers' Aid-China Committee organized by nonparty intellectuals of different countries. One of the English signatures is that of Bernard Shaw, whose name is known to all Chinese interested in world literature. Among the French names is that of Henri Barbusse, whose works have also been translated into Chinese. His mother is English, which may account for the fact that he writes with such realism, with no trace of the hedonism common to French writers. Now all these men are coming out to demand justice for the Chinese, so I feel there is still much we can learn from the English—I do not, of course, include those policemen and merchants, or those "ladies" who clapped and jeered from their balconies when the student demonstrators marched past.

I do not mean that we should "love our enemies." All I mean is that so far we have not looked upon anyone as our enemy. Recent articles, it is true, occasionally contain such phrases as "We must see our enemy clearly." But this is a case of literary exaggeration. If there really is an enemy, we should have risen long ago with our swords to demand "blood for our blood." But instead what are we demanding? After clearing ourselves, all we want is some slight compensation. Though there are some dozen clauses in our demands, all they amount to is "We shall sever relations," and "have no more to do with you." Even the closest friends might do the same.

But the fact of the matter is: because might and right are not yet one, and all we have on our side is right, we are friends with everyone, even if they slaughter us wilfully.

As long as we have right only and no might, we shall always be busy defending ourselves, and exerting ourselves for nothing. During the last few days, posters have been stuck on some walls advising people not to read the *Shuntian News*.[1] I seldom read that paper, not from any "anti-foreign" feeling, but because its views of right and wrong are so very different from mine. Occasionally, though, it hits the nail on the head, and says things which we Chinese ourselves would not say. Two or three years ago, during some patriotic movement, I happened to read one of its editorials to the effect that, when a country is declining, men always hold two conflicting opinions. Some advocate "national spirit," others "national strength." When the former are in the majority, the country will grow weak; while when the latter are in the majority, the country will grow strong. I think this is quite right, and we should constantly bear this fact in mind.

In China, unfortunately, we have always had a majority in favour of "national spirit," and that is the case today. If we do not change, we shall go downhill until we

---

1. A Chinese paper sponsored by Japanese imperialists in Beijing. Started in 1901, it ceased publication in 1928.

have no strength left even to defend ourselves against false charges. So while we are forced to encourage the people empty-handed, we should do all we can at the same time to build up our country's strength. Indeed, we should continue all our lives to do so.

Hence young Chinese have a much heavier responsibility than young people in other countries. For our forbears devoted so much energy to being mysterious and unfathomable, balanced and smooth, they left all the real, difficult jobs for those after them. So now that one man has to do the work of several, if not of ten or a hundred, we have a chance to prove our worth. And our opponents are the stubborn Britishers, who are a good whetstone on which to improve our mettle. Assuming that the average age of these youngsters who have woken up to the facts is twenty, and paying due consideration to the fact that the Chinese age prematurely, we can still resist, work for reforms, and struggle together for at least thirty years. If this is not enough, another generation or two can continue after us. . . . So many years may seem rather frightening from the point of view of one individual; but if we are so easily frightened, then we are incurable, and all we can do is resign ourselves to death. For in the history of a nation this is a very brief period, and there is no short cut. Let us, then, not hesitate, but make trial of ourselves, and struggle for our existence with malice towards none.

There are three dangers, however, that might destroy this movement. The first is the fact that we pay too much attention all the time to superficial propaganda and despise other tasks. The second is impatience with our fellow-men, which makes us call them traitors or slaves of foreign masters whenever we have the least difference of opinion. The third is that there are many clever people who seize every opportunity to snatch any immediate advantage for themselves.

June 11, 1925

14.3 A PATIENT NAMED TAIWAN: CHIANG WEI-SHUI'S "CLINICAL NOTES," 1921

From the Shimonoseki Treaty of 1895 to the end of World War II, Japan's colonial rule in Taiwan exploited the island's abundant natural resources in support of its imperial ambitions. Promoting Japan's "model colony," the colonial government invested in Taiwan's education and economic development, even while maintaining tight political control. In the 1920s, a more liberal political climate in Tokyo opened the door to overtures for "home rule."

Chiang Wei-shui (1890–1931) was one of the most important political activists of the interwar period. Born in Yilan, on the northeast coast of Taiwan, Chiang developed a passion for politics while attending Taiwan

Imperial Medical College. After his graduation, he became a founding member of the Taiwan Cultural Association. With the approval of the colonial authorities, the association focused on elevating the "cultural level" of the Taiwanese through reading groups, lectures, drama performances, and other social activities. As more activist members called for measures promoting political reforms and greater local autonomy, the association splintered into groups advocating varying degrees of anti-Japanese resistance. Chiang Wei-shu's subsequent participation in organizations such as the Taiwan People's Party and the Taiwan Workers League landed him in prison more than ten times.

In the following essay, originally written in Japanese and published in the *Bulletin of the Taiwan Cultural Association,* Chiang delivers a trenchant diagnosis of the ailments of Taiwanese society. The doctor prescribes maximum doses of education and predicts a slow but full recovery. His narrative of Taiwan's history invokes an ancient lineage, with a complicated history of cultural impoverishment under Qing and Japanese rule.

Prepared for the patient named Taiwan

NAME: Island of Taiwan

GENDER: Male

AGE: Since moving to current place of residence, twenty-seven years

PLACE OF ORIGIN: Taiwan District, Fujian Province, Republic of China

PRESENT ADDRESS: The Government-General of Taiwan, Empire of Greater Japan

OCCUPATION: Prime strategic point guard for world peace

LINEAGE: Obvious lineal ties to the bloodline of the Yellow Emperor, Duke Zhou, Confucius, Mencius, and others

TALENTS: As noted above, the descendant of sages and worthies, strong and healthy with natural endowments of wisdom

PAST MEDICAL HISTORY: In his childhood, during the times of Zheng Chenggong, he was strong in stature, keen of mind, strong in will, lofty in moral character, and nimble of action. Since the Qing Dynasty, because of having been poisoned by political policies, he grew weaker by the day, his will deteriorated, his moral character grew despicable, and his moral integrity became increasingly debased. After relocating to the Japanese Empire, he received unsound medical care and, although there was some improvement, after about two hundred years of slow poisoning, it has been difficult to successfully treat him with drug therapy.

CURRENT SYMPTOMS: Moral values decayed, sense of humanity spoiled, excessive desire for material goods, lacking the spiritual in life, customs polluted, submerged in superstition, thickheaded and stubborn, completely lacking in basic hygiene, shallow in knowledge, no sense of a long-range plan, concerned only with seeking short-term profit, degenerate and indolent, corrupt, debased, neglected, vain, lacking in modesty and a sense of shame, exhaustion and slackness in all four limbs, overcome by inertia, dejected in spirit, and no vitality to speak of.

PATIENT'S COMPLAINT: Neck pain, dizziness, and hunger pains

For the most part this is an accurate assessment of the patient. During the examination it was discovered that, given his size, he should have quite a large head, which presumably would indicate a strong capacity for reasoning. Several questions were posed to test his general knowledge, but his answers failed to grasp the main points of the questions and suggest that the patient is either foolish or mentally retarded. Although he has a large skull, its contents are suspect and he seems to lack sufficient intelligence. When he was asked more challenging questions about philosophy, arithmetic, science, and world affairs, he became dizzy.

Yet his arms and legs are well-developed, due, perhaps, to excessive hard labor. Further examination of his abdomen reveals it to be small and sunken, with the surface covered by row upon row of wrinkles shaped by the intestinal walls, which look exactly like the stretch marks on women who have just given birth. This presumably is attributed to the Great War that began in Europe in 1916 [1914]. For a time the abdomen had expanded, but last summer's news of peace talks led to a bout of intestinal flu that worsened and became dysentery, which caused the abdomen to contract.

DIAGNOSIS: A mentally retarded child of world culture

ETIOLOGY: Poor intellectual nutrition

COURSE OF ILLNESS: Contracted a long-term chronic illness

PROGNOSIS: Because his basic constitution is good, if given proper medical treatment, he should recover quickly. If, however, the wrong treatment is given or proper treatment is delayed, the disease will attack the vital organs and will likely lead to death.

TREATMENT: Causal treatment will cure the problem radically.

PRESCRIPTION: Normal school education: maximum dose; supplementary education: maximum dose; kindergarten: maximum dose; library: maximum dose; newspaper reading club: maximum dose.

If the treatment regimen outlined above is immediately taken as instructed, a full recovery can be expected in twenty years.

Other effective medications are omitted.

14.4–14.6 PURGING THE COMMUNISTS: THREE DOCUMENTS

The purge of the Communists from the United Front in the spring of 1927 drastically altered the character of the Guomindang. The Party began almost immediately to retreat from the radical social programs it had grudgingly endorsed since 1924. Instead, Guomindang leaders sought to promote the

Three Principles of the People as a panacea for all of China's ills and forsook the path of class struggle for good. In the weeks that followed Chiang Kai-shek's attack on his former allies, civilian and military spokesmen for the Guomindang were obliged to justify their actions, whip up enthusiasm for the purge policy, and send warnings to workers and others who still admired and supported the Communists.

The three documents that follow, all published within days of the start of roundups and summary executions of Communists in Shanghai and Guang-zhou, show how the Nationalists attempted to carry out these political goals. The party statement outlines the rationale for expulsion, the slogans are designed to motivate correct thought, and the army division's proclamation provides ominous suggestions of the fate awaiting Chinese workers who forsake "endurance and obedience" to take part in strikes, walkouts, and other political activities.

14.4 *Official Statement by the Guomindang, April 1927*

To understand clearly the objects of the movement for the purification of the Guomindang Party, it is necessary to know first the actual conditions of the present time. We have not yet accomplished the aims of the Revolution. We are only at the beginning of the task; and while victory is already in sight, it is of the utmost importance at this juncture to carry on the Revolution to a successful end. We must stand together and face the common cause with a united mind. The slightest neglect on our part will not only defeat the Revolution, but will also make it impossible to attain the objects of liberty and equality for the Chinese nation.

Therefore, all members of the party must know the gravity of their responsibility. At this critical moment, the undesirable elements are unscrupulously and untiringly doing the work of destruction, and if we do not check it in an effective manner, it will not only mean the fall of the Party but also the failure of the Revolution. With this in view, we adopt the following for the purification of the Party. First, to purge the Party of the Communists, and secondly, to purge the Party of the opportunists and other undesirable elements.

It will be remembered that when Dr. Sun Yat-sen admitted members of the Communist Party into the Guomindang, he was quite aware of the fact that Communism was not fit for China. But as the Communist Party members were ready to give up their Communistic belief, and willing to be directed by the Guomindang in order to cooperate in the work of the Revolution, it was only natural that they should be admitted into the Party. But since the beginning of the Northern Expedition, while members of the Guomindang have been labouring faithfully either on the field of battle or elsewhere, and while the militarists of the country have been gradually eliminated, the Communists, taking advantage of our success, have seized important cities as their centres for propaganda and usurped the power of the Party. Our military successes are being utilized by them to inflame the undesirable sections of the populace to undermine our forward move and to create disturbances in the rear.

Aside from the Communistic members who are to be condemned, there are also the opportunists and other undesirable elements in the Party. It is they who shamefully steal the name of the Party for their selfish gains, and it is also they who falsely use the power of the party for their personal activities and aggrandizement. Theirs is a crime no less serious than that of the Communists.

For the welfare of the Revolution as well as that of the Guomindang, we are forced to adopt this strong measure to purge the Party of all the undesirable elements.

14.5 "Purge the Party" Slogans for the Chinese People, May 1927

THE FOLLOWING SLOGANS, PREPARED BY THE PUBLICITY COMMITTEE OF THE GUANGDONG PROVINCIAL SPECIAL GUOMINDANG, ARE AN EMBODIMENT OF THE AIMS AND SPIRIT OF THE NATIONALIST MOVEMENT.

(MAY 1927)

1. Down with the Chinese Communist Party which is treacherous to our late director, Dr. Sun Yat-sen.
2. Down with the Chinese Communist Party which is against the San-Min Chu-I, "The Three Principles of the People."
3. Down with the Chinese Communist Party which is destroying the People's Revolution.
4. Down with the Chinese Communist Party which is undoing the work of the Northern Expedition.
5. Down with the Chinese Communist Party which is utilizing bandits and labor usurpers to oppress the Peasants and Labourers.
6. Down with the Chinese Communist Party which is insulting and disgracing our late Director, Dr. Sun.
7. Down with the Chinese Communist Party which is plotting the downfall and destruction of the Guomindang.
8. To be against "The Three Principles of the People" is to be a Counter-Revolutionary.
9. To be against the Guomindang is to be a Counter-Revolutionary.
10. All power and authority belong to the Guomindang.
11. All true and loyal comrades of the Guomindang must unite and rise.
12. Down with all Counter-Revolutionaries.
13. Down with all Opportunists.
14. Concentrate the powers of the Guomindang.

254 | THE FRACTURED ALLIANCE

15. Down with all forms of Imperialism.
16. Down with the Fengtien[2] clique of Militarists.
17. Eradicate all corrupt officials, greedy gentry, and unscrupulous merchants.
18. Purge the Guomindang of all anti-revolutionists.
19. To call a Strike against the Guomindang is Counter-Revolutionary.
20. Those who refuse to come under the direction and guidance of the Guomindang are not Revolutionaries.
21. The masses of the people must rise and clean up the Counter-Revolutionary Chinese Communist Party.
22. The masses of the people must rise and support the Chinese Guomindang.
23. Support the Central Government at Nanking.
24. Support the advancing Nationalist Forces.
25. Down with the bogus governments at Wuhan and at Peking. . . .

14.6 A Proclamation, Headquarters of the Twenty-sixth Nationalist Army, April 22, 1927

Our Chinese workmen have been admired by the world for their endurance and obedience, but with the increase in industrial activity there has come a menace in the form of strikes and walkouts.

When Shanghai was recently taken by our armies, many workmen were induced or forced by mutineers to leave their employment and to parade and join various unlawful associations, and to otherwise countenance unlawful activities.

Through my advice to workers and other steps which have been taken many factories are again running. These are cases, however, where simple-minded workers are still deluded by agitators. To them I wish to offer this advice:

1. The manufacturing and commercial conditions of China are quite different from those of Europe and America. Because of this difference the treatment accorded to workmen must be different. Chinese workmen, consequently, cannot expect the same treatment as that accorded to workmen in other countries.
2. Chinese workmen are fortunate in that they can if they wish make China a real industrial nation by gaining full knowledge of the industries with which they are affiliated. This fact has apparently been lost sight of in following professional agitators who are very selfish and who are seeking to sacrifice the laboring classes only for their own benefit.
3. If, in following the advice of these agitators and law violators, a strike occurs, the loss of valuable time and the money which that valuable time would bring

2. A Manchurian warlord army under Zhang Zuolin.

to the workmen is the only result. Although some of the workmen who go on strike have money for the rainy day, others have not. These last starve themselves and starve their families. It is absolutely foolish to strike, for it is both unlawful and a loss of livelihood.

4. When a strike is in effect the factories are closed. Consequently the Nationalist government and the Nationalist armies are forced to buy foreign made goods merely because there are no native productions. This is death not only to the country's commerce, but to patriotism as well.

From the above four points it is plain that strikes are not only harmful, but they have not a single advantage.

The Nationalist Government is now facing and executing the task of clearing away the bacteria which causes the disturbances in the laboring classes—and making the source of this disturbance clear.

Hereafter when professional agitators or others in the laboring classes plan to induce otherwise good workmen to strike, commit unlawful acts, or violence we ask that the factories and the good workmen report them to the headquarters of this army that they may be severely punished. Only by doing this may we be able to protect the good workmen and see that they are well treated.

> April 22, 1927.
> Chow Vung Chee,
> Commander of the Twenty-Sixth
> Nationalist Army; and
> Vice-Commander of the Shanghai
> and Sungkiang Defence Area.

14.7 MADAME SUN YAT-SEN DEFENDS THE LEFT, AUGUST 1927

After the collapse of the Wuhan government, the left wing of the Guomindang disintegrated into squabbling factions. Madame Sun Yat-sen and others who had supported the United Front policy were dismayed when Wuhan leaders began their own purges of Communists, and expressed their opposition by following Borodin and other Comintern representatives into exile in the U.S.S.R.

Madame Sun Yat-sen (Song Qingling, 1892–1981) was nearly thirty years younger than her late husband. After his death she became an increasingly outspoken critic of Chiang Kai-shek and the Guomindang right wing, who she believed were attempting to appropriate Sun's name to justify their own political program. As her public statement, issued shortly before she left for Moscow, indicates, Madame Sun considered the leaders of the Nationalist Party unworthy of her husband's legacy.

If China is to survive as an independent country in the modern struggle of nations, her semi-feudal conditions of life must be fundamentally changed and a modern state created to replace the medieval system which has existed for more than a thousand years. This task needs to be done by the method of revolution, if only because the alternative method of gradualness postulates a period of time which is denied the nation by both the cancerous force of Chinese militarism eating from inside and foreign imperialism ravaging from outside.

To forge a fit instrument of revolution, Sun Yat-sen reorganized the Guomindang on a revolutionary basis in the winter of 1924, and reinforced the Three People's Principles by formulating the Three Great Policies of action. The first of these policies calls for the inclusion and support of the nation's workers and peasants in the work of the revolution. These two massive elements of the national population—one carrying on and sustaining the life of organized society and the other producing food on which man lives—represent nearly 90 percent of the nation. And, in view of their numerical strength and the fact that the masses ought to be the chief beneficiaries of the revolution, they must be drawn into it if there is to be life and reality in the movement.

The second of the policies laid down by Sun recognizes the necessity of cooperation between the Guomindang and members of the Chinese Communist Party during the period of revolutionary struggle with Chinese militarism and foreign imperialism. The Chinese Communist Party is indubitably the most dynamic of all internal revolutionary forces in China; and its influence over the masses and power of propaganda enabled the Guomindang to control its military elements and subordinate them to the civil authorities.

The third of Sun Yat-sen's policies deals with the profoundly important question of the connection of the Soviet Union with the Guomindang. The connection is sometimes justified on the ground that the Soviet Union has no unequal treaties with China. This, however, was a minor consideration in Sun's view of the matter. In formulating the third policy, he was moved by larger reasons. Just as he regarded the Chinese Communist Party as the most active revolutionary force in China, so he envisaged the Soviet Union as the most powerful revolutionary force in the world; and he believed that a right correlation by the Guomindang of these two outstanding revolutionary forces would signally assist the revolution to realize national independence for China. Sun was not afraid or ashamed to avow this revolutionary thesis, since he knew that the revolutionary role played by France, in the person of Lafayette, in the American revolution was repeated in many a chapter in the history of freedom.

It was a statesmanlike application of these three policies of Sun and the correlation of the forces deriving from them that enabled the Guomindang power to put an end to ten years of disorder and confusion in Canton, and to create and finance revolutionary armies that conquered their way to the historic line of the Yangtze and—after shattering the main force of the Fengtien army in Honan—penetrated to the bank of the Yellow River. Besides its striking administrative work at Canton and the great military achievement of the Northern Expedition, the Guomin-dang scored memorable successes in a field in which China has always known defeat and humiliation. It raised the international status of China to a point never attained before, compelling the representatives of great powers to meet the foreign minister of Nationalist China as an equal in council, and causing men in high as well as in the scattered places of the earth to heed his statements on Nationalist aims and aspirations. In those days—it is but three months since—the Guomin-dang may have been hated and even feared, but none dared to despise it.

Today it is otherwise. The famous name of the Nationalist Government is now sunk to the level of other semi-feudal remnants in the North; and those who have been entrusted by the revolution with leadership are allowing the new militarist clique in the Yangtze to capture and utilize the Guomindang; and they themselves are now becoming or are about to become, the secretaries and clerks of the new Caesar. No one fears and no one respects the Guomindang, which is now despised even by foes who used to blanch and flee at the sound of its armies on the march.

What is the cause for this startling change in values and in men's opinions? The answer is to be found in the work of the reaction in Canton, in Nanking and Shanghai, in Changsha, and lastly in Wuhan. Peasants and their leaders, workers and their leaders, Communists and their leaders, who labored in order that the Guomindang power might reach the Yangtze, have been ruthlessly and wantonly killed; and Soviet workers who gave of their best to the Guomindang and who men, in later and juster days, will adjudge to have deserved well of Nationalist China, have been forced to leave, because so-called "leaders" of the Guomindang—petty politicians reverting to type—believe that they can violate Sun Yat-sen's Three Policies and rely on the new militarism to carry out the stupendous task of the revolution.

They will fail and go the way of those before them who have sought to rule in like fashion. But they must not be permitted to involve in their own ultimate ruin the heritage left to us by Sun. His true followers must seek to rescue the real Guomin-dang from the degradation of becoming a mere secretariat of the new militarist clique emerging out of the intrigues and disloyalties now afoot.

My own course is clear. Accepting the thesis that the Three Policies are an essen-tial part of the thought and technique of the revolution, I draw the conclusion that real Nationalist success in the struggle with Chinese militarism and foreign impe-rialism is possible only by a right correlation, under Guomindang leadership, of the revolutionary forces issuing from the Three Policies. As the reaction led by pseudo-leaders of the Guomindang endangers the Third Policy, it is necessary for the revo-lutionary wing of the Guomindang—the group with which Sun would today be identified had he been alive—to leave no doubt in the Soviet mind that, though some have crossed over to reaction and counterrevolution, there are others who will continue true and steadfast to the Three Policies enunciated by him for the guid-ance and advancement of the work of the revolution.

I go, therefore, to Moscow to explain this in person.

CHAPTER 15

The Guomindang in Power

15.1 AND 15.2 LAW IN THE NANJING DECADE

During the Nanjing decade (1928–1937), Chiang Kai-shek's government aspired to build a monolithic Party dictatorship. The main goals were to strengthen the central armies, enforce ideological unity, and gain territories controlled by anti-Nationalist groups. To achieve these aims the Nationalists formed an extensive civil and military internal security apparatus. Judicial and military courts had maximum flexibility to punish and suppress the Party's enemies during the period of "Political Tutelage" that officially commenced in March 1929.

Hu Shi's article on the "failure of law" was published originally in the liberal journal *Xinyue* (the crescent moon) in the spring of 1929 and was reprinted almost simultaneously in Shanghai's *North China Herald*. It criticized the imprecision of Guomindang (GMD) definitions of legal and human rights and suggested that the government had created a legal framework that invited arbitrary manipulation. The article was one of a series of sharply critical pieces that Hu Shi published on this topic. Cumulatively, they aroused the ire of GMD authorities and resulted in a temporary ban on Hu Shi's writings.

The "Emergency Law for the Suppression of Crimes Against the Safety of the Republic" is a specimen of the special or provisional legislation used by the Nanjing government to facilitate its "bandit extermination" campaigns against the Communists. By this time, the alliance of warlords Yan Xishan (1883–1960) and Feng Yuxiang (1882–1948) had been defeated and the primary targets of the new martial law decree were clearly the Communist "rebels" of the Jiangxi Soviet. The intentionally imprecise language and the harsh punishments prescribed by this law gave Nationalist jurists the broadest discretion in adjudicating cases involving "counterrevolutionaries."

15.1 *Hu Shi Appeals for Legal Rights, 1929*

FAILURE OF LAW IN NATIONALIST CHINA

Rights of the Individual Destroyed Under the Provisional Constitution, By Dr. Hu Shi

The National Government on April 20, 1929, promulgated a decree aiming at the protection of the Rights of Man. The decree reads:

> In all countries in the world the Rights of Man receive the protection of law. The tutelage period having now commenced, a solid foundation should be laid for government by law. No persons, individual or corporate body residing within the domain of the National Government of China, shall, by an illegal act, be permitted to violate another man's person, liberty and property. Any violation of this kind shall be severely punished according to law. Let all governmental organs, executive and judicial, publish this order for general observance.

The above order issued at the present period during which personal rights are being least respected, cannot but be welcomed by the people. When, however, our first enthusiasm for its reception is over and when we scrutinize the order in a more sober state of mind, we are greatly disappointed in at least three aspects:

1. While the order recognizes the rights of man under three headings—person, liberty and property—these rights are not defined. For instance, under liberty, the order omits to say what kinds of liberty, nor does it say what will be the form of guarantee which will be given to property. The absence of definition of any sort is a serious defect.

2. This order only forbids violation of these rights by a private individual or a corporation but fails to restrict governmental organs. It is true that a private person or a corporation must be prohibited from attempting acts of encroachment upon another man's person, liberty and property, but the country is suffering very much more through and from illegal acts of the governmental organs, or acts done in the name of the government and the party. For example, all interference with the liberty of speech and publication, confiscation of private property, and recent attempts at nationalization (which is another form of confiscation) of electrical and industrial plants in several

cities—all these have been done in the name of some government organ. The order in question seems to have accorded no protection or guarantee to the people against these acts of the government itself. "A public officer may indeed start a conflagration, but the people must not light their tiny lamps."

3. The order is of a mandatory nature carrying a penalty, "according to law." It omits to state what law, or kind of law will be applicable in a case of this sort. There is indeed a special provision in the criminal code for an offence against personal liberty. But should an act of unlawful violation be perpetrated under and in the name of the government or the party, then the aggrieved party would be without a redress of guarantee.

NOT AFFECTED BY THE ORDER

Shortly after the promulgation of the order, the local press in Shanghai began to question whether or not the activities of the Anti-Japanese Boycott Society would be covered by it. The Japanese press answered the question in the affirmative, but Chinese papers like the "Shishi Xinbao" argued that this order did not cover the acts of the patriotic boycotters.

The Anti-Japanese Boycott Society is not the only exception. All those who are branded as "Reactionaries," "Local Bullies and Wicked Elders," "Counter-Revolutionaries" and "Suspected Communists" are not within it, so that their persons may be insulted, liberty curtailed, and property seized at pleasure. These acts would not be illegal. Any publication may be banned as reactionary and the banning would be no violation of the liberty of thought or the press. A foreign-controlled school may be closed down as an organ of "cultural invasion," and a Chinese-controlled school may meet the same fate, if someone sees fit to style it a reactionary center. Are these not acts of unlawful violation of personal rights? What guarantee do people have against such unlawful acts of encroachment?

DEMAND FOR MORE RIGOUR

On March 26, 1929, the Shanghai papers contained in their telegram columns, a report that Mr. Chen Decheng[1] of the Shanghai Municipality had submitted a proposal before the Third Congress of the Party, in which Mr. Chen moved for a stronger policy in dealing with the counter-revolutionaries. Mr. Chen felt that the courts of justice had been too lenient, having, in his opinion, too much regard for

---

1. Chen Decheng was the head of the Propaganda Department of the Guomindang Headquarters in Shanghai. He and Hu Shi were frequently at odds in 1929 as Hu became a vocal critic of elements of Sun Yat-sen's Three Principles of the People and, as in this document, Guomindang experiments in controlling dissent through draconian laws and state mandates. See Jerome Grieder, *Hu Shih and the Chinese Renaissance: Liberalism in the Chinese Revolution, 1917–1937* (Boston: Harvard University Press, 1970), pp. 240–241.

proof and were inclined to technicalities, thus enabling many counter-revolutionaries to escape from their merited punishments. The proposal he submitted was that anyone who had been certified by a provincial branch of the Guomindang, or of a special Municipality as a counter-revolutionary, should be accepted as such by all courts of justice with the local GMD's certification as conclusive evidence of his guilt without further evidence being adduced. On his appeal against the judgment, a similar certificate issued by the Central Guomindang Party would constitute a sufficient ground for dismissing the appeal. In other words, Mr. Chen wanted to vest in the Party judicial authority to determine the question of guilt of one who is charged with being a counter-revolutionary, and the court had only to perform its ministerial duty in the execution of the Party's order. Such a suggestion is preposterous and totally inconsistent with the doctrine of government by law.

A LETTER THAT WAS BANNED

After reading the press report, I immediately wrote a letter addressed to Dr. Wang Zhonghui, President of the Judicial Council, asking his opinion on the subject, and inquiring if he, with his profound knowledge of the legal history of the world, had known of anything like it in the history of jurisprudence in any civilized country. I considered Mr. Chen's proposal as something deserving public attention, so I sent a copy of my letter to the Guowen News Agency for publication.

The agency after a few days wrote back saying that the letter had been duly forwarded to various newspapers, but its publication had been banned by the censor, and the copy was therefore returned. I failed to see any legal grounds justifying the censor to suppress the publication of a document having no reference whatsoever in military affairs. It was written in my own name for which I was prepared to assume full responsibility. Why may not a private citizen discuss a question of national importance and interest when he is prepared to take the responsibility? What protection have we against this kind of unreasonable interference? . . .

NEED OF A CONSTITUTION

If there is a real desire to protect the rights of man and to have a true government by law, the first prerequisite should be a Constitution of the Chinese Republic. The least . . . should be the promulgation of a Provisional Constitution for the period of tutelage.

Dr. Sun Yat-sen in his work entitled *Revolutionary Tactics* [1906] divided his national construction program into three distinct periods: (1) the Military Era, scheduled to last for three years, (2) the era of the Provisional Constitution, which is to last six years during which all the rights and obligations of the military government towards the people as well as the people's rights and obligations towards the government shall be definitely fixed by the Provisional Constitution. This law should be rigidly obeyed by the military government and the local assemblies as well as private citizens, [and] (3) the era of Constitutional Rule.

... In 1919 when Dr. Sun wrote his *Sun Wen's Philosophy* the author in no mistakable manner repeatedly emphasized the importance of the transitional stage during which "the government should rule in accordance with the Provisional Constitution in order to guide the people towards local self-government." In his later work, *The History of Chinese Revolution*, published in January 1923, the second stage assumed a new name and was termed "the transitional stage," which, said Dr. Sun,

> is an era of rule under the Provisional Constitution (not the one promulgated in Nanjing in 1912). This stage shall devote itself to instituting local self-government, and to the development of popular government. Taking a *xian* as a unit, each *xian* or district shall see to it that as soon as all disbanded soldiers are expelled and all military operations ceased, the Provisional Constitution shall be proclaimed and enforced, in which people's rights and obligations as well as the authority of the revolutionary government shall be clearly defined. This era is to have a duration of three years, on expiration of which, the people shall elect their own district officials. The revolutionary government shall only exercise a tutelage supervision, within the limits of the Provisional Constitution, over all self-government functionaries.

FUNDAMENTAL LAW INDISPENSABLE

One year later, in 1924, when Dr. Sun commenced writing his *Program for National Construction*, he again divided the rehabilitation into three stages. The second stage was now called the tutelage era, but no mention was made of the Provisional Constitution nor of the length of the tutelage period. Unfortunately, another year later, Dr. Sun died. People who read the last *Program* without a knowledge of his previous works, are likely to think that the tutelage era may be prolonged indefinitely, and may not need any convention or constitution. This I think is a grave mistake. ...

What we want to-day is a Provisional Constitution or convention, the kind which, in the words of Dr. Sun, "would define the rights and obligations of the people as well as the governmental powers of the revolutionary government." We want some law to fix the proper limits of the government beyond which all acts become illegal. We ask for a convention that will define and safeguard man's person, liberty, and property. Any violator of these rights, be he the Chairman of the National Government, or the Colonel of the 152nd Brigade, may be prosecuted and adjudicated by law.

15.2 *Guomindang "Emergency Laws," 1931*

(I)

EMERGENCY LAW FOR THE SUPPRESSION OF CRIMES AGAINST THE SAFETY OF THE REPUBLIC

PROMULGATED BY THE NATIONAL GOVERNMENT ON JANUARY 31 OF THE TWENTIETH YEAR OF THE REPUBLIC OF CHINA (1931) AND ENFORCED IN MARCH THE SAME YEAR.

ARTICLE 1.   Whoever, with a view to subvert the Republic, commits one of the following acts, shall be punished by death:

1. Disturbing peace and order,
2. Entering into a secret relationship with a foreign country in order to disturb peace and order,
3. Associating with rebels in order to disturb peace and order,
4. Instigating a military person to commit a non-disciplinary [*sic.*, insubordinate] act or cause him to fail in the performance of his duty, or to associate with rebels.

ARTICLE 2.   Whoever, with a view to subvert the Republic, commits one of the following acts, shall be punished with death or life imprisonment:

1. Instigating another person to disturb peace and order or to associate with rebels,
2. Conducting a campaign of propaganda against the State by writing, sketching, or speech-making.

ARTICLE 3.   Whoever, with a view to subvert the Republic, commits one of the following acts, shall be punished by life imprisonment, or imprisonment for more than ten years:

1. Committing a non-disciplinary [*sic.*, insubordinate] act, failing in the performance of his duty, or associating with rebels on the instigation of the criminal indicated in [Part] 4 of Article 1,
2. Disturbing peace and order or associating with rebels on the instigation of the criminal indicated in Part 1 of Article 2,
3. Conducting propaganda on the instigation of the criminal indicated in Part 2 of Article 2.

Whoever, having committed one of the crimes specified in the preceding paragraphs, on immediately and voluntarily reporting, shall receive an attenuation or exoneration of the penalty.

ARTICLE 4.   Whoever, having knowledge that a certain individual is a rebel, shelters him without giving notification to the competent authorities, shall be punished by imprisonment for more than five years.

Whoever, having committed the crime specified in the preceding paragraph, immediately and voluntarily reports, shall receive an attenuation or exoneration of the penalty.

ARTICLE 5.   Whoever, with a view to subvert the Republic, commits one of the following acts, shall be punished with death, or life imprisonment or imprisonment for more than ten years:

1. Obtaining or transporting military supplies for rebels,
2. Revealing or transmitting to rebels military and political secrets,
3. Destroying means of communication.

ARTICLE 6.   Whoever, with a view to subvert the Republic, organizes associations or unions or spreads doctrines incompatible with the Three Principles of the People, shall be punished by imprisonment of from five to fifteen years.

ARTICLE 7.   Whoever, commits one of the crimes specified by the present law in a region under a state of siege shall be tried by the highest military organ in that region: If he commits the crime within the limits of the suppression of banditry, he shall be tried by a provisional court composed of the magistrate of the district and two judicial officials.

The provisional court shall be established in the district and the magistrate shall be designated as the president of the court.

ARTICLE 8.   In case a suspect is tried by a military organ in conformity with the present law, that organ shall submit a statement of the trial to the competent superior military organ and the sentence shall be executed only after approval by the latter. If the suspect is tried by a provisional court, the court shall submit a statement of the trial to the superior court and the sentence shall be executed only after approval by the latter; the case shall also be reported to the provincial government for reference.

The competent superior military organ or the superior court, if it doubts the judgment passed by the organ which is its subordinate, can give to that organ an order for re-examination, or designate a special delegate to be present at the reconsideration of the judgment.

ARTICLE 9.   The military organ or police which arrests a person suspected of having committed one of the infractions specified by the present law, shall report the matter immediately to the interested competent authorities.

ARTICLE 10.   To all offenses that do not fall within the limits of the present law, the provisions of the Penal Code are applicable.

ARTICLE 11.   The duration of the application of the present law and the date of its enforcement shall be fixed by ordinance.

The provisional law suppressing anti-revolutionary plots shall be repealed from the date of the enforcement of the present law.

15.3–15.5 THE MUKDEN INCIDENT AND MANCHUKUO

After the Sino-Japanese War (1894–1895) Manchuria became a key zone of international competition. Its vast resources and strategic position made it a tempting target for both Russian and Japanese expansion, and the Qing government was forced to strike compromises with both sides to retain its sovereignty over the region. After its defeat of Russia in 1905, Japan greatly expanded its military position in Manchuria, establishing the southern part of the region as a Japanese "sphere of influence."

Following the signing of the Portsmouth Treaty on September 5, 1905, Japan's Guandong Army (Kantō gun) was posted to Manchuria, ostensibly to guard the Southern Manchurian Railroad (SMR). It soon became the dominant army in China's northeast.

To justify war against the Chinese garrisons in Manchuria, the Guandong Army needed a pretext. The first document, excerpted from a Japanese foreign ministry report on the Manchurian Incident, describes a provocation that never occurred. In fact, the bombing incident this document describes was entirely invented by conspirators of the Guandong Army. The "bomb" was a tiny explosive charge planted by Captain Imada Shintaro of the Guandong Army's Special Service Agency. It caused little physical damage to the SMR tracks, but it gave the conspirators the "emergency" they needed to launch their invasion of Manchuria. Soon nearly one-sixth of the land mass of China, at least as it existed prior to 1911, was controlled by Japan.

The League of Nation's response to Japan's aggression in southern Manchuria was far less forceful than Nationalist politicians hoped it would be. In December 1931 the League organized a commission headed by Lord Lytton, the acting viceroy of India, to investigate the Manchurian Incident. During this investigation, Japanese spokesmen did their best to justify the takeover of Manchuria. They invited the last reigning emperor of the Qing dynasty, Henry Puyi, to come to Mukden to claim the throne of the "independent" state of Manchukuo, and tried to round up international recognition for the new government. Surrounded and coached by ex-Qing officials, Japanese politicians, and Manchu clansmen, Puyi took a predictably ultraconservative approach to rule. His statement, made at the time of his installation as "Chief Executive" of Manchukuo, pledged to bring about "benevolent rule" and the "kingly way." This enabled Japanese politicians to create a veneer of political legitimacy for the new Manchurian state.

The satirical poem "The Naughty Japanese," published in Mukden shortly after the foundation of Manchukuo, expressed what for the Japanese was a real grudge: other countries, including France, Britain, and the United States, had built up their colonies without a word of condemnation, but when Japan attempted to do likewise it became the whipping boy of the international community.

15.3 *Japan on the Mukden Incident*

A few minutes past 10 o'clock on the evening of September 18, a lieutenant and six privates of the railway guards stationed at Hushitai were proceeding southward on patrol practice along the railway track. When they reached a point about six or seven hundred meters south of the North Barracks of the Fengtien army, they suddenly heard the sound of an explosion in the rear. They hurriedly retraced their steps to the spot where the explosion had occurred, and found a number of Chinese soldiers running in the direction of the North Barracks after destroying a section of the track.[2] They gave chase to them, when they were suddenly fired upon by Chinese troops, four or five hundred strong, [who] appeared in *gaoliang* [sorghum] fields to the north of the North Barracks and opened a fierce fire upon them. They hurried 120 men to the scene and engaged and defeated the enemy, who fled into the North Barracks pursued by the Japanese troops. Upon attempting to enter the barracks, they were greeted with a hail of bullets and shells from rifles, machine-guns and infantry guns, but succeeded occupying part of the barracks. They had, however, to fight hard for a time as they were pitted against overwhelming numbers, until they were reinforced by the main strength of the battalion then stationed at Mukden. Subsequently with the help of reinforcements hurried from Tieling the Japanese succeeded in clearing the North Barracks of their assailants by daybreak of the following day.

Now that regular troops of Japan and China had thus come to an armed collision, it was at once realized that it was quite different in nature from encounters of our railway guards with Manchurian bandits, such as had very frequently taken place in the past,—that the situation was extremely critical, and that in view of the

2. Cases of obstruction done by Chinese to the operation of the South Manchuria Railway have occurred frequently of late, cases of heavy stones being laid on the track, stones thrown at passenger trains, rivets of rails or sleepers removed, sticks inserted in the points, etc., having been experienced one after another. In spite of the vigilant watch kept by the railway guards and the employees of the South Manchuria Railway Company such attempts at dislocating the traffic service were gradually on the increase in recent years causing delay of the service and endangering the lives of passengers.

attitude the Chinese troops in Mukden were adopting against our army and fellow countrymen prior to the present occurrence, the Chinese troops in other places would also commence active hostilities. The total strength of the Japanese army in service in Manchuria at that time was only 10,400, while that of the Chinese was as high as 220,000 (of the 330,000 officers and men constituting the total strength of Zhang Xueliang's[3] army, 110,000 were then in service in North China inside the Great Wall). If, therefore, the Chinese army attacked ours, not only would our men find it difficult to discharge their duty of defending the Guandong Leased Territory and protecting 1,100 kilometres of the South Manchuria Railway, but the lives of one million Japanese subjects resident in Manchuria would be exposed to great danger. For this reason it was imperative for the Japanese army to act promptly, to concentrate the troops scattered about in small numbers at various points of strategic importance and to forestall the hostile forces by taking advantage of the efficient training of the men and the railway facilities that could be commanded. In other words, it was the only course left open to our army, in confronting the numerically far superior hostile forces, to attack them first and eliminate the troops immediately opposed to it as quickly as possible, and to find a means of discharging its duties by securing scope for active operations. Accordingly as soon as a report of the incident reached them, the higher command of our army promptly commenced operations for removing all causes of danger by disarming the Chinese troops in its vicinity.

After helping their comrades who had come to a collision with Chinese troops to drive the latter away from the North Barracks, our troops in Mukden promptly occupied all points of strategic importance in that city such as the Government offices, arsenal and wireless station. On the other hand our troops stationed at Tieling, Kaiyuan, Sipingkai and Liaoyang moved to Mukden on the 19th, leaving skeleton forces at their respective posts. The headquarters of our army at Port Arthur were also removed to Mukden the same day.

At various places along the South Manchuria Railway . . . our troops for the purpose of removing immediate danger, as well as for the defence of the railway zone and the protection of Japanese subjects resident in their neighbourhood, disarmed the Chinese troops and police and occupied the strategic points. . . . It was reported that simultaneously with the occupation of various points, our army proclaimed military administration and seized customs-houses. This report is, however, absolutely devoid of foundation. Only in Mukden and one or two other cities, the Chinese authorities having fled, our army, in cooperation with leading Chinese citizens, took temporary charge of the preservation of peace and order, but in no instance did it interfere with Chinese local administration.

3. Commander of the pro-Guomindang Fengtian army (b. 1898).

15.4 *Japan's Expansion: A Satirical Poem*

THE NAUGHTY JAPANESE

> *I am bad*
> *All others good;*
> *O wherefore should this be?*
> *Strong nations have their lovers*
> *—Except the Japanese.*

Look upon the cheery Indo-Chin,
For brunet Senegal spare but a glance;
Syria too considers with a grin
How deep her debt to kindly rule of France.

> *For I am bad*
> *All others good;*
> *O wherefore should this be?*
> *There's place for you in heaven*
> *—But not the Japanese.*

Children of the jewel Irish Isle
Johnny Bull their tender homage give;
Gandhi's natives likewise fondly smile,
Grateful they have still a right to live.

> *Yes I am bad*
> *All others good;*
> *O wherefore should this be?*
> *Make way for all the righteous*
> *—This bars the Japanese.*

Mongol Herder murmurs "Vive La Russe"!
Master's voice is heard at every campfire.
Who would care to make the smallest fuss.
In Soviet Union's gentle empire?

> *I am bad*
> *All others good;*
> *O wherefore should this be?*
> *Hell is closed to everyone*
> *—Except the Japanese.*

Benevolent the pious hand of Sam:
Europe for his loans is full of praise;
Hawaii, Haiti, blacks in Alabam
Bless his rule that brings delirious days.

> *Ugh! I am bad*
> *All others are good;*
> *O wherefore should this be!*
> *Faultless are the empires*
> *—Except the Japanese.*

Destiny has marked us on the stage,
Villain part as foil against the rest;
How else could sanctified and sage
Except by contrast rate themselves the best!
So I am bad
All others are good;
O wherefore should this be?
All mankind's in union
—But the naughty Japanese.

15.5 *Puyi's Proclamation*

CHIEF EXECUTIVE'S PROCLAMATION

Mankind should respect Morality. Since there exists racial discrimination, one race attempts to exalt itself by oppressing the others; thus comes about the weakness of Morality.

Benevolence should be highly esteemed by mankind. But on account of international strife, one nation strives to benefit herself at the expense of others, which causes Benevolence to lose its value.

Our new State is established on Morality and Benevolence. As a result of the removal of racial discrimination and the termination of international strife, this State will, as a matter of course, become a land of peace and happiness under "Wang-tao," the Way of Benevolent Rule.

Endeavor, therefore, all people for the attainment of these noble objectives.

Pu Yi
Chief Executive of Manchukuo
9th March, the First Year of Tatung (1932).

15.6 AND 15.7 SOCIAL INNOVATIONS IN THE NANJING DECADE

Marion Yang (Yang Chongrui, 1891–1983) was an important pioneer of modern medicine in China. Born to a Christian family near Peking, Yang attended missionary schools and graduated from Peking Union Medical College (P.U.M.C.), specializing in obstetrics, gynecology, and public health. In 1929, she helped establish the First National Midwifery School, funded by the Rockefeller Foundation and affiliated with P.U.M.C. As she explains in Document 15.6, compared with other countries China's infant and maternal mortality rates were deplorably high. The training of midwives with modern scientific standards, Yang asserted, would be a long-term project. In the mean time, "old-type" midwives could be educated to adopt simple changes to reduce mortality rates.

James "Jimmy" Yen (1890–1990) was born Yan Yangchu in Sichuan. After attending missionary schools and Hong Kong University, Yen graduated from Yale in 1918. He found his calling in France during World War I, when he taught Chinese laborers, sent to work in France in support of the Allied war effort, to read and write. In the 1920s Yen spearheaded the Mass Education Movement in China, developing a national program of basic literacy. His *People's 1,000 Character Primer* sold millions of copies and spawned numerous imitators. In the 1930s, with the support of international donors, Yen expanded his efforts to a large-scale experimental program in Ding county, about two hundred miles south of Peking. As Yen explains in Document 15.7, education was the starting point for a comprehensive project of rural reconstruction. China's rural citizens were key to the nation's future, and in Ding county Yen and his colleagues searched for solutions to the daunting cultural, economic, health, and political problems of the countryside.

15.6 "Control of Practising Midwives in China," 1930

Midwifery is a branch of Medicine. Midwifery is one of the medical professions. It is unfortunate that organization of midwifery training did not occur in history until the last century. It has been found impossible to produce high grade midwives in the absence of high standard midwifery schools. Economic conditions in China and the small number of applicants make it impossible to train the number of personnel required for the country in less than half a century. Meanwhile, in order to meet the present demands as many suitable training and refresher courses should be established as possible with certification of successful candidates. In the meantime, the community has to utilize what is obtainable, and the medical administrative authorities have to make use of what exists. Since the establishment of the Ministry of Health, midwifery control comes directly under its jurisdiction. The enforcement of the regulations largely depends upon how the local health authorities are going to carry them out. It seems that the normal procedure would be the registration of the present practising midwives, both old-type and modern-trained.

It is estimated there are 200,000 old-type and 500 modern trained midwives in China. To make registration possible, one should lower the requirements to include all the former group but even then about one third of the deliveries will be done by "helpers" who do not practise as a profession. One should be content under present conditions to secure 85 percent completeness of registration. Most of the midwives depend upon their profession as a means of livelihood, in which case there exists little difficulty in requesting them to register. Registration, however, at times is impossible, as some midwives, realizing their poor qualifications and lack of training, occasionally refuse to register. Also, those who take midwifery work merely as a kind of voluntary service will not register. With an incomplete registration it is useless to enforce rules governing their practices, and thus we cannot expect 100 percent perfection with unregistered midwives practising secretly.

China's present high maternal and infant mortality rate as compared with other countries is most deplorable. The principal causes are puerperal infection and *tetanus neonatorum*. There is a maternal mortality of about 15 per 1,000 births in China as against 3 in England and Wales and 5 in the United States, thus giving a ratio of one to five and three respectively. The infant mortality in the United States and England and Wales is less than 75 per 1,000 births, while it reaches as high as 250 in China, again being about three times higher. If compared with Japan, the latter has only a maternal death rate of 4 and an infant mortality of 187, or a ratio of 1 to 4 and 1 to 2. Thus the urgent need for midwifery training has come up to the attention of the Government. As a preliminary step and in order to meet the most pressing need, steps had been taken locally by the Peiping Midwifery Commission to train the old-type midwives who were practising without the slightest knowledge of the theory of their profession. In a year's time 163 old-type midwives in Peiping have been trained especially as to cleanliness in order to wipe out the mortality caused by puerperal infection and tetanus neonatorum. Those who passed the examination have been given "baskets" and are allowed to continue their profession. It has been found to be an excellent measure to utilize these old-type midwives as a means of publicity, as their talk and demonstrations will influence the mass of the people for traditional reasons. Furthermore, it gives the community a chance to recognize the need of modern midwifery, thus creating a demand for modern-trained midwives. Peiping is estimated to have 270 old-type midwives and 35 modern trained ones, who, however, are not thoroughly trained and also lack practical experience. Out of an estimated 220 practising midwives of both groups, 193 (163 old-type) are registered, thus giving Peiping 87 percent completeness of registration. 62 percent of the 163 old-type midwives have satisfactorily passed examinations of the special course.

Supervisors are engaged to observe whether the graduated midwives are undertaking their profession on a satisfactory basis, to encourage them in case of difficulties, to gain the patients' confidence and to learn of their reactions. The supervisor also has an opportunity of learning the standards of living of the patients visited, and to form an opinion towards the improvement of the midwifery profession preparatory to its control.

The following recommendations are suggested for the effective control of midwives:

1. Enforcement of registration of certified midwives (old-type and modern trained).
2. Age of practising midwives must be under 65, above which practice should be prohibited.

Perhaps because of the relatively simple conditions under which the Chinese farmers lived, it might be possible so to reconstruct rural life in China as to make a positive contribution to the problem of rural life in other nations of the world.

XIAN-UNIT LABORATORY. As we were ourselves ignorant about the rural problem, our approach to it was that of the research student. For the purpose of our research, we needed a laboratory, and selected Ding Xian, a typical North China county, with a population of about 400,000 representing one-thousandth of the population of China. China is a vast country, but it is made up of some 1,900 *xian*; and the problem is reduced to manageable proportions when it is taken on the *xian*-unit basis. Also since the Chinese are a homogeneous people with a uniform culture, manner of life and organization, a positive program found to be workable in one district will in general hold good for the country.

DING XIAN EXPERIMENT. With the approach of the student to our living laboratory of Ding Xian, we conducted a social survey in order to secure facts. Literacy work, supported by the villages, brought us into friendly relationship with the people, at the same time paving the way for future programs by raising the general level of intelligence. We began to conduct agricultural experiments to improve production, and established a small experiment station on land donated by the people. Gradually we became acquainted with rural life and its problems.

RECONSTRUCTION PROGRAM WITH FOUR ASPECTS. Our experience convinced us that the four fundamental weaknesses of Chinese life were ignorance, poverty, disease, and civic disintegration; that they mutually react upon one another in the life of the people; and that all must be tackled in a correlated manner if any one is to be overcome. Through study and practical experimentation, a workable reconstruction program has been evolved, with four aspects, Cultural, Economic, Health, and Political, to deal specifically with the four weaknesses, but to be applied as a whole.

EDUCATION OF THE PEOPLE THROUGH THREE CHANNELS. While the importance of formulating a rural reconstruction program based on actual conditions cannot be overemphasized, the training of the people should not be neglected. A reform program superimposed on the people without their participation is bound to be short-lived, if it ever lives at all. Reconstruction can be realized only if a new mentality is created in the people, and new habits and skills are acquired by them, through the infusion of the Fourfold Program into their lives. For this purpose, Three Types of Education have been evolved, to reach the people through the three channels of School, Home, and Community.

RESEARCH COMMUNITY. While the *xian* is the unit for the practical application of a reconstruction program, it proved too large for intensive research. In 1931 a "Research Community" was demarcated, consisting of 61 villages with a total population of about 44,000. During the past three years all the intensive studies of the Movement, in the content and techniques of the Fourfold Program and the Three Types of Education, have been conducted in this area....

No. of villages	472
Area	480 sq. mi.
Population	397,000
No. of families	68,000
Average farm holding	23 *mou*
Average per capita income	$30
Percent of *xian* income from agriculture	80%
Percent of *xian* income from rural industries	8.4%
Income from principal crops	1931
Millet	$3,308,000
Wheat	2,354,000
Sweet potato	2,250,000
Beans	2,180,000
Cotton	1,674,000
Value of cotton yarn & cloth production (1931)	2,766,000
Current monthly rate of interest	2.5%
No. of village primary schools	447
No. of children of school age (6–12)	51,000
No. of children in school (1930)	
Male	15,500
Female	2,100
No. of villages without medical facilities (1930)	226
No. of old-style physicians	430
Annual per capita expenditures for medical purposes	30¢

Ding Xian Facts

IV. THE FOURFOLD RECONSTRUCTION
PROGRAM

A. CULTURAL DIVISION

Chinese scholars and artists working under the Cultural Division are striving to adapt the various cultural media to make them effective for the reconstruction program. Literature, drama, painting, the great historical characters of Chinese history, and the modern medium of radio, are to be marshalled for the intellectual and spiritual nourishment of the people as well as for their recreation, to create a reconstruction mentality in the people, and ultimately, to rediscover the "soul of the race" and revitalize it for the modern world.

1. PEOPLE'S LITERATURE.   A corollary of the inability of the people to read is the lack of a people's literature. China's rich and voluminous literature is written in "wen-li," the classical language, and is for the aristocracy of scholars. It is far beyond the comprehension of the masses, for whom practically no literature exists. The creation of a people's literature implies, on the one hand, the preparation of language tools for teaching the people to read, and on the other, the training of scholars, in technique, "mentality," and subject matter, to write for them.

Vocabulary study is basic, and includes the selection and systematization of single words, and compound words or phrases, to make up the foundation vocabulary for the Thousand Character Lessons. The National Phonetic Script is studied by this Department in collaboration with the Department of School Type Education as an aid to learning Chinese characters, and appears beside all new characters in the texts to indicate pronunciation. Improvements made in the Script as a result of our studies have been accepted by the National Language Unification Commission. A People's Pocket Dictionary is being compiled containing from two to three thousand characters in addition to the foundation vocabulary, intended for the use of People's School graduates in self-education.

In order to equip and discipline themselves to create a vigorous "People's Literature," members of the Department of People's Literature live and work in the rural districts, aiming to bridge the gap between the traditionally secluded literati and the masses. About 350 booklets have been prepared, covering a wide range of subjects, historical, scientific, biographical, general information, plays, poems, stories and songs, all in line with the ideas and ideals of the Fourfold Program of the Movement. For technical subjects the specialists of the various lines of the Movement give their cooperation. These are the beginnings of a People's Library, soon to contain one thousand titles. . . .

2. PEOPLE'S DRAMA.   The Chinese stage, which penetrates every village and town, reaching the literate and illiterate alike, has exerted a more powerful influence over the thinking and living of the masses than any other single cultural institution. The old plays have done a great deal of good in helping to inculcate the four "cardinal virtues" of loyalty, filial piety, chastity, and friendship. They have also done

considerable harm, however, in fostering superstitious beliefs and hindering the development of a scientific attitude toward natural phenomena and the problems of everyday life. If drama is to become a force for the education of the masses for the new day, it must be reconstructed in content and infused with new life.

Like the members of the People's Literature Department the dramatists must also live and work in the rural district in order to "catch the soul of the farmer," for only through a knowledge of the people's life would they be equipped to create a drama dynamic enough to remake life. . . .

3. PAINTING.   For the intellectual and spiritual development of the farmers, most of whom are at present unlettered, no medium of expression could be more effective than that of color and imagery. Much like Chinese literature, however, painting has been for centuries chiefly a sort of pastime for the aristocracy and the literati and it has had little influence upon the life of the people. Nevertheless it had its cultural roots in the nation and ought to be made effective for the cultural objective of reconstruction.

Up to the present the members of the Department of Art and Visual Education have been devoting most of their time to illustrative work and have prepared a total of more than a thousand pictures, posters, and cartoons for the various activities of the Movement. At the same time, they are making tests to discover the most effective technique not only of expressing a concrete idea, but of awakening the latent artistic sense of the farmers. In connection with developing a true "people's art," a study of the folk art of the district is being made, of frescoes on the temple walls, of the detail of design in homes and public buildings, of sculpture and pottery, and of the art symbolism of the festivals.

4. HISTORICAL CHARACTERS.   This project may be said to be the core and heart of our whole study of the culture of our nation. A nation's history is the most valuable material it possesses for the fashioning of its future. Certainly, the personalities who have made China's history ought to be explored for the making of a great modern people. This is to be done not by copying down their moral sayings, but by presenting national ideals as actually lived by them. It is to be a discovery of the soul of the race as expressed in the noblest lives.

This study has been carried on by the Movement for a number of years. So far the period from ancient times to the Sung Dynasty has been covered, selecting as national heroes those great men and women who embody the qualities that are vital for the regeneration of the race. These personalities have been used extensively as the central themes for textbooks, biographical writings, dramas, paintings, lectures, and songs. Through these various channels it is calculated that the enduring qualities of these great lives, reinterpreted in the light of modern needs, may be integrated and become flesh and blood in the lives of men and women of today.

5. PEOPLE'S RADIO.   Radio is potentially a highly effective medium for the education of the masses, and we have been conducting a broadcasting experiment to determine its best use as a cultural tool for rural reconstruction. As in most other activities undertaken in connection with the Four Fundamentals, the

Alumni Association in a village is given the responsibility of carrying out the experiment. Its members care for and operate the instrument, keep records of attendance, of the reception of the broadcast, of the audience's reaction to the program. They also interpret talks to the listeners, as those whose minds have not yet been opened up through education find it extremely difficult to grasp what they hear through the strange mechanism.

The programs which have proved most effective consist of five items:

(i) Education—to give reconstruction knowledge. The talks are drafted by the technical members of the various Departments and after revision to make them suitable for broadcasting, are spoken over the radio by a man who speaks in the local idiom.

(ii) Projects—to inform the people of the plans of the *xian* government and the projects it is launching for reconstruction.

(iii) Activities—to report on the achievements or efforts of villages or individuals along the lines of reconstruction.

(iv) News—to keep the people in touch with current events, international, national, and local. Next to news of the activities of the Japanese, market reports are perhaps the most interesting item.

(v) Recreation—which includes "community singing," phonograph records of operatic songs, and such simple entertainment as jokes and conundrums.

Special studies have been made for the purpose of bringing the radio within the economic reach of the people. It has been demonstrated in our workshop that it is possible to manufacture a 4-tube receiver with loudspeaker for $26. The monthly running expenses for each receiving set is $1.00, and for the broadcasting station, $36, which would be economically possible for rural districts if taken up by the government.

With the materials and methods being developed in Ding Xian, a radio broadcasting system reaching into all parts of the country should be possible, motivated by the ideal of mass education and rural reconstruction. . . .

B. ECONOMIC DIVISION[5]

The Economic Division is concerned primarily with finding ways and means of helping to improve the standard of livelihood of the farmers. This involves agricultural research and a study of village industries with a view to improving production; a new rural economic organization based on rural needs and adapted to modern conditions; a practical training for farmers in scientific agriculture and in rural economics.

5. Partly supported by the China Foundation for the Promotion of Education and Culture (1929–1934).

1. AGRICULTURE   Most of our agricultural schools and colleges, especially in North China, emphasize teaching, and little if any attention is given to questions of practical application. To be effective, both research and practical application must be undertaken from the standpoint of the farmer, and results must meet the farmer at his own level. Because of the avenues of approach that the Movement has to the farmers in the all-round educational and social program, the vital problems are revealed and the results of research may be tested for their adaptability to the conditions of rural life.

Owing to lack of personnel and funds, our researches in agriculture have been confined to two major lines, namely, agronomy and animal husbandry. . . .

2. VILLAGE INDUSTRIES   While China is primarily an agricultural nation, her farmers are extensively engaged in small industries preparing the fundamental necessities of life. Through farming, they produce the raw materials; through the industries, usually carried on in the home, they manufacture foodstuffs, clothing, implements and utensils, both for home use and for export. The purpose of our experiment is to improve and organize those industries which are the most important in the district with respect both to home consumption needs and to increasing the cash income of the farm family. Through effective development of the village industries, the unproductive idle months of the farmer would be made productive, and he would have something to fall back upon in case of crop failures. Through centralization of management in finance, purchasing, and marketing, some of the most important benefits of mass production will accrue to the village industries, while they retain at the same time the social and economic advantages of small producing units. . . .

The chief contribution of the Movement is not in the invention of processes or equipment, but in finding a solution for the problem of making the improved techniques available for the people through organization and training, and in developing a system whereby the village industries can be carried on economically and efficiently without divorcing the workers from agriculture, which must remain the mainstay of Chinese economy for many years to come.

3. ECONOMIC ORGANIZATION   While it is important that production in the rural districts be improved, the rural economic system is even more fundamental to the people's livelihood, and must be reorganized on a more efficient basis.

Self-Help Societies.   The Self-Help Society is a temporary organization for bringing financial relief to the farmers, until a positive program creating a new economic system can be developed. Two leading banks, the Bank of China and the Kincheng Bank, are cooperating with the Movement in this project for "credit in combination with warehousing." . . .

Integrated Cooperative Societies.   The more positive economic development that should follow the Self-Help Societies is the organization of Integrated Cooperative Societies. An Integrated Cooperative is constructed with the object of serving the village in its major economic activities. It extends credit to its members as needed for purchasing, production, and marketing; and it provides the structure by means of which these three operations may be conducted cooperatively.

Through the Integrated Cooperative, the liquid capital resources of a village are concentrated in a single organization for the all-year-round productive uses of the entire village. This is an important point, first, because liquid capital is scarce; and second, because of the diversification of Chinese farming, which results in a large number of products, and a relatively small volume of business for any one product. This type of organization is also suitable in its conservation of managing personnel; for in a farming population of about 600, sufficient personnel could hardly be found for the management of various cooperative societies with specialized functions, such as there are in the West. . . .

An essential feature of the Integrated Cooperative is the quality of its membership. In the first place, only active producers, real dirt farmers, are eligible. In the second place, literacy is a requirement. The result is that the graduates of the People's Schools are the nucleus in this as in other reconstructive undertakings. Thirdly, all candidates for membership receive an intensive training in the principles and meaning of cooperation and the operation of an Integrated Cooperative Society; and selected members are then given a specialized technical training (in bookkeeping, management, etc.) equipping them to be managing officers.

The *xian* cooperative system as it is being developed in Ding Xian consists of *Village Cooperatives*, which combine to form a *Cooperative Union*, two or more Unions combining to form a *Xian Federation of Cooperatives*. The Union gives supervision to its member Societies, and assists in making favorable marketing and purchasing arrangements. The *Xian* Federation is to maintain a Farmers' Cooperative Bank, thereby strengthening the credit position of the individual Societies; and it will have a "Trade Board" to act as a *xian*-unit economic planning commission, in touch with both the wider market conditions and the local Ding Xian situation. . . .

Through such a rural economic system based upon the principles of mutual cooperation, it is hoped that new habits and a new mentality will be created in the farmers that will enable them to carry out the reconstruction of their own life and environment.

4. FARMERS' INSTITUTE   The purpose of the Farmers' Institute is to train farmer-leaders to carry out simple and practical projects for the economic reconstruction of their villages. It is organized in such a way as to help solve the farmers' current problems. Its schedule and curriculum are worked out in accordance with a "farmer's calendar," which is based on the old Chinese "Almanac," with the dates transferred to the solar calendar. The farmer's calendar notes such events as ploughing, sowing, and harvesting of the various crops, and further, the proper times (for example) for controlling the insect pests and plant diseases that may be expected.

The Farmers' Institute has been held in Ding Xian in five village centers, serving in one year altogether 32 villages and over 300 students. The staff consists of one technically trained teacher, assisted by a local "demonstrator" who had completed the course the previous year. The teacher gives the classroom instruction, and passes on to the next village center, the "demonstrator" taking charge of the "field session" to show how the projects are actually handled.

The Institute may last from two days in the busy farming season to two or three weeks in winter, when the major attention is given to the organization and management of Integrated Cooperative Societies.

The Institute is composed mainly of graduates of the People's Schools, but leading literate farmers who may have had other schooling are also admitted. The farmers who complete the one year's course become "Demonstration Farmers," who are expected to put into practice at least ten projects on their own farms, and teach them to the ordinary "extension" farmers in their villages. The Demonstration Farmers receive supervision from the technical staff of the Agricultural Station, and give supervision to the extension farmers.

The Institute is an integral part of an education system which aims to *develop a new race of farmers* imbued with the right ideas and ideals and equipped with the techniques and skills to improve their own livelihood.

C. HEALTH DIVISION[6]

A survey of medical and health conditions prevailing in Ding Xian was made in 1930, by the Department of Social Survey in collaboration with the Department of Public Health, to serve as a basis for the inauguration of a health experiment. According to the data secured, nearly 30% of the people who die in Ding Xian receive no medical attention whatsoever. Of the 472 villages in the district, 220 possess no medical facilities of any kind, and the other 252 can boast of little more than a self-made (and not infrequently illiterate) physician of the old type who prescribes drugs which he himself sells. Yet it is revealed that the annual per capita expenditure of the people in the district for medicines and medical attention of such an unreliable type is about 30 cents.

The most pressing problem in connection with health in rural China today would seem to be the evolution of a system, practicable under existing conditions, to make elementary medical relief and health protection available for the masses. The system now being developed in Ding Xian is built according to the resources of the three rural administrative units, the village, the subdistrict, and the district (*xian*), and provides for three classes of service, the Village Health Worker, the Sub-District Health Station, and the District Health Center.

6. This phase of the Experiment made possible through the financial support of the Milbank Memorial Fund, New York. For further details of the work, see published reports.

Village Health Worker.　The average village, with a population of about 700 and not more than $150 available for medical purposes, could not possibly support any known type of regular medical personnel; and yet under present conditions in the rural districts, the foundation of a community health system must be in the village.

The Village Health Worker is a member of the People's School Alumni Association of his village. He has been recommended by the Village Elder for the position, and has completed a ten-day course of health training at a Sub-District Health Station. He is expected to do the following:

(i)   record the births and deaths in his village;

(ii) vaccinate his village against smallpox;

(iii) reconstruct his own well, as a demonstration, according to an approved design to reduce the danger of surface pollution;

(iv) give simple treatments according to the facilities of his "First Aid Box," which contains ten essential and safe drugs;

(v)   "introduce" to the Sub-District Health Station patients whose ailments do not come within his scope;

(vi) serve as "health extension agent," giving every possible assistance to the higher grades of health personnel in making contacts with the people and transmitting ideas.

Thus is provided in the village the foundation for vital statistics, epidemic control, sanitation, and medical relief.

Vital Statistics.　The statistical work in 1933 was carried on by a system of supervised registration, using the police in the city and 16 Village Health Workers in 16 villages. The method is fairly accurate, and is inexpensive. A birth or death certificate costs at present 13 cents, which eventually, as the system expands, should be reduced to 3 cents.

Birth rate (per 1,000 population)	40.1
Death rate (per 1,000 population)	27.2
Infant mortality (per 1,000 live births)	199.0
Maternity mortality (per 1,000 live births)	13.0

Vital Statistics in Research Community 1933

Medical Relief.　The Village Health Workers give an average of 5 treatments per day, at a cost of 1.1 cents per treatment, including material and labor. The treatments as given by them are found to be over 95% correct. In June 1934 there are in Ding Xian 61 health workers in 58 villages.

While the Village Health Worker's training course is exceedingly brief, he receives regular supervision (at least once a week) from the physician at the Sub-District Health Station, which is considered to be the most valuable part of his training. Other factors which make for the effectiveness of the Village Health Workers are these: They realize, and their neighbors also know, the limitations of their training; their membership in an organized group, the Alumni Association, subjects them to group opinion and censure; and they could easily be replaced if they should prove incompetent or should attempt too much.

Sub-District Health Station. To supplement the work of the Village Health Workers with a higher type of service, a qualified physician ("B-Grade") and dresser or nurse are located in the Sub-District Health Station. Under the health system it is possible for the Health Stations to serve a population of approximately 30,000 each, carrying on both curative and preventive work. To enable them to do this, special supplementary training is given to the Station staff at the District Health Center.

Graduates of "B-Grade" medical schools are the type of medical personnel ordinarily available today, and this is likely to be the case for many years to come. Furthermore, the graduates of the highest type of school are beyond the economic reach of rural communities.

It may be of interest to mention in this connection that in Ding Xian there are no less than 16 graduates of "B-Grade" schools, but only three of them are even attempting to practice. Two reasons may be offered in explanation: the training they have received does not equip them for service in the rural districts; and isolated as they are, they are not able to obtain the confidence of the people, and cannot make a living out of such meager practice as they might secure.

A daily clinic is conducted at the Health Station. Other duties and activities are: supervision of Village Health Workers, local "midwives" (old type retrained) and midwifery helpers, and school health; popular health education, and vaccination against smallpox. There is a weekly conference for the physicians at the District Health Center.

Medical Relief. In 1933 the average daily attendance at each clinic was 29. Of the new patients, over 3% were referred by the Village Health Workers. The average cost of treatment was about 9 cents.

School Health. An experiment conducted in 25 village primary schools within a radius of six miles from the Sub-District Health Stations included physical examinations by the physicians. It was shown that 58.5% of the children had trachoma, 26.2% ringworm of the scalp. Treatment was given by teachers and nurses. The program included also attention to personal and environmental cleanliness, and special efforts are being made to have the schools reconstruct their drinking wells and latrines. Health instruction was given in the early stages by the nurses, later by the teachers themselves.

There are at present four Health Stations, two in the villages maintained by the Movement for experimental purposes, and one city Station and one village Station under the auspices of the local government. With the supervision and help of the District Health Center, the physicians in these Stations are able to do a great deal of work that could not be expected of isolated physicians.

District Health Center.   For the entire *xian* a Health Center, housing a hospital with fifty beds, and a laboratory, as well as administrative offices and classrooms, is established. It coordinates and supplements all the activities of the Sub-District Health Stations so that they will be free from administrative conflicts and maintain a requisite professional standard. The Health Center also takes up such activities as control of epidemics, and special studies in connection with school health, sanitation, maternity and child health, birth control, training of physicians, nurses, dressers, etc., as well as giving intensive training courses to medical students and other personnel. . . .

The entire health system, including Health Center, Health Stations, and Health Workers, is well within the economic reach of the people. The people's acceptance of it, however, depends on the effectiveness not of the health program alone, but of the all-round reconstruction program, raising the general intellectual and economic level of the people.

D. POLITICAL DIVISION

INTEGRAL PART OF RECONSTRUCTION.   A rural reconstruction program is incomplete and ineffective unless it takes up the government of the rural districts as well as the cultural, economic, and health aspects of rural life.

1. The *xian* government is the logical and only effective agency for practical application on a *xian*-wide scale, from the point of view of both authority and administrative machinery.
2. The *xian* government affects vitally and directly practically all aspects of rural life. A social reconstruction program which fails to take account of the local government is likely to find itself obstructed.
3. Without the *xian* government, certain studies in the field of social reconstruction cannot be conducted with any degree of thoroughness, because they come within the sphere of government control. Examples are: land tenure and taxation, the system of rural education, the *xian* judicial system.

OUTSIDE MOVEMENT'S SPHERE.   A vital piece of research into the political aspect of reconstruction cannot be conducted by a non-governmental institution. A study of the government conducted by outsiders, or social investigators merely, would touch only the periphery of the problem. "Unless you enter the tiger's den, you cannot get the cubs." The essential realities of the political problem are only to be grasped by getting into the very life of the *xian* government, as "research officials," and studying it from the inside out. The Mass Education Movement, as a private institution, is not in a position to make an adequate study of the *xian* government and its functions. The political aspect of reconstruction is therefore outside its proper sphere.

ATTENTION OF CENTRAL GOVERNMENT. Because of the general awakening in China to the importance of rural reconstruction, the Central Government is paying increasing attention to the rural district. Toward the end of 1932 the Ministry of the Interior sent Vice-Minister Kan to make a tour of the rural experiment centers in North China, during the course of which he spent four days in studying the Ding Xian work. Through his survey, he became impressed by the need for *xian* government reorganization in order to facilitate and accelerate rural reconstruction programs such as that developed at Ding Xian.

NATIONAL CONFERENCE ON HOME AFFAIRS—DECEMBER 1932. Subsequently at the National Conference on Home Affairs, called by the Ministry of the Interior and held at Nanking in December 1932, *xian* government reform was the central theme of discussion. The major resolution presented to the Conference by the Ministry was one based on Vice-Minister Kan's report of his investigations and observations. The resolution recommended that the problem of rural reconstruction be approached in the provinces *experimentally* and *on a xian unit basis*; specifically, that an "Institute of Political and Social Reconstruction" be established in each province to conduct the experimentation, and that an Experiment Area be set aside as "laboratory," the Experiment Area to be under the direct and complete control of the Institute. The Conference, which was attended by the Provincial Commissioners of Civil Affairs, other Provincial and Central Government officials, and a number of invited specialists in rural work, adopted the resolution unanimously. It later became law by the final sanction of the Central Political Council.

HEBEI PROVINCIAL INSTITUTE ESTABLISHED. Soon after the Conference, those provinces which were in a position to do so, and whose high officials were interested, began to make plans for the experimental study of *xian*-unit reconstruction. In Hebei Province, General Yü, Chairman of the Provincial Government, and the members of the Provincial Committee, succeeded through persistent efforts during the period of Japanese invasion, in having an Institute of Political and Social Reconstruction inaugurated in the spring of 1933.

COOPERATION WITH MOVEMENT. In order to take advantage of the foundation work already done, and to profit by the experiences of the Mass Education Movement, Ding Xian was selected as the location for the Institute. For the sake of assuring a close cooperation between two institutions, the General Director of the Movement was invited to become President of the Institute, and other experienced personnel of the Movement were also appointed to responsible positions, serving concurrently the Movement and the Institute. They act in the Institute in an honorary capacity, but assume full responsibility for directing its program and development.

While the Institute and the Movement are separate, independent institutions, they nevertheless have an organic cooperative relationship with each other. Since the program of the Movement is incomplete without that of the Institute, a brief account of the Institute is necessary here, and is given in the following section.

VI. A NATIONAL RURAL RECONSTRUCTION MOVEMENT

NATIONAL AWAKENING. During the past few years the country has become "rural conscious." Social, educational, and political leaders have begun to look upon the rural district as a field for their activities. Even intellectuals have turned to the rural problem as a subject for their writings. As a result, many rural centers have sprung up, and lately experiment *xians* have been started in different parts of the country. Appeals for technical assistance and trained leadership are received in Ding Xian almost daily from government and people's institutions. No less than three thousand visitors have come to Ding Xian during the past year from as far as Sichuan, Inner Mongolia, Guangdong, and Yunnan. The majority of them came to study the program in order to apply it through the institutions which they represent.

A CRITICAL SITUATION. This enthusiasm and earnestness for rural reconstruction makes us hopeful, but at the same time apprehensive. Ever since the "Opium War" many national reform movements have sprung up in China, but they have borne little fruit. Enthusiasm for rural reconstruction is good and necessary, but with enthusiasm alone, it will become a mere fad, without real meaning. Unless serious and painstaking study of it is made by scholars and scientists on the one hand, and administrative and technical personnel are systematically trained for it on the other, the rural reconstruction movement which is sweeping over the country just now is bound to dwindle away as many other movements have done in the past.

Creative genius is required at the source, for the direction and development of the program. Men who combine the highest possible technical qualifications for scientific research with an intimate knowledge of the realities of Chinese life, are also eminently fitted for training younger leadership for rural reconstruction in the *xian*-unit and in the Provinces.

TOWARD NATIONAL UNITY AND STABILITY. In the midst of political differences and conflict of social theories, "Rural Reconstruction" appears as a real *unifying force*, the one outstanding national platform upon which all China, north and south, can agree. Rural reconstruction is national reconstruction, and national reconstruction, rural reconstruction. Promoted by the governments, central, provincial, and local, with the participation of colleges and research institutions, it is bound to have also a *stabilizing influence* in the country. Energy and creativity now dissipated in civil strife will be turned into constructive channels, and the shouting of empty *isms* and slogans will give way to competition in achievements in rural reconstruction.

The rural reconstruction movement is both dynamic and basic and, provided with scientific techniques and competent leadership, is able to meet the needs of the China of today and lay the foundation for the China of tomorrow. . . .

15.8 POLITICS OF POWER: GENERAL VON FALKENHAUSEN'S ADVICE TO CHIANG KAI-SHEK, 1936

Between 1934 and 1937, the Nanjing regime developed a close relationship with the Third Reich of Adolf Hitler. China, like Germany, was attempting to establish a state unified around a single party and a single leader, and the German model seemed an attractive model to many of Chiang Kaishek's followers and, quite probably, to the Generalissimo himself. Many adherents of the Guomindang, including Chiang's own son, were sent to Germany to receive military and police training. There were those who dreamed that China's "Revival Society" (*Fuxingshe*), a paramilitary group also known as the Blueshirts, would ultimately emerge as an elite political clique that would wield great power in the Guomindang.

Another symbol of the mutual interest and sympathy of Germans and Chinese in the 1930s was the arrival of numerous German advisors in China. Several Germans in sequence served as Chiang's chief foreign military advisors; Captain Walter Stennes trained Chiang's personal bodyguard; and Colonel-General Hans von Seeckt and General Alexander von Falkenhausen, both outstanding staff officers of the First World War, were the architects of the positional warfare tactics that led to the destruction of the Jiangxi Soviet in October 1934. Von Falkenhausen, as this top secret memorandum to Chiang indicates, also had strong ideas in the political realm and was anxious to see Chiang emerge as a president with powers similar to those enjoyed by Hitler.

Office of the General Adviser
Tbg. No. 5972/I.
Top Secret!
Nanjing, September 6, 1936
    . . . . The history of all times has taught us that leaders are needed by states and nations in times of distress, when only the concerted application of *all* state and national power can provide the necessary control over their destiny. Absolute power made possible the great deeds of such historical figures, from Julius Caesar to Genghis Khan, such as Cromwell, Frederick the Great, and Napoleon I. Though history has examples of leadership shared by several persons, *one* person always was clearly in the leadership, and the others subordinate; such as recently Bismarck who, with the support of the King, found in Moltke and Roon the necessary complement to himself.

Limited power, however, or a division of power, but also the inadequacy of the leader, have almost invariably brought struggles for national existence to an unsuccessful end; from Hannibal to the Great War of 1914–18. . . .

The recent period has everywhere shown tendencies to return to practical absolutism. For example in Italy and Germany, but also in Russia, all power is concentrated in one hand, while in some instances no constitutions even exist, and no control organ such as, legally, in Italy the King and in Germany Hindenburg until his death.

Therein lies the natural striving to have a personality at the head of the state endowed with ultimate responsibility, a person independent from elections, party politics, and public mood, and capable to provide a stability immune to the turnover of individual personalities. But this is the essence of monarchy.

[But] we must distinguish leaders [Führer] from dictators. Leaders are those who command the allegiance of the masses of the people and who provide for some check through occasional plebiscites. Dictators derive authority from material power, supported by a minority. Dictators can nevertheless be historically justifiable at a time when no consensus is possible among the people and the state is in need of firm guidance in order to survive.

Most dictators come to a violent end, unless they found a dynasty (Ming Dynasty). . . . For in every pure dictatorship there comes the moment when the dictator has become blind to the signs of the time, or is no longer in the position to heed them. What is missing is control through a healthy, objective opposition. For this reason, Bismarck once said, that in the absence of an opposition he would create one. The dictator who has no responsibility but to himself needs a source of control that is independent without interfering with his freedom of making the final decision in times of great emergency. *The opposition also, must be selfless and national-minded* in order to fulfill purpose in the state. . . .

In applying the supreme power of command of the President care must be taken not to limit the instruments of power of the state to the traditional armed forces on land, sea, and air, but to note that modern warfare requires the combined strength of the whole state and its people, down to the smallest detail.

As a precaution, the whole nation must be prepared for war; this is the only way to provide for its security in its entirety. This consideration must apply to every state measure concerning the economy, finances, and above all popular education and propaganda. Every powerful modern state today does this; they represent "nations in arms." Most states have laws regulating in every detail the "mobilization of the nation in case of war."

This fact leads naturally to the preeminent importance of military consideration in all government actions, and requires that the leading statesman possess unfettered powers in this so vital area for the state and nation. Generally speaking, this task no longer can be left to the individual government departments. Instead, it calls for firm consolidation and single-minded leadership.

"War is the continuation of politics by other means." Policies must be coordinated with the realities of the state's power, its "potential de guerre." This means: the state's policies must be based on a just assessment of the power instruments available, and the instruments of power must be so ordered to suit the political situation.

Thus the ideal is a chief of state who is both statesman and commander in chief (e.g., Frederick the Great, Pilsudski, Mustapha-Kemal-Atatürk, et al.), and who *already in time of peace so organizes and staffs the national instruments of power* that the whole machine functions smoothly at all times.

At the same time we must remember that no single person in today's world has the energy to direct and lead everything. As division of labor becomes necessary, the unity of concept and the loyal cooperation of all must be secured above all.

Thus the whole organization of the state must be basically adapted to modern warfare in time of peace, for modern warfare requires that everything be prepared in peace time down to the smallest detail, so that it can automatically begin to function at the outbreak of hostilities.

Three major areas are affected:

a) All branches of the armed forces, on land, water, and in the air must be organically coordinated, also their missions.
b) The whole task of preparing for national economic mobilization.
c) The [need for an] unanimous attitude on the part of the true public, i.e., unanimous national support.

To subordinate the three areas—armed forces, economy, people—to the supreme leader is the ultimate end of all preparation for mobilization. They are closely related to one another. . . .

We [in China] have also tried centralization through the person of the Generalissimo and the creation of the National Military Commission. But since the highest offices of the armed forces continue to exist unchanged, there is in practice a lack of clarity in the division of spheres of competence and responsibility. This gives rise to duplication of work, interferes with cooperation, leads to higher expenditures.

Thus to create a clear and unitary organization is important. It must assure in peace time the shaping and the coordination of all the direct and indirect elements that make up the state and the nation's defensive capacity, so that they work automatically in time of war. . . .

CHAPTER 16

Communist Survival

16.1 THE JIANGXI SOVIET LAND LAW, 1932

After the failure of the Autumn Harvest Uprisings in 1927, Mao Zedong went into hiding with the survivors in the Jinggang Mountains. In 1928, attacks from Guomindang armies forced Mao to move again, this time to a mountainous area on the border of Jiangxi and Fujian provinces. There he would stay until 1934, building the Jiangxi Soviet into a sizeable stronghold.

The centerpiece of Mao's experiments with social reform in Jiangxi was a sweeping land reform law that called for the redistribution of property to tenant farmers and "poor" and "middle peasants." As the following document shows, the calculus of land confiscation and redistribution was complex, with numerous permutations and exceptions to be considered. While a radical land policy attracted landless peasants to the Communist cause, it also alienated the wealthier peasants who dominated local society.

A. WHOSE LAND SHOULD BE CONFISCATED?

1. Land (including land rented to tenants), houses, and all other forms of property, including household items, that belonged to members of the gentry and landlords are to be confiscated.

2. Land, houses, and all other forms of property, including household items, that belong to family shrines, Buddhist or Taoist temples, clan or social organizations are to be confiscated.

3. Land and farm implements owned by those rich peasants who have been verified as members of counterrevolutionary organizations (e.g., the

A-B [Anti-Bolshevik] League and the Social Democratic Party) are to be confiscated. As for houses, only those of the poorest kind or in the worst conditions are allowed to be continually occupied by them. If the Soviet Government has found to its satisfaction that their relatives have neither joined any counterrevolutionary organization nor engaged in any counter-revolutionary activities and if, in the meantime, these relatives have inti-mated to the government that they will sever all relations with the counterrevolutionaries in question, the government can return part of the confiscated land to these relatives in accordance with their rich peasant sta-tus, provided that all other peasants in the community do not raise objections.

4. Land owned by rich peasants should be confiscated.

B. WHO SHOULD RECEIVE LAND?

5. The amount of land to be distributed is the same for all tenant farmers and poor peasants. Whether the land of the middle peasants should be redis-tributed so as to assure that they have the same amount as that of tenant farmers and poor peasants depends upon the decision to be made by the middle peasants themselves. If the majority of them so desires, the land of the middle peasants will be redistributed, even though the minority does not agree. If the majority of the middle peasants does not want its land to be redistributed, its land will not be redistributed and it can keep the land it presently has; but its decision, in this case, does not bind the minority of the middle peasants which, if it so chooses, can participate in the redistribution program. This provision, however, does not affect land distribution among the middle peasants that had been completed before December 31, 1931. The completed distribution should remain effective and should not be altered in any fashion.

6. The relatives of a farm laborer shall receive land. He himself should also receive land if he is unemployed. (By unemployment is meant the lack of employment for most of the year. It does not include temporary unemploy-ment that lasts only a short period of time.)

7. Independent artisans (including artisans who have apprentices working for them but excluding those who have hired workers), physicians, and teachers are to receive land if they have been unemployed for six months or longer. (Their relatives, if they are poor or middle peasants, shall of course receive land as other poor or middle peasants do. If they are not poor or middle peasants, they shall be subsidized in accordance with their actual need. Under no circumstances, however, should the subsidy be more than two-thirds of the land received by others.)

8. Shop owners and their relatives shall not receive any land.

9. Rich peasants will receive poor land in accordance with the size of their respective households as well as the number of able-bodied workers in them. If a rich peasant household has able-bodied workers, each of them will receive a certain amount of poor land as his share. If none of its members can work, a subsidy in the form of poor land will be provided, but this subsidy shall not be more than two-thirds of the land granted to others.

10. Beginning with the operation of this statute, members of the gentry landlords, and members of counterrevolutionary organizations will not be entitled to land distribution. Nor are former wives, daughters-in-law, or daughters of rich peasants who have in the past assumed the leadership in opposing land distribution of their own accord, even though they are presently married to farm laborers, tenant farmers, poor or middle peasants.

11. There are cases in which members of the gentry, landlords, and counterrevolutionary rich peasants have adopted the method of "invitation marriage" by marrying their wives or daughters to farm laborers, tenant farmers, poor or middle peasants for the sole purpose of preserving their own properties. The properties in question, including houses, shall be confiscated by the government forthwith. However, the farm laborers, tenant farmers, poor or middle peasants who have been thus married will receive their fair share when the confiscated properties, including houses, are redistributed.

12. As for the adopted sons or daughters of members of the gentry, landlords, and those rich peasants who have in the past been members of counterrevolutionary organizations, they are not entitled to land distribution if they have lived the same kind of life and have had the same kind of education as their foster parents. If on the other hand they have been treated like slaves even though they are adopted sons or daughters, they are entitled to land distribution.

13. As for Buddhist monks and nuns, Taoist priests, magicians and sorcerers, fortunetellers, geomancers, and other feudal remnants as well as Protestant ministers and Catholic priests, they are not entitled to land distribution if religion is their main means of earning a livelihood. If land has been granted to them, it should be returned. If on the other hand religion is only their avocation and farming is in fact their main occupation, they are entitled to land distribution if people in their respective communities approve. If the relatives of the aforesaid monks, nuns, etc. do not depend upon religion for their respective livelihood and are in fact farm laborers, tenant farmers, middle or rich peasants, they are entitled to land distribution in accordance with their class differentiation, that is, farm laborers, tenant farmers, etc.

14. Beginning with the operation of this statute, the sons or daughters of the members of the gentry or landlords are no longer entitled to land distribution

even though they have been adopted by poor laborers or peasants as their own children.

15. Members of the gentry, landlords, and those rich peasants who have in the past assumed the leadership in opposing land distribution of their own accord, together with all of their relatives, are not entitled to land distribution. If land has been granted to them, it shall be returned to the government.

16. Rural merchants who, prior to the revolution, had been able to support their families through trade and commerce are not entitled to land distribution. If land has been granted to them, it shall be returned to the government. They will be granted land in the same fashion as independent artisans, however, had they become unemployed after the revolution.

17. Unemployed peddlers are entitled to land distribution.

18. A woman can dispose of her land the way she wishes when she is married.

C. HOW IS LAND TO BE DISTRIBUTED?

19. The geographical unit whereby land is distributed should be the township. If the majority of the middle and poor peasants so desire, a village can be used as a unit for land distribution purposes.

20. Insofar as tenant farmers, poor and middle peasants, unemployed farm laborers, and unemployed independent artisans are concerned, population and land productivity shall be taken into consideration when land is being distributed. But middle peasants have the option not to participate in land distribution.

21. Hills that are economically productive (such as those that produce tea, firewood, bamboo, and miscellaneous grains) are to be regarded as "land" for the purpose of land distribution. They should be assessed a cash value and be equitably distributed according to local conditions. Rich peasants, however, are to be given the least productive hills only. All the large forests are to be managed and controlled by the Soviet Government.

22. All mines are owned by the government. For working purposes, the government can either lease these mines to others or organize its own cooperatives. At the moment leasing should be the major means to achieve these purposes.

23. Fish ponds can be either divided in the same way as land or assessed a cash value before distribution takes place. As an alternative, a cooperative may be formed in charge of the fish ponds, and in this case, only the fish are to be distributed, not the ponds. The main purpose of maintaining water ponds is to irrigate adjacent fields.

24. Surplus oxen, houses, and farm implements owned by rich peasants are to be confiscated by the government. The confiscated items will then be divided up among poor laborers and peasants in accordance with their needs.

25. Houses, personal properties, farm implements, and household items that are confiscated from members of the gentry, landlords, and those rich peasants who have in the past assumed the leadership in opposing land distribution are to be distributed among poor peasants and farm laborers. Before this distribution takes place, however, two portions should be set aside: one for the Soviet Government and other revolutionary organizations for their own uses and the other for the relatives of Red soldiers and also of those who have suffered greatly during the war.

26. No governmental official or staff member in any of the revolutionary organizations is entitled to land distribution if he is not a tenant farmer, poor or middle peasant, unemployed farm laborer, coolie, or independent artisan.

D. HOW IS LAND TO BE DISTRIBUTED AMONG MEMBERS OF THE RED ARMY?

27. The relatives of a Red soldier will receive land in the same manner as poor and middle peasants. The land they receive shall not be located too far from the place where they live.

28. In a township where each person has received land that yields 5 piculs of grain per year, the common land administered for the support of the Red Army shall be equivalent to the total amount received by three to five persons in the said township. The total amount of common land in each township increases in proportion to the amount received by each individual person. The government may lease this common land to individual peasants for cultivation purposes, and in such cases is obligated to provide farm implements, oxen, fertilizers, and seeds for the peasants concerned. The amount of rent to be paid to the government is subject to negotiation between the parties involved.

E. LEASING, TRADE, INHERITANCE, AND OTHER RELATED MATTERS

29. Distributed land can be leased to others for cultivation purposes. It cannot be leased, however, to members of the gentry, landlords, and their relatives. The amount of rent to be paid by the cultivator is subject to negotiation between the parties involved.

30. Distributed land can be bought and sold, but it cannot be sold to members of the gentry, landlords, and their relatives. The price is subject to negotiation between the parties concerned, but must be registered with the local government once decided upon.

31. Distributed land can be inherited by the grantee's heirs. The government will not take land away upon the death of the grantee; nor will it grant additional

land upon the enlargement of his family. If a grantee dies without an heir, the distributed land will be returned to the government.

32. There should not be any redistribution of landownership in an area where tenant farmers, poor and middle peasants have already benefited from land distributions carried out in the past, and redistribution, in this case, can only take place if the majority of the people involved demand it. However, corrections (in the form of either addition or subtraction) will be made in those areas where land distributions in the past are incompatible with the provisions of the newly enacted land statute or decisions relating to them. If on the other hand it is the rich peasants who have benefited from land distributions in the past, the government shall mobilize tenant farmers, poor and middle peasants for redistribution purposes.

33. With the exception of their leaders, those who have opposed land distribution in the past will nevertheless receive land like others. If they have not yet returned home, their relatives will till the distributed land on their behalf. Upon their return they will take over ownership as if the distributed land had been temporarily leased to their relatives for cultivation purposes. The distributed land will be returned to the government if they fail to return home at the end of a one-year period.

34. Those who have been serving as militiamen or self-defense guards for the White Army shall receive land like others. They are not entitled to land distribution, however, if they have also been members of the gentry or landlords. The above-mentioned militiamen or self-defense guards must return home to cultivate the distributed land within a specified period of time. If they fail to return within this specified period, the distributed land will be returned to the government.

35. Artisans, tenant farmers, poor and middle peasants who have been duped in joining counterrevolutionary organizations (such as the A-B League, the Revisionist Group, and the Social Democratic Party) but are now willing to admit their errors will receive land like others. A proportional amount of land shall be set aside for those presently in prison awaiting trial. A rich peasant, however, is not entitled to this consideration.

36. Priority should be given to tenant farmers, poor and middle peasants for the cultivation of abandoned fields, and the government, in such cases, should grant the cultivators tax and rent exemptions for a specific number of years. Rich peasants will be allowed to till those abandoned fields which the government has not been able to lease to tenant farmers, poor and middle peasants. Depending upon circumstances, they may or may not be exempt from tax and rent obligations. If they are exempt from these obligations, the period of exemption should be shorter than that for tenant farmers, poor and middle peasants. After all the peasants mentioned above have been taken care of, if there are still abandoned fields which cannot be utilized through the means of migration, or if abandoned fields continue to exist even after migration,

they may, in this case, be leased for cultivation purposes to members of the gentry, landlords, and their families under the strict supervision of the township government and the people in the township. The cultivators, in this case, are not entitled to tax or rent exemption, and the abandoned fields in question must be located in the central section of the Soviet region rather than its border areas. The amount of tax and rent to be paid and the length of the period during which the lease is effective are to be determined by the government.

16.2 THE LONG MARCH: THE TALE OF LUDING BRIDGE, 1935

Between 1928 and 1934, the Nanjing government launched five "bandit extermination" campaigns against the Jiangxi Soviet. Although the Red Army successfully countered the first four attacks, by the late summer of 1934 the fifth such campaign adopted a strategy of encirclement and mobilized an army of nearly two million men to steadily reduce the size of the Communist stronghold. To the escape the tightening noose, Chinese Communist Party leaders decided to launch a breakout. In October 1934, some one hundred thousand men and women fought their way through a vulnerable part of the Nationalist blockade and began the Long March. In a grim year-long journey, most of the Long Marchers died—only ten thousand survived to begin anew in Yan'an, in the remote northwest.

As the years passed, the epic story of the Long March was evoked again and again to symbolize, with mythic force, the commitment, self-sacrifice, and courage of the CCP. In this selection, commander Yang Chengwu describes an especially harrowing moment during the Long March. Although his account undoubtedly embroiders the heroism of the Communist army, it nonetheless captures the drama of the river crossing, an episode memorialized for posterity.

On May 25, 1935, the First Regiment of the Red Army's First Division made a successful crossing of the Dadu River at Anshunchang. The current was too rapid to permit the building of a bridge there, and it would take many days to transfer our thousands of men to the other side, as only a few small boats were available to serve as ferries.

Chiang Kai-shek had ordered Yang Sen and other Sichuan warlords to rush up their troops and prevent our crossing. . . . Decades before, the famous general of the Taiping Revolution, Shih Dakai, and his army had been annihilated by the Qing soldiers at Anshunchang. Chiang Kai-shek had dreams of causing the Red Army to meet a similar fate. It was imperative to capture the bridge at Luding and ensure swift crossing of the river to prevent encirclement by the enemy. At such a critical moment, this task was given to the vanguard Fourth Regiment of our left-route army. The First Division, our right-route army, which had already crossed the river, would advance north along the east bank of the river in co-ordination with our efforts to capture Luding Bridge. . . .

After we had occupied several buildings and a Catholic church to the west of the bridge, our men prepared for the coming battle. When Regimental Commander Wang and I went out with the battalion and company officers to study the location, we were taken aback by the difficulties to be overcome. The reddish waters, cascading down the mountain gorges of the river's upper reaches, pounded against ugly boulders rising from the river bed and tossed white foam high into the air. The roar of the rushing torrent was deafening. In such a current even a fish could not keep steady for long. Fording or crossing in boats was out of the question.

We examined the bridge. It was made of 13 iron chains, each link as thick as a rice bowl. Two chains on each side served as hand-railings, while the other nine formed a cat-walk. Planks had originally been laid across the nine chains but were now gone, taken away by the enemy, and only the black swinging chains remained. At the head of the bridge two lines of a poem were inscribed on a stone slab:

> *Towering mountains flank Luding Bridge,*
> *Their summits rising a thousand* li *into the clouds.*

The town of Luding was built half along the shore and half on the mountain slope, located directly beyond the eastern end of the bridge and surrounded by a wall more than seven meters high. Its west gate faced the end of the bridge. Luding was garrisoned by two enemy regiments, and strong fortifications had been built along the mountain slope. Machine-gun emplacements close to the bridge kept us in continual fire, and mortar shells rained down on us.

The enemy soldiers were confident that their position was impregnable and yelled sneeringly: "Let's see you fly over! We'll give you our arms if you can do it!"

Our soldiers shouted back: "We don't want your weapons. It's the bridge we want!"

Back from our survey we soon set a battalion in position to seal off the narrow path and prevent the movement of any enemy reinforcements on the eastern bank of the river. That was the only path between the mountainside and the river along which they could come. Then we went among our companies to begin our battle rallies. Enthusiasm ran high, each company submitting a list of volunteers for an assault party, and each wanting the men of their particular unit to be given the task of taking the bridge.

All the officers of the regiment met in the church at noon to decide on the composition of the assault party. Discussion had just started when enemy mortar shells blew a big hole in the roof of the building where we gathered. Shell fragments and bits of broken tile showered down on us, but not one of us moved.

"The enemy is urging us on," I said. "We must drive across the bridge immediately. Now let's decide which company shall be responsible for the assaults."

Liao Dazhu, commander of the Second Company, jumped to his feet. A taciturn man, he forced himself to speak, his dark, sunburned face flushed with the effort, and his short wiry frame trembled with excitement as he said:

"The First Company was commended as a model for their forced crossing of the Wujiang River. We'd like to emulate them and distinguish ourselves in the battle to take Luding Bridge."

"You've got to give the assault mission to the Third Company," interrupted Wang Yuzai, the quick-tempered commander of that company, spluttering like a machine-gun. "Our Third Company has done well in every battle. We guarantee to take Luding Bridge." Standing as solid as an iron turret, he added plaintively, "If you do not give the assault mission to the Third Company, I dare not go back and face my men."

A heated debate followed, no company willing to yield to another. It was left to the leaders to decide. Commander Wang and I talked it over. Then he stood up and announced that the Second Company would be given the mission. I then rose and said:

"If it's fighting you want, there's plenty more to come. You'll each get your chance. At the Wujiang River it was the First Company that led off; this time we'll let the Second Company start. The assault party will be formed of twenty-two men, Communists and non-Party activists, and will be led by Company Commander Liao. It seems like a good arrangement to me. What do the rest of you think?"

The response was a burst of applause from all present. Commander Liao jumped for joy. Only the Third Company commander was not satisfied. "The Third Company's job is not easy either," I assured him. "You have to go over directly behind the Second Company and lay planks across those chains so that the rest of the men can charge into the town. Is that all right?" The commander smiled.

Men fight better on a full stomach, so I told the company commanders to give each man a good meal. After the meeting, Luo Huasheng, secretary of the general Party branch, went to the Second Company to help with their preparations for the assault.

The attack began at four in the afternoon. The regimental commander and I directed it from the west end of the bridge. The buglers of the regiment gathered together to sound the charge, and we opened up with every weapon we had. The blare of the bugles, the firing and the shouts of the men reverberated through the valley. The 22 heroes, led by Commander Liao, crept across on the swaying bridge chains in the teeth of intense enemy fire. Each man carried a tommy-gun or a pistol, a broadsword and 12 hand-grenades. Behind them came the men of the Third Company, each carrying a plank in addition to full battle gear. They fought and laid planks at the same time.

Just as the assault party reached the bridgehead on the opposite side, huge flames sprang into the sky outside the town's west gate. The enemy was trying to throw a fire barrier across our path. The blaze, reddening the sky, licked fiercely around the end of the bridge.

The outcome of the attack hung by a hair. Our assault party hesitated for a few seconds and the men standing by the regimental commander and me shouted in unison: "It's a critical moment, comrades! Charge in! The enemy is crushed!" The shouts gave the heroes courage, confidence and strength. With the clarion call of the bugles, our assault party swiftly plunged into the flames. Commander Liao's cap caught fire. He threw it away and fought on. The others also dashed through the flames, closely behind Liao. In the street fighting that followed, the enemy brought their full weight to bear, determined to wipe out our assault party. Our gallant men fought until all their bullets and grenades were spent. There was a critical pause as the Third Company came charging to their rescue. Then Regimental Commander Wang and I sped across the bridge with our reinforcements and entered the town. Within two hours we had destroyed the greater part of the two enemy regiments while the remainder fled in panic. By dusk we had completely occupied the town of Luding and were in control of the bridge.

16.3–16.5 THREE ACCOUNTS OF THE NEW LIFE MOVEMENT

The New Life movement was launched with a torchlight parade in Nanchang on February 19, 1934. This date was selected by Guomindang planners to coincide with the Lantern Festival and the start of the new lunar year.

One of the cherished goals of the New Life movement was to inculcate propriety, righteousness, incorruptibility, and a sense of shame (*liyilianchi*) in all Chinese. These clichéd neo-Confucian virtues, now carried to the masses for the first time by radio, in propaganda broadsides, slogans, and via other mechanisms at the disposal of the Party state, were to be the formulae for national revival. Guomindang officials believed that these and other New Life moral and behavioral concepts, once assimilated by ordinary Chinese, would transform China into a strong and forward-looking nation state.

In the following documents, Madame Chiang Kai-shek's idiosyncratic description of the meaning and application of *liyilianchi* was designed to persuade American readers of the 1930s, in terminology they could identify with, of the high purposes of New Life. The list of rules for New Life described the behaviors and values the movement tried to promote.

C. W. H. Young's elegiac description of the accomplishments of the New Life movement in Jiangxi suggests how it was perceived by some members of the American missionary community active in China in the mid-1930s.

16.3 *Mme. Chiang on the New Life Movement, 1935*

China, like almost every other nation during the past few years, has felt the tremendously enervating effects of world depression. Each nation, according to its lights, has sought to find a way out of stagnation into normalcy. Italy has its Fascism, Germany its Nazism, the Soviet Union its first and second five-year plans, and America its New Deal. The primary aim of each is to solve the economic problems involved and to bring material prosperity to the people. China, like the rest of the nations, is confronted with a similar problem, added to which is the necessity of rescuing the people from the cumulative miseries of poverty, ignorance, and superstition, combined with the after effects of communistic orgies and natural calamities, and last but not least, the grave consequences of external aggression.

To this end, what is known as the New Life movement has been launched, to strike at the very roots of the several evils. . . .

FOUR ANCIENT VIRTUES

The idea of the New Life movement became crystallized in the mind of Generalissimo Chiang Kai-shek during the anti-communist campaign. He realized that military occupation of recovered territory was not enough; that it must be followed up by social and economic reconstruction in the divested areas; and that, to be effective, a national consciousness and spirit of mutual co-operation must be aroused. He saw that the immediate need was the development of the vitality of the spirit of the people, which seemed to have been crushed. He contemplated the perspective of history in the light of existing conditions about him; he realized how much depended upon the people's consciousness of their heritage from the past and conviction came to him that the four great virtues of old China, *Li, I, Lien*, and *Chih* constituted a remedy that could rescue the country from stagnation and ruin, because at the time when those principles were practiced, China was indeed a great nation. He decided then and there to base a New Life movement upon them, to try to recover what had been lost by forgetfulness of this source of China's greatness. For it has become obvious that mere accumulation of wealth is not sufficient to enable China to resume her position as a great nation. There must also be a revival of the spirit, since spiritual values transcend mere material riches.

What significance lies behind these four principles which hold so much good in them for China, if they can be carried out in the spirit intended?

First the *Li*, which in the ordinary and most accepted form of translation means courtesy. And by courtesy is meant that which emanates from the heart— not a formality which merely obeys the law.

The second is *I*, which, roughly translated, means duty or service, toward the individual's fellow men and toward himself.

The third is *Lien*, meaning a clear definition of the rights of the individual and of the degree in which those rights may be enforced without infringing upon those of others. In other words, honesty. A clear demarcation between what is public and what is private, what is yours and what is mine.

The fourth is *Chih*, which denotes high-mindedness and honor.

Some people have criticized the New Life movement on the ground that, since there is not sufficient food for everyone in the land, it is useless to talk about or seek spiritual regeneration. We reject the argument by pointing out the very evident fact that, if everyone from the highest official to the lowest wheel-barrow-man would conscientiously practice these principles in everyday life, there would be food for all. If we have the right conception of *Li*, we recognize not outward pomp but the sterling native qualities in our fellow men. If we practice *I*, we feel an obligation not to hold wealth and enjoy it wastefully while our fellow country-men may be on the verge of starvation or suffering from sickness or other misfortunes. Again with *Lien*: if officials recognize the rights of the people under them, they do not try to benefit themselves at the expense of the people just because the latter are too powerless and ignorant to fight in their own defense. And, if *Chih* is a reality, no one is shameless or stoops to mean or underhanded deeds.

Being a realist, the Generalissimo recognized that conditions in China are entirely different from what they were centuries ago when China was a great nation. At that time China could well afford to stand aloof, shut herself within the confines of her own boundaries, and keep out all intruders; but today she is part of a worldwide scheme of things, and, in order to maintain and improve her present position, she must keep in step with world progress.

So the New Life movement is based upon the preservation of these four virtues, and it aims to apply them to actual, existing conditions, in order that the moral character of the nation shall attain the highest possible standard. The Generalissimo observed that communism crushed the spirit of the people in addition to robbing them of material things; that it struck at all the fundamental principles of moral character. He found the people bereft of ideas or ideals concerning either humanity in general or their fellow men in particular. Communism was, indeed, the last abrasive in the destruction of a sense of law and order, unselfishness, loyalty, and those other qualities necessary for the development of human kindness and the maintenance of a high national consciousness. It tortured and degraded the status of man and dispossessed human life of value. In the face of this dismal prospect, the Generalissimo decided that the New Life movement could sow the first seeds of an effort to awaken in the people an urge for a more satisfying life.

THE MOVEMENT SPREADS

Not content with organizations specially delegated to these divested areas to work toward a better community life, the Generalissimo, before the end of the spring school season, called a meeting of all the middle-school students in Nanchang. He spoke at length to them of the conditions in the country at large and particularly in their own districts. He pointed out to them the necessity of recognizing the sacrifices their parents were making to give them educations and the fact that such sacrifices entailed a proportionate responsibility on the part of the students to repay the community for what they were receiving. . . .

As a direct result of this talk the students pledged themselves to return to their homes to take active part in giving a practical impetus to the principles of the New Life movement. Some pledged themselves to open up kindergartens for the village children; others, to teach night classes for the adults; others, to lecture on hygiene and sanitation; and still others, to make fly swatters and to rid their communities of breeding places of insects which carry malarial infections. The reports have just arrived, and these show that the students take their work seriously.

Out of all this is emerging a new citizen, a contented farmer and artisan, on the one hand, and, on the other, a teacher with new ideals, born of the contentment he is producing. The response of the people to the new movement on their behalf has been significant. Finding that those who have come so suddenly to work among them are working for them, they cooperate to the full and have complete confidence in their leaders. Progress is noticeable immediately. The neglect and filth which characterized the villages go quickly. Personal cleanliness is replacing erstwhile indifference to dirt and disease, and the villagers' participation in the many schemes for their good develops a feeling of happiness. Corruption is being fearlessly exposed when detected; soldiers have been shorn of domineering attitudes by strict punishment for proved offenses.

The New Life movement has already come within the reach of the humblest citizen and had much to contribute to the most enlightened. As it operates in Jiangxi, so it is spreading and flourishing all over the country. In the twelve provinces recently toured by the Generalissimo, noticeable advances were seen in the general cleanliness and orderliness of the cities as well as in the recovery of spirit by the people and in a new sense of responsibility in officials. They, in contradistinction to other days, are manifesting lively concern for the well-being of the people and contributing in every way possible to the effective application of the principles of the New Life movement.

In the large centers, the missionary bodies were assembled and were addressed by the Generalissimo and by myself. In every case they signified an immediate wish to work with the leaders of the movement in their respective regions, and joint committees were at once formed under the chairmanship of the Governor of the Province. While the government is enforcing stringent measures for opium suppression, these committees will do their part in establishing opium-curing clinics and teaching the people its evil effects. They will carry on campaigns against foot-binding, tuberculosis, trachoma, and other more local evils. . . .

In conclusion let me quote from a letter just received from one of the foreign missionaries, now in Jiangxi, on his reaction to the work sponsored there by the New Life movement:

> The suppression of the communist-bandits and the work of the New Life Movement are proving to be the first stage of a long battle against ignorance, dirt, carelessness, unsuitable dwellings, and the corruption that has for so long cost so much in human suffering. Like the program of Christ this movement is concerned with the poor, the oppressed, the sick, and the little children who have never been given a chance to enjoy life. Out of it will come a strong and united China, which will command the respect of the world, and that new China, like the very old one, will be based firmly upon the four cardinal virtues, with the addition of those desirable elements which go to make a modern world.

16.4 *"New Life" in Brief*

RULES FOR BEHAVIOR

Clothing should be tidy and clean.
Buttons should be well buttoned.
Hats should be worn straight.
Shoes should be worn correctly.
Food should be eaten in an orderly manner.
Sit upright.
Do not throw food on the ground.
Bowls and chopsticks should be set in order.
Do not make noise while eating and drinking.
Rooms should be kept clean.
Do not write on walls.
Furniture should be simple.
The home should be tranquil.
Walk and sit with erect posture.
Be punctual for appointments.
Speak after others have finished speaking.
Help your neighbor if a fire breaks out.
Do not laugh when others have funerals.
Try to mediate the quarrels of others.
Aid others who have fallen.

Keep silent in meetings or at the theater.
Do not scold, swear at, or hit others.
Do not laugh or talk loudly on boats or in buses.
Do not call out in restaurants or teahouses.
Be polite in conversation.
Keep to the left when walking on the street.
Do not overtake others while walking.
Stay in line at the station when buying tickets.
Stay in line when entering a public place.
Say good morning to others every morning.
Say goodbye when you leave your friends.
Do not gamble or visit prostitutes.
Do not smoke opium.
If you pick up something on the street, return it to its owner.
Be careful of public property and try to make use of scrap materials.
Salute the national flag when it is raised and brought down.
Stand while singing the Party song or the National anthem.
Salute your elders.
Be polite and courteous to women and children.
Help old people, women, and the weak in getting off boats and buses.
Be filial to your parents and love your brothers and sisters.
Take off your hat in meeting places.
Do not wear your hat indoors.
Be loyal to your friends.
Be fair in business transactions.
Reduce the number of meaningless parties or gatherings.
Be frugal at weddings, funerals, and on festive occasions.

HYGIENE

Go to bed early and rise early.
Keep your face clean.
Keep your hands clean.
Wash out your mouth and keep your hair clean.
Breathe fresh air.
Comb your hair.
Cut your nails frequently.
Clothes should be kept clean.
Holes in clothing should be patched.
Bedding should frequently be washed and dried outdoors.
Children should be kept clean.
Do not eat snacks.
Do not eat unclean food.
Do not drink unboiled water.

Do not get drunk.

Do not smoke.

Sweep and clean your rooms frequently.

Drain ditches and gutters frequently.

Keep windows open as often as possible.

Keep tables and chairs clean.

Keep bowls and chopsticks clean.

Keep bathrooms clean.

Exterminate flies.

Exterminate mosquitoes.

Exterminate rats.

Do not spit on the ground.

Do not urinate as you please.

Dump garbage in garbage cans.

Do not throw waste paper on the street.

Do not throw fruit peels on the street.

Do not hang your clothes and dry them on the street.

Do not post advertisements everywhere.

Get vaccinated.

Keep bus stations and docks clean.

Keep parks and theaters clean.

Restaurants, hotels, and tea houses should be clean.

Bath houses and barber shops should be clean.

Every household should clean the street in front of its door each day.

Everyone should keep himself clean all the time.

16.5 *"New Life" for the Reds*

VARIOUS PHASES OF NEW LIFE MOVEMENT

The New Life movement, the aim of which is the social regeneration of China, is within reach of the humblest citizen but it has contributed much towards the most enlightened. It is reconstruction through a widespread social movement that promises rapidly to remold the life of the entire Chinese people. Progress is achieved through discipline and order, rather than through violent revolution.

It is concerned with the materials out of which life is made and it further stresses the use that shall be made of these materials. In doing so, it emphasizes both the material and spiritual in life and desires a happy blending of the two. Respect for personality and a desire to prevent the exploitation of man by man—these are the factors that are at the heart of the movement.

In the province of Jiangxi, the heart of the movement, New Life has penetrated government offices, public utilities, schools, bus lines, wharves, railways, and even the army. It will first establish itself in the heart of the administration and gradually it will extend its influence to the people. Indeed, it has already made considerable headway towards influencing the masses.

On the trains and motor buses, and on the ferries, I found cleanliness and orderliness that one hardly expected to find in the heart of an interior province. Members of the staffs were extremely courteous and gave the passengers every assistance possible: indeed, they were comparable in their courtesy to the staffs of some of the best run trains in western countries. They were courteous not because they wanted to be "tipped" ("tipping" being a practice which is not encouraged) but because they had been influenced by the New Life movement. . . .

The train between Jiujiang and Nanchang is, as a result of the operation of the New Life movement, probably the best train in the whole of China. It always keeps to time, except, of course, in case of accidents. It starts punctually on time and its third class carriages and conveniences are as scrupulously clean as the first-class. It is a train run for the benefit of the people, as a whole, not for the privileged classes alone. . . .

REFORM PROGRAM FOR CONVERTED REDS

Many have heard of what the Generalissimo and Madame Chiang Kai-shek are doing and have been doing for the past two years towards bringing about the reformation of Communists who have surrendered but few actually know the lines on which this program is being carried out as those in charge of the "repentance" camps which have been established at Jiujiang have been reluctant to discuss their activities with outsiders, much less with members of the press. Hence, nothing has appeared in print concerning this aspect of the Generalissimo's fine work.

In the Red camp, the inhabitants and soldiers are given to believe that, should they escape from the Communist areas and flee to Government territory, they will immediately be slaughtered for aiding the Soviets. Nothing could be further from the truth, as inmates of the repentance camps will tell you. As a matter of fact, the contrary is the case.

Those who have fled into Government territory have been agreeably surprised to find that they are received with open arms, like the Prodigal Son of the Biblical tale.

As soon as they surrender, they are at once taken to the repentance camps. Here they are informed that the Government has pardoned them for their former "faults" and they are given small rewards for surrendering their arms, if they possess any.

In these camps, they are taught the error of their former ways and emphasis is placed on the fact that the Communist doctrine is one which is not suitable for China and the Chinese people. They are taught a way of earning a livelihood and, at the end of their term, they may elect either to return to their native homes or remain in the service of the Government. Not a few choose the latter alternative and they are now bitter enemies (to use their own words) of Communism and devoted followers of the Generalissimo. They are taught to see things in a new light and their policy of "first realize your own faults, then try to teach others to realize theirs. Love others as yourselves," is one which they are attempting to put into practice.

REPENTANCE CAMPS

Here in these repentance camps, they are given an elementary education, a factor which apparently was omitted from the Soviet "equality" program and they are taught to become good citizens in every sense of the word.

The repentance camps, well arranged and well equipped, luxurious from a Red viewpoint, have been established in the barracks of the huge military field at Jiujiang. All of the buildings are built on western lines and contain many commodious class-rooms, sanitary bed-rooms and bath-rooms. Emphasis is placed on the word sanitation and not a thing has been left undone to ensure that absolutely clean conditions prevail. In addition to the rooms mentioned, there are rooms for laundry work, hair-dressing saloons, clinics and a hospital, a number of recreation halls (for games, such as ping-pong, etc.), a gymnasium, several libraries and a cinema hall. In addition, the huge drill ground in front is utilized for football, basketball, volley-ball and other outdoor games, as well as Chinese boxing and calisthenics.

Clean and wholesome food is provided for all inmates. True, this is not elaborate but it is thoroughly appetizing and most palatable. The old rags worn in the Communist districts have been discarded and the inmates appear distinctive in neat uniforms presented by the Generalissimo himself.

INTELLECTUAL IMPROVEMENT

The living quarters are very good indeed and those visiting the camps consider that they look like superior Chinese village hotels, with the exception that conditions are much cleaner. Each inmate is provided with a bed, matting, pillows, and blankets. In addition, they are supplied with towels, soap, socks and shoes, things which, they say, are seldom to be seen in the Communist territories.

Along the lines of education, the inmates are, as already mentioned, given elementary lessons with books provided by the Special Educational movement of Jiangxi under Mr. Zheng Shigui, and lectures are given on the New Life Movement and other worthy subjects, capable of transforming the erstwhile Red men and women into useful citizens of China. Debates and discussions on useful subjects are held regularly in which all are expected to take part. Prizes are offered at regular intervals for the best literary efforts and everything is done to improve these talents and to improve the intellects of those in the camps.

University students led the way raising high a huge banner and flags that read: "Oppose the Hebei-Chahar Political Council!,"[2] "Down with all Chinese traitors!," "Down with Japanese imperialism." All of the other schools followed in order and waved the banners that remained after the attacks of the police. On the flanks were each school's student marshals and the bicycle communication teams. As they marched, the students cried out: "Down with Chinese traitors!," "Oppose all false organizations!," "Down with Japanese imperialism!," "Expand the national revolutionary war!" They also passed out leaflets and pasted slogans on electrical poles.

When the marchers arrived at Qianmen (the Zhengyang Gate), they found that the police had shut one of the huge doors of the gate (the other door was broken and could not be shut). The Special Service Police brandished the sabres they had used at the battle of Xifengkou[3] and dashed in among the marchers as though they were confronting a strong enemy with whom they had decided to fight to the death. When the students arrived here the police suddenly fired dozens of shots and as the crowd looked for cover the rear portion of the march unit was thrown into chaos. The police continued to fire shots and all of the shopkeepers along the street began to close up their shops and pedestrians ran wildly in all directions. In the melee three rickshaws were overturned and crushed. The marchers then turned back and went into the empty square in front of the Pinghan Railroad Station. Many of the students were now badly hurt and the two sides were locked in a tense face-off for a long time. Gradually, however, things began to quiet down. Then the students began to negotiate informally with the police. The students said to the policemen: "You are Chinese, why are you helping people to beat up other Chinese? We are not your enemy." A small number of police showed some sympathy but the face-off was maintained.

In the meantime, on Qianmen Avenue a crowd of about ten thousand people had gathered. Everyone wanted to know the reason for the shooting. Everywhere the students had put up posters and slogans, scores of people gathered around to read them in order to understand what was going on. After Qianmen was sealed off, many pedestrians were not permitted to pass through it and so gradually about two hundred people gathered before the gate. They raised a great clamor and opposed the police's opening fire on the students. Some police went over to hold them in check and the crowd roared: "Beat them! Beat the running dogs!" Because there were only a few police, they felt scared and scuttled back to their lines. More police were sent and they used clubs and their belts to disperse the masses.

2. Sponsored by Nanjing and set up in Peking in December 1935 to counter the Japanese "autonomist" organization in East Hebei.

3. A battle between Song Zheyuan's Chinese army and the Japanese outside the Great Wall. Song (1885–1940) was a former subordinate of Feng Yuxiang who, by mid-1930, served the Nanjing government. On July 7, 1937, Song's troops clashed with the Japanese near the Marco Polo Bridge, which led to the outbreak of large-scale fighting in China.

It was already three o'clock in the afternoon. Student representatives began negotiating with the police. The police insisted that they would not permit all of the students to pass through the Zhengyang Gate. Early that morning many policemen had been posted to guard the Hebei-Chahar Political Council Building but they were still afraid that the students would attempt to destroy it. The police then permitted the students to divide themselves into three groups; a small group could enter the city through the Zhengyang Gate while the majority would enter through the Shunzhi Gate (the West Gate). The remaining students would wait where they were until the other two groups dispersed and then a decision would be made about them. Moreover, they were not permitted to circulate leaflets.

As the students were negotiating with the police, they declared the opening of a student congress and elected a chairman on the spot. They used three bicycles to form an impromptu speaker's platform and student marshals protected it on all sides. They passed the following eight resolutions: (1) "Autonomy" or any political "autonomist" organization[4] is not in accord with the will of the people; (2) The government must apologize to and compensate students who were wounded and beaten, or stabbed; (3) The government must refuse Japan's political and economic demands; (4) Telegrams should be sent to students of the entire nation asking them to go on strike immediately and stay on strike until the government meets student demands; (5) Oppose the government's recognition of the Three Principles of Hirota;[5] (6) Demand that the government immediately halt the civil war and abolish the Hebei-Chahar Political Council; (7) Expand the people's revolutionary war; (8) Swear to fight to the death for absolute freedom to be a patriot.

After the meeting, the chairman and student leaders led the crowd in shouting slogans. When the gathering dispersed, one group of five or six hundred students from Peking University, Zhicheng Middle School, and other schools passed through Qianmen Gate and entered the city. They passed Rongxian *hutong* [narrow alleys] and as they walked they shouted slogans and passed out leaflets. After one more attack by the police, they arrived at Shunzhi Gate. The students' original intention was to join forces with other students who were to enter the city through the Shunzhi Gate but when they arrived at the gate it was still closed. It was already four o'clock and soon the more than two thousand students who were marching

---

4. The formation of a Japanese-sponsored "autonomist" organization in north China and Inner Mongolia was seen by Peking students as an attempt by Tokyo to gain further control of north China through pulling Hebei, Chabar, Suiyuan, and Shandong into the Eastern Hebei Autonomous Council, organized in the winter of 1935.

5. Hirota Koki (1878–1948), foreign minister of Japan in 1934. He proposed three principles (the so-called *sangensoku*) for Manchuria and north China in October 1935, including the formation of a Japan-China-Manchukuo block, the quelling of anti-Japanese activities in China, and the formation of a Sino-Japanese front to combat communism.

here from the Pinghan Railroad Station arrived. The sound of slogans shouted from inside and without the city walls echoed and re-echoed.[6]

The one thousand or so students who were outside Qianmen, insisting that they would certainly be tricked, refused to be led into the city by the police. They returned, instead, to Tianqiao and continued their speeches for about half an hour before they were again stopped by the police. They then turned about and walked to the outer side of Shunzhi Gate and joined forces with the other students already there. At five o'clock, the police and city firemen rushed up and again used sabres and bayonets to slash at the students and, finally, to force them to disperse. Three wounded girl students were all junior students from the Second Girl's Middle School. . . . There were many male students whose clothing was slashed to ribbons and who had been cut on the arms or head. They were all taken to Shoushan Hospital and Peking Union Hospital. The majority of the wounded students, however, simply returned home.

The students outside the Shunzhi Gate, feeling terribly cold and hungry, waited until eight o'clock or so but the authorities still refused to open the gate. The students from Yanjing University and Jingde Middle School then left the city through Xibian Gate. (But according to a report from the Yanjing University student union, only a few of these students had returned by the morning of the seventeenth. . . . According to students who telephoned from the city, a large number were wounded and still trapped inside the city.) . . .

Students from Yanyi Middle School and the middle school affiliated with Peking Normal University and local residents formed various relief teams to send water, rolls, and steamed buns to the hungry students [gathered at the city gate]. At nine thirty it was decided that they would go to the Normal University and spend the night there. The chill wind cut at them like a knife and the police watched them attentively. The students continued to behave as they had before and some new students, hearing of all of this, came to join them. When their march passed the Chunming Girls Middle School, the police again swept the student ranks with fire hoses and swarmed out with sabres and clubs from all directions to attack them. The students were already so tired and hungry they seemed about to topple over and many of them simply fell to the ground. It was already the middle of the night; there were very few passersby and the police beat them even more brutally than they had during the day. Pounding them with frenzied blows, the police pursued them in all directions and innumerable students were wounded. This finally halted at about ten o'clock. When the Peking Union Hospital heard of this, they immediately sent four ambulances to the rescue. They were halted, however, and constrained to return. According to reports on the sev-

6. The activity described here took place on the edge of the "Tartar City." The Shunzhi Gate was one of the gates of the city wall southwest of Tiananmen (the Gate of Heavenly Peace). The Pinghan Railroad Station was the terminus of the Peking-Hankow railroad line.

enteenth, thirteen students were carried to Union Hospital but there were no clear reports from other hospitals. It is impossible to calculate how many students were arrested.

16.7 AND 16.8 MUTINY IN XI'AN, 1936

After the survivors of the Long March reached Shaanxi in October 1935, Chiang Kai-shek continued his quest to eliminate his Communist rivals. The only troops loyal to the Guomindang stationed in the northwest region were soldiers under the command of Young Marshal Zhang Xueliang and General Yang Hucheng. The Manchurian soldiers of Zhang's army, who had been forced out of their homeland by the Japanese in 1931 and 1932, were particularly reluctant to participate in Chiang's "bandit extermination" campaign, and advocated forming a new united front with the Communists to fight Japanese encroachment.

Concerned about the army's will to fight, Chiang Kai-shek flew to Xi'an in early December 1936 to supervise Generals Zhang and Yang as they launched a new offensive against the Communists. On December 12, a mutiny broke out and Chiang was placed under house arrest. The first document selected here, a telegram sent to the nation by Zhang Xueliang and Yang Hucheng immediately after Chiang's arrest, articulates the professed patriotic motives and demands of the mutinous generals. The second document is an excerpted passage from Chiang's admonition of Zhang and Yang, issued after his sudden release on Christmas Day 1936.

16.7 *Zhang Xueliang and Yang Hucheng's Eight-Point Program*

It is now over five years since Japan occupied China. National sovereignty has been infringed upon, and more and more of our territory lost to the enemy. The humiliating Shanghai Armistice Agreement of early 1932 was followed by the signing of the Tang'gu and He-Umezu Agreements.[7] All our fellow countrymen feel distressed at these events. Recently, a great change has taken place in the international situation with some forces working hand in glove to make a sacrifice of our country and people. The start of fighting in east Suiyuan has thrown

---

7. The Tang'gu Truce of May 1933 and the He-Umezu Agreement of June 1935 removed Nationalist armies from Hebei.

the whole country into a ferment and the morale of our troops has never been so high.

At this very moment, the central authorities should do their utmost to encourage the army and people to launch nationwide resistance against Japan. But while our officers and men are engaged in bloody fighting against the enemy at the front, our diplomats have been doing their best to reach a compromise with alien invaders. The imprisonment of the Shanghai patriots has shocked the whole world besides paining the entire Chinese nation. It distresses everyone to see patriots treated as criminals. Generalissimo Chiang, misled by mean officials and divorced from the masses of people, has made our nation suffer greatly. We—Zhang Xueliang and Yang Hucheng—have repeatedly offered him our earnest remonstrances, only to be harshly reproached. When the students in Xi'an demonstrated for national salvation, police were ordered to open fire at these patriotic youths. Anyone with a conscience could not have let things go so far! Having for long years been colleagues of the Generalissimo, we could hardly sit by idly. So we offered him our last remonstrance for the sake of his personal safety and in order to stimulate his awakening.

Now the army and people in northwest China unanimously demand:

1. Reorganize the Nanjing government to admit representatives of all parties and groups to jointly share the responsibility of saving the nation;
2. End all civil war;
3. Immediately release all the imprisoned leaders of the patriotic movement in Shanghai;
4. Release all political prisoners in the country;
5. Give a free hand to the patriotic mass movement;
6. Safeguard the political freedom of the people, including the freedom of assembly;
7. Earnestly carry out Dr. Sun Yat-sen's Will; and
8. Immediately convene a conference on national salvation.

The above eight points are what we and the army and people in the northwest stand for with respect to national salvation. It is hoped that all of you, in compliance with public opinion, will endorse the aforesaid in true earnest so that there will be a ray of hope for the nation, and past wrongs will be righted. For the sake of this our just cause, we feel duty-bound to act, our sole purpose being the thorough implementation of the program of national salvation which, we believe, will benefit our nation. As for ourselves, we leave it to our compatriots to judge whether our act is a merit or crime.

Anxiously we look forward to your response.
Zhang Xueliang
Yang Hucheng

16.8 *Chiang Kai-shek's Admonition to Zhang Xueliang and Yang Hucheng*

This coup d'état is an act which gravely affects both the continuity of Chinese history of five thousand years and the life and death of the Chinese nation, and it is a criterion whereby the character of the Chinese race may be judged. Since today you have shown due regard for the welfare of the nation and have decided to send me back to Nanjing and no longer try to make any special demands or force me to make any promise or give any orders, it marks a turning point in the life of the nation and is also an indication of the high moral and cultural standard of the Chinese people.

It is an ancient Chinese saying that a gentleman should correct his mistakes as soon as he realizes them. The present outcome of the coup d'état shows that you are both ready to correct your own mistakes, and that is creditable to you as well as auguring a bright future for the Chinese race. Since you are now so convinced by my sincerity towards you that you have the courage to acknowledge your wrongdoing you are entitled to remain as my subordinates. Furthermore, since you can be so readily converted it will certainly be easier for your subordinates to follow suit.

Formerly you were deceived by reactionaries and believed that I did not treat the people fairly and squarely and that I was not loyal to our revolutionary ideals. But now you have read my private diary for this whole year, the public and private telegrams and documents numbering some fifty thousand words that have passed through my hands during the past two months as well as my plans for the salvation of the nation and those relating to internal administration, foreign affairs, military finance and education, numbering some one hundred thousand words, you must now know that there is not a single word which could condemn me of any self-interest or insincerity on my part.

In fact since I took military command and began to take charge of military training there are two principles which I have always emphasized to my students and subordinates, namely:

(1) That if I have any selfish motives or do anything against the welfare of the country and the people, then anybody may consider me a traitor and may shoot me on that account.
(2) If my words and deeds are in the least insincere and I neglect the principles and revolutionary ideals, my soldiers may treat me as their enemy and may also shoot me.

From my diary and the other documents you can see whether you can find one word which is to the detriment of the revolution. If you can find one such word here I am still in Xi'an and you are at liberty to condemn and kill me. On my part

I am glad that I have always done what I have taught other people to do, namely, to be sincere and disinterested, and I can say in all confidence that I have done nothing of which I need be ashamed.

The responsibility of this coup d'état naturally rests with you two, but I consider myself also responsible for the causes which led up to the crisis. I have always worked for the country and always believed that my sincerity and teaching would reach all my subordinates. Hence I have not paid any attention to my personal safety. I have taken no precautions on that account and have therefore tempted the reactionaries to take advantage of the situation. Everything has its remote causes. My own carelessness was the remote cause of this coup d'état and gave rise to this breakdown of discipline, causing the Central government as well as the people much worry and the nation much loss. On this account I feel I am to be blamed and must apologize to the nation, the party and the people.

A country must have law and discipline. You two are military officers in command of troops, and when such a coup d'état has taken place you should submit to the judgment of the Central government. However, I recognize that you were deceived by propaganda of reactionaries and misjudged my good intentions to be bad ones. Fortunately immediately after the coup you realized that it was harmful to the country and expressed your deep remorse to me. Now you have further realized your own mistake in listening to reactionaries and are now convinced that not only have I had no bad intentions towards you, but that I have always had every consideration for you.

I have always told my subordinates that when they make mistakes their superiors must also be blamed for not having given them adequate training. As I am in supreme command of the army, your fault is also my fault, and I must ask for punishment by the Central Authorities. At the same time I will explain to them that you sincerely regret what you have done. As you have rectified your mistake at an early stage, the crisis has not been prolonged, and I believe the Central Authorities should be able to be lenient with you. . . .

The policy of the Central government for the last few years has been to achieve peace in and unification of the country and to increase the strength of the nation. Nothing should be done to impair this strength. During the present crisis, as you engineered the coup, you are responsible for bringing about warfare in the country. But as you have expressed remorse, I shall recommend the Central government to settle the matter in a way that will not be prejudicial to the interests of the nation.

In short you now know the situation of our country as well as my determination to save it. I always give first thought to the life and death of the nation as well as the success or failure of the revolution and do not pay any attention to personal favours or grudges. Questions of personal danger or loss are of no interest to me. I have had the benefit of receiving personal instruction from Dr. Sun concerning broad-mindedness, benevolence and sincerity, and am not vindictive with regard to things that have passed. As you felt remorse very early, it shows that you know that the welfare of the nation is above everything else. That being the case, you ought to obey unreservedly the orders of the Central government and carry out whatever decisions it may make. This is the way to save the nation from the dangers it is facing, and this is the way to turn a national calamity into a national blessing.

campaign to stir up hate against Japan be discontinued and that the Central Government renounce the union with Communism which was solemnized at Xi'an, in Shaanxi Province, when General Chiang Kai-shek was released from imprisonment last Christmas Day.

Premier Konoye, Foreign Minister Hirota and War Minister Sugiyama have all stated that Japan is not bent on conquest and has no desire to detach or annex any part of China. What our government and people want is peace and security in the Far East. If only in our own selfish interests we seek the welfare of the colossal nation beside which we must continue to live for all time.

In a number of North China cities temporarily local governments have grown up to replace the military administrations which have disappeared with the retreating Chinese armies. These "Peace Preservation Committees," formed by local Chinese leaders, are successfully maintaining civil order. But they have been given to understand that Japan will not support them in any move to secede from the rest of China. Indeed, the commanders of the Japanese garrisons not only permitted but encouraged the people of North China to celebrate what the Chinese call the "Double-Tenth" holiday on October 10, the anniversary of the founding of the Chinese Republic. This is evidence of our intentions. . . .

With China's millions Japan has no quarrel—nor have those millions anything to fear from Japan. In fact, even at this moment several thousand Chinese students are attending Japanese schools and tens of thousands of Chinese businessmen are conducting their trades as usual in Japan. At no time since the present trouble began has there been a single case of violence against any Chinese living in Japan.

VII

The underlying accord of our peoples prompts in me high hope that when the leaders of the Nanjing regime and the Chinese Nationalist Party adopt a reasonable policy toward Japan, it will not take long to spin close ties of friendship and harmony of incalculable benefit to both China and Japan, and of much also to the rest of the world. With permanent peace between Japan and China, progress will be made in East of Asia that will redound to the benefit of others in a spread of the feeling of security and an expansion of general and profitable trade and cultural relations. The progress of Japan has brought an enormous increase of trade to Western Countries, particularly the United States, and the peace of China cannot fail to bring progress to the industrious and well-meaning masses of her people.

17.3 CHIANG REPLIES, 1938

By the end of 1938, the Japanese army controlled the eastern half of China, having pressed the Chinese Nationalists into the interior. The occupation authorities actively encouraged the Chinese to collaborate with the new regime, articulating a grandiose vision of a "Greater East Asia Co-Prosperity Sphere." Accusing the Guomindang government of being not only anti-Japanese but also pro-Communist, the Japanese hoped to strengthen support for the war at home, and deflect the hostile public opinion of the West.

In response to Japan's call for Chinese collaboration, Chiang Kai-shek reiterated that he would fight to the end. In this address, given before a meeting of the Central Guomindang Headquarters in Chongqing on December 26, 1938, Chiang sought to expose Japan's design of subjugating China and dominating East Asia. Specifically, he assails a statement made by Prince Konoe (Konoye) on December 22, 1938, which Chiang believed illuminated Japan's true intentions.

GENERALISSIMO CHIANG ASSAILS PRINCE KONOYE'S STATEMENT

Comrades, our resistance has now entered a new phase. I have recently pointed out on several occasions that the past eighteen months may be called the first period of our resistance of the preliminary period. We have now entered upon the second or latter period. At present, on both northern and southern warfronts the excellence of our soldiers' morale and fighting spirit provides an auspicious sign unprecedented since the war commenced. Our soldiers are fully aware that in this war our enemy is bent on subjugating China completely and that we must take the most drastic measures to save our country. Their determination is, therefore, extraordinarily strong and their spirit roused to the uttermost.

Our people also understand that the enemy will not pause until he has fully realized his malevolent designs and the ultimate aim of his aggression in the destruction of China. If we do not seek life by braving death we cannot expect to survive in any fortuitous way. . . .

Konoye's statement is intrinsically nothing more than sheer wearisome repetition of canting phrases. Solemnly engaged in our resistance as we are, it would seem unnecessary for us to pay any attention to it, let alone refute it. Considering it, however, together with the enemy's deeds and words of the past months, we perceive that the statement, though superficially vague and incoherent, has a keen edge hidden beneath. It might be called, in short, a complete exposure of the fantastic Japanese programme to annex China, dominate East Asia and further even to subdue the world. It is also a complete revelation of the contents of the enemy. . . .

What I wish to draw the attention of all to is the barbarism of the Japanese militarists, their insanity, their practice of deceiving themselves and others, and their gross ignorance. What is most urgent is that all should realize that Japan is determined to swallow China entirely. Taking Konoye's statement on December 22 as the pivot for my observations, I shall now recall what Japanese popular sentiment has championed during the past few months and what cabals and slogans have been actually put into practice. By analysis, a comprehensive understanding may be gained. For convenience of narration I shall first draw attention to the following four points:—

(1) THE SO-CALLED "CREATION OF A NEW ORDER IN EAST ASIA!"

The Japanese take special pride in this slogan. According to the Japanese Foreign Minister, Arita, in his explanation of December 19: "The new order in East Asia consists in Japan, Manchukuo and China assisting and cooperating with each other closely in politics, economics and culture to combat the Red Peril, to protect Oriental civilization, to remove economic barriers, and to help China rise from her semi-colonial status so as to secure peace in the Far East." On December 14, Konoye also said: "The ultimate objective of the China Incident lies not merely in achieving military triumph but in a rebirth of China and the erection of a new order in East Asia. This new order will be based on tripartite cooperation of a new China with Japan and Manchukuo."

Let all observe that what he meant by a China reborn was that independent China was to perish and in its place an enslaved China created, which would abide by Japan's word from generation to generation. The so-called new order would be based on the intimate relations that would tie the enslaved China to the Japanese-created Manchukuo and Japan herself. What is the real aim? Under the pretext of opposition to the "Red Peril," Japan seeks to control China's military affairs; claiming to uphold Oriental civilization, Japan seeks to uproot China's racial culture; and by urging the elimination of economic barriers, she aspires to exclude American and European influence and dominate the Pacific. Again, the so-called "economic unity" of Japan, Manchukuo and China is the instrument she intends to use for obtaining a stranglehold on China's economic arteries. Let us try to realize the immense evils with which the words "creation of a new order in East Asia" are pregnant. In a word, it is a term for the overthrow of international order in East Asia, and the enslavement of China as the means whereby Japan may dominate the Pacific and proceed to dismember other states of the world.

(2) THE SO-CALLED "UNITY OF EAST ASIA,"
"INDIVISIBILITY OF JAPAN, MANCHUKUO AND CHINA,"
"LINKED RELATIONS OF MUTUAL ASSISTANCE BETWEEN
JAPAN, MANCHUKUO AND CHINA."

To make a "homogeneous body" of East Asia has been a much-touted Japanese slogan during the past few months. The application of this slogan is broader, vaguer and more general than that of the so-called "economic unity" or "economic bloc."

Advancing the theme of an "indivisibility of Japan, Manchukuo and China," the Japanese aim to absorb China politically, economically and culturally into one body with their own country. Japanese periodicals have maintained that the structural relationship of the "East Asia unity" should be vertical with Japan at the summit, and not in any sense horizontal; the system of relationship should be patriarchal, with Japan as patriarch and Manchukuo and China as offspring. In other words, the former is to be the governor and master while the latter are to be the governed and underlings.

What is it if it is not annexation? What is it if it is not the total extinction of China? Konoye's phrase, "the establishment of linked relations of mutual assistance in matters political, economic and cultural between Japan, Manchukuo and China," puts me in mind only of links and manacles and shackles. His "linked relations" would be the forged chains which would drag us down into a pit from which we would never escape.

(3) THE SO-CALLED "ECONOMIC UNITY" AND "ECONOMIC BLOC."

This has been promoted for many years by the Japanese, and the thesis has recently been as prevalent as ever and has even made rapid headway. It is essential to the proposed "homogeneity of East Asia." They have rung many changes on the wording of the slogan: they have called it on occasion "economic reciprocity" and "economic co-operation." In the manifesto of the Japanese Government issued on November 3, it was described as "economic union." In the latter part of November enemy newspapers printed the headline "Japan, Manchukuo and China are to form an economic unity and henceforth share a common fate." Subsequently Arita in his statement of December 19 said: "Japan has resolved to convene an economic conference to bring about an intimate economic confederation between Japan, Manchukuo and China and to invigorate the resulting economic monad."

Japan has, in fact, already installed such instruments of economic aggression as the "North China Development Company" and the "Central China Development Company." Economic conversations have already been held more than once by self-styled representatives of Manchukuo and China with those of Japan. What the Japanese call their "Planning Bureau" adopted, two days after Konoye's statement was made, a resolution urging "the expansion of the productive capacity of Japan, Manchukuo and China." The "economic bloc" is designed to be the means of not only taking control over our customs revenue and finance and of monopolizing our production and trade, but also of gradually limiting the individual freedom of our people even in regard to what they eat and wear, where they live and whither they move. The Japanese are to do as they please: to have power among us over life and death, the power of binding and losing; we are then to become their slaves and cattle, and the whole of our nation will thus be dissolved beneath the lash of tyranny.

(4) THE CREATION OF THE SO-CALLED "ASIATIC DEVELOPMENT BUREAU."

This organ was introduced after much agitation for a medium through which to deal with China. A "China Bureau" was once projected, which has now given way to this "Asia Development Bureau." The former term is insulting and dreaded enough, but the comprehensiveness of the latter is a flagrant insult to all the peoples of Asia. Japan is set not only on ruining and dismembering China alone, but her ambition embraces the entire Asiatic Continent.

On the day before the official inauguration of this "Asia Development Bureau" on December 15, Konoye stated that "a new executive organ should be constituted for creating a new order in East Asia: this organ in conjunction with other organs abroad will maintain coherent relations between Japan and China: it will become the key to executing our China policy, the fulfillment of which is our final object in regard to the China Incident." This should serve to acquaint all with the true function of the organ: to be the means of executing a policy designed to destroy China. For it may be described as Japan's highest special service organ combining all the special service branches long set up all over China for the working of all manner of villainy, which formerly operated with the greatest stealth because it was regarded premature to work openly. Now, however, they boldly unmask themselves and are accorded official status. By establishment of the "Asia Development Bureau" a concentrated light is thrown upon the means and ends of Japanese policy; the tortuous and obscure devices pursued for years are seen with their supreme aim openly confessed. All concealment is at an end. . . .

On our part, the war for a year and a half has laid for us a solid foundation for national regeneration. We fear no problems, nor are we concerned over impending dangers. We merely lament the fate of Japan, the present status of which was brought about by the hard efforts and sacrifices of her reformist patriots. Today, her people are powerless, her throne without prerogative, and her politicians without integrity and knowledge, thus allowing a few hot-headed young militarists to do as they please. They are sapping Japan's national strength, shaking her national foundations and advancing savagely on the infamous road of self-seeking at the expense of others. In the eyes of these young Japanese militarists, China does not exist, nor do the other countries of the world. They have regard neither for discipline, nor for law, nor yet for their own government. Guided by their greed, cruelty and violence, they do as they please. If such conduct be allowed to continue, the future of Japan is indeed full of danger. Although we are sworn enemies of the Japanese militarists, yet we are still neighbors to the Japanese people, who share with us a language of a common origin. Reviewing Japan's history and looking forward to her future, we not only see danger in her path but lament her lot. . . .

China as a state is founded on the principles not to oppress the undefended, nor fear the aggressive. More particularly, she is not willing to violate pacts or break faith and thus destroy the righteous principles governing the relations of mankind. I remember the meeting of Tanaka and our late Tsungli (Dr. Sun Yat-sen) in Shanghai in the third year of the Republic which coincided with the outbreak of the Great War in Europe. Tanaka proposed that East Asiatics should at the time denounce all rationed relations with foreign countries and erect a new order in East Asia. Dr. Sun queried: "Would it not involve the breaking of international treaties?" To which Tanaka retorted: "Is not the denunciation of treaties and termination of unequal obligations advantageous to China?" "Unequal treaties should be terminated by straightforward and legitimate procedure," solemnly declared Dr. Sun, "and China is not prepared to become a party to the illegal denunciation of treaties even though advantageous to our country." Comrades, such is China's spirit. It is also the spirit of the Three People's Principles. We have relied on this spirit to resist invasion; we have depended on this spirit to resist all forms of domination, force and violence. We should be sustained by this spirit to restore order in East Asia and offer it as a contribution towards enduring world peace. . . .

A Chinese proverb says: "Virtue never lacks company; it will ever find support." The force of world justice will rise, and men of goodwill ultimately cooperate in the interests of rectitude. On our part, we should hold fast to our goal, and be firm in our determination. Our firmness should increase with greater difficulties, and our courage should rise with prolonged resistance. The entire nation should carry on with oneness of heart. The final victory will be ours. I urge my comrades, our army and our people to redouble their efforts in order to attain success.

17.4 AND 17.5 THE RAPE OF NANJING

On December 13, 1937, one month after the Japanese army had taken Shanghai, the first elements of General Iwane Matsui's attacking forces entered Nanjing. A few days before, in a message calling upon the Chinese garrison commander of the Nationalist capital to surrender, Matsui had declared: "Though harsh and relentless to those who resist, the Japanese troops are kind and generous to noncombatants and to Chinese troops who entertain no enmity to Japan." In reality, the officers and men of the Imperial Army were to show neither kindness nor generosity to the helpless citizens of Nanjing. The capture of the city was the prelude for a month-long reign of terror. During this time, unarmed Chinese prisoners of war were used as targets for bayonet and rifle practice; drunken mobs of Japanese infantry roamed the streets looting, murdering, and raping; and large parts of Nanjing were burned to the ground by deliberately set fires. By the time martial law was finally imposed by the Japanese command, the streets of Nanjing were in ruins, and its prewar population of nearly one million had been reduced to fewer than two hundred thousand.

The following letter from an anonymous foreign resident of Nanjing, and excerpts of a diary kept by the same author during the grim days of December 1937, were reprinted in a volume on the "Rape of Nanjing" compiled by H. J. Timperley, China correspondent for the *Manchester Guardian*. They provided foreign readers with an eyewitness account describing violence that was at once random and deliberate.

In an appendix, Timperley also reprinted copies of two short articles published respectively on December 7 and 14, 1937, by the *Japan Advertiser*, an English daily printed in Tokyo, that described the competition between two young Japanese officers to kill Chinese.

17.4 *Bearing Witness*

On Tuesday the 14th [December 1937] the Japanese were pouring into the city— tanks, artillery, infantry, trucks. The reign of terror commenced, and it was to increase in severity and horror with each of the succeeding ten days. They were the conquerors of China's capital, the seat of the hated Chiang Kai-shek government, and they were given free rein to do as they pleased. The proclamation on the handbills which airplanes scattered over the city saying that the Japanese were the only real friends of the Chinese and would protect the good, of course meant no more than most of their statements. And to show their "sincerity" they raped, looted and killed at will. Men were taken from our refugee camps in droves, as we supposed at the time for labor—but they have never been heard from again, nor will they be. A colonel and his staff called at my office and spent an hour trying to learn where the "six thousand disarmed soldiers" were. Four times that day Japanese soldiers came and tried to take our cars away. Others in the meantime succeeded in stealing three of our cars that were elsewhere. On Sone's[1] they tore off the American flag, and threw it on the ground, broke a window and managed to get away all within the five minutes he had gone into Prof. Stanley's[2] house. They tried to steal our trucks—did succeed in getting two—so ever since it has been necessary for two Americans to spend most of their time riding trucks as they delivered rice and coal. Their experience in dealing daily with these Japanese car thieves would make an interesting story in itself. And at the University Hospital they took the watches and fountain pens from the nurses. . . .

At our staff conference that evening word came that soldiers were taking all 1,300 men in one of our camps near headquarters to shoot them. We knew there were a number of ex-soldiers among them, but Rabe[3] had been promised by an

1. Reverend Hubert L. Sone, American, Nanjing Theological Seminary.
2. Professor C. Stanley, American, Nanjing Theological Seminary.
3. Hans Rabe was a German businessman who tried to protect Chinese civilians in Nanjing. He left an illuminating diary which describes the sacking of the city.

officer that very afternoon that their lives would be spared. It was now all too obvious what they were going to do. The men were lined up and roped together in groups of about a hundred by soldiers and bayonets fixed; those who had hats had them roughly torn off and thrown on the ground—and then by the light of our headlights we watched them marched away to their doom. Not a whimper came from the entire throng. Our own hearts were lead. Were those four lads from Canton who had trudged all the way up from the south and yesterday had reluctantly given me their arms among them, I wondered; or that tall, strapping sergeant from the north whose disillusioned eyes, as he made the fatal decision, still haunt me? How foolish I had been to tell them the Japanese would spare their lives! We had confidently expected that they would live up to their promises, at least in some degree, and that order would be established with their arrival. Little did we dream that we should see such brutality and savagery as has probably not been equalled in modern times. For worse days were yet to come.

The problem of transportation became acute on the sixteenth, with the Japanese stealing our trucks and cars. I went over to the American Embassy where the Chinese staff were still standing by, and borrowed Mr. Atcheson's car for Mills[4] to deliver coal. For our big concentrations of refugees and our three big rice kitchens had to have fuel as well as rice. We now had twenty-five camps, ranging from two hundred to twelve thousand people in them. In the University buildings alone there were nearly thirty thousand and in Ginling College, which was reserved for women and children, the three thousand were rapidly increased to over nine thousand. In the latter place even the covered passageways between buildings were crowded, while within every foot of space was taken. We had figured on sixteen square feet to a person, but actually they were crowded in much closer than that. For while no place was safe, we did manage to preserve a fair degree of safety at Ginling, to a lesser degree in the University. Miss Vautrin,[5] Mrs. Twinem[6] and Mrs. Chen[7] were heroic in their care and protection of the women.

That morning the cases of rape began to be reported. Over a hundred women that we knew of were taken away by soldiers, seven of them from the University library; but there must have been many times that number who were raped in their homes. Hundreds were on the streets trying to find a place of safety. At tiffin [tea] time Riggs,[8] who was associate commissioner of housing, came in crying. The Japanese had emptied the Law College and Supreme Court and taken away

4. Reverend W. P. Mills, American, Northern Presbyterian Mission.
5. Miss Minnie Vautrin, American, Ginling College.
6. Mrs. Paul DeWitt Twinem, formerly American but then a Chinese citizen, University of Nanjing.
7. Mrs. Chen, matron and superintendent of dormitories, Ginling College.
8. Charles H. Riggs, American, University of Nanjing.

practically all the men, to a fate we could only guess. Fifty of our policemen had been taken with them. Riggs had protested, only to be roughly handled by the soldiers and twice struck by an officer. Refugees were searched for money and anything they had on them was taken away, often to their last bit of bedding. At our staff conference at four we could hear the shots of the execution squad nearby. It was a day of unspeakable terror for the poor refugees and horror for us. . . .

Friday, Dec. 17. Robbery, murder, rape continued unabated. A rough estimate would be at least a thousand women raped last night and during the day. One poor woman was raped thirty-seven times. Another had her five months infant deliberately smothered by the brute to stop its crying while he raped her. Resistance means the bayonet. The hospital is rapidly filling up with the victims of Japanese cruelty and barbarity. Bob Wilson,[9] our only surgeon, has his hands more than full and has to work into the night. Rickshas, cattle, pigs, donkeys, often the sole means of livelihood of the people, are taken from them. Our rice kitchens and rice shop are interfered with. We have had to close the latter.

After dinner I took Bates[10] to the University and McCallum[11] to the hospital where they will spend the night, then Mills and Smythe to Ginling, for one of our group has been sleeping there each night. At the gate of the latter place we were stopped by what seemed to be a searching party. We were roughly pulled from the car at the point of the bayonet, my car keys taken from me, lined up and frisked for arms, our hats jerked off, electric torches held to our faces, our passports and purpose in coming demanded. Opposite us were Miss Vautrin, Mrs. Twinem and Mrs. Chen, with a score of refugee women kneeling on the ground. The sergeant, who spoke a little French (about as much as I do), insisted there were soldiers concealed there. I maintained that aside from about fifty domestics and other members of their staff there were no men on the place. This he said he did not believe and said he would shoot all he found beyond that number. He then demanded that we all leave, including the ladies, and when Miss Vautrin refused she was roughly hustled to the car. Then he changed his mind: the ladies were told to stay and we to go. We tried to insist that one of us should stay too, but this he would not permit. Altogether we were kept standing there for over an hour before we were released. The next day we learned that this gang had abducted twelve girls from the school.

Saturday, Dec. 18. At breakfast Riggs, who lives in the Zone a block away but has his meals with us, reported that two women, one a cousin of a Y.M.C.A. Secretary, were raped in his house while he was having dinner with us. Wilson reported a boy of five years of age brought to the hospital after having been stabbed with a bayonet five times, once through his abdomen; a man with eigh-

9. Dr. Robert O. Wilson, American, University of Nanjing Hospital.
10. Dr. M. S. Bates, American, University of Nanjing.
11. Reverend James H. McCallum, American, University of Nanjing Hospital.

teen bayonet wounds, a woman with seventeen cuts on her face and several on her legs. Between four and five hundred terrorized women poured into our headquarters compound in the afternoon and spent the night in the open.

Sunday, Dec. 19. A day of complete anarchy. Several big fires raging today, started by the soldiers, and more are promised. The American flag was torn down in a number of places. At the American School it was trampled on and the caretaker told he would be killed if he put it up again. The proclamations placed on all American and other foreign properties by the Japanese Embassy are flouted by their soldiers, sometimes deliberately torn off. Some houses are entered from five to ten times in one day and the poor people looted and robbed and the women raped. Several were killed in cold blood, for no apparent reason whatever. Six out of seven of our sanitation squad in one district were slaughtered; the seventh escaped, wounded, to tell the tale. Toward evening today two of us rushed to Dr. Brady's[12] house (he is away) and chased four would-be rapers out and took all women there to the University. Sperling[13] is busy at this game all day. I also went to the house of Douglas Jenkins[14] of our Embassy. The flag was still there; but in the garage his house boy lay dead, another servant, dead, was under a bed, both brutally killed. The house was in utter confusion. There are still many corpses on the streets. All of them civilians as far as we can see. The Red Swastika Society would bury them, but their truck has been stolen, their coffins used for bonfires, and several of their workers bearing their insignia have been marched away.

Smythe[15] and I called again at the Japanese Embassy with a list of fifty-five additional cases of violence, all authenticated, and told Messers. Tanaka[16] and Fukui[17] that today was the worst so far. We were assured that they would "do their best" and hoped that things would be better "soon," but it is quite obvious that they have little or no influence with the military whatever, and the military had no control over the soldiers. . . .

Wednesday, Dec. 22. Firing squad at work very near us at 5 a.m. today. Counted over a hundred shots. The University was entered twice during the night, the policeman at the gate held up at the point of a bayonet, and a door broken down. The Japanese military police recently appointed to duty there were asleep. Representatives of the new Japanese police called and promised order by January 1. They also asked for the loan of motorcars and trucks. Went with Sperling to see fifty corpses in some ponds a quarter of a mile east of headquarters. All obviously

12. Dr. Richard F. Brady, American, acting superintendent of the University of Nanjing Hospital.
13. Eduard Sperling, German businessman.
14. Douglas Jenkins, Jr., third secretary, American Embassy.
15. Lewis S.C. Smythe, American missionary.
16. Sueo Tanaka, attaché, Japanese Embassy (now Consul).
17. Kiyoshi Fukui, Japanese consul-general, Nanjing.

civilians, hands bound behind backs, one with the top half of his head cut completely off. Were they used for sabre practice? On the way home for tiffin stopped to help the father of a Y.M.C.A. writer who was being threatened by a drunken soldier with the bayonet, the poor mother frantic with fear, and before sitting down had to run over with two of our fellows to chase soldiers out of Gee's[18] and Daniel's[19] houses, where they were just about to rape the women. We had to laugh to see those brave soldiers trying to get over a barbed wire fence as we chased them!

Bates and Riggs had to leave before they were through tiffin to chase soldiers out of the Sericulture building—several drunk. And on my arrival at office there was an S.O.S. call, which Rabe and I answered, from Sperling and Kroeger[20] who were seriously threatened by a drunk with a bayonet. By fortunate chance Tanaka of the Embassy together with some general arrived at the same moment. The soldier had his face soundly slapped a couple of times by the general but I don't suppose he got any more than that. We have heard of no cases of discipline so far. If a soldier is caught by an officer or M.P. he is very politely told that he shouldn't do that again. In the evening I walked home with Riggs after dinner—a woman of fifty-four had been raped in his house just before our arrival. It's cruel to leave the women to their fate, but of course it is impossible for us to spend all our time protecting them. Mr. Wu, engineer in the power plant which is located in Hsiakwan, brought us the amusing news that forty-three of the fifty-four employees who had so heroically kept the plant going to the very last day and had finally been obliged to seek refuge in the International Export Company, a British factory on the river front, had been taken out and shot on the grounds that the power plant was a government concern—which it is not. Japanese officials have been at my office daily trying to get hold of these very men so they could start the turbines and have electricity. It was small comfort to be able to tell them that their own military had murdered most of them.

17.5 The Nanjing "Murder Race"

SUB-LIEUTENANTS IN RACE
TO FELL A HUNDRED CHINESE
RUNNING CLOSE CONTEST

Sub-lieutenant Toshiaki Mukai and Sub-lieutenant Takeshi Noda, both of the Katagiri unit of Kuyung, in a friendly contest to see which of them will first fell a

18. C. T. Gee, Chinese, resident architect and engineer, University of Nanjing.
19. Dr. J. H. Daniel, American, superintendent, University of Nanjing Hospital.
20. Christian Kroeger, German engineer.

hundred Chinese in individual sword combat before the Japanese forces completely occupy Nanjing, are well in the final phase of their race, running almost neck to neck. On Sunday when their unit was fighting outside Kuyung, the "score," according to the newspaper the *Asahi*, was: Sub-lieutenant Mukai, 89, and Sub-lieutenant Noda, 78.

On December 14, 1937, the same paper published the following additional report:

CONTEST TO KILL FIRST 100 CHINESE WITH SWORD EXTENDED WHEN BOTH FIGHTERS EXCEED MARK

The winner of the competition between Sub-lieutenant Toshiaki Mukai and Sub-lieutenant Takeshi Noda to see who would be the first to kill 100 Chinese with his Yamato sword has not been decided, the *Nichi Nichi* reports from the slopes of Purple Mountain, outside Nanjing. Mukai has a score of 106 and his rival has dispatched 105 men, but the two contestants have found it impossible to determine which passed the 100 mark first. Instead of settling it with a discussion, they are going to extend the goal by 50.

Mukai's blade was slightly damaged in the competition. He explained that this was the result of cutting a Chinese in half, helmet and all. The contest was "fun," he declared, and he thought it a good thing that both men had gone over the 100 mark without knowing that the other had done so.

Early Saturday morning, when the *Nichi Nichi* man interviewed the sublieutenant at a point overlooking Dr. Sun Yat-sen's tomb, another Japanese unit set fire to the slopes of Purple Mountain in an attempt to drive out the Chinese troops. The action also smoked out Sub-lieutenant Mukai and his unit, and the men stood idly by while bullets passed overhead.

"Not a shot hits me while I am holding this sword on my shoulder," he explained confidently.

17.6 FENG ZIKAI: "BOMBS IN YISHAN"

Feng Zikai (1898–1975) was one of the most celebrated cartoonists of the twentieth century. Born in Zhejiang province, Feng attended a teacher training college in Hangzhou and spent ten months studying Western painting and music in Japan. His drawings first appeared in commercial publications and literary journals in the 1920s, and in this time he was primarily known for a series of whimsical cartoons portraying mischievous children at play.

The outbreak of the war against Japan in 1937 profoundly changed both Feng's life and his attitude toward art. He fled west to Guangxi, first to

Guilin and then Yishan (where Zhejiang University had temporarily relocated), before settling in Chongqing. Feng became politically active and produced numerous patriotic cartoons designed to inspire anti-Japanese resistance. "Bombs in Yishan" is Feng's memoir of Japanese air raids during the war. "A Mother's Severed Head" is his most famous drawing, depicting the horrific death of a mother while nursing her baby.

"BOMBS IN YISHAN"

The first time Yishan was bombed would have been in the autumn of 1938, when I was in Guilin. It was said the target was Zhejiang University, and countless bombs were dropped. The university dormitories were out in Biaoying, a district which is criss-crossed by ditches, and the students knew what to do in air raids. By lying low in the ditches, they escaped without a single casualty. One student, however, was suffering from a mental illness; in his deranged condition, he refused to take cover, and stayed in a building that was bombed. The shock brought an immediate end to his symptoms, and he afterwards was restored to health and was able to resume classes. His story was often told at Zhejiang University, as a matter for celebration.

I encountered the second bombing, which took place in the summer of 1939. This time, though, it was anything but a matter for celebration. Quite a lot of people were killed near the bus station, quite a lot injured, and quite a lot more were frightened out of their wits. Ever afterwards I blanched at the sound of an iron wok lid being banged, or the hiss of steam from a kettle. I was such a bundle of nerves that when the old lady next door called her little boy Jingbao, I used to think she was shouting 'Jingbao' (Air raid warning!), and was poised to jump to my feet and run for cover. Now that it is over and I can lick my wounds, I still get angry at the thought of the vileness of the Japanese warlords. Thankfully, our final victory has been won, the Japanese have surrendered, and their warlords are being executed. And I have come through safe and sound. If I look back here on bygone days, it may actually help to lay some old ghosts and contribute to the festive mood.

We ran into trouble when we first arrived in Yishan. When the Zhejiang University bus carrying my own family of ten and a few other passengers, plus a load of baggage, got to the East Gate we were stopped by two policemen, who said an air raid alert was in force and we weren't alowed into the city. That explained why the gate was completely deserted. The driver immediately turned the bus round and drove back a mile or so, stopping under a big tree out in the country. We all got out and sat on some rocks in a gully. By then it was past noon, and stomachs were rumbling. Luckily we had a basket of *zongzi* to stave off our hunger.[21] It hap-

---

21. *Zongzi* are little packets of sticky rice with meat and vegetable flavouring wrapped in bamboo leaves; they are normally eaten during the Dragon Boat Festival.

pened to be the Qingming holiday time, and though we were travelling we still kept to our old custom of making some 'Qingming *zongzi*' to take with us. So now all of us, that is my whole family of ten, the driver and the other passengers, tucked into the *zongzi* and sat around talking. The sun was shining, the breeze was gentle, the day was perfect. If we had been able to forget we were in Yishan taking cover from an air raid, and imagine we were picnicking by the West Lake in Hangzhou, that afternoon would have been pure bliss! The whole family mustered, from the two-year-old to the over seventies, out on a spring excursion, and a few friends along besides—how exhilarating, how civilized! Alas, the sad truth is that in this life we are sometimes obliged to make believe like that.

When we had finished the *zongzi* the sun was slanting in the sky, as if to tell us we could enter the city now. Thereupon we got back on the bus and headed back. This time we were indeed allowed to go through the East Gate. But no sooner had we alighted than a crowd of people started rushing in our direction. When we asked in alarm what was up, we discovered it was another air raid alert! Being newcomers we did not know the geography of the place, and had to flee blindly in the wake of the crowd. Our children and old folk were not very mobile, so they made for the nearest cover of a thicket outside the East Gate. I fled with other people across the river and hid in a cave. The all clear did not sound till it was nearly dark. Fortunately when we got back to the bus we found the luggage was all still intact, and the rest of the family eventually straggled back, all accounted for. Then we had to find lodgings and somewhere to eat. We did not get to bed till late at night. We learned that there had been three alerts that day, those that we encountered being the second and third. We were also told that the thickets outside the East Gate concealed the station and the military command post. These would have been the prime targets for the bombers. Imagine, my family was hiding from an air raid right in the target area!

Our relationship with Yishan was measured in air raid alerts: we became acquainted in the middle of one and afterwards parted in one. In between we had alerts practically every day, and experienced one bombing.

To begin with we lived over the Kaiming Bookshop in town. Later on we could not put up with all the running about occasioned by the great number of air raid alerts, so we rented a small cottage some distance from the city, and the family moved out, leaving me and one small son in the Kaiming Bookshop. One day—it happened to be market day—I was idly gazing down from an upstairs window on the hawkers' pitches at the roadside when I saw a crepe fabric seller suddenly pack up his goods. The hawker on the neighbouring pitch, without inquiring into the reason why, did likewise. A third followed suit, then a fourth, and in no time all the hawkers along the street were packing up, telling each other 'It's an air raid!' They all made off helterskelter in search of safety. Quite befogged, I took my son downstairs to look for shelter myself. But once outside, I found everyone all smiles. In fact there was no air raid warning; it was only much ado about nothing. The alarm was sparked off, it transpired, by the fabric seller packing up early for reasons of his own. His movements were quite hasty and abrupt, which led the hawker next to him to think an air raid was coming, with the farcical consequences I have described. As the old saying goes, if three people say there is a tiger, there is a tiger. But behind the farce could be seen the real fear of air raids at that time. I found it impossible to settle down to anything in this jittery atmosphere, where people were afraid of their own shadows, so I took my son to join the rest of the family in the cottage in the country.

This thatched cottage was pitifully small: just three rooms, each ten feet square. We needed to buy two bunk beds to sleep the ten of us. The beds doubled as seats, the dining table doubled as a desk, without too much trouble. If you looked upon it as a boat rather than a house, it was in fact rather spacious. And there was the scenery as well: pavilion, terrace, escarpment, hills, stands of bamboo. These were originally the Dragon Ridge Gardens, and where we lived was originally the gardener's cottage. The escarpment was quite rugged, with lots of clefts and fissures. We hid in those clefts during the air raid alerts. At the first alarm we all stayed put, and waited for the emergency alert before taking cover in the clefts. But the enemy planes never came, and every time we returned peacefully to our little cottage. But later on, some days before the fall of Nanning, the neighbouring county was bombed and Yishan took fright. We ourselves came to think the rock clefts gave inadequate protection, and we ought to find a safer refuge. But inertia prevailed and we did nothing about it.

One day I fully intended to go out and look for a cave, but the weather was quite unsettled, alternating very oddly between sunshine and rain. Everyone said it was unlikely there would be an alert. My native indolence persuaded me to put off my expedition. Suddenly the alarm bell sounded. The people taking flight past our house seemed unusually panicky, and the changing of the bell was unusually ominous. On top of that, the emergency alert followed swiftly. I had to stop an acquaintance of mine to find out that reliable report had it that the enemy planes were especially active that day, and the chances were Yishan would be bombed.

Applying the test of air raid alerts to my family, they could be divided into two factions: the bold faction, namely my wife, my mother-in-law, and the youths over sixteen; and the timid faction, my older sister and the two girls. I could be said to be sandwiched in between, belonging to no faction; or you could say I was a fence-sitter, a misfit, or a member of both factions, because after a drink I belonged to the bold faction, but before I'd had a drink I belonged to the timid faction. That day the bold faction took cover in the nearby rock clefts. As I hadn't had a drink I joined the timid faction in going further afield.

Going further afield did not mean we had a safer objective in mind, it was just a belief akin to that of people who bought joss-sticks to worship the Buddha, namely, 'to fork out money is a virtue in itself.' Likewise we thought to go further afield must be a good thing in itself. We happened to fall in with some people we knew who were making resolutely for the open fields; they assured us there were caves up ahead. So we pushed on with our guides, getting bootfuls of water. Our cross-country trek ended in a spot where there really was a formation of towering rocks, and we hurriedly searched for the cave. These rocks were in the shape of a V laid out horizontal on the ground, allowing you to pass through the open end to the apex, but there was no cover overhead—actually it was no cave at all! Still, by this stage we could not move on elsewhere; if we were to die, we would die here.

Lots of men and women squeezed into the V. I crouched at the mouth of the V. Now able to take in the surroundings, I uttered an exclamation of dismay. In fact we were only a few hundred feet from the prime targets of the station and the sports field! It was a whole lot more dangerous here than among the rocks of the Dragon Ridge Garden. As I was getting all worked up I heard a heavy droning noise, and the people in the V shouted, 'The Jap bombers are coming!' whereupon they all ducked down and camouflaged themselves with the ferns that sprouted from the rocks. What was I to do, stuck outside the opening, with no protection at all? Suddenly I spotted on the outer slope of the V formation a slight depression overgrown with ferns. On the inspiration of desperation, I laid myself flat in the hollow underneath the ferns.

I lay still and watched the sky through the leaves of the ferns above me. A squadron of enemy bombers appeared in the distant sky heading towards me, the drone of their engines growing louder all the time. I thought to myself, there are only three possible outcomes today: one, I will get up and go home unharmed; two, I will be injured and be carried to hospital; three, I will be killed in this hollow. Any way, I had to take what came. I seemed to see one of those shakers used for drawing lots in front of me, with three spills in it: one marked 1, one marked 2, one marked 3. I stretched out my hand and drew one. . . .

As this thought was going through my mind, three bombers came up over my head. Suddenly they slowed and hovered. Then a black spherical object fell from the aircraft straight towards me. I could not bear to look, and covered my face, waiting for it to explode. First there came a whistling noise, followed by a 'crump.' The earth shook and the rocks shook. The blast lifted me from the ground. Yet I seemed not to have been injured. Peeping out, all I could see was a spreading pall of smoke, and the three planes circling over it. Another black spherical object fell from a plane, and a second whistled down from a different plane. The objects were right overhead. I covered my face with my hands, and heard 'crump,' 'crump' all around me.

I pictured a bomb landing right in the middle of the V, going off bang, and all of us—men, women, young and old—blown to smithereens in a flash: an end like this would have been clean and straightforward, and would have put us out of our misery at least. But the latest bombs did not do that: they just demoralized us with their more powerful blasts. This proved the bombs were getting closer, and our danger was increasing. Suddenly I heard a woman howl from inside the V, followed by the sound of whimpering. I could not work out what was going on. Fortunately the enemy planes were moving on, the drone of their engines fading. We all began to breathe again. I got up, covered in dust, and crept over to the opening of the V. They were surprised to see me, not knowing where I had got to, or whether I was safe or not. Seeing them all unscathed, I asked why the howl. It turned out there was a wasp's nest in the V. One young woman had knocked against it, and had been stung, hence the howl and whimpering.

The enemy planes dropped a dozen or so bombs and, their blood lust satisfied, returned to base. Long afterwards the all clear sounded. We filed out of the V but could not see far for the dust and smoke, which still hung in the air. The girl who had been stung by the wasp set off home through the haze, her hand held to her swollen face. My terror had dissipated by the time I got home after my false alarm, but it had been replaced by a sense of grievance. This just wouldn't do! I hated to have my right to life controlled by the enemy! But what could I do about it? I was still pondering when my daughter came back and reported that numerous bombs had fallen around the station, on the sports field, by the river, and in the park; so many people had been killed and so many injured. One woman had been killed under a tree, her head half blown off while her body remained sitting erect. Lots of people had been carted off to the hospital shrieking and groaning. When I heard this report I realized how lucky we had been. It was clear the enemy had deliberately bombed the outskirts rather than the city centre, anticipating that the city would have been evacuated by the time they arrived. In that case our V had presented them with a nice target! I don't know what good deeds our little band had done to have saved us from harm. Thinking back on it now, perhaps that V foreshadowed the V that appeared on the night of 10 August 1945, the symbol of final victory.[22]

That night I could not contain my indignation. I felt that to kill people by 'air raid' was too unmanly. If there is honour among thieves, there is also an honourable way of killing. If we are both on level ground, and you come to kill me, I run. If I can't get away, I am killed by you. This kind of killing, simply in terms of killing, is fair enough, and one would die without complaint. But if they come to kill you from above and you have to get away from below, they are bound to have the upper hand, and you are bound to be on the losing end. The matter of dying was secondary, what was intolerable was the moral injustice and affront to one's feelings. I had to think of a way to render the killers from the air powerless against me and to save myself from further indignity.

The next day I had my solution. After breakfast I gathered together some fellow spirits from my family, and we set out for the hills, taking with us reading matter and victuals. We walked over a mile to the Nine Dragon Cliffs, sat in the entrance of a big cave, and read.

22. The actual date of the Japanese unconditional surrender was 14 August 1945; the signing of the documents of surrender took place on 3 September.

Having spent a carefree day, we returned at dusk. I was totally unaware of whether there had been an air raid or not. This style of life continued for over a month, during which time I was indeed free from further subjection to indignity. Nor was the city bombed again. But before long there came the news of the fall of Nanning. I had no choice but to take the refugee trail, carrying my sense of injustice along with me.

1946

"A MOTHER'S SEVERED HEAD"

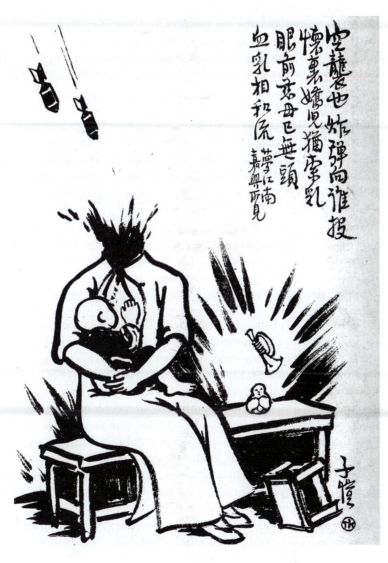

17.7 WANG JINGWEI: ON COLLABORATION, 1941

It is a sad irony that Wang Jingwei's career as a revolutionary and patriot ended in collaboration with the Japanese. After the Mukden Incident, Wang was briefly one of the most outspoken critics of Chiang Kai-shek's appeasement policy. After he joined the Guomindang government as the head of the Executive Yuan (in 1932), however, Wang ceased his attacks on Chiang. In the aftermath of the Marco Polo Bridge Incident and Japan's occupation of much of coastal China, Wang urged Chiang to open negotiations, but his advice was ignored. Convinced that the war policy of the Chongqing government would bleed China dry, Wang Jingwei fled to Hanoi in December 1938, where he announced his support for a negotiated settlement to the war. In March 1940, he agreed to return to China to head a "national" government under Japanese sponsorship.

Wang Jingwei's Faustian bargain with the Japanese repeatedly forced him to assume self-abasing positions. By 1941, as the following radio address illustrates, the language of submission had replaced the brave and often visionary rhetoric that had once distinguished Wang. Although his defenders have maintained that during the war years Wang continued to fight for Chinese interests in secret, his public stance was indistinguishable from that of other collaborationist leaders.

RADIO ADDRESS BY MR. WANG JINGWEI, PRESIDENT OF THE CHINESE EXECUTIVE YUAN, BROADCAST ON JUNE 24, 1941

I am deeply moved as I speak to you today in Tokyo, the capital of your great country. I studied in your country 38 years ago. My stay then was short, and due particularly to my limited abilities I could not master your language and learning. However, if, fortunately, I know something, I owe it to my old teachers and classmates. I can never forget what they have done for me. To have been able to come to your great country again and meet you, the people of Japan, is like meeting my old teachers and classmates and I am filled with the warm feeling. . . .

When the slogan of "the construction of a new order in East Asia" was heard in your country, our people found a gleam of hope in the darkness. When the Konoe Statement was issued, in particular, how the two nations can cooperate was made clearly and concretely known to us, and we have been led to take steps looking to the realization of the hope.

The significance of the construction of a new order in East Asia lies, on the one hand, in endeavoring to eliminate from East Asia the evils of Western economic imperialism from which this part of the world has suffered for the past century and, on the other, in checking the rising tide of Communism which has been threatening our prosperity for these twenty years. Japan was the only country in the East who could shoulder the responsibility for such undertakings single-handedly. Although we have Dr. Sun Yat-sen's Pan-Asianism, his followers and compatriots have failed to make united efforts for the attainment of that ideal.

There may be causes for the recent unfortunate conflict between our two countries. If, however, we examine ourselves as to why we have failed in our efforts to purge the country of the evils of Western economic imperialism and to check the rise of Communism, thereby leaving the country to deteriorate into a semi-colonial status and the people in the deepest distress, we cannot but blame ourselves. When we heard of the slogan of the construction of a new order in East Asia put forth by Japan, we immediately opened our eyes to the fact that it was not time for quarreling among ourselves, and realized that we should revert to our essential character founded upon the moral principles of the East, breaking down the old order consisting of a chain of pressures brought to bear upon us by economic imperialism and Communism, and establish a new order based on independence, freedom, co-existence and co-prosperity. China could not but hesitate to take up such a heavy responsibility when she thought of her limited spiritual and material resources. Moreover, the conditions in which she found herself were too difficult for her to readily undertake such a heavy responsibility. This hesitation, however, was overcome when she heard the Konoe Statement; she knew for the first time that Japan had already surmounted such difficulties on behalf of China.

The most important significance of the Konoe Statement, I believe, lies in the fact that Japan will give aid to China in providing such conditions as are necessary for her development into a modern State if China herself will participate with determination and sincerity in the construction of a new order in East Asia. The reason why Japan adopted this definite policy was that if Japan and China unite and proceed with the construction, it will result not only in the establishment of permanent peace between the two countries but also in the reconstruction of East Asia. . . .

I and my colleagues in the National Government of China have never failed to examine ourselves constantly as to our responsibilities for increasing strength; and at the same time we are making efforts to induce Chongqing leaders to join in the peace movement. As a matter of fact, we have been and are ceaselessly making every effort to induce them through various channels to join us in the peace movement; we will continue to do so in the future.

I should like to add that not only number but also quality is important in the development of the peace movement. The basic objective of peace is to realize Pan-Asianism and to establish a new order in East Asia. In our efforts to attain that objective the peace movement should be purified in quality as it grows in numbers; its quality should not be changed or weakened by an increase in numbers. Not to give economic imperialism any chance to recover its influence and not to give Communism an opportunity to succeed are two main points which we should not neglect.

I was deeply moved when I paid a visit to His Imperial Minister, the Emperor, who granted me His gracious words concerning Sino-Japanese friendship. Yesterday Prime Minister Prince Konoe and I issued a joint statement as a result of our conversations for several days. We are firmly determined to strive hereafter for the accomplishment of the purpose in accordance with the statement. I want to tell you tonight of this inflexible determination of mine, and taking this occasion I want to express my deep appreciation of your expectations for our future and for your warmest sympathy for and powerful aid to our cause. Certainly I am moved by your kindness; I shall never forget to the end of my life all that you have done for me. At the same time, however, I cannot but be ashamed to think of the fact of how little I have accomplished; I am not worthy of all your kindness. Only let me take back with me your kindness and sympathy to the people at home, so that they may fully appreciate your earnest wishes for Sino-Japanese friendship. All our people will unite with you, I am sure, for the performance of the high task to which the peoples of East Asia are called. My friends, no one knows what new developments may take place tomorrow in the international situation. Whatever happens, the attitude of our two countries to reconstruct East Asia in the friendly relationship of co-existence and co-prosperity will be forever unchangeable.

In conclusion, let me wish you health and prosperity. *Banzai* [ten thousand years] for the Empire of Japan! *Banzai* for the Republic of China!

17.8 LIU SHAOQI: HOW TO BE A GOOD COMMUNIST, 1939

During the war years the Chinese Communist Party, like other governments, parties, and protogovernments in China's history, labored to devise an ideal model for behavior with which to inspire its followers. The invasion of China's coastal regions had driven millions of refugees into the hinterlands of China. The new recruits who had come to Yan'an from Shanghai, Tianjin, Peking, and other parts of China had to be taught to adhere to party discipline and to serve as reliable cogs in the political machinery being constructed in the "liberated zones." Many of the new arrivals from urban areas were intellectuals who may have worked on the fringes of clandestine leftist organizations, but were by no means accustomed to behaving in docile accord with party dictates.

In July 1939, in lectures delivered at the Institute of Marxism-Leninism Yan'an, Liu Shaoqi, a former Shanghai labor organizer and senior party official, attempted to synthesize notions of what was meant by a "good Communist" for newcomers to the ranks of the Party and also for veteran Party members.

The short excerpt from Liu's long theoretical speech on the theme of being a good Communist that is included here stresses self-cultivation and a mode of personal remolding very much in harmony with traditional Confucian mores. Communist and revolutionary standards replaced, of course, the benchmarks provided by the neo-Confucian tradition, but the idea of creating individual behavior in perfect harmony with ethical models provided by the party and state was all too familiar.

WHY COMMUNISTS MUST UNDERTAKE SELF-CULTIVATION

Why must Communists undertake to cultivate themselves?

In order to live, man must wage a struggle against nature and make use of nature to produce material values. At all times and under all conditions, his production of material things is social in character. It follows that when men engage in production at any stage of social development, they have to enter into certain relations of production with one another. In their ceaseless struggle against nature, men ceaselessly change nature and simultaneously change themselves and their mutual relations. Men themselves, their social relations, their forms of social organization, and their consciousness change and progress continuously in the long struggle which as social beings they wage against nature. In ancient times, man's mode of life, social organization, and consciousness were all different from what they are today, and in the future they will again be different.

Mankind and human society are in process of historical development. When human society reached a certain historical stage, classes and class struggle emerged. Every member of a class society exists as a member of a given class and lives in given conditions of a class struggle. Man's social being determines his consciousness. In class society the ideology of the members of each class reflects a different class position and different class interests. The class struggle constantly goes on among these classes with their different positions, interests, and ideologies. Thus it is not only in the struggle against nature but in the struggle of social classes that men change nature, change society and at the same time change themselves. . . .

When we say that Communists must remold themselves by waging struggles in every sphere against the counter-revolutionaries and reformists, we mean that it is through such struggles that they must seek to make progress, and must enhance their revolutionary quality and ability. An immature revolutionary has to go through a long process of revolutionary tempering and self-cultivation,

A few days ago, as we are all aware, one of the most despicable and shameful events of history occurred here in Kunming. What crime did Mr. Li Gongpu commit that would cause him to be murdered in such a vicious way? He merely used his pen to write a few articles, he used his mouth to speak out, and what he said and wrote was nothing more than what any Chinese with a conscience would say. We all have pens and mouths. If there is a reason for it, why not speak out? Why should people be beaten, killed, or, even worse, killed in a devious way? [Applause]

Are there any special agents [Guomindang spies] here today? Stand up! If you are men, stand up! Come forward and speak! Why did you kill Mr. Li? [Enthusiastic applause] You kill people but refuse to admit it and even circulate false rumors that the murder happened because of some sexual scandal or as the result of Communists killing other Communists. Shameless! Shameless! [Applause] This is the shamelessness of the Guomindang but the glory belongs to Mr. Li. Mr. Li participated in Kunming's democratic movement for a number of years. Now he has returned to Kunming and sacrificed his own life. This is Mr. Li's glory, it is the glory of the people of Kunming!

Last year, at the time of the December First Incident, the young students of Kunming were slaughtered for demonstrating against the civil war and that was a case of the younger generation sacrificing its precious lives. Now, Mr. Li, striving for democracy and peace, has also suffered assassination by the reactionaries. Let me proudly say, an old comrade-in-arms has now sacrificed his precious life for my generation. Both of these incidents happened here in Kunming and this will be an eternal glory for Kunming. [Applause]

After the news of the reactionary's assassination of Mr. Li spread, everyone was indignant and outraged. I certainly can't understand the heart of those shameless creatures; under these circumstances how can they fabricate false rumors to insult Mr. Li? But in fact it is very simple. The reason they are madly creating terror is because they themselves are in a panic! They are afraid! They create terror because they feel terrified!

Special agents, think about it, how many days are left for you?

Do you really think that if you hurt a few or kill a few, that you can intimidate the whole people? In fact, you cannot beat all of the people or kill all of the people. For every Li Gongpu you kill, hundreds of millions of Li Gongpus will stand up! [Applause] In the future you will lose the support of hundreds of millions of people.

The reactionaries believe that they can reduce the number of people participating in the democratic movement and destroy its power through the terror of assassination. But let me tell you, our power is great, our power is enormous! [Applause] Look! All of these people today are our people and their power is our power. [Applause]

The power of the people will win and truth will live forever! [Applause] Throughout history, all who have opposed the people have been destroyed by the people! Didn't Hitler and Mussolini fall before the people? Chiang Kai-shek, you are so rabid, so reactionary, turn the pages of history, how many days do you think you have left? You're finished! It is over for you! [Enthusiastic applause]

Bright days are coming for us. Look, the light is before us. Just as Mr. Li said as he was dying: "Daybreak is coming!" Now is that darkest moment before dawn. We have the power to break through this darkness and attain the light! The coming of our light marks the final moment for the reactionaries! [Applause]

Mr. Li's blood was not shed in vain! Mr. Li gave his life and we shall demand a price in return. We have this confidence and we must have this confidence. . . .

Reactionaries, you have seen one man fall but have you seen hundreds of millions stand up!

Justice can never be killed because truth lives forever! . . . [Applause]

To attain democracy and peace, we must pay a price. We are not afraid of making sacrifices. Each of us should be like Mr. Li. When we step through the door, we must be prepared never to return. [Long, enthusiastic applause]

18.2 GENERAL MARSHALL: THE MEDIATOR'S VIEW, 1947

After VJ (Victory over Japan) Day, the United States government was eager to see the Guomindang and the Communist Party unite in a coalition to govern China. In December 1945, President Truman sent George Marshall to Nanjing to work out a cease fire and help convene a Political Consultative Conference (PCC) to establish the foundation for one national government and army. Initially, Marshall believed that both sides were receptive to the idea of a unity government. He was received cordially by both Chiang and Mao, and steps were underway in January 1946 to form the PCC.

In the end, however, the previous decades of political opposition, civil war, and deep feelings of mutual suspicion doomed the Marshall mission to failure. By the spring of 1946 armed clashes had already erupted. Marshall continued in his attempts to forestall civil war, but by the end of that year he was forced to acknowledge the futility of further American mediation.

Marshall's statement below, released on January 7, 1947, just before his departure, reflected his conviction that efforts to unify the two sides were undermined by their intransigence and the absence of any moderate force capable of acting as a buffer. When Marshall subsequently became the secretary of state, he adopted a wait-and-see policy for the United States that precluded an active search for solutions to the deepening crisis in China.

The greatest obstacle to peace [in China] has been the complete, almost overwhelming suspicion with which the Chinese Communist Party and the Guomindang regard each other.

On the one hand, the leaders of the Government are strongly opposed to a communistic form of government. On the other, the Communists frankly state that they are Marxists and intend to work toward establishing a communistic form of government in China, though first advancing through the medium of a democratic form of government of the American or British type.

The leaders of the Government are convinced in their minds that the Communist-expressed desire to participate in a government of the type endorsed by the Political Consultative Conference last January had for its purpose only a destructive intention. The Communists felt, I believe, that the government was insincere in its apparent acceptance of the PCC resolutions for the formation of the new government and intended by coercion of military force and the action of secret police to obliterate the Communist Party. Combined with this mutual deep distrust was the conspicuous error by both parties of ignoring the effect of the fears and suspicions of the other party in estimating the reason for proposals or opposition regarding the settlement of various matters under negotiation. They each sought only to take counsel of their own fears. They both, therefore, to that extent took a rather lopsided view of each situation and were susceptible to every evil suggestion or possibility. . . .

I think the most important factors involved in the recent breakdown of negotiations are these: On the side of the National Government, which is in effect the Guomindang, there is a dominant group of reactionaries who have been opposed, in my opinion, to almost every effort I have made to influence the formation of a genuine coalition government. This has usually been under the cover of political or party action, but since the Party was the Government, this action, though subtle or indirect, has been devastating in its effect. They were quite frank in publicly stating their belief that cooperation by the Chinese Communist Party in the government was inconceivable and that only a policy of force could definitely settle the issue. This group includes military as well as political leaders.

On the side of the Chinese Communist Party there are, I believe, liberals as well as radicals, though this view is vigorously opposed by many who believe that the Chinese Communist Party discipline is too rigidly enforced to admit of such differences of viewpoint. Nevertheless, it has appeared to me that there is a definite liberal group among the Communist ideology in the immediate future. The dyed-in-the-wool Communists do not hesitate at the most drastic measures to gain their end as, for instance, the destruction of communications in order to wreck the economy of China and produce a situation that would facilitate the overthrow or collapse of the Government, without any regard to the immediate suffering of the people involved. They completely distrust the leaders of the Guomindang and appear convinced that every Government proposal is designed to crush the Chinese Communist Party. I must say that the quite evidently inspired mob actions of last February and March, some within a few blocks of where I was then engaged in completing negotiations, gave the Communists good excuse for such suspicions.

However, a very harmful and immensely proactive phase of the Chinese Communist Party procedure has been in the character of its propaganda. I wish to state to the American people that in the deliberate misrepresentation and abuse of the action, policies and purposes of our Government this propaganda has been without regard for the truth, without any regard whatsoever for the facts, and has given plain evidence of a determined purpose to mislead the Chinese people and the world and to arouse a bitter hatred of Americans. It has been difficult to remain silent in the midst of such public abuse and wholesale disregard of facts, but a denial would merely lead to the necessity of daily denials, an intolerable course of action for an American official. In the interest of fairness, I must state that the Nationalist Government publicity agency has made numerous misrepresentations, though not of the vicious nature of the Communist propaganda. Incidentally, the Communist statements regarding the Anping incident[1] which resulted in the death of three Marines and the wounding of twelve others were almost pure fabrication, deliberately representing a carefully arranged ambuscade of a Marine convoy with supplies for the maintenance of Executive Headquarters and some UNRRA supplies, as a defence against a Marine assault. The investigation of this incident was a tortuous procedure of delays and maneuvers to disguise the true and privately admitted facts of the case.

Sincere efforts to achieve settlement have been frustrated time and again by extremist elements of both sides. The agreements reached by the Political Consultive Conference a year ago were a liberal and forward-looking charter which then offered China a basis for peace and reconstruction. However, irreconcilable groups within the Guomindang, interested in the preservation of their own feudal control of China, evidently had no real intention of implementing them. Though I speak as a soldier, I must here also deplore the dominating influence of the military. Their dominance accentuates the weakness of civil government in China. At the same time, in pondering the situation in China, one must have clearly in mind not the workings of small Communist groups or committees to which we are accustomed in America, but rather of millions of people and an army of more than a million men. . . .

Between this dominant reactionary group in the Government and the irreconcilable Communists who, I must state, did not so appear last February, lies the problem of how peace and well-being are to be brought to the long-suffering and presently inarticulate mass of the people of China. The reactionaries in the Government have evidently counted on substantial American support regardless of their actions. The Communists by their unwillingness to compromise in the national interest are evidently counting on an economic collapse to bring about the fall of the Government, accelerated by extensive guerrilla action against the long lines of rail communications—regardless of the cost of suffering to the Chinese people.

1. A clash between U.S. Marines and Communist troops that occurred near Tianjin, on July 29, 1946.

The salvation of the situation, as I see it, would be the assumption of leadership by the liberals in the Government and in the minority parties, a splendid group of men, but who as yet lack the political power to exercise a controlling influence. Successful action on their part under the leadership of Generalissimo Chiang Kai-shek would, I believe, lead to unity through good government.

In fact, the National Assembly has adopted a democratic constitution which in all major respects is in accordance with the principles laid down by the all-party Political Consultative Conference of last January. It is unfortunate that the Communists did not see fit to participate in the Assembly since the constitution that has been adopted seems to include every major point that they wanted.

Soon the Government in China will undergo major reorganization pending the coming into force of the constitution following elections to be completed before Christmas Day 1947. Now that the form for a democratic China has been laid down by the newly adopted constitution, practical measures will be the test. It remains to be seen to what extent the Government will give substance to the form by a genuine welcome of all groups actively to share in the responsibility of government.

The first step will be the reorganization of the State Council and the executive branch of Government to carry on administration pending the enforcement of the constitution. The manner in which this is done and the amount of representation accorded to liberals and to non-Guomindang members will be significant. It is also to be hoped that during this interim period the door will remain open for Communists or other groups to participate if they see fit to assume their share of responsibility for the future of China.

It has been stated officially and categorically that the period of political tutelage under the Guomindang is at an end. If the termination of one-party rule is to be a reality, the Guomindang should cease to receive financial support from the Government.

I have spoken very frankly because in no other way can I hope to bring the people of the United States to even a partial understanding of this complex problem. I have expressed all these views privately in the course of negotiations; they are well known, I think, to most of the individuals concerned. I express them now publicly, as it is my duty, to present my estimate of the situation and its possibilities to the American people who have a deep interest in the development of conditions in the Far East promising an enduring peace in the Pacific.

18.3 THE 2-28 INCIDENT IN TAIWAN

Peng Ming-min was born in 1923 in a small coastal town in central Taiwan, the son of a respected doctor. Like many children of the Taiwanese elite during the period of Japanese colonial rule, Peng received his secondary education in Tokyo. He returned to Taiwan to study law in 1945, and later received his Ph.D. from the University of Paris.

In 1964, after serving as an advisor to Taiwan's U.N. delegation, Peng
wrote a manifesto calling for democracy in Taiwan. He and his coconspirators were arrested and imprisoned. Released to serve a life sentence under
house arrest, Peng fled to Sweden with the help of friends who engineered a
daring escape. While in exile Peng became a leading spokesman for the cause
of "Formosan independence." He returned to Taiwan in 1992, and in 1996
became the Democratic Progressive Party's first candidate for president.

In the following excerpt from his memoir, published in 1972, Peng
describes the events leading up to the February 28 Incident of 1947 and its
bloody aftermath. The uprising and the clash with Nationalist authority
launched a period of martial law that did not end until 1987, and the bitter
memories of the event continue to be a flashpoint of political controversy
in Taiwan.

Formosa's legal status was peculiar. China had ceded Formosa and the Pescadores
to Japan in 1895. Tokyo then gave the inhabitants two years in which to choose
nationality, and a few thousand Formosans chose to leave or to register as Chinese
subjects. The great majority did not, however, and for fifty years thereafter they
and their children and grandchildren were Japanese subjects by law. Had they
wished to migrate to China at any time, they could arrange to do so. Some did,
but the vast majority remained. Under the Japanese they enjoyed the benefits of a
rule of law. The police were strict, often harsh, and the Japanese colonial administration treated Formosans as second-class citizens. However, under Japanese
reorganization and direction our island economy had made spectacular gains, and
our living standard rose steadily until among Asian countries we were second
only to Japan in agricultural and industrial technology, in communications, in
public health, and in provisions for the general public welfare. Our grandparents
had witnessed this transformation from a backward, ill-governed, disorganized
island nominally dependent on the Chinese. They did not like the Japanese, but
they appreciated the economic and social benefits of fifty years of peace which
they enjoyed while the Chinese on the mainland proper endured fifty years of
revolution, warlordism, and civil war.

In our father's generation, and in our own, hundreds of well-educated young
Formosans had supported a home rule movement. This was first organized during World War I when they were encouraged by the American president's call for
the universal recognition of the rights of minority people. Throughout the 1920s
Formosan leaders pressed the Japanese government for a share in island government, and, at last, in 1935, Tokyo began to yield. Local elections were held for
local assemblies, the voting rights were gradually enlarged, and in early 1945 it
was announced that Formosans at last would be granted equal political rights
with the Japanese.

But it was too late. By then Japan faced defeat and young Formosan home rule
leaders were reading and listening to promises broadcast to them by the American

government, promises of a new postwar life in a democratic China. To us this meant freedom to participate in island government at all levels and to elect Formosans to represent the island in the national government of China.

Japan surrendered Formosa to the Allied Powers at Yokohama on September 3, 1945. Transfer of sovereignty to China would not take place, however, until a peace conference produced a formal treaty. In view of promises made by President Roosevelt to Generalissimo Chiang at Cairo in 1943, promises then reaffirmed by President Truman at Potsdam, Washington decreed that the island of Formosa and the Pescadores should be handed over to the Nationalist Chinese for administration pending legal transfer. There was no reservation of Allied rights during this interim period and no reservation of Formosan interests. There was no provision offering Formosans a choice of citizenship as there had been in 1895. The Formosans, whether they liked it or not, were to be restored to China.

Formosa was a rich prize for the ruling Nationalists. Keelung and Kaohsiung had been heavily damaged and Taipei city had suffered, but the basic industrial and agricultural structure was there. Warehouses were full of sugar, rice, chemicals, rubber, and other raw materials that had not been shipped to Japan. The power plants and sugar mills were not badly damaged. The Japanese prepared an elaborate and carefully detailed report of all public and private properties handed over to General Chen Yi on October 25. It was estimated that these confiscated Japanese properties had a value of some two billion American dollars at that time. At Chungking and Nanking the factions around Generalissimo Chiang, the armed forces, the civil bureaucracy, the party, and the powerful organizations of Madame Chiang's family had competed fiercely to gain immediate control of this island prize. A temporary provincial administration was set up, and the Generalissimo made Lieutenant General Chen Yi the new governor general, carefully surrounding him with representatives of other leading factions, principally of the army, the air force, and Madame Chiang's interests. T. V. Soong had hired representatives of an American firm to survey Formosan industrial resources on his behalf, and the surveying team reached the island even before Chen Yi arrived to accept the formal local surrender and transfer.

American planes and ships ferried the Nationalists from China to the new island possession. Formosans welcomed them enthusiastically in October 1945, thinking that a splendid new era was at hand. Within weeks we found that Governor Chen Yi and his commissioners were contemptuous of the Formosan people and were unbelievably corrupt and greedy. For eighteen months they looted our island. The newcomers had lived all their lives in the turmoil of civil war and of the Japanese invasion. They were carpetbaggers, occupying enemy territory, and we were being treated as a conquered people.

In the nineteenth century, Formosa had been controlled by a disorderly garrison government, notorious even in China for its corruption and inefficiency, but after a half-century of strict Japanese administration we had learned the value of the rule of law. People made contracts and kept them. It was generally assumed that one's neighbor was an honest man. In the shops a fixed price system had made it possible for every merchant to know where he stood. We had learned that modern communications, scientific agriculture, and efficient industries must operate within a system of honest measurement, honored contracts, and dependable timing.

All these standards were ignored by our new masters. We were often treated with contempt. Incoming government officials and the more intelligent and educated carpetbaggers made it evident that they looked upon honesty as a laughable evidence of stupidity. In the dog-eat-dog confusion of Chinese life during the war years, these men had survived and reached their present positions largely through trickery, cheating, and double-talk, often the only means of survival in the Chinese cities from which they came. To them we were country bumpkins and fair game.

The continental Chinese have traditionally looked upon the island of Formosa as a barbarous dependency. Addressing a large gathering of students soon after he arrived, the new commissioner of education said so, with blunt discourtesy, and this provoked an angry protest. On the other hand, Formosans laughed openly and jeered at newcomers who showed so often that they were unfamiliar with modern equipment and modern organization. I witnessed many examples of Chinese incompetence myself and heard of other extraordinary instances. There were well-advertised incidents when officials insisted upon attempting to drive automobiles without taking driving lessons, on the assumption that if a stupid Formosan could drive any intelligent man from the continent could do so. The conscript soldiers from inland Chinese provinces were the least acquainted with modern mechanisms. Many could not ride bicycles, and having stolen them or taken them forcibly from young Formosans, they had to walk off carrying the machines on their backs.

The year 1946 was one of increasing disillusionment. At all levels of the administration and economic enterprise Formosans were being dismissed to make way for the relatives and friends of men in Chen Yi's organization. The secretary general, Chen Yi's civil administrator, had promptly placed seven members of his family in lucrative positions. One of them was given charge of Formosa's multimillion dollar tea export industry. The new manager of the Taichung Pineapple Company, one of the world's largest producers before World War II, was a Y.M.C.A. secretary from Shanghai who had never seen a pineapple plant. The new police chief in Kaohsiung was believed to have more than forty members of his family and close associates on the payroll. The commissioner of agriculture and forestry attempted to sequester a large number of privately owned junks on the East Coast on the pretext that they would be "better kept" under government management at Keelung, when in fact it was common knowledge that his subordinates were operating a smuggling fleet.

At the beginning of 1947 tension had reached a breaking point. The governor general had a direct family interest in the management of the Trading Bureau to which many producers were obliged to sell their products at fixed prices, after which they were sold in turn at great profit within Formosa or on the continent. The commissioners of finance, communications, and industry developed between them an elaborate network of rules and regulations which gave them a stranglehold on the total island economy. Nothing could move out of the island or be imported without some payment of fees, percentages, or taxes.

For a time we students of law, economics, and political science, the *San-San Kai* group, continued to devote ourselves to books, theories, and abstract discussions. We were not yet politicized, but it was impossible to close our eyes and ears to evidence of a mounting crisis. The Generalissimo's representatives on Formosa were extending to our island the abuses that weakened his position throughout China and brought about his ultimate downfall. By the end of 1946, Chen Yi's commissioners were acting with unlimited and desperate greed. They wanted to become as rich as possible before the Nationalist government collapsed. They called it "necessary state socialism."

All this directly affected our own interests or the interests of our families. My father, Speaker of the Kaohsiung City Council, was not molested but he was well acquainted with countless incidents of extortion and illegitimate confiscation of Formosan property, and of properties and businesses in which Formosans and Japanese had developed shared interests during the preceding fifty years. The "collaborationist" charge was used by any unscrupulous Chinese who thought he saw a chance to dispossess a Formosan of attractive property.

During the first weeks of 1947 while we were concentrating on our work for degrees, a series of acts by the Chen Yi administration provoked a violent protest. The commissioners of finance, communications, and industry, working with the Trading Bureau, issued a series of new regulations that drastically tightened the monopolies, the "necessary state socialism," that was draining Formosa's wealth into the pockets of these commissioners, the governor general, and their patrons on the continent. These regulations provoked heated discussion among the students in our group. Concurrently the central government announced adoption of a new constitution for "democratic China," but Governor Chen Yi, on Chiang Kai-shek's orders, informed the people of Formosa that since they were unfamiliar with democratic processes, the provisions would not apply in Formosa until after a period of political tutelage. In other words, we would not be able to have an effective voice in the island administration until the Nationalist party leaders were ready to take the risk. According to us, students of law and political science, the true reason was that Formosa was not yet legally Chinese territory, and the local administration could not take the risk of exposing itself to a public vote of confidence. Then followed a third provocation, and the consequences of this action nearly blasted Chen Yi and the Nationalists from the island.

On the night of February 28, 1947, several of Chen Yi's Monopoly Bureau police savagely beat an old woman who was peddling a few packs of cigarettes without a license in the street market of Round Park. A riot followed. The Monopoly agents were chased to a nearby police station, and their cars were burned. On the next day the whole of Taipei was seething, and by nightfall a great confrontation between the Formosan people and the occupying Chinese had begun. The first wave of angry protests were directed against the Tobacco Monopoly Bureau. Its branch offices were ransacked and burned and its employees beaten in the streets. Demonstrators marched on the Monopoly Bureau headquarters to demand moderation of Monopoly policies. Getting no satisfaction there, they marched toward the governor's office to protest and present their petition. As they approached the gates, the unarmed marchers were mowed down by machine-gun fire before they could enter the compound.

Pent-up public anger immediately burst forth. By nightfall next day Chen Yi's administration was virtually paralyzed. The principal officials and more influential carpetbaggers had established an armed camp in the northern suburbs to which they sent wives, children, and truckloads of private possessions, under heavy guard. A majority of newcomers from the continent hid in their homes, fearing a general massacre.

There was actually no threat of this. The Formosans were unarmed and police functions were taken over temporarily by students who were observing strict discipline. In the first two days there had been some violence on both sides, for Governor Chen's roving patrols were shooting at random in an attempt to terrorize the people, and the Formosans sometimes resorted to clubs and stones. Several Monopoly Bureau employees were beaten so severely that they died of injuries. Greater public anger was provoked by the disappearance of a number of middle school students who had entered the Railway Bureau offices to ask when service would be resumed on the main line so that they could leave the city for their homes south of Taipei.

On the third day Governor General Chen Yi announced that he was ready to hear the people. He appointed a committee of prominent Formosans to meet with his own representatives to settle the "incident" by drawing up a program of reforms which he promised to submit to the central government for consideration. He promised to withdraw roving patrols from the city streets and pledged that no troops would be brought into Taipei. This widely representative committee included members of the emergency and temporary police force that had assumed the duties of Chen Yi's men, now in hiding. Among his own representatives on the committee, I am ashamed to say, were several men who were Formosans by birth but had gone to China in the 1920s and had worked there for the Nationalist government. They had come back to serve under Chen Yi, and can only be described as "professional Formosans," men who were well paid by the government and who were always brought forward as "native Formosans" to talk convincingly with foreign visitors on behalf of Chen's administration.

In setting up the committee, the governor announced he wished to receive the recommendations for a program of reform on March 14. Seventeen branch committees were set up in cities and towns throughout the island. At each of these, local Formosan grievances were discussed, recommendations drawn up, and forwarded to the central committee at the capital. The Settlement Committee met on the stage of the city auditorium, and the seats in the large hall were crowded at every session.

Within five days after the initial uprising, Taipei was quiet, although tense. Shops reopened and supplies began to come in from the countryside to city markets. Despite the governor's pledges, he tried to bring troops up from the south, hoping to forestall the necessity of receiving the reform proposals. Fortunately word of the events of February 28 and March 1 had spread rapidly throughout the island. Alert citizens in the Hsinchu area prevented troop movements by tearing up the rails at certain places and stalling the troop trains. Governor Chen's attempt at deception heightened the anger and mistrust of the Taipei people. Riots occurred in some of the principal towns where the governor's men attempted to maintain control. A handful of communists, men and women released from local Japanese prisons in late 1945 on General MacArthur's orders, attempted to take advantage of the confusion. They failed to attract a following. Formosans had become accustomed to fear communism ever since Japan adopted its determined anticommunist policies at the close of World War I.

During the height of the excitement at Taipei, we students at the university gathered at the medical school auditorium to discuss the situation. There was no organization, and the meetings were inconclusive. Our situation on the campus was a favorable one, and we still thought we lived in a detached world. We would have liked a better and larger faculty, but we had no real academic grievance. Our only grievances were both personal and general, the troubles, injuries, and losses suffered by our families and by Formosans in general. When our meetings broke up, we each went our own way with the tacit understanding that each would do what he wanted in the crisis.

Chen Yi and his principal officers addressed the people from time to time on the radio, urging them to be calm, saying that their demands for reform were justified, and that their proposals would be given careful consideration. But we began to hear rumors that a large military force was being assembled in Fukien, a hundred miles away across the straits. The committee therefore hastened to finish the Draft Reform Program, knowing that if Nationalist troops arrived in force, Governor Chen would never bother to consider it.

All through the week our local papers issued regular and special editions to keep us informed of the committee's work, and from time to time the proceedings in the city auditorium were broadcast. Occasionally some of our university group attended these sessions, and we talked of nothing else throughout the first week of March. On March 7, after consulting with all the seventeen local committees, such as the one which my father was a member of, the spokesmen for the committee transmitted to the governor the reform proposals he had requested them to make.

One politically active group of students drew up a written petition for reforms and addressed it to General Chen. It was phrased with restraint, and when taken to the governor's offices it was politely received. The governor's officers called it very useful advice, and politely asked the petitioners to write down their names and addresses. This they did, in all innocence.

Meanwhile my father experienced a cruel ordeal at Kaohsiung. Kaohsiung was one of the seventeen cities and towns to form a Settlement Committee and he was asked to be its local chairman. In this strange interim period it was charged with maintaining local law and order and formulating proposals for consideration by the Central Committee at Taipei. The committee therefore decided to call on the local garrison commander, General Peng Meng-chi, to ask that he restrain the soldiers who were attempting to terrorize the city and intimidate the committee. His roving patrols were shooting at random whenever they spotted small groups of Formosans gathered in the streets discussing the crisis. My father's deputation was to ask General Peng to withdraw these patrols and to keep his soldiers in barracks while local leaders debated reform in response to the governor's invitation for recommendations.

The Kaohsiung garrison headquarters is located on a hill overlooking city and harbor. As soon as my father and his companions reached the compound there, they were seized and bound with ropes. Unfortunately one committee member, a man named Tu, was an impulsive man recently returned from China, who had at one time served under Wang Ching-wei, Chiang Kai-shek's bitter rival in the Nationalist Party. This man now burst out in a violent tirade against the Generalissimo as well as against his appointee, General Chen.

After this he was taken from the others and bound with bare wires instead of ropes. The wires were twisted with wire-pliers until Tu screamed in agony. After a night of torment, he was shot.

My father and the other committee members were then bound with ropes looped around their necks and were threatened by soldiers with bayonets. They too expected to be shot at any moment, but on the second day my father was released and sent home. General Peng had intervened and shown clemency saying that he knew my father well. He said, "We know this man Peng is a good man. There is no reason to hurt him."

Totally exhausted, Father went home. He had nothing to eat for two days and he was emotionally shattered. His disillusionment was complete. Henceforth he would have nothing more to do with politics and public affairs under the Chinese. His was the bitterness of a betrayed idealist. He went so far as to cry out that he was ashamed of his Chinese blood and wished that his children after him would always marry foreigners until his descendants could no longer claim to be Chinese.

At Taipei I knew nothing of this at this time. We students were listening to radio reports of fighting here and there, of the action along the railway lines near Miao-li that had kept Chen Yi's troops out of the city, and rumors that the aborigines were coming down from the hills to help us confront the Chinese.

My grandmother from Patou village was keeping house for me in Taipei, as she had done for my brothers and sisters so many years ago. She had many relatives and friends in Keelung, and on the afternoon of March 10 a terrified visitor from Patou relayed the news that troop ships were coming in from China, and that soldiers on deck had begun strafing the shoreline and docking area even before the ships had reached the pier.

This began a reign of terror in the port town and in Taipei. As the Nationalist troops came ashore they moved out quickly through Keelung streets, shooting and bayoneting men and boys, raping women, and looting homes and shops. Some Formosans were seized and stuffed alive into burlap bags found piled up at the sugar warehouse doors, and were then simply tossed into the harbor. Others were merely tied up or chained before being thrown from the piers.

By late evening military units had entered Taipei city and from there began to move on through the island. At the same time other troop ships from China arried at Kaohsiung where Nationalist army units joined General Peng's garrison and repeated there the ferocious behavior of the troops at Keelung and Taipei. General Chen Yi was determined to intimidate the Formosan people and to destroy all Formosans who had dared criticize his administration.

Until March 8 the Formosans who were members of the Settlement Committee and many others who were not, continued to call for reform and tried again and again to appeal to Generalissimo Chiang to recall Chen Yi and replace his commissioners with honest men. By March 10 most of these leading Formosans were dead or imprisoned or in hiding, seeking a way to escape from the island. On March 12 Nationalist planes flew low over the principal towns, scattering leaflets bearing a message from the Generalissimo, "President of the Republic, Commander-in-Chief of the Armed Forces, and Leader of the Party." These carried the text of his comments on the "incident" delivered to a body of high officials at Nanking. He fully endorsed Chen Yi's actions. The leaders of the riots, he said, were "Communists" and "people spoiled by the Japanese." He said the Formosan people owed a great debt to the continental Chinese who had "struggled for fifty years to recover Taiwan."

Nobody knows how many Formosans died in the following weeks, but the estimates ranged from ten to twenty thousand. Members of the Settlement Committee were the first to disappear. Editors and teachers, lawyers and doctors who had dared criticize the government were killed or imprisoned. The university students who had carried a petition to the governor's office and had so naïvely given their true names and addresses were sought out and killed. Many of the middle school students who had taken the place of the cowardly Chinese policemen during the previous week were killed. After that it seemed that anyone who had dared laugh at any Chinese at any time since 1945 was in danger of his life.

During these terrifying weeks I remained quietly within my grandmother's house, frightened and worried. I had not been a member of any politically active group on the campus, and my name was on no petition or manifesto. No soldiers came to search our house, and I was not called out in the middle of the night as were some friends who disappeared. For all my hard work toward a degree in political science at the university, I was still far removed from practical politics and very naïve. I had not yet fully realized how much more threatened our personal freedom was now than it had been under the Japanese. In several letters to my father at this time I expressed an angry reaction to the terrible things taking place at Taipei. I did not then know that my father's mail was being censored until one day the chief of police at Kaohsiung quietly warned my father to tell his son not to write such letters, and that my name too was now on a blacklist.

Kaohsiung had suffered terribly during the incident and the weeks following the arrival of Chiang's troops. In these days the garrison commander, General Peng, earned his reputation as "the Butcher of Kaohsiung." For example, when a large number of leading Kaohsiung citizens had gathered in the city auditorium to debate the crisis, the doors were closed and the chamber swept with machine-gun fire. Families were compelled to watch the public execution of fathers and sons in the square before the railway station. There were many stories of torture inflicted on prisoners before their execution. My father, who had been an idealist all his life, became more bitter and more depressed.

Throughout Formosa prominent men or men with property were being intimidated and blackmailed by petty Nationalist officials who threatened to charge them with "antigovernment sentiment." The deputy speaker of the Kaohsiung City Council, for example, was subjected to extortion by several young Nationalist army officers, and barely managed to evade a demand that he hand over a young daughter to one of them. He had been a wealthy man, but was soon bankrupt. It was rumored at one time that my father would soon be arrested and tried for having been chairman of the local Kaohsiung Committee for Settling the Incident. He was closely watched for a long period and only narrowly escaped the hard fate of many friends.

Gradually Taipei became quiet. General Chen Yi was recalled to Nanking, made a senior advisor to the government, and soon President Chiang made him governor of the large and important province of Chekiang. His successor at Taipei was a lawyer, Dr. Wei Tao-ming, who had once been Chinese ambassador to Washington and had many American friends.

We students gradually returned to the campus one by one. We did not dare meet in groups anywhere at any time but confined our angry discussions to moments when we could walk together in twos and threes across the broad university grounds. We quickly realized that there were informers planted among us in the classrooms, and that it was never safe to speak out frankly before a mere acquaintance or before any university group. Occasionally the dreaded secret police, the military police, or the city police raided university dormitories apparently following up leads given to them by members of the student body. Among those arrested in these campus raids were liberal and outstanding Chinese students who were as severely critical of the government as we were. By now we were fully aware that one of the most common Chinese practices was the use of paid informants and the offering of rewards ranging from a few Formosan dollars in cash to promises of lucrative jobs and offices. . . .

18.4 AND 18.5 MAO TAKES CHARGE

After the surrender of Peking, the Communist armies advanced rapidly south, forcing their way across the Yangzi River. Nanjing, the Guomindang capital, fell on April 21, 1949. By the beginning of the summer, it was clear that the Communists would prevail in the civil war.

The two documents below capture the mood in the Chinese Communist Party camp as soldiers of the People's Liberation Army advanced to take Nanjing. Like Prince Dorgon in 1644, Mao Zedong was no longer obliged to coddle his enemies. With victory clearly in sight, conciliatory words and the rhetoric of compromise were not needed. Instead, Mao sought to reassure the residents of cities newly under Communist administration and promised a quick restoration of order. Simultaneously, knowing that a rapid victory in the southeast would prevent the destruction of the industrial base built by the Nationalists, Mao spurred on his army commanders to complete the military consolidation quickly.

18.4 *The Army Advances*

ORDER TO THE ARMY FOR THE COUNTRY-WIDE ADVANCE (APRIL 21, 1949)

Comrade commanders and fighters of all field armies, comrades of the People's Liberation Army in the guerrilla areas of the south!

The Agreement on Internal Peace, drafted after long negotiations between the delegation of the Communist Party of China and the delegation of the Nanjing Guomindang government, has been rejected by that government. The responsible members of the Nanjing Guomindang government have rejected the agreement because they are still obeying the orders of U.S. imperialism and Chiang Kai-shek, the chieftain of the Guomindang bandit gang, and because they are trying to block the progress of the cause of the Chinese people's liberation and prevent the internal problem from being solved by peaceful means. The Agreement on Internal Peace, comprising eight sections with twenty-four articles formulated by the two delegations in the negotiations, is lenient on the problem of war criminals, is lenient towards the Guomindang officers, soldiers and government personnel and provides appropriate solutions for other problems, all proceeding from the interests of the nation and the people. The rejection of this agreement shows that the Guomindang reactionaries are determined to fight to the finish the counter-revolutionary war which they started. The rejection of this agreement shows that in proposing peace negotiations on January 1 of this year the Guomindang reactionaries were only trying to check the advance of the People's Liberation Army and thus gain a breathing space for a later comeback to crush the revolutionary forces. The rejection of this agreement shows that the Li Zongren government at Nanjing was utterly hypocritical in professing to accept the Chinese Communist Party's eight terms for peace as the basis for negotiations. Inasmuch as the Li Zong-ren government had already accepted such fundamental terms as the punishment of war criminals, the reorganization of all the reactionary Guomindang troops on democratic principles and the handing over of all power and authority by the Nanjing government and its subordinate governments at all levels, it had no reason to reject the specific measures which were drawn up on the basis of these fundamental terms and which are most lenient. In these circumstances, we order you as follows:

1. Advance bravely and annihilate resolutely, thoroughly, wholly and completely all the Guomindang reactionaries within China's borders who dare to resist. Liberate the people of the whole country. Safeguard China's territorial integrity, sovereignty and independence.
2. Advance bravely and arrest all the incorrigible war criminals. No matter where they may flee, they must be brought to justice and punished according to law. Pay special attention to arresting the bandit chieftain Chiang Kai-shek.
3. Proclaim to all Guomindang local governments and local military groups the final amended version of the Agreement on Internal Peace. In accordance with its general ideas, you may conclude local agreements with those who are willing to cease hostilities and to settle matters by peaceful means.
4. After the People's Liberation Army has encircled Nanjing, we are willing to give the Li Zongren government at Nanjing another opportunity to sign the Agreement on Internal Peace if that government has not yet fled and dispersed and desires to sign it.

Mao Zedong
Chairman of the Chinese People's
Revolutionary Military Commission

Zhu De
Commander-in-Chief of the Chinese
People's Liberation Army

18.5 *Takeover Details*

PROCLAMATION OF THE CHINESE PEOPLE'S LIBERATION ARMY
(APRIL 25, 1949)

The Guomindang reactionaries have rejected the terms for peace and persist in their stand of waging a criminal war against the nation and the people. The people all over the country hope that the People's Liberation Army will speedily wipe out the Guomindang reactionaries. We have ordered the People's Liberation Army to advance courageously, wipe out all reactionary Guomindang troops who dare to resist, arrest all the incorrigible war criminals, liberate the people of the whole country, safeguard China's territorial integrity, sovereignty and independence, and bring about the genuine unification of the country, which the whole people long for. We earnestly hope that people in all walks of life will assist the People's Liberation Army wherever it goes. We hereby proclaim the following eight-point covenant by which we, together with the whole people shall abide.

1. Protect the lives and property of all the people. People in all walks of life, irrespective of class, belief or occupation, are expected to maintain order and adopt a co-operative attitude towards the People's Liberation Army. The People's Liberation Army on its part will adopt a co-operative attitude towards people in all walks of life. Counter-revolutionaries or other saboteurs who seize the opportunity to create disturbances, loot or sabotage shall be severely dealt with.

2. Protect the industrial, commercial, agricultural and livestock enterprises of the national bourgeoisie. All privately owned factories, shops, banks, warehouses, vessels, wharves, farms, livestock frames and other enterprises will without exception be protected against any encroachment. It is hoped that workers and employees in all occupations will maintain production as usual and that all shops will remain open as usual.

3. Confiscate bureaucrat-capital. All factories, shops, banks, and warehouses, all vessels, wharves and railways, all postal, telegraph, electric light, telephone and water supply services, and all farms, livestock farms and other enterprises operated by the reactionary Guomindang government and the big bureaucrats shall be taken over by the People's Government. In such enterprises the private shares held by national capitalists engaged in industry, commerce, agriculture or livestock raising shall be recognized, after their ownership is verified. All personnel working in bureaucrat-capitalist enterprises must remain at their posts pending the take-over by the People's Government and must assume responsibility for the safekeeping of all assets, machinery, charts, account books, records, etc., in preparation for

the check-up and take-over. Those who render useful service in this connection will be rewarded; those who obstruct or sabotage will be punished. Those desiring to go on working after the take-over by the People's Government will be given employment commensurate with their abilities so that they will not become destitute and homeless.

4. Protect all public and private schools, hospitals, cultural and educational institutions, athletic fields and other public welfare establishments. It is hoped that all personnel in these institutions will remain at their posts; the People's Liberation Army will protect them from molestation.

5. Except for the incorrigible war criminals and counter-revolutionaries who have committed the most heinous crimes, the People's Liberation Army and the People's Government will not hold captive, arrest or subject to indignity any officials, whether high or low, in the Guomindang's central, provincial, municipal and county governments, deputies to the "National Assembly," members of the Legislative and Control Yuans, members of the political consultative councils, police officers and district, township, village and *baojia*[2] officials, so long as they do not offer armed resistance or plot sabotage. All these persons are enjoined, pending the take-over, to stay at their posts, abide by the orders and decrees of the People's Liberation Army and the People's Government and assume responsibility for the safekeeping of all the assets and records of their offices. The People's Government will permit the employment of those among them who can make themselves useful in some kind of work and have not committed any grave reactionary act or other flagrant misdeed. Punishment shall be meted out to those who seize the opportunity to engage in sabotage, theft or embezzlement, or abscond with public funds, assets or records, or refuse to give an accounting.

6. In order to ensure peace and security in both cities and rural areas and to maintain public order, all stragglers and disbanded soldiers are required to report and surrender to the People's Liberation Army or the People's Government in their localities. No action will be taken against those who voluntarily do so and hand over their arms. Those who refuse to report or who conceal their arms shall be arrested and investigated. Persons who shelter stragglers and disbanded soldiers and do not report them to the authorities shall be duly punished.

7. The feudal system of landownership in the rural areas is irrational and should be abolished. To abolish it, however, preparations must be made and the necessary steps taken. Generally speaking, the reduction of rent

2. The Guomindang's *baojia* was based on the Qing system of the same name. In 1932, the Nationalist government promulgated "Regulations for the Organization of *Bao* and *Jia*," which required neighbors to report each other's activities to the authorities. All were subjected to punishment if one was found guilty.

and interest should come first and land distribution later; only after the People's Liberation Army has arrived at a place and worked there for a considerable time will it be possible to speak of solving the land problem in earnest. The peasant masses should organize themselves and help the People's Liberation Army to carry out the various initial reforms. They should also work hard at their farming so as to prevent the present level of agricultural production from falling and should then raise it step by step to improve their own livelihood and supply the people of the cities with commodity grain. Urban land and buildings cannot be dealt with in the same way as the problem of rural land.

8. Protect the lives and property of foreign nationals. It is hoped that all foreign nations will follow their usual pursuits and observe order. All foreign nationals must abide by the orders and decrees of the People's Liberation Army and the People's Government and must not engage in espionage, act against the cause of China's national independence and the people's liberation, or harbour Chinese war criminals, counter-revolutionaries or other law-breakers. Otherwise, they shall be dealt with according to law by the People's Liberation Army and the People's Government.

The People's Liberation Army is highly disciplined; it is fair in buying and selling and is not allowed to take even a needle or a piece of thread from the people. It is hoped that the people throughout the country will live and work in peace and will not give credence to rumors or raise false alarms. This proclamation is hereby issued in all sincerity and earnestness.

Mao Zedong
Chairman of the Chinese People's
Revolutionary Military Commission

Zhu De
Commander-in-Chief of the Chinese
People's Liberation Army

18.6 DEMOCRATIC DICTATORSHIP

During the last days of civil war and on the eve of the twenty-eighth anniversary of the founding of the Chinese Communist Party (CCP), Mao Zedong took time to reflect on the turbulent pattern of modern Chinese history and the revolutionary experiences that he and others of his generation had shared. The product of these ruminations was his famous essay "On the People's Democratic Dictatorship."

This work, like Lenin's *The State and the Revolution*, was the expression of a lifetime of sacrifice and labor on the behalf of the revolutionary ideal. The practical problems of bringing about revolution and the unification of China were at an end. The time was at hand for construction of the revolutionary state that Party visionaries had dreamed of since the formation of the earliest Marxist study groups in China.

Mao suggested that it was the "correct world outlook" of the Communist Party that enabled it to triumph in the historical process. In the future, the "scientific" understanding of history would provide the framework of CCP rule and the dictatorship of the Party would lead the way to a classless society and the extinction of parties, governments, and, of course, social classes. Enemies of the revolutionary order would be silenced and democracy would be the property of "the people," i.e., the peasantry, the working class, the national bourgeoisie, and the urban petty bourgeoisie. The dialectic process had foretold the demise of the CCP's enemies and dictatorship would henceforth be an instrument to crush the landlord class, Nationalist reactionaries, and bureaucratic capitalists.

In subsequent years, the Communist Party would succumb to the temptation of using the dictatorship proclaimed by Mao in 1949 in cruel and capricious ways. But in the summer of 1949, the abuses to which a monopoly of political power and single-party rule could lead were only dimly glimpsed. The war was at an end, Chiang Kai-shek had skulked off to Taiwan, U.S. and British imperialism were at bay, and Chairman Mao and his comrades-in-arms strode forward to place their imprint on the future of China.

On the People's Democratic Dictatorship

IN COMMEMORATION OF THE TWENTY-EIGHTH
ANNIVERSARY OF THE COMMUNIST PARTY OF CHINA
JUNE 30, 1949

The first of July 1949 marks the fact that the Communist Party of China has already lived through twenty-eight years. Like a man, a political party has its childhood, youth, manhood and old age. The Communist Party of China is no longer a child or a lad in his teens but has become an adult. When a man reaches old age, he will die; the same is true of a party. When classes disappear, all instruments of class struggle—parties and the state machinery—will lose their function, cease to be necessary, therefore gradually wither away and end their historical mission; and human society will move to a higher stage. We are the opposite of the political parties of the bourgeoisie. They are afraid to speak of the extinction of classes, state power, and parties. We, on the contrary, declare openly that we are striving hard to create the very conditions which will bring about their extinction. The leadership of the Communist Party and the state power of the people's dictatorship are such conditions. Anyone who does not recognize this truth is no communist. Young comrades who have not studied Marxism-Leninism and have only recently joined the Party may not yet understand this truth. They must understand it—only then can they have a correct world outlook. They must understand that the road to the abolition of classes, to the abolition of state power and to the abolition of parties is the road all mankind must take; it is only a question of time and conditions. Communists the world over are wiser than the bourgeoisie, they understand the laws governing the existence and development of things, they understand dialectics and they can see farther. The bourgeoisie does not welcome this truth because it does not want to be overthrown. To be overthrown is painful and is unbearable to contemplate for those overthrown, for example, for the Guomindang reactionaries whom we are now overthrowing and for Japanese imperialism which we together with other peoples overthrew some time ago. But for the working class, the laboring people and the Communist Party the question is not one of being overthrown, but of working hard to create the conditions in which classes, state power and political parties will die out very naturally and mankind will enter the realm of Great Harmony. We have mentioned in passing the long-range perspective of human progress in order to explain clearly the problems we are about to discuss.

As everyone knows, our Party passed through these twenty-eight years not in peace but amid hardships, for we had to fight enemies, both foreign and domestic, both inside and outside the Party. We thank Marx, Engels, Lenin and Stalin for giving us a weapon. This weapon is not a machine-gun, but Marxism-Leninism.

In his book *"Left-Wing" Communism, an Infantile Disorder* written in 1920, Lenin described the quest of the Russians for revolutionary theory. Only after several decades of hardship and suffering did the Russians find Marxism. Many things in China were the same as, or similar to, those in Russia before the October Revolution. There was the same feudal oppression. There was similar economic and cultural backwardness. Both countries were backward, China even more so. In both countries alike, for the sake of national regeneration progressives braved hard and bitter struggles in their quest for revolutionary truth.

From the time of China's defeat in the Opium War of 1840, Chinese progressives went through untold hardships in their quest for truth from the Western countries. Hong Xiuquan, Kang Youwei, Yan Fu and Sun Yat-sen were representative of those who had looked to the West for truth before the Communist Party of China was born. Chinese who then sought progress would read any book containing the new knowledge from the West. The number of students sent to Japan, Britain, the United States, France, and Germany was amazing. At home, the imperial examinations were abolished and modern schools sprang up like bamboo shoots after a spring rain; every effort was made to learn from the West. In my youth, I too engaged in such studies. They represented the culture of Western bourgeois democracy, including the social theories and natural sciences of that period, and they were called "the new learning" in contrast to Chinese feudal culture, which was called "the old learning." For quite a long time, those who had acquired the new learning felt confident that it would save China, and very few of them had any doubts on this score, as the adherents of the old learning had. Only modernization could save China, only learning from foreign countries could modernize China. Among the foreign countries, only the Western capitalist countries were then progressive, as they had successfully built modern bourgeois states. The Japanese had been successful in learning from the West, and the Chinese also wished to learn from the Japanese. The Chinese in those days regarded Russia as backward, and few wanted to learn from her. That was how the Chinese tried to learn from foreign countries in the period from the 1840s to the beginning of the 20th century.

Imperialist aggression shattered the fond dreams of the Chinese about learning from the West. It was very odd—why were the teachers always committing aggression against their pupil? The Chinese learned a good deal from the West, but they could not make it work and were never able to realize their ideals. Their repeated struggles, including such a country-wide movement as the Revolution of 1911, all ended in failure. Day by day, conditions in the country got worse, and life was made impossible. Doubts arose, increased and deepened. World War I shook the whole globe. The Russians made the October Revolution and created the world's first socialist state. Under the leadership of Lenin and Stalin, the revolutionary energy of the great proletariat and laboring people of Russia, hitherto latent and unseen by foreigners, suddenly erupted like a volcano, and the Chinese and all mankind began to see the Russians in a new light. Then, and only then, did the Chinese enter an entirely new era in their thinking and their life. They found Marxism-Leninism, the universally applicable truth, and the face of China began to change.

It was through the Russians that the Chinese found Marxism. Before the October Revolution, the Chinese were not only ignorant of Lenin and Stalin, they did not even know of Marx and Engels. The salvoes of the October Revolution brought us Marxism-Leninism. The October Revolution helped progressives in China, as throughout the world, to adopt the proletarian world outlook as the instrument for studying a nation's destiny and considering anew their own problems. Follow the path of the Russians—that was their conclusion. In 1919, the May 4th Movement took place in China. In 1921, the Communist Party of China was founded. Sun Yat-sen, in the depths of despair, came across the October Revolution and the Communist Party of China. He welcomed the October Revolution, welcomed Russian help to the Chinese and welcomed cooperation of the Communist Party of China. Then Sun Yat-sen died and Chiang Kai-shek rose to power. Over a long period of twenty-two years, Chiang Kai-shek dragged China into ever more hopeless straits. In this period, during the anti-fascist Second World War in which the Soviet Union was the main force, three big imperialist powers were knocked out, while two others were weakened. In the whole world only one big imperialist power, the United States of America, remained uninjured. But the United States faced a grave domestic crisis. It wanted to enslave the whole world; it supplied arms to help Chiang Kai-shek slaughter several million Chinese. Under the leadership of the Communist Party of China, the Chinese people, after driving out Japanese imperialism, waged the People's War of Liberation for three years and have basically won victory.

Thus Western bourgeois civilization, bourgeois democracy and the plan for a bourgeois republic have all gone bankrupt in the eyes of the Chinese people. Bourgeois democracy has given way to people's democracy under the leadership of the working class and the bourgeois republic to the people's republic. This has made it possible to achieve socialism and communism through the people's republic, to abolish classes to render a world of Great Harmony. Kang Youwei wrote Datongshu, or the *Book of Great Harmony*, but he did not and could not find the way to achieve Great Harmony. There are bourgeois republics in foreign lands, but China cannot have a bourgeois republic because she is a country suffering under imperialist oppression. The only way is through a people's republic led by the working class.

All other ways have been tried and failed. Of the people who hankered after those ways, some have fallen, some have awakened and some are changing their ideas. Events are developing so swiftly that many feel the abruptness of the change and the need to learn anew. This state of mind is understandable and we welcome this worthy desire to learn anew.

The vanguard of the Chinese proletariat learned Marxism-Leninism after the October Revolution and founded the Communist Party of China. It entered at once into political struggle and only now, after a tortuous course of twenty-eight years, has it won basic victory. From our twenty-eight years' experience we have drawn a conclusion similar to the one Sun Yat-sen drew in his testament from his "experience of forty years"; that is, we are deeply convinced that to win victory, "we must arouse the masses of the people and unite in a common struggle with those nations of the world which treat us as equals." Sun Yat-sen had a world outlook different from ours and started from a different class standpoint in studying and tackling problems; yet, in the 1920s he reached a conclusion basically the same as ours on the question of how to struggle against imperialism.

Twenty-four years have passed since Sun Yat-sen's death, and the Chinese revolution, led by the Communist Party of China, has made tremendous advances both in theory and practice and has radically changed the face of China. Up to now the principal and fundamental experience the Chinese people have gained is twofold:

1. Internally, arouse the masses of the people. That is, unite the working class, the peasantry, the urban petty bourgeoisie and the national bourgeoisie, form a domestic united front under the leadership of the working class, and advance from this to the establishment of a state which is a people's democratic dictatorship under the leadership of the working class and based on the alliance of workers and peasants.

2. Externally, unite in a common struggle with those nations of the world which treat us as equals and unite with the peoples of all countries. That is, ally ourselves with the Soviet Union, with the People's Democracies and with the proletariat and the broad masses of the people in all other countries, and form an international united front.

"You are leaning to one side." Exactly. The forty years' experience of Sun Yat-sen and the twenty-eight years' experience of the Communist Party have taught us to lean to one side, and we are firmly convinced that in order to win victory and consolidate it we must lean to one side. In the light of the experiences accumulated in these forty years and these twenty-eight years, all Chinese without exception must lean either to the side of imperialism or to the side of socialism. Sitting on the fence will not do, nor is there a third road. We oppose the Chiang Kai-shek reactionaries who lean to the side of imperialism, and we also oppose the illusions about a third road.

"You are too irritating." We are talking about how to deal with domestic and foreign reactionaries, the imperialists and their running dogs, not about how to deal with anyone else. With regard to such reactionaries, the question of irritating them or not does not arise. Irritated or not irritated, they will remain the same because they are reactionaries. Only if we draw a clear line between reactionaries and revolutionaries, expose the intrigues and plots of the reactionaries, arouse the vigilance and attention of the revolutionary ranks, heighten our will to fight and crush the enemy's arrogance can we isolate the reactionaries, vanquish them or supersede them. We must not show the slightest timidity before a wild beast. We must learn from Wu Song on the Jingyang Ridge.[3] As Wu Song saw it, the tiger on Jingyang Ridge was a man-eater, whether irritated or not. Either kill the tiger or be eaten by him—one or the other. . . .

"You are dictatorial." My dear sirs, you are right, that is just what we are. All the experience the Chinese people have accumulated through several decades teach us to enforce the people's democratic dictatorship, that is, to deprive the reactionaries of the right to speak and let the people alone have that right.

Who are the people? At the present stage in China, they are the working class, the peasantry, the urban petty bourgeoisie and the national bourgeoisie. These classes, led by the working class and the Communist Party, unite to form their own state and elect their own government; they enforce their dictatorship over the running dogs of imperialism—the landlord class and bureaucrat-bourgeoisie, as well as the representatives of those classes, the Guomindang reactionaries and their accomplices—suppress them, allow them only to behave themselves and not

3. Mao here refers to a celebrated episode from the novel *Water Margin* (fourteenth century) by Shi Nai'an. This novel was one of Mao Zedong's favorites as a boy and it is characteristic of him that Wu Song's single-handed struggle to defeat a ravenous tiger should be remembered here as a metaphor for the CCP's struggle against its enemies.

to be unruly in word or deed. If they speak or act in an unruly way, they will be promptly stopped and punished. Democracy is practiced within the ranks of the people, who enjoy the rights of freedom of speech, assembly, association and so on. The right to vote belongs only to the people, not to the reactionaries. The combination of these two aspects, democracy for the people and dictatorship over the reactionaries, is the people's democratic dictatorship.

Why must things be done this way? The reason is quite clear to everybody. If things were not done this way, the revolution would fail, the people would suffer, the country would be conquered.

"Don't you want to abolish state power?" Yes, we do, but not right now; we cannot do it yet. Why? Because imperialism still exists, because domestic reaction still exists, because classes still exist in our country. Our present task is to strengthen the people's state apparatus—mainly the people's army, the people's police and the people's courts—in order to consolidate national defence and protect the people's interests. Given this condition, China can develop steadily, under the leadership of the working class and the Communist Party, from an agricultural into an industrial country and from a new-democratic into a socialist and communist society, can abolish classes and realize the Great Harmony. The state apparatus, including the army, the police and the courts, is the instrument by which one class oppresses another. It is an instrument for the oppression of antagonistic classes; it is violence and not "benevolence." "You are not benevolent!" Quite so. We definitely do not apply a policy of benevolence to the reactionary classes. Our policy of benevolence is applied only within the ranks of the people, not beyond them to the reactionaries or to the reactionary activities of reactionary classes.

The people's state protects the people. Only when the people have such a state can they educate and remold themselves by democratic methods on a country-wide scale, with everyone taking part, and shake off the influence of domestic and foreign reactionaries (which is still very strong, will survive for a long time and cannot be quickly destroyed), rid themselves of the bad habits and ideas acquired in the old society, not allow themselves to be led astray by the reactionaries, and continue to advance—to advance towards a socialist and communist society.

Here, the method we employ is democratic, the method of persuasion, not of compulsion. When anyone among the people breaks the law, he too shall be punished, imprisoned or even sentenced to death; but this is a matter of a few individual cases, and it differs in principle from the dictatorship exercised over the reactionaries as a class.

As for the members of the reactionary classes and individual reactionaries, so long as they do not rebel, sabotage or create trouble after their political power has been overthrown, land and work will be given to them as well in order to allow them to live and remold themselves through labour into a new people. If they are not willing to work, the people's state will compel them to work. Propaganda and educational work will be done among them too and will be done, moreover, with as much care and thoroughness as among the captured army officers in the past.

This, too, may be called a "policy of benevolence" if you like, but it is imposed by us on the members of the enemy classes and cannot be mentioned in the same breath with the work of self-education which we carry on within the ranks of the revolutionary people.

Such remolding of members of the reactionary classes can be accomplished only by a state of the people's democracy dictatorship under the leadership of the Communist Party. When it is well done, China's major exploiting classes, the landlord class and the bureaucrat-bourgeoisie (the monopoly capitalist class), will be eliminated for good. There remain the national bourgeoisie; at the present stage, we can already do a good deal of suitable educational work with many of them. When the time comes to realize socialism, that is, to nationalize private enterprise, we shall carry the work of educating and remolding them a step further. The people have a powerful state apparatus in their hands—there is no need to fear rebellion by the national bourgeoisie.

The serious problem is the education of the peasantry. The peasant economy is scattered, and the socialization of agriculture, judging by the Soviet Union's experience, will require a long time and painstaking work. Without socialization of agriculture, there can be no complete, consolidated socialism. The steps to socialize agriculture must be co-ordinated with the development of a powerful industry having state enterprise as its backbone. The state of the people's democratic dictatorship must systematically solve the problems of industrialization. Since it is not proposed to discuss economic problems in detail in this article, I shall not go into them further. . . .

To sum up our experience and concentrate it into one point, it is: the people's democratic dictatorship under the leadership of the working class (through the Communist Party) and based upon the alliance of workers and peasants. This dictatorship must unite as one with the international revolutionary forces. This is our formula, our principal experience, our main programme.

Twenty-eight years of our Party is a long period, in which we have accomplished only one thing—we have won basic victory in the revolutionary war. This calls for celebration, because it is the people's victory, because it is victory in a country as large as China. But we still have much work to do; to use the analogy of a journey, our last work is only the first step in a long march of ten thousand *li*. Remnants of the enemy have yet to be wiped out. The serious task of economic construction lies before us. We shall soon put aside some of the things we know well and be compelled to do things we don't know well. This means difficulties. The imperialists reckon that we will not be able to manage our economy; they are standing by and joking on, awaiting our failure.

We must overcome difficulties, we must learn what we do not know. We must learn to do economic work from all who know how, no matter who they are. We must esteem them as teachers, learning from them respectfully and conscientiously. We must not pretend to know when we do not know. We must not put on bureaucratic airs. If we dig into a subject for several months, for a year or two, for three or five years, we shall eventually master it. At first some of the Soviet Communists also were not very good at handling economic matters and the imperialists awaited their failure too. But the Communist Party of the Soviet Union emerged victorious and, under the leadership of Lenin and Stalin, it learned not only how to make the revolution but also how to carry on construction. It has built a great and splendid socialist state. The Communist Party of the Soviet Union is our best teacher and we must learn from it. The situation both at home and abroad is in our favour, we can rely fully on the weapon of the people's democratic dictatorship, unite the people throughout the country, the reactionaries excepted, and advance steadily to our goal.

CHAPTER 19

The Birth of the People's Republic

19.1 TREATY WITH THE SOVIET UNION, FEBRUARY 1950

In the first decade of Communist rule, the Soviet Union was the primary ally of the People's Republic of China. The legal basis for Sino-Soviet cooperation was set in place in 1949 and 1950 in a series of diplomatic and economic accords. After the proclamation of the new Chinese state, Moscow dispatched thousands of Soviet advisors to assist in the construction of socialist China. In this era of cordial relations with the USSR, Stalinist models were adopted in almost every sphere of Chinese life, including industry, law, education, and art. Even the Chinese system of collectivized agriculture was influenced by the Soviet *kolhoz* (collective farm).

The Treaty of Friendship of February 1950 was the cornerstone of the Sino-Soviet alliance. It tied China's international interests to those of the Soviet Union and would serve as a defining framework after the outbreak of the Korean War in June 1950. For cold war warriors in the West, already hostile to "people's China," this treaty substantiated the existence of an "international communist conspiracy."

TREATY OF FRIENDSHIP, ALLIANCE AND MUTUAL ASSISTANCE BETWEEN THE UNION OF SOVIET SOCIALIST REPUBLICS AND THE PEOPLE'S REPUBLIC OF CHINA

(FEBRUARY 14, 1950)

The Presidium of the Supreme Soviet of the Union of Soviet Socialist Republics and the Central People's Government of the People's Republic of China.

ARTICLE 24.   After divorce, debts incurred during the period of marriage shall be paid out of the property acquired by husband and wife during this period. In the case where no such property has been acquired or in the case where such property is insufficient to pay off such debts, the husband shall be held responsible for paying these debts. Debts incurred separately by the husband or wife shall be paid off by the party responsible.

ARTICLE 25.   After divorce, if one party has not remarried and has difficulties in maintenance, the other party should render assistance. Both parties shall work out an agreement with regard to the method and duration of such assistance; in case an agreement cannot be reached, the people's court shall render a decision.

ARTICLE 26.   Persons violating this law shall be punished in accordance with law. In the case where interference with the freedom of marriage has caused death or injury, the person guilty of such interference shall bear criminal responsibility before the law.

ARTICLE 27.   This law shall come into force from this date of its promulgation. In regions inhabited by national minorities, the Military and Political Council of the Administrative Area of the provincial people's government may enact certain modifications of supplementary articles in conformity with the actual conditions prevailing among national minorities in regard to marriage. But such measures must be submitted to the Government Administration Council for ratification before enforcement.

19.3 DING LING'S FICTION: *THE SUN SHINES OVER THE SANGGAN RIVER*

In the summer of 1946, the CCP issued a detailed directive on land reform and dispatched thousands of cadres to liberated zones to launch the redistribution campaign. Acclaimed writer Ding Ling was an observer of these early land reform efforts in the Chahar countryside, northwest of Peking. Later, she used this material as the basis for her novel *The Sun Shines over the Sanggan River,* first published in 1948. In 1951 it became the first Chinese novel to win the Stalin Prize.

One important component of land reform was the "speak bitterness" (*suku*) meeting, where peasants were encouraged to confront the landlords and rich peasants who had once abused them. In some cases, in the emotional airing of grievances that followed, these "class enemies" were beaten to death. Chapter 50 of Ding Ling's novel describes one such "speak bitterness" meeting in Nuanshui, where villagers confronted a local bully named "Schemer Qian." In this piece it is possible to glimpse the depth of rural dissatisfaction, and the energies that the CCP was able to harness as it built its revolutionary movement.

THE SUN SHINES OVER
THE SANGGAN RIVER

When they heard the footsteps of the children who had followed the militia out, the men on the stage glanced at each other, knowing what it meant. The crowd stood still, straining their necks for a sight. The militia looked even sterner, and stopped talking. Yumin, Orchard-keeper Li and Young Guo posted themselves in the middle of the stage and Freckles Li started shouting slogans: "Down with the local despots!" "Down with feudal landlords!" The crowd shouted too, at the same time pressing forward, watching and waiting in an agony of impatience, so that when they were not shouting slogans they were absolutely still.

With a smart movement the militia obeyed the order to stack their rifles, and the crowd's tension increased even more. Then three or four militiamen took Schemer Qian up to the platform. He was wearing a lined gown of grey silk and white trousers, his hands tied behind him. His head was slightly lowered, and his small beady eyes were screwed up, searching the crowd. Those reptilian eyes of his which used to strike fear into people's hearts still cast a blight and quelled many of those present. His pointed mustaches made him look more sinister. Nobody said a word.

Members of the presidium looked at each other anxiously. Old Dong and other members of the work team exchanged anxious glances too and looked expectantly at Freckles Li, who in turn was looking expectantly at the members of the crowd. The crowd was looking at Schemer Qian, and still not a word was said.

For thousands of years the local despots had the power. They had oppressed generation after generation of peasants, and the peasants had bowed their necks under their yoke. Now abruptly they were confronted with this power standing before them with bound hands, and they felt bewildered, at a loss. Some who were particularly intimidated by his malevolent look recalled the days when they could only submit, and now, exposed to this blast, wavered again. So for the time being they were silent.

All this time Schemer Qian, standing on the stage gnawing his lips, was glancing round, wanting to quell these yokels, unwilling to admit defeat. For a moment he really had the mastery. He and his many years of power had become so firmly established in the village it was difficult for anyone to dislodge him. The peasants hated him, and had just been cursing him; but now that he stood before them they held their breath and faltered. It was like the pause before two game-cocks start fighting, each estimating the other's strength. The longer the silence lasted, the greater Qian's power became, until it looked as if he were going to win.

At this point a man suddenly leapt out from the crowd. He had thick eyebrows and sparkling eyes. Rushing up to Schemer Qian he cursed him: "You murderer! You trampled our village under your feet! You killed people from behind the scenes for money. Today we're going to settle all old scores, and do a thorough job of it. Do you hear that? Do you still want to frighten people? It's no use! There's no place for you to stand on this stage! Kneel down! Kneel to all the villagers!" He

Schemer Qian's silk gown was torn. His shoes had fallen off, the white paper hat had been trampled into pieces underfoot. All semblance of order was gone and it looked as though he was going to be beaten to death, when Yumin remembered Comrade Pin's last instructions and pushed his way into the crowd. Having no other way of stopping them, he shielded Qian with his body, and shouted: "Don't be in such a hurry to beat him to death! We've got to ask the county authorities!" Then the militiamen started checking the people.

The crowd was furious at seeing Yumin shelter Schemer Qian. They pressed forward together. Yumin was considerably knocked about but still he said to them: "I swear, there was a time I was afraid we couldn't get the better of him! Now you want to beat him to death, of course I'm pleased. I've long wanted to beat him to death to clean up our district! Only, there's been no order from our superiors and I don't dare. I daren't take the responsibility. A man can only be executed with the county court's approval. I'm asking you to delay it for a few days. Do it as a favour for me! Don't kill him yet; we'll punish him suitably later."

By now quite a few others had come over to help him keep the crowd back, and they said: "Yumin's quite right. A sudden end is too good for him. Let's make him suffer." A lot of people were persuaded, feeling that it was best to consult the county court before killing anyone, and since it was certain the county would grant the people's request, it did not matter waiting a few days. But still some of them were dissatisfied. "Why can't we kill him? The people want to kill him, what's to stop them?"

Old Dong stepped forward and addressed the crowd:

"Schemer Qian owes you money and lives. Just killing him won't make it up to you, will it?"

"If he died several deaths he couldn't make it up," someone said.

By this time Qian had already been carried back onto the stage. He lay there panting like a dying dog, and someone said: "Kill the dog."

"Bah! Killing's too good for him. Let's make him beg for death. Let's humble him for a few days, how about it?" Old Dong's face was red with excitement. He had started life as a hired labourer. Now that he saw peasants just like himself daring to speak out and act boldly, his heart was racing wildly with happiness.

"Right," someone agreed.

"If you don't pull the roots, a weed will always make trouble," another said.

"Are you still afraid of him? Don't be afraid. As long as we're united like today we can keep him in order. Think of a way to deal with him."

"Yes, I've a proposal. Let's have the whole village spit at him, what about that?"

"I say his property should be divided up among us all."

"Make him write a statement, admitting his crimes, and if he opposes us again, we'll have his life."

"Yes, let him write a statement. Make him write it himself."

Schemer Qian crawled to his feet again and kneeled to kowtow to the crowd. His right eye was swollen after his beating so that the eye looked even smaller. His lip was split and mud was mixed with his blood. His bedraggled mustaches drooped disconsolately. He was a wretched sight, and as he thanked the villagers his voice was no longer clear and strong, but he stammered out: "Good people! I'm kowtowing to you good folks. I was quite wrong in the past. Thank you for your mercy . . ."

A group of children softly aped his voice: "Good people! . . ."

Then he was dragged over to write a statement. He took the brush in his trembling hand and wrote line by line. Then everyone discussed the question of confiscating his property and decided to appropriate all, including that of Qianli. But they could not touch Yi's twenty-four *mou*. The peasants were dissatisfied, but this was an order from above, because Yi was a soldier in the Eighth Route Army! So they had to put up with it.

By now the sun was sinking. Hunger made some of the children so restless, they were kicking pebbles at the back of the meeting, and some of the women went quietly home to prepare a meal. The presidium urged Schemer Qian to hurry up and finish writing, saying everybody was tired of waiting for him, and asking where his usual ability had gone to.

When the chairman started reading the statement the crowd grew tense again, and shouted, "Let him read it himself!"

Qian knelt in the middle of the stage, his lined gown hanging in shreds, shoeless, not daring to meet anyone's eyes. He read: "In the past I committed crimes in the village, oppressing good people! . . ."

"That won't do! Just to write 'I' won't do! Write 'local despot, Qian.'"

"Yes, write 'I, local despot Qian.'"

"Start again!"

Schemer Qian started reading again: "I, Qian, a local despot, committed crimes in the village, oppressing good people, and I deserve to die a hundred times over; but my good friends are merciful . . ."

"Who the devil are you calling your good friends?" An old man rushed forward and spat at him.

"Go on reading! Just say all the people of the village."

"No, why should he call us his people."

"Say all the gentlemen."

"Say all the poor gentlemen. We don't want to be rich gentlemen! Only the rich are called gentlemen."

Qian had to continue: "Thanks to the mercy of all the poor gentlemen in the village . . ."

"That's no good. Don't say poor gentlemen; today we poor people have stood up. Say 'the liberated gentlemen,' and it can't be wrong."

"Yes, liberated gentlemen."

Someone chuckled. "Today we're liberated gentlemen!"

"Thanks to the mercy of the liberated gentlemen, my unworthy life has been spared . . ."

"What? I don't understand." Another voice from the crowd interrupted Qian. "We liberated gentlemen aren't going to pass all this literary stuff. Just put it briefly: say your dog's life has been spared."

"Yes, spare your dog's life!" the rest agreed.

Qian had to go on: "Spare my dog's life. In future I must change my former evil ways completely. If I transgress in the slightest or oppose the masses, I shall be put to death. This statement is made by the local despot, Qian, and signed in the presence of the masses. August 3."

The presidium asked the crowd to discuss it, but very few further amendments were proposed, although a few people still felt he was getting off too lightly and they ought to beat him some more.

Schemer Qian was allowed to go back. He was only permitted to live in Yi's house for the time being. All his property apart from his land was to be sealed up immediately by the peasants' association. As to the question of how much should be left him, that was left to the land assessment committee to decide.

Last of all a land assessment committee was elected. Everybody shouted Liuman's name. Young Guo was elected too. Orchard-keeper Li had made quite a good chairman, and he was elected too. Quan was an old peasant who knew more than anyone else about the acreage in the village, so he was also elected. He rubbed his bristling mustaches and said with embarrassment: "If you don't think I'm too old, and want me to do a job, how can I refuse!"

Co-op Tian was elected too, because he was good at using the abacus and quick-witted. Without him they would be in the soup with their accounts. Young Hou could calculate too, and he was young and not afraid of offending people, so he was nominated and elected. Last of all they elected the chairman of the peasants' association, Young Cheng. Cheng had refused Schemer Qian's bribe, staunchly leading them all in the struggle; they all supported such a peasants' association chairman.

By now land reform here could be considered as well under way. Although the peasants still had certain reservations, at least they had passed one large hurdle, and overthrown their greatest enemy. They intended to continue the struggle against the bad powers in the village, settling accounts with each in turn. They meant to stand up properly. They had the strength, as the events of the day made them realize. Their confidence had increased. Nuanshui was no longer the same as the previous day. As the meeting broke up they shouted for joy, a roar like thunder going up into the air. This was an end, it was also a beginning.

19.4 HU SHI AND HU SIDU: FATHER AND SON

Hu Shi (1891–1962) was one of the most influential intellectuals of the May Fourth Movement and an important proponent of Anglo-American democracy. Throughout his career as an educator, writer, and diplomat, Hu frequently criticized the authoritarianism of the Nationalist government

(Document 15.1), and rejected the CCP's ideology of class struggle. Despite his differences with Chiang Kai-shek's regime, Hu did serve the Guomindang in a series of official and quasi-official positions. From 1938 to 1941, he was Chongqing's ambassador to the United States and later an advisor to the Executive Yuan.

After the Communist victory, Hu Shi fled initially to the United States before settling in Taiwan. His younger son, Hu Sidu, remained in China and was forced to undergo "thought reform," to purge himself of his bourgeois upbringing and worldview. Hu Sidu's 1950 criticism of his father was part of his reformation process. In writing this blistering condemnation, he "drew a line" between himself and his father. But despite demonstrating his loyalty to the Communist Party by rejecting his family, Hu Sidu was branded a "rightist" and persecuted. He committed suicide in 1957.

HU SIDU'S DENUNCIATION OF HIS FATHER

In the old society, I considered my father as an "aloof" and "clean" good man. Even after the liberation I felt deeply insulted whenever my father was being criticized. Within my heart I strongly objected to Premier Zhou Enlai's calling my father a man who never understood what imperialism means. After I had read the *History of Social Development, State and Revolution, History of Chinese Revolution* and many other books written by Communists, my concept of my father began to change. Now I shall analyze his effect on historical development.

My father came from a fallen family of bureaucrats. He was a student from 1904 to 1910. When he went to the United States at the age of 20, the American material and spiritual civilization dazzled him and swiftly conquered him. His educational environment changed him as a man from a semi-feudal, semi-colonial country to a bourgeois. His article on "The Improvement of Chinese Literature" won him popularity in China because it was anti-feudalistic. He was considered as a progressive.

When he returned in 1917, China was under the despotic rule of Yuan Shikai and Duan Qirui. He made up his mind "not to talk politics in 20 years" and buried himself in books. But during the period of "May 4" he could no longer escape from politics. So he published his *Problem and Doctrine*, to attack the growing socialistic ideas with evolutionism. He believed that China could have progress without making fundamental changes. His opinion represented the entire class of bourgeois intellectuals when confronted with the "May 4" and "June 3" movements. What he objected to was a revolution that would demolish the warlords, bureaucrats, landlords, and state machine.

THE WRONG WAY

After 1919 he drifted farther down the wrong way. He praised Ibsenism and battled materialism with experimentalism. He himself was wandering among the rulers of those days, hoping his "evolutionism" would be adopted by them. Weak capitalist intellectuals never dared resist the "government." Hu Shi, like all other members of his class, bowed his head to the reactionary government, and turned to Chiang Kai-shek to practice his doctrine of reforms.

. . . [In 1931] he voluntarily became the dean of the Arts School of Peking University. It was in that job that he laid down his foundation as a political and cultural ruler. He became one of the pillars of the Rockefeller Foundation and the Sino-American Cultural Fund Society. He turned out to be the docile tool of the imperialists.

GREATER POWER

When the reactionary government was campaigning against the Communists, he praised it as a "good men's government." Wang Wenhao and Jiang Tingfu[3] under his "inspiration" all joined the reactionary government. The people who had long suffered under the oppression of the reactionaries thought that the government might change for the better after such "liberal" professors had joined it. The reason why my father refused to become the Minister of Education under Chiang at that time was because he thought that by remaining "aloof" he would enjoy greater power.

In 1937, when the Japanese invading hordes began to storm into East and South China and the rich compradores of the Anglo-American imperialists were forced to take up their cudgel against the aggressor, the interests of his class were gravely threatened. In 1938, he finally became Chiang's ambassador to the United States. In his post as the ambassador to the American imperialists, he signed all kinds of trade agreements and was greatly instrumental in obtaining loans from the American government to fight the Communists.

BOOMING TIDE

In 1946, when the booming tide of the people's revolution was threatening the ruling class, he considered it as a sacred duty to serve for his class. He returned to his country and worked faithfully for the Chiang government. At that time he was carrying out the orders of the reactionary government as the president of Peking University on the one hand and was deceiving the people by writing middle-of-the-road articles on the other. He more or less had given the people an impression of a "worldly man."

But his loyalty to the reactionary government had not saved the common enemy of the people from extinction. At a time when final victory was about to descend

---

3. Important associates of Hu Shi and leading intellectual figures of the 1930s. Both men served on the editorial board of the famous journal *The Independent Critic* (*Duli pinglun*) published in Peking from 1932 to 1937 and joined the Guomindang government in 1935.

to the people, he left Peking and China to become a "White Chinese" living a life of exile.

Today, after my education in the Party, I begin to recognize his true qualities. I have come to know that he is a loyal element of the reactionary class and an enemy of the people. Politically, he has never been progressive. After his publication of *Problem and Doctrine* in 1919, he wandered on the road in indecision. For 11 years, he groped in the labyrinth of darkness. In 1930, he began to participate actively in the work of strengthening the reactionary government.

This time he went to the United States in an endeavor to form a third party and took care of the U.S. $4,000,000 relief fund for Chinese students in the United States on behalf of the American State Department. He was willing to serve for the United States and for those reactionary individualistic students.

ENSLAVEMENT EDUCATION

In the past, I was subjected to a long period of enslavement education by the reactionaries, and I was ignorant about the policies of the people. A friend of mine who came to Peking from Hong Kong on business asked me what attitude I would adopt toward my father. I replied that perhaps he could never learn about "group doctrine" and would probably stay in the United States.

Today I realize the lenient policy of the People's government. It gives a chance to all those who have acted against the interests of the people to live down their past and start life anew, only if they can come to realize their past misdeeds.

Until my father returns to the people's arms, he will always remain a public enemy of the people, and an enemy of myself. Today, in my determination to rebel against my own class, I feel it important to draw a line of demarcation between my father and myself. . . .

19.5 CHIANG KAI-SHEK: BACK TO THE MAINLAND, OCTOBER 10, 1954

The Korean War and the consequent posting of the U.S. Seventh Fleet to the Taiwan Straits thwarted the reunification of Taiwan with China and gave a new lease of life to Chiang Kai-shek's government-in-exile. After Chiang consolidated his control over Taiwan, he purged dissident elements in his officer corps and began rebuilding his shattered armies. Institution for institution, the Nanjing government was reconstituted in Taipei and a separate provincial government for Taiwan was set up in the city of Taichung.

Throughout the remaining years of Chiang Kai-shek's life, he regarded the Peking regime of Mao Zedong as a temporary "bandit" government that would be replaced when Chiang returned to the mainland in triumph with his armies. Each year on the Double Ten anniversary of the founding of the

Republic of China, Chiang would reiterate the legitimacy of his government as the government of all of China and would restate his promise to rescue the Chinese people from Communist bondage. For decades after 1949, Chiang promised the people of Taiwan and the mainland that the "decisive phase" of the war to reclaim China was at hand, and, as in this document, he excoriated Communist mismanagement of natural disasters, social reform, and a panoply of other dilemmas. But despite cries in some quarters in the United States for the "unleashing" of Chiang, no American support was forthcoming for new Nationalist military adventures on the mainland.

PRESIDENT CHIANG KAI-SHEK'S MESSAGE TO THE NATION ON NATIONAL DAY (OCTOBER 10, 1954)

Fellow Countrymen and Members of the Armed Forces:

It is 60 years since the founder of the Chinese Republic, Dr. Sun Yat-sen, started the national revolution and organized the Xingzhonghui [Revive China Society].[4] It is 43 years since the revolution of 1911 and, today, we find ourselves engaged in an anti-Communist and resist-Russia struggle. It is a struggle that will decide the outcome of our national revolution. It is also a struggle which will decide whether we as a nation are to survive or perish. This struggle has now entered into its crucial stage. The Chinese people must stand united as one and demonstrate their patriotism by dedicating themselves to the achievement of final victory in order to make this day a glorious occasion to be remembered as the National Day of the Republic of China.

On this National Day, the thing that comes to our mind is that millions of our compatriots, including our own parents, our children, our relatives and our friends on the mainland, are being subjected to greater suffering than ever before at the hands of the Russian and Chinese Communist bandits. This thought has filled our hearts with pain and sorrow.

In the last five years, the Communist bandits have, in their propaganda, been boasting that they had benefited from the experience of the Russian Communists and that they had undertaken a great piece of engineering work in water conservancy along the Huai, the Yellow and the Yangtze Rivers. They claimed that they had succeeded in harnessing these rivers and that floods had become a thing of the past. But last summer, the basins of the Yangtze, the Huai, the Yellow and the Han Rivers were all inundated by floods of unprecedented ferocity. Breaches in the dikes of these rivers have resulted in the flooding of twelve provinces, making millions of our compatriots homeless and starving. What is the cause of such unprecedented natural and man-made calamities? This is, as the Communists have been

---

4. Sun Yat-sen's first revolutionary organization, formed in November 1894.

telling people, the "miracle" created by the Communist party, "which, by representing and safeguarding the vital interest of the people, would lead the people to a life of freedom and happiness." This is also what they have been boasting as "the grand achievement of farm irrigation and conservancy" and "raising the standard of living of the people."

As is to be expected, the Communist bandits under Zhu De and Mao Zedong have shown no sympathy for the hapless flood victims. The surprising thing is that they have seen fit at this particular moment to compel our compatriots on the mainland to toe what they call "the general line of the transition period." By using such phrases as "transition period" and "general line," it is their intention to drive our compatriots on the mainland further along the road to create a tightly integrated "unbreakable alliance between the USSR and the People's Republic of China." In other words, it is the intention of Zhu De and Mao Zedong to hand over our people and territory on the mainland to the Russian imperialists. Fellow Countrymen: Can we allow "transition" to come to pass? Can we bear to see the ruin of our country and the extermination of our race? No, we must stand united; we must rise up and work for the downfall of both the Russian and Chinese Communist bandits.

In the past five years, we have not relaxed our efforts in prosecuting the war against the Communists in the Taiwan Straits and along the mainland coast. But these on and off operations are merely small-scale engagements of a long-term all-out war. Now the Communist bandits are about to embark on a new adventure and start a new war. They have initiated hostile action against Quemoy and Tachen [islands] off the mainland coast and have boasted about their determination to "liberate" Taiwan. The Russian Communist bosses have openly stated they would do their best to support the Chinese Communists. They have said that the Soviet Union is deeply concerned with the "liberation" of Taiwan. Why is Soviet Russia so much concerned with this war? The answer is that it might thwart her attempt to enslave 1,100,000,000 people in Asia. This why the Russian Communist bosses stated emphatically that they would support the Chinese Communist bandits to fight for further consolidation and development. It is possible that the objective of the Russian Communists is not limited to the "liberation" of Taiwan. It will in due course include the "liberation" of all the nations in Asia and eventually the entire human race. The "liberation" of Taiwan is but a foretaste of what the Russian Communists have in store for the world. . . .

Fellow Countrymen: The Communist bandits have started hostile action against the islands off the mainland. They are in fact knocking on the front door of this island. All our military forces and civilians must be mobilized for war. We must intensify our mobilization and speed up our preparation for our counter-offensive, in order to discharge our heavy responsibility to recover our country and save the people.

Now I would like to take this opportunity to acquaint our compatriots on the mainland with the fundamental principles by which the Government will be guided upon the recovery of the mainland. First, we shall safeguard all freedoms

20.3 AND 20.4 THE HUNDRED FLOWERS CAMPAIGN, MAY 1956

During the first seven years of the People's Republic, widespread enthusiasm for the new era of peace brought about by the Communist unification of China insulated the new government from criticism. In this "honeymoon" phase, the Party elite ruled with a self-assurance rarely challenged from below.

In 1953 and 1954, cracks began to appear in the edifice of Communist control. As power struggles and internal purges shook the Party, regional leaders were removed from power and intellectuals were persecuted. In addition, the death of Stalin in 1953 initiated a reassessment of Soviet history, culminating in Khrushchev's renunciation of the Stalinist system. In May 1956, Lu Dingyi, the director of the powerful Propaganda Department of the Central Committee, delivered a speech (Document 20.3) calling for a careful opening to dissent and for more creative freedom for intellectuals working in all fields. After almost a year of reticence and prodded by cadres to speak out, intellectuals began launching sharp attacks against the Party. The 1957 denunciation of the leadership by two university professors (Document 20.4) was mild in comparison to some critiques. Its challenge to fundamental aspects of Communist rule, however, suggests why Party leaders felt threatened by the expressions of discontent that were unleashed.

20.3 Lu Dingyi: "Let Flowers of Many Kinds Blossom, Diverse Schools of Thought Contend!" May 26, 1956

Mr. Guo Morou, President of the Chinese Academy of Sciences and Chairman of the All-China Federation of Literary and Art Circles, has asked me to speak on the policy of the Chinese Communist Party on the work of artists, writers and scientists.

To artists and writers, we say, "Let flowers of many kinds blossom." To scientists we say, "Let diverse schools of thought contend." This is the policy of the Chinese Communist Party. It was announced by Chairman Mao Zedong at the Supreme State Conference.

In applying this policy we have gained some further experience, but it is still far too scanty. Furthermore, what I am saying today is merely my own personal understanding of this policy. You here are scientists specializing in the natural and social sciences, doctors, writers and artists; some of you are members of the Communist Party, some friends from democratic parties, and others non-Party friends. You will readily see how immensely important this policy is in the development of Chinese art, literature and scientific research—the work you yourselves are engaged in—so if you think I am mistaken on any point, please don't hesitate to correct me. Then we can all do our bit to promote the common cause.

I. WHY THIS POLICY, AND WHY THIS EMPHASIS ON IT NOW?

If we want our country to be prosperous and strong, we must, besides consolidating the people's state power, developing our economy and education and strengthening our national defense, have a flourishing art, literature and science. That is essential.

If we want art, literature and science to flourish, we must apply a policy of letting flowers of many kinds blossom, letting diverse schools of thought contend.

Literature and art can never really flourish if only one flower blooms alone, no matter how beautiful that flower may be. Take the theatre, an example which readily comes to mind these days. Some years back there were still people who set their face against Peking opera. Then the Party decided to apply the policy summed up in the words "let flowers of many kinds blossom side by side, weed through the old to let the new emerge" to the theatre. Everybody can see now how right it was to do so, and the notable results it led to. Thanks to free competition and the fact that the various kinds of drama now all learn from one another, our theatre has made rapid progress.

In the field of science, we have historical experience to draw on. During the period of the Spring and Autumn Annals (722–481 B.C.) and of the Warring States (403–221 B.C.) more than two thousand years ago, many schools of thought vied with each other for supremacy. That was a golden age in the intellectual development of China. History shows that unless independent thinking and free discussion are encouraged, academic life stagnates. And conversely, when they are encouraged, academic growth speeds up. But, of course, the state of affairs existing in those ancient times was very different from what it is in present-day China. At that time, society was in turmoil. The various schools of thought did vie with each other, spreading their ideas; but they did so spontaneously, with no sort of conscious, organized leadership. Now the people have won a world of freedom for themselves. The people's democratic dictatorship has been set up and consolidated. There is a popular demand that nothing should be allowed to impede the onward march of science. That is why we consciously map out an all-embracing plan for scientific development and adopt a policy of letting diverse schools of thought contend to give vigor to academic growth.

One cannot fail to see that in class societies art, literature and science are, in the last analysis, weapons in the class struggle.

This is quite clear in the case of art and literature. Here we can see things that are obviously pernicious. The stuff written by Hu Feng[1] is one such example. Pornographic and gutter literature that debauches people and turns them

---

1. Marxist literary critic (1903–1985). Hu was heavily criticized in the 1950s and later as a counterrevolutionary and imperialist.

into gangsters is another. Still another example is the so-called literature summed up in phrases like "let's play mah-jong and to hell with state affairs," "the moon in America is rounder than the moon in China," etc. It is perfectly right and proper for us to look on literature of this pernicious kind as a par with flies, mosquitoes, rats and sparrows and rid ourselves of it all. This can only benefit, not harm our literature. Thus we say there is art and literature, for instance, that serves the workers, peasants and soldiers, and art and literature that serves the imperialists, landlords and bourgeoisie. What we need is art and literature that serves the workers, peasants and soldiers—art and literature that serves the people.

The existence of class struggle is also fairly clear in the philosophy and the social sciences. Hu Shi's views on philosophy, history, education and politics have been held up to public odium. The repudiation of his views is a reflection of class struggle in the field of the social sciences. We are perfectly justified in denouncing Mr. Liang Shuming's[2] ideas. We are also right in criticizing other philosophical schools of bourgeois idealism and bourgeois sociology.

Now let us see how things stand in the field of natural science. All scientists have their own political viewpoint, although natural science itself has no class character. Formerly some who specialized in the natural sciences blindly worshipped the United States, while others tended to be "non-political." It is right and proper to criticize all such things as undesirable—and such criticism is a reflection of class struggle.

We cannot fail to notice too that although art, literature and scientific research have a close bearing on the class struggle, they are not, after all, the same thing as politics. Political struggle is a direct form of class struggle. Art, literature and the social sciences give expression to the class struggle sometimes in a direct, and sometimes in a roundabout way. It is a one-sided, rightist way of looking at things to assume that art, literature and science have nothing to do with politics and that "art for art's sake," or "science for science's sake" is a justified standpoint. To look at things in that way is certainly wrong. On the other hand, it is one-sided and "leftist" to oversimplify things and equate art, literature and science with politics. This view is equally wrong.

"Letting flowers of many kinds blossom, diverse schools of thought contend" means that we stand for freedom of independent thinking, of debate, of creative work; freedom to criticize and freedom to express, maintain and reserve one's opinions on questions of art, literature or scientific research. . . .

---

2. Leading opponent of the New Culture movement and exponent of cultural preservation in the May Fourth period.

II. STRENGTHEN UNITY

Let flowers of many kinds blossom, diverse schools of thought contend: that is a policy to mobilize all the positive elements. It is also, therefore, a policy that will in the end strengthen unity.

On what basis are we to unite? On the basis of patriotism and socialism.

What do we unite for? To build a new, socialist China and combat our enemies both at home and abroad.

There are two kinds of unity: one is built on mechanical obedience and the other on our own conscious, free will. What we want is the latter.

Are those engaged in art, literature and science united? Yes, they are. Compare the situation in the days when the Chinese People's Republic was just founded with what we have now and you find we now have a far closer unity among artists, writers and scientists. This has come about as a result of our work for social reforms and changes in our ways of thought. It would be wrong to deny or ignore this. But even so, we cannot say that our unity is all it should be: there is still room for improvement. . . .

We hope, too, that writers, artists and scientists who are not Party members will also pay attention to the question of securing closer unity. And here I would like to repeat part of what Comrade Zhou Enlai said in his "Report on the Question of Intellectuals."

"We have already pointed out that there is still a certain distance between some intellectuals and our Party. We must take the initiative to remove this. For this distance, both sides usually bear responsibility. On the one hand, our comrades do not approach to try to understand the intellectuals; on the other, certain intellectuals still have reservations regarding socialism or even oppose it. There are such intellectuals in our enterprises, schools, government offices and society as a whole. Failing to differentiate between friend and foe, between the Communist Party and the Guomindang, between the Chinese people and imperialism, they are dissatisfied with the policies and measures of the Party and the People's Government and hanker after capitalism or even feudalism. They are hostile to the Soviet Union and unwilling to learn from her. They refuse to study Marxism-Leninism, and sneer at it. Despising labour, the laboring people and government workers who come from families of working people, they refuse to mix with workers and peasants or government cadres of worker or peasant origin. Unwilling to see growth of new forces, they consider progressives as opportunists, and often stir up trouble and hostility between intellectuals and the Party as well as among intellectuals themselves. They have enormous conceit, thinking themselves Number One in the world, and refusing to accept anyone's leadership or criticism. Denying the interests of the people or of society as a whole, they view everything only from their personal interests. What is to their personal advantage they accept, what is not to their personal advantage they oppose. Of course, there are very few intellectuals today who have all these faults; but not a small number have one fault or another. Even some of the middle

and the Party has no need to observe it. Outwardly we have democratic elections, a united front policy and non-Party people exercising leadership; actually, the Party exercises dictatorship and a few persons of the Political Bureau of the Party centre exercise absolute power. Since the election of people's deputies is not democratic, elections are actually a variety of appointment. Although some non-Party people occupy leading posts, they perform duties but have no power. . . . Nor is there democracy within the Party. The convening of the 8th National Congress, for instance, was a great event, but which Party member could put his views to the congress? . . . As to freedom of assembly, association and publication, that is just something written in the Constitution; actually, citizens can only become obedient subjects or, to use a harsh word, slaves. The Party is the emperor and an august and sacred body. Who dares to oppose it when it holds the bible of Marxism-Leninism in the one hand and the sword of state power in the other? You would either be labeled an anti–Marxist-Leninist or handcuffed with 'unfounded charges.'

"If this state of affairs is to be changed, a system of general election campaigns should be put into effect alongside the abolition of the absolute leadership of the Party. The people should be allowed freely to organize new political parties and social bodies, and to put out publications so as to open the channels of public opinion, supervise the government, combat cheap praises and encourage them to oppose an undesirable *status quo* even if it meant opposition to the Communist Party, provided they do not stand against the people and socialism. The Communist Party, if it really represents the people, will not be kicked out; if the Communist Party is kicked out, it means it no longer represents the people. Is it pitiable to have such a Party kicked out?"

Chang Po-sheng went on: "Whose words count in connection with state affairs? The Constitution lays down that the words of the National People's Congress and its Standing Committee count, but actually the National People's Congress is nothing but a mud idol while all power is in the hands of the Party centre. The National People's Congress merely carries out the formality of raising hands and passing resolutions. In all these years, one has seldom seen a Standing Committee member putting forward an important motion, though occasionally one has seen some of them publishing unimportant notes on inspection tours in the Press. Is this not laughable? Why did the National People's Congress deputies see no contradictions among the people during their inspection tours? They saw only what the Party said and saw nothing when the Party did not say anything. They did not see or they dared not say? Even more laughable is that the Chinese People's Political Consultative Conference, which is said to be representing the united front, spends most of its energy on work connected with organization of studies . . . Like two paper flowers the National People's Congress and the People's Political Consultative Conference decorate the facade of democracy . . . All kinds of important questions are decided upon by six persons—Chairman Mao, Liu Shaoqi, Premier Zhou Enlai and those above the rank of the secretary general of the Party centre—at their table. The destiny of 600 million people is dictated by the pen of these six persons. And how can they know the actual situation? At best they can make an inspection tour of the Yellow River and swim in the Yangtze [in 1956]. Even if they talked with the peasants, the peasants would not tell the truth and could only say: 'Chairman Mao is great.' How can mistakes be avoided when such a small number of people take arbitrary action and recklessly issue orders? The Party centre has never criticized itself publicly since the founding of the Republic. If this dictatorial obstruction to national affairs is to be changed, the Party must be removed from its position of superiority to the National People's Congress and the government, the government must be placed below the National People's Congress and the National People's Congress must be made an organ exercising genuine power. . . ."

Chang Po-sheng said: "Personnel work is in a complete mess. Incompetent persons become leaders and competent ones become men without official standing . . . Full-time Party cadres should be drastically reduced. . . . One hears that the Young Communist League of Yugoslavia has only some 170 full-time cadres throughout the country, whereas our First Motor Car Plant alone has more than 100 full-time League cadres. This is indeed a laughing matter, a big laughing matter! . . . If a person is a Party member, he is made a leading cadre; if he is not a Party member, he is placed at a lower level. . . .

"Whether a post should be high or low should be determined by whether the person is equal to the post. How about the veteran revolutionary cadres who have worked for the revolution for several decades but whose cultural level is very low? They may be employed as grooms but, since they have rendered meritorious service to the revolution, we should respect them and grant them a service allowance. . . ."

In conclusion, Chang Po-sheng explained that the views as expressed in their speeches were at the stage of fermentation in December 1956 and were only written down yesterday.

[*Shenyang Daily*, June 11, 1957]

20.5 DENG XIAOPING: THE ANTIRIGHTIST CAMPAIGN, SEPTEMBER 23, 1957

In late summer 1957, Mao Zedong, in a revised version of his speech "On the Correct Handling of Contradictions among the People," stated strict limits on dissent and took aim at critics who were too aggressive in their attacks on the Party and Communist state. In the months that followed, a "rectification" campaign against "rightists" was launched in every city and every work unit in China. As a result of the campaign, many of the bold critics, within and outside of the Party, who exposed their real feelings about politics and other issues were denounced and obliged to undergo either "thought reform" or "reform through labor." Others paid for their outspokenness with terms in prisons or labor camps.

Deng Xiaoping, who was general secretary of the CCP during the anti-rightist campaign, was given responsibility for pursuing the policy set out by Mao Zedong in "On the Correct Handling of Contradictions among the People." And it was Deng who oversaw the implementation of anti-rightist activities. The excerpt that follows, from Deng's report in September 1957 to an enlarged Plenum of the Central Committee of the CCP, suggests how the campaign was viewed in Party circles, and illustrates how Mao's rather abstract analysis of the problem of "rightists" emerged as policy.

ON THE COMMUNIST PARTY AND THE YOUNG COMMUNIST LEAGUE

At present our Party has 12,712,000 members (including 2,800,000 probationary members). Among them are more than 1,740,000 workers, more than 8,500,000 peasants, more than 1,880,000 intellectuals and more than 600,000 members with other backgrounds.

During the rectification campaign and the struggle against the rightists, the majority of the Party members behaved well. However, many problems have also been exposed.

Large volumes of matter relating to bureaucracy, sectarianism and subjectivism have been exposed during the campaign. One section of the Party members possess bourgeois individualism to a serious degree, zealously craving for personal enjoyment and keeping their minds on honor and position. There are also a very small number of Party members who have lost their revolutionary spirit or have even degenerated, become corrupt, and offended against the law and against discipline.

In the course of the campaign, the rightists within the Party have come into the open. The discovery of these spokesmen of the bourgeois class is of great significance for the consolidation and purification of our Party. In addition, there are still some Party members who have serious rightist ideology and are extremely discontented with the Party. Their views diverge from those of the Party over some important policy questions and they have shown political vacillation in the current struggle.

The rise of these serious problems within the Party has social and ideological origins: (1) The majority of the Party members are not from the working class; (2) The Party has grown rapidly without adequate attention having been paid to quality and the ideological and political work has lagged behind; and (3) What is more important is that the majority of Party members joined the Party in the days after victory. At the time when they joined, they lacked genuine socialist consciousness. After joining the Party, they have been in an environment of cooperation with the bourgeoisie for a long time without experiencing direct and acute class struggle against the bourgeoisie. The majority of the 1,880,000 intellectuals among the Party members have not experienced training in productive labor, nor have they gone through serious tests of the class struggle.

In the struggle against the rightists, the rightists within the Party must be treated equally and as seriously as the non-Party rightists. However, there are now some comrades who, in the struggle against inner-Party rightists, have exhibited to a more serious extent the trend of sentimentalism, and this is especially noticeable in the expressions of regret, the show of weakness, and the reluctance to take action in dealing with some veteran Party members who should be demarcated as rightists.

When the campaign proceeds into the third and fourth stages, it is more necessary to tackle carefully the task of rectification within the Party than outside. Apart from the errors of bureaucracy, subjectivism and sectarianism (including sectionalism and group exclusiveness) among leading functionaries which must be corrected in all seriousness, the rightist ideas among rank and file Party members must also be criticized. All kinds of bourgeois and petty-bourgeois ideology must be criticized.

The work of ideological and political education must be strengthened. During the current rectification campaign, a comprehensive ideological and political survey of every Party member must be made. The weaknesses of inadequate attention to ideological and political education, unhealthy organizational life and loose discipline must be seriously corrected.

During the rectification campaign, except for renegades and those who have gravely offended against the law and disciplinary rules, consideration should be shown to all Party members and Young Communist League members. Great efforts must be made to help them correct their errors and overcome their shortcomings, improve their working methods, and raise their working ability, their ideological and political level. The Party members and cadres must be educated to be vigorous, to have revolutionary will and to have the attitude of serving the people selflessly and whole-heartedly.

It is necessary to have a conscientious check-up of all the basic organizations of the Communist Party in conjunction with the rectification campaign. Through the rectification campaign, the purity of the ranks of the Communist Party and the consolidation of the Party organization must be achieved.

Rightists inside the Party should be dismissed from the Party. If their cases are less serious and they make a showing in changing for the better, and are not dismissed from the Party, their rightist "label" may be taken away.

All kinds of bad elements who have infiltrated into the ranks of the Party, elements who have seriously violated the law and Party discipline, those who have degenerated to the point beyond salvation, and those with serious bourgeois individualist thinking and acts who fail to repent after repeated education must be purged from the Party.

People who have lost their revolutionary will and cannot play the role of the Communist Party member and fail to reform after criticism and education, should be persuaded to resign from the Party or else be purged from the Party.

In deciding on the expulsion of a member of the Party, his mistakes must be verified, the prescribed procedure must be followed, and after his dismissal, concern should continue to be given to him politically and ideologically, special personnel assigned to maintain contact with him, to place him under observation and to educate him.

We must strengthen the education of probationary Party members, and carry out a rigid examination to prevent those who do not possess the full qualifications for Party membership from becoming full members of the Party.

To ensure a constant readjustment of the composition of the Party membership and to infuse fresh blood into the Party, people who are really qualified for membership, particularly veteran workers and outstanding higher intellectuals, may be accepted into the Party in a selective manner on the basis of the rectification campaign and the anti-rightist struggle and on the condition that the quality of the membership is assured.

The rectification campaign and the anti-rightist struggle place each Party member, and particularly each functionary, to a test. It is necessary here to say something about the work of the Party relating to its functionaries.

Our Party has paid consistent attention to selecting outstanding workers, peasants and intellectuals closely linked with the masses of workers and peasants for various leading positions. This is the line of the Party's work regarding functionaries.

During a certain period in the past, we had assigned to leadership organs of various levels too large a number of young intellectuals who had not been steeled in production labor or tested in actual struggles. This was a defect.

Hereafter, we should continue to choose functionaries from among the excellent elements of the workers and peasants but these should be workers and peasants with a certain cultural level. We should likewise select functionaries from among the better elements of intellectuals, but they should be intellectuals who have been steeled in production work and struggle and maintain close connection with the workers and peasants. Those intellectual functionaries who have not been tempered in practical struggle and have no experience of working in an organization at the lowest level should be systematically sent to do production work in villages and factories for a few years, or to do practical work in an organization at the lowest level for a few years. All leading personnel in the Party, government and the mass organizations at various levels should be tempered in practical struggle and equipped with the experience of working at the lowest level. Those who are not should make up for it. This is also true of those working in the fields of literature, the arts, press, theoretical work and in other fields of propaganda.

An appropriate scheme should be worked out to enable graduates from universities and colleges and technical schools first to do manual work in organizations of production which are suited to their specialties. Only after one or more years of work, can they be assigned to jobs according to their specialties and their record in manual work.

Serious efforts should be made to create conditions to enable manual workers in production work to have opportunities to raise their cultural and technical knowledge and to enable part of them who can proceed to advanced education to enter universities and colleges.

Only by seriously carrying through this working line regarding functionaries can the Party and the state do the work of selecting functionaries on a reliable basis, and establish a force of functionaries dedicated to the cause of Communism and capable of weathering storms.

CHAPTER 21

Deepening the Revolution

21.1–21.3 THE GREAT LEAP FORWARD

The propaganda campaign in the spring of 1958 that prepared the way for the Great Leap Forward emphasized the originality and revolutionary contributions of Mao Zedong. Supporters of Mao considered the methods deployed in this campaign to be unique in the history of Marxism. Chen Boda's[1] speech at Peking University in July 1958, with its emphasis on Mao's creativity and genius, was a standard evocation of the themes that undergird the cult of Maoist leadership.

Two concrete goals of the Great Leap Forward, launched in the fall of 1958, were the increase of Chinese steel production and the formation of "people's communes." Throughout China a campaign to construct "backyard furnaces" was actively pursued by local Party authorities. Propagandists of the movement announced that in fifteen years China would be able to overtake Great Britain's steel production, stimulating frenzied efforts to collect and smelt iron in the crude, earthen furnaces constructed by almost all work units. Yin Zeming's account of accomplishments in central Hunan suggests how the steel production movement was promoted, suffused with the sense that anything was possible.

Undoubtedly, the most sweeping program of the Great Leap was the Party's plan to fully collectivize agriculture. The "people's commune" was designed to centralize economic, political, cultural, and military affairs. According to Party theorists, private property would virtually cease to exist

---

1. Secretary to Chairman Mao and party specialist in ideological matters (1905–1989). With the fall of the Gang of Four in 1976, Chen was toppled from his party positions and sentenced to sixteen years in prison. He was released in 1988 and died in October the following year.

and the countryside would enter a new utopian age of socialist production. The September 3, 1958, *People's Daily* editorial reproduced below was a statement on collectivization derived directly from the writings of Mao Zedong. Its extreme optimism and disregard of any difficulties were typical aspects of the rhetoric of the Great Leap era.

21.1 Chen Boda: "Under the Banner of Comrade Mao Zedong," July 16, 1958

July 1 is the birthday of our party. It has been 37 years since the founding of our party. In these 57 years, the Chinese people and our party have traversed a tortuous path and won a series of great victories under the banner of Comrade Mao Zedong. Thirty-seven years is not a long time in the history of China but one can see that under the leadership of our party and the banner of Comrade Mao Zedong the Chinese people have realized an epoch-making revolution on their land and are creating their own life by leaps and bounds at such a rate that "twenty years are concentrated in one day. . . ."

Comrade Mao Zedong is able to examine and explore the characteristics of China without being the least bound by formalism. Practice instead of formula is his point of departure. The most striking feature of Comrade Mao Zedong's thought is his ability to integrate the universal truth of Marxism-Leninism closely with the creativeness of the masses. He puts faith in the masses, relies on the masses, and respects the intelligence of the ordinary masses, thereby to increase the invincible power of Marxist-Leninist theory under new conditions and in new surroundings. . . .

The problems solved by Comrade Mao Zedong were many sided. Here I will take up several problems that were important to the cause of the Chinese people as a whole.

The primary and outstanding contribution Comrade Mao Zedong made to the Democratic Revolution was his theory of building and developing revolutionary bases in the countryside as the main form of alliance between the working class and the peasantry under the leadership of the Communist Party in the political, military, and economic fields, and of taking such bases as the starting points of revolution and nation-wide victory. In the past, many people, basing their view on the French bourgeois revolution of the eighteenth century and on the 1911 revolution and Northern Expedition in China, established the idea that revolution always began from big cities. And it was generally held that guerrilla warfare was merely a supplement of regular warfare. Comrade Mao Zedong rejected these old ideas that were not applicable to the conditions of the Chinese revolution. He set forth the new idea of placing guerrilla warfare in a strategic position in the Chinese revolution, and the new idea of arming all the people in revolution. These new ideas put forward by Comrade Mao Zedong gave the party leadership a new direction of struggle after the 1927 revolutionary failure. Later, during the period of anti-Japanese war Comrade Mao Zedong developed and enriched these ideas, and eventually the Chinese people and our party were enabled to win a nation-wide victory during 1949.

During the period of socialist revolution in our country, Comrade Mao Zedong creatively solved a series of fundamental problems of socialist transformation arising from transition from individual ownership to collective ownership, from capitalist ownership to popular ownership. During the time of establishing revolutionary bases, Comrade Mao Zedong had summed up the experiences of the mutual-aid organizations of the peasant masses. He saw germs of socialism in such mutual-aid organizations and popularized these mutual-aid organizations in his belief that such mutual-aid organizations could raise labor productivity to a considerable degree. After the nation-wide liberation, Comrade Mao Zedong continued to sum up new experiences of this and, shortly after conclusion of the agrarian reform, urged widespread establishment of temporary mutual-aid teams and year-round mutual-aid teams on a voluntary basis, and the gradual and massive development of agricultural producer cooperatives semi-socialist in character (land share, common labor, and unified administration) on the basis of mutual-aid teams. He took the view that such agricultural producer cooperatives semi-socialist in character were the main form of guiding the peasants voluntarily to full socialism, thereby breaking down the old view of some comrades that without agricultural machinery large-scale cooperativization of agriculture could hardly be realized.

On the question of capitalist ownership, Comrade Mao Zedong drew a distinction between ownership by bureaucratic capitalists and ownership by the national capitalists. Towards the former, a policy of expropriation was adopted at the time of liberation; towards the latter, methods of gradual transformation and various forms of state capitalism were adopted in order to transform capitalist enterprises steadily into socialist enterprises.

In short, whether in the case of agriculture and handicrafts or in the case of capitalist industry and commerce, coordination was achieved between revolution from the top and revolution from the bottom, and diversified forms of transition and different methods of transition were massively adopted. As a result, the socialist transformation of economy won an unexpected and rapid victory.

Comrade Mao Zedong broke down the old view that the solution to the problem of ownership would answer the question of outcome of struggle between socialism and capitalism. He held that, besides solving the question of outcome of struggle as regards ownership, we must go a step further and solve the question of the outcome of struggle on the political and ideological fronts—otherwise the results of socialist transformation as regards ownership could not be consolidated. The big debate held by the people over socialism and capitalism during 1957, when the bourgeois rightists launched a ferocious attack on the party, bore out Comrade Mao Zedong's viewpoint. When the masses have waged an all-out struggle against the rightists and the people have distinguished right and wrong through the rectification campaign, contention, and blossoming, a new situation has arisen in which the Communist ideology is set free.

As far back as the time when Jiangxi was used as a revolutionary base, Comrade Mao Zedong laid down a correct policy of combining revolution and construction. During the Anti-Japanese War, Comrade Mao Zedong continued to adhere to this policy. Following the rectification campaign which began in 1942, Comrade Mao Zedong promoted a large-scale production drive during 1943, which considerably increased the material strength of the people in liberated areas and provided a material basis for wiping out Chiang Kai-shek's counter-revolutionary army during the liberation war. Over the economic and financial problems Comrade Mao Zedong always placed the mass development of production in the leading position and criticized the error of one-sided financial and distribution viewpoints divorced from the development of production.

After the nation-wide liberation, socialist transformation and socialist construction are interlocked in their progress. In the course of socialist transformation, observing the signs that began in agricultural cooperation, Comrade Mao Zedong pointed to the inexhaustible and immense latent power of the Chinese working people to develop the productive force. Comrade Mao Zedong said in his comments in the *Upsurge of Socialism in China's Countryside* "There will appear various things never conceived before and high yield of crops several, ten and scores of times greater than at present. The development of industry, communications, and exchange will be beyond the imagination of the predecessors. This will also be the case with science, culture, education, and public health." Therefore, he pointed out in the preface to the *Upsurge of Socialism in China's Countryside* that the questions confronting the party and the whole nation after solution of the problem of socialist transformation were the question of scale and rate of economic and cultural construction, the question of doing things regarded as impossible, and the question of criticizing the rightist conservative ideas. . . .

Mao Zedong's banner is a banner combining the Chinese Communists and the people, a banner integrating the universal truth of Marxism-Leninism with the concrete practice of the Chinese revolution, and a banner creatively developing Marxism-Leninism under the conditions of China. Therefore, Mao Zedong's banner is a banner of victory of the Chinese people's revolution and socialist construction.

Mao Zedong's banner is a red flag held aloft by the Chinese people. Guided by this great red flag the Chinese people will in the not distant future enter in the great Communist society.

21.2 Yin Zeming: "The Strength of the Masses Is Limitless," 1958

Iron smelting and steel making in the Shaoyang Special Administrative Region, Hunan Province, are rapidly developing on a mass scale. In a short period in the

advanced co-operatives. They are undoubtedly far superior to individual farming, mutual-aid terms, and even the elementary agricultural producers' co-operatives, and have contributed enormously to the steady increase of China's farm out-put in the past few years. With the growth of agricultural production, especially the great leap forward in agriculture since last winter, these co-operatives have, however, gradually become inadequate to meet fully the needs of the day. The reason is as follows. These co-operatives are comparatively small in size. Averaging less than one hundred households in membership, they have but a small amount of manpower. The amount of their public reserve funds is small and the rate of accumulation slow. With these handicaps it is difficult for them to engage in many kinds of production.

To achieve a high-speed advance in agriculture, enable the countryside to assume a new aspect at an early date, and improve the peasants' living standards as quickly as possible, as facts show, it is necessary to carry out large-scale capital construction that will fundamentally change the natural conditions; to apply new farming techniques; to develop forestry, animal husbandry, side-occupations and fishery side by side with agriculture; to build industries that serve agriculture and the needs of the peasants as well as big industries; gradually to carry out mechanization and electrification; to improve transport, communications and housing conditions in rural areas; and set up educational, health and cultural establishments—to do all this is beyond the power of an agricultural producers' co-operative consisting of a few dozen or hundreds of households.

The agricultural producers' co-operatives which merged into the present Zhaoying People's Commune in Shangzheng, Henan Province, previously had little industry though they abound in natural resources. After the formation of the commune 2,500 cadres and 17,500 members were allocated to the work and in ten days steel and iron plants, and factories making machinery, chemical fertilizer, cement, etc.—4,530 all told—were built, of which 3,250 enterprises soon went into operation. Here, the superiority of people's communes is clearly visible.

In the work of building water-conservancy projects, afforestation, combating drought, and flood prevention since last winter, the agricultural producers' co-operatives in many places acutely felt the inferiority of small co-operatives and the incompetency of their original labour organization to develop potential power and raise labour efficiency. Hence many small co-operatives spontaneously joined hands, and socialist co-operation between co-operatives of different townships, different counties, and even different provinces was carried out. A series of measures have also been taken to "get organized along military lines, work with a fighting spirit, and live in a collective way." This shows that the agricultural co-operatives, which are small in size, meager in items of production and low in the degree of collectivization, are becoming handicaps to the further development of the productive forces.

It must be pointed out that the rapid growth of the people's communes definitely does not stem solely from economic causes. The keenness shown by the mass of peasants towards the people's communes speaks first of all of their greatly increased socialist and communist consciousness.

Through the 1957 debate among the rural population on the socialist and capitalist roads of development in the countryside, the Communist Party smashed the attack launched by the bourgeois rightists, landlords, rich peasants, and counter-revolutionaries, and overcame the capitalist trend among the well-to-do middle peasants. Later, through the rectification campaign, it fundamentally changed the relations between the cadres and the masses and eliminated the rightist conservative ideas in agricultural production. During the current leap forward in agricultural production and rural work the mass of peasants have witnessed not only a several-fold increase in agricultural production but also the happy future of industrialization and urbanization of rural areas. As a result, the prestige of the Party has become more consolidated than ever among the peasants. The peasants have shown an unprecedentedly firm determination to achieve socialism at an earlier date and to prepare conditions for the gradual transition to communism. While striving for the quickest advance in production and in culture and education, the peasants are trying to establish new relations of production and new organizational forms best suited to the development of the productive forces. Without political consciousness as a basis, development of the people's commune movement would be impossible and inconceivable.

The establishment of people's communes has provided good conditions for the further development of the relations of production in the countryside. The expansion of the people's communes and the merger of people's communes and townships into one entity, which facilitates the rapid advance of industry, mining, communications, culture and education in the rural areas, makes it possible gradually to eliminate the differences between rural and urban areas, between peasants and workers, between peasants and intellectuals, as well as between collective ownership and ownership by the whole people.

The present people's commune movement does not, however, require the immediate transformation, in all cases, of collective ownership into ownership by the whole people. Even less does it mean the transition from the lower stage of socialism which is based on the principle "from each according to his ability, to each according to his work," to its higher stage, i.e., communism, which is based on the principle "from each according to his ability, to each according to his needs."

Some people's communes may have gone farther than others, but generally speaking, the transformation of collective ownership into ownership by the whole people is a process that will take three or four years, even five or six years, to complete in the rural areas. Then, after a number of years, production will be greatly increased. The people's communist consciousness and morality will be highly improved. Education will be made universal and elevated among the people. Differences between workers and peasants, urban and rural areas, mental and manual labour—left over from the old society and inevitably existing in the socialist society—as well as the remnants of unequal bourgeois rights which are the reflection of these differences, will gradually vanish, the function of the state will be limited to protecting the country from external aggression; it will play no role in domestic affairs. By that time Chinese society will enter the era of communism, the era when the principle "from each according to his ability, to each according to his needs" will be realized.

Now the development of people's communes is growing into a mass movement more gigantic than the co-operative movement of 1955. The Party committees of various places must work out appropriate plans and give active guidance to the development according to local conditions. The development of people's communes will doubtlessly be different in time, scale, pace, and method in different places. Uniformity should not be imposed. People's communes must be set up on the basis of full discussion by the people concerned and it must be a matter of the people's own choice. No rash, impetuous, or domineering attitude should be taken, especially on the question concerning change in the ownership of the means of production.

At present, work in the autumn fields allows for no delay while preparations must be made for the farm work of the coming winter and next spring. We must give first priority to work related to production in all places, regardless of the condition whether people's communes have or have not been established.

21.4 HEROINE OF THE GREAT LEAP FORWARD: "A BRIEF BIOGRAPHY OF LI SHUANGSHUANG"

Li Shuangshuang, the fictional protagonist of this short story first published in 1959, became an icon of female empowerment during the Great Leap Forward. In the original version, excerpted below, Shuangshuang is a spirited young peasant who inspires her commune to create a public canteen, freeing women from time-consuming domestic duties to participate in the Great Leap. She also motivates her unenlightened husband to change his attitudes about women's abilities. United by their common purpose, the couple forge a closer relationship and become models for emulation. Subsequent adaptations of the story into drama, comic strips, and film introduced new plot twists. But the central message remained consistent, capturing the utopian possibilities at the beginning of the Great Leap, before the visions of plenty were fatally shattered.

1

Li Shuangshuang is the wife of Sun Xiwang of the Sun Family Village Brigade of our commune and is twenty-six or -seven years old this year. Before the establishment of the commune and the Great Leap Forward, there were very few in the village who knew her name was Shuangshuang, because she already had two or three children when still very young. In the days of the agricultural collectives, she was seldom able to head out to the fields to do any work. Even when she put in a few days of labour during the busy season around the wheat harvest, these would all be entered on Xiwang's work record. Among their village neighbours, when the elder generation mentioned her it was as 'Xiwang's wife' or 'Xiwang's woman,' and the younger ones would just call her 'Auntie Xiwang.' As for Xiwang himself, when he spoke of her in front of others years ago he would just refer to her as 'the one in my home,' but in recent years, after she had children, he changed to 'Little Chrysanthemum's mother.' He also had another name for her which didn't sound as good, 'the one that cooks for me.'

Since there were so many alternative forms of address, of course the name Shuangshuang seldom made an appearance. But all things change in their due time, and in the spring of 1958 the Great Leap Forward allowed Shuangshuang to 'leap' out. Not only did her name leap before the entire commune, it also leaped onto the pages of the county and provincial newspapers. The name Li Shuangshuang was pronounced resoundingly among the people. We must, however, take a step back. The first time her name appeared before the people was after the Spring Festival of 1958, on a big-character poster during a Mass 'Blooming and Contending' Meeting at Sun Family Village. Our story must also begin at that point.

Early in the spring of 1958, the masses of the entire township broke with their traditional Spring Festival celebrations and launched a mighty drive to create an irrigation system. Hoisting large flags and beating gongs and drums, the young men and women of Sun Family Village headed up Black Hill to build a reservoir. The workforce that was left in the village was kept busy gathering fertilizer and spreading manure, doing the spring hoeing and planting sweet potato shoots. But because of the shortage of labour, there was just no way to take care of the wheat fields as well.

At this time, the commune's Party branch called on the masses to 'Bloom and Contend' in discussion of this issue, asking everyone to come up with ways to solve the problem. A Mobilization Meeting was held at commune headquarters, and on the first day big-character posters were pasted up along the streets. That day Comrade Luo Shulin, the secretary of the rural party committee, came to Sun Family Village, and he and the commune's Old Party Secretary Uncle Leap read the colourful posters pasted up on the walls of the houses on both sides of the street. One poster in particular caught their attention.

The characters on this poster were oversized, and the handwriting was just a little crooked, but the content of what was written on it was exceptionally novel:

> Household chores
> are such a bore!
> We've got the drive
> but can't mobilize!
> If we're stuck home to cook all day,
> how can Great Leap plans get under way?

We have to start a canteen and then
we women will show we can take on the men!

The name signed at the bottom was Li Shuangshuang.

Putting up this poster may not seem that big a deal, but Secretary Luo was thrilled with it. He read it out loud over and over again and slapped Uncle Leap on the shoulder: 'Hey, old friend, we might just have something here! This poster is really important! If we can get the housewives out of their homes, then this Great Leap of ours could really take off!' He then asked which household this Li Shuangshuang belonged to.

Uncle Leap thought about it and replied: 'These young women nowadays, I just can't keep track of them all. None of them come out to the meetings that much.'

'Go and make some enquiries,' Secretary Luo said. 'This is someone we should seek out and cultivate. To be able to come up with something like this is not easy, it's really got some kick to it!'

At the mention of 'kick,' Uncle Leap said: 'Now that you mention it, it's probably Xiwang's wife.'

Secretary Luo asked: 'How can you tell?'

Uncle Leap replied: 'It's possible that young woman could come up with something like this! During the Great Contending last year, she went up on stage and gave a speech. It's just that she usually doesn't make it to many meetings. A couple of days ago I saw her scrapping with Xiwang!'

As the two men were talking, the sun had worked its way directly overhead and the shadows of the trees had shortened. People returning from the fields gathered round to read the poster. Uncle Leap asked them: 'Is this Li Shuangshuang Xiwang's wife?' Some of them said it was while others said it wasn't.

Someone said: 'This was written by Xiwang's wife. During last winter's literacy campaign, Li Shuangshuang was the name she used to register at the community school.'

Someone else said: 'That young woman is smart as a whip and good at her studies, she could have written that.'

Just as everyone was deliberating, Xiwang happened to return from the fields pushing a small cart. Xiwang was thirty-four, seven or eight years older than Shuangshuang. He also came from a poor background, and before Liberation he spent two years as an apprentice cook at a restaurant in the county town. But later, because he broke a couple of dishes when he was serving food and was afraid of being beaten by the manager, he skipped town and drifted around with a musical troupe for a couple of years, only getting back to the village after liberation.

Everyone saw Xiwang and called out: 'Xiwang, who do you think wrote this big-character poster? Could it be your Little Chrysanthemum's mother?'

When Xiwang heard that Shuangshuang had pasted up a big-character poster, his first reaction was alarm. He thought to himself: 'That fool never thinks before she acts. She'd better not have let on about that fight we had a couple of days ago!'

Seeing both Secretary Luo from the township and the Old Party Secretary there reading the poster, he was all the more reluctant to admit to it. Hemming and hawing, he walked over to the poster and read it over, and he felt as relieved as if a stone had been lifted from his heart. Again he heard Secretary Luo exclaim: 'Well written! This poster is really well written!' He finally mumbled: 'Yes, that was written by the one who cooks for me.'

As soon as Xiwang's words were out, everyone exploded with laughter. Xiwang thought they were laughing at him for bragging about his wife, so he hurriedly provided confirmation: 'You don't believe me? It really was written by my Little Chrysanthemum's mother. Her name is Li Shuangshuang, and she knows how to write! She doesn't just put up big-character posters here, she's always scribbling little notes, they're pasted up all over our house.' As he said this, the crowd laughed even harder. Chuckling, Secretary Luo asked him: 'And just what does she usually write on those little notes?'

Xiwang blushed: 'She's just a woman, what does she know. She writes stuff like what's on this poster: "I really want to study, but I just don't have the time," "When will I be able to stop cooking and participate in the Great Leap?" Then there's: "The character for trousers, *ku*, remove the clothing radical, *yi*, and it becomes the character for reservoir, *ku*." . . . all sorts of them! They're pasted all over the head of the bed, on the window-papers, I can't remember what they say. Anyway, that one who cooks for me, she's all talk, she's got no sense of what effect what she says can have. You don't need to be bothered with her.' As he was speaking, Xiwang went to tear the poster Shuangshuang had written from the wall, but the Old Party Secretary held him back: 'Just what do you think you're doing? She's written a poster and you think you can just tear it down? She's Blooming and Contending!'

When he heard this was 'Blooming and Contending,' Xiwang quickly withdrew his hand. Secretary Luo looked him over and chuckled: 'Xiwang my friend, your wife Li Shuangshuang's poster is excellently written. Her suggestion will be really useful for our entire township's Great Leap Forward. It's not the case that she doesn't know anything, actually she knows a great deal. I'm going to take this poster with me. The rural party committee will hold a special meeting to discuss this idea.' Patting Xiwang on the shoulder he continued, '*Ai*, and from now on you have to change your old ways. Why do you always call her, "the one who cooks for me"? Her posters are pasted at the head of your bed, shouldn't you be a bit more democratic?'

When Secretary Luo had finished speaking, he took down the poster, folded it up and put it in his pocket, then headed off to commune headquarters with the Party Secretary. For the moment, Xiwang was dumbstruck, unable to make head or tail of it.

2

Xiwang was deep in thought as he headed for home, pushing his empty wheelbarrow.

He thought, that woman of mine writes a couple of lines of doggerel, and secretary Luo of the rural party committee thinks that what she wrote is a thing of great value! But this is pretty risky too! It's just as well she didn't let on about that fight we had. If she'd really written a big-character poster about me and stuck that up by the roadside, it's likely everyone would have been 'disputing' with me! *Ai*, with an outspoken woman like that, I'll have to be a bit more careful in the future.

Actually there was a whole series of reasons for the fight that Xiwang and Shuangshuang had had a couple of days before. Shuangshuang's family had been destitute peasants before liberation, and she had been given in marriage to Xiwang the year she turned seventeen. For the first few years after she came into his house, Shuangshuang was just a kid, she didn't know anything about anything, and she got beaten by Xiwang on a regular basis. After the land reform, the government implemented the new marriage law, and Xiwang didn't dare to hit her all the time. For one thing, life was getting a bit better, and he was afraid she would divorce him; for another, now that Shuangshuang had the children, she had more of a temper than before. Sometimes when Xiwang hit her, she would fight back for all she was worth. Xiwang had picked a fight with her a couple of times and hadn't been able to get the better of her. The village cadres criticized him for his unreasonableness, and after that he hadn't used his fists on her again. He was still in charge of the affairs of their family, at home and outside. After collectivization, the principle of equal pay for equal work was brought in, and although Shuangshuang didn't work that much, she still received a share. Now Xiwang was supposed to consult her whatever he did, but Shuangshuang had the children to look after and so didn't go to many meetings or get out to the fields much. Xiwang was happy to put in a little extra work himself; from his point of view, it saved him a good deal of trouble.

Xiwang actually did like Shuangshuang. He liked her fiery personality, and he liked the way she had turned into someone with a forthright nature, always daring to talk and laugh. Shuangshuang was good-looking, skilled with a needle, and quick and neat about her work. In recent years she'd been able to spin half a catty of thread a day from the coarsest of cotton fibres and could weave thirteen or fourteen feet of cloth in a day. Even now that there were more children, Xiwang never went without new cloth shoes, and the children always had clean cotton-padded clothing to change into when the wind turned cold in the autumn. But there were also things about her that Xiwang didn't like, such as that in his opinion she talked too much, she tended to mind other people's business outside the house, and to talk about things that did not concern her. Because she was interfering, she inevitably got into fights with people, so that sometimes Xiwang had to make apologies for her. Whenever this sort of thing happened, Xiwang would always angrily lament: '*Ai*, that woman of mine is just too quick-witted. If she wasn't so bright, she'd be easier to get along with.'

The winter before last, the village expanded the community school and Shuangshuang enrolled. While at school she concentrated on her studies and didn't get into as many quarrels, which put Xiwang's mind at ease. He thought to himself: 'This is fine, she can learn to write a couple of characters a day, and it will keep her mind occupied. After all, everyone needs to have an interest.'

When the village provided each household with access to a radio broadcasting network a couple of years ago, Xiwang also installed a loudspeaker. Xiwang enjoyed listening to the local *bangzi* opera and music played on the *suona*, while Shuangshuang preferred news and reports. With each of them taking turns, things went along quite smoothly. But Xiwang hadn't anticipated that with Shuang-shuang getting an education and then listening to news broadcasts and reading newspapers, she would stir up more trouble. Not only was she posting up little notes all over the house, she had even got into a fight with Xiwang a couple of days before.

The fight happened on the seventh day of the first lunar month. Shuangshuang watched as all the young villagers headed up to the reservoir on Black Hill. She had heard that they were also going to redirect Red Rock River into the village and were digging a large irrigation ditch east of the village. She put in a request to go and work on the ditch.

Xiwang said: 'Forget it. The team didn't assign you any work there.'

Shuangshuang replied: 'Assigned or not, I still want to go. I'm bored stiff stuck at home. Everyone is out there taking part in the Great Leap Forward and I can't even leave this house!'

Xiwang said: 'What's all this about a "Great Leap Forward," they're just digging.'

Pursing her lips, Shuangshuang glowered at Xiwang and said: 'Enough of your conservative talk, I'm going!'

Xiwang couldn't change her mind and just had to do as she wanted, taking the children round to their neighbour, Fourth Auntie, while Shuangshuang went off to the east of the village to work on the irrigation ditch.

After a couple of days working, Shuangshuang's cheeks were rosy from the wind, she was more talkative and laughed more loudly, but she was also busier than ever, especially with having to cook three meals a day. Each day she would need to race home before quitting time and hurriedly cook a meal while the fire was still smoky. But before the food even reached her mouth, the bell would go in the team to summon them back to work.

At noon on the seventh day of the lunar month, Shuangshuang returned home a little late, and as she came in she saw the children crying for food. She was utterly exhausted, and with the children yelling, Shuangshuang got really flustered. She parted the curtains hanging in the doorway and went into the house to have a look, only to find Xiwang already home and lying on the bed having a smoke.

Seeing this made Shuangshuang furious: 'The kids are crying like this and you don't take care of them? It's all very well for you to relax!'

But Xiwang just puffed on his pipe, not saying a word.

Shuangshuang took two steamed buns out of the basket and gave them to the children, washed her hands, and then kneaded the dough: 'It's not like you can't cook. When you get home just get the dough ready ahead of time and I'll roll it out when I get back. This will save some time. All you do is lie on the bed and smoke!'

At that, Xiwang extended two fingers to dismiss this idea: *'Ai!* I couldn't do that. Cooking is a woman's job. If I cook for you now, before you know it you'll be getting me to wash diapers!'

Hearing this, Shuangshuang's heart seethed with anger: 'You need to realize the difference between being busy and being idle. Haven't you noticed how busy I am?'

Xiwang replied: 'You've brought this on yourself. I can't be looking after you.'

As she sliced the dough into noodles, she rapped the cutting-board with the knife and snapped: 'When we turn the commune's dry fields into paddy-fields, don't you bother eating any of the food we grow.'

Xiwang retorted: 'So you're saying you don't want to let me eat, that's fine! But in the future it's still going to be you who has to cook for me.'

Hearing him say this, Shuangshuang's eyes flared. She threw down the knife with a clang: 'Eat! You won't get to eat!' And with that, she slumped down furiously on the doorstep and began to cry.

While Shuangshuang sat there in tears, Xiwang acted as though nothing had happened. He lay down for a while and then, with pretended unconcern, he went over to the chopping board to look at the noodles Shuangshuang had sliced. 'This is enough for me, I'll cook them myself,' he said, walking over to the pot and dropping in the noodles. While the noodles were boiling, he found a couple of cloves of garlic, minced them with a knife, added a little vinegar and got ready to eat his dish of noodles.

In the house, Shuangshuang's howling became more anguished as Xiwang pounded away at the garlic.

Shuangshuang ground her teeth as she watched him prepare the noodles so casually, thinking to herself: 'Here I am crying while you're there eating. You won't get your fill!' At that point, she rushed over and delivered two vicious punches to Xiwang's spine.

After taking these two blows, Xiwang yelled: 'Fine! You asked for it!' Grabbing the garlic pestle, he turned and was about to hit her back, when Shuangshuang grabbed hold of it and gave him a shove that pushed him out of the house and left him squatting down on the ground in the courtyard.

Once she'd pushed Xiwang to the ground, Shuangshuang couldn't help herself from bursting out laughing. She laughed so hard she shook the tears off her face and onto the ground.

Xiwang pulled himself up off the ground and was about to explode when Shuangshuang came over and grabbed hold of him: 'Let's go! We're going to get the Old Party Secretary to sort this out! How can you be like this? I'm taking part in the Great Leap Forward but you don't want me to. You're upset, you're grumpy, and you're purposely making it hard for me. What are you thinking! Let's go!'

Xiwang had wanted to give Shuangshuang a couple of really good whacks, but hearing her say this he knew he was in the wrong. Besides, he really had been trying to make life difficult for Shuangshuang. So he didn't dare to hit her again, much less go to see the Old Party Secretary with her. He quickly pulled his hands away and, standing right in front of the door, said angrily: 'Go on! You go there first and I'll follow!'

That may have been what he said, but actually he just slipped away.

3

Their scrap left Shuangshuang feeling both angry and amused. There was however, actually something else on her mind. She thought to herself: 'Just fighting like that is getting us nowhere. We've got to do something.'

That night, after Shuangshuang got the children to sleep and adjusted the wick on the lamp, she sat alone by the window stitching soles for cloth shoes and thinking about what was bothering her. Then suddenly, light from a fire east of the village turned the window-paper a glowing red. Like raindrops, the sounds of pickaxes and shovels digging into stone pattered in the distance, interspersed with bursts of excited shouting and laughter from the villagers.

Shuangshuang peered eastward through the window, knowing it was the night shift on the Red Rock River irrigation project. Lanterns were strung out in a row, like a fiery dragon; the lanterns lit up a long line of dark figures, their pickaxes and shovels in constant motion, rising and falling. The sound of the stone-tamper falling pounded out a rhythm, while the clear notes of young men and women singing work-songs flowed like a tide that swept through the window into Shuangshuang's home.

'The Great Leap Forward is turning the sky red outside,' Shuangshuang thought, 'Can I let myself be tied down by this household for the rest of my life?' She felt her heart race and her cheeks burn and was no longer in the mood to work.

Just then, the door creaked open and somebody came in. Shuangshuang assumed it was just Xiwang and purposely refused to look at him.

'Yo! You're putting on airs, ignoring me like that! Or are you nodding off?'

Shuangshuang quickly looked up to see Guiying, the wife of Changshui from the South Courtyard. Laughing, she said: 'I thought it was my "Lord and Master" returning home, but it's you!'

Guiying said: 'What's up, don't you want to see him?'

Shuangshuang replied: 'I don't want to have anything to do with him for the next ten lifetimes!'

'Don't be like that,' said Guiying, 'Haven't you heard the proverb?

> Like rain from the sky that sinks in the soil,
> Couples who quarrel make peace as they toil,
> They eat from the same pot when the day's work is done,
> Then on the same pillow two heads lie as one.

Shuangshuang retorted: 'We're not even able to eat together!'

As the two women spoke they began to giggle, making so much noise that the children tossed and turned in bed. They quickly suppressed their laughter.

Shuangshuang softly asked Guiying: 'How about your kids?'

'I just got them to sleep too,' said Guiying.

'Why aren't you asleep?'

'Can't sleep. What about you?'

'I can't sleep either,' Shuangshuang said, 'I heard that in a few days the water in the irrigation ditch will flow right by the village.'

Guiying said: 'Auntie Xiwang, tell me, what are people like us going to do? Everyone else is Leaping Forward, but how are we going to make the Great Leap? The day before yesterday my husband Changshui went to the reservoir on Black Hill. I wanted to go too, but he said people like us with lots of children aren't allowed. I told him I would go to the reservoir to cook, but he said there would be nobody to look after the children!'

Shuangshuang stood up suddenly and asked: 'Have they set up a canteen at the reservoir?'

Guiying replied: 'Sure. The day before yesterday they took all the big pots and steamers up there with them.'

Shuangshuang then threw down a shoe sole: '*Hei*! If they can set up a canteen at the reservoir, why can't we have a canteen in the village?' Clapping her hands, Guiying said: 'Yeah! Now that's an idea!'

As the two young wives cheered up, they became more energetic and resourceful. They discussed how they would run the canteen and how they could make arrangements for the children. The more they talked, the more enthusiastic they became, chatting well into the middle of the night. Still not satisfied, Shuangshuang then dragged Guiying off to find the Old Party Secretary that very night.

They arrived at the home of the Old Party Secretary before he got back from the work-site; Auntie Leap was the only one at home. When they talked to her about wanting to set up a canteen in the village, Auntie Leap said: 'You two have come up with this at just the right time. There is a meeting being held tonight to investigate how to get more people into the workforce. Your idea is great! Bring it up, go ahead and Bloom and Contend, it's sure to go over well!'

Shuangshuang asked: 'But how are we going to Bloom and Contend?'

Auntie Leap replied, 'Paste up a big-character poster! You can both write. Take your idea, write it out in big characters and paste it up in the street if you want! . . .'

While Auntie Leap was still speaking, Shuangshuang grabbed hold of Guiying: 'Come on! Don't worry what anyone says, we'll worry about what happens after we paste it up!' Full of enthusiasm, the two women headed out.

Shuangshuang got home to find Xiwang already fast asleep. She lit the lamp again, found a sheet of paper and began writing out her big-character poster. As she was writing, Xiwang woke up to see Shuangshuang concentrating intently on what she was writing. He called out to her: '*Wei!* Get to sleep. Don't stay up all night.

It doesn't matter how many characters you write out, you're never going to be a scholar!'

Shuangshuang just ignored him and focused on her writing. She wrote until the light was rising in the east before she finally had her rhyme written. Then she took it out and pasted it up by the road.

It had never occurred to Xiwang that the big-character poster Shuangshuang wrote would be of such value.

After he had pushed his empty wheelbarrow back home, he sat in the courtyard and giggled like a fool looking at Shuangshuang. Shuangshuang became impatient with his laughing and scolded him: 'Just what are you giggling at? You're sitting there laughing like you've eaten a clucking chicken and started clucking yourself!'

Xiwang grimaced: 'Little Chrysanthemum's mother, you're a hard one to figure out.'

'What are you talking about "hard to figure out," if you have something to say just go ahead and say it, quit beating around the bush!'

Xiwang said: 'That big-character poster of yours caught the eye of Secretary Luo from the township, and he said the rhyme you wrote is really important. The rural party committee is going to hold a special meeting to discuss it.'

'Really?' Shuangshuang was so happy she was practically jumping for joy.

But Xiwang continued: 'I'm telling you, in the future try not to make so much trouble for me! You can't just paste posters up whenever you feel like it. What do you understand about policies! What kind of an idea is this canteen business, can the commune just open up a restaurant?'

Shuangshuang replied: 'All you can think about is running a restaurant. What I'm talking about is setting up a public canteen where all the households in the village pool their food supply, and a couple of talented cooks are selected to make meals. Just like up there at the reservoir, it will save manpower and fuel. As for you, my good man, in the future don't even think about trying to make things hard for me. I'm not just going to obey you blindly any more. I've had enough of that.'

Hearing her say this, Xiwang forced a laugh: 'It sounds to me like you want to grow wings and fly away! How is that going to work? A bunch of families eating together, that's something different! If the township approves that poster of yours, huh . . .'

Shuangshuang said: 'It's not certain yet, but if they want to go ahead with it, what are you going to have to say about it?'

Xiwang said: 'If they go for your idea, I'll walk around in circles on my head!'

Before Xiwang finished speaking, the speaker hanging from the eaves of the house started up. The broadcast began: 'Good news to report to all commune members! In order to get us Leaping Forward even more, and based on the request from the masses, the rural party committee will establish a mass public canteen in Sun Family village. . . .'

Hearing these words, Shuangshuang was so delighted she took off at once into the street. As she reached her doorway a group of women including Auntie Leap, Fourth Auntie and Guiying were surging toward her house shouting and yelling: 'Shuangshuang! Our big-character poster worked! The rural committee wants us to start a canteen!'

'Let's go, we've got to find a place to build a stove!'

'Who knows how to build a stove?'

'There's an ideal person! Xiwang! He knows how. He can set up a big powerful stove!'

'We have to borrow a big pot. The Ermao family from the eastern side of the village has a big pot they used when they slaughtered cattle!'

Within moments, the Xiwang family courtyard was as thronged with people as though they were rushing to a New Year's gathering. This noisy group of women, laughing and shouting, dragged Xiwang off in search of a place to set up the stove.

4

A location was found for the canteen to the south of the village crossroads, in the courtyard where the wealthy middle peasant Sun You's family used to keep their carts. They whitewashed the three north-facing rooms a sparkling snowy white, and they built two large coal-fired cooking stoves under the window on the southern wall. Two large cast-iron pots had been placed on the stovetop, while on either side sat pairs of cooking pots, each as big around as a bull's waist. Then, at the eastern end of the room, they put together a twelve by eight foot chopping board made of persimmon wood.

After they had borrowed all of the hardware and utensils they needed, Sun Family Village Agricultural Co-operative Masses Public Canteen was ready for the fires to be lit in the stoves.

Within the courtyard, over 100 families had gathered together in the new canteen premises to select the canteen cooks and superintendent.

During the meeting, the Old Party Secretary talked about how the rural party committee supported everyone's request to set up a canteen, and that this suggestion was being acted on as soon as it was raised. When it finally came around to selecting the kitchen staff, everyone erupted in a noisy clamour.

Shuangshuang was the first to speak. Her face blushing red, she shouted: '*Wei*! I propose we call upon Fourth Auntie to be a cook. Fourth Auntie is a poor peasant, she's neat and tidy and reliable in her work. Not only that, we all know Fourth Auntie's heart's in the right place!'

As soon as Shuangshuang finished speaking, the crowd cried in support: 'Fourth Auntie's our first cook! She can do it!'

'She certainly won't waste any rice or noodles.'

'But we have so many heavy pots and big steamers, we still need somebody big and strong.'

'Let's pick a man this time!'

Xiwang was at the meeting that day. He'd come by to watch and was off to one side puffing on his pipe and certainly hadn't expected anybody to bring up his name . . . but Guiying did.

Guiying stood up and made a suggestion: 'Ai, I've got somebody, Brother Xiwang. We all know that Brother Xiwang is an ace in the kitchen. He used to work in a restaurant. Stir-fry or quick-fry, he can do it all. But we've never actually seen him cook! What do you say, everyone?'

'All right,' the crowd responded in agreement. Someone added: 'With someone as strong as he is working in the canteen, fetching water won't be a problem!'

'With Xiwang working here, if we want to eat chicken or fish nothing will stop us!'

'Xiwang will be great, he's a good guy.' The wealthy middle-peasant Sun You hadn't been very keen on the idea of a canteen to start with, but after hearing what everyone had to say, he also expressed his agreement.

Someone from the crowd continued: 'With Xiwang doing the cooking for the canteen, even the turnip dishes will be tasty.'

Everyone in the crowd chipped in, all of which delighted Shuangshuang. In the time since she was married to Xiwang, she had yet to see so many people praising him. She thought to herself: 'This Great Leap Forward is really making good use of people's skills. Just look at all the support Xiwang's getting.'

Just as she was thinking this, Xiwang stood up to speak. He seemed very full of himself. Instead of smoking his pipe, he pulled a cigarette from behind his ear and cleared his throat a couple of times before speaking: 'Everyone has just nominated me to go and work in the canteen, but I can't do this kind of canteen work. I know people will say, "You used to work in the restaurant at Cedar Inn in the North Mountains, so this village canteen of ours would be no problem for you." But that's exactly the reason. It's just as people say, you can only understand what's written down if you've studied the right books. The apprentices at the restaurant were separated into the bun and noodles section, the cooked dishes section and the food-prep section. I studied in the cooked dishes section. If you want chicken or fish, I can do it steamed or braised. But steaming buns and making noodles, that was a different section . . .' Xiwang had not yet finished what he was going to say when the crowd shouted out, 'We picked you because you know how to cook!'

'If you can work a grinder you can turn a millstone; it's all the same kind of work! It won't be long before we'll have fish and chicken to serve in our canteen, you have to look ahead!'

'The fish in the reservoir are all over a catty!'

At that moment, Shuangshuang laughed and pointed at Xiwang: 'He knows how to steam buns. He also knows how to make noodles. At home he often makes himself a snack if he feels like it.'

Realizing Shuangshuang had called his bluff, Xiwang glared at her: 'You've got some mouth on you! When have you ever seen me cook for myself?'

Not letting up, Shuangshuang replied, 'You just cooked the other day! How can you say you don't know how to make noodles or steamed buns. You're being honoured but you won't accept it! I can't stand people who "won't go forward when they're dragged and go the wrong way when they're hit," people who say they're "dog meat and not good enough to be set on the table."'

Shuangshuang's cutting remarks elicited great laughter from the crowd at the scene. Xiwang rolled up his sleeves as if wanting to say something more, but then the Old Party Secretary took over: 'The establishment of this canteen is for the benefit of all commune members, it's to allow our commune's production to Leap Forward even further. If we're selected by everyone, it's because people think we can be of service. We can't go turning it down.' Even though the Old Party Secretary didn't say much, every word of it was aimed at Xiwang. Xiwang was often self-important, but he was extremely deferential towards the Old Party Secretary. He blushed: 'In that case, ignore what I just said. You can take the word of the one who cooks for me!'

As soon as these words left his mouth, the crowd erupted in laughter and even the Old Party Secretary had to laugh. Blushing scarlet, Xiwang scratched his head, realizing that this form of address really was behind the times!

5

The first meal served in the canteen was sorghum and green beans with noodles, a dish everybody called 'carp flitting through the sand.' Because it was the canteen's inaugural meal, both the Old Party Secretary and team leader Yushun were personally on hand in the kitchen.

As for the cooks, besides Xiwang and Fourth Auntie, Guiying had also been chosen. They hadn't been able to find a superintendant for the time being, so this responsibility was given to the eldest son of Sun You's family, Jinqiao. Jinqiao had graduated from primary school, but later, because of his age and his failure to pass the middle school entrance examinations, had to labour in the commune. On this day, the Old Party Secretary arrived at the canteen early and got a fire going. He then grabbed a shoulder pole with water buckets and hurried back and forth filling up the water vats. Watching the Party Secretary work so hard at his advanced age made Xiwang feel a little guilty. After he had rolled out a few lumps of noodle dough, he passed them on to Guiying and the other women for cutting and took the Old Party Secretary's carrying pole and water buckets and went off to fetch water. Without stopping he hauled more than thirty loads of water, filling up two large vats to the brim before he considered his work finished.

When it was time to eat, the entire village, men, women, old and young, all came to the canteen. Shuangshuang also brought her three children, Little Chrysanthemum, Little Whistle and Little Reed-pipe. She watched Xiwang wearing his chef's hat and his snow-white uniform embroidered with large red characters, as he rushed about serving people and taking their meal tickets. Everyone was calling out to him and searching him out; it looked as if he could laugh and chat with them all, as though he was suddenly ten years younger.

While they were eating, Shuangshuang glanced over at him from a distance and smiled. She made a point of lifting the noodles high out of her bowl and into her mouth and called over to him appreciatively, teasing him, as if to say now I can eat food you prepared! Xiwang saw what she was up to but turned away and pretended not to notice.

Before the Old Party Secretary had his meal, he went from table to table asking everyone for their opinions on the canteen. He approached Shuangshuang and asked: 'Shuangshuang, is the food in this canteen any good?' Laughing, Shuangshuang replied: 'It's excellent! And this saves so much time: when you've finished eating, you just wipe your mouth and go. Now we can just focus on Leaping Forward, with nothing to fuss or worry about!' As she spoke she looked at Xiwang, and he thought to himself: 'OK then, so now you're really a somebody!'

When the meal was over, Xiwang cleaned up the canteen and returned home. He saw that Shuangshuang was looking after their two boys Little Whistle and Little Reed-pipe, washing their faces, putting on powder and face-cream, and changing their clothes before sending them off to kindergarten. Xiwang entered the room but ignored all the fuss. Letting out a long, deep sigh he said, 'Goddamn, all that work is really killing me. My whole body is just exhausted.' And as he spoke he collapsed onto the bed.

Shuangshuang knew that he liked to boast about how much work he had done, and so she just ignored him, letting him sit there moaning and complaining ceaselessly. When the children were ready to go, Auntie Leap, the head of the kindergarten, came by to pick the boys up. After they were gone, Shuangshuang returned to the room and poured a glass of hot water from the thermos. She pursed her lips into a smile and with both hands carried the glass over to Xiwang, placing it in front of him.

'Are you worn out?' she asked softly.

'Feels like my spine's been pulled out,' exaggerated Xiwang, putting on his most long-suffering face. Shuangshuang then prepared a basin of warm water and carried it over to Xiwang, chiding him: 'Just look at your face, all smeared with dirt so you look like General Jingde in the operas! You're always going on about how you worked in a big fancy restaurant, but you don't know the first thing about hygiene. Now we're trying to Destroy the Four Pests, if we go up one and Destroy the Five Pests, we'll be getting rid of you as well!'

At this, Xiwang rolled himself over and sat up proclaiming: 'I carried forty loads of water today, you go and try that!'

Shuangshuang replied: 'I don't need to, I know how hard that kind of work is. But if I came home after cooking in the canteen, I certainly wouldn't be grumbling and groaning like you. *Aiya* . . .'

Washing his face, Xiwang retorted: 'It isn't big talking that tires a person out! These days you seem to think you're above everyone else.'

To which Shuangshuang said: '*Ai*, it's not like I'm not busy, work is work! Old Zhao said cooking for the canteen is an important job.'

Happy now, Xiwang asked: 'Little Chrysanthemum's mother, tell me, just how were my noodles?'

'Delicious. Nice and long and thin,' praised Shuangshuang.

Xiwang was delighted at this compliment: '*Hai*, and you haven't even tried any of my specialties yet. If I take those noodles, add a little chicken broth and some shredded chicken, dried shrimps and seaweed . . . wait till you try that! But right now the canteen doesn't have everything I need. When I used to . . .' He was just about to continue but Shuangshuang interrupted: 'I don't want to hear about it! I just don't want to hear about it!'

'I didn't finish, how do you know what I was going to say?'

'You think I don't know!?' Shuangshuang said. 'You were going to go on about when you were at the Cedar Inn in the North Mountains again.'

Xiwang gulped back his spittle: 'That's not it at all.'

Shuangshuang saw that he was no longer happy and tried to talk him round: 'How come you always bring up that Cedar Inn? I just don't want to hear about it. That was the old society, and you were bullied and beaten there. However good the things you made there were, they were all made to serve to landlords, despots and no-gooders. What did our own families have to eat? Bowls of soup so thin you could see your reflection in the bottom, rice-husk dumplings so coarse that you couldn't keep them from falling apart. Even at New Year, you'd never see white steamed rolls. Our canteen may only provide simple home cooking right now, but at least it's made for us working people. You don't have to go on bragging about that place of yours. I think that if we can continue to Leap Forward like this, then in the future we will harvest bumper crops of grain and raise plenty of pigs and fish. Certainly there will be a day when the food from our canteen will be better than that restaurant of yours. Besides all that, do you realize how many pairs of hands you are freeing up with your two hands working in the canteen? I got assigned to the pig-farm today, we're only raising thirty-eight pigs right now, but by the end of the year we plan to have 150. Before this, I just had to stay home and wait on you.'

Xiwang nodded his head and thought to himself: 'What she's saying makes sense.' . . .

21.5 "DECISION APPROVING COMRADE MAO ZEDONG'S PROPOSAL TO STEP DOWN," DECEMBER 10, 1958

The catastrophic failures of the Great Leap Forward sharpened the conflict between Mao Zedong and other leaders of the Communist Party. Despite the mounting problems of collectivization and the ill-conceived steel production campaign, Mao refused to retreat from the overambitious plans. Liu Shaoqi and Deng Xiaoping had made their careers in Party circles as loyal supporters of Chairman Mao; they had served in important capacities at the pinnacle of the Chinese state throughout the first decade of Communist rule and had been enthusiastic and unqualified supporters of the Hundred Flowers campaign, the Anti-Rightist campaign, and the Great Leap Forward itself. In 1958, Mao was vulnerable due to the economic crisis brought about by his misguided policies. Liu and Deng exercised their influence in the Central Committee to pressure Mao Zedong to step down as head of state. Mao Zedong remained the Party chairman but was deprived of actual participation in decision making. Liu Shaoqi replaced Mao as head of state and the chairman was encouraged, as the following document suggests, to concentrate on "Marxist-Leninist theoretical work." Mao Zedong was unhappy with this forced departure from the frontline of political work and later complained that Liu and Deng treated him like a "dead man at his own funeral." Between 1958 and 1966, Mao restively inhabited the historical shrine constructed for him by his comrades-in-arms, but the struggle for control of the state was still very much alive.

In the past few years, Comrade Mao Zedong has more than once expressed to the Central Committee of the Party the wish that he should not continue to hold the post of Chairman of the People's Republic of China. Following full and all-round consideration, the Plenary Session of the Central Committee has decided to approve this proposal of Comrade Mao Zedong, and not to nominate him again as candidate for Chairman of the People's Republic of China at the First Session of the Second National People's Congress. The Plenary Session of the Central Committee deems this to be a completely positive proposal, because, relinquishing his duties as Chairman of the state and working solely as Chairman of the Central Committee of the Party, Comrade Mao Zedong will be enabled all the better to concentrate his energies on dealing with questions of the direction, policy and line of the Party and the state; he may also be enabled to set aside more time for Marxist-Leninist theoretical work, without affecting his continued leading role in the work of the state. This will be in the better interests of the whole Party and of all the people of the country. Comrade Mao Zedong is the sincerely beloved and long-tested leader of the people of various nationalities of the whole country. He will remain the leader of the entire people of various nationalities even when he no longer holds the post of Chairman of the state. If some special situation arises in the future which should require him to take up this work again, he can still be nominated again to assume the duties of the Chairman of the state in compliance with the opinion of the people and the decision of the Party. Party committees at all levels should, in accordance with these reasons, give full explanations to the cadres and masses both inside and outside the Party at appropriate meetings of the Party, sessions of the people's congresses of various levels, meetings of workers in industrial and mining enterprises, and meetings in people's communes, offices, schools and armed units, so that the reasons for this may be understood by all that there may be no misunderstanding.

21.6 STATEMENT OF THE GOVERNMENT OF THE PEOPLE'S REPUBLIC OF CHINA ON THE SUCCESSFUL EXPLOSION OF THE ATOMIC BOMB, 1964

Despite his brash dismissal of the American nuclear arsenal (Document 20.1), after the confrontation with the United States in the Taiwan Straits crisis of 1954–1955, Mao decided that building an atomic bomb was a strategic imperative for the PRC. Throughout the late 1950s, Chinese scientists worked with Soviet technical advisors to install research facilities and develop the necessary skills. When the project was interrupted by the withdrawal of Soviet assistance in 1960, Mao characteristically turned to "self-reliance," exhorting the project teams to master the complex technology without foreign help. The news that Chinese scientists had successfully tested its first nuclear weapon on October 16, 1964, was greeted with national jubilation.

As the following announcement makes clear, the Chinese government viewed its nuclear capability as a form of self-defense against American imperialism. While reiterating the idea of the atomic bomb as a "paper tiger," for the PRC, acquiring such a strategic weapon broke the nuclear monopoly of its adversaries.

China exploded an atom bomb at 15:00 hours on October 16, 1964, and thereby conducted successfully its first nuclear test. This is a major achievement of the Chinese people in their struggle to increase their national defence capability and oppose the U.S. imperialist policy of nuclear blackmail and nuclear threats.

To defend oneself is the inalienable right of every sovereign state. And to safeguard world peace is the common task of all peace-loving countries. China cannot remain idle and do nothing in the face of the ever increasing nuclear threat posed by the United States. China is forced to conduct nuclear tests and develop nuclear weapons.

The Chinese Government has consistently advocated the complete prohibition and thorough destruction of nuclear weapons. Should this have been realized, China need not develop the nuclear weapon. But this position of ours has met the stubborn resistance of the U.S. imperialists. The Chinese Government pointed out long ago that the treaty on the partial halting of nuclear tests signed by the United States, Britain and the Soviet Union in Moscow in July 1963 was a big fraud to fool the people of the world, that it tried to consolidate the nuclear monopoly held by the three nuclear powers and tie up the hands and feet of all peace-loving countries, and that it not only did not decrease but had increased the nuclear threat of U.S. imperialism against the people of China and of the whole world. The U.S. Government declared undisguisedly even then that the conclusion of such a treaty does not at all mean that the United States would not conduct underground tests, or would not use, manufacture, stockpile, export or proliferate nuclear weapons. The facts of the past year and more fully prove this point.

During the past year and more, the United States has not stopped manufacturing various nuclear weapons on the basis of the nuclear tests which it had already conducted. Furthermore, seeking for ever greater perfection, the United States has during this same period conducted several dozen underground nuclear tests, thereby further perfecting the nuclear weapons it manufactures. In stationing nuclear submarines in Japan, the United States is posing a direct threat to the Japanese people, the Chinese people and the peoples of all other Asian countries. The United States is now putting nuclear weapons into the hands of the West German revanchists through the so-called multilateral nuclear force and thereby threatening the security of the German Democratic Republic and the other East European socialist countries. U.S. submarines carrying Polaris missiles with nuclear warheads are prowling the Taiwan Straits, the Tonkin Gulf, the Mediterranean Sea, the Pacific Ocean, the Indian Ocean and the Atlantic Ocean, threatening everywhere peace-loving countries and all peoples who are fighting against imperialism, colonialism and neocolonialism. Under such circumstances, how can it be considered that the U.S. nuclear blackmail and nuclear threat against the people of the world no longer exist just because of the false impression created by the temporary halting of atmospheric tests by the United States?

The atom bomb is a paper tiger. This famous saying by Chairman Mao Zedong is known to all. This was our view in the past and this is still our view at present. China is developing nuclear weapons not because we believe in the omnipotence of nuclear weapons and that China plans to use nuclear weapons. The truth is exactly to the contrary. In developing nuclear weapons, China's aim is to break the nuclear monopoly of the nuclear powers and to eliminate nuclear weapons.

The Chinese Government is loyal to Marxism-Leninism and proletarian internationalism. We believe in the people. It is the people who decide the outcome of a war, and not any weapon. The destiny of China is decided by the Chinese people, and the destiny of the world by the peoples of the world, and not by the nuclear weapon. The development of nuclear weapons by China is for defence and for protecting the Chinese people from the danger of the United States launching a nuclear war.

The Chinese Government hereby solemnly declares that China will never at any time and under any circumstances be the first to use nuclear weapons.

The Chinese people firmly support the struggles for liberation waged by all oppressed nations and people of the world. We are convinced that, by relying on their own struggles and also through mutual aid, the peoples of the world will certainly win victory. The mastering of the nuclear weapon by China is a great encouragement to the revolutionary peoples of the world in their struggles and a great contribution to the cause of defending world peace. On the question of nuclear weapons, China will neither commit the error of adventurism nor the error of capitulationism. The Chinese people can be trusted.

The Chinese Government fully understands the good wishes of peace-loving countries and people for the halting of all nuclear tests. But more and more countries are coming to realize that the more the U.S. imperialists and their partners hold on to their nuclear monopoly, the more is there danger of a nuclear war breaking out. They have it and you don't, and so they are very haughty. But once those who oppose them also have it, they would no longer be so haughty, their policy of nuclear blackmail and nuclear threat would no longer be so effective, and the possibility for a complete prohibition and thorough destruction of nuclear weapons would increase. We sincerely hope that a nuclear war would never occur. We are convinced that, so long as all peace-loving countries and people of the world make common efforts and persist in the struggle, a nuclear war can be prevented.

The Chinese Government hereby formally proposes to the governments of the world that a summit conference of all the countries of the world be convened to discuss the question of the complete prohibition and thorough destruction of nuclear weapons, and that as a first step, the summit conference should reach an agreement to the effect that the nuclear powers and those countries which may soon become nuclear powers undertake not to use nuclear weapons, neither to use them against non-nuclear countries and nuclear-free zones, nor against each other.

If those countries in possession of huge quantities of nuclear weapons are not even willing to undertake not to use them, how can those countries not yet in possession of them be expected to believe in their sincerity for peace and not to adopt possible and necessary defensive measures?

The Chinese Government will, as always, exert every effort to promote the realization of the noble aim of the complete prohibition and thorough destruction of nuclear weapons through international consultations. Before the advent of such a day, the Chinese Government and people will firmly and unswervingly march along their own road of strengthening their national defences, defending their motherland and safeguarding world peace.

We are convinced that nuclear weapons, which are after all created by man, certainly will be eliminated by man.

CHAPTER 22

The Cultural Revolution

22.1 LIFE AND DEATH OF LEI FENG, AN ADMIRABLE "FOOL"

In September 1959, veteran general of the People's Liberation Army (PLA) Lin Biao succeeded Peng Dehuai as minister of defense. During the years prior to the opening of the Cultural Revolution, the army remained a powerful bastion of support for Mao Zedong and the Maoist line. As minister of defense, Lin Biao played a central role in organizing PLA support for Mao. He was rewarded for his loyalty by being designated as Mao's successor.

One aspect of Lin Biao's political work was the creation of a cult around the figure of a PLA soldier named Lei Feng, epitomizing the highest virtues of a socialist man. He was devoted to Chairman Mao, he loved the people, he was frugal, he did good deeds, and he was, in general, great because of his sheer ordinariness. Everyone could imitate Lei Feng, a "rust-proof screw" in the machinery of revolution. In fact, even Lei's death was humdrum: he died when a heavy pole, propelled by a skidding truck, crashed down on his head. The model of Lei Feng was designed to promote personal submission to the Party's leadership and incorporation of Mao Zedong Thought into everyday life. After 1963, a "Learn from Lei Feng" campaign became a central element of army political training. The following excerpts, purportedly from Lei Feng's diary, create a vivid sense of the values Lin Biao and the PLA would promote with great energy before and during the Cultural Revolution.

I want to be of use to our people and our country. If that means being a "fool," I am glad to be a "fool" of this sort. (From Lei Feng's Diary)

Lei Feng made a box in which to keep the screws, bits of wire, toothpaste tubes, rags, worn-out gloves, and other scraps that he collected. He called this his "treasure chest."

And that treasure chest was extremely useful.

If a screw was missing from the truck or a part broke down, Lei Feng searched through his treasure chest and made do if possible with something there. Only in case of extreme necessity did he ask the leadership for a replacement. He washed the rags and old gloves and used them as dusters, returning the new dusters that were issued to him. As for the toothpaste tubes and wire, when he had collected a sufficient amount he sold it as scrap and handed in the proceeds to his unit.

When summer uniforms were issued, each man received two uniforms, two shirts, and two pairs of shoes. From 1961 on, however, Lei Feng drew only one uniform, one shirt, and one pair or shoes.

"Why not take two?" asked the officer-in-charge.

"There's still plenty of wear in this uniform I have on, if it's patched and mended. The patched clothes I'm wearing now are a thousand times better than the rags I wore as a child. I'd rather hand back the other clothes to the state."

It hurt him to see the least waste of state property. There was a time when their job was loading cement. During the loading and unloading, some of the paper sacks invariably burst, so that at the end of each trip the bottom of the trucks would be covered by a layer of cement. Lei Feng always fetched a brush to sweep this up. The others followed suit, with the result that by the time this particular job was finished, they had salvaged nearly 1,800 kilos of cement.

Lei Feng lived extremely simply, never spending a cent more than necessary. Every month, after paying his Party dues and keeping a small sum to buy more of Chairman Mao's writings or some daily necessities, he banked all the rest of his pay. His socks were darned and re-darned until little of the original material was left, yet still he did not like to throw them away. His basin and mug have lost nearly all their enamel, exposing large patches of the iron beneath, yet he refused to buy new ones.

One of the men asked. "Why skimp yourself, Lei Feng? You've no family to support."

"Who says I have no family?" Lei Feng retorted. "There are hundreds of millions of people in my family—the big family of the motherland. Chairman Mao has called on every one of us to go all out and struggle hard to change our country's poverty and backwardness. Am I wrong to economize?"

"What difference will those few yuan of yours make to a big country like ours?"

"Every little bit counts. If everyone saved ten cents a day, just figure out for yourself how much the whole country would save. Now that we're masters of the state, we ought to be good managers."

Another man said, "Lei Feng is a fool—and so stingy!"

He did not let himself be influenced by these taunts. In the past, he had wanted to dress smartly and live well. But his standards had changed. He had realized that labor and creation were true beauty, that lofty moral qualities were beautiful. To spur himself on, he made the following entry in his diary:

> True beauty can be found in a soldier's faded, patched yellow uniform, a worker's grease-stained blue overalls, a peasant's rough, calloused hands, and the laboring people's swarthy, sun-burned faces, clamorous work chants, and tireless work for the building of socialism. All these things make up the beauty of our age. And anyone who sees no beauty in them does not understand our age.

After being called a "fool" he told himself, "If that's being a 'fool,' I'm glad to be a fool. The revolution needs 'fools' of this sort."

In reality, Lei Feng's actions were the best reply to those who called him "stingy" or a "fool."

Summer was just coming in all its loveliness when the people near the base held a rally, beating gongs and drums to celebrate the establishment of urban People's Communes. To support the communes, Lei Feng drew out of the bank the whole 200 yuan he had saved in the past few years in the factory and the army, and took it to the Party committee office of the Heping People's Commune in Wanghua.

"I've been looking forward to this day," he cried, putting a pile of bank notes on the table. "Please take this small contribution as a token of my warm support for the people of Wanghua."

"We'll accept your good wishes, comrade," said the people in the office, deeply stirred. "But we can't take this money. Keep it to use yourself, or send it home."

The word "home" touched Lei Feng to the quick.

"The People's Communes are my home!" he exclaimed. "I'm bringing my money home. I was an orphan in the old days, but I've grown up in good times. Everything I have I owe to the Party and the people. Because this money comes from the Party, let it play a small part now for the cause of the people."

When they still would not take the money, Lei Feng went on pleading until he burst into tears. Then the comrades there, moved to tears themselves, agreed to take half. The commune Party committee, in a later report, wrote, "Comrade Lei Feng's love for the commune is an immense inspiration to all our cadres and commune members. It has made some of our members pledge to run the commune well to show our appreciation to the PLA...."

The 100 yuan that the commune would not accept was the sum Lei Feng sent for flood relief to the Liaoyang Municipal Party Committee....

AN IMMORTAL FIGHTER

I must always remember these words:
Treat comrades with the warmth of spring,
Treat work with the ardor of summer,

> Treat individualism like the autumn wind blowing down dead leaves,
> Treat the enemy with the ruthlessness of winter.
> (From Lei Feng's Diary)

At eight a.m. on August 15, 1962, a fine rain was falling when Lei Feng and his assistant brought their truck back from a mission. Lei Feng jumped out and asked the assistant to park the truck where he could overhaul it and wash the mud off.

The assistant slid across to the driver's seat and started up. The truck vibrated as the engine roared and churned up mud as it began backing. Lei Feng stood behind, signaling directions: "Left, left! Back, back . . ."

The puddles of rain on the ground were very slippery. As the truck turned, it skidded into a post in a barbed-wire fence. Lei Feng was absorbed in giving directions and did not see the post, which crashed down on his head. He fell unconscious . . .

The assistant company commander himself drove at top speed from Fushun to Shenyang, aware that there was not a moment to lose. A first-rate driver, he covered the distance in record time, bringing back the best doctors in Shenyang.

But it was too late to save Lei Feng. The local doctors had done all they could, but he had lost so much blood from his head injuries that he could not hear the assistant company commander calling his name, could not hear the anguished sobs of his assistant, could not hear the weeping of his comrades-in-arms.

Lei Feng gave his life in the execution of his duty.

He lived only twenty-two short years, but his life was a glorious one.

He was born in bitterness, but he grew up in sweetness, and his every action shed radiance in this age of Mao Zedong!

His whole life was militant. He was the living embodiment of the Communist spirit of loyalty to the motherland, to the people, and to the Party, of utter devotion to others without thought of self. He expressed his philosophy in these words: "I believe we should live so that others may have a better life . . . I will gladly put up with a few hardships myself if I can thereby help others and do some good deeds." This was his world outlook, his rule of life, his lofty revolutionary ideal.

The people honored him, but he never let it go to his head. He wrote in his diary:

> Lei Feng, Lei Feng! Remember this warning: On no account be complacent. Don't ever forget that it was the Party that rescued you from the tiger's mouth, it was the Party that gave you everything . . . Any little job you can do is no more than your duty. Each trifling achievement or any slight progress you may make should be attributed to the Party. The credit must go to the Party. Water has its sources, a tree its roots.

The source and roots of Lei Feng's spirit were Mao Zedong's thought and the teaching of the Party. He was keenly aware that "The more we study and the more deeply we delve into Chairman Mao's writings, the clearer our ideas will be, the broader our vision, the firmer our stand, and the more farsighted our views."

He compared Mao Zedong's thought to food, to a soldier's weapon, to the steering wheel of a truck. He studied avidly and put all he learned into practice, making a creative study and application of Chairman Mao's works. This was the basic reason why Lei Feng—an orphan in the old society—developed into a hero and a Communist fighter in the new society.

Lei Feng was immortal. In the words of a poet:

> Death, do you boast that you have killed Lei Feng?
> In a hundred million hearts he still lives on.

To commemorate Lei Feng, our beloved and honored leader Chairman Mao wrote an inscription, calling on us to "Learn from Comrade Lei Feng!"

22.2 Lin Biao: "Long Live the Victory of People's War!," September 1965

Lin Biao also pledged his devotion to the Maoist vision of "people's war." Like Mao, Lin believed that human beings, rather than complicated weapons systems or atomic bombs, were the essential element in warfare. Written in 1965, just as the United States was expanding its role in Vietnam, "Long Live the Victory of People's War!" was Lin Biao's attempt to crystallize his notions of revolutionary warfare and the contradictions existing between advanced industrial and rural countries. Extending Chairman Mao's military and political ideas to the international arena, Lin Biao argued that revolutionary forces in Asian, African, and Latin American countries would soon isolate, surround, and defeat U.S imperialism.

Overall, Lin Biao's political work promoted the idea of a world revolution sponsored by China that would be of great value as the Maoist group opposed "revisionists" in the party. As the Maoists triumphed over rivals in the Party in 1966 and 1967, the style of Lin Biao's political work in the PLA was utilized throughout society.

The International Significance of Comrade Mao Zedong's Theory of People's War

In Commemoration of the Twentieth Anniversary of Victory in the Chinese People's War of Resistance Against Japan. . . .

The Chinese revolution is a continuation of the Great October Revolution. The road of the October Revolution is the common road for all people's revolutions.

The Chinese revolution and the October Revolution have in common the following basic characteristics: (1) Both were led by the working class with a Marxist-Leninist party as its nucleus. (2) Both were based on the worker-peasant alliance. (3) In both cases state power was seized through violent revolution and the dictatorship of the proletariat was established. (4) In both cases the socialist system was built after victory in the revolution. (5) Both were component parts of the proletarian world revolution.

Naturally, the Chinese revolution had its own peculiar characteristics. The October Revolution took place in imperialist Russia, but the Chinese revolution broke out in a semicolonial and semifeudal country. The former was a proletarian socialist revolution, while the latter developed into a socialist revolution after the complete victory of the new-democratic revolution. The October Revolution began with armed uprisings in the cities and then spread to the countryside, while the Chinese revolution won nationwide victory through the encirclement of the cities from the rural areas and the final capture of the cities.

Comrade Mao Zedong's great merit lies in the fact that he has succeeded in integrating the universal truth of Marxism-Leninism with the concrete practice of the Chinese revolution and has enriched and developed Marxism-Leninism by his masterly generalization and summary of the experience gained during the Chinese people's protracted revolutionary struggle.

Comrade Mao Zedong's theory of people's war has been proved by the long practice of the Chinese revolution to be in accord with the objective laws of such wars and to be invincible. It has not only been valid for China, it is a great contribution to the revolutionary struggles of the oppressed nations and peoples throughout the world.

The people's war led by the Chinese Communist Party, comprising the War of Resistance and the Revolutionary Civil Wars, lasted for twenty-two years. It constitutes the most drawn-out and most complex people's war led by the proletariat in modern history, and it has been the richest in experience.

In the last analysis, the Marxist-Leninist theory of proletarian revolution is the theory of the seizure of state power by revolutionary violence, the theory of countering war against the people by people's war. As Marx so aptly put it, "Force is the midwife of every old society pregnant with a new one."

It was on the basis of the lessons derived from the people's wars in China that Comrade Mao Zedong, using the simplest and the most vivid language, advanced the famous thesis that "political power grows out of the barrel of a gun. . . ."

Comrade Mao Zedong's theory of people's war solves not only the problem of daring to fight a people's war, but also that of how to wage it.

Comrade Mao Zedong is a great statesman and military scientist, proficient at directing war in accordance with its laws. By the line and policies, the strategy and tactics he formulated for the people's war, he led the Chinese people in steering the ship of the people's war past all hidden reefs to the shores of victory in most complicated and difficult conditions.

It must be emphasized that Comrade Mao Zedong's theory of the establishment of rural revolutionary base areas and the encirclement of the cities from the countryside is of outstanding and universal practical importance for the present revolutionary struggles of all the oppressed nations and peoples, and particularly for the revolutionary struggles of the oppressed nations and peoples in Asia, Africa, and Latin America against imperialism and its lackeys.

Many countries and peoples of Asia, Africa, and Latin America are now being subjected to aggression and enslavement on a serious scale by the imperialists headed by the United States and their lackeys. The basic political and economic conditions in many of these countries have many similarities to those that prevailed in old China. As in China, the peasant question is extremely important in these regions. The peasants constitute the main force of the national-democratic revolution against the imperialists and their lackeys. In committing aggression against these countries, the imperialists usually begin by seizing the big cities and the main lines of communication, but they are unable to bring the vast countryside completely under their control. The countryside, and the countryside alone, can provide the broad areas in which the revolutionaries can maneuver freely. The countryside, and the countryside alone, can provide the revolutionary bases from which the revolutionaries can go forward to final victory. Precisely for this reason, Comrade Mao Zedong's theory of establishing revolutionary base areas in the rural districts and encircling the cities from the countryside is attracting more and more attention among the peoples in these regions.

Taking the entire globe, if North America and Western Europe can be called "the cities of the world," then Asia, Africa, and Latin America constitute "the rural areas of the world." Since World War II, the proletarian revolutionary movement has for various reasons been temporarily held back in the North American and West European capitalist countries, while the people's revolutionary movement in Asia, Africa, and Latin America has been growing vigorously. In a sense, the contemporary world revolution also presents a picture of the encirclement of cities by the rural areas. In the final analysis, the whole cause of world revolution hinges on the revolutionary struggles of the Asian, African, and Latin American peoples who make up the overwhelming majority of the world's population. The socialist countries should regard it as their internationalist duty to support the people's revolutionary struggles in Asia, Africa, and Latin America. . . .

Vietnam is the most convincing current example of a victim of aggression defeating U.S. Imperialism by a people's war. The United States has made south Vietnam a testing ground for the suppression of people's war. It has carried on this experiment for many years, and everybody can now see that the U.S. Aggressors are unable to find a way of coping with people's war. On the other hand, the Vietnamese people have brought the power of people's war into full play in their struggle against the U.S. Aggressors. The U.S. Aggressors are in danger of being swamped in the people's war in Vietnam. They are deeply worried that their defeat in Vietnam will lead to a chain reaction. They are expanding the war in an attempt to save themselves from defeat. But the more they expand the war, the greater will be the chain reaction. The more they escalate the war, the heavier will be their fall and the more disastrous their defeat. The people in other parts of the world will see still more clearly that U.S. Imperialism can be defeated, and that what the Vietnamese people can do, they can do too.

History has proved and will go on proving that people's war is the most effective weapon against U.S. Imperialism and its lackeys. All revolutionary people will learn to wage people's war against U.S. Imperialism and its lackeys. They will take up arms, learn to fight battles and become skilled in waging people's war, though they have not done so before. U.S. Imperialism, like a mad bull dashing from place to place, will finally be burned to ashes in the blazing fires of the people's wars it has provoked by its own actions.

22.3–22.5 THE FUTURE DIRECTION OF THE CULTURAL REVOLUTION

On August 5, 1966, while the Eleventh Plenum of the Central Committee of the CCP was debating the future direction of the Cultural Revolution, Mao Zedong launched his attack on Liu Shaoqi and Deng Xiaoping. His famous big-character poster, put up at the site of the plenum meeting, indirectly but clearly denounced his rivals and set the tone for the subsequent decisions taken by Party leaders attending the meeting.

In the days that followed, the Plenum issued a sixteen-point decision that would serve as the charter for the Cultural Revolution and a constant point of reference for Red Guards and other radicals. The meeting was a crushing defeat for Liu Shaoqi and Deng Xiaoping. The radical line was ascendant and the official communiqué of the Plenum left no doubt about how Mao Zedong and his contribution to Marxism should be viewed:

> Comrade Mao Zedong is the greatest Marxist-Leninist in the contemporary world. He has ingeniously, creatively, and totally inherited, defended, and developed Marxism-Leninism and elevated it to a brand-new stage. Mao Zedong Thought is the Marxism-Leninism of an age in which imperialism is approaching complete collapse and socialism is approaching total global victory. Mao Zedong Thought is the guiding principle for all the work of the entire party and nation.[1]

In the aftermath of the Eleventh Plenum, Liu, Deng, and their allies came under attack from all sides. As the cult of Mao Zedong grew, Lin Biao consolidated his power within the regime, and Red Guard organizations became

1. Yan Jiaqi, *Zhongguo Wenge Shinianshi* vol. 1, (Hong Kong, 1986), p. 42.

active throughout China. In October 1966, Mao gathered national and provincial Party leaders in Peking to instruct them about the future direction of the Cultural Revolution. The meeting lasted far longer than originally anticipated. In its concluding days, Liu and Deng issued self-criticisms that were, in fact, symbolic declarations of political defeat.

The three documents that follow—Mao's big-character poster, selections from the "Sixteen-Point Decision," and Deng Xiaoping's self-criticism—trace this sequence of events. Cumulatively, they provide a sense of the process that brought radicals to the forefront of Party work and overthrew key "revisionist" leaders like Liu and Deng. For the Cultural Revolution to go on at the grassroots level, these changes were first necessary within the highest tier of the Party.

22.3 Mao Zedong's Big-character Poster: "Bombard the Headquarters"

China's first Marxist-Leninist big-character poster and Commentator's article on it in *Renmin Ribao* (People's Daily) are indeed superbly written! Comrades, please read them again. But in the last fifty days or so some leading comrades from the central down to the local levels have acted in a diametrically opposite way. Adopting the reactionary stand of the bourgeoisie, they have enforced a bourgeois dictatorship and struck down the surging movement of the great cultural revolution of the proletariat. They have stood facts on their head and juggled black and white, encircled and suppressed revolutionaries, stifled opinions differing from their own, imposed a white terror, and felt very pleased with themselves. They have puffed up the arrogance of the bourgeoisie and deflated the morale of the proletariat. How poisonous! Viewed in connection with the Right deviation in 1962 and the wrong tendency of 1964 which was 'Left' in form but 'Right' in essence, shouldn't this make one wide awake?

22.4 The "Sixteen-Point Decision"

1. A NEW STAGE IN THE SOCIALIST REVOLUTION

The great Proletarian Cultural Revolution now unfolding is a great revolution which touches the very soul of the people; it is a new and deeper phase of the socialist revolution in China.

At the Tenth Plenary Session of the Eighth Central Committee of the CCP Comrade Mao Zedong said: "To overthrow a political power, it is always necessary to first of all, create public opinion, to do ideological work. This is true both for the revolutionary classes as well as for the counterrevolutionary classes." Practice has proven Comrade Mao Zedong's thesis to be entirely correct.

Although the bourgeoisie has been overthrown, it is still trying to use the old ideas, culture, customs and habits of the exploiting classes to corrupt the masses, capture their minds and endeavour to stage a comeback. The proletariat must do the exact opposite: it must meet every ideological challenge posed by the bourgeoisie head-on. Our present aim is to topple those in power who are taking the capitalist road, to criticize reactionary scholarly 'authorities,' criticize the ideology of the bourgeoisie and all exploiting classes. We must reform art and literature, reform all parts of the superstructure that do not accord with the socialist base of our country. Our purpose in doing this is to stabilize and develop our socialist system.

2. THE MAIN CURRENT AND THE TWISTS AND TURNS

The broad sectors of workers, peasants, soldiers, revolutionary intellectuals and revolutionary cadres make up the principal forces in this Great Cultural Revolution. Large numbers of revolutionary young people, previously unknown, have become courageous and daring pathbreakers. They are vigorous and intelligent. Through the media of big-character posters and through great debates, they argue things out, expose and criticize thoroughly, and launch resolute attacks on the open and hidden representatives of the bourgeoisie. In such a great revolutionary movement, it is unavoidable that they should show shortcomings of one kind or another; however, their general revolutionary orientation has been correct from the beginning. This is the main current in the Great Proletarian Cultural Revolution. It is the general direction along which this revolution continues to advance.

Since the Cultural Revolution is a revolution, it inevitably meets with resistance. This resistance comes chiefly from those in authority who have found their way into the Party and are taking the capitalist road. It also comes from the force of habits from old society. At present, this resistance is still fairly strong and stubborn. However, the Great Proletarian Cultural Revolution is, after all, an irresistible trend and there is abundant evidence that such resistance will be quickly broken down once the masses are fully aroused.

Because the resistance is fairly strong, there will be reversals and even repeated reversals in this struggle. There is no harm in this. It tempers the proletariat and other working people, especially the younger generation, teaches and gives them experience, and makes them see that the revolutionary road zigzags and does not run smoothly. . . .

4. LET THE MASSES EDUCATE THEMSELVES IN THE MOVEMENT

In the great Proletarian Cultural Revolution, the masses must liberate themselves, this is the only way and any other method must not be used.

Trust the masses, rely on them and respect their initiative. Cast out fear. Don't be afraid of disturbances. Chairman Mao has often told us that revolution cannot be so very refined, so gentle, so temperate, kind, courteous, restrained and magnanimous. Let the masses educate themselves in this great revolutionary movement and learn to distinguish between right and wrong and between the correct and incorrect way of doing things.

Make full use of big-character posters and mass debates to argue matters out, so that the masses can clarify the correct views, criticize the wrong views and expose all the witches and goblins. Thus, the masses will be able to raise their political consciousness in the course of the struggle, enhance their abilities and talents, distinguish right from wrong and draw a clear line between ourselves and the enemy.

5. FIRMLY APPLY THE CLASS LINE OF THE PARTY

The primary question of any revolutionary movement, including the Cultural Revolution is, who are our friends and who are our enemies.

Party leadership should be good at discovering the Left and developing and strengthening the ranks of the Left; it should firmly rely on the revolutionary Left. This is the only way to isolate the most reactionary Rightists thoroughly, win over the middle forces and unite with the great majority in the course of the movement so that in the end we shall achieve the unity of more than 95 percent of the cadres and more than 95 percent of the masses.

Concentrate all forces to strike at the handful of ultrareactionary bourgeois rightists and counter-revolutionary revisionists, and expose and criticize to the full their crimes against the Party, against socialism and against Mao Zedong Thought so as to isolate them as much as possible.

The main target of the present movement is those within the Party who are in power and are taking the capitalist road.

Greatest care should be taken to distinguish between the anti-Party, antisocialist rightists and those who support the Party and socialism but have said or done something wrong or have written bad articles or other works.

Greatest care should be taken to distinguish between the reactionary bourgeois scholar-despots and 'authorities' on the one hand and those who have the ordinary bourgeois academic ideas on the other. . . .

8. THE QUESTION OF CADRES

Cadres fall roughly into four categories:

1. good;
2. comparatively good;

3. those who have made serious mistakes but have not become anti-Party, anti-socialist rightists;
4. the small number of anti-Party, anti-socialist rightists.

In general, the first two categories (good and comparatively good) are the great majority.

The anti-Party, anti-socialist rightists must be fully exposed, refuted, overthrown and completely discredited and their influence irradicated. At the same time, they should be given a chance to turn over a new leaf. . . .

10. EDUCATIONAL REFORM

One of the most important tasks of the Great Proletarian Cultural Revolution is to transform the old educational system and the old principles and methods of teaching.

In this great Cultural Revolution, the phenomenon of our schools being dominated by bourgeois intellectuals must be completely changed.

In every kind of school we must apply thoroughly the policy advanced by Comrade Mao Zedong of education serving proletarian politics and education being combined with productive labour, so as to enable those receiving an education to develop morally, intellectually and physically and to become labourers with social consciousness and culture.

The period of schooling should be shortened. Courses should be fewer and better. The teaching material should be thoroughly transformed, in some cases beginning with simplifying complicated material. While their main task is to study, students should also learn other things. That is to say, in addition to their studies they should also learn industrial work, farming and military affairs, and take part in the struggles of the Cultural Revolution to criticize the bourgeoisie as these struggle occur. . . .

14. GRASP REVOLUTION AND PROMOTE PRODUCTION

The aim of the Great Proletarian Cultural Revolution is to revolutionize people's ideology and as a result achieve greater, faster, better and more economical results in all fields of work. If the masses are fully aroused and proper arrangements are made, it is possible to carry on both the Cultural Revolution and production without one hampering the other, while guaranteeing high quality in all our work.

The Great Proletarian Cultural Revolution is a powerful driving force for the development of the productive forces in our country. Any idea of counterposing the great Cultural Revolution to the development of production is incorrect.

15. THE ARMED FORCES

In the armed forces, the Cultural Revolution and the Socialist Education Movement should be carried out in accordance with the instructions of the Military Commission of the Central Committee of the Party and the General Political Department of the People's Liberation Army.

16. MAO ZEDONG THOUGHT IS THE GUIDE TO ACTION IN THE GREAT PROLETARIAN CULTURAL REVOLUTION

In the Great Proletarian Cultural Revolution, it is imperative to hold aloft the great red banner of Mao Zedong Thought and put proletarian politics in command. The movement for the creative study and application of Chairman Mao Zedong's works should be carried forward among the masses of the workers, peasants and soldiers, the cadres and the intellectuals, and Mao Zedong Thought should be taken as the guide to action in the Cultural Revolution.

In the complexities of the current Cultural Revolution, Party committees at all levels must study and apply Chairman Mao's works all the more conscientiously and in a creative way. In particular, they must study over and over again Chairman Mao's writings on the Cultural Revolution and on the Party's methods of leadership, such as *On New Democracy, Talks at the Yenan Forum on Literature and Art, On the Correct Handling of Contradictions Among the People, Speech at the Chinese Communist Party's National Conference on Propaganda Work, Some Questions Concerning Methods of Leaderships*, and *Methods of Work of Party Committees*.

Party committees on all levels must abide by the directions given by Chairman Mao over the years, that is, that they should thoroughly apply the mass line of "from the masses, to the masses" and that they should be pupils before they become teachers. They should try to avoid being one-sided or narrow. They should foster materialist dialectics and oppose metaphysics and scholasticism.

The Great Proletarian Cultural Revolution is sure to achieve brilliant victory under the leadership of the Central Committee of the Party headed by Comrade Mao Zedong.

22.5 *Deng Xiaoping: Self-Criticism*

. . . My recent errors are by no means accidental or disconnected; they have their origins in a certain way of thinking and a certain style of work which has developed over a considerable period of time. Ideologically, I must confess that not only have I not raised high the banner of Mao Zedong Thought, but that I have not even lifted this banner up. As my office is very close to the Chairman, theoretically I should have ample opportunity to receive personal direction and help from him. However, I have a very inadequate grasp of Mao Zedong Thought, do little to propagate it and am not practiced at applying it in my work. Mao Zedong Thought is the soul of all of our work, and an aptitude in it or otherwise is the standard by which to judge the depth of a person's knowledge of Marxism-Leninism and the amount of a person's proletarian thinking. If one does not make progress, then one will retrogress. If one does not study Mao Zedong Thought, then it is inevitable that the non-proletarian things in one's thinking will increase. The results of this is that one will make mistakes, and if unchecked, one will commit errors of a right opportunist tendency. In retrospect, my last few years have been marked by a steady regression and due to my laxity in the study and use of Mao Zedong Thought, I have made a number of mistakes. As the person in charge of the Secretariat of the Central Committee I must admit that the work of this department has been very badly done and that the areas of greatest error and fault are those departments under the direct leadership of the Secretariat. In matters concerning class struggle and struggle within the Party, I have consistently shown rightist tendencies. I am partly responsible for the rightist tendencies commited in 1962 which Chairman Mao mentioned in his big-character poster. Similarly, I must take some responsibility for the seemingly leftist but in essence rightist excesses of 1964, for though I was not in full agreement at the time, my objections were still not in compliance with Mao Zedong Thought. I also want to take this opportunity to make a thorough criticism of the numerous errors I made prior to 1962. My distancing myself from the masses and lack of contact with reality is directly connected with my failure to follow Chairman Mao and my lack of proper study. As a result, I have become accustomed to lording it over others and acting like someone special, rarely going down among the people or even to make the effort to contact cadres and other leaders so as to understand their working situation and problems. I have not been exacting in the execution of my office, continually failing to mix with the people and carry out investigatory work. The manner in which I deal with everyday problems has been too simplistic and sometimes quite inflexible. It is due to the above attitude that I have imprisoned myself in a mesh of subjectivism and bureaucracy over the past years. As a corollary to this 'imprisonment' I have made ideological and administrative errors with greater frequency and of increased gravity. A prolonged neglect of Mao Zedong Thought in the past has now developed into a salient opposition to it. Till recently I have not been aware of my attitude and still felt myself superior and infallible. Affected by such a viewpoint, I naturally have not taken great care in doing my work. Rarely did I ask for help or advice from other comrades or the people. Worse yet still is that I have rarely reported to and asked advice from the Chairman. Not only is this one of the main reasons for my errors, but is also a serious breach of Party discipline. In late 1964, Chairman Mao criticized me for being a kingdom unto myself. At first, somewhat shaken by this, I, however, consoled myself with the thought that I was neither a greedy person nor a power seeker, therefore delved no further into the origins of my faults. Thus unchecked, it was inevitable that I would commit an error involving political line, now or in the future. In the final analysis, my way of thinking and style of work is completely incompatible with Mao Zedong Thought. I have not raised high the great banner of Mao Zedong Thought, nor have I followed Chairman Mao closely, therefore I cut myself off from the leadership; in addition, my contact with the masses is infrequent and I am isolated from reality. I have shown myself not to be a good student of Chairman Mao and am absolutely unsuited to my present position of responsibility. Recent events have revealed me as an unreformed petit-bourgeois intellectual who has failed to pass the tests posed by socialism. Seeing myself thus reflected in my actions I am overwhelmed. I feel it would be damaging to the Party and the people for a person with my ideological level and political understanding to continue in my present position. What I need to do is reflect on my past actions, I need to earnestly study Chairman Mao's works, reform myself and correct my mistakes. By so doing, I hope to be of some use to the Party and the people in the latter years of my life and make up, in some way, for my past misdeeds. I firmly believe that with the help of my comrades and with my own determination, I will be able to correct my mistakes. Though I have gone astray on the road of politics, with the radiance of Mao Zedong Thought lighting my forward path, I should have the fortitude to pick myself up and go on. . . .

The above is a preliminary self-criticism. I hope all comrades present will give their criticisms and suggestions.

Long live the Great Proletarian Cultural Revolution!

Long live invincible Mao Zedong Thought!

Long live the great teacher, the great helmsman and the great leader Chairman Mao!

22.6 AND 22.7 "I SAW CHAIRMAN MAO!!!"

At the beginning of the Cultural Revolution in the summer of 1966, Bei Guancheng was a twenty-six-year-old teacher at Jianguang Junior Middle School in Shanghai, where he participated with fervor in the denunciation of Wang Xingguo, the school's Party Secretary. After a confrontation with a group of Red Guards who ransacked his home, Bei was the subject of a "struggle session" and labeled a "black element." In early September Bei traveled to Peking, intending to petition "the central" for redress. When he returned to Shanghai at the end of the month, Red Guards at his school took him into custody. He committed suicide on October 2.

In the first document below, Bei Guancheng wrote to his colleagues from Peking, describing the feverish joy of seeing Chairman Mao in the flesh. In the second document, eyewitnesses described in graphic detail how Bei was tortured when he returned to Shanghai.

22.6 Bei Guancheng: "I Saw Chairman Mao!!!"

Comrades:

Let me tell you the great news, news greater than heaven. At five minutes past seven in the evening on the 15th of September 1966, I saw our most most most most dearly beloved leader Chairman Mao! Comrades, I have seen Chairman Mao! Today I am so happy my heart is about to burst. We're shouting "Long live Chairman Mao! Long live! Long live!" We're jumping! We're singing! After seeing the Red Sun in Our Hearts, I just ran around like crazy all over Beijing. I so much wanted to tell everyone the great news! I wanted everyone to join me in being happy, jumping, and shouting.

It was like this: Last night I knew that today Chairman Mao would receive the teachers and students who had come to Beijing, and so this afternoon I pleaded over and over again with the pickets to let me pass. I figured they never would, so I really did not make that much of an effort, and at first I did indeed have to remain on the outside. But by seven o'clock, the pickets finally let me pass. At that very moment, an ocean of people surged forward in the direction of the Tiananmen rostrum, and I also pushed like mad from the side to get in. Finally I managed to get to the visitor's stand, and by a stroke of luck just then Chairman Mao came over to the east side of the rostrum. I could see him ever so clearly, and he was so impressive. Comrades, how can I possibly describe to you what that moment was like? In any case, I together with everyone else just exploded in shouts of "Long live Chairman Mao!" Having seen Chairman Mao, I made a silent pledge to definitely become Chairman Mao's good pupil.

> Comrades, join us in our joy and in our singing!
> Greetings,
> Bei Jr.
> 15 September 1966, under the midnight lamp

PS: Later I heard that Chairman Mao was coming forward for the second time when I saw him, after repeated pleas from the masses. In any case, what luck! How can I possibly go to sleep tonight! I have decided to make today my birthday. Today I started a new life!!!

22.7 "As We Watched Them Beat Him . . ."

[Original editor's comment:] These are extracts from big-character posters written by teachers and students who themselves either took part in or witnessed the violence. The extracts forcefully expose [School Party Secretary] Wang Xingguo as the instigator of these criminal acts of violence.

1. Fei Zhensheng (elderly staff worker):

I saw some twenty students surrounding Bei Guancheng on the terrace of Building No. 5. Three or four students were beating him up. And Bei himself? He did not utter a sound, but just let them go on beating him. A student by the name of XXX was most vicious and threw Bei to the concrete floor maybe five or six times. When Bei refused to get up by himself, they pulled him to his feet and hit and kicked him until once again he was lying on the floor. At one point he was lying face up when student XXX came forward and kicked him on the head. Once he managed to sit up, students XXX and XXX stepped forward to slap him in the face for about two minutes. They took turns, one taking over when the other had to rest, their slapping producing a sound like exploding firecrackers . . .

Later I watched through the window in Room 401 how Bei Guancheng was in a sort of frog-like position—his face pressed against the floor, his arms supporting him on the sides, and his behind up in the air. Only later did I find out that he had been enduring a form of punishment . . .

2. Chen Dongsheng (teacher) and Liu Xueqing (Red Guard):

At that point we heard the noise and excitement outside so we walked up to the window and looked in the direction of the North Sports Ground, where we saw a group of students dragging Bei Guancheng through a crowd that had gathered at the entrance of the main building. The students were violently beating and kicking Bei Guancheng. Finally they dragged him off to the ping-pong table (under the trees next to the North Sports Ground) and propped him up against it, his arms and legs already limp. Then some students ordered him to crawl onto the table, and they began hitting him in the face and on the head with their fists. From afar you could hear the noise and the "slam, bam, slam, bam" sound of him being beaten. Then the students ordered Bei Guancheng to lift his arms and lower his head and admit to being a counter-revolutionary, an ox-monster and a snake-demon. Then we saw one student kicking the legs out from under Bei Guancheng. At that point we could not bear to watch the violence any more, and so we walked away from the window.

3. Yin Honghai (Red Guard in the third grade):

I was also present when Bei Guancheng was beaten. That afternoon we returned from a meeting when we saw them dragging Bei Guancheng onto the terrace. I did not actually witness the violence on the terrace, but I saw it with my own eyes when they dragged him off to Room 401 to beat him up. I saw it when they told him to lift his arms up in the air and lower his head. Then later some people kicked his behind, others punched him on the back with their clenched fists, others twisted his arms, yelling over and over again: "You went to Beijing to establish counter-revolutionary contacts, didn't you?" By far the most vicious part was when they made him bend over and lean forward against the edge of the [concrete] ping-pong table and then pushed his head with full force against its edge. They did this not just once. Just as they were beating him, I saw Wang Xingguo coming out of

Room 403. After she had taken a quick look at what was happening in Room 401, she walked off smiling with a triumphant look on her face. That's what I saw at the time. At the time, I too joined in the beating, which was wrong of me. I had been influenced by Wang Xingguo's bourgeois reactionary line.

4. Fu Xiaokang (Red Guard in the second grade, class 7):

Around 2:30 in the afternoon on 2 October, I and some of my classmates including Ji Zhengliu were preparing to return home when a smiling Wang Xingguo came through the school gate and said, "Students, don't go away. Just now Wang Xiongxiang, Huang Longmin, and some others went to fetch Bei Guancheng." Since we are all rather mischievous students who don't mind a fight or beating up on somebody now and then, and since we had heard that some people had already beaten Bei Guancheng, we said right away in unison: "So we can beat him up too then?" Having said that, we got some bamboo sticks and other weapons to thrash him with and got all fired up. Wang Xingguo saw all of this but did nothing to stop us. On the contrary, she was laughing loudly. From what we were able to tell at the time, Wang Xingguo was highly supportive of our "revolutionary action."

It is only now that we have seen through Wang Xingguo's vile personality, how she provoked us into beating Bei Guancheng. Wang Xingguo is Bei Guancheng's executioner. She must take the blame for what happened. We were duped.

5. Chen Yong (Red Guard in the first grade, class 1):

Under the leadership of the Party branch headed by Wang Xingguo, I carried out the bourgeois reactionary line of the Shanghai municipal party committee and branded the revolutionary masses "counter-revolutionaries," "fake Leftists," "genuine Rightists," "demanders" (shenshoupai), etc. Under the circumstances, many students were hoodwinked, and I am one of them.

I am a worker's son. I have boundless love for the Party and for Chairman Mao.

The Red Guard organization at our school had barely been established when I joined. But because it was controlled and dominated by Wang Xingguo, it ended up doing many things in contravention of the "Sixteen Points." Our language teacher, Bei Guancheng, developed a bad attitude after some Red Guards had ransacked his home. He went to Beijing to tell on Wang Xingguo, the powerholder in our school. As a result, he was branded a "counter-revolutionary." After teacher Bei left for Beijing, everybody was gossiping, saying that he had "absconded to Beijing to avoid punishment for his crimes," etc.

At the time, we were all really furious. On 29 September, when teacher Bei came back from Beijing, my classmate XXX and I went to look for him. We told him, "The Cultural Revolution Committee is looking for you!" He said, "I have already spoken to Zhang Li on the Cultural Revolution Committee and made my attitude clear." Soon after that, Bei Guancheng was dragged off by us to the roof of Building No. 5 to be given a beating. I said we should not beat him, but student XXX said that teacher XXX (leader of the Red Guards and a member of the Cultural Revolution Committee) had said: "You just go ahead and beat him up. Even if you kill him, you won't be held responsible." Words like that actually gave us the courage, ordering us to go and beat him, which is what we did next. In the course of the beating, student XXX tried to force Bei Guancheng to commit suicide by jumping off the roof, but I pleaded with him, "What if he commits suicide and drags you with him? You'd die too." Because I said that, students XXX and XXX no longer tried to force him to commit suicide by jumping off the roof. Then later quite a few students who had attended a city district Red Guard Company meeting returned to beat him up. I pleaded with XXX not to let teacher Bei return home, as I was convinced if allowed to return home, he would commit suicide. That is all I witnessed, and as for what happened later I don't know. Nobody came forward to try and stop the beating. That's what happened.

There is a mountain of hard evidence, and Wang Xingguo will not escape responsibility for her crimes!

Bei Guancheng was a revolutionary comrade and not a counter-revolutionary!

It was Wang Xingguo who hounded Bei Guancheng to death!

CHAPTER 23

Reopening the Doors

23.1 AND 23.2 RAPPROCHEMENT WITH THE UNITED STATES

While the Cultural Revolution resulted in domestic chaos and constant purges within the Party hierarchy, Premier Zhou Enlai struggled, at first with mixed results, to take charge of state affairs. China's foreign relations were greatly disrupted from 1967 to 1969. Many of China's ambassadors were called back to China and embassies were left with skeleton staffs; relations with the United States were extremely hostile; and in 1969, border conflicts with the Soviet Union seemed about to erupt into a full-scale war.

In 1969 and 1970, this situation began to change. Mao Zedong, alarmed by the collapse of China's global position, was prepared to permit Zhou to play a more active role as the primary architect of China's foreign policy. At the same time, the new Nixon administration sought to consolidate a relationship with China and find a multilateral solution to the Vietnam conflict. The net result of ping-pong diplomacy and Kissinger's secret visit to China was Richard Nixon's historic visit to China in February 1972.

The documents presented here, the Shanghai Communiqué and Deng Xiaoping's speech at the United Nations, illuminate the shape of China's foreign policy as it emerged in the early 1970s. In the Shanghai Communiqué, the United States and China agreed to disagree while pursuing mutually beneficial endeavors. This agreement established a basis for the normalization of relations with China during the Carter administration and a nonconfrontational American approach to the question of Taiwan's future. Deng's enunciation of Mao's theory of "three worlds" suggested the role China would seek to play among the nonaligned states of the world and in its competition with the United States and the Soviet Union.

23.1 *The Shanghai Communiqué*

JOINT COMMUNIQUÉ

The Chinese and U.S. sides reached agreement on a joint communiqué on February 27 in Shanghai. Full text of the communiqué is as follows:

President Richard Nixon of the United States of America visited the People's Republic of China at the invitation of Premier Zhou Enlai of the People's Republic of China from February 21 to February 28, 1972. Accompanying the President were Mrs. Nixon, U.S. Secretary of State William Rogers, Assistant to the President Dr. Henry Kissinger, and other American officials.

President Nixon met with Chairman Mao Zedong of the Communist Party of China on February 21. The two leaders had a serious and frank exchange of views on Sino-U.S. relations and world affairs.

During the visit, extensive, earnest, and frank discussions were held between President Nixon and Premier Zhou Enlai on the normalization of relations between the United States of America and the People's Republic of China, as well as on other matters of interest to both sides. In addition, Secretary of State William Rogers and Foreign Minister Qi Pengfei held talks in the same spirit.

President Nixon and his party visited Peking and viewed cultural, industrial, and agricultural sites, and they also toured Hangchow and Shanghai where, continuing discussions with Chinese leaders, they viewed similar places of interest.

The leaders of the People's Republic of China and the United States of America found it beneficial to have this opportunity, after so many years without contact, to present candidly to one another their views on a variety of issues. They reviewed the international situation in which important changes and great upheavals are taking place and expounded their respective positions and attitudes.

The Chinese side stated: Wherever there is oppression there is resistance. Countries want independence, nations want liberation, and the people want revolution—this has become the irresistible trend of history. All nations, big or small, should be equal; big nations should not bully the small and strong nations should not bully the weak. China will never be a superpower and it opposes hegemony and power politics of any kind. The Chinese side stated that it firmly supports the struggles of all the oppressed people and nations for freedom and liberation and that the people of all countries have the right to choose their social systems according to their own wishes and the right to safeguard the independence, sovereignty, and territorial integrity of their own countries and oppose foreign aggression, interference, control, and subversion. All foreign troops should be withdrawn to their own countries. The Chinese side expressed its firm support to the peoples of Viet Nam, Laos, and Cambodia in their efforts for the attainment of their goal and its firm support to the seven-point proposal of the Provisional Revolutionary Government of the Republic of South Viet Nam and the elaboration of February this year on the two key problems in the proposal, and to the Joint Declaration of the

Summit conference of the Indochinese Peoples. It firmly supports the eight-point program for the peaceful unification of Korea put forward by the Government of the Democratic People's Republic of Korea on April 12, 1971, and the stand for the abolition of the "U.N. Commission for the Unification and Rehabilitation of Korea." It firmly opposes the revival and outward expansion of Japanese militarism and firmly supports the Japanese people's desire to build an independent, democratic, peaceful, and neutral Japan. It firmly maintains that India and Pakistan should, in accordance with the United Nations resolutions on the India-Pakistan question, immediately withdraw all their forces to their respective territories and to their own sides of the ceasefire line in Jammu and Kashmir and firmly supports the Pakistan government and people in their struggle to preserve their independence and sovereignty and the people of Jammu and Kashmir in their struggle for the right of self-determination.

The U.S. side stated: Peace in Asia and peace in the world requires efforts both to reduce immediate tensions and to eliminate the basic causes of conflict. The United States will work for a just and secure peace: just, because it fulfills the aspirations of peoples and nations for freedom and progress; secure, because it removes the danger of foreign aggression. The United States supports individual freedom and social progress for all peoples of the world, free of outside pressure or intervention. The United States believes that the effort to reduce tensions is served by improving communication between countries that have different ideologies so as to lessen the risks of confrontation through accident, miscalculation or misunderstanding. Countries should treat each other with mutual respect and be willing to compete peacefully, letting performance be the ultimate judge. No country should claim infallibility and each country should be prepared to re-examine its own attitudes for the common good. The United States stressed that the peoples of Indochina should be allowed to determine their destiny without outside intervention; its constant primary objective has been a negotiated solution; the eight-point proposal put forward by the Republic of Viet Nam and the United States on January 27, 1972, represents a basis for the attainment of that objective; in the absence of a negotiated settlement the United States envisages the ultimate withdrawal of all U.S. Forces from the region consistent with the aim of self-determination for each country of Indochina. The United States will maintain its close ties with and support for the Republic of Korea; the United States will support efforts of the Republic of Korea to seek a relaxation of tension and increased communication on the Korean peninsula. The United States places the highest value on its friendly relations with Japan; it will continue to develop the existing close bonds. Consistent with the United Nations Security Council Resolution of December 21, 1971, the United States favors the continuation of the ceasefire between India and Pakistan and the withdrawal of all military forces to within their own territories and to their own sides of the ceasefire line in Jammu and Kashmir; the United States supports the right of the peoples of South Asia to shape their own future in peace, free of military threat, and without having the area become the subject of great power rivalry.

There are essential differences between China and the United States in their social systems and foreign policies. However, the two sides agreed that countries regardless of their social systems should conduct their relations on the principles of respect for the sovereignty and territorial integrity of all states, non-aggression against other states, equality and mutual benefit, and peaceful coexistence. International disputes should be settled on this basis, without resorting to the use or threat of force. The United States and the People's Republic of China are prepared to apply these principles to their mutual relations.

With these principles of international relations in mind the two sides state that:

—progress toward the normalization of relations between China and the United States is in the interests of all countries.
—Both wish to reduce the danger of international military conflict;
—neither should seek hegemony in the Asia-Pacific region and each is opposed to efforts by any other country or group of countries to establish such hegemony; and
—neither is prepared to negotiate on behalf of any third party or to enter into agreements or understandings with the other directed at other states.

Both sides are of the view that it would be against the interests of the peoples of the world for any major country to collude with another against other countries, or for major countries to divide up the world into spheres of interest.

The two sides reviewed the long-standing serious disputes between China and the United States. The Chinese side reaffirmed its position: The Taiwan question is the crucial question obstructing the normalization of relations between China and the United States; the Government of the People's Republic of China is the sole legal government of China; Taiwan is a province of China which has long been returned to the motherland; the liberation of Taiwan is China's internal affair in which no other country has the right to interfere; and all U.S. Forces and military installations must be withdrawn from Taiwan. The Chinese Government firmly opposes any activities which aim at the creation of "one China, one Taiwan," "one China, two governments," "two Chinas," an "independent Taiwan" or advocate that the "status of Taiwan remains to be determined."

The U.S. side declared: The United States acknowledges that all Chinese on either side of the Taiwan Strait maintain there is but one China and that Taiwan is a part of China. The United States Government does not challenge that position. It reaffirms its interest in a peaceful settlement of the Taiwan question by the Chinese themselves. With this prospect in mind, it affirms the ultimate objective of the withdrawal of all U.S. Forces and military installations from Taiwan. In the meantime, it will progressively reduce its forces and military installations on Taiwan as the tension in the area diminishes.

The two sides agreed that it is desirable to broaden the understanding between the two peoples. To this end, they discussed specific areas in such fields as science, technology, culture, sports, and journalism, in which people-to-people contacts and exchanges would be mutually beneficial. Each side undertakes to facilitate the further development of such contacts and exchanges.

Both sides view bilateral trade as another area from which mutual benefit can be derived, and agreed that economic relations based on equality and mutual benefit are in the interest of the peoples of the two countries. They agree to facilitate the progressive development of trade between their two countries.

The two sides agreed that they will stay in contact through various channels, including the sending of a senior U.S. Representative to Peking from time to time for concrete consultations to further the normalization of relations between the two countries and continue to exchange views on issues of common interest.

The two sides expressed the hope that the gains achieved during this visit would open up new prospects for the relations between the two countries. They believe that the normalization of relations between the two countries is not only in the interest of the Chinese and American peoples but also contributes to the relaxation of tension in Asia and the world.

President Nixon, Mrs. Nixon, and the American party expressed their appreciation for the gracious hospitality shown them by the Government and the people of the People's Republic of China.

February 28, 1972

23.2 Deng Xiaoping: Speech at the United Nations, April 10, 1974

Mr. President,

.... This is the first time in the 29 years since the founding of the United Nations that a session is held specially to discuss the important question of opposing imperialist exploitation and plunder and effecting a change in international economic relations. This reflects that profound changes have taken place in the international situation. The Chinese Government extends its warm congratulations on the convocation of this session and hopes that it will make a positive contribution to strengthening the unity of the developing countries, safeguarding their national economic rights and interest and promoting the struggle of all peoples against imperialism, and particularly against hegemonism.

At present, the international situation is most favourable to the developing countries and the peoples of the world. More and more, the old order based on colonialism, imperialism and hegemonism is being undermined and shaken to its foundations. International relations are changing drastically. The whole world is in turbulence and unrest. The situation is one of "great disorder under heaven," as we Chinese put it. This "disorder" is a manifestation of the sharpening of all the basic contradictions in the contemporary worlds. It is accelerating the disintegration and decline of the decadent reactionary forces and stimulating the awakening and growth of the new emerging forces of the people.

In this situation of "great disorder under heaven," all the political forces in the world have undergone drastic division and realignment through prolonged trials of strength and struggle. A large number of Asian, African and Latin American countries have achieved independence one after another and they are playing an ever greater role in international affairs. As a result of the emergence of social-imperialism, the socialist camp which existed for a time after World War II is no longer in existence. Owing to the law of the uneven development of capitalism, the Western imperialist bloc, too, is disintegrating. Judging from the changes in international relations, the world today actually consists of three parts, or three worlds, that are both inter-connected and in contradiction to one another. The United States and the Soviet Union make up the First World. The developing countries in Asia, Africa, Latin America and other regions make up the Third World. The developed countries between the two make up the Second World.

The two superpowers, the United States and the Soviet Union, are vainly seeking world hegemony. Each in its own way attempts to bring the developing countries of Asia, Africa and Latin America under its control and, at the same time, to bully the developed countries that are not their match in strength.

The two superpowers are the biggest international exploiters and oppressors of today. They are the source of a new world war. They both possess large numbers of nuclear weapons. They carry on a keenly contested arms race, station massive forces abroad and set up military bases everywhere, threatening the independence and security of all nations. They both keep subjecting other countries to their control, subversion, interference or aggression. They both exploit other countries economically, plundering their wealth and grabbing their resources. In bullying others, the superpower which flaunts the label of socialism is especially vicious. It has dispatched its armed forces to occupy its "ally" Czechoslovakia and instigated the war to dismember Pakistan. It does not honour its words and is perfidious; it is self-seeking and unscrupulous.

The case of the developed countries in between the superpowers and the developing countries is a complicated one. Some of them still retain colonialist relations of one form or another with Third World countries, and a country like Portugal even continues with its barbarous colonial rules. An end must be put to this state of affairs. At the same time, all these developed countries are in varying degrees controlled, threatened or bullied by one superpower or the other. Some of them have in fact been reduced by a superpower to the position of dependencies under the signboard of its so-called "family." In varying degrees, all these countries have the desire of shaking off superpower enslavement or control and safeguarding their national independence and the integrity of their sovereignty.

The numerous developing countries have long suffered from colonialist and imperialist oppression and exploitation. They have won political independence, yet all of them still face the historic task of clearing out the remnant forces of colonialism, developing the national economy and consolidating national independence. These countries cover vast territories, encompass a large population and abound in natural resources. Having suffered the heaviest oppression, they have the strongest desire to oppose oppression and seek liberation and development. In the struggle for national liberation and independence, they have demonstrated immense power and continually won splendid victories. They constitute a revolutionary motive force propelling the wheel of world history and are the main force combating colonialism, imperialism, and particularly the superpowers.

Since the two superpowers are contending for world hegemony, the contradiction between them is irreconcilable; one either overpowers the other, or is overpowered. Their compromise and collusion can only be partial, temporary and relative, while their contention is all-embracing, permanent and absolute. In the final analysis, the so-called "balanced reduction of forces" and "strategic arms limitation" are nothing but empty talk, for in fact there is no "balance," nor can there possibly be "limitation." They may reach certain agreements, but their agreements are only a facade and a deception. At bottom, they are aiming at greater and fiercer contention. The contention between the superpowers extends over the entire globe. Strategically, Europe is the focus of their contention, where they are in constant tense confrontation. They are intensifying their rivalry in the Middle East, the Mediterranean, the Persian Gulf, the Indian Ocean and the Pacific. Every day, they talk about disarmament but are actually engaged in arms expansion. Every day, they talk about "détente" but are actually creating tension. Wherever they contend, turbulence occurs. So long as imperialism and social-imperialism exist, there definitely will be no tranquillity in the world, nor will there be "lasting peace." Either they will fight each other, or the people will rise in revolution. It is as Chairman Mao Zedong has said: The danger of a new world war still exists, and the people of all countries must get prepared. But revolution is the main trend in the world today. . . .

The hegemonism and power politics of the two superpowers have also aroused strong dissatisfaction among the developed countries of the Second World. The struggles of these countries against superpower control, interference, intimidation, exploitation and shifting of economic crises are growing day by day. Their struggles also have a significant impact on the development of the international situation.

Innumerable facts show that all views that overestimate the strength of the two hegemonic powers and underestimate the strength of the people are groundless. It is not the one or two superpowers that are really powerful; the really powerful are the Third World and the people of all countries uniting together and daring to fight and daring to win. Since numerous Third World countries and people were able to achieve political independence through protracted struggle, certainly they will also be able, on this basis, to bring about through sustained struggle a thorough change in the international economic relations which are based on inequality, control and exploitation and thus create essential conditions for the independent development of their national economy by strengthening their unity and allying themselves with other countries subjected to superpower bullying as well as with the people of the whole world, including the people of the United States and the Soviet Union. . . . .

Mr. President,

History develops in struggle, and the world advances amidst turbulence. The imperialists, and the superpowers in particular, are beset with troubles and are on the decline. Countries want independence, nations want liberation and the people want revolution—this is the irresistible trend of history. We are convinced that, so long as the Third World countries and people strengthen their unity, ally themselves with all forces that can be allied with and persist in a protracted struggle, they are sure to win continuous new victories.

23.3 THE LOST GENERATION

During the Cultural Revolution, more than sixteen million urban educated youths were sent to the countryside. The campaign, known as going "up to the mountains, down to the villages" (*shangshan xiaxiang*), demobilized warring factions of Red Guards and eased overcrowding in the cities. Many went as volunteers with fervent revolutionary ideals, only to become disillusioned by rural life and feel betrayed by the Communist Party. Known as "sent-down youths" (*zhiqing*), many of these educated urbanites were separated from their families for more than a decade.

In the late 1980s, Laifong Leung interviewed a group of Chinese writers about their experiences as sent-down youths during the Cultural Revolution. Excerpts from two of these interviews appear below. Wang Anyi (b. 1954), a writer acclaimed for her short stories and novellas, remembers the two years she spent in Anhui with cynicism. Liang Xiaosheng (b. 1949), who spent more than five years on a military farm near the Russian border, explains how his *zhiqing* experience influenced his writing.

WANG ANYI

I was born in Nanjing in 1954, and my parents moved to Shanghai when I was one year old. Except for those two years I spent in the countryside, I have always lived in Shanghai.

When did you go to the countryside?

I went to the countryside in 1970 right after I graduated from junior high school. In fact, I had not learned anything in school because it was closed during the Cultural Revolution. I muddled through those three years.

What did you do in those three years?

We had to attend mass meetings and parades and yell slogans. At that time, we elementary school students were very enthusiastic about the Cultural Revolution.

We wanted to do something, but we were not allowed. I particularly admired those older than us who could participate in the Red Guard Movement and go to other cities to join the "Mass Exchange of Revolutionary Experiences." Writers a few years older, like Liang Xiaosheng, Lu Xing'er, and many others, were Red Guards. If I were only two years older, I might have had different experiences.

Were your parents attacked during the Cultural Revolution?

Yes, but not too severely. My father was labeled a "rightist" during the Anti-Rightist Campaign in 1957. On top of that he was discriminated against because he was a returned overseas Chinese. My mother at that time had lost her leading position in the Shanghai Municipal Branch of the Writers' Association. Soon after the Red Guard Movement was over, I could not wait to go to the countryside.

Where did you go?

I went to Wuhe (Five Rivers) County, Anhui Province. It is located north of the city of Bangbu and along the Huai River. It is called Five Rivers because there are five rivers in this county.

Did you choose this place?

Some time ago my friends and I were talking about how *zhiqing* chose their place of rustication. We came to the conclusion that those who had high ideals tended to choose the Great Barren North; those who were ordinary and spoiled at home tended to choose Anhui. I belonged to the latter category. The reason I chose this place was because my mother thought that Heilongjiang was too far away, whereas Anhui was much closer and I could return home often. In fact, my mother did not want me to leave home, because my older sister had been sent to Anhui Province. But I was very insistent, and, in my adolescent mind, I thought that if I could not go, I would have no future.

Why did you think that way?

By 1970, the Cultural Revolution had been going on for four years. I had been very bored at home doing nothing. I was at my adolescent stage and was quite unsteady. When I read my old diaries, I found that at that time I was really restless, wanting eagerly to change my environment. My mother asked me, "Why do you want to leave? If you don't leave, I can support you for the rest of your life." But I insisted I wanted to go. On the date of departure, my mother was very upset; she cried bitterly at the train station.

Did you regret your decision when you got there?

I regretted it deeply the first day I arrived there. I thought, how could I do this to my mother? How could I, so spoiled at home and without ideals to transform the countryside, come to such a backward and poor place?

Did you live with the local peasants?

The production team where I was rusticated was very poor. The government allocated two hundred yuan to each *zhiqing* for the expense of building a house. It was called a "settling-in fee." But the peasants thought differently. They just did not believe that a Shanghai girl would stay long in the village. They did not use the money on me; instead, they gave it to the production team. Then they arranged to have me stay with a peasant's family.

How did you adjust yourself to their lifestyle?

It was very difficult, almost impossible. I was not used to living with them at all. From the very start, I had been requesting to have a house of my own. But they didn't listen to me. As my patience ran out, I became angry and said strongly that I was entitled to have the settling-in fee. After I said this I felt embarrassed because I was supposed to receive reeducation from the poor and lower-middle peasants. Coincidentally an old woman next door died, so they gave me her house. I slept right beneath her memorial tablet.

It must have been frightening!

It was, because there was no electricity. But it was strange that at that time I would rather be afraid than live with the peasants. I was really at odds with them; I had no room to think my thoughts and had to put up a front with them all day.

How long did you live in that old woman's house?

A few months. Then I returned to Shanghai for a stay, and went back to the village again. My mother did not want me to leave. But I became restless if I stayed home too long. In fact, some Shanghai girls simply did not return to the places they were sent.

I have heard that people from the Neighborhood Revolutionary Committee (jiedao geming weiyuan hui) would come to hassle you and urge you to go back to the countryside.

In the beginning they were very fierce to me. Later, they cooled off somewhat because my older sister had already gone to Anhui. At least one of us had gone there.

Did you return to Shanghai often?

I returned to Shanghai every half a year. If I calculated the number of months I stayed in the countryside, I would feel embarrassed. *Zhiqing* writers such as Liang Xiaosheng and Lu Xing'er were very devoted to transform the countryside.

Do you think life might have been better on the military farm where you could live with other zhiqing?

That's true. They did not have to live with the peasants.

What impact did the rustication have on you?

Rustication was a horror to me; therefore when I left, I left with the feeling of escaping from hell. I didn't send any letters back, nor do I ever want to go back again. Recently many people have told me to go back for a visit, saying that things there might have changed and that would evoke my feelings. But I don't want these kind of feelings and I just don't want to go!

Many zhiqing writers have returned to the places where they were rusticated and have come up with works based on their visits. Shi Tiesheng, for instance, has written the novella—"A Story of Rustication"—that looks at rustication in a new light.

People of Shi Tiesheng's age are different from mine. They are a few years older and were more mature; they had participated in the Red Guard Movement; they had joined the "Mass Exchange of Revolutionary Experiences," and they had already graduated from senior middle school. By the time they were sent to the countryside, they had already formed their worldview. But for me, I was thrust to the countryside before my worldview was formulated. Therefore, the days of rustication were particularly horrifying to me. Some people said that rustication still had its good points; I don't agree with this view at all.

What good points?

They said that rustication could make our generation mature faster. But to sacrifice so much for the sake of speeding up maturity, I don't want it.

Despite the misfortune, many zhiqing *writers since 1982 have written nostalgic works about rustication. What is your view on this?*

This is only a kind of nostalgia. Recently, I came across a criticism of Liang Xiaosheng's novel *Snow City* by a student from Fudan University. The student criticized Liang Xiaosheng, wondering how he could yearn for his past, which was made up of the sacrifices of millions of educated youths. I could not agree with him more. In my case, I was full of hope and enthusiasm, but my hopes and enthusiasm were shattered by rustication.

Many zhiqing *writers said to me that if they had not been sent to the countryside, they would not have been able to become writers. What do you think?*

I don't think this is the way that writers should be made. If one becomes a writer only by rustication, I would rather not be a writer. I would say ninety-nine percent were sacrificed. My cousin was a case in point. Having gone through the Cultural Revolution and rustication, she became mentally ill and died. One really cannot say that rustication was a good policy because of some fortunate individuals. It was truly a great loss. We can only say that it tempered a generation of people and it brought some modern civilization to rural China. For instance, people there thought we were strange when they saw us brushing our teeth. Girls there did not use handkerchiefs. When I gave them a handkerchief as a gift, they were thrilled.

After you stayed in Wuhe Country for two years, you went to join a local performing arts troupe. How did it happen, and what did you actually do in this troupe?

It performed dance and song. When I was in Wuhe County, I heard about the recruitment. Because I had learned cello at home I was accepted into the Xuzhou Performing Arts Troupe. I was there for six years.

Many zhiqing *writers told me they were very eager to attend university when they were in the countryside. Why did you choose a performing arts troupe? Did you have any desire to go to university?*

I really wanted to attend university. In those days, one needed a recommendation to attend university; it was not based on academic achievements. I had always wanted to be a medical doctor; I tried very hard to obtain a recommendation, but I failed. The only opportunity open to me was the performing arts troupe.

You wrote quite a number of stories about the performing arts troupe. You must have a deep feeling for it.

I had a sense of belonging to this group. The reason was that working there I didn't have to worry about food or lodging. The sense of security enabled me to do some writing; I managed to publish some prose essays.

Was it based on these prose essays that you were transferred back to Shanghai?

No. I came back with the "return to the city wind." My mother had always felt that I shouldn't have gone to the countryside and she took the opportunity to try all she could to get me transferred to Shanghai.

How were you transferred back to Shanghai?

Because I had published something, and because the performing arts troupe was classified as a cultural unit, I was able to obtain a post at *Childhood*, a Shanghai children's literature magazine. The process of my transfer was quite smooth.

Your mother, Ru Zhijuan, is a famous writer. Are you influenced by her in any way?

Many things have influenced me. However, I must say that the atmosphere at home provided me with a familiarity with art and literature since childhood. In the beginning I did not like literature, and my parents also wanted me to learn science. My father was inclined to think that science is good for the nation and good for me. After the fall of the Gang of Four, when I was still working in the performing arts troupe, I began to study for the university examination, wanting very much to further my education in either physics or medicine. My first choice was to study medicine. This was because at that time, Bangbu Medical College had begun recruiting students, and someone I knew in Wuhe County had already been accepted to it. I was very eager to enter that medical institute.

How did you study science subjects without a laboratory?

I concentrated on mathematics. I was hoping that I would make up chemistry after I entered university. I was only eighteen, and I thought I could still catch up. But my dreams were not realized. I was terribly disappointed and depressed. I really wanted to be a doctor.

LIANG XIAOSHENG

I know that you went to a military farm by the Amur River in Heilongjiang Province. How did you decide to go there?

I joined one of the earliest groups of *zhiqing* going to the countryside. I went there in June 1968, and Chairman Mao did not proclaim his order that educated youths should go to the countryside until 23 December 1968. I was a "monitor" (*qinwuyuan*) when I was in third-year senior middle school. The title "*qinwuyuan*" (literally diligent server) was a new title coined for Chairman Mao's slogan "Serve the People." My ultimate responsibility was to mobilize all my classmates to go to the countryside.

Why do you think that Mao wanted to mobilize the urban educated youths to go to the countryside?

In the beginning Chairman Mao was very supportive of the Red Guards. He received millions of them at Tiananmen Square. The Red Guards played an important role in the Cultural Revolution by dragging down Liu Shaoqi and

Deng Xiaoping. However, once their mission was over Mao was aware that as a political force the Red Guards had completed their task. That was the reason Mao said, "Now, the little revolutionary generals [Red Guards] have committed a mistake." At that time, many Red Guards could not figure out why, having participated in the revolution for two years and having still a great number of tasks to be completed, they suddenly were discarded. Of course, the impending danger of mass urban unemployment also influenced Mao's decision. But the countryside was not quite prepared for the urban youths.

When you went to the countryside, did you have any idea that the rustication program was meant to be permanent?

At that time we were very naive and had no idea that it was supposed to be permanent. No doubt the whole operation was deceptive. To us middle school students, the term "establish roots" (*zhagen*) was vague and beyond comprehension.

After we went to the military farm we lived a very harsh and puritanical life in the first four years. We really lived up to the standard of not being afraid of hardship and of fatigue. The way we lived was a kind of sadomachism.

Did you have any idea what the military farm was going to be like?

Vaguely. We were told that we would be given a military uniform. To tell you the truth, it was not until June (1968) when I was on the train going to the countryside that I heard Mao's order that military farms should be established and that soldiers there should work with the Nanniwan Spirit of the Yan'an period of the early forties to reclaim land, build farms, and grow food.

How many zhiqing *were sent there and how were these military farms established?*

A total of four hundred and eighty thousand *zhiqing* were sent to the military farms in Heilongjiang. Strictly speaking, from the time we went there up to the time we left, no military farm in the true sense was ever established. After Mao gave his order, several state farms in Heilongjiang Province that had originally been built with the assistance of Soviet experts—for example, the Friendship State Farm, the Red Reclamation State Farm, and a number of small labor camps—were amalgamated to form military farms.

What was the population on these military farms?

There were two million people in these farms. This figure includes people entering at different stages. In the early fifties, there were already discharged soldiers. After the Korean War (1951), one hundred thousand discharged soldiers were sent there. Later, particularly in 1963, about two hundred thousand immigrants from Shandong Province poured in due to the famine caused by the Great Leap Forward, and then, in the late 1960s four hundred and eighty thousand *zhiqing* were sent there.

Because of the large population, more and more agricultural land had to be reclaimed through a process called *tahuang*, which literally means "to tread on the uncultivated land." That is, after ascertaining that the soil was suitable for agriculture, tents were set up and a new company was founded. Many *zhiqing* companies were established in this manner.

How did you adapt to life on the military farm?

When we first arrived there, we lived in an abandoned mill which was built of tree branches. Our beds were also made of branches. The beds were not ordinary beds, but long ones on which a few dozen people could sleep.

The conditions were particularly hard for city girls. The younger ones were fifteen and the oldest twenty-two. They were not used to the food or the cold weather. Some of them had never done any domestic work at home, not even mending their own buttons.

It seems that the entire rustication program was particularly cruel for women.

Indeed. Even after they returned to the city, they encountered more problems than the males. Most of them had passed their prime and it was very difficult for them to find suitable mates. In China, unmarried women over thirty suffer from tremendous social pressure. Some of those in this situation married hastily. I am certain that there will be many future divorces among these marriages. There were also those female *zhiqing* who were so desperate that they married in the countryside shortly before the relaxation of the rustication policy (1979).

How was the relationship between males and females on the military farm?

People of our generation missed one stage of growth. We jumped straight from adolescence to middle age. Therefore, emotionally, we sometimes want to relive the youthful stage that we missed. I personally have suffered deeply from this. I was on the military farm for seven years. From the age of eighteen to twenty-five I did not have any romance. In such a restrictive environment it was impossible to have any, not even the desire. Normally, eighteen to twenty-two is the best age for love. But for us, during those years, we suppressed consciously or unconsciously all our own desires, and spent all our energy on striving for the titles of "model worker" or outstanding Youth League member, or striving to enter a Study Group of Chairman Mao's Works. External rewards became the replacement for personal feelings. Most of us became aware of the desire for the opposite sex by our late twenties. But any thought of it was immediately dampened by practical questions: can I still leave after I marry? How can I maintain a family here? Thus, when some *zhiqing* succeeded in obtaining permits to leave, the others began to feel restless.

What other factors made the zhiqing *restless?*

Another factor was the fear of being abandoned. From the beginning, we had thought that Chairman Mao was always concerned about us. We even heard a rumor that Chairman Mao wanted to introduce a rotational system under which the *zhiqing* would be replaced every few years. However, this did not materialize. More and more *zhiqing* were being sent there, but very few could leave. Those who left were the children of high-ranking cadres and those with connections. Everybody felt discouraged and abandoned. Every day we hoped good news would come. The *zhiqing* from Beijing, especially, tried all they could to find out the most up-to-date news from the government. Rumors were going around that the first group of *zhiqing* would soon be sent back home. This gave everybody hope.

Because of the Sino-Soviet conflict on the border at Zhenbao Island in 1969, Mao seemed to change his thinking about the *zhiqing*. He said, "Don't move them; I want to use them." We again felt that we were of some use and prepared to go to war. We made preparations for the onset of the battle with the Soviet Union. At that time we did not think about ourselves. We did not have the sense of self-value. The term "value of the self" is a concept that has only recently emerged in China. For us then, we only thought of the collective and the nation. Later, this selflessness disappeared and feelings of discontent and loss spread quickly.

Looking back, what do you think that the zhiqing *contributed to the Great Barren North?*

I have always felt that we made two contributions to the Great Barren North. First, we built an electric network for all the military farms; secondly, we reclaimed much land. After all, the *zhiqing* brought new knowledge, education, and lifestyles to the long-closed communities. A couple of hundred *zhiqing* could bring vitality to a once dull and backward village. And these *zhiqing* were not ordinary young people. They had gone through the Cultural Revolution and were well trained in making propaganda. Almost all companies had their own art performance groups, producing many types of entertainment. The clothing of the *zhiqing* also influenced the local people. I remember local people asked the *zhiqing* to buy them shoes from Beijing. Years later, after the *zhiqing* had left, the local people felt that they had lost the inspiration to make themselves look better. This was particularly the case for the local girls.

People of your generation have sacrificed so much. Do you think the contribution can compensate for the sacrifices?

When one considers the large number of four hundred and eighty thousand *zhiqing* and a period of ten years, we have sacrificed much more than we have contributed. With all this manpower and time, a mid-sized city could have been built. . . .

In your fiction about rusticated life you tend to depict one or two zhiqing *who choose to remain in the Great Barren North. Why?*

I personally know of a small number of them who chose to remain there. The reasons were two-fold: pure idealism, which of course could be very painful, and the career purpose of becoming a leading cadre on a military farm.

Now the military farms have been dismantled. What could they still be doing there?

Since the military farms have been turned into state farms they still need cadres to manage them. In fact, these cadres have good pay and big living space; some even have the privilege of using cars. They wouldn't have all this in the city.

What is your motive in writing zhiqing *fiction?*

I hope I can write about aspects of the life of the *zhiqing*. Putting many aspects together, we then have a more comprehensive picture of this generation.

I consider Snow City *(a two-volume novel about one million characters in length) the most comprehensive treatment of the lives of the* zhiqing *generation. The setting of the novel is after the* zhiqing *characters have returned to the city. Do you think that this setting was the best choice?*

The reason I chose this setting is that after the *zhiqing* returned to the city they had to start from scratch again. The already very limited space in their parents' homes became even more crowded. It was impossible for them to have their own places. All these factors led ten thousand *zhiqing* to participate in a large demonstration in Shanghai in the spring of 1979. Actually, it was not limited only to Shanghai, as there were demonstrations in Xinjiang. A common song that they sang goes like this [Liang Xiaosheng waved his arm and started singing]:

Brothers, sisters.

No jobs. . . .

When this novel was made into a television series, the demonstration scene was cut because of its sensitive nature.

That is too bad. Did you have any trouble in getting the first volume of the novel published?

There were some difficulties, mainly because I depicted the sharp confrontation between the *zhiqing* generation and the older bureaucrats. In Beijing, the situation was more acute because some of the *zhiqing* from Shanxi province were on their way to Beijing to protest. Therefore, the first volume was abridged somewhat when it was published.

I was asked to depict more ex-*zhiqing* characters as factory managers, scholars, and writers. They also wanted my male characters to be more masculine and to be more in the mold of a reformer. I didn't agree with them, because I didn't think that these types of people were representative of the *zhiqing* generation. Most of them in fact are leading an ordinary life.

How did you write such a voluminous work?

Before I began writing I had thought about it for a long time. I did not write drafts, because one draft would mean one million words.

How did you handle so many characters?

At the start, I did not decide on the fates of the characters. It was impossible, so I modified them as they developed.

In your fiction you tend to endow your female characters with idealized qualities, such as the beautiful and passionate Li Xiaoyan (in "A Land of Wonder and Mystery") and the pure and gentle Pei Xiaoyun (in "The Snowstorm Is Coming Tonight"). What was the reason for this tendency?

Some literary critics have said that male *zhiqing* writers tend to portray gentle and romantic females because it reflects the attitude of the *zhiqing* generation. I totally agree with this observation. This represents our search for what we have lost; this is also an examination of the self.

After 1982, there was a trend for zhiqing *writers to be nostalgic about the country-side. Why was that?*

I have always had such a feeling. Sometimes I wish I could sense the Great Barren North in this room. I wish I was by a river; or I wish it was raining or snowing outside. This kind of feeling arises out of the disgust and fatigue caused by life in the city. Even though people of the *zhiqing* generation are only in their late thirties, they are very tired. Some of them do not want to be so ordinary. They attend evening college, and they struggle for a better life. But they are very tired. The nostalgia for the Great Barren North is a search for peace and solitude, as well as a search for the self.

In *Snow City* I write about an old maid who is an ex-*zhiqing* in Beijing. The editor expected that I would make her into an enterprising woman who has a happy marriage. But the character does not develop that way. As she grows older, the Great Barren North becomes more and more attractive. She writes her ex-neighbors there and tells them that she wants to go back. But her neighbors reply that their daughter wants to visit Beijing. When the young woman comes to Beijing, she asks her about that willow tree in the village. The young woman says that there is no willow tree there. Later, the young woman is seduced by a young man, and she has no intention to go home. The plain fact is the land in the Great Barren North has been divided up among individual households; how can the ex-*zhiqing* survive there?

Some say that your fiction is characterized by heroism and idealism. What do you think?

It is true. When I wrote "The Snowstorm Is Coming Tonight" and the first volume of *Snow City,* I did include heroism and idealism. That was why I depicted those *zhiqing* who chose to remain in the countryside. But in less than a year when I wrote the second volume of *Snow City*, I had said good-bye to heroism and idealism.

Do you continue to write about the zhiqing *generation?*

It seems that by 1986 there is not much to be written about the *zhiqing*. But I feel obliged to do my best to write about this generation. After that, I will turn to something else.

People of your generation have suffered so much. How different do you think you are from the younger generation?

I am prejudiced; I love my generation very much. I think that for a long time to come there won't be a generation as strong and tough as the *zhiqing* generation. After all, we have gone through the Cultural Revolution and the Rustication Movement. Young people nowadays still complain even if they receive all the care from their parents and all the education they want. They cannot take hardship. I have heard that one college student committed suicide just because his roommate said something bad about him in front of his girlfriend.

How would you evaluate the Rustication Movement?

To be honest, the Rustication Movement gained very little. People of each nation should have a pioneering spirit. However, there must first be a certain level of material well-being. Only when such a living standard is achieved can the opening up of new land be possible.

23.4 AND 23.5 BAREFOOT DOCTORS

During the Cultural Revolution, the call for self-reliance expanded into the nation's healthcare system. In rural areas without access to formally trained physicians, "barefoot doctors" took on the burden of providing medical care to the peasants. As the first document below describes, such practitioners, celebrated as models of selfless devotion, received only the most rudimentary training and relied on improvised treatments for serious illnesses. The second document is drawn from *A Barefoot Doctor's Manual,* published in 1970 by the Institute of Traditional Chinese Medicine in Hunan province. The contents of this lengthy compendium ranged from explanations of basic human anatomy, prescriptions of Chinese herbs, and directions for delivering babies. In the excerpts included here, hygiene practices and diagnostic and treatment techniques are explained.

23.4 *Barefoot Doctors: Giving Medical Treatment While Taking Part in Farm Work*

"Barefoot doctor" has become a familiar term to more and more readers abroad. Just what are these doctors? How are they trained? And what role do they play in China's medical and public health work? The following stories offer some answers.

TO MEET THE PRESSING DEMAND

The name "barefoot doctor" first appeared in the Jiangzhen People's Commune on Shanghai's outskirts.

In 1965 when Chairman Mao issued the call "In medical and health work, put the stress on the rural areas," a number of mobile medical teams formed by urban medical workers came to Jiangzhen. Though it was near the metropolis, this commune had only one health clinic with about a dozen medical personnel serving a population of 28,000. When the medical teams arrived, the local peasants were glad to see them. While curing and preventing commune members' diseases, the doctors from Shanghai helped the clinic give a group of young peasants some medical training.

Later when the teams left, these peasants took their place and since then have gradually become full-fledged doctors. Taking medical kits with them, they worked barefooted alongside the peasants in the paddyfields, and they treated peasants in the fields, on the threshing grounds or in their homes. They were at once commune members and doctors, doing farm work and treating patients. Like other commune members, they receive their pay on the basis of work-points, and their income was more or less the same as that of able-bodied peasants doing the same amount of work. The peasants warmly welcomed them and affectionately called them "barefoot doctors."

Renmin Ribao [*People's Daily*] devoted much coverage on September 14, 1968, to this new-born thing. This set off nationwide efforts to train "barefoot doctors" from among the peasants.

Eight out of every ten people in China are in the countryside. But the vast rural areas had been short of medical workers and medicines for centuries under reactionary rule before liberation. Over a fairly long period of time after liberation, medical personnel, medical and public health funds, medicines and medical equipment were mainly concentrated in the cities and medical conditions in the rural areas had not improved rapidly due to the effects of Liu Shaoqi's counter-revolutionary revisionist line. Changing this situation was an urgent task confronting medical and public health work. Thus after Chairman Mao issued his call to stress medical and health work in the rural areas, prompt action was taken throughout the country. The People's Government allocated special funds for the rural areas. Factories turned out more medical equipment and medicines suited to rural conditions. Urban medical personnel and large numbers of graduates from medical schools went to work in the countryside. It was under these circumstances that the "barefoot doctors" emerged.

BUILDING A NEW SOCIALIST COUNTRYSIDE

Wang Guizhen was one of the Jiangzhen Commune's first "barefoot doctors." After graduating school in Shanghai, she worked in a towel factory for three years. Anxious to build a new socialist countryside, she returned to her village to do farm work in 1961.

A group of city medical workers arrived at the height of the early rice harvest in mid-July to inoculate the peasants against summer diseases and help them improve environmental sanitation. Wang Guizhen took an active part in this work which helped keep the peasants fit during the busy farming season. She learnt that building up the rural areas meant much more than just working with hoe or sickle.

In 1965, Wang Guizhen who was 21 that year was chosen to attend a training course for "barefoot doctors" run by the commune's clinic. The first lesson was given by an old poor peasant who recounted his past sufferings and spoke of today's happy life. Two instances he talked about left a deep impression on her, daughter of an impoverished rural carpenter.

The first was about a poor peasant's son who had acute ulceration of the gum and cheeks before liberation. Blood and pus continually oozed from the ulcers and the child's case got worse and worse. The father went to town to get a doctor who demanded an amount of money far beyond what he could pay. He went back and borrowed the money from his fellow villagers. But by the time the doctor came that night, the child had died.

Another poor peasant's child contracted encephalitis B several years ago. There was no hospital near the village and the boy's condition rapidly worsened. He was rushed to town and hospitalized for a month. Though the family spent more than 300 yuan, the child became disabled because of delayed treatment.

These examples made a deep impression on Wang Guizhen and heightened her determination to do what she could for the peasants' well-being.

During her four months of training, Wang Guizhen and 27 other young men and women were taught to cure scores of common diseases and prescribe some 100 medicines and they learnt the fundamentals of acupuncture treatment at 30 major points on the human body. This ABC of medical science was of great use to these young people who have deep feelings for the peasants.

Back from the training course, Wang Guizhen continued doing farm work such as transplanting rice-shoots, weeding and harvesting together with the villagers. Wherever she worked, in the fields, at construction sites of water conservancy projects or other places, she always had her medical kit at hand. She and two other "barefoot doctors" took charge of handling all the diseases and injuries they could among the more than 1,500 brigade members. After giving prescriptions, she made it a rule to call on the patients and ask them about the effects of the medicine so as to sum up experience and improve her work. As to cases she could not handle, she always went with the patients to the city hospital.

All this was not just for the purpose of learning, but, more important, her aim was to look after the patients still better. In summer, villagers sometimes were bitten by snakes. When she was told that a worker in a factory several kilometres away could treat snake-bites with herbal medicine, she immediately went to see him. Combining what she learnt from the worker with Western medicine, she has treated more than a dozen snake-bite cases in the last two years.

Affectionately called their "close friend" by the villagers, Wang Guizhen was elected deputy secretary of the commune Party committee and a member on the county Party committee. Despite the change in her position, she is still a "barefoot doctor."

She has also made rapid progress in medical technique. She and other "barefoot doctors" took turns working in the commune's health clinic or getting further training in advanced courses. Last year, she spent two months studying anatomy, physiology and biochemistry in a medical college and later went to the county hospital's internal medicine department for advanced study in combination with clinical treatment.

TO SERVE THE PEASANTS

"Barefoot doctor" Jentso who belongs to the Tibetan nationality lives on the Qinghai Plateau some 4,500 metres above sea level, an area with very low temperatures and only one or two snow-free months. In addition to strong winds all year round, there is snow, hail or sandstorms in different seasons. What with the herdsmen living far apart, a "barefoot doctor" has to overcome many difficulties to see the patients. From the day she began practising medicine, Jentso has made light of journeys across mountains, valleys and grasslands to treat 36,000 patients.

A homeless orphan, Jentso started tending the herd-owners' flocks at the age of seven. Because of malnutrition, her hair turned brown. The herd-owners and so-called "living Buddhas" regarded this as an ominous sign and cursed her as a devil.

She was not even allowed to stand near the livestock sheds. After liberation, she was sent to many medical training courses run by the commune, county and autonomous *zhou*. She is now able to cure local common diseases, give acupuncture treatment and deliver babies. "Though there are difficulties in my work," she said, "they are nothing compared with what we herdsmen and women suffered in by-gone days." She always shows warm concern for the patients on her calls. Apart from helping them boil water and cook meals, she encourages them to build up their confidence in conquering illness.

A Communist Party member, Jentso seldom mentions the difficulties she encounters or gets conceited about her achievements. She takes an active part in collective productive labour, milking, spinning wool and doing other work, and is paid according to her work-points just as other commune members. Time and again she has declined subsidies offered her by the production brigade.

At the county's Party congress in May 1971, Jentso was elected a member of the county Party committee.

STUDY IN THE COURSE OF PRACTICE

Generally speaking, "barefoot doctors" are given three to six months of short-term training before starting to work. Training classes with fewer but well-selected courses are run by the commune's clinic, county hospital, mobile medical teams from the cities or medical schools, according to the principle of linking theory with practice. The aim is to give the trainees the ability to do practical work as quickly as possible and to lay the foundation for advanced study.

For "barefoot doctors," in addition to taking part in short-term advanced study (one to several months) by turns and with full pay, most of their study is always tied in with problems that crop up in their everyday work. Many of them have made rapid progress through hard work and diligent study.

Chulaimu Niyatse who is of Uighur nationality returned to her native village in Xinjiang's Kuche county after graduating from junior middle school. Before becoming a "barefoot doctor," she had studied for only 35 days in the class run by the commune's clinic and she could only handle injections and minor injuries.

After 1966, she began studying medicine in the clinic every Wednesday while learning from the doctors and the medical team members whenever there was the opportunity to do so. She and the "barefoot doctors" from other brigades were required to report on the villagers' health conditions and the clinic's experienced doctors gave them lectures on how to prevent, diagnose and cure diseases. There once were five cases of diphtheria in her brigade and she administered medicine to the sick children and at the same time isolated them from the others whom she inoculated against the disease, thus checking it. Another time she used the same method to prevent meningitis from spreading. She now not only can use Western medicine to cure the local common diseases, but can prescribe traditional Chinese medicine and give acupuncture treatment. She also has learnt to deliver babies.

Together with four other "barefoot doctors," she took charge of a medical centre for a production brigade of 1,600 people. Last year, they gave medical treatment on over 7,000 occasions, including complicated cases such as tuberculosis of the bones and paralysis. There was one woman whose placenta was retained after giving birth and whose uterus bled profusely. Chulaimu brewed some medicinal herbs for her and got her out of danger.

"Barefoot doctor" Zhang Xianghua in the countryside around Yenan in northwest China had only learnt some elementary knowledge and technique of Western medicine in a training class. In the course of practice, he found that there were many effective prescriptions of traditional Chinese medicine used by the local people who lived in a hilly village where many medicinal herbs grew. If these traditional methods were put to good use, he thought, it would produce very good results in curing certain diseases and save the patients much expense. So he and his colleagues set about learning from veteran practitioners of traditional Chinese medicine and experienced herb-pickers in the locality. As a result, they were able to recognize 240 herbs and learnt to give herbal prescriptions and cure diseases by acupuncture. They themselves picked the needed herbs and later planted them. Last year, they went a step further. Based on efficacious herbal prescriptions, they processed herbs into easy-to-use pills, powders and liquid medicines to stop bleeding and coughing, induce lactation and cure burns.

In 1970, Zhang Xianghua had the opportunity to learn from a traditional Chinese doctor of a medical team that had come from Peking for six months. He worked together with this old doctor every day, diagnosing and curing patients. He also spent one to two hours listening to his talks on the theories of traditional Chinese medicine. Studying this way helped Zhang quickly increase his ability.

For a period of time, he and other "barefoot doctors" in the brigade co-operated closely with medical teams from Peking, making an overall investigation of an endemic disease. They learnt to give every brigade member a cardiographic checkup and carried out auscultatory and oral investigations from house to house. They gave decoctions of herbal medicine twice a day to 28 patients who had varying symptoms. Carefully observing the effects, they continued studying ways to improve the prescription's ingredients. After 150 days, all the patients were better. In this way, the young "barefoot doctors" learnt how to diagnose, cure, treat and prevent this disease.

Study through practice, as shown by the abovementioned examples, is the basic way "barefoot doctors" are trained. This quick and effective method makes up for the drawbacks due to medical schools being unable to train large numbers of doctors in a short time. In a developing country like China, the first step to change backwardness in medical work in the rural areas is, so to speak, "sending charcoal in snowy weather," not "adding flowers to the embroidery." "Barefoot doctors" are a new-born force which has bright prospects.

Every rural people's commune today has its "barefoot doctors" who are either children of the once impoverished peasants and herdsmen or city-bred middle school students who have settled in the countryside. These peasant-doctors are playing an important role in the rural areas where doctors and medicine are in great demand.

23.5 *A Barefoot Doctor's Manual*

NOTES ON THE PREPARATION
OF THIS MANUAL

1. All effort has been made to adapt the contents of this book—the signs and symptoms of diseases described, and their diagnosis and treatment with the drugs listed—to actual rural conditions in Hunan Province and to the educational level of the rural barefoot doctors. For this reason, diagnosis begins with a recognition of signs and symptoms, and descriptions of special tests (such as X-rays, laboratory examinations) are largely omitted. In an attempt to integrate traditional Chinese medicine and western medicine in diagnosis, the names of disease and their type forms [according to traditional Chinese medicine] are described together to facilitate treatment of cause and use of discriminative therapy [treatment based on recognition of disease form/type]. In the sections on treatment, the use of Chinese herbs and new therapeutic techniques are emphasized with the selective use of western medicines appropriately mentioned (for the actual dosage and use of related western medicines, and precautions connected with them, please consult section on "Classification of Commonly Used Western Medicines" in the Appendix).

2. To cut down on the size of the manual and to simplify the use of subdivisions, descriptions of the various diseases in Chapter 6 follows a general pattern. The first section of each description covers the name of disease [and synonyms], etiology, pathology, signs and symptoms, important diagnostic features, differential diagnosis and type/form classification of the disease without any great detail. It is followed by subsequent sections on "Prevention" and "Treatment" which go into greater detail.

3. In principle, the amounts of herbs given in the [cooked in water] concoction-prescriptions listed for treating various diseases are for the prescribed daily dosage, taken in two divided doses, the number of daily-dosage prescriptions used based on the severity of illness. Where not specifically noted, the herbs called for are dried. If the fresh product is used, the amounts are generally doubled, but an explanation is given.

4. This handbook records the prevention and treatment of illnesses we are concerned with, and includes 338 illustrations describing common herbs seen in Hunan Province. Another 184 drugs (including some Chinese herbs, other

herbs rarely grown in Hunan Province, animal-origin drugs, minerals etc.) which were not illustrated only had their properties and action, the conditions they were most used for, and preparation and usage mentioned briefly.

5. Characteristic of Chinese-herb treatment of disease is the approach of discriminative therapy [that treats according to the recognition of disease condition]. Selection of tested single- and compound-ingredient prescriptions used is based on the patient's actual condition such as his general physical health, severity of illness, nature of the disease and its course of development [whether rapid or slow]. The amount of herbs used in each prescription is also based on the severity of the patient's conditions, his age, and the state of the herb [whether fresh or dried]. There is no need for blind adherence to the original amounts stated.

6. The appendix at the end of the book lists in tables Chinese patent medicines and the commonly used western medicines by categories, for treatment and reference use. One index lists Chinese herbs by their proper names and synonyms, and another one groups the plants into herbs, vines and shrubs/trees (limited to these Chinese herbs with illustrations) to facilitate search and gradual standardization of the herb terminology, while reducing confusion caused by the same drug having different names or the same name being assumed by several different drugs. For reference use, another table lists the normal values of some common clinical laboratory tests.

CHAPTER II. HYGIENE

SECTION 1. THE PATRIOTIC HEALTH MOVEMENT

To realize an effective Patriotic Health Movement, we must observe the following guidelines:

1. Carry out a policy emphasizing prevention.
2. Mobilize the masses on a large scale. Hygiene and disease prevention work must depend on the large masses of workers, peasants, and soldiers who fight unsanitary practices.
3. Popularize disease prevention knowledge.

Drinking Water Sanitation

Dirty drinking water can easily cause disease. Many gastrointestinal tract infections such as typhoid, acute gastroenteritis, dysentery etc., and many parasitical infections are due to contamination of the water supply. To assure that drinking water is sanitary and clean, the following measures must be observed.

1. *Protection of water supply source*

    (1) Place barns, latrines, manure pits, outhouses and waste water drains as far away as possible from the water supply source. They are located best below the source of water supply.

    (2) Wherever possible, line wells with bricks and cover the bottoms with gravel or coarse sand. It is best to build a platform for the well and to place a cover over it.

    (3) Do not pour garbage or excreta, nor wash night-waste buckets or diapers in ponds and rivers [that supply drinking water]. Drinking water ponds and other-usage ponds should be separate. If river water must be used for all purposes, delineate usage zones, with the upstream zone designated for drinking water supply, and the downstream zone designated for other uses. This way, the introduction of waste matter and disease parasites into the drinking water is kept to a minimum.

2. *Disinfection of drinking water*

    The best method for disinfecting water is by boiling it. However, boiling must be maintained for 15 minutes to meet sterilization (disinfection) requirements. Advocate the drinking of boiled water, and not untreated water.

    (1) *To purify water*: Place finely crushed alum, half an ounce to every 10 *dan* [man load of 2 buckets to each *dan*] in the water tank and stir well. After a while, the impurities will settle to the bottom, and the water become clear. If some impurities still remain, add a little lime to hasten the settling process.

    (2) *To disinfect with bleaching powder*: The use of bleaching powder to disinfect drinking water is the most extensive and comparatively economical and effective method used at present. When the bleach breaks down in water, it has a germicidal effect. However, the tanks should still be tightly covered when water is stored. It is best to disinfect the water as it is being used up. If it is possible to disinfect the water twice a day, results will be even better.

    (3) *To disinfect with traditional Chinese drugs*: Wrap in cloth and place in water tank the following:

    Place 1 *liang* of "guanzhong," (*Cyrtomium fortunei* J. Sm.)
        3 *qian* of "shichangpu" (*Acorus gramineus*, soland)
        3 *qian* of realgar

    After 1 hour, water is ready for use. Water so treated will prevent against gastrointestinal tract infections.

Excreta Management

Human and animal excreta are both used as agricultural fertilizers. To increase agricultural production, manure composting must be practiced, though certain infectious diseases and parasitical infections are transmitted because of improper excreta management. "Excreta management" is a measure designed to curtail multiplication/propagation of flies. It is also a measure that prevents disease transmission by curtailing the dispersal/loss of excreta (retained as fertilizers made effective for increasing production) and by eliminating/killing disease-causing bacteria and parasite ova.

Food Sanitation

Since disease enters by the mouth, attention should be given to cleanliness and ygiene in food handling, in order to maintain high on-the-job attendance and productivity. To accomplish this, the following points are raised:

1. Do not eat raw and cold food. Food should only be eaten after being cooked, and cooked food kept overnight should be reheated or steamed again before eating. Fermented food should not be eaten.
2. Select food stuffs including fish, meat, eggs, etc., for freshness. Any rotten or spoiled food should not be eaten.
3. If possible, do not eat meat taken from animals who have died of disease. Do not eat wild plants and mushrooms that are not identifiable nor consume cultivated plants freshly sprayed with insecticide, to avoid food poisoning.
4. Remember to wash hands—after work, before, and after bathroom use.

CHAPTER III. INTRODUCTION TO DIAGNOSTIC TECHNIQUES

The physician's basic task is protection and improvement of the people's health and prevention, early diagnosis and proper treatment of disease, so that the sick can early regain their health.

SECTION 1. HOW TO UNDERSTAND DISEASE

Under certain conditions, the human body is affected internally and externally by disease-causing factors that cause the balance between the body and the environment or the balance between body components to be disturbed, and become sick.

To recognize and understand disease we must be in close contact with the patients and study them with care. Through case histories and thorough physical examinations, the physician is able to obtain significant data. On the basis of this data, he can apply medical theories of disease differentiation to carefully analyze and evaluate the etiology, pathology, diagnosis, treatment, and prognosis of disease in gradual steps. Using such techniques as interviewing, observation, auscultation, (listening, "hearing,") touching, and percussion, the physician makes a correct diagnosis through comprehensive analysis and deduction of the data collected. Again, the treatment carried out on the basis of the diagnosis obtained must not be isolated, restricted, or based on a static metaphysical approach to disease analysis and recognition. Under most conditions, the physician must repeat and follow up his studies, and accumulate some practical experience before he can better understand disease and its management.

CHAPTER IV. THERAPEUTIC TECHNIQUES

SECTION 1. TREATMENT WITH CHINESE HERBS

Traditional Chinese medicine is the sum total of the Chinese working people's experience in their struggle against disease over the last several thousand years. It contains the rich experiences and theoretical knowledge of their fight against disease over a long period of time.

Great numbers of barefoot doctors, workers, peasants, soldiers, and workers have promoted, on a large scale, the use of Chinese herbs to treat disease. Not only have they obtained very good results toward the control of commonly seen rural ailments, they have also obtained valuable experience in treating difficult-to-treat diseases. From this, they have stengthened the development of cooperative medical therapeutics and contributed immensely to creating a new medicine and a new pharmacology for China based on a combination of the traditional Chinese and western medicine approaches. Chinese herb resources in Hunan Province are plentiful. For daily emergencies, they are valuable for treating disease; for wartime emergencies, good for treating wounds. Simple and easy to use, they are well received by the large masses of people.

Precautionary measures that should be taken in the use of Chinese herbs to treat disease are discussed in Chapter VII. For detailed information on medicinal plant recognition and identification, collection, processing, storage and use, please consult Chapter VII.

The use of Chinese herbs to treat disease generally takes eight approaches:

1. The perspiration method (*jiebiaofa*): Literally meaning "to release externally," this method is suited for "superficial" or external exposure ailments. Chinese medicines used for this purpose are externally releasing drugs (*jiebiaoyao*), which are perspiration inducers. Divided into warm (*xinwen*) and cool (*xinliang*) perspiration inducers, the warm inducers are suited for wind-cold illnesses; the cool inducers, for wind-heat illnesses.

Mourning with Deepest Grief the Passing Away of the Great Leader and Great Teacher Chairman Mao Zedong

MESSAGE TO THE WHOLE PARTY, THE WHOLE ARMY AND THE PEOPLE OF ALL NATIONALITIES THROUGHOUT THE COUNTRY

The Central Committee of the Communist Party of China, the Standing Committee of the National People's Congress of the People's Republic of China, the State Council of the People's Republic of China and the Military Commission of the Central Committee of the Communist Party of China announce with deepest grief to the whole Party, the whole army and the people of all nationalities throughout the country: Comrade Mao Zedong, the esteemed and beloved great leader of our Party, our army and the people of all nationalities in our country, the great teacher of the international proletariat and the oppressed nations and oppressed people, Chairman of the Central Committee of the Communist Party of China, Chairman of the Military Commission of the Central Committee of the Communist Party of China, and Honorary Chairman of the National Committee of the Chinese People's Political Consultative Conference, passed away at 00:10 hours on September 9, 1976, in Beijing as a result of the worsening of his illness and despite all treatment, although meticulous medical care was given him in every way after he fell ill.

Chairman Mao Zedong was the founder and wise leader of the Communist Party of China, the Chinese People's Liberation Army and the People's Republic of China. Chairman Mao led our Party in waging a protracted, acute and complex struggle against the Right and "Left" opportunist lines in the Party, defeating the opportunist lines pursued by Chen Duxiu, Qu Qiubai, Li Lisan, Luo Zhanglong, Wang Ming, Zhang Guotao, Gao Gang-Rao Shushi, and Peng Dehuai and again, during the Great Proletarian Cultural Revolution, triumphing over the counter-revolutionary revisionist line of Liu Shaoqi, Lin Biao and Deng Xiaoping, thus enabling our Party to develop and grow in strength steadily in class struggle and the struggle between the two lines. Led by Chairman Mao, the Communist Party of China has developed through a tortuous path into a great, glorious and correct Marxist-Leninist Party which is today exercising leadership over the People's Republic of China.

During the period of the new-democratic revolution, Chairman Mao, in accordance with the universal truth of Marxism-Leninism and by combining it with the concrete practice of the Chinese revolution, creatively laid down the general line and general policy of the new-democratic revolution, founded the Chinese People's Liberation Army and pointed out that the seizure of political power by armed force in China could be achieved only by following the road of building rural base areas, using the countryside to encircle the cities and finally seizing the cities, and not by any other road. He led our Party, our army and the people of our country in using people's war to overthrow the reactionary rule of imperialism, feudalism and bureaucrat-capitalism, winning the great victory of the new-democratic revolution and founding the People's Republic of China. The victory of the Chinese people's revolution led by Chairman Mao changed the situation in the East and the world and blazed a new trail for the cause of liberation of the oppressed nations and oppressed people.

In the period of the socialist revolution, Chairman Mao comprehensively summed up the positive as well as the negative experience of the international communist movement, penetratingly analysed the class relations in socialist society and, for the first time in the history of the development of Marxism, unequivocally pointed out that there are still classes and class struggle after the socialist transformation of the ownership of the means of production has in the main been completed, drew the scientific conclusion that the bourgeoisie is right in the Communist Party, put forth the great theory of continuing the revolution under the dictatorship of the proletariat, and laid down the Party's basic line for the entire historical period of socialism. Guided by Chairman Mao's proletarian revolutionary line, our Party, our army and the people of our country have continued their triumphant advance and seized great victories in the socialist revolution and socialist construction, particularly in the Great Proletarian Cultural Revolution, in criticizing Lin Biao and Confucius and in criticizing Deng Xiaoping and repulsing the Right deviationist attempt at reversing correct verdicts. Upholding socialism and consolidating the dictatorship of the proletariat in the People's Republic of China, a country with a vast territory and a large population, is a great contribution of world historic significance which Chairman Mao Zedong made to the present era; at the same time; it has provided fresh experience for the international communist movement in combating and preventing revisionism, consolidating the dictatorship of the proletariat, preventing capitalist restoration and building socialism.

All the victories of the Chinese people have been achieved under the leadership of Chairman Mao; they are all great victories for Mao Zedong Thought. The radiance of Mao Zedong Thought will for ever illuminate the road of advance of the Chinese people.

Chairman Mao Zedong summed up the revolutionary practice in the international communist movement, put forward a series of scientific theses, enriched the theoretical treasury of Marxism and pointed out the orientation of struggle for the Chinese people and the revolutionary people throughout the world. With the great boldness and vision of a proletarian revolutionary, he initiated in the international communist movement the great struggle to criticize modern revisionism with the Soviet revisionist renegade clique at the core, promoted the vigorous development of the cause of the world proletarian revolution and the cause of the people of all countries against imperialism and hegemonism, and pushed the history of mankind forward. . . .

Chairman Mao Zedong was the greatest Marxist of the contemporary era. For more than half a century, basing himself on the principle of integrating the universal truth of Marxism-Leninism with the concrete practice of the revolution, he inherited, defended and developed Marxism-Leninism in the protracted struggle against the class enemies at home and abroad, both inside and outside the Party, and wrote a most brilliant chapter in the history of the movement of proletarian revolution. . . .

The passing away of Chairman Mao Zedong is an inestimable loss to our Party, our army and the people of all nationalities in our country, to the international proletariat and the revolutionary people of all countries and to the international communist movement. His passing away is bound to evoke immense grief in the hearts of the people of our country and the revolutionary people of all countries. The Central Committee of the Communist Party of China calls on the whole Party, the whole army and the people of all nationalities in the country to resolutely turn their grief into strength:

We must carry on the cause left behind by Chairman Mao and persist in taking class struggle as the key link, keep to the Party's basic line and persevere in continuing the revolution under the dictatorship of the proletariat.

We must carry on the cause left behind by Chairman Mao and strengthen the centralized leadership of the Party, resolutely uphold the unity and unification of the Party and closely rally round the Party Central Committee. We must strengthen the building of the Party ideologically and organizationally in the course of the struggle between the two lines and resolutely implement the principle of the three-in-one combination of the old, middle-aged and young in accordance with the five requirements for bringing up successors to the cause of the proletarian revolution.

We must carry on the cause left behind by Chairman Mao and consolidate the great unity of the people of all nationalities under the leadership of the working class and based on the worker-peasant alliance, deepen the criticism of Deng Xiaoping, continue the struggle to repulse the Right deviationist attempt at reversing correct verdicts, consolidate and develop the victories of the Great Proletarian Cultural Revolution, enthusiastically support the socialist new things, restrict bourgeois right and further consolidate the dictatorship of the proletariat in our country. We should continue to unfold the three great revolutionary movements of class struggle, the struggle for production and scientific experiment, build our country independently and with the initiative in our own hands, through self-reliance, hard struggle, diligence and thrift, and go all out, aim high and achieve greater, faster, better and more economical results in building socialism.

We must carry on the cause left behind by Chairman Mao and resolutely implement his line in army building, strengthen the building of the army, strengthen the building of the militia, strengthen preparedness against war, heighten our vigilance, and be ready at all times to wipe out any enemy that dares to intrude. We are determined to liberate Taiwan.

We must carry on the cause left behind by Chairman Mao and continue to resolutely carry out Chairman Mao's revolutionary line and policies in foreign affairs. We must adhere to proletarian internationalism, strengthen the unity between our

Party and the genuine Marxist-Leninist Parties and organizations all over the world, strengthen the unity between the people of our country and the people of all other countries, especially those of the third world countries, unite with all the forces in the world that can be united, and carry the struggle against imperialism, social-imperialism and modern revisionism through to the end. We will never seek hegemony and will never be a superpower.

We must carry on the cause left behind by Chairman Mao and assiduously study Marxism–Leninism–Mao Zedong Thought, apply ourselves to the study of works by Marx, Engels, Lenin and Stalin and works by Chairman Mao, fight for the complete overthrow of the bourgeoisie and all other exploiting classes, for the establishment of the dictatorship of the proletariat in place of the dictatorship of the bourgeoisie and for the triumph of socialism over capitalism, and strive to build our country into a powerful socialist state, make still greater contributions to humanity and realize the ultimate goal of communism.

Long live invincible Marxism–Leninism–Mao Zedong Thought!

Long live the great, glorious and correct Communist Party of China!

Eternal glory to the great leader and teacher Chairman Mao Zedong!

| # Redefining Revolution

24.1 DENG XIAOPING: "EMANCIPATE THE MIND, SEEK TRUTH FROM FACTS AND UNITE AS ONE IN LOOKING TO THE FUTURE," DECEMBER 13, 1978

In the two years after the fall of the Gang of Four, Deng Xiaoping emerged as the most important leader within the Party hierarchy. During the reshuffling that occurred in the top leadership ranks in 1978, Mao's successor, Hua Guofeng, was increasingly marginalized. When a dramatic program of reform was launched at the end of 1978, it was clear that Deng was its major proponent.

The following speech was given by Deng Xiaoping at the closing session of a Central Committee meeting in preparation for the Third Plenum. The Third Plenum announced details for the Four Modernizations in agriculture, science and technology, national defense, and industry, establishing them as the guiding blueprint for reform. Deng's speech laid the groundwork for the decisions that followed. With its emphasis on pragmatism and the reversal of the verdict on the 1976 Tiananmen Incident, the speech seemed a hopeful departure from the CCP's recent past. However, the insistence on the importance of Mao Zedong Thought and Marxism-Leninism and the stress on adherence to the Party line were clear signals that Deng subscribed to the authoritarian mode of governance.

Comrades,

This conference has lasted over a month and will soon end. The Central Committee has put forward the fundamental guiding principle of shifting the focus of all Party work to the four modernizations and has solved a host of important problems inherited from the past. This will surely strengthen the determination, confidence and unity of the Party, the army and the people of all of China's nationalities. Now we can be certain that under the correct leadership of the Central Committee, the Party, army and people will achieve victory after victory in our new Long March. . . .

Today, I mainly want to discuss one question, namely, how to emancipate our minds, use our heads, seek truth from facts and unite as one in looking to the future.

I. EMANCIPATING THE MIND IS A VITAL POLITICAL TASK

When it comes to emancipating our minds, using our heads, seeking truth from facts and uniting as one in looking to the future, the primary task is to emancipate our minds. Only then can we, guided as we should be by Marxism-Leninism and Mao Zedong Thought, find correct solutions to the emerging as well as inherited problems, fruitfully reform those aspects of the relations of production and of the superstructure that do not correspond with the rapid development of our productive forces, and chart the specific course and formulate the specific policies, methods and measures needed to achieve the four modernizations under our actual conditions.

The emancipation of minds has not been completely achieved among our cadres, particularly our leading cadres. Indeed, many comrades have not yet set their brains going; in other words, their ideas remain rigid or partly so. That isn't because they are not good comrades. It is a result of specific historical conditions.

First, it is because during the past dozen years Lin Biao and the Gang of Four set up ideological taboos or "forbidden zones" and preached blind faith to confine people's minds within the framework of their phoney Marxism. No one was allowed to go beyond the limits they prescribed. Anyone who did was tracked down, stigmatized and attacked politically. In this situation, some people found it safer to stop using their heads and thinking questions over.

Second, it is because democratic centralism was undermined and the Party was afflicted with bureaucratism resulting from, among other things, overconcentration of power. This kind of bureaucratism often masquerades as "Party leadership," "Party directives," "Party interests" and "Party discipline," but actually it is designed to control people, hold them in check and oppress them. At that time many important issues were often decided by one or two persons. The others could only do what those few ordered. That being so, there wasn't much point in thinking things out for yourself.

Third, it is because no clear distinction was made between right and wrong or between merit and demerit, and because rewards and penalties were not meted out as deserved. No distinction was made between those who worked well and those who didn't. In some cases, even people who worked well were attacked while those who did nothing or just played it safe weathered every storm. Under those unwritten laws, people were naturally reluctant to use their brains.

Fourth, it is because people are still subject to the force of habit, the small producer, who sticks to old conventions, is content with the status quo and is unwilling to seek progress or accept anything new.

When people's minds aren't yet emancipated and their thinking remains rigid, curious phenomena emerge.

Once people's thinking becomes rigid, they will increasingly act according to fixed notions. To cite some examples, strengthening Party leadership is interpreted as the Party monopolizes and interferes in everything. Exercising centralized leadership is interpreted as erasing distinctions between the Party and the government, so that the former replaces the latter. And maintaining unified leadership by the Central Committee is interpreted as "doing everything according to unified standards." We are opposed to "home-grown policies" that violate the fundamental principles of those laid down by the Central Committee, but there are also "home-grown policies" that are truly grounded in reality and supported by the masses. Yet such correct policies are still often denounced for their "not conforming to the unified standards."

People whose thinking has become rigid tend to veer with the wind. They are not guided by Party spirit and Party principles, but go along with whatever has the backing of the authorities and adjust their words and actions according to whichever way the wind is blowing. They think that they will thus avoid mistakes. In fact, however, veering with the wind is in itself a grave mistake, a contravention of the Party spirit which all Communists should cherish. It is true that people who think independently and dare to speak out and act can't avoid making mistakes, but their mistakes are out in the open and are therefore more easily rectified.

Once people's thinking becomes rigid, book worship, divorced from reality, becomes a grave malady. Those who suffer from it dare not say a word or take a step that isn't mentioned in books, documents or the speeches of leaders: everything has to be copied. Thus responsibility to the higher authorities is set in opposition to responsibility to the people.

Our drive for the four modernizations will get nowhere unless rigid thinking is broken down and the minds of cadres and of the masses are completely emancipated.

In fact, the current debate about whether practice is the sole criterion for testing truth is also a debate about whether people's minds need to be emancipated. Everybody has recognized that this debate is highly important and necessary. Its importance is becoming clearer all the time. When everything has to be done by the book, when thinking turns rigid and blind faith is the fashion, it is impossible for a party or a nation to make progress. Its life will cease and that party or nation will perish. Comrade Mao Zedong said this time and again during the rectification movements. Only if we emancipate our minds, seek truth from facts, proceed from reality in everything and integrate theory with practice, can we carry out our socialist modernization programme smoothly, and only then can our Party further develop Marxism-Leninism and Mao Zedong Thought. In this sense, the debate about the criterion for testing truth is really a debate about ideological line, about politics, about the future and the destiny of our Party and nation. . . .

People both at home and abroad have been greatly concerned recently about how we would evaluate Comrade Mao Zedong and the Cultural Revolution. The great contributions of Comrade Mao in the course of long revolutionary struggles will never fade. If we look back at the years following the failure of the revolution in 1927, it appears very likely that without his outstanding leadership the Chinese revolution would still not have triumphed even today. In that case, the people of all our nationalities would still be suffering under the reactionary rule of imperialism, feudalism and bureaucrat-capitalism, and our Party would still be engaged in bitter struggle in the dark. Therefore, it is no exaggeration to say that were it not for Chairman Mao there would be no New China. Mao Zedong Thought has nurtured our whole generation. All comrades present here may be said to have been nourished by Mao Zedong Thought. Without Mao Zedong Thought, the Communist Party of China would not exist today, and that is no exaggeration either. Mao Zedong Thought will forever remain the greatest intellectual treasure of our Party, our army and our people. We must understand the scientific tenets of Mao Zedong Thought correctly and as an integral whole and develop them under the new historical conditions. Of course Comrade Mao was not infallible or free from shortcomings. To demand that of any revolutionary leader would be inconsistent with Marxism. We must guide and educate the Party members, the army officers and men and the people of all of China's nationalities and help them to see the great service of Comrade Mao Zedong scientifically and in historical perspective.

The Cultural Revolution should also be viewed scientifically and in historical perspective. In initiating it Comrade Mao Zedong was actuated mainly by the desire to oppose and prevent revisionism. As for the shortcomings that appeared during the course of the Cultural Revolution and the mistakes that were made then, at an appropriate time they should be summed up and lesson should be drawn from them—that is essential for achieving unity of understanding throughout the Party. The Cultural Revolution has become a stage in the course of China's socialist development, hence we must evaluate it. However, there is not need to do so hastily. Serious research must be done before we can make a scientific appraisal of this historical stage. It may take a rather long time to fully understand and assess some of the particular issues involved. We will probably be able to make a more correct analysis of this period in history after some time has passed than we can right now. . . .

The four modernizations represent a great and profound revolution in which we are moving forward by resolving one new contradiction after another. Therefore, all Party comrades must learn well and always keep on learning.

On the eve of nationwide victory in the Chinese revolution, Comrade Mao Zedong called on the whole Party to start learning afresh. We did that pretty well and consequently, after entering the cities, we were able to rehabilitate the economy very quickly and then to accomplish the socialist transformation. But we must admit that we have not learned well enough in the subsequent years. Expending our main efforts on political campaigns, we did not master the skills needed to build our country. Our socialist construction failed to progress satisfactorily and we experienced grave setbacks politically. Now that our task is to achieve modernization, our lack of the necessary knowledge is even more obvious. So the whole Party must start learning again.

What shall we learn? Basically, we should study Marxism-Leninism and Mao Zedong Thought and try to integrate the universal principles of Marxism with the concrete practice of our modernization drive. At present most of our cadres need also to apply themselves to three subjects: economics, science and technology, and management. Only if we study these well will we be able to carry out socialist modernization rapidly and efficiently. We should learn in different ways—through practice, from books and from the experience, both positive and negative, of others as well as our own. Conservatism and book worship should be overcome. The several hundred members and alternate members of the Central Committee and the thousands of senior cadres at the central and local levels should take the lead in making an in-depth study of modern economic development.

So long as we unite as one, work in concert, emancipate our minds, use our heads and try to learn what we did not know before, there is no doubt that we will be able to quicken the pace of our new Long March. Under the leadership of the Central Committee and the State Council, let us advance courageously to change the backward condition of our country and turn it into a modern and powerful socialist state.

24.2 AND 24.3 WEI JINGSHENG: "THE FIFTH MODERNIZATION"

On December 5, 1978, a former Red Guard named Wei Jingsheng posted a big-character poster on Democracy Wall, calling for a "Fifth Modernization." For several weeks, crowds had gathered along a main thoroughfare to the west of the Forbidden City, to read wall posters, append comments to them, and exchange copies of underground journals. Initially, the poems and essays posted on Democracy Wall expressed thinly veiled criticisms of the Communist Party, as well as support for Deng Xiaoping's reform program. Wei's bold declaration intensified the conversation and broached the line of tolerable dissent. Before his arrest in March 1979, Wei published other sharply critical essays, in which he assailed Deng by name and questioned the CCP's commitment to reform.

During Wei Jingsheng's trial in November 1979, a fellow Democracy Wall activist named Liu Qing smuggled a tape recorder into the proceedings and published the transcript, to sensational effect. For this, Liu was arrested and imprisoned for more than ten years, frequently in solitary confinement. His account of taping the trial and the aftermath are excerpted from his prison memoirs.

24.2 *"The Fifth Modernization"*

Newspapers and television no longer assail us with deafening praise for the dictatorship of the proletariat and class struggle. This is in part because these were once the magical incantations of the now-overthrown Gang of Four. But more importantly, it's because the masses have grown absolutely sick of hearing these worn-out phrases and will never be duped by them again.

The laws of history tell us that only when the old is gone can the new take its place. Now that the old is gone, the people have been anxiously waiting to see what the new will bring; gods never betray the faithful, they thought. But what they've long awaited is none other than a grandiose promise called the Four Modernizations. Our wise leader, Chairman Hua Guofeng, along with Vice Chairman Deng Xiaoping, whom many consider even wiser and grander, have finally crushed the Gang of Four. There is now the possibility that those brave souls whose blood flowed over Tiananmen Square might have their dreams of democracy and prosperity realized.

After the arrest of the Gang of Four, the people eagerly hoped that Vice Chairman Deng Xiaoping, who might possibly "restore capitalism," would rise up again like a magnificent banner. Finally, he did regain his position in the central leadership. How excited the people felt! How inspired they were! But alas, the old political system so despised by the people remains unchanged, and the democracy and freedom they longed for has not even been mentioned. Their living conditions remain the same and "increased wages" have far from kept up with the rapid rise in prices. There was talk of "restoring capitalism" and instituting a bonus system, but after careful consideration, it was determined that such measures would simply be "invisible whips" of the type once cursed by our Marxist forefathers as "the greatest form of worker exploitation."

There are reports confirming that "deceptive policies" will no longer be implemented and that the people will no longer follow a "great helmsman." Instead, "wise leaders" will lead them to "catch up with and surpass the most advanced nations of the world" such as Britain, the United States, Japan, and Yugoslavia(!). It's no longer fashionable to take part in the revolution, a college education will take you further in the world. Cries of "class struggle" no longer need fill people's ears, the Four Modernizations will take care of everything. Of course, in order to realize this beautiful dream, we must still follow the guiding central spirit passed down from the "April Fifth Society" as well as the guidance and direction of a unified leadership.

There are two ancient Chinese sayings that go: "Sketch cakes to allay your hunger" and "Think of plums to quench your thirst." People of ancient times had such wit and sarcasm, and they've even been said to have progressed since then. So now no one would ever actually consider doing such ridiculous things, would they?

Well, not only did some consider doing such things, they actually did.

For decades, the Chinese people faithfully followed the Great Helmsman while he used "Communist idealism" to sketch cakes and offered up the Great Leap Forward and the Three Red Banners as thirst-quenching plums. People tightened their belts and forged ahead undaunted. Thirty years flew by and the experience taught them one lesson: For three decades we've been acting like monkeys grabbing for the moon's reflection in a lake—no wonder we've come up empty-handed! Therefore, when Vice Chairman Deng called for "practicality," the people's enthusiasm surged forth like a rolling tide and swept him back into power. Everyone expected him to employ the maxim "Seek truth from facts" to review the past and lead the people toward a promising future.

But once again there are people warning us that Marxist–Leninist–Mao Zedong Thought is the foundation of all things, even speech; that Chairman Mao was the "great savior" of the people; and that "without the Communist Party, there would be no new China" actually means "without Chairman Mao, there would be no new China." Official notices will clear things up for anyone who refuses to believe this. There are even those who seek to remind us that Chinese people need a dictator; if he is even more dictatorial than the emperors of old, this only proves his greatness. The Chinese people don't need democracy, they say, for unless it is a "democracy under centralized leadership," it isn't worth a cent. Whether you believe it or not is up to you, but there are plenty of empty prison cells waiting for you if you don't.

But now someone has provided us with a way out: Take the Four Modernizations as your guiding principle; forge ahead with stability and unity; and bravely serve the revolution like a faithful old ox and you will reach your paradise—the prosperity of Communism and the Four Modernizations. And these kind-hearted someones have warned us that if we are confused, we must undertake a serious and thorough study of Marxist–Leninist–Mao Zedong Thought! If you're still confused, it's because you don't understand, and not understanding only reflects just how profound the theory is! Don't be disobedient or the leadership of your work unit will be uncompromising! And so on and so on.

I urge everyone to stop believing such political swindlers. When we all know that we are going to be tricked, why don't we trust ourselves instead? The Cultural Revolution has tempered us and we are no longer so ignorant. Let us investigate for ourselves what should be done!

1. WHY DEMOCRACY?

People have discussed this question for centuries. And now those who voice their opinions at Democracy Wall have carried out a thorough analysis and shown just how much better democracy is than autocracy.

"People are the masters of history." Is this fact or merely empty talk? It is both fact and empty talk. It is fact that without the effort and participation of the people there can be no history. No "great helmsman" or "wise leader" could exist, let alone any history be created. From this we can see that the slogan should be "Without the new Chinese people, there would be no new China," not "Without Chairman Mao, there would be no new China." It's understandable that Vice Chairman Deng is grateful to Chairman Mao for saving his life, but why is he so ungrateful to all of those whose "outcries" propelled him back into power? Is it reasonable for him to say to them: "You must not criticize Chairman Mao, because he saved my life"? From this we can see that phrases like "people are the masters of history" are nothing but empty talk. Such words become hollow when people are unable to choose their own destiny by majority will, or when their achievements are credited to others, or when their rights are stripped away and woven into the crowns of others. What kind of "masters" are these? It would be more appropriate to call them docile slaves. Our history books tell us that the people are the masters and creators of everything, but in reality they are more like faithful servants standing at attention and waiting to be "led" by leaders who swell like yeasted bread dough.

The people should have democracy. When they call for democracy they are demanding nothing more than that which is inherently theirs. Whoever refuses to return democracy to them is a shameless thief more despicable than any capitalist who robs the workers of the wealth earned with their own sweat and blood.

Do the people have democracy now? No! Don't the people want to be the masters of their own destiny? Of course they do! That is precisely why the Communist Party defeated the Nationalists. But what became of all their promises once victory was achieved? Once they began championing a dictatorship of the proletariat instead of a people's democratic dictatorship, even the "democracy" still enjoyed by a tenth of a millionth of the population was displaced by the individual dictatorship of the "great leader." Even Peng Dehuai was denounced for following the orders of the "great leader" and airing complaints.

A new promise was made: If a leader is great, then blind faith in him will bring greater happiness to the people than democracy. Half forced, half willingly, people have continued to believe in this promise right up until the present. But are they any happier? No. They are more miserable and more backward. Why, then, are things the way they are? This is the first question the people must consider. What should be done now? This is the second. At present, there is absolutely no need to assess the achievements and failures of Mao Zedong. When Mao himself suggested this be done, it was only out of self-defense. Instead, the people should be asking themselves whether without the dictatorship of Mao Zedong China would have fallen into its current state. Are the Chinese people stupid? Are they lazy? Do they not want to live more prosperous lives? Or are they unruly by nature? Quite the opposite. How, then, did things get the way they are? The answer is obvious: The Chinese people should not have followed the path they did. Why, then, did they follow this path? Was it because a self-glorifying dictator led them down it? The truth is, even if people had refused to follow this path, they would still have been crushed by the dictatorship. And when no one could hear any other alternative, the people felt that this was the one and only path to take. Is this not deceit? Is there any merit in this at all?

What path was taken? It's often called the "socialist road." According to the definition formulated by our Marxist forefathers, the premise of socialism is that the masses, or what is called the proletariat, are the masters of everything. But let me ask the Chinese workers and peasants: Aside from the few coins you receive each month to feed yourselves with, what are you the masters of? And what do you master? It's pitiful to say it, but the truth is, you are mastered by others, even down to your own marriages!

Socialism guarantees that the producer will receive the surplus fruits of his labor after he has fulfilled his duty to society. But is there any limit to the amount of this duty? Are you getting anything more than the meager wage necessary to sustain your productive labor? Can socialism guarantee the right of every citizen to receive an education, to make full use of his abilities, and so forth? We can observe none of these things in our daily lives. We see only "the dictatorship of the proletariat" and "a variation of Russian autocracy"—that is, Chinese-style socialist autocracy. Is this the kind of socialist road the people need? Does dictatorship, therefore, amount to the people's happiness? Is this the socialist road Marx described and the people aspired to? Obviously not. Then what is it? As ridiculous as it may sound, it actually resembles the feudal socialism referred to in *The Communist Manifesto* as feudal monarchy under a socialist cloak. It's said that the Soviet Union has been elevated to socialist imperialism from socialist feudalism. Must the Chinese people follow the same path?

People have suggested that we settle all our old accounts by blaming them all on the fascist dictatorship of feudal socialism. I completely agree with this because there is no question of right or wrong. In passing, I would like to point out that the correct name for the notorious German fascism is "national socialism." It too had an autocratic tyrant; it too ordered people to tighten their belts; and it too deceived the people with the words: "You are a great people." Most importantly, it too stamped out even the most rudimentary forms of democracy, for it fully recognized that democracy was its most formidable and irrepressible enemy. On this basis, Stalin and Hitler shook hands and signed the German-Soviet Pact whereby a socialist state and a national-socialist state toasted the partition of Poland while the peoples of both countries suffered slavery and poverty. Must we go on suffering from this kind of slavery and poverty? If not, then democracy is our only choice. In other words, if we want to modernize our economy, sciences, military, and other areas, then we must first modernize our people and our society.

II. THE FIFTH MODERNIZATION: WHAT KIND OF DEMOCRACY DO WE WANT?

I would like to ask everyone: What do we want modernization for? Many might still feel that the times depicted in *Dream of the Red Chamber* were just fine. One could do some reading, dabble in poetry, cavort with women, and be fed and clothed effortlessly. These days such a person might even go to see foreign movies as well—what a godlike existence! It's not bad to live like a god, but such a life-style remains irrelevant to ordinary people. They want simply to have the chance to enjoy a happy life, or at least one that is no less than what people enjoy in other countries. A prosperity that all members of society can enjoy equally will only be achieved by raising the level of social productivity. This is quite obvious, but some people have completely overlooked one important point: When social productivity increases, will the people be able to enjoy prosperous lives? The problems of allocation, distribution, and exploitation still remain.

In the decades since Liberation, people have tightened their belts and worked hard to produce a great deal of wealth. But where has it all gone? Some say it's gone to plump up small-scale autocratic regimes like Vietnam, while others say it's been used to fatten the "new bourgeois elements" like Lin Biao and Jiang Qing. Both are correct, but the bottom line is, none of it has trickled down into the hands of the working people of China. If powerful political swindlers, both big and small, have not squandered the wealth themselves, then they have given it to scoundrels in Vietnam and Albania who cherish ideals similar to their own. Shortly before his death, Mao Zedong got upset when his old lady asked him for several thousand yuan, but did anyone ever know him to feel any pain as he threw away tens of billions of yuan earned with the sweat and blood of the Chinese people? And this was all done while the Chinese people were building socialism by tightening their belts and begging on the streets for food. Why, then, can't all those people who keep running to Democracy Wall to praise Mao Zedong open their eyes and see this? Could it be that they are deliberately blind to it? If they genuinely can't see it, I would ask them all to use the time they spend writing wall posters to go over to Beijing or Yongdingmen Train Station, or to any street in the city, and ask those country folk arriving from the provinces whether begging for food is such a rare occurrence where they come from. I can also bet that they aren't that willing to give away their snow-white rice to aid "friends in the Third World"! But does their opinion matter? The sad thing is that in our people's republic all real power is in the hands of those people who live like gods and have nothing better to do after stuffing their faces than to read novels and write poetry. Are not the people completely justified in seizing power from the hands of such overlords?

What is democracy? True democracy means placing all power in the hands of the working people. Are working people unable to manage state power? Yugoslavia has taken this route and proven to us that people have no need for dictators, whether big or small; they can take care of things much better themselves.

What is true democracy? It is when the people, acting on their own will, have the right to choose representatives to manage affairs on the people's behalf and in accordance with the will and interests of the people. This alone can be called democracy. Furthermore, the people must have the power to replace these representatives at any time in order to keep them from abusing their powers to oppress the people. Is this actually possible? The citizens of Europe and the United States enjoy precisely this kind of democracy and can run people like Nixon, de Gaulle, and Tanaka out of office when they wish and can even reinstate them if they so desire. No one can interfere with their democratic rights. In China, however, if a person even comments on the "great helmsman" or the "Great Man peerless in history," Mao Zedong, who is already dead, the mighty prison gates and all kinds of unimaginable misfortunes await him. If we compare the socialist system of "centralized democracy" with the "exploiting class democracy" of capitalism, the difference is as clear as night and day.

Will the country sink into chaos and anarchy if the people achieve democracy? On the contrary, have not the scandals exposed in the newspapers recently shown that it is precisely due to an absence of democracy that the dictators, large and small, have caused chaos and anarchy? The maintenance of democratic order is an internal problem that the people themselves must solve. It is not something that the privileged overlords need concern themselves with. Besides, they are not really concerned with democracy for the people, but use this as a pretext to deny the people of their democratic rights. Of course, internal problems cannot be solved overnight but must be constantly addressed as part of a long-term process. Mistakes and shortcomings will be inevitable, but these are for us to worry about. This is infinitely better than facing abusive overlords against whom we have no means of redress. Those who worry that democracy will lead to anarchy and chaos are just like those who, following the overthrow of the Qing dynasty, worried that without an emperor, the country would fall into chaos. Their decision was to patiently suffer oppression because they feared that without the weight of oppression, their spines might completely collapse!

To such people, I would like to say, with all due respect: We want to be the masters of our own destiny. We need no gods or emperors and we don't believe in saviors of any kind. We want to be masters of our universe; we do not want to serve as mere tools of dictators with personal ambitions for carrying out modernization. We want to modernize the lives of the people. Democracy, freedom, and happiness for all are our sole objectives in carrying out modernization. Without this "Fifth Modernization," all other modernizations are nothing but a new lie.

Comrades, I appeal to you: Let us rally together under the banner of democracy. Do not be fooled again by dictators who talk of "stability and unity." Fascist totalitarianism can bring us nothing but disaster. Harbor no more illusions; democracy is our only hope. Abandon our democratic rights and we shackle ourselves again. Let us have confidence in our own strength! We are the creators of human history. Banish all self-proclaimed leaders and teachers, for they have already cheated the people of their most valuable rights for decades.

I firmly believe that production will flourish more when controlled by the people themselves because the workers will be producing for their own benefit. Life will improve because the workers' interests will be the primary goal. Society will be more just because all power will be exercised by the people as a whole through democratic means.

I don't believe that all of this will be handed to the people effortlessly by some great savior. I also refuse to believe that China will abandon the goals of democracy, freedom, and happiness because of the many difficulties it will surely encounter along the way. As long as people clearly identify their goal and realistically assess the obstacles before them, then surely they will trample any pests that might try to bar their way.

III. MARCHING TOWARD MODERNIZATION: DEMOCRACY IN PRACTICE

To achieve modernization, the Chinese people must first put democracy into practice and modernize China's social system. Democracy is not merely an inevitable stage of social development as Lenin claimed. In addition to being the result of productive forces and productive relations having developed to a certain stage, democracy is also the very condition that allows for the existence of such development to reach beyond this stage. Without democracy, society will become stagnant and economic growth will face insurmountable obstacles. Judging from history, therefore, a democratic social system is the premise and precondition for all development, or what we can also call modernization. Without this precondition, not only is further development impossible, but even preserving the level of development already attained would be very difficult. The experience of our great nation over the past three decades is the best evidence for this.

Why must human history follow a path toward development, or modernization? It is because humans need all of the tangible advantages that development can provide them. These advantages then enable them to achieve their foremost goal in the pursuit of happiness: freedom. Democracy is the greatest freedom ever known to man. Therefore, isn't it quite apparent why the goal of all recent human struggles has been democracy?

Why have all the reactionaries in modern history united under a common banner against democracy? It is because democracy gives their enemy—the common people—everything, and provides them—the oppressors—no weapons with which to oppose the people. The greatest reactionaries are always the greatest opponents of democracy. The histories of Germany, the Soviet Union, and "New China" make this very clear and show that these reactionaries are also the most formidable and dangerous enemies of social peace and prosperity. The more recent histories of these countries make it apparent that all the struggles of the people for prosperity and of society for development are ultimately directed against the enemies of democracy—the dictatorial fascists. When democracy defeats dictatorship, it always brings with it the most favorable conditions for accelerating social development. The history of the United States offers the most convincing evidence of this.

The success of any struggle by the people for happiness, peace, and prosperity is contingent upon the quest for democracy. The success of all struggles by the people against oppression and exploitation depends upon achieving democracy. Let us throw ourselves completely into the struggle for democracy! Only through democracy can the people obtain everything. All illusions of undemocratic means are hopeless. All forms of dictatorship and totalitarianism are the most immediate and dangerous enemies of the people.

Will our enemies let us implement democracy? Of course not. They will stop at nothing to hinder the progress of democracy. Deception and trickery are the most effective means they have. All dictatorial fascists tell their people: Your situation is truly the best in the entire world.

Does democracy come about naturally when society reaches a certain stage? Absolutely not. A high price is paid for every tiny victory; even coming to a recognition of this fact will cost blood and sacrifice. The enemies of democracy have always deceived their people by saying that just as democracy is inevitable, it is doomed, and, therefore, it is not worth wasting energy to fight for.

But let us look at the real history, not that fabricated by the hired hacks of the "socialist government." Every small branch or twig of true and valuable democracy is stained with the blood of martyrs and tyrants, and every step taken toward democracy has been fiercely attacked by the reactionary forces. The fact that democracy has been able to surmount such obstacles proves that it is precious to the people and that it embodies their aspirations. Therefore the democratic trend cannot be stopped. The Chinese people have never feared anything. They need only recognize the direction to be taken and the forces of tyranny will no longer be invincible.

Is the struggle for democracy what the Chinese people want? The Cultural Revolution was the first time they flexed their muscles, and all the reactionary forces trembled before them. But at that time the people had no clear direction and the force of democracy was not the main thrust of their struggle. As a result, the dictators silenced most of them through bribes, deception, division, slander, or violent suppression. At the time, people also had a blind faith in all kinds of ambitious dictators, so once again they unwittingly became the tools and sacrificial lambs of tyrants and potential tyrants.

Now, twelve years later, the people have finally recognized their goal. They see clearly the real direction of their fight and have found their true leader: the banner of democracy. The Democracy Wall at Xidan has become the first battlefield in the people's fight against the reactionary forces. The struggle will be victorious— this is already a commonly accepted belief; the people will be liberated—this slogan has already taken on new significance. There may be bloodshed and sacrifice, and people may fall prey to even more sinister plots, yet the banner of democracy will never again be obscured by the evil fog of the reactionary forces. Let us unite together under this great and true banner and march toward modernization of society for the sake of the tranquillity, happiness, rights, and freedom of all the people!

24.3 Liu Qing: Sad Memories and Prospects: My Appeal to the Tribunal of the People

ON THE TAPE RECORDING OF WEI JINGSHENG'S TRIAL

On 14 October 1979, I heard that the public trial of Wei Jingsheng was to begin the following morning. I passed the news to some journals and groups in the Beijing democratic movement, and we arranged to meet at seven o'clock the next day outside the courthouse at No. 1 Zhengyi Street and to try to attend the trial. When I got there, there were already a few foreign journalists and people from the democratic movement shivering in the fresh morning wind. A notice had been pasted up on the fence in front of the court building: "Wei Jingsheng's trial has been postponed." When we asked at the reception how long the trial would be postponed, we were told that it was not yet known. We assumed from previous experience that it would be postponed indefinitely. But to our surprise we learned the same evening that the trial would begin at eight o'clock the following day (the 16th). At the same time we heard that only a handpicked audience would be allowed to attend the trial. Why so much secrecy surrounding a public trial?

The whole country was closely following what would happen to Ren Wanding (of the Human Rights League), Wei Jingsheng, Fu Yuehua, Chen Lü, Zhang Wenhe, and others arrested in March 1979. Even the world press was interested, and it seems that the United Nations and Amnesty International corresponded with the Chinese Government about them. Why this concern about the fate of a few ordinary Chinese? It was because the arrests had created a cold March wind that was blowing across the Chinese political horizon. It was not only a question of these few individuals. Even more important was what the arrests implied for the political situation as a whole in China.

Now the authorities had filled all the seats in the public auditorium where the trial was to be held (why was that necessary?), we had to work out another strategy. That same evening I visited an acquaintance who was among those officially invited. I gave him a tape recorder to record the trial.

On the evening of the 16th I got my tape recorder back and together with a few friends spent four or five hours listening to the recording. We all thought that Wei Jingsheng had been sentenced for leaking secrets, but it turned out that the court had found him guilty of two serious crimes and had sentenced him to fifteen years in jail and three years' deprivation of political rights. We were not going to take that lying down. It was an attack on democracy and in open contempt of the principles of legality that were just beginning to win ground in China. This sentence shows that in China it is still not possible to speak one's mind. Genuine freedom of conscience and expression remains something for the future. Progress in this direction will depend on the efforts of individuals who have the courage to challenge injustice. If everyone averts their eyes and pretends that nothing is happening, there can be no progress. A people that acquiesces in injustice will be destroyed, and deserves to be. But the Chinese people have thrown up individuals who even in periods of darkest dictatorship speak the truth fearlessly.

As a result of the wide interest in the case and the obvious irregularities in the judgment, Wei Jingsheng's trial became a main topic of conversation. All the democratic journals in Beijing shared the view that it was our job to publicize the truth and get more people interested in the affair. We hoped in this way to exercise some influence on those national leaders who were serious about wanting to reform the Chinese system. Duplicating the entire recording turned out to be less work than we expected, so that it was not necessary to call on the assistance of people from the various Beijing democratic journals. Moreover, it was rather dangerous to expose the authorities in this way. Later we discovered that our premonitions were justified. It was essential to involve as few people as possible in this work. I therefore took responsibility myself, and used the help of a few good friends.

MY DIFFERENCES WITH WEI JINGSHENG

From the very first time *April Fifth Forum* (Siwu luntan) hit the streets we have always openly stated our political views, and these differed in significant ways from the views expressed in Wei Jingsheng's *Explorations* (Tansuo). As editor of *April Fifth Forum*, I repeatedly debated Wei Jingsheng. When *Explorations* published Wei Jingsheng's "Democracy or a New Dictatorship" I answered with a critical article.

Although the authorities were very irritated by Wei Jingsheng's articles, to my knowledge they never once seriously countered them. At Democracy Wall some people honored Wei Jingsheng as a hero, while others cursed him. I am probably the only one who, however clumsily, actually criticized his arguments in an article. And I was not thanked for doing so. One friend told me to my face: "I'd like to tear that damned article of yours off the Wall." So some people see me as an enemy of Wei Jingsheng, and at the very least I cannot be considered his cothinker. Even my worst enemy would find it hard to put me in the same camp as Wei Jingsheng, so I was naive enough to think that I could go ahead and plead his case. The unofficial journals and groups in Beijing had set up a "joint conference" at the beginning of 1979. In it all currents were represented, and they signed a four-point agreement the most important point of which was that in the case of individual or collective arrests on the grounds of opinions or beliefs the surviving groups would come to the aid of those arrested. They would then have the duty to mobilize public opinion, to console the relatives of those arrested and to support them financially as far as possible, and to approach the authorities with requests to visit those held prisoner. The participating groups named me as contact person. The job was actually too much for me, but when Ren Wanding, Wei Jingsheng, and the others were arrested I had no choice but to carry out the four-point agreement. Although the "joint conference" no longer existed, it was up to me, the contact person, to do what had been promised.

WEI JINGSHENG ASKS ME TO DEFEND HIM

In June 1979 I heard from a court official, Luo Kejun, that Wei Jingsheng had asked whether I would defend him or find another lawyer to do so. I talked over his request with people in the law department of the University and with some other experts. At the time the penal code had not yet been promulgated, so I finally had to tell Luo Kejun:

> Since there is no penal code, there is no basis for a defense. That means that I cannot agree to Wei Jingsheng's request. But I am prepared to defend him if the court cooperates by announcing what legal provisions will be followed in this case. We request the court for permission to visit Wei Jingsheng and discuss the entire case with him, so that he can really defend himself during his trial. Finally I request the court in the name of all the democratic magazines and a great many individuals to conduct the trial in public.

Later the penal code was published, and with a few others we decided to set up a defense committee for Wei Jingsheng, Ren Wanding, and the others. Unfortunately the sentence was already passed before we had the chance to tell the court that we now agreed to Wei Jingsheng's request. Our national sickness—the inability to make decisions—had struck once again; we had acted too late. Although the trial's outcome was obvious even in advance, it was my moral duty to stand by Wei Jingsheng and not to dishonor the trust that had been placed in me. In early November, with the help of friends, I transcribed the entire trial proceedings. We carefully checked the transcript against the original, and the result can be considered a complete and literal rendering of what was said during the trial. The only exceptions are a few unintelligible words and short gaps while the tape was being changed. At first we intended to put the text up on Democracy Wall in the form of a wall poster, but later we decided to make stencils of it, and to duplicate between one and two thousand copies.

ARRESTS DURING THE SALE
OF THE TRIAL REPORT

In early November we put up a notice on Democracy Wall that the transcript of Wei Jingsheng's trial would go on sale on the 11th. That day several thousand people had gathered by the early afternoon. At the request of many of those present we began selling earlier than planned. We tried to keep order with the help of some twenty people, but things still became rather chaotic. Potential buyers saw that the edition was limited and everyone began to press forward to make sure of getting a copy. While I was busy trying to restore order a friend tugged at my sleeve and told me that he had some important news for me. I followed him to a quieter place and then he told me that the security police were on their way and would arrive within half an hour. I hurried back but it was already too late. The crowd had grown so thick that I could no longer reach the sales point.

Someone told me that there had been arrests and that the publication had been confiscated. This person took me to one side and I saw a lorry packed with people and a sort of ambulance which began to drive off with its siren on.

Later I heard what had happened after my departure. Suddenly the police had appeared on the scene. Some said that there were between seventy and eighty, others spoke of a hundred. The street in front of Democracy Wall was sealed off and some of the agents forced their way into the crowd, seized the transcripts, and arrested one seller, who was taken off in handcuffs. A few bystanders who protested at these arrests were also shackled hand and foot and put into a police vehicle. Altogether some four or five people were said to have been arrested. [Later Liu Qing was himself arrested when he tried to get these people released from custody.]

24.4 HE SHIGUANG: "ON A VILLAGE MARKET STREET," AUGUST 1980

The Four Modernizations had an immediate impact on the rural economy and the life of the peasantry. The decisions of the Third Plenum allowing profit-making enterprises marked a return to the partial privatization experiments of the 1950s and early 1960s, and were greeted with enthusiasm throughout the countryside.

In both rural and urban areas, however, the corruption and nepotism of the Party elite, although diminished, remained a central feature of everyday life. In many places, those who had used the upheaval of the Cultural Revolution to enhance their own power remained in positions of authority. Tensions persisted between people, living as neighbors and working as colleagues, whose relationships had been poisoned by violence and recriminations in the tumultuous movements of the past decades.

He Shiguang's short story "On a Village Market Street" captures this facet of the process of modernization. The protagonist Uncle Feng, feeling emboldened by the government's new economic polices, speaks out against those who have tormented him in the past. In a startling reversal, the formerly invincible Mrs. Luo becomes the laughingstock of the entire village. While the story ends on a rather syrupy note of optimism, it both reflects the hopeful mood of the early reform period and shows how political skepticism had become part of everyday life.

On our small market street in Pear Blossom village in the Wumeng Mountains, Uncle Feng, a tall man over forty, is a notorious drunkard and good-for-nothing farm hand. Only the devil knows how he manages to survive day after day, all these years. But no one cares. Just now, who knows why, he has been brought here. Grinning in embarrassment, he stands between two women as he waits for questions from the brigade Party Secretary. He is to testify as witness of a quarrel between the women and suddenly has an air of importance. It seems so funny!

"Uncle Feng, just a little while ago, at breakfast time—that's to say, at primary school morning break time—were you going along the market street with your ox?" Secretary Cao Fugui asks him.

The incident took place on the market street and so of course either Secretary Cao or Secretary Song should act as the arbitrator. But everyone here knows that Secretary Cao is on Mrs. Luo's side. In appearance this Secretary looks not much older or different from Uncle Feng. Cao also seems like just another farm hand wearing a loose shirt and a bandana wrapped around his head. But don't be fooled by appearances; he's a very wily character! Pear Blossom village has only this one street, so short you can see it all in a glance, and living here is like being part of a big clan household. Everyone knows all there is to know about everyone else.

Uncle Feng narrows his eyes and scratches his tousled hair. He giggles in an ingratiating way and replies:

"We all live on this street, why fuss?"

The bystanders burst into laughter. It's the leisurely time just after breakfast and nearly half the people living on the street have gathered here. Just as a little stone can disturb quiet reflections on the surface of a pond, so any small matter on this market street arouses the concern of everyone. Partly that's because the street is so small that anything happening here will probably pull you in and partly it's just because there's too little to see on the street. Uncle Feng's just playing tricks, right? He can't be a good witness!

"Well, did you go by or not? Speak up."

"You mean. . . . breakfast?"

"At the time of the morning break for breakfast!"

"Pulling my ox?"

"Yes!"

Uncle Feng scratches his head again and starts laughing. He opens his wide mouth and feigns shyness. This evokes another guffaw from the crowd.

Mrs. Luo, the short, fat woman standing by his side, sneers at the thin woman standing opposite her and says:

"Uncle Feng, everyone insists that you were there. You saw everything. Could you have seen a kid belonging to the Luo family acting so low class he wanted something not worth two cents? Did he really need to be beaten. . . ."

When this woman opens her mouth, Uncle Feng's liveliness is dampened. As memories flood back, people feel stifled. In recent years, when people hear her voice, they feel as depressed and desolate as a harvested cornfield with broken stalks left soaked by the rain. To look at this woman you would think she was grimy and ridiculous, right? About thirty, it looks like she never washes her hair or face, and her two wadded flannel shirts are spotted with grease. Elsewhere she would be laughable. But here in Pear Blossom village, she appears to be an important woman because her husband is the accountant of the food station on the street and also the butcher. No one believes that the thin woman or her child would dare provoke the Luo family. Her man is Big Ren, the honest but drab schoolteacher who has been teaching at the village primary school for many years. How can they measure up to the Luo family? Everyone has just lived through some bleak years and knows how differently honor and humiliation have been doled out to these two women on this little street. Although the past now seems as bizarre as a nightmare, the reality of it is like a stone. Everyone knows that Mrs. Luo is tormenting Big Ren's woman and they feel worried.

"Please say something fair, Uncle Feng! My kid really didn't. . . ."

Big Ren's woman watches Uncle Feng in a timid, imploring way. This ill-fated woman is married to a teacher and has no clout on this street. Her clothing, like her house standing forlornly at the corner, always needs mending. Her face is so shriveled that people only see her pointed chin and a pair of large, lusterless eyes. She has always been weak and submissive and, if it was not necessary, she would have never involved Uncle Feng. . . .

As for Uncle Feng, he pulls his head lower and lower and still says nothing. Oh, Uncle Feng is really being crushed and everyone feels sorry for him.

Mrs. Luo keeps swearing. This evil hen demon puts her hands on her hips, stamps the ground, and then slaps her thighs. She purses her lips and spits repeatedly at the ground in front of Uncle Feng.

"If I were you, Uncle Feng," Secretary Cao speaks again, "I would 'seek the truth from facts' and speak out! It has been four years since we smashed the Gang of Four. Everyone should 'seek truth from facts'!"

Goaded by this continuous persuasion, Uncle Feng finally stands up.

"That's right," the Secretary says, "it's not your business anyway."

Uncle Feng nods his head. Dragging his feet, he walks back and seems to be on the verge of crying. He looks very strange. The saying goes that "you go against your conscience when you cannot do otherwise"; will he really harm the family of the poor and timid teacher?

"Secretary Cao," his voice quivers in a strange way, "you . . . want me to speak out?"

"Yes, we have been waiting for you for a long time."

Uncle Feng nods his head again and stands still.

Feeling quite uncomfortable and facing the crowd, he speaks slowly: "As everyone knows, I'm a nobody on this street. . . . I'm like a dog here. . . . I am so poor I can't help it! . . . Everyone has seen it, I have lost all face. . . ."

What's happening to him? People feel strange, they're silent and watch him.

"Last year," he continues, "if you add up the millet and corn combined, I got several hundred catties more than before. I figure that my family will have food until the Dragon Boat festival. I also have several dozen catties of glutinous millet and my woman has said that this year we could wrap a few millet patties with bamboo leaves for the kids. By that time the potatoes will be ready. . . . For our vegetable seed garden, the government promises to sell some rice as a reward. In our private plots there is some wheat to harvest. . . . Last year we insisted that we should pull water into the wet fields to plant fast growing crops. The fields are full of water and so the responsibility falls on individuals and it is easy to make up the fields and transplant rice seedlings. . . . As long as the seedlings can be planted, there will be millet and corn to pick in the future. . . ."

Mrs. Luo interrupts him: "You're going from the southern mountains to the northern sea; how far are you going to go?"

All of a sudden Uncle Feng whirls around. He stamps his feet, and, with both eyes turning red, roars with all his might: "Secretary Cao, it's up to you whether I get my grain ration. But I don't care! This year, even without it, I can still survive."

The people have never seen Uncle Feng so ferocious. Everyone is dumbfounded. His broad face is suddenly sunken and steely gray and he grinds his teeth. He is truly terrifying. "Do I want to have a few ounces of meat?" He pounds his chest and replies: "I do! What about it? I'll buy it. After I sell my vegetable seed, I'll buy a few catties to feed my kids but I promise not to buy it from you, Luo. Anyway, country people can now slaughter their own pigs and sell them. It's no longer a monopoly for your food station. It's open. It's only a few dimes more and you can even choose between the lean and fatty meat as you like. . . . Let me tell you, now it's different than it was before. Whoever refuses to sell this or that or whoever hides this under the counter or that behind the door can't even fulfill his sales quota. This year, your old dad . . ."

"Uncle Feng! You better watch your mouth. Whose old dad are you?"

"What can you do? Do you dare to touch me? If you want to have a fight, try it today! For the past few years, your old dad has been neither a man nor a ghost! But I've had enough! It's fortunate that in these two years the government has untied us farmers' hands and feet. Who dares curse me? I won't be polite today!"

Secretary Cao cuts in: "Now then, Uncle Feng—"

Uncle Feng immediately interrupts him. "Don't give me this! Pack up your nasty tricks and beat it! Send me to the correction camp? Send me to do irrigation work on New Year's eve? Forget it! You can't do it anymore. . . . Be a little official; if you're an official for ten years then I won't steal a cow for ten years. I can make a living; the government allows it this time. Let's see what you can do to me."

"You, you . . ."

"You what? Didn't you ask me to come to be a witness? I was there all the time. You can't say only the Luo kid was raised by human beings. He took something from Big Ren's kid. When people asked him to give it back he got nasty and cursed everybody out. *Who* beat him? The Ren kid didn't fight back or curse. Now am I speaking clearly?"

All of this comes so suddenly that everyone is stunned. Then laughter bursts from the crowd like thunder on a dry day and shakes the whole street. The thunder changes into the sound of noisy discussions which follow like the patter of rain on the market street. To use another figure of speech, it's like the dragon dance on the Lantern Festival that brings the happy sound of firecrackers to the little market street. All the time this fellow Uncle Feng was squatting there he was figuring this out! We always misunderstood him in the past. . . .

Now he turns around and speaks solemnly to Big Ren's woman: "Tell Teacher Ren, your kid didn't hit Luo. I saw it with my own eyes. We farm hands are not like those bastards . . ."

Mrs. Luo screeches: "All right, Uncle Feng, just you remember . . ."

But the grating sound of her voice is lost in the raucous laughter of the crowd. Only Uncle Feng's voice is clear and loud:

"As long as the government's policy does not go back to what it was in the past few years and so long as it doesn't change back and forth against us farm hands, with my strength and energy, what do I have to fear?"

And so, tramping off with his big feet, saying he is busy, Uncle Feng walks away. Watching his broad-shouldered back, the people begin to remember that since last year Uncle Feng has changed. He drinks less and works harder. Didn't he buy that big pair of Liberation sneakers last winter? It's said that "when food is at hand, the heart is not anxious; with two feet on solid ground, one is truly happy." When he put on those Liberation sneakers, he liberated himself. The unfair days of the past are like a mist now scattering day by day. On this market street, sunshine is piercing through the gray fog. Things are changing for the better and the backbones of the farm hands are straightening. This most ordinary quarrel has delighted the people of Pear Blossom village. No matter how Mrs. Luo fusses, they laugh and disperse, feeling happy. The spring is certainly a busy season; there is lots to be done and the whole group, men and women, all walk rapidly away.

CHAPTER 25

Levels of Power

25.1 AND 25.2 THE ONE-CHILD POLICY

The attempt to check the alarming rate of population growth through the one-child policy transformed the social fabric of Chinese society in the 1980s. The 1982 constitution enshrined the obligation to follow the state's family planning policy as a duty of citizens. Although many exceptions were allowed (to rural residents and national minority groups, among others), family planning cadres were tasked with enforcing birth quotas and improving the "quality" of the population through "eugenic" practices. In the countryside, the government mandate to marry later and have fewer children (usually two) clashed against enduring preferences for large families and sons. With decollectivization and the implementation of the household responsibility system, the need for agricultural labor also compelled many to defy the birth control policy.

In the following "Open Letter" sent to the members of the Communist Party in 1980, the Central Committee reiterated the critical importance of family planning to the nation's modernization drive, urging all Party members to take responsibility for population control. At the same time, the government's instructions acknowledged that many problems were in the making: coercive implementation, an aging workforce, gender inequality, and the future fate of a society full of singletons. As the 1984 Work Report describes in detail, the implementation of the policy at the grassroots level was exceedingly complicated, and many of the forecasted problems did indeed become reality.

25.1 Open Letter of the Central Committee of the Communist Party of China to the General Membership of the Communist Party and the Membership of the Chinese Communist Youth League on the Problem of Controlling Population Growth in Our Country, September 25, 1980

Comrade Members of the Communist Party of China and the Chinese Communist Youth League:

To strive for the goal of holding the total population in our country under 1.2 billion by the end of the century, the State Council has made an appeal to the people of the entire country to promote the policy of each couple having only one child. This is a major measure that has significant bearing on the speed and future of the construction of the Four Modernizations, on the health and happiness of all future generations, and is in line with both the long-term future interests and the immediate interests of the people of the country as a whole. The Central Committee now calls on all Communist party members and all Chinese Communist Youth League members, and especially the cadres at all levels, to take the lead in responding to the State Council's appeal with positive and practical action, and to carry out enthusiastically and responsibly the necessary propaganda and education among the broad masses with patience and care.

Since the founding of the People's Republic, owing to improvements in public health work and in the people's living conditions, the mortality rate in our country, and especially the infant mortality rate, has been greatly reduced and life expectancy has been extended significantly. On the other hand, however, the birth rate has not been appropriately controlled for a long time in this country, which has led to a far too rapid increase in the overall population. In the 109 years from 1840 to 1949, in the period of Old China, the population of the country increased only by 130 million. In contrast, in the thirty-odd years after the founding of the People's Republic of China, more than 600 million people were born; taking into consideration the attrition by deaths in the same period, the net increase in the population is more than 430 million people. With the population growing at such a tremendous rate, we have come to encounter increasingly severe problems in such areas as feeding the entire people, clothing them, housing them, providing adequate transportation, education, public health care, and employment for our people. This makes it difficult for the country as a whole to transform its state of poverty and backwardness over a short time. In particular, the most severe period was the time from 1963 to 1970, when the population increase was most rapid. At the moment, the category of people who are below the age of thirty make up approximately 65 percent of the entire population. From here on out, there will be, on average, more than 20 million people entering the age of marriage and childbearing each year. Unless we start now to implement and promote a general policy of having each married couple bear only one child, and thus hope to control and arrest the growth of the population, within the next thirty to forty years, and especially in the next twenty to thirty years, the total population in our country, based on the current rate of an average of 2.2 children per couple, will reach the 1.3 billion mark in twenty years, and exceed the 1.5 billion mark in forty years. This would greatly increase the difficulty for us to realize the goals of the Four Modernizations, and create a very severe situation in which we could hardly expect to make any appreciable improvement in the lives of the people at large.

The most effective way to resolve this problem would be for all of us to carry out the appeal of the State Council, and for every couple in the country to have no more than one child.

For the individual family or household, the way to take account of this is very clear—if the population of the household is increased, and before the new members could make a living for themselves, more money would have to be spent on them by the household, more food would be consumed, and this would affect the improvement of family life. Even after the new family members have reached the age when they could make a living, while on the one hand they would indeed be making contributions to society, on the other hand, they would also be consuming the material resources produced by the society. As far as the country as a whole is concerned, as long as the rate of labor productivity in industry and agriculture is still rather low, and as long as we have not reached a state of abundance in the production of material resources, the rate of population growth will directly affect the accumulation of the capital funds necessary for the construction of modernization. A much too rapid growth of population will mean a reduction in the accumulation of capital funds, while a slowdown in population growth could mean an increase in the accumulation of capital funds. With the growth of the population, in addition to the fact that the families and households would need to expend an increased amount of money to take care of the children, in order to resolve the problems of their education and employment and so on, the state would also need to increase its budget for education, and its investment in equipment and in the society's public facilities, and so on. Consider this: if we could save up the money expended in these areas, and spend it on developing the economy and the cultural and educational enterprises, what an impact that would have!

If the population grows at an excessive pace, it would be very difficult to improve people's standards of living. Consider the food supply, for example. To ensure the adequacy of the food rations and the industrial-use grain and other types of grain usage in the cities and in the countryside at large, in the future we would have to expect the average per capita per annum grain use to reach at least 800 catties. At that rate, if we gave birth to an additional 100 million people, we would have to produce an additional 80 billion catties of grain. Right now, we have approximately an average of 2 *mou* of arable land per capita; if the population increases to 1.3 billion, the per capita arable land acreage would decrease to less than 2 *mou*. Under current conditions, it would be a matter of significant difficulty to produce an average of 800 catties of grain for each person in the country and also produce an adequate amount of cash crops, on the basis of such a small amount of land. Moreover, in addition to increasing the difficulties in educational and employment opportunities, an overly rapid increase in the population will also increase excessively the consumption of natural resources, such as energy resources, water, and forests. It will also aggravate the pollution of the environment and severely worsen the conditions for production and the people's living environment, making it difficult to improve these in the long run.

In that case, can the appeal of having each couple bear only one child be realized? We believe that as long as we all pull together and strive to reach this goal with our common efforts, it is possible for us to attain this objective. From 1971 to 1979, we made a strong effort to control the population increase in our country, and in those nine years, by accumulation, we gave birth to 56 million fewer babies, so to speak. Since 1979, millions of young married couples in our country have responded positively to the appeal of the Party and volunteered to give birth to only one child. In 1979 alone, 10 million fewer babies were born as compared to 1970. The facts show that our people are reasonable and have a concern for the bigger picture; they are able to understand the state's difficulty and also care about their children and later generations.

Some comrades are worried that if each couple gave birth to only one child, other new types of problems would appear in the future: For instance, a general aging of the population as a whole in terms of average age, shortage of labor, a greater number of males than females, an increase in the number of old people being taken care of by each young couple, and so on. Some of these issues come out of a misunderstanding of the situation and the policy; others are simply resolvable.

The phenomenon of the "aging" or, as some people call it, "graying" of the population is not likely to appear within this century. This is because at this time, about half of the total population of the country is under the age of twenty-one, whereas the number of old people over the age of sixty-five make up less than 5 percent of the population. Thus, the phenomenon of the graying of the population, at the very earliest, would appear in forty years' time. In the meantime, it is entirely possible for us to take measures ahead of time to prevent this phenomenon from taking place.

At this moment, there are approximately 500 million laborers in our country, and we estimate that in twenty years the number will increase to 600 million. Even when we get to the early twenty-first century, more than 10 million laborers will be added each year. After thirty years, the problem of the growth of the population, which is especially severe at the present time, will most likely have become relaxed, and we will be able to adopt a different population policy. Therefore, we really need not worry about the problem of not having a large enough labor force.

The population statistics of our country for all the years since Liberation show that in general the sex ratio of the population—that is, the ratio between the births of male children and the births of female children—remains generally equal, with just a slight margin of advantage to the number of boys. Since we promoted the one-child-per-couple policy, the related departments have conducted surveys regarding the sex ratio of first-birth babies in a number of areas, and the results show, in general, that there is only a slight advantage in the number of male babies. We should remember that when girls grow up they work in labor just like boys, they are very skillful and proficient at some special professions and areas of work, and they are even better at domestic labor. Furthermore, it is permissible for husbands to live with their wives' families. The people of New China, and especially the younger generation, absolutely must overcome the old-fashioned mentality of believing males are superior to females; if a couple gives birth to a single female child, then they must bring her up properly and well, just as they would a boy.

If we implement the one-child-per-couple policy, it is true that in forty years' time, a problem of older people not having anybody by their side to take care of them would likely appear with some families and households. This problem, in fact, is ubiquitous in many countries, and we must pay attention to it and find ways to resolve it. In the future, when production is more developed, and the people's lives improved, there ought to be continuous increase and improvement in social welfare and social insurance. We should be able to gradually move toward attaining a situation in which all the old people will be taken care of, so that the livelihood of the elderly will be guaranteed. Respecting and honoring the elderly, caring for them and taking care of their livelihood, so that they may enjoy their latter years, these are all responsibilities that children must bear. This is also a good tradition in our society. The people of our country must continue and further enhance this fine social custom. Behavior that results in not taking care of one's parents in their old age, or even tormenting and abusing parents, should be severely criticized, and those actions that violate the law in this regard must be subjected to penalty.

At the same time that we promote the one-child-per-couple policy, we should also, to an appropriate extent, emphasize the virtues of late marriages and late childbearing. The age of marriage stipulated by the Marriage Law is in fact not late. For the sake of the people's education and work, however, an appropriate later age of marrying is something we still need to promote, and even more so, we should emphasize a later age for childbearing. Let us look at the situation in this way. If young women began their childbearing at the age of twenty, within one hundred years' time, they would be giving birth to five generations of people. If they started their childbearing around the age of twenty-five instead, then in a hundred years they would only be giving birth to four generations. Therefore, late marriages and especially late childbearing have tremendous significance for reducing the amount of population increase and slowing down the rate of population growth. As for the young couples themselves, an appropriately later age of childbearing and child-rearing would also have many benefits.

In order to control population growth, the party and the government have already resolved to adopt and carry out a series of specific policies. In such aspects as arranging places for children to be admitted to nurseries, to schools, in terms of providing medical attention and care, in terms of employment recruitment, housing in the cities, and rural residence base allocations, these policies will take care of single children and their families. We must earnestly carry out the policy of equality of work and equality of wages between men and women. We must greatly expand and develop the work of scientific research in the fields of childbirth physiology and eugenics (that is, ensuring that people do not give birth to handicapped or diseased children) and birth-control technologies. We aim to train a large number of qualified and certified technical personnel to engage in the work of birth-control technology instruction, gynecological and pediatric health care and child education, and to do these well, so as to ensure the safety and quality of birth-control technology and reduce the number of births of infants that carry genetically inherited or inheritable diseases and handicaps. The related departments must swiftly take effective measures to produce high-quality birth-control medication and devices to satisfy the needs of the masses.

Family planning involves the immediate and personal interests of every household and family in this country. We must put ideological work in the first place of importance. We must maintain our efforts in carrying out the work of educating the people by persuasion patiently and carefully. Some people who indeed have practical difficulties as stipulated in the policy regulations may be allowed to give birth to two children, but not three. With regard to certain minority nationalities, we should permit a certain degree of relaxation in the policy according to the stipulations within the policy. With regard to birth-control measures, contraception should be primary, with specific methods chosen voluntarily by the masses.

To carry out the policy of one child per couple is a major undertaking of changing the customs and transforming cultural attitudes among the people. The Central Committee calls on all Communist party members and Communist Youth League members, and especially the cadres at all levels, to care about the country's future, act responsibly for the people's interests, have a sense of responsibility to our children's happiness and that of all future generations, thoroughly understand the significance and necessity of this major undertaking, and therefore set personal examples with their own actions. Party members and the cadres must take the lead in overcoming the feudal ideas in their own heads, and get rid of the erroneous concept that unless they give birth to boys they have no one to carry on their family line. As for younger comrades, they should start with themselves; as for older comrades, they must educate and urge their own children to do so. Each comrade must enthusiastically and patiently work at persuading the masses around him or her. Every comrade who is engaged in the work of family planning must become an effective propagandist, to help the masses resolve both ideological problems and practical questions. Furthermore, all comrades must be firmly resolved not to engage in coercion or commandism, or act in violation of the law and discipline, and they must also persuade other people not to do such things, so that we can fully realize the appeal of the State Council, and promote the realization of the socialist Four Modernizations.

25.2 *Report on the Conditions Regarding the Work of Family Planning, March 22, 1984*

To the Secretariat of the Central Committee of the Chinese Communist Party: We hereby submit our report on various problems related to the work of family planning, as follows:

I. THE OVERALL SITUATION REGARDING THE WORK OF FAMILY PLANNING, AND THE TASK FOR THE FUTURE

Since the Third Plenum of the CCP Eleventh Central Committee was held, the work of controlling population growth has been carried out and accomplished with relatively good results, and much achievement has been made. In comparison with the eight years from 1971 to 1978, in which the average per annum births was 21.66 million, the figure was reduced to 19.03 million in the five years from 1979 to 1983. The rate of natural population growth, therefore, has been reduced from 18.71 per thousand to 13.28 per thousand. Furthermore, it is estimated that the number of births in 1983 could be more than 2 million less than the more than 21 million of 1982, and the natural growth rate could drop from 14.49 per thousand to less than 13 per thousand between those two years.

In the last year or so, under the Central Committee's and the State Council's leadership, we have primarily concentrated on six areas of work: (1) Launching the national family planning propaganda month activities, of which the core content was to propagandize the directives regarding family planning issued by the Twelfth Congress of the party. In the latter part of the month, in accordance with the opinion suggested by Comrade Hu Qiaomu, we promoted a policy of competitive comparison and accounting at each level, so that this basic national policy of family planning would increasingly sink more deeply into people's minds. (2) Convening the nationwide on-the-spot conferences family planning work. Summing up and introducing to the public the so-called three primaries experience (that is, "propaganda/education as primary; routine work as primary; contraception as primary") of Rongcheng County of Shandong Province. (3) Having the various localities launch activities that give recognition to advanced collectives and progressive individuals, thus bringing forth a torrent of examples of model figures who speak directly to and for the problems of women of childbearing age, such as

Tan Yuling of Jilin Province and Cui Peihua of Shandong Province. (4) Forcefully promoting contraceptive surgery and technical measures for those with second or additional childbirths beyond the plan. The number of family planning operations carried out in 1983 exceeded the number for previous years. (5) Carrying out a million-person survey of the population birth rate, thus setting up examination and test points for regional population planning. (6) New developments in the areas of work in foreign affairs and scientific research.

There were also problems in family planning work. From the perspective of the party group of the State Family Planning Commission, the chief problems are the following: (1) People lack an overall understanding of the guidelines, policies, and instructions that the Central Committee has formulated with regard to family planning, and therefore do not implement these with significant effort or vigor. They have not continued to improve and concretize these guidelines, policies, and directives in accordance with practicality and reality. (2) While taking hold of population control and reducing the birth rate, they have neglected to improve their workstyle, to improve the relationship between the Party and the masses, or to consolidate unity and stability and, in allocating tasks and stipulating targets, they have neglected to give account of their work methods. (3) They have not adopted forceful and effective measures to correct the phenomena of coercion and commandism and violation of law and discipline that still exist in certain areas; the demands for carrying out sterilization have been far too extreme. (4) Not enough work has been done in surveying and studying problems in order to expose them and resolve them; people have not seriously taken hold of grassroots work; there is a lack of specific and concrete guidance; and the work is not quite solid yet. With regard to these problems, we shall try earnestly to resolve them in accordance with the Central Committee's spirit of Party rectification.

In 1984 and 1985 we must carry out the directives of the Secretariat of the Central Committee related to this subject, and, under the guidance of the Central Committee's spirit of Party rectification, unify our ideological positions, improve and implement policy, improve our workstyle and methods, raise our standards of science and technology, strengthen the grassroots work and ideological education, striving to improve our work in accordance with the principle of seeking truth from facts and proceeding from practical reality in all matters. We must strive to limit the population to less than 1.2 billion by the end of the century, to ensure that the population growth rate is kept under 13 per thousand within the Sixth Five-Year Plan period; control the size of the population while at the same time enhancing its quality.

II. UNIFY OUR IDEOLOGICAL POSITIONS, IMPROVE AND IMPLEMENT POLICY

In the work of family planning we absolutely must obey the general mission and overall objective of the Party as a whole and serve its interests. We must understand fully and correctly implement the guidelines and policies formulated by the

Central Committee, and consciously maintain political unity with the Central Committee.

The policy of childbearing. The Central Committee of the Communist Party of China and the State Council stipulate the following: "Except for those who have received permission for special circumstances, among state employed cadres and workers and urban residents, each couple may only give birth to one child." "In the countryside, the policy of having each couple give birth to one child will be universally promoted, but with regard to certain people among the masses who do indeed have practical difficulties that require of them to petition to have two children, such may be arranged in a planned way after the petition has been thoroughly examined and permission has been given. Under no circumstances will permission be given for couples to have a third child." Whether it be one child, two, or more, we must give comprehensive, total consideration to all these situations. Concrete requirements must be proposed on the basis of different circumstances in different areas and localities, and we must carry out instruction and guidance accordingly.

Single childbirth. In 1982, there were, throughout the country, more than thirty million women of childbearing age who had only one child. Most of them are between twenty and twenty-nine years of age, which is precisely the peak childbearing period. The majority of the families that had only one child reflected that they had only one child "in response to the appeal issued by the Party and because they understood the country's difficulties." It is also reflected in the statistics that quite a sizable segment among these people have not yet become ideologically enlightened. From this moment until the end of the century, on average there will be more than eleven million young couples each year entering into their marrying and childbearing years, but, on the other hand, we can only allow for an annual net increase of ten million in our population. Therefore, it remains a major task for us to take further steps to carry out propaganda and education in the countryside, especially among the masses in regions where the work of family planning has been relatively ineffective, and we must continue to promote the policy of only one child per couple.

Two or multiple childbirths. Among the infants born in 1982, those that are second children and those that are third or higher-order births make up 24.2 percent of the total. We endorse "opening a small hole to close a large hole" (referring to second or multiple births in excess of the plan). In 1982 the state stipulated that in the countryside there are ten types of circumstances under which a second child may be permitted. According to estimates, the number of couples who could give birth to a second child under these stipulations make up less than 5 percent of the number of couples that have only one child. We are giving consideration to adding a few more types of extenuating circumstances, so as to expand the second child preference to about 10 percent [of single-child couples]. We really have not studied and surveyed this problem adequately, and consequently we cannot consider ourselves as having taken hold of the problem seriously and earnestly. When we suggest 10 percent, we are referring to a general requirement for the countryside as a whole, but each locality must strengthen the work of ideological guidance in its own area in accordance with the actual conditions, and gradually promote the policy first through a detailed auditing of population growth, through spot experimentation, and through gaining firsthand experience. In the future, as the number of third or higher-order births is reduced, the opening for a second child can continue to be enlarged somewhat. In some places it has been stipulated that in the cases in which the husband and the wife are both themselves single children, they should be permitted to give birth to two children. We intend to continue to carry out this method. In this way, in about twenty-odd years, we shall be able to gradually transform the childbirth policy as it exists today, because by then the number of single children will be in the majority. If we operate in this way, it will not affect the goal of reaching the population target we have set for the end of the century, and yet the masses will be happier.

With regard to second or multiple births that are beyond the limits of the plan, we must resolutely stop them and yet, at the same time we cannot handle the matter simplistically. In general, a high birth rate is a reflection of economic and cultural backwardness. The reasons the masses want to have more children are manifold, however. We must correspondingly resolve them by adopting many different methods—ideological education, economic sanctions, administrative measures, providing technical service, children's health care, taking care of elderly people, correcting improper "winds" and behavior, and so on. In the area of birth control measures, we should still take contraception as primary. We should promote comprehensive procedures and measures so that the masses have room for choice. In view of the current circumstances, in which there are many localities where rural third births are numerous, we still must promote the policy that, on a voluntary basis, either the husband or wife should undergo sterilization when a couple has two or more children. Nonetheless, on this issue we must differentiate among specific conditions, and we must absolutely not carry out a "one cut of the knife" policy. We must also not use high targets that exceed the realm of practical possibility to put pressure on people at the grassroots level. People who have already passed the peak age of childbearing, for instance, need not undergo sterilization, and those who have adopted other contraceptive methods with effectiveness also need not undergo sterilization; instead, we would permit them simply to sign a birth control agreement.

The problem of family planning among minority nationalities. The Central Committee of the Chinese Communist Party and the State Council instruct that: "Family planning must also be promoted among minority nationalities, but the requirements may be relaxed a bit where it is appropriate to do so." Currently, these instructions have not yet been carried out fully. We are giving consideration to the following: For the minority nationalities with a population of more than ten million, the requirements, in principle, shall be the same as those stipulated for the Han nationality. For those with a population less than ten million, in accordance with population density and other circumstances, permission may be given for couples to give birth to a second child, and in individual cases, to a third child. Under no circumstances should a fourth child be permitted. The specific stipulations should be formulated by the local people's congress and government of the nationalities' autonomous region in conjunction with related provincial and autonomous region authorities in accordance with the actual conditions in those localities, and may be carried out after they are reported to the standing committee of the people's congress, or the people's government at the next higher level and have received approval.

On the policies regarding rewards and sanctions. Each province, autonomous region, and centrally administered municipality has stipulated certain methods regarding rewards and sanctions. These have played a positive role in promoting family planning work when implemented. The current problem is that the local authorities cannot afford to reward people, and the higher the one-child rate of a locality, the heavier the burden; in some localities, the rewards have been too high and the penalties too severe. When we draft the law on family planning, we shall study the issues and attempt to resolve them in accordance with the specific experiences of each place. The stipulations already in place for the provinces, autonomous regions, and centrally administered municipalities need not be changed for now but we must not have additional burdens added on level by level. In terms of penalties, we must not permit any violation or undermining of the masses' basic means of production and means of living. People who have not adopted any contraception must not be punished in the same way as those who have given birth to excess numbers of children. Overall, work must be grasped tightly and done well, the work in the areas of propaganda and technical service must be done at a deeper level and with a greater concern for details, and we must do the best we can to reduce the scope of penalization.

On the policy of late marriage and late childbearing. The ages of late marriage currently promoted (for men, twenty-five years old; for women, twenty-three years old) are inconsistent with the marriage ages stipulated by the Marriage Law (which are twenty-two years old for men and twenty years old for women) and consequently there have been occasions in which contradictions have emerged in the process of carrying out the policies. Our recommendation is that from now on we should continue to promote late marriage, and strictly prohibit early marriages where people get married before they reach the legal age, those who have reached the legal marriage age, and, after dissuasion has been attempted, still insist on getting married, ought to be permitted to get married, but we must mobilize them to practice late childbearing. For those who are getting married at the ages of late marriage, their timing for childbearing should not be further restricted.

III. IMPROVE WORKSTYLE

The mission of family planning is difficult and arduous. The broad ranks of the cadres who are engaged in the work of family planning have done in-depth work and have given full consideration to practicality, relied on the masses, and have done their work well by courageously overcoming many difficulties, thus achieving great success. Nonetheless, in some places there are instances of coercion and commandism, which have not been resolved in a timely manner, and the main responsibility is ours. We believed that, given the weight of the mission of family planning work, it would be unavoidable that instances of coercion and commandism would appear, but that only a minority would engage in coercion and commandism. For that reason, we did not adequately understand the harmfulness of this situation and we failed to provide strong guidance on this issue.

To correct the instances of coercion and commandism is chiefly a question of education. We should start with leading organs at the upper levels, have leading cadres conduct more self-criticism, take the initiative to bear responsibility, and pay attention to protect the enthusiasm of the vast number of grassroots cadres and active elements. Our Party group must earnestly take steps to resolve this problem during this Party rectification. With regard to the broad ranks of cadres and active elements involved with the work of family planning, we must guide and lead them with methods of strengthening ideological education, summing up experiences, and giving recognition to advanced examples, and we must continue to improve work style and work methods.

Actions that wrongfully show favoritism or violate law and discipline must be strictly prohibited.

IV. PUT FORTH GREAT EFFORT INTO ENHANCING THE STANDARDS OF SCIENCE AND TECHNOLOGY AND THE QUALITY OF MEDICAL DEVICES

To further enhance the technical standards of the technical cadres involved in the work of family planning is a major problem we now face in this area of work. We must, in cooperation with the department of public health, take a firm grasp of their training, and raise the standards of their knowledge of birth control technology and skills. We must also make them improve their attitude of service, so that they will be responsible to the people. They must carry out their duties in strict compliance with the "General Rules of Birth Control Operations," gradually reduce abortions, especially late-term abortions, raise the quality of the surgical operations, and prevent the occurrence of surgical accidents, ensure the health of the recipients of the surgery, and produce a sense of security on the part of the masses. We must also take a serious attitude toward handling collateral illnesses and side-effects that occur after surgery. We must, in cooperation with the pharmaceutical/medical and chemical industry departments, further improve the quality of contraceptive medicine and devices, and open up the channels of supply more broadly and ensure that they be distributed in the proper numbers and specifications and in a timely fashion into the hands of couples of childbearing age. We must strengthen the work of scientific research in family planning, and place the greatest concentration of energy and effort on those problems that most urgently need to be resolved in the practice of family planning. We should pay attention to discovering effective contraceptive and birth control medicines and methods from

Chinese herbal medicine and from among the masses' lore and practices, propagate the new technologies and new results achieved domestically in China's own scientific research in family planning, and actively introduce and import, as well as apply, advanced technology, medicines, and devices from abroad, so that the masses will receive better and safer and more effective, high-quality services.

V. STRENGTHEN GRASSROOTS WORK

Grassroots work is the foundation for doing family planning work well. The Party committees and governments of the provinces, autonomous regions, and centrally administered municipalities must pay extremely serious attention to this, and must grasp the situation at every level, with each level taking hold of the work at the next lower level all the way down. We must take a firm hold, a good grasp, according to local conditions, and we must do it continuously for several years. We must perfect the structure and equipping of the leading organs of family planning at every level, outfitting them with specialized cadres. The production brigades (the villagers' committees) must, under the unified leadership of Party branch offices, form ranks with a women team leader as the backbone, complete with the participation of the village physicians, Communist Party members and the Communist Youth League members and active elements among the masses. We must perfect the system of job responsibility, firm up the relationship between the Party and the masses, do the routine ideological, organizational, and technical service work, so as to strive to meet the state-stipulated population plans for the various localities. The leading organs must serve the basic levels, strengthen concrete guidance, and we must, as quickly as possible, develop the routine work at the grassroots level. We must strive to hold a conference in the fall of 1984 for the exchanging of experiences of family planning at the grassroots. To ensure that grassroots cadres do a good job in family planning work, we should let them go through, in a planned way, a rotating training session at least once a year. The local financial department should support and resolve the problem of the proper compensation for them in a reasonable and appropriate way.

Family planning is a major undertaking that impinges on the changing customs and habits of the people. We should make family planning a component of all sorts of activities, such as the launching of "civilized villages"; of "the Five-Good Families"; and so on.

VI. WITH EARNEST AND CONCRETE EFFORT, DO THE WORK OF IDEOLOGICAL EDUCATION WELL

At every link in the chain of the work of family planning and in the process as a whole, there is a need to insist on and maintain in-depth and carefully done ideological education in order to continue to enhance the cadres' and the masses' consciousness in carrying out family planning. There are many possible and permissible forms and methods for carrying out ideological education, and we must maintain the principle of carrying it out regularly, frequently, and repeatedly. We must prevent oversimplification, as well as rashness. We must earnestly sum up the experiences of the "Propaganda Month" activities. In all future propaganda activities we must, from first to last, take hold of this central link which is ideological education. We must be solid and practical; we must emphasize actual effects, and not engage in superficial rhetoric. We must have the leadership and the masses join together in carrying out the auditing and comparisons. We must carry out the "Five Visitings and Five Inquiries" purposefully (that is, visiting couples that, after giving birth to one child, do not request to be permitted second children; visiting family planning role models and active elements; visiting comrades who have undergone birth control surgical operations; visiting comrades who, for all sorts of reasons, have been subjected to punishment; visiting newlyweds; inquiring about people's conditions in the winter, when it's cold, or when it's warm; inquiring after the health of the mother and her daughter or son; inquiring about the financial difficulties in the family; inquiring about people's opinions on the work that is being done), and we simply must tighten up our relationships with the masses. To do so we must constantly carry out the work of giving recognition to the advanced collectives and advanced individuals, and continue to discover and cultivate advanced prototypes in all areas.

As far as the county-level propaganda and guidance stations are concerned, they are something that we can gradually establish and perfect in accordance with the spirit of the "Directive on Further Improving the Work of Family Planning" issued by the Central Committee of the Chinese Communist Party and the State Council (Central Document no. 11 [1982]) and the "Minutes of the National Conference on Family Planning Work," transmitted and approved by the Office of the Central Committee of the Chinese Communist Party and the Office of the State Council (Central Committee and State Council Office Document no. 37 [1982]).

VII. ON THE TASK OF THE FAMILY PLANNING COMMISSION

The tasks of the State Family Planning Commission and the local family planning committees must be made clear. The chief energies and efforts should be put into striving to meet the goal of population control by carrying out the Party's guidelines and policies, formulating plans, conducting investigative surveys and research, summing up and exchanging experiences, and going down to the lower levels to solve problems. At the moment we have to take a firm hold of the work of drafting the Family Planning Law, and organizing the cadres to penetrate to the grassroots and the masses to take a good hold of "pilot" work.

The State Family Planning Commission must promote unity and cooperation with all related departments. Technical service work is primarily the responsibility of the public health department. The family planning committees at all levels shall, from now on, no longer transfer technical personnel away from the public health departments; they must build up their own technical ranks. The technical service stations that the family planning departments have already established must be reorganized and improved earnestly. The major part of the work of scientific research is done in the public health departments, the pharmaceutical departments, the educational departments, and in the Academy of Sciences. The production and supply of contraceptive and birth-control medication and devices are mainly the responsibility of the State Pharmaceutical Bureau and the Ministry of Chemical Industries. The State Family Planning Commission must tighten up its relationship with all the aforementioned departments, bring forth its requests and requirements, and do the work well together in harmony and unanimity of purpose. In order that its relationship with the other departments may be strengthened, we propose that comrades in these departments who are responsible for or in charge of related areas could be absorbed into the family planning committee as part-time committee members, so that the committee may have consistent access to their opinions and therefore be able to coordinate its work with them.

We would like to ask that the Central Committee examine the above report and send us its instructions.

The Chinese Communist Party Group of
the State Family Planning Commission

25.3 THE BACKGROUND TO *BITTER LOVE*, APRIL 1981

Born in 1930, Bai Hua joined the Communist Party in 1949 and became a writer for the People's Liberation Army. Labeled as a "rightist" in 1957, Bai was finally rehabilitated and allowed to return to creative work in the late 1970s. His screenplay for *Bitter Love* (Kulian) was one of the first works of art to explore the plight of intellectuals during the Cultural Revolution. A stark portrayal of the fate of Chinese who returned abroad to serve the Revolution, *Bitter Love* was widely criticized and banned.

The article below, published in the *Liberation Army Daily* (Jiefangjun bao) in April 1981, attacked Bai Hua for suggesting that the socialist system—and perhaps the Communist Party itself—caused the suffering of individuals during the Maoist era. The controversy over *Bitter Love* provided one clear indication that the Party was willing to examine the past only on its own terms, with a line of dissent drawn at works that dared to suggest, however indirectly, that the Gang of Four and other renegades were not the only culprits responsible for the suffering of the past decades.

As everyone knows, since the founding of New China, the Party has made tremendous achievements in its work concerning intellectuals. The Party Central

Committee and Mao Zedong, Zhou Enlai and other leading comrades devoted a great deal of their energies and efforts to uniting with, winning over, transforming and training the intellectuals.

Of course, the Party has also made mistakes in policies towards the intellectuals since the founding of New China and should seriously sum up experience and draw lessons from them. Particularly during the "Great Cultural Revolution," vast numbers of intellectuals, as well as the Party's leading cadres at all levels and the masses of the people, suffered ruthless persecution by Lin Biao and the Gang of Four. This is a fact that remains fresh in people's memories.

. . . . Since the downfall of the Gang of Four, the Party and State have redressed many cases in which people were framed, falsely charged and wrongly sentenced and then cleared their names. Facts have proved that the motherland [literally *zuguo*, the "ancestral land"] and the Party are concerned about and take good care of intellectuals and that the hearts of the masses of intellectuals have always turned to the motherland, the Party and socialism.

However, this is not the way "Bitter Love" describes them. One of the themes of the story is the relationship between intellectuals and the motherland. On the surface, the story does seem to describe the intellectuals' patriotism with bold strokes and striking colours. It describes how several intellectuals, filled with patriotic passion, returned to the motherland and how deeply each one of them was attached to the motherland. The author indeed has imparted to these characters quite a few patriotic words and deeds, even to the point of sometimes being touching.

However, this is not the point. The point is that by taking great pains to describe the love of a few intellectuals for the motherland, the author intends to contrast it with the motherland's lack of love for the intellectuals. Under the author's pen, not one of the returned intellectuals has had a happy experience and come to a good end. In short, the intellectuals' love for the motherland is merely one-sided, unrequited love. You love the motherland, but the motherland does not love you. The more deeply you love the motherland, the more bitter your end will be. Thus, the more vividly the story plays up the intellectuals' patriotic words and deeds, the sharper its condemnation of the motherland. This is the so-called "bitter love."

The depiction of this part of history is not intended to denounce and castigate Lin Biao and the Gang of Four but to accuse the ancestral land which suffered together with its 1,000 million sons and daughters. It is intended to equate Lin Biao and the Gang of Four, the handful of traitors, with the motherland and to sum up the crimes of Lin Biao and the Gang of Four in trampling on the patriotic intellectuals in the conclusion that the motherland does not love intellectuals. Thus, the intention is to reach the objective conclusion that the motherland is not worthy of love. How can this be called a hymn of patriotism? . . . .

Second, "Bitter Love" confuses the essential distinction between the counter-revolutionary crimes of Lin Biao and the Gang of Four and the mistakes made by the great Marxist, Comrade Mao Zedong, in his later years. It points the spearhead of criticism not at Lin Biao and the Gang of Four but at Comrade Mao Zedong, the Party and the socialist system as a whole.

The story not only arranges for Xingxing, the painter's daughter, to flee the country in order to criticize the motherland's failure to love her sons and daughters but takes great pains to describe the tragic experience of the painter Ling Chenguang in the motherland in order to place the blame for the tragedy on the Party, the leader and the socialist system.

The finale as depicted in the script is a scene that develops like this: The time seems to be some time after the downfall of the Gang of Four. People are running in search of the missing painter. However the painter has already died a tragic death on the snow-covered ground. In the last moment of his life, he is seen carving with all his remaining strength a big question mark in the snowy ground, his cold body substituting for the dot of the question mark.

Thus, with its enormous question mark as the end, the script raises a question of major political importance before the audience. That is, who is to be blamed for the tragic life of Ling Chenguang? Although the author has not answered this question in so many words, he has offered a clear explanation through his overall portrayal. The work depicts Chinese society during the decade of the cultural revolution as a dark kingdom with no ray of light. What perplexes people even more, despite their repeated pondering over the matter, is that while the author has maintained that his work is about the 10 chaotic years, there is no scene in the entire script that can arouse hatred among the people for Lin Biao and the Gang of Four. Why is this? Instead, many devices like metaphors and insinuations are employed in the script to direct its spearhead squarely at the Party, Party leaders and at the socialist system.

Third, "Bitter Love" not only draws no distinction between socialist New China and semi-feudal and semi-colonial Old China, but it does not distinguish either between the different intrinsic characteristics of the socialist system and the capitalist system. As a result, while debasing the socialist motherland, it also enhances capitalist society and advertises the bourgeois idea of humanism. By employing methods peculiar to film-making, the work alternately describes Ling Chenguang's escape both in the period of the old society and in the period of the new society to liken New China to Old China and show that the new society is just as dark as the old society. . . .

To portray the great and tortuous course we have traversed in the 31 years since the founding of our country is undoubtedly an important task for the writers and artists of China. Yet it is also a very complex and arduous task. The Party Central Committee has earnestly given us this admonition: With regard to the appraisal of the Party's work since the founding of our country, we must fully affirm the tremendous achievements made over the past 31 years. Shortcomings and mistakes should be criticized seriously, but they must not be described as utterly hopeless. . . .

25.4 Liu Binyan: A Case of Persecution in Xi'an in Disregard of Central Instructions, August 25, 1984

After 1979, a number of prominent "rightist" intellectuals who had disappeared from public life in 1957 were rehabilitated and again permitted to work in cultural fields within which they had earned their fame some twenty years before. One such intellectual was Liu Binyan (1925–2005), an investigative journalist and ace practitioner of the genre known as "reportorial literature" (*baogao wenxue*). Liu had been a major target in the anti-rightist campaign, and the reappearance of his byline on the pages of *People's Daily* was an indication that the Party was willing to forgive those previously castigated for political errors.

Liu Binyan emerged from obscurity with a critical spirit undiminished by years of persecution and hardship. His reports once again established him as a controversial figure in Chinese journalism and provided some of the most searching and acid portraits of everyday life that had ever appeared during China's years "under the red flag."

The following article, written between March and June 1984, describes the problems faced by China—in this case in the setting of the Xi'an local government—as the legal system addressed grievances inherited from previous eras. As Liu's report indicates, former victims of Maoist-era politics, like Guo Jianxing and his family, were often at a disadvantage in court as networks of *guanxi* (relationships) came into play to prevent the reversal of confiscations of property and other illegal acts that occurred in the context of political movements of earlier decades. The article illustrates the imperfect separation of the Party and judiciary that continued to frustrate legal reformers in the 1980s. This article provoked an enormous controversy when it appeared and contributed to Liu's expulsion from the CCP in 1987.[1]

"THE RIGHTS AND WRONGS OVER THE PAST 38 YEARS"

A reversal:

Because of China's enormous size many stories go unheard. Lately a seventy-two year old man named Guo Jianying became a defendant and the No. 2 branch of the Xi'an housing and land management bureau, which 12 years ago occupied the backyard of Guo Jiangying's house and robbed him of his property, took on the role of plaintiff. On 7th December 1983, the branch bureau gathered people together and

---

1. Liu Binyan's investigation of Guo Jianying and its results are described in Liu Binyan, *A Higher Kind of Loyalty* (New York: Random House, 1990), pp. 179–190.

sent dozens of armed men and a prison van to pull down a shed in the backyard of Guo's house (142, Qingnian Street, Xi'an city). By order of Liang Ping, Vice President of the Lianhu district court, they also brutally raided Guo's family.

There was a bigger reversal: Another reason why old Guo became the defendant was that in 1946, he lent a large sum of money to the New Fourth Army, which was in a difficult position in southern Shaanxi at that time, to help it solve a pressing need.

In 1958 [at the time of the antirightist campaign], the following logic was employed: If Guo Jianying could find so much money to support the revolution, was it possible that he was not a capitalist? The answer was no: He had to have been a capitalist.

This was the original theoretical basis for "transforming" his private house. In 1966, yet a new logic was applied: Why would a capitalist be willing to take out so much money to support the revolution? His support must have been insincere. And so Guo was thrown into a "cowshed" on the charge of "perpetrating a political fraud by misrepresenting himself." He and his family were in dire straits.

In 1972, a looter named Gu Laigen of the No. 2 branch of the Xi'an housing and land management bureau took over the backyard of the Guo house and built a posh five-room house with an exclusive courtyard for Zhang Jintang, a section-chief who controlled the city materials bureau. During the construction, the seepage pit in the backyard was filled in, two brick toilets were destroyed, eight trees were felled and Guo Jianying's property was stripped from him.

After ten years China entered a new historical period. But Gu Laigen was still able to ride roughshod over the Guos. Supported by a friend named Shi Zhaoyi, who was chief of the financial section of the city housing and land management bureau, Gu Laigen had the house with its exclusive courtyard pulled down. He wanted to construct a building for the provincial timber company by expanding the area of construction to the north. This meant occupying nearly the whole courtyard. Guo Jianying was driven beyond forebearance and, encouraged by the line of the third plenary session of the 11th CCP Central Committee, he rose in resistance against these people. He claimed an "unfulfilled correction."

Knowing that Leftist errors were often at the root of private legal interests and that in many cases houses and property were at stake, Vice Mayor Li Tingbi, who has been in charge of Xi'an urban construction for many years, decided to investigate six families. An investigation group led by Wang Jianpeng conducted a careful and practical investigation for four months and a conclusion was made that the socialist transformation of four of the houses in 1958, including that of the Guos, was wrong. At a routine affairs meeting of mayors on 16th June 1983, mayors and vice mayors maintained that mistakes should be corrected and property rights should be restored to the owners. But Zhang Huaide, chief of the city housing and land management bureau, who attended the meeting, raised an objection and proposed that the returning of two private houses should be postponed. Guo Jianying's house was one of the two.

In the twenty-six years since 1958, the members of the Guo family grew more numerous and Guo Jianying's children were now adults. Since 1980, the Guos applied twice to build a house in the courtyard. But the housing and land management bureau did not approve their application. The family had no choice but to build a twelve square meter shed in the backyard for the youngest son to dwell in.

Although this wretched little shed was far from the construction site [of the building for the provincial timber company], Gu Laigen insisted that the shed was hampering the progress of construction. Guo's family maintained that the construction was in itself illegal and that the property ruined and taken away in 1972 should be returned. Vice Mayor Li Tingbi supported Guo's family's reasonable and legal request. He instructed both sides to talk the matter over and suggested that construction projects should be suspended until the dispute was solved. Having strong backing, Shi Zhaoyi and Gu Laigen turned a deaf ear to the vice mayor's instruction. They lodged a suit with the Lianhu district court against Guo Jianying. Thus, a tug-of-war with great disparity in strength began.

"EVEN IF THE DECISION IS WRONG, IT MUST BE CARRIED OUT"

The plaintiff's superiority was clear: "It" was a "unit" and "organisation" safeguarding "state interests"; whereas the defendant was a family pursuing its private affairs.

Guo Jianying, however, had a rare, favourable condition: President Li Xiannian issued two instructions with regard to his appeal.[2] On many occasions, Comrade Ma Wenrui, First Secretary of the Shaanxi Provincial CCP Committee, instructed the Xi'an city CCP Committee seriously to implement President Li Xiannian's instructions. Comrade Wang Feng, a member of the Central Advisory Commission . . . was the most authoritative person who could stand witness to the problem concerning Guo Jianying's lending money. He instructed a responsible comrade to advise Comrade He Chenghua, Secretary of the Xi'an city CCP Committee, not to violate Comrade Li Xiannian's instructions so as to avoid committing mistakes.

On the night of 5th December 1983, Comrade Wang Feng, who was then at Xi'an, learned that the Xi'an city court had made a decision to pull down the shed in Guo's backyard the following day. He called Secretary He Chenghua, telling him to put off the decision. However, Secretary He Chenghua resolutely took the opposite step. He told Li Tianshun, his personal secretary, to inform Guo Jianying: "Even if the decision is wrong, it must be implemented. In the future, if the verdict passed on you is reversed, I will have the building which has been constructed pulled down. But for now the decision must be implemented." The reason was that "the Party must not interfere in judicial affairs."

2. Here we see that intervention from the highest level of the central government failed to deter local authorities.

What Secretary He Chenghua said was contrary to the fact. Without the interference by some Xi'an leaders, the case would not have been placed on file for prosecution. From the beginning, some comrades of the Lianhu district court maintained that the case was a dispute over property rights, involved the problem of implementing policies and should be handled by the Party and government departments concerned. They placed the case on file for investigation only after they had received instructions from some "city leaders." Also, only after the district court submitted the files to Secretary He Chenghu for approval was the judgment made.

With a high sense of organisation and discipline, the district court and the intermediate court fulfilled their tasks exceptionally fast. Not only did they turn a blind eye to the plaintiff's violation of civil lawsuit procedures, but they themselves also violated the procedures. They shortened the process of examination and approval so as to enable Gu Laigen and his followers to continue the projects as soon as possible, as Gu Laigen and his followers had been waiting impatiently. . . .

In late December, Secretary He Chenghua wanted to implement President Li Xiannian's instructions. He formed an investigation group for Guo Jianying's case. To investigate what? First, to investigate the problem of Guo Jianying lending the money in 1948. The three investigations made over the past twenty years and more, Comrade Li Xiannian's instructions and Comrade Wang Feng's testimony did not count. Second, to investigate the problem of transforming Guo Jianying's private house. The former investigation was to be carried out by an investigation group of the city government and the conclusion made by the vice mayors of the city did not count.

By selecting testimony which had been negated by a witness who possessed first-hand materials and by relying on other testimony inappropriately obtained by a lawyer engaged by the housing and land management bureau, the city CCP Committee investigation group tried to prove that Guo Jianying was forced to "deliver" the money to the New Fourth Army instead of willingly lending the money to the army. To arrive at this conclusion, the investigation group distorted history and brought shame on the New Fourth Army. It asserted that the southern Shaanxi Party and army adopted the policy of "beating rich people" and the method of "canvassing votes," which in fact they never did. It even went so far as to say that because Guo Jiangying informed against a guerrilla leader, the guerrilla leader was killed by the enemy. It did so in disregard of the fact that since 1958, this allegation was negated twice by a more reliable witness and that recently Comrade Wang Feng testified that the killing of the guerrilla leader had nothing to do with Guo Jianying.

In its scrutiny of the matter of private houses, the city CCP Committee's investigation group did no more than to negate the investigation carried out by the city government and to affirm the mistake in 1958, that is, houses in a compound with an entrance or entrances commonly used by the dwellers were regarded as houses being rented. The purpose of this regulation was to make up the figure of

150 sq.m., which was the minimum area fixed for "transformation." [This technicality made it possible to take over the Guo property.] So the site in Guo's backyard was "transformed." Otherwise, the occupation of Guo's backyard would have been unreasonable.

To be perfectly safe, it was necessary to make an alteration on the class status of Guo Jianying. In 1980, in line with the Central (1979) Document No. 84, the Lanzhou motor transport company of Gansu Province, where Guo Jianying worked, determined Guo's class status as "petty proprietor," which belongs to the category of the working people. But the city CCP Committee investigation group maintained that the classification was a little biased toward the "Right." So it started collecting materials concerning Guo Jianying in an attempt to prove that the classification had been carried out in a "minor key." It would be a good idea to determine Guo's class status as capitalist, as this would legalise the transformation of his private house in 1958 and would make unassailable everything done by the housing and land management bureau, by Gu Laigen, by the court and by the city CCP Committee.

This was how the principal leaders of the Xi'an city CCP Committee implemented the "practical" spirit of the third plenary session of the 11th CCP Central Committee and President Li Xiannian's instructions with regard to Guo Jianying's problem. A person is invincible if he has the power to distribute houses.

In this drama, which was focused on Guo Jianying, Gu Laigen played a very important part. Gu was a low-level cadre of the housing and land management bureau. Everybody knew that during the "cultural revolution," he commanded an attack on the city CCP Committee and that he was a "two-gun" tyrant. But in his files, there is not even a single line carrying records of his activities during the "Cultural Revolution," nor can a trace of his several years' imprisonment be found (it was also struck off the table of contents). He often used the "house distribution tickets" he possessed to threaten or bribe people. He was good at using hard and soft tactics to force families out of the sites to be used for capital construction. Because of all this, many people dared not offend him, as he was quite useful to them.

In this affair, Gu Laigen just demonstrated his power. He could instruct the public security bureau to threaten Guo's family. He could hire some twenty gangsters to beat the Guo family and to carry out kidnappings. He could also control judicial departments. Why did Xu Pei, judge of the Lianhu district court, side with Gu Laigen, ignore the most rudimentary legal proceedings and shorten the process of examination? His purpose was to get a house, and indeed, he got one with two large rooms. Why did Yang Qingxiu of the city intermediate court overstep his authority to remove obstacles for Gu Laigen and to engage Liu so and so, lawyer of the Legal Advisory Department? And why did Liu so and so, a part-time lawyer, illegally open an introduction letter and take risks (because it was illegal) in investigating Guo Jianying's history and class status, which had nothing to do with the case? . . . Obviously, each had his own purpose.

What did Gu Laigen and his behind-the-scenes backer—Shi Zhaoyi, chief of the financial section of the housing and land management bureau—intend to have? The provincial timber company had long agreed to provide them with 15 houses and a fund of 300,000 yuan. In addition, Gu Laigen got another thing: He and his wife were transferred back to Shanghai to work in a Shanghai-based Shaanxi office. Dark forces and dirty tricks

Now we can faintly see a "united front" encircling Guo's family. . . .

Of course, Guo Jianying is not a hero. But, after all, he made some contributions to the victory of the liberation war. Also, he was a victim of "Leftist" mistakes. The CCP Central Committee has issued explicit policies and instructions with regard to his rewards and the way to treat him. But why does the Xi'an city CCP Committee still adhere to their "Leftist" principles in handling his case? Why does the Xi'an city CCP Committee persist in their Rightist principles in dealing with Gu Laigen and his followers, who have serious problems both in politics and morality and who rode roughshod in the 10 years of internal disorder? Can creators and supporters of this affair be regarded as persons keeping abreast with the CCP Central Committee politically?

25.5 THE JOINT AGREEMENT BY BRITAIN AND CHINA DEFINING THE FUTURE OF HONG KONG, SEPTEMBER 26, 1984

After 1949, Hong Kong and its tiny neighbor Macao remained the final colonial possessions on Chinese soil controlled by foreign powers. For decades they were permitted by the PRC to continue to exist because they played a useful role in the trade and commerce of China. Hong Kong, in particular, served as a door to the external world that could be opened and closed at will.

The some four hundred square miles that constitute Hong Kong and the New Territories were defined by a set of treaties signed in 1842, 1860, and 1898. The last of these gave Great Britain a ninety-eight year lease on the New Territories, due to expire in 1997. The imminent expiration of this lease triggered the negotiations between Peking and London that culminated in the Joint Declaration of 1984, which defined how Hong Kong would be reincorporated into Chinese society after July 1, 1997.

In these negotiations the Chinese stressed that Hong Kong would be treated, per the Chinese constitution, as a Special Administrative Region (SAR); it would maintain its own laws and economic system without interference from China. Two slogans that summarized Peking's approach were: "No changes for fifty years" and "One country, two systems." As Hong Kong was restored to China, the world watched expectantly to see whether the city's anomalous path to a postcolonial future would follow the guidelines outlined in the joint agreement.

The Government of the United Kingdom of Great Britain and Northern Ireland and the Government of the People's Republic of China have reviewed with satisfaction the friendly relations existing between the two Governments and peoples in recent years and agreed that a proper negotiated settlement of the question of Hong Kong, which is left over from the past, is conducive to the maintenance of the prosperity and stability of Hong Kong and to the further strengthening and development of the relations between the two countries on a new basis. To this end, they have, after talks between the delegations of the two Governments, agreed to declare as follows:

(1)

The Government of the People's Republic of China declares that to recover the Hong Kong area (including Hong Kong Island, Kowloon and the New Territories, herein after referred to as Hong Kong) is the common aspiration of the entire Chinese people and that it has decided to resume the exercise of sovereignty over Hong Kong with effect from 1 July 1997.

(2)

The Government of the United Kingdom declares that it will restore Hong Kong to the People's Republic of China with effect from 1 July 1997.

(3)

The Government of the People's Republic of China declares that the basic policies of the People's Republic of China regarding Hong Kong are as follows:

1. Upholding national unity and territorial integrity and taking account of the history of Hong Kong and its realities, the People's Republic of China has decided to establish, in accordance with the provisions of Article 31 of the Constitution of the People's Republic of China, a Hong Kong Special Administrative Region upon resuming the exercise of sovereignty over Hong Kong.
2. The Hong Kong Special Administrative Region will be directly under the authority of the Central People's Government of the People's Republic of China. The Hong Kong Special Administrative Region will enjoy a high degree of autonomy except in foreign and defense affairs, which are the responsibilities of the Central People's Government.
3. The Hong Kong Special Administrative Region will be vested with executive, legislative and independent judicial power, including that of final adjudication. The laws currently in force in Hong Kong will remain basically unchanged.

The Hong Kong Special Administrative Region shall retain the status of a free port and continue a free trade policy, including the free movement of goods and capital. The Hong Kong Special Administrative Region may on its own maintain and develop economic and trade relations with all states and regions.

The Hong Kong Special Administrative Region shall be a separate customs territory. It may participate in relevant international organizations and international trade agreements (including preferential trade agreements) such as the General Agreement on Tariffs and Trade and arrangements regarding international trade in textiles. Export quotas, tariff preferences and other similar arrangements obtained by the Hong Kong Special Administrative Region shall be enjoyed exclusively by the Hong Kong Special Administrative Region. The Hong Kong Special Administrative Region shall have authority to issue its own certificates of origin for products manufactured locally, in accordance with prevailing rules of origin.

The Hong Kong Special Administrative Region may, as necessary, establish official and semiofficial economic and trade missions in foreign countries, reporting the establishment of such missions to the Central People's Government for the record.

FINANCIAL CENTER

The Hong Kong Special Administrative Region shall retain the status of an international financial center. The monetary and financial systems previously practiced in Hong Kong, including the systems of regulation and supervision of deposit-taking institutions and financial markets, shall be maintained.

The Hong Kong Special Administrative Region government may decide its monetary and financial policies on its own. It shall safeguard the free operation of financial business and the free flow of capital within, into and out of the Hong Kong Special Administrative Region. No exchange control policy shall be applied in the Hong Kong Special Administrative Region. Markets for foreign exchange, gold, securities and futures shall continue.

The Hong Kong dollar, as the local legal tender, shall continue to circulate and remain freely convertible. The authority to issue Hong Kong currency shall be vested in the Hong Kong Special Administrative Region government. Hong Kong currency bearing references inappropriate to the status of Hong Kong as a Special Administrative Region of the People's Republic of China shall be progressively replaced and withdrawn from circulation.

The Exchange Fund shall be managed and controlled by the Hong Kong Special Administrative Region government, primarily for regulating the exchange value of the Hong Kong dollar.

The Hong Kong Special Administrative region shall maintain Hong Kong's previous systems of shipping management and shipping regulation, including the system for regulating conditions of seamen. . . .

DIPLOMATIC RELATIONS

Subject to the principle that foreign affairs are the responsibility of the Central People's Government, representatives of the Hong Kong Special Administrative Region government may participate, as members of delegations of the Government of the People's Republic of China, in negotiations at the diplomatic level directly affecting the Hong Kong Special Administrative Region conducted by the Central People's Government. The Hong Kong Special Administrative Region may on its own, using the name "Hong Kong, China," maintain and develop relations and conclude and implement agreements with states, regions and relevant international organizations in the appropriate fields, including the economic, trade, financial and monetary, shipping, communications, touristic, cultural and sporting fields.

The application to the Hong Kong Special Administrative Region of international agreements to which the People's Republic of China is or becomes a party shall be decided by the Central People's Government, in accordance with the circumstances and needs of the Hong Kong Special Administrative Region, and after seeking the views of the Hong Kong Special Administrative Region government. . . .

POLICE POWER

The maintenance of public order in the Hong Kong Special Administrative Region shall be the responsibility of the Hong Kong Special Administrative Region government. Military forces sent by the Central People's Government to be stationed in the Hong Kong Special Administrative Region for the purpose of defense shall not interfere in the internal affairs of the Hong Kong Special Administrative Region. Expenditure for these military forces shall be borne by the Central People's Government.

Religious organizations and believers may maintain their relations with religious organizations and believers everywhere, and schools, hospitals and welfare institutions run by religious organizations in the Hong Kong Special Administrative Region and those in other parts of the People's Republic of China shall be based on the principles of non-subordination, noninterference and mutual respect. . . .

25.6 – 25.8 FANG LIZHI AND THE PARTY

To achieve the Four Modernizations, the Party had to win back the sympathy of China's intellectuals. Their expertise was a precondition for the success of the regime's ambitious reform scheme. But after the oppressions of the Cultural Revolution, intellectuals were understandably wary of the Party's overtures. Some considered the Four Modernizations to be an incomplete reform agenda, and advocated for fundamental changes to the legal and political framework of governance.

Fang Lizhi, an astrophysicist and, for a time, vice-chancellor of the prestigious University of Science and Technology in Hefei, Anhui, emerged in the mid-1980s as one of the most outspoken proponents of radical change. As his 1987 interview with Italian journalist Tiziano Terzani, given shortly after Fang's expulsion from the Communist Party, shows, Fang's criticisms were clearly calculated to jangle the nerves of China's leaders. His views directly inspired pro-democracy demonstrations on the campus of the University of Science and Technology and other schools in 1986.

Fang Lizhi argued that Marxism-Leninism was an outdated pseudoscience and that democracy was the only hope for a thorough reform. He vigorously criticized corruption in high places and called for laws to guarantee fundamental human rights. His articulate platform for change became an inspiration for the Tiananmen demonstrations in the spring of 1989. After the suppression of this popular movement, Fang Lizhi sought refuge in the American embassy in Peking.

In addition to Fang Lizhi's interview with Terzani, we have included two criticisms of Fang printed in *People's Daily* in January 1987. They suggest the extreme irritation that his efforts to promote democracy and human rights provoked within officialdom. For the Party leaders, Fang Lizhi's thinking was an intolerable type of heterodoxy striking at the very foundation of their power.

25.6 *Fang Lizhi's Interview with Tiziano Terzani, 1987*

Professor Fang, among Chinese students you are a hero. The international press has hailed you as China's Sakharov. Deng Xiaoping, on the other hand, calls you a "bad element." China's Communist Party maintains you are a victim of the disease called "bourgeois liberalization." What are you really?

A little bit of all of these. But in the first place I am an astrophysicist. The natural sciences are my religion. Einstein once said something of the sort. Previously I did not understand him. Now I know: we scientists have a belief and an aim, we have an obligation towards society. If we discover a truth and society does not accept it, this weighs on us. This is what happened to Galileo. That is when, as scientists, we have to intervene. With this mission I step into society.

What kind of mission do you have in China?

Democratization. Without democracy there can be no development. Unless individual human rights are recognized there can be no true democracy. In China the very ABC of democracy is unknown. We have to educate ourselves for democracy. We have to understand that democracy isn't something that our leaders can hand down to us. A democracy that comes from above is no democracy, it is nothing but a relaxation of control. The fight will be intense. But it cannot be avoided.

First you have attacked local Party cadres, then the Municipal Party Committee of Peking. Recently you attacked the Politburo. What is your next target?

Next I will criticize Marxism itself.

You go very far.

It is an undeniable truth that Marxism is no longer of much use. As a scientist I can prove it. Most answers given by Marxism with regard to the natural sciences are obsolete, some are even downright wrong. That is a fact. What Marxism has to say about the natural sciences stems from Engels' book *Natural Dialectics*. On nearly every page of this book one can find something that is either outdated or completely incorrect.

For example?

In the 1960s, with the aid of Marxism, the USSR and China repeatedly criticized the results of modern natural sciences. In biology they criticized genetics, in physics they criticized the theory of relativity and extended their criticism from cosmology to the development of the computer. Not even once has their criticism been proved correct. Therefore, how can one say today that Marxism should lead the natural sciences? It's a fallacy.

Have you ever believed in Marxism?

I certainly have! Immediately after Liberation [1949] and in the 1950s I firmly believed in Marxism. In 1955, when I joined the Party, I was convinced that Marxism would lead the way in every field and that the Communist Party was thoroughly good.

When, in 1958, during the Anti-Rightist Campaign, I was expelled from the Party, I made a very sincere self-criticism. I was convinced that I had wronged the Party. Now the Party has expelled me a second time, but this time I know that I was not in the wrong. Therefore I have refused to make a self-criticism.

Deng stated in 1979 that, in conformity with the Chinese Constitution, every citizen should be guided by the Four Basic Principles: the socialist road, the people's democratic dictatorship, leadership of the Party, and Marxism-Leninism and Mao Zedong Thought.

Marxism is a thing of the past. It helps us to understand the problems of the last century, not those of today. The same is true in the case of physics. Newton developed his theory 300 years ago. It is still valuable, but it does not help to solve today's problems, such as those related to computer technology. Marxism belongs to a precise epoch of civilization and that era is over. It is like old clothing that must be put aside. . . .

In 1978 something similar was said when the worker Wei Jingsheng wrote on a wall in Peking, which later became known as Democracy Wall: "Without democracy, there will be no modernization!" He got 15 years in prison for it. You, Professor Fang, are still free. Is it because you are a well-known scientist, whereas Wei Jingsheng was nothing but an electrician?

Of course. That's how things are in China. A worker who says something objectionable can easily be removed. Workers' unrest does not worry the government; workers are easily dealt with. Right now there are quite a few [workers'] disturbances, but the public is not aware of them. One knows nothing of them overseas, for these people have no international contacts.

Are things different in the case of the intellectuals?

Whenever it is students who demonstrate, the government is more concerned. It does not dare to take action as easily against students. That is why I maintain that the power of the intellectuals is relatively great. That is why I keep telling my students: he who has knowledge also has influence, and cannot be disregarded by the government. I advise my students not to say too much at first, but to study diligently. Those, however, who have successfully completed their studies must speak out. Wei Jingsheng spoke out ten years ago. Today I speak like he did. In another ten years perhaps other scholars may also speak up. People should be allowed to criticize their leaders without fear. This is a sign of democracy. . . .

What about human rights in China?

It is a dangerous topic. The question of human rights is taboo in China. Things are far worse than in the Soviet Union. Wei Jingsheng is a famous case, but there are thousands of others whose names are not even known. At least in the Soviet Union there are name lists. Not so in China. . . .

What is going to happen after Deng Xiaoping dies?

In the short run we might be worse off; in the long run, better. It's possible that after Deng's death Mao Zedong Thought will no longer be considered valid and then we will finally be able to make a radical reassessment of the past thirty years. That is probably just what General Secretary Hu Yaobang, who was demoted in January, planned to do. He once said that not one portrait of Mao should be left hanging in China. The last one hangs on the Tiananmen Gate, but Mao's Thought continues to dominate us.

Could the army play an important role in the future?

In our society, the army does play an important role. But it is no monolith. People at different levels hold different views. I, for one, have received numerous letters of support from members of the army.

How many have you received in all?

Thousands. Often simply open postcards with the name and address of the sender—a brave deed in China. On one it even said: "If this postcard does not reach its destination, then there is no democracy in China." When, on the day of my departure, I passed through customs, the policemen on duty in the booths stopped working and came over to talk to me. "Are you Fang Lizhi? Are you all right now? Are you allowed to travel overseas? That's good!"

Are you sure that after you return to China you will not be arrested or exiled to some far away place?

I'm prepared for that possibility.

You could emigrate. . . .

I have seriously considered it in the past. Now it is impossible. Should I leave now, I would be abandoning my students and friends in China. I have been denounced by high-level cadres, yet I haven't emigrated, whereas the children of high-level cadres go abroad to study although they've never been criticized. . . .

What's happened to the students who took part in the demonstrations?

As far as I know, no students from the well-known universities have been arrested. However, we do known that all of them have been photographed and had their names registered [by the police]. Later, they will make them "wear small shoes,"[3] as we say in China.

The campaign against "bourgeois liberalization" continues. . . .

That campaign has shown us just how strong the resistance to the reforms is. It has shown us that we badly underestimated the strength of our opponents. We have been too optimistic. On the other hand, the campaign has convinced more and more people of the necessity of reform. We do not want a revolution, which would in the first place be very difficult to achieve, and secondly would not necessarily be a good thing. Therefore, the only option that is left for China is reform. Democracy, education and intellectual freedom are the absolute and indispensable prerequisites of this reform. Without these last—be it with or without democracy—China has no future.

Professor Fang, we thank you for this interview.

25.7 On Fang Lizhi's Expulsion, January 20, 1987

On January 17 [1987], the Disciplinary Inspection Committee of the Anhui Branch of the Communist Party of China came to the decision that Fang Lizhi should be stripped of his Party membership.

Fang Lizhi was formerly the Vice-President of the Chinese University of Science and Technology. On January 12 he was dismissed from his post. In their report, "Regarding the Decision to Expel Fang Lizhi from the Party," the Disciplinary Inspection Committee pointed out that in recent years Fang Lizhi has on various occasions publicly encouraged bourgeois liberalization, opposed the Four Basic Principles, defied the leadership of the Party, denied the socialist system, caused dissension between intellectuals and the Party, and incited student demonstrations, resulting in serious disturbances.

---

3. To persecute them by making life as uncomfortable as possible.

25.8 *Explanation of Fang Lizhi's Errors, January 21, 1987*

With regard to Fang Lizhi's errors of word and deed, the relevant Party organizations have subjected him to severe criticism many times, but he has always merely feigned compliance, admitting to some mistakes on one hand and on the other continuing in his bad old ways, becoming in fact even more unbridled in his attacks on the Four Basic Principles and in his advocacy of Bourgelib (bourgeois liberalism). He has thrown Party discipline to the winds. Not to eliminate from the Party someone who has been so outspoken in his opposition is something that neither the Party nor the people can tolerate. Fang Lizhi is a middle-aged intellectual who has been nurtured by the Party. The Party had high expectations of him and had, moreover, entrusted him with an important post. He has disappointed the Party and disappointed his people, however, by falling into the muddy ditch of error, from which he is incapable of extricating himself. Now, although he has been dismissed from his post and expelled from the Party, the Party and government have arranged a position in scientific research for him, thus allowing him to bring his specialized vocational skills into play. If his actions indicate he has made a genuine change for the better, he will be welcomed back by the Party and the people.

Even though people like Fang are only a tiny minority within the Party, their negative example reminds us of the importance and urgent necessity of educating Party members at large to abide by the Party Regulations, and to implement Party discipline, particularly within the new historical conditions created by the policies of Reform and the Open Door to the outside world.

CHAPTER 26

Testing the Limits

26.1 AND 26.2 DEMONSTRATIONS FOLLOWING THE DEATH OF HU YAOBANG

The death of Hu Yaobang on April 15, 1989, initiated a cycle of massive demonstrations in Peking. This popular movement took as its model the April Fifth incident of 1976, in which thousands of residents and students assembled on Tiananmen Square to mourn the death of Zhou Enlai were dispersed by troops and security forces loyal to the "Gang of Four." After the fact, Deng Xiaoping had deplored this use of force and used it to discredit Hua Guofeng in his own ascent to power in 1978.

In 1989 tens of thousands of students from Peking's universities and training institutes launched demonstrations that used Tiananmen Square, in the political heart of the city, as their hub. Almost from the outset, the strongest theme was the demand for freedom of speech and greater participation in China's political life. Demonstrators also implored the country's leaders to reverse the verdict on Hu Yaobang's dismissal in 1987. In their eyes, Hu's fall symbolized the Party's rejection of popular participation in government.

Sharpening the division between government and demonstrators was the publication of a harsh and perhaps intentionally provocative editorial in *People's Daily* on April 26. In the editorial, some demonstrators were attacked as "conspirators," and their political activities were declared to be a destructive and illegal form of "turmoil." In the political parlance of the Party, these were fighting words that escalated the tension already prevailing in Peking.

Reaction to the Party's view of the democracy movement came swiftly. On April 27, a new wave of demonstrations brought over one million Peking residents, including factory workers, to the streets in sympathy with the

and the very few people who created the turmoil, and we will not penalize students for their radical words and actions in the student movement.

Moreover, dialogue will continue in an active way through various channels and at different levels between the party and the Government on one hand and the students and people from other walks of life on the other, including dialogue with those students who have taken part in demonstrations, class boycott and hunger strike, so as to take full heed of opinions from all fields.

We will give clear-cut answers to the reasonable demands raised by the students, we will pay close attention to and accept their reasonable criticism and suggestions, such as punishing profiteering officials, getting rid of corruption and overcoming bureaucratization, so as to improve the work of the party and the Government.

Under extremely complicated conditions in this period, leaders, teachers and students of many colleges and universities have taken pains to try to prevent demonstrations and keep order for teaching and studying.

Public security personnel and armed policemen have made great contributions in maintaining traffic, social order and security under extremely difficult conditions. Government offices, factories, shops, enterprises and institutions have persisted in production and work, taking pains to keep social life in order. For all this, the party and the Government are grateful and the people will never forget.

Now, to check the turmoil with a firm hand and quickly restore order, I urgently appeal on behalf of the party Central Committee and the state council:

To those students now on hunger strike on Tiananmen Square to end the fasting immediately, leave the square, receive medical treatment and recover their health as soon as possible.

ORDERS TO END STRIKE

To students and people in all walks of life to immediately stop all demonstrations, and give no more so-called support to the fasting students in the interest of humanitarianism. Whatever the intent, further "support" will push the fasting students to desperation.

On behalf of the party Central Committee and the state council, I now call on the whole party, the whole army and the whole nation to make concerted efforts and act immediately at all posts so as to stop the turmoil and stabilize the situation.

Party organizations at all levels must unite the broad masses, carry out painstaking ideological work and play a role of the core leadership and fighting fortress.

All the Communist Party members must strictly abide by the party's discipline. They should not only stay away from any activities harmful to stability and unity but also play a vanguard role in curbing the turmoil.

THE PARTY'S DISCIPLINE

Governments at various levels must enforce administrative discipline and law, strengthen leadership and administration over their regions and departments and earnestly carry out the work of stabilizing the situation, reform and economic construction.

All Government functionaries must stick to their own positions and maintain normal work order.

All the public security personnel and armed policemen should make greater efforts to maintain traffic and social order, intensify social security, and resolutely crack down on criminal activities.

All the industrial and commercial enterprises and Government institutions should abide by work discipline and be engaged in normal production.

And schools of various kinds and at various levels should maintain normal teaching order. Those on strike should resume classes unconditionally.

MAINTAINING LEADERSHIP

Comrades, our party is a party in power and our Government, a people's government. To be responsible to our sacred motherland and to the entire Chinese people, we must adopt firm and resolute measures to end the turmoil swiftly, maintain the leadership of the party as well as the socialist system.

We believe that our actions will surely have the support of all members of the Communist Party and the Communist Youth League, workers, peasants, intellectuals, democratic parties, people in various circles and the broad masses, and have the backing of the People's Liberation Army which is entrusted by the Constitution with the glorious task of safeguarding the country and the peaceful work of the people.

At the same time, we also hope the people in the capital will fully support the People's Liberation Army, police and armed police in their efforts to maintain order in the capital.

Comrades, we must, under the conditions of resolutely safeguarding stability and unity, continue to adhere to the four cardinal principles, persist in the reform and opening up to the outside world, strengthen democracy and the legal system, eliminate all kinds of corruption and strive to advance the cause of socialist modernization.

26.5 Deng Xiaoping's Explanation of the Crackdown, June 9, 1989

After the imposition of martial law, student hunger strikers and their supporters ignored the government's order to clear Tiananmen Square and impeded the movement of troops into the heart of Peking. Tense confrontations took place almost every day and rumors abounded as to the "real" attitude of army commanders and their troops. The protesters and the PLA circled each other warily; yet, despite the fact that millions of people were involved in overt defiance of government orders and the active obstruction of PLA deployments, no fatal accidents or serious injuries occurred prior to June 3.

At the same time, massive demonstrations of support took place throughout China, in Hong Kong, and among Chinese living abroad. To many analysts of Chinese affairs, it seemed that the government would be forced to seek a compromise solution or run the risk of civil war.

But in the end, the cruelly prophetic words of the *People's Daily* editorial of April 26 became reality as the Party decided to halt "turmoil" with the full weight of its armed forces. Under orders from Li Peng and President Yang Shangkun, troops, tanks, and armored personnel carriers forced their way into the heart of Peking. The first clashes occurred on June 3. After midnight on June 4, tanks and soldiers armed with AK-47 assault rifles fired indiscriminately on demonstrating crowds. The demonstrators were methodically herded out of Tiananmen Square and in a day, the pro-democracy movement was over. The human cost was high. Peking's hospitals were swamped with civilian casualties and makeshift morgues were set up at Peking University and elsewhere. The protest ended, and a period of active repression and arrests began.

For several days after June 4, it was unclear whether Deng Xiaoping was behind the massacre. Any doubt about Deng's role was dispelled, however, by his speech on June 9 to the commanders of the martial law forces. In this speech, Deng applauded the "martyrs" of the army who had been killed in the fighting. The speech provided a sense of the apocalyptic fears of aging veterans of the Party and suggested the sources of their willingness to use violence to crush dissent.

You comrades have been working hard.

First of all, I'd like to express my heartfelt condolences to the comrades in the People's Liberation Army, the armed police and police who died in the struggle— and my sincere sympathy and solicitude to the comrades in the army, the armed police and police who were wounded in the struggle, and I want to extend my sincere regards to all the army, armed police and police personnel who participated in the struggle.

I suggest that all of us stand and pay a silent tribute to the martyrs.

I'd like to take this opportunity to say a few words. This storm was bound to happen sooner or later. As determined by the international and domestic climate, it was bound to happen and was independent of man's will. It was just a matter of time and scale. It has turned out in our favor, for we still have a large group of veterans who have experienced many storms and have a thorough understanding of things.

They were on the side of taking resolute action to counter the turmoil. Although some comrades may not understand this now, they will understand eventually and will support the decision of the Central Committee.

The April 26 editorial of the *People's Daily* classified the problem as turmoil. The word was appropriate, but some people objected to the word and tried to amend it. But what has happened shows that this verdict was right. It was also inevitable that the turmoil would develop into a counterrevolutionary rebellion.

We still have a group of senior comrades who are alive, we still have the army, and we also have a group of core cadres who took part in the revolution at various times. That is why it was relatively easy for us to handle the present matter. The main difficulty in handling this matter lay in that we had never experienced such a situation before, in which a small minority of bad people mixed with so many young students and onlookers. We did not have a clear picture of the situation, and this prevented us from taking some actions that we should have taken earlier.

It would have been difficult for us to understand the nature of the matter had we not had the support of so many senior comrades. Some comrades didn't understand this point. They thought it was simply a matter of how to treat the masses. Actually, what we faced was not just some ordinary people who were misguided, but also a rebellious clique and a large quantity of the dregs of society. The key point is that they wanted to overthrow our stand and the party. Failing to understand this means failing to understand the nature of the matter. I believe that after serious work we can win the support of the great majority of comrades within the party.

OVERTHROW OF THE PARTY

The nature of the matter became clear soon after it erupted. They had two main slogans: to overthrow the Communist Party and topple the socialist system. Their goal was to establish a bourgeois republic entirely dependent on the West. Of course we accept people's demands for combating corruption. We are even ready to listen to some persons with ulterior motives when they raise the slogan about fighting corruption. However, such slogans were just a front. Their real aim was to overthrow the Communist Party and topple the socialist system.

During the course of quelling the rebellion, many comrades of ours were wounded or even sacrificed their lives. Some of their weapons were also taken from them by the rioters. Why? Because bad people mingled with the good, which made it difficult for us to take the firm measures that were necessary.

Handling this matter amounted to a severe political test for our army, and what happened shows that our People's Liberation Army passed muster. If tanks were used to roll over people, this would have created a confusion between right and wrong among the people nationwide. That is why I have to thank the P.L.A. officers and men for using this approach to handle the rebellion.

The P.L.A. losses were great, but this enabled us to win the support of the people and made those who can't tell right from wrong change their viewpoint.

They can see what kind of people the P.L.A. are, whether there was bloodshed at Tiananmen, and who were those that shed blood.

Once this question is made clear, we can take the initiative. Although it is very saddening that so many comrades were sacrificed, if the event is analyzed objectively, people cannot but recognize that the P.L.A. are the sons and brothers of the people. This will also help people to understand the measures we used in the course of the struggle. In the future, whenever the P.L.A. faces problems and takes measures, it will gain the support of the people. By the way, I would say that in the future, we must make sure that our weapons are not taken away from us.

PASSING THE TEST

In a word, this was a test, and we passed. Even though there are not so many veteran comrades in the army and the soldiers are mostly little more than 18, 19 or 21 years of age, they are still true soldiers of the people. Facing danger, they did not forget the people, the teachings of the party and the interests of the country. They kept a resolute stand in the face of death. They fully deserve the saying that they met death and sacrificed themselves with generosity and without fear.

When I talked about passing muster, I was referring to the fact that the army is still the People's Army. This army retains the traditions of the old Red Army. What they crossed this time was genuinely a political barrier, a threshold of life and death. This is by no means easy. This shows that the People's Army is truly a great wall of iron and steel of the party and country. This shows that no matter how heavy the losses we suffer and no matter how generations change, this army of ours is forever an army under the leadership of the party, forever the defender of the country, forever the defender of socialism, forever the defender of the public interest, and they are the most beloved of the people.

At the same time, we should never forget how cruel our enemies are. For them we should not have an iota of forgiveness.

The outbreak of the rebellion is worth thinking about. It prompts us to calmly think about the past and consider the future. Perhaps this bad thing will enable us to go ahead with reform and the open-door policy at a more steady, better, even a faster pace. Also it will enable us to more speedily correct our mistakes and better develop our strong points. I cannot elaborate on this today. I just want to raise the subject here.

CLEAR ANSWERS SOUGHT

The first question is: Are the line, goals and policies laid down by the Third Plenum of the 11th Central Committee, including our "three-step" development strategy, correct? Is it the case that because this riot took place there is some question about the correctness of the line, goals and policies we laid down? Are our goals "leftist"? Should we continue to use them for our struggle in the future? These significant questions should be given clear and definite answers.

makes it possible for us to understand each other and to develop friendship and closeness.

Thinking over what I might say today, I decided to share with you some of my thoughts concerning the common problems all of us face as members of the human family. Because we all share this small planet earth, we have to learn to live in harmony and peace with each other and with nature. That is not just a dream, but a necessity. We are dependent on each other in so many ways that we can no longer live in isolated communities and ignore what is happening outside those communities. We need to help each other when we have difficulties, and we must share the good fortune that we enjoy. I speak to you as just another human being, as a simple monk. If you find what I say useful, then I hope you will try to practice it.

I also wish to share with you today my feelings concerning the plight and aspirations of the people of Tibet. The Nobel Prize is a prize they well deserve for their courage and unfailing determination during the past forty years of foreign occupation. As a free spokesman for my captive countrymen and -women, I feel it is my duty to speak out on their behalf. I speak not with a feeling of anger or hatred towards those who are responsible for the immense suffering of our people and the destruction of our land, homes and culture. They too are human beings who struggle to find happiness and deserve our compassion. I speak to inform you of the sad situation in my country today and of the aspirations of my people, because in our struggle for freedom, truth is the only weapon we possess. . . .

The awarding of the Nobel Prize to me, a simple monk from far-away Tibet, here in Norway, also fills us Tibetans with hope. It means that, despite the fact that we have not drawn attention to our plight by means of violence, we have not been forgotten. It also means that the values we cherish, in particular our respect for all forms of life and the belief in the power of truth, are today recognized and encouraged. It is also a tribute to my mentor, Mahatma Gandhi, whose example is an inspiration to so many of us. This year's award is an indication that this sense of universal responsibility is developing. I am deeply touched by the sincere concern shown by so many people in this part of the world for the suffering of the people of Tibet. That is a source of hope not only for us Tibetans, but for all oppressed peoples.

As you know, Tibet has, for forty years, been under foreign occupation. Today, more than a quarter of a million Chinese troops are stationed in Tibet. Some sources estimate the occupation army to be twice this strength. During this time, Tibetans have been deprived of their most basic human rights, including the right to life, movement, speech, worship, only to mention a few. More than one-sixth of Tibet's population of six million died as a direct result of the Chinese invasion and occupation. Even before the Cultural Revolution started, many of Tibet's monasteries, temples and historic buildings were destroyed. Almost everything that remained was destroyed during the Cultural Revolution. I do not wish to dwell on this point, which is well documented. What is important to realize, however, is that despite the limited freedom granted after 1979 to rebuild parts of some monasteries and other such tokens of liberalization, the fundamental human rights of the Tibetan people are still today being systematically violated. In recent months this bad situation has become even worse.

If it were not for our community in exile, so generously sheltered and supported by the government and people of India and helped by organizations and individuals from many parts of the world, our nation would today be little more than a shattered remnant of a people. Our culture, religion and national identity would have been effectively eliminated. As it is, we have built schools and monasteries in exile and have created democratic institutions to serve our people and preserve the seeds of our civilization. With this experience, we intend to implement full democracy in a future free Tibet. Thus, as we develop our community in exile on modern lines, we also cherish and preserve our own identity and culture and bring hope to millions of our countrymen and -women in Tibet.

The issue of most urgent concern at this time is the massive influx of Chinese settlers into Tibet. Although in the first decades of occupation a considerable number of Chinese were transferred into the eastern parts of Tibet—in the Tibetan provinces of Amdo (Qinghai) and Kham (most of which has been annexed by the neighboring Chinese province)—since 1983 an unprecedented number of Chinese have been encouraged by their government to migrate to all parts of Tibet, including central and western Tibet (which the PRC refers to as the so-called Tibet Autonomous Region). Tibetans are rapidly being reduced to an insignificant minority in their own country. This development, which threatens the very survival of the Tibetan nation, its culture and spiritual heritage, can still be stopped and reversed. But this must be done now, before it is too late.

The new cycle of protest and violent repression, which started in Tibet in September of 1987 and culminated in the imposition of martial law in the capital, Lhasa, in March of this year, was in large part a reaction to this tremendous Chinese influx. Information reaching us in exile indicates that the protest marches and other peaceful forms of protest are continuing in Lhasa and a number of other places in Tibet despite the severe punishment and inhumane treatment given to Tibetans detained for expressing their grievances. The number of Tibetans killed by security forces during the protest in March and of those who died in detention afterwards is not known but is believed to be more than two hundred. Thousands have been detained or arrested and imprisoned, and torture is commonplace.

It was against the background of this worsening situation and in order to prevent further bloodshed, that I proposed what is generally referred to as the Five Point Peace Plan for the restoration of peace and human rights in Tibet. I elaborated on the plan in a speech in Strasbourg last year. I believe the plan provides a reasonable and realistic framework for negotiations with the People's Republic of China. So far, however, China's leaders have been unwilling to respond constructively. The brutal supression of the Chinese democracy movement in June of this year, however, reinforced my view that any settlement of the Tibetan question will only be meaningful if it is supported by adequate international guarantees.

The Five Point Peace Plan addresses the principal and interrelated issues, which I referred to in the first part of this lecture. It calls for (1) Transformation of the whole of Tibet, including the eastern provinces of Kham and Amdo, into a Zone of *Ahimsa* (non-violence); (2) Abandonment of China's population transfer policy; (3) Respect for the Tibetan people's fundamental human rights and democratic freedoms; (4) Restoration and protection of Tibet's natural environment; and (5) Commencement of earnest negotiations on the future status of Tibet and of relations between the Tibetan and Chinese peoples. In the Strasbourg address I proposed that Tibet become a fully self-governing democratic political entity.

I would like to take this opportunity to explain the Zone of Ahimsa or peace sanctuary concept, which is the central element of the Five Point Peace Plan. I am convinced that it is of great importance not only for Tibet, but for peace and stability in Asia.

It is my dream that the entire Tibetan plateau should become a free refuge where humanity and nature can live in peace and in harmonious balance. It would be a place where people from all over the world could come to seek the true meaning of peace within themselves, away from the tensions and pressures of much of the rest of the world. Tibet could indeed become a creative center for the promotion and development of peace.

The following are key elements of the proposed Zone of Ahimsa:

—the entire Tibetan plateau would be demilitarized;
—the manufacture, testing, and stockpiling of nuclear weapons and other armaments on the Tibetan plateau would be prohibited;
—the Tibetan plateau would be transformed into the world's largest natural park or biosphere. Strict laws would be enforced to protect wildlife and plant life; the exploitation of natural resources would be carefully regulated so as not to damage relevant ecosystems; and a policy of sustainable development would be adopted in populated areas;
—the manufacture and use of nuclear power and other technologies which produce hazardous waste would be prohibited;
—national resources and policy would be directed towards the active promotion of peace and environmental protection. Organizations dedicated to the furtherance of peace and to the protection of all forms of life would find a hospitable home in Tibet;
—the establishment of international and regional organizations for the promotion and protection of human rights would be encouraged in Tibet.

Tibet's height and size (the size of the European Community), as well as its unique history and profound spiritual heritage make it ideally suited to fulfill the role of a sanctuary of peace in the strategic heart of Asia. It would also be in keeping with Tibet's historical role as a peaceful Buddhist nation and buffer region separating the Asian continent's great and often rival powers.

In order to reduce existing tensions in Asia, the President of the Soviet Union, Mr. Gorbachev, proposed the demilitarization of Soviet-Chinese borders and their transformation into a "frontier of peace and good-neighborliness." The

Nepal government had earlier proposed that the Himalayan country of Nepal, bordering on Tibet, should become a zone of peace, although that proposal did not include demilitarization of the country.

For the stability and peace of Asia, it is essential to create peace zones to separate the continent's biggest powers and potential adversaries. President Gorbachev's proposal, which also included a complete Soviet troop withdrawal from Mongolia, would help to reduce tension and the potential for confrontation between the Soviet Union and China. A true peace zone must, clearly, also be created to separate the world's two most populous states, China and India.

The establishment of the Zone of Ahimsa would require the withdrawal of troops and military installations from Tibet, which would enable India and Nepal also to withdraw troops and military installations from the Himalayan regions bordering Tibet. This would have to be achieved by international agreements. It would be in the best interest of all states in Asia, particularly China and India, as it would enhance their security, while reducing the economic burden of maintaining high troop concentrations in remote areas. . . .

Let me end with a personal note of thanks to all of you and our friends who are not here today. The concern and support which you have expressed for the plight of the Tibetans has touched us all greatly, and continues to give us courage to struggle for freedom and justice; not through the use of arms, but with the powerful weapons of truth and determination. I know that I speak on behalf of all the people of Tibet when I thank you and ask you not to forget Tibet at this critical time in our country's history. We too hope to contribute to the development of a more peaceful, more humane and more beautiful world. A future free Tibet will seek to help those in need throughout the world, to protect nature, and to promote peace. I believe that our Tibetan ability to combine spiritual qualities with a realistic and practical attitude enables us to make a special contribution in however modest a way. This is my hope and prayer.

In conclusion, let me share with you a short prayer which gives me great inspiration and determination:

> For as long as space endures,
> And for as long as living beings remain,
> Until then may I, too, abide
> To dispel the misery of the world.

Thank you.

27.2 WEI JINGSHENG: "THE WOLF AND THE LAMB," NOVEMBER 18, 1993

Wei Jingsheng became one of China's most well known dissidents after his call for a "Fifth Modernization" (Document 24.2) during the Democracy

Wall movement of 1978–1979 earned him a lengthy prison sentence. When he was released in September 1993, after serving fourteen years of his term, he was just as outspoken and acerbic in his criticisms of the CCP. The following op-ed appeared in the *New York Times* just weeks after Wei's release. It reflected his view that human rights in China had not improved in the intervening years. Wei also addressed the issue of American attitudes and policies toward engagement with China. Shortly after the essay's publication, Wei was again arrested.

Most Americans don't really understand China, just as most Chinese don't understand America. This leads the two Governments to make numerous miscalculations in their relations and leads the two peoples toward numerous misunderstandings of the opposing regime's conduct.

For example, the Chinese Government holds that America cares nothing for the fate or future of the Chinese people; this means that raising human rights issues becomes nothing but a political tactic used in laying siege to the Communist Party or merely an economic bargaining tool.

So China treats human rights as a problem of foreign relations. And the primary pretext for refusing to bend under international pressure on human rights is that China "will not allow interference in its internal affairs."

Furthermore, there is a tendency on the part of China to view the detention and release of dissidents as a hostage transaction, in which freedom for the prisoner is just a bargaining chip in an economic poker game.

The reason the Chinese Government is willing to make such unclean transactions is that it does not understand why the U.S. might be unwilling to continue lucrative trade relations if China's human rights environment does not improve. China doesn't understand, because it thinks this way: Is it really likely that Americans would befriend a people they are not at all familiar with?

Is it really likely that Americans would abandon an opportunity to make money just to protect the human rights of those they have befriended?

Is it really likely that the American people's determinations of right and wrong could ever influence the judgment of the U.S. Government?

It looks as if the Communist Party has answered these questions in the negative. So even though it may have realized that its own conduct might have been in error, it still firmly pursues a strategy of brinksmanship, giving ground only when absolutely necessary and always in the last five minutes of negotiations. For example, Chinese officials last week agreed to give "positive consideration" to allowing the International Committee of the Red Cross to inspect prisons.

The party holds that in such ways it will save face, and in the end will debunk Yankee protestations of seriousness over human rights, which the party believes are just an affectation. Pursuing this strategy, Beijing believes, will free it to deprive the people of their freedom. It also seems that the U.S. Government has misunderstood the true mind-set of the Chinese Government. Washington evidently believes that the Communist Party resembles a bunch of slow-witted rulers of a backward culture and that China doesn't comprehend that violations of human rights are evil.

Therefore, the Clinton Administration now plans to abandon policies of pressure in favor of a policy of persuasion and "enhanced engagement"—a misguided shift to be symbolized in Seattle today by the handshake between Presidents Clinton and Jiang Zemin. Unfortunately, the reality is more like the Aesop's fable in which a lamb tries to reason with a wolf. After the wolf accuses the lamb of fouling his drinking water, the lamb protests: "I could not have fouled your water because I live downstream from you." The wolf eats the lamb anyway.

I fear that no matter how much the two countries debate, the old wolf in China will still complain about its drinking water. China not only doesn't understand reason but also does not intend to reason.

I'm unclear about the American people's understanding of changes in China-U.S. relations, but the Chinese people's understanding of their own Government is very precise. The present leaders were the most outspoken group of men, shouting their support of human rights and democracy before they ascended to power. But their subsequent dictatorship made clear that they have no intention of making good on the promises they once made to the masses.

The Chinese people's understanding of the new direction of U.S. policy toward China leads them to believe that the party was right all these years in saying that the American Government is controlled by rich capitalists. All you have to do is offer them a chance to make money and anything goes.

27.3 PRESIDENT CLINTON REEVALUATES HUMAN RIGHTS AS ELEMENT OF CHINA POLICY, MAY 27, 1994

In his first years in the White House President Clinton stressed human rights as an element of American foreign policy. However, when it came to pursuing this policy in the framework of the debate about the renewal of China's Most Favored Nation (MFN) status in the spring of 1994, the Clinton administration changed its stance. It decided to "delink" human rights and instead pursue a policy of "engagement" designed to expand economic ties with China, while promising to use moral suasion to address rights violations.

Our relationship with China is important to all Americans. We have significant interests in what happens there and what happens between us.

China has an atomic arsenal and a vote and a veto in the U.N. Security Council. It is a major factor in Asian and global security. We share important interests, such as in a nuclear-free Korean peninsula and in sustaining the global environment.

China is also the world's fastest-growing economy. Over $8 billion of United States exports to China last year supported over 150,000 American jobs.

I have received Secretary Christopher's letter recommending, as required by last year's executive order—reporting to me on the conditions in that executive order. He has reached a conclusion with which I agree, that the Chinese did not achieve overall significant progress in all the areas outlined in the executive order relating to human rights, even though clearly there was progress made in important areas, including the resolution of all immigration cases, the establishment of a memorandum of understanding with regard to how prison labor issues would be resolved, the adherence to the Universal Declaration of Human Rights, and other issues.

Nevertheless, serious human rights abuses continue in China, including the arrest and detention of those who peacefully voice their opinions and the repression of Tibet's religious and cultural traditions.

The question for us now is, given the fact that there has been some progress but that not all the requirements of the executive order were met, how can we best advance the cause of human rights and the other profound interests the United States has in our relationship with China?

I have decided that the United States should renew Most Favored Nation trading status toward China. This decision, I believe, offers us the best opportunity to lay the basis for long-term sustainable progress in human rights, and for the advancement of our other interests with China.

Extending MFN will avoid isolating China and instead will permit us to engage the Chinese with not only economic contacts but with cultural, educational and other contacts, and with a continuing aggressive effort in human rights—an approach that I believe will make it more likely that China will play a responsible role, both at home and abroad.

I am moving, therefore, to delink human rights from the annual extension of Most Favored Nation trading status for China. That linkage has been constructive during the past year, but I believe, based on our aggressive contacts with the Chinese in the past several months, that we have reached the end of the usefulness of that policy, and it is time to take a new path toward the achievement of our constant objectives. We need to place our relationship into a larger and more productive framework.

In view of the continuing human rights abuses, I am extending the sanctions imposed by the United States as a result of the events in Tiananmen Square. And I am also banning the import of munitions, principally guns and ammunition, from China.

I am also pursuing a new and vigorous American program to support those in China working to advance the cause of human rights and democracy. This program will include increased broadcasts for Radio-Free Asia and the Voice of America, increased support for nongovernmental organizations working on human rights in China, and the development, with American business leaders, of a voluntary set of principles for business activity in China.

I don't want to be misunderstood about this. China continues to commit very serious human rights abuses. Even as we engage the Chinese on military, political and economic issues, we intend to stay engaged with those in China who suffer from human rights abuses.

The United States must remain a champion of their liberties.

I believe the question, therefore, is not whether we continue to support human rights in China but how we can best support human rights in China and advance our other very significant issues and interests. I believe we can do it by engaging the Chinese. . . .

The actions I have taken today to advance our security, to advance our prosperity, to advance our ideals, I believe are the important and appropriate ones. I believe, in other words, this is in the strategic economic and political interests of both the United States and China, and I am confident that over the long run this decision will prove to be the correct one.

27.4 AND 27.5 THE THREE GORGES

Designed to be the world's largest hydroelectric dam, the Three Gorges project was a historic engineering feat mired in controversy from its inception. With an installed capacity of 22,500 megawatts, the dam promised to produce electricity to meet the nation's growing energy needs and solve the Yangzi River's perennial flooding problems. The enormous financial costs and potentially devastating ecological consequences, however, spurred opposition from many quarters, both domestic and foreign.

In the two documents below, a strong proponent and a vocal critic of the project discuss population resettlement, one of the most controversial issues. In an excerpt from his book *Developmental Resettlement Is Good*, Li Boning, a government expert on resettlement, argues that the region is particularly well suited to absorb the more than one million people to be moved. In an essay written for the English-language edition of her banned book *Yangtse! Yangtse!,* journalist Dai Qing[1] challenges Li's facts and figures and accuses the government of papering over myriad problems and concealing the truth.

27.4 *Li Boning: General Plan for Population Resettlement, September 1991*

The success or failure of resettlement will ultimately determine the success or failure of the Three Gorges project. Both the Central Committee of the Chinese

---

1. Dai Qing is the adopted daughter of Ye Jianying, a veteran of the Long March and a senior commander in the People's Liberation Army. She was trained as a missile engineer but became an investigative journalist in the 1980s. Dai published a volume of essays critical of the Three Gorges project in 1989, just before the student demonstrations erupted in Beijing. She resigned her membership in the CCP on June 5, 1989, and subsequently spent ten months in prison.

Communist Party and the State Council consider resettlement to be a very important issue and have adopted the policy of "Developmental Resettlement." This new approach to resettlement includes lump-sum reimbursement for lands lost to inundation, rural resettlement, township and factory relocation, personnel training, and other issues pertinent to relocation.

Trial projects have shown that although it is very difficult, resettlement in the Three Gorges area is environmentally feasible. If the Central Committee's resettlement policy is carried out fully and in a timely fashion, it will be possible to move most local populations back from the river and settle them in nearby areas. They need not be moved far away. What follows is an introduction to the issues germane to resettlement and a discussion of trial projects carried out over the past five years.

PROBLEMS WITH RESETTLEMENT

When the Three Gorges dam is complete, 19 counties and municipalities will be partially or completely submerged, including two county-level municipalities, 11 county seats, 140 towns, 326 townships, and 1,351 villages. As of 1985, inundation is expected to affect the following:

- Population of areas to be inundated: 725,500
  From townships: 392,900
  From rural areas: 332,600
- Amount of arable land to be inundated: 356,900 *mou* [23,800 hectares]
  Of rice paddies: 110,700 *mou*
  Of dry land: 240,200 *mou*
  Of orange groves: 74,400 *mou*
- Number of factories to be inundated: 675
  Value of fixed assets of the factories: 819 million yuan
- Number of power stations to be inundated: 139
  Total installed capacity: 77,000 KW
- Length of highways and roads to be submerged: 956.1 km
- Length of high-tension wires to be flooded: 1106.4 post [wires] km
- Length of telephone lines lost: 2,729.5 post [wires] km
- Broadcast (nonwireless) communications lines: 5,276.2 post [wires] km
- Number of primary cultural antiquity sites flooded: 6

As these figures indicate, the Three Gorges project is unprecedented in Chinese dam-building history. The difficulties faced in construction, especially those related to resettlement, are therefore equally unprecedented.

Population density is very high in the reservoir area, with an average of 1.1 *mou* of land per capita. There is a lack of irrigation facilities and very little planning for flood prevention. Education levels are quite low. Moreover, during the many decades of uncertainty over the project, there was little economic investment in the region, creating considerable poverty among the locals. Of the 18 million people in the region, more than three million live in poverty, and many counties in the region rely on government subsidies just to get by.

Previous resettlement operations are likely to provide little comfort for potential Three Gorges relocatees. In the past, resettlement was not handled properly; many people were left stranded without employment or adequate shelter and in a state of destitution, creating considerable social and political instability in reservoir areas. These experiences have left people feeling wary of resettlement. Whenever the issue is brought up, people react with fear, and they refuse to discuss why previous efforts failed and how the Three Gorges is different. Once bitten, twice shy.

Certainly, successful resettlement will be difficult and must be taken seriously, but critics' assumptions that resettlement in the Three Gorges area will be a disaster are not credible.

WHY THE THREE GORGES AREA IS WELL SUITED FOR RESETTLEMENT

The Three Gorges area is particularly well suited to accommodate a large resettled population for a number of reasons. The area has abundant natural resources (especially land); most of the resettlers are from townships and are therefore easier to move than are rural people; the project is a long one and will allow sufficient time for proper resettlement; the new Developmental Resettlement policy will ensure that resettlers are well taken care of; and, finally, the central government is firmly committed to the resettlement program and to the project overall.

The Three Gorges area's abundant land resources and burgeoning agriculture, fishing, mining, tourism, and processing and service industries make it particularly well suited to receive settlers. In fact, many of these industries have emerged as a result of the dam's construction. The dam will submerge more than 350,000 *mou* of land, including 70,000 *mou* of orange groves, but studies have shown that there is upward of 20 million *mou* of undeveloped land in the 19 counties and municipalities where people must be resettled, 3.89 million *mou* of which is found in the 361 townships where resettlement will take place. About 4.2 million *mou* of the undeveloped land in the area is arable, and 40 percent of it is low-grade sloping land. For each rural relocatee, one-half *mou* of highly productive land for grain, and one *mou* of land for orange groves or other cash crops (fruit, tea, mulberry leaves, or herbs) is needed. This means that 500,000 *mou* of land will be required to accommodate the 300,000 rural resettlers. An additional 30 to 50 percent of this amount must be developed and given to the locals as compensation for lands allocated to resettlers. In total then, 800,000 to one million *mou* of land will have to be developed to resettle people successfully and assure them adequate grain production, a stable life, and higher incomes than they enjoyed before.

Although it is both possible and feasible to develop the needed land in the 361 townships, if necessary, the areas slated to receive relocatees can be expanded to include other territories within these same counties. It will also be possible to develop some areas that lie below the submersion line. By building dikes to protect arable land in Kaixian, Zigui, Badong, and Wanxian counties, an additional 25,000 *mou* of farmland can be saved. Moreover, if the dam's normal pool level is reduced to 160 from 175 meters, another 160,000 *mou* of land can be saved from inundation and used by local farmers to supplement their incomes. Finally, there are also vast grasslands in the Three Gorges area that can be used by relocatees to graze animals and to begin an animal husbandry industry for local markets.

The Three Gorges area also contains abundant stores of natural resources—salt, natural gas, coal, phosphorous, limestone, and marble—the exploitation of which will create thousands of jobs for resettlers. As a start, the government has approved construction of a 60,000 ton-capacity alkaline facility near Wanxian Municipality, which will create 39,000 jobs. Projects like this one not only contribute to job creation and economic growth, they also reduce the cost of resettlement; in effect, killing two birds with one stone. If national and local governments can provide similar opportunities for rural relocatees during the dam's construction, then the cost of resettlement can be reduced substantially. This is in line with the general policy laid out by Comrade Deng Xiaoping, who has said on many occasions that "we should strive to provide more projects in this area," and also with Article 19 of the State Council announcement titled "Land Reimbursement and Resettlement Procedures for Large and Medium-Sized Hydroelectric Projects," which declares that the construction of new production facilities must be combined with resettlement work.

Rural relocatees will be able to continue working in the agricultural sector after they have been resettled. Trial resettlement projects have proven the viability of this approach, and rural relocatees and relevant local governments have guaranteed that the projects will be successful. Finally, where continued work in the agricultural sector is no longer possible, other occupations can be considered, though a large-scale conversion from agricultural to nonagricultural employment will not be necessary.

A second reason why the Three Gorges area is so well suited to receive relocatees is the relative proportion of people being moved from townships as compared with those being moved from rural areas. Just over half of those to be moved (54 percent) are from townships—a much higher percentage than in most resettlement efforts. This is important because resettling people from townships is a simple affair; generally, after moving people work at similar jobs as they did before (and, therefore, do not require retraining), and officials need only expand urban services and functions to the new areas in order to accommodate them. Resettling rural people is more difficult. It often means converting them to an entirely new way of life in fundamentally different occupations.

The rural dwellers who will be moved are scattered throughout 19 counties and municipalities, from Sandouping in Yichang Municipality, to Mudong Township in Ba County. They constitute only 2.6 percent of the total rural population of the Three Gorges area, while the arable land to be flooded constitutes only 2.5 percent of the total. And, significantly, only 2 percent of the rice paddies in the Three Gorges area will be lost to the dam. (Because the region is hilly, much of the arable land is on hillsides above the projected submersion line.)

None of the 326 towns that will be affected by the reservoir will be completely submerged, and only a very small number of villages will be totally inundated. Studies indicate that in 291 of the townships, resettlers will simply have to move to other parts of the town, and in only 35 of them will people have to move to other towns altogether. This is why local conditions are so favorable for carrying out the policy of moving back from the river and settling in nearby areas rather than having to move relocatees over great distances, something which is unique to the Three Gorges project. These studies show that the Three Gorges project will not repeat the problems of previous large-scale hydroelectric projects which required the resettlement of large numbers of people to remote and distant areas.

The fact that the dam will take many years to build is a third factor that will help facilitate successful resettlement. Unlike previous projects in which rivers were diverted quickly, driving people from the area without adequate preparation or planning, the Three Gorges project will give people enough time to adapt to their new environments and employment possibilities.

A fourth factor is the Developmental Resettlement policy, which is designed to provide economic benefits to rural resettlers through the government-financed reclamation of higher-elevation land, the cultivation of cash crops, and the creation of industrial jobs along with lump-sum reimbursements for relocatees' losses. Trial projects over the last five years have proven the success of this approach, and the policy ensures that migrants will be protected by the central government from the start of the project to its finish.

A final factor contributing to the feasibility of resettlement in the Three Gorges area is the central government's firm commitment to the project and resettlement program. Government leaders not only formulated the Developmental Resettlement policy, but also allocated ¥100 million for trial projects over the past five years and formed the Leading Group of the State Council Overseeing Trial Resettlement Projects. None of these steps was taken for previous hydroelectric projects: Moreover, the Economic Development Office of the Three Gorges Project has worked with relevant local governments to coordinate the various aspects of Developmental Resettlement. Together they have made great progress. Over the course of the five-year trial projects, cadres, masses, and migrants have come to appreciate the benefits of the dam and support its speedy construction. Together, the cooperation of the masses, the support of the central government, and the five-year experience with trial projects guarantee that resettlement will be done well.

Still, despite all this evidence that resettlement will be successful, some comrades are concerned that developing more land in the Three Gorges region will contribute to soil erosion and destroy the local environment. This is an issue that deserves attention, but it can be resolved. Strict planning procedures and adherence to stringent quality control standards will be followed in opening lands to grain and citrus fruit tree production. This is not a case of unplanned and haphazard development of barren lands. Indeed, the orange groves which were developed as part of the trial projects required the construction of stone wall terraces [on the mountains] that actually improved soil retention. The same is true where grasses and trees were planted to help in soil conservation.

TRIAL PROJECTS IN TOWNSHIP RESETTLEMENT

In planning for new towns over the past five years, we have focused our efforts on building road, water, and electricity projects. These projects, called "three dimensional infrastructure construction projects" (santong gongcheng), have created favorable conditions for township resettlement and development.

Through various studies and the experience of the trial projects, we have learned that the long delay in launching the Three Gorges project has had an especially adverse effect on the development of some township economies. Now these towns are so saturated by recent population growth and urban sprawl that there is little room for further development. If the resettlement programs are not implemented soon, given population growth and peoples' desire to escape poverty, the locals may start building projects below the submersion line. In fact, we know that millions of yuan have already been spent on these types of projects in counties all along the river. According to resettlement experts, by 1986, 11 billion yuan had been invested in projects below the submersion line. By 1990, the figure was up to 18.5 billion yuan and was increasing by an average of 1.8 billion yuan per year. If this situation persists, the cost and complexity of successfully resettling people will increase dramatically. Therefore, it is extremely important to carry out the "three dimensional projects" in order to create an environment favorable to investment, to reduce future investments below the submersion line, and to lay a solid foundation for future large-scale resettlement and development.

Over the past few years, we have invested more than 9 million yuan in 13 "three dimensional projects," and most are already showing considerable benefits. For instance, Fuling Municipality took advantage of reconstruction work on the Wu River bridge and built a three-level overpass. In three years, 300,000 square meters of new housing and 7.5 kilometers of new roads have been built in the area. Fuling relied primarily on its own resources and funds for the trial projects and received only 1.6 million yuan from the government. The projects will greatly reduce the costs incurred by inundation.

Another county received 2.1 million yuan for its program to build roads, relocate ten factories, and build an alkaline plant with an annual production capacity of 60,000 tons. Badong County used resettlement funds from the Gezhouba dam and 800,000 yuan from the government to help with its project—building 7.7 kilometers of roads and 600 cubic meters of water storage tanks for newly developed areas.

Actor Gu Yue, in Tiananmen Square.

None of the films I've worked on have touched on these questions. None have dealt directly with the Cultural Revolution. I can hardly be blamed if it's not in the script. If, in the future, the script calls for it, then I'll do what is required of me.

What did you think when, as you were working on developing your Mao character, you came across his dark side?

Mmm. Nobody's perfect after all, and Mao Zedong is no exception to that. Mistakes and errors were inevitable given the long and protracted struggles in which he was involved. The Party Central line on this at the present time is quite correct. I wouldn't speculate on how he'll be seen in the future. I do feel, however, that Comrade Deng Xiaoping has been magnanimous in the way he has dealt with this matter. Despite the numerous attacks made on him personally, Deng has not treated Mao Zedong in a vengeful fashion. Western journalists often ask me what I think of Mao's errors. Once in Ji'nan [the capital of Shandong Province] I responded to an American journalist with a question of my own: What do you think of the statue of Venus? Her arms may be broken but she's still beautiful. I see Mao Zedong in the same way. Flawed beauty is more alluring.

The MaoCraze in China leads one to reflect on the Soviet Union. They not only negated Stalin, now they've even dumped Lenin. Do you think that one day China will act like this?

If we support the Four Basic Principles as formulated by Deng Xiaoping, China will not change. If, however, we abandon those principles, China will naturally go the way of the Soviet Union.

Will China abandon the Four Basic Principles after the generation of Older Revolutionaries has died?

That's just what the prognosticators of Western imperialism are hoping for. It depends entirely on the next generation of leaders.

If there is a change, Mao will be the first to get it. Are you prepared for that possibility?

One can understand that some people hold fears for China becoming like the Soviet Union after our Older Revolutionaries pass away. But the Soviet Union didn't change overnight and we are presently taking precautions.

A report in Sing Pao today claims that Mao's daughter thinks of you as her father. Is that true?

Not exactly. When I was filming *The Final Conflict* at Xibaipo, Li Na [Mao and Jiang Qing's daughter] happened to make a trip there. She had lived there with Mao when she was seven. She asked to see me. I recall that we met in a conference room. She held me by the hand, and said: "Your hand's big and soft just like my father's." She's only a little younger than me, but she's had a hard life. After her father died, her mother had certain difficulties. Li Na must have been deeply disturbed and affected by all of that. When I was seeing them off she ran over, hugged me, and burst into tears. I was taken completely by surprise. I realized that there were no words that could express what she was feeling at that moment. I cried too. Everyone present became tearful. Finally I said to her: "I understand."

Have you met all of Mao's family?

I see Li Min [the other of Mao's daughters] and her husband, Kong Linghua. Since first meeting them in 1984, she always invites me to spend December 26 [Mao's birthday] at their house. I invariably meet a number of old comrades who knew Mao very well there. So, if I'm free, I go every year and, through her, I've met Mao's secretaries, doctors, nurses, and personal guards. They all remember Chairman Mao with great affection and it has been a valuable learning experience for me. Through them, I've also been able to find out a great deal about the Chairman's private life. I've also met Mao Anqing and his wife.

Have you ever met Zhang Yufeng?

Someone told me she was in the same theater when I went to see a performance of some description, but I did not search her out.

There's a rumor that she had a child by Mao. Is that true?

As far as I know it's just that, a rumor. Someone wrote about it in a book, and a leader in the Central government remarked that if such gossip persists legal action can be taken for defamation. I believe people who have a grudge against the Chairman made the story up. If it were really true, there's no way it could be kept a secret these days. So many people hate him, and there's been all this material pointing out his errors that you can't tell me you could keep a thing like that secret. Zhang Yufeng is presently a Section Head in the Ministry of Rail Transportation.

Lin Biao and Liu Shaoqi rarely make an appearance in the films about Party leaders. Is this intentional?

No. From what I understand there is a central plan for the production of such films. Initially, we are making films about the historical events everyone can agree on, like *The Final Conflict* and *The Three Great Campaigns,* and various periods before the Cultural Revolution. A lot of water has passed under the bridge and people can reflect on the past more calmly. It will be easier to make such films from now on.

Are there deliberate attempts to emphasize Deng Xiaoping's role?

No. It is a matter of historical fact. *The Final Conflict* is about a period during which Liu Bocheng and Deng Xiaoping were equally important but, after Liberation, Liu didn't play as major a role as Deng. In the same token, Liu Shaoqi doesn't have a large role in *The Final Conflict*, and that's a matter of historical fact too.

What do you know about Jiang Qing?

She really was an ambitious woman. I've read some things that show she didn't start out that way. But she revealed a typically feminine kind of jealousy from the time she became an actress. The moment she got into power she wanted revenge. I've been told that when she and Mao were married, Zhou Enlai proposed that she be kept out of politics. As a result her political ambitions were frustrated for years and she harbored a grudge against the Premier. She had a real lust for power.

Do you have access to classified material?

Only limited access. For example, I've read top-secret military telegrams related to the Three Great Campaigns (now stored in the Academy of Military Science). Mao Zedong directed the campaigns by telegram and there are more than 400 telegrams in the files, of which he composed 360. I made reams of notes as background research.

What does Deng think of your acting?

Every time I've seen him he's praised my work. I've met the state leaders on various national holidays.

Who's in charge of films related to Party leaders? Is the funding particularly good?

Li Ruihuan [then the Politburo leader in charge of ideological matters] is the highest authority. All the films are vetted by "The Steering Committee on Major Revolutionary Historical Themes" which is chaired by Ding Qiao [a former government minister in charge of cinema]. Wang Renzhi [then head of the Department of Propaganda] and Ai Zhisheng [then head of the Ministry of Film and Television] are also involved. Budgets for revolutionary epics are pretty big, but they're based on box office projections. It really depends on the film.

Mao films are so predominantly political, do you think there's any chance they can reach an international audience?

I believe there are great possibilities. There's a well-known American director by the name of Oliver Stone who wants to make a film about Mao Zedong. If he wants to find an actor in China for the role I'm confident that I can do it since I've played Mao [in all stages of his life] from youth to old age. If Stone wants me, I'll do my utmost for the role. Mao Zedong is, after all, a national hero. *Gandhi* made it internationally, so there is no reason Mao can't do the same. As long as you have a good script and the film is performed and filmed well, there's a real chance of success. *The Final Conflict* could be an international war epic.

But such films have a hard time even making it to Taiwan.

That goes without saying. But people on both sides of the Straits want an accurate portrayal of history. We no longer present a caricature of Chiang Kai-shek in our films; we try to be as convincing as possible.

How do you compare your work to Soviet films about Party leaders?

Our films are an advance on the style of filmmaking developed from 1928 by Soviet directors like Eisenstein. I'm particularly impressed by the work of the actor who portrayed Lenin as a great yet also ordinary man.

As you're such a successful Mainland film star, do you make much more than other actors?

Let me be frank. Although I'm politically advantaged in that I've often been given audiences with Central leaders, something unheard of for most actors, financially I'm at a distinct disadvantage. I can't negotiate my own terms. According to the regulations of the Ministry of Film and Television, an actor on loan [to another studio] should receive four times their usual wage. But all that money goes to their film studio, in my case, the 1 August Studio. I don't make any extra money. My monthly wage is about three hundred yuan. Many other famous actors can get seven or eight times their basic wage when they work for another studio, but I do it for nothing. At most, I get an extra living allowance. To play a leader you have to be prepared to make some sacrifices. What can I do about it? If you play a hero, you have to act the hero in real life. If I haggled about such things, I could damage Mao's image.

Has there been any adverse effect on your family life?

No. My wife and I still make more than most people. We do okay. But, of course, we can't compare to movie stars overseas.

CHAPTER 28 | # Breakthrough?

28.1 CHINA CAN SAY NO

A seminal text of popular nationalism, *China Can Say No* was first published in 1996, in the immediate aftermath of the confrontation between China and the United States in the Taiwan Straits. The first edition of 130,000 copies sold out quickly and caused a major stir. Soon a cottage industry of "say no" books appeared, including a hastily assembled sequel, *China Can Still Say No*, by the original team of authors. The U.S. bombing of the Chinese embassy in Belgrade in 1999 prompted another wave of "say no" publications. Inspired by similar works from Japan, the "naysayer" phenomenon in China reflected popular sentiment stoked by government encouragement. With confrontational statements and salacious charges, these books both channeled and provoked a rising tide of passionate and often xenophobic nationalism.

As the following excerpts from the original 1996 volume illustrate, the authors were incensed by the machinations of the United States, plotting to sabotage China's rise. The issue of Taiwan inspired special vitriol, the most obvious evidence of American duplicity and aspirations to world hegemony.

PREFACE

This is not another nationalist manifesto, nor is it a strategic plan to establish China's position in world politics.

What it should be taken as is an attempt to elucidate and give some precision to widespread popular sentiment.

Many signs point to the fact that after the end of the Cold War, as the only remaining large socialist nation, China's path has garnered significant attention.

Emerging from deep-rooted mentalities and conflicting viewpoints, and owing to their desire to dominate the world as the sole superpower, America has expressed much consternation and unease at the phenomenon of China's sudden rise to power. In their view, in the not too distant future, perhaps China will be the only nation with the power to check and balance America's cultural, economic, and military hegemony. Therefore, the "Free World" has started to brew up a grand scheme directed against China.

The reason why I call it a scheme is because America says one thing and does another.

For example, even as Americans reaffirm that Taiwan is part of China's territory, their Seventh Fleet nonetheless patrols near Taiwan. Meanwhile, they pompously declare to the world, "Let no one forget that America's navy is the world's finest."

Moreover, while they sing pleasant tunes about their desire to help China enter the World Trade Organization as soon as possible, a high-ranking official of the European Union indicated privately, "We have no serious problems. The major issue is that America is obstructing the process."

Furthermore, China has repeatedly clarified its own position on the issue of human rights, expressing the wish for dialogue, not antagonism, in this sphere. And yet, America's Geraldine Ferraro,[1] blind to her own hypocrisy, said at the annual meeting of the United Nations Human Rights Committee, that China's motion of "not granting consideration" to the issues raised by Western nations was an act of antagonism.

Finally, at the same time that America was clamoring all around about how the spread of China's arms manufacturing was deepening crises in vulnerable areas of the world, America became embroiled in its own Iran-Contra scandal.

In sum, "containing" China in every domain has become one of America's fundamental national policies. America has launched a new Cold War against China.

As one of the authors of this book says, "I was originally a believer in internationalism, but when I saw the actions of America, Britain, and other countries in response to China's bid to host the Olympics I was truly upset. Ever since then I have slowly become a believer in nationalism." I believe that there are many people in China who have the same or similar trains of thought.

In passing, let me just say that all five authors of this book are young people around thirty years old—newspaper reporter, university professor, poet, and freelance writer. Regardless of if you look at their qualifications, identity or status, they have nothing in common with Morita Akio, Ishihara Shintarō, and Mahathir bin Mohamad, the authors of *The Japan That Can Say No* and *The Asia That Can Say No*. The decision to write this book was in large part an emotional one—the authors are not experts on international problems. But it is precisely that fact that gives this book its broad and robust base of popular sentiment.

1. Geraldine Ferraro was the U.S. ambassador to the U.N. Commission on Human Rights from 1993 to 1996.

China saying no is, in fact, not the same as seeking confrontation. Rather, saying no is about seeking dialogue in a more equal environment—this is one of the main themes that runs throughout the book. With America taking the lead among Western nations fondly remembering the days of the Cold War, and with politicians infatuated with establishing policies of "confrontation" and "containment," they ought to understand that they have driven Chinese people, and especially the youth of China, to a point of extreme frustration and disgust.

We need to lay out a few conclusions:

America can't lead everyone—it can only lead itself
Japan can't lead everyone—it sometimes can't even manage to lead itself
China doesn't want to lead anyone else—China only wants to lead itself

Please continue and read the main body of the text.

April 26, 1996

HOW MUCH IS AMERICA WILLING TO PAY FOR TAIWAN?

Ever since Taiwan's authorities gave signs clearly indicating their desire for independence, they have received increasing levels of commitment from all over America. But how much are Americans really willing to pay for Taiwan? This is something about which Taiwan's authorities really have no way to be sure. But there is one thing that is absolutely clear—it is a mistake for Taiwan to put all of its eggs in the American basket. History makes perfectly clear that Americans will easily abandon allies in pursuit of their own self-interest. Just as how China's government has made many overtures of trade to America, Taiwan may easily repeat the fate of Chiang Kai-shek in 1949.

The problem is that we absolutely cannot propose a compromise with America that would be harmful to our honor. America has not been realistic in its thinking and they will have to abandon Taiwan. Here and now, Taiwan must not make the mistake of continuing to walk down the path toward independence. In Taiwan's calculations, America's interests are greater in Taiwan than in the mainland. They therefore think that in a time of crisis, America will support Taibei. But Taiwan's rough calculation only looks at the benefits to be found in American political and military arenas. True, it is because of Taiwan's existence that America can impede the Chinese government's activities in international affairs. But at the same time, this is clearly wishful thinking by the authorities in Taiwan. It is true that Taiwan's existence gives America an excuse to interfere in China's domestic affairs. Yet, the actual extent of their power to impede China is something that must be carefully analyzed going forward.

In fact, China's course of modernization has already forced America to face this Eastern Giant. The fact that America continues to harass China about Taiwan,

Tibet, and other questions just goes to show that America can't get a hold of any "new goods." On the contrary, China's development will progressively contain America's hegemony in Asia.

America naturally views China as the biggest threat to its hegemony in Asia. America has established bases for its Pacific Fleet in Japan, Korea, Taiwan and the Philippines. In doing so, they envision creating a crescent shaped encirclement so as to control Southeast Asia. In spite of international norms as well as Sino-American joint communiqués, America continues to ship arms to Taiwan. But no matter what, as long as Taiwan sees itself as simply a card for someone else to play, sovereignty will never be in its own hands. This is a truly sorrowful matter.

Taiwan's authorities have a naive mindset. They think they can simply rely on existing economic power to walk the path toward independence. But they are obviously pulling the wool over their eyes and are blind to the reality of the situation. Taiwan is China's territory. If 1.2 billion people disagree with their stance, then Taiwan's authorities are betraying both the people and the homeland. As the loss of the DPP's candidate and independence advocate Peng Mingmin shows, the people of Taiwan have no desire to split the homeland. Splitting the homeland is simply not in accord with popular sentiment. Even the members of the American central administration most supportive of Taiwan have unequivocally declared that they do not wish to see China divided.

One Country Two Systems is an excellent framework. The Chinese people are able to stand on their own two feet and have absolutely no use for foreign interference. It is obvious that seeking American protection is like inviting a wolf into the room. The countries of Southeast Asia are, in fact, not happy about American political, economic, cultural and military interference in the region. That Taiwan draws American power into the area actually leads to regional conflict and upheaval. This furthermore has an effect on Taiwan's relationship with other countries throughout Asia. Aside from countries ruled by Western colonial powers, who is still willing to return to the era of colonialism?

In truth, of all the factors in the history of the creation of economic disparity between the East and West, colonialism is the principal root of this misfortune. The people of many Eastern countries have deep personal experiences with the crimes of the West. Furthermore, without exception, Eastern countries have achieved periods of economic development only after having first thrown off colonial rule. We believe that it is impossible for Eastern countries to forget the pain of this history, just like people in Taiwan cannot forget the trauma of Japanese colonial rule.

The opposition to Western military presence is rising among people in Asia because this region of the world has no desire for conflict and turmoil. From the perspective of the impending new world order, no matter from what angle you look, it is clear that Taiwan should not place too much of its hopes on America. They need to give themselves an escape route. Some people in Taiwan look at the annual twenty billion dollars in American imports and exports and the nearly forty-five billion dollars of deposits in American bank accounts and conclude that

America has a significant interest in Taiwan's trade and economy—even greater than its involvement with the mainland economy. But this is clearly a shortsighted and utilitarian point of view. The mainland, with Reform and Opening Up and the development of a market economy, has a latent market power with which Taiwan simply cannot compete. In the very near future, the mainland market will have the capacity to absorb several hundred billion dollars. Furthermore, the mainland is progressively establishing good economic relations with countries around the world, bringing significant benefits to which America cannot afford to remain indifferent. Therefore, in the area of economy and trade, Taiwan shouldn't set its hopes too high.

In this showdown between China and America, having Taiwan as a card in its hand has already brought many benefits to the U.S.—but America can't expect heaven to bestow such good fortune forever. On the base of its current pace of development, going into the next century China will have enough international influence to compel America to abandon its illegitimate positions. Those who support independence for Taiwan should take careful note of this point. On the other hand, if Taiwan were to persist on the road of unification with the homeland, open up positive dialogue, and enact the policy of One Country Two Systems, then the Chinese people—tied together by blood and by history—and the expansive mainland market will be enough to stimulate rapid development in Taiwan's economy as they gain the most precious of resources. Just by looking at the current volume of transshipping trade in Hong Kong, it is obvious that Taiwan is not living up to its full potential. It ought to be clear to those in Taiwan engaged in industry and commerce exactly where the road forward lies.

In the coming century, how much will America still be willing to pay for Taiwan? America's interference with China's domestic affairs has not brought the gains it had hoped for in the international arena. On the contrary, America's actions have made more and more countries anxious and dissatisfied. Even the White House is clear: they don't actually have the courage of their convictions. America's meddling can only bring about regional conflict and a tumultuous situation, benefiting absolutely no one. On this point we ought to be clear: no matter how powerful the military is, it will never be able to preserve the final victory. . . . The most crucial point is that America cannot abandon the progress made in diplomatic relations with the mainland and the benefits they bring. While Newt Gingrich, Bob Dole and others express anger over the mainland's military exercises in the Straits, the question remains just how much of their anger is hyperbole. This is an election year in America, and we all know that it is an American tradition for politicians to say whatever it takes to win support leading up to an election. When Clinton was campaigning against Bush, didn't Clinton fiercely criticize Bush's weak position and lack of accomplishments in regard to China? . . . The fact is that in America, before an election you should discount 20 percent of everything politicians say, even more if there is a debate. If you want to believe the promises they make and take all their strategic thinking seriously, then in the end they'll just make a fool out of you. Americans don't play by the same rules as everyone else.

It's best not to participate in this type of game.

America had better not "play the world." Beware of frightening your children.

—Translated by Daniel Barish

28.2 AND 28.3 EARTHQUAKE IN SICHUAN, MAY 2008

On May 12, 2008, an earthquake registering 7.9 on the Richter scale shook Sichuan province, with reverberations felt across the country. In the aftermath, the world watched as rescuers desperately dug into thousands of crumpled buildings in search of survivors, and as the death toll climbed to nearly seventy thousand.

Liao Yiwu (b. 1958) was in the town of Wenjiang when the earthquake struck. A native of Sichuan, Liao had spent many years writing about ordinary people in Chinese society. He was particularly interested in the lives of the dispossessed, and his writings (frequently banned) typically featured the socially marginalized, presenting their stories as an implicit rebuke of the inequalities in contemporary society. A few days after the earthequake, Liao struck up a conversation with a factory worker who had just narrowly escaped with his life. "The Survivor" is the transcript of their conversation, which was translated into English and first published in the *Paris Review*. The second document, "Fortitude in Adversity," appeared in *Beijing Review* one week after the earthquake. It describes the government's rescue and relief efforts and praises the people's resolve and courage in a time of tragedy.

28.2 *"The Survivor"*

On the afternoon of May 12, I was walking to my home in the town of Wenjiang, in Sichuan Province, China, when the ground began to shake. I didn't realize it was an earthquake until I saw all the buildings around me vibrating.

After the tremors subsided, security guards began patrolling the neighborhood, urging people to leave their homes and seek shelter in the parks. I could see giant cracks in many buildings. All the main thoroughfares had been blocked and policemen were busy directing traffic and pedestrians. Inside Wenjiang Park, people set up tents or put down sheets on the lawn. Garbage piled up.

Clouds gathered and the wind started to blow. There were long lines in front of all the grocery stores and restaurants. I found a small noodle shop and waited for ten minutes. The line didn't move. I yelled at the top of my voice. Nobody paid any attention. People buried their faces in their bowls, eating and eating. I snatched a couple of cakes at a bakery, then I wandered through the streets.

At eleven P.M. a large crowd of people gathered around a television set on the street. The government announced an initial death toll of eight thousand. A friend called from Dujiangyan, one of the most damaged cities in Sichuan Province. He screamed into the phone: The entrance to Erwang Temple has collapsed. Rubble is everywhere. Dead bodies are everywhere. As he was yelling, our call cut off.

I felt guilty that I had survived. On television I watched babies and students being pulled out of the debris. I wished I could be there helping, or at least record-ing their despair. I thought of the professional mourner I'd interviewed ten years ago. He spent his whole life crying and playing the *suona* at other people's funer-als. What would happen to him now?

Four days later, a friend and I decided to visit Dujiangyan. I wanted to interview survivors. Since Premier Wen Jiabao was in the city helping to organize the rescue work, the local government had set up several checkpoints along the road. Only rescue workers and government-sanctioned journalists were allowed to enter.

After a couple of phone calls, my friend, who is well connected, managed to gain us access. Crumbled houses and makeshift tents were everywhere we looked. I met a forty-year-old man named Yang Wenchang, who had bruises all over his body, and his wife, Zhou Zehua. Yang had just returned the day before from Wenchuan County, the epicenter of the magnitude-eight earthquake.

LIAO YIWU: *You were born here in Dujiangyan. How did you end up in Wenchuan County?*

YANG WENCHANG: About a month and a half ago, a friend told me about a job in the town of Shaohuoping. My wife's been sick for a while. My kids need money to attend school. I'm the family's sole breadwinner. It's hard to make money here. So I went to Shaohuoping and worked at a factory that made steel and iron wires. My job was to take care of the furnaces, and my monthly salary was supposed to be about a hundred and seventy dollars. I worked hard, hoping to see some money come in. Before I got my first paycheck, the earthquake hit.

Were you inside the factory when it happened?

YANG: We had the day off because the factory had a power outage. Eight of us migrant workers were on the top floor of our apartment building, sleeping in. It was a three-story building. There was no warning beforehand. As I was sleeping, my bed, which was in the middle of the room, started to shake violently. It was as if an army of blacksmiths were hitting me with their meaty fists from under the mattress. I was tossed off the bed. Before I could stand up, everything began to shake sideways. I struggled to claw my way to the door. Then I looked outside. I found myself perched on the edge of an abyss, hundreds of miles deep.

It was only a three-story building. You couldn't have been that high off the ground.

YANG: It certainly felt that way. It was like getting seasick on a boat in the middle of an ocean. I tried to hold on to the edge of the door. I looked back inside and saw the center of the room suddenly collapse. All that was left was a big hole. Three people and four beds fell through the hole, right in front of my eyes. Pieces of steel-reinforced concrete followed them, falling from the ceiling, plunging through the second floor until they hit the ground.

Didn't you just say there were eight of you? What happened to the other four people?

YANG: They lived next door and had plunged down to the bottom too. All the walls around me started to crumble—boom, boom—with ashes shooting up seventy or eighty feet. All seven of my coworkers were buried under the building. The next day, one was dug out. He had suffered severe injuries but survived. When I left the area yesterday, the other six were still missing.

How did you manage to escape the collapsing building?

YANG: As the ceiling and the surrounding walls were collapsing, I lost my balance and fell. Thank heavens, before I hit the ground, my feet landed on a supporting wall that was still standing on the first floor. I managed to balance myself and then jump one flight to the ground. My body landed on a pile of debris. I hurt my head, my arms, and my legs, but not seriously. If it hadn't been for that supporting wall, I would have been buried like the others.

What happened next?

YANG: About thirty people spent all day digging nonstop. They were able to locate the guy I talked about. His body had been hit hard by falling concrete. When rescue workers tried to give him water, he spat blood. It looks like he'll live, but I think he'll be disabled.

You were lucky.

YANG: I guess God spared my life and let me get away this time because I've been good. A few minutes after I got out, the whole building came down. The noise was so loud that I lost my hearing for a long time. Soon after the earthquake we had a terrible landslide. Shaohuoping is sandwiched between two mountains. A river runs through the middle of the town. Within that narrow space between the two mountains, there used to be several factories. Luckily, on my side of the river, there is a hill next to the mountain. The hill slowed down the landslide and diverted it to either side of where I was. The people who worked in factories on the opposite side of the river were less fortunate. Chunks of rocks tumbled down

How did you get out of Yingxiu?

YANG: Initially, everyone was so busy digging in the rubble that nothing was done to help those inside the tents get back home. Once the rescue workers arrived, everything was done properly. I left Yingxiu around noon on May 15. I was assigned to a large group. We walked in a single file and used bamboo sticks as walking canes. We looked just like those refugees you see in movies. We walked along a badly damaged road for three hours before we reached a ferry station. About a thousand people were already waiting on the riverbank, but each boat could carry only six people at a time. We let young children, old folks, and the disabled get on first. I lucked out. I was given a bottle of water during my wait, and finally the boat carried me across the river, where I boarded a truck that carried me home.

ZHOU ZEHUA: When he suddenly showed up at our village, my kids and I were shocked to see him. We had tried to phone him but couldn't get through. I thought he must have been killed. I cried every day. I didn't know what to do or how to support this family without him. I've been sick for a long time. My whole body, from head to toe, is filled with bumps. I thought I had cancer. I went to the hospital. The doctor said I had noncancerous cysts. The cysts don't hurt but they're all over me. We don't have money to see a doctor and I can't do any labor-intensive work. Before the earthquake, we had opened up a tea shop here, trying to earn money from tourists to support the family. I was selling tea when the earthquake happened. My kids and I clutched at a big tree and held on to it. The tables tipped over and all the teacups shattered. About a dozen or so people in our village lost their lives.

Did your house suffer any damage during the earthquake?

ZHOU: Our house collapsed. We are now living in a tent. This is nothing compared to other places. The most important thing is that my man—the pillar of our household—is back. No matter how poor and difficult our lives might be, we can handle it. Life will gradually get better.

—Translated by Wen Huang

28.3 *"Fortitude in Adversity"*

On the afternoon of May 12, a sudden trembling startled office workers in high-rise buildings in cities of central and west China. As the floors and walls of their buildings shook, people rushed out into the streets. As the shaking passed, relief began to set in that the earthquake had been relatively mild, but thousands of miles away the same quake had already claimed tens of thousands of lives. Later, as news of the event spread across the country, people would unite in grief and determination to save as many people as possible.

A major earthquake measuring 7.8 on the Richter scale jolted Wenchuan County in southwestern Sichuan Province at 2:28 p.m. With a population of 111,800, Wenchuan lies in the southeastern part of the Aba Tibetan-Qiang Autonomous Prefecture, 146 km northwest of Chengdu, the provincial capital of Sichuan. As the county with the largest economy under Aba, Wenchuan is also home to the Wolong Nature Reserve, China's leading research and breeding base for endangered giant pandas.

The earthquake was so strong that the shocks were felt in 16 provinces, municipalities and autonomous regions in western, northern, central and eastern areas of China. Forty-four counties and districts in Sichuan were severely affected by the quake. About half of the 20 million population in these areas were directly affected by the quake. The earthquake had also led to casualties in neighboring provinces of Gansu, Shaanxi, Henan, Yunnan and Chongqing Municipality.

In two hours, Chinese President Hu Jintao issued an order to make saving lives the top priority of relief work. Premier Wen Jiabao immediately boarded a plane bound for Chengdu in the evening.

RESCUE WORK HINDERED

Explaining the destructiveness of the earthquake, Zhang Guomin, a researcher at the Institute of Earthquake Science under the China Earthquake Administration, said the focus of the intraplate earthquake was close to the earth's surface.

Zhang said there is an average of 18 earthquakes each year measuring at or above 7 magnitude on the Richter scale around the world, with one or two above a magnitude of 8. China, located on the plate interface between the Indian Ocean and the Pacific Ocean, is an earthquake-prone country. Wenchuan is located on a north-south earthquake belt that runs from northwest Ningxia Hui Autonomous Region to southwest Yunnan Province.

Wang Erqi, a researcher at the Institute of Geology and Geophysics under the Chinese Academy of Social Sciences, said the reason that people in a vast region sensed the earthquake is that Wenchuan is located on solid rock, which enables the aftershocks to spread very far.

Frequent aftershocks posed another challenge to rescue work. Immediately after the earthquake, the China Earthquake Administration revised the rating of the earthquake from 7.6 magnitude to 7.8 magnitude on the Richter scale. Sun Shihong, Chief Forecaster at the China Earthquake Networks Center, said during an interview on May 14 that there was a possibility the official rating could be revised again.

Sun said that unlike earthquakes caused by two neighboring tectonic plates slipping relative to each other, which produce few aftershocks, the Wenchuan earthquake did not release tectonic energy during the first major quake, so the aftershocks could last for one to two months. According to a report by the China National Radio, by the morning of May 14 over 3,000 aftershocks had occurred, three of which were over 6 magnitude on the Richter scale.

In less than three days after the earthquake, 119 aftershocks above 4 magnitude on the Richter scale had been monitored in Wenchuan, which hampered rescue work, causing more casualties and injuries.

A strong aftershock jolted Yingxiu Town in the epicenter of Wenchuan County on the morning of May 14.

Rocks rolled down from the hills and some dilapidated houses, already damaged by the main earthquake, collapsed completely, according to an on-the-spot reporter from Xinhua News Agency.

Traffic disruption caused by the earthquake was particularly serious because most of the devastated areas are mountainous. This hindered the transportation of rescue workers, medicine, water, food and digging vehicles that were badly needed in the quake-hit regions. The earthquake closed several major highways, including expressways to Wenchuan that were struck by rocks rolling off the mountains during the earthquake. The army was clearing rocks on the highways to the county headquarters of Wenchuan, three days after the earthquake.

Traffic was interrupted along several national and provincial highways through Aba, and landslides struck several highways in neighboring Shaanxi Province.

The first batch of 100 soldiers of the People's Liberation Army was parachuted soon after into the cut-off Maoxian County, northeast of the epicenter in Wenchuan. Disaster relief goods were airdropped to major quake-hit areas, including Wenchuan County and Mianzhu City.

The government had dispatched 110 helicopters from the armed forces and the civil aviation industry to quake-hit areas for reconnaissance, food and water airdrops, transporting injured people and delivering rescuers by May 15.

By May 15, military transporters and helicopters had taken 300 flights to transport or airdrop rescuers and relief supplies. As the prime time for rescuing survivors, 72 hours after the quake, passed, rescuers were desperate to find survivors. Sniffer dogs were also dispatched to the quake-hit areas to assist in search and rescue.

Heavy rain in the earthquake hit areas slowed down rescue work by hindering repair work on the power grid and telecommunication network, causing landslides and making the landing of rescue aircraft and parachutists impossible.

Communication failures to the outside world in the worst-hit counties in Sichuan due to damage to the cellphone network also added to the woes. Telecommunications cables connecting Wenchuan County with other parts of the country had been repaired by the afternoon of May 15.

LIFE LARGER THAN HEAVEN

During Premier Wen's inspection of the rescue work in a middle school in Dujiangyan City, where over 100 students were buried in collapsed buildings, on the first night after the earthquake, he said, "Life is larger than heaven. As long as there is a slim hope, we will try our best to save everyone buried in the debris."

At a high-profile meeting of the Political Bureau of the Central Committee of the Communist Party of China on May 14, President Hu Jintao stressed that saving lives should be taken as the top priority during quake relief.

Immediately after the earthquake, rescue and medical forces across the country were mobilized and quickly shipped to earthquake-devastated areas. Emergency response systems were quickly activated in various ministries.

Wang Yongping, Ministry of Railways spokesman, said at a press conference that the railways were used to ship in soldiers and relief aid. Of the 56 trains carrying 28,000 troops to quake-hit areas, 21 trains, or more than 10,000 soldiers, arrived before the morning of May 15.

A total of 844 railcars filled with relief materials were also en route, including 79,700 tents, 828,600 boxes of water, 18,870 pieces of medicine, and 351,100 cotton-padded coats and blankets, said Wang.

Also on the way were 157 railcars full of rescue machinery and ambulances, seven railcars of oil and 69 railcars of steel and other materials.

The ministry collected plenty of empty passenger cars, boxcars and container flatcars that are standing by for emergency use, Wang said.

"As far as I am concerned, this is the most efficient mobilization of the Central Government. Premier Wen arrived at the disaster areas in a matter of hours and the Standing Committee of the Political Bureau of the Central Committee of the Communist Party of China held an overnight meeting to elaborate on the relief work. In less than a day, a large number of rescue workers had arrived in devastated areas," said Vice Minister of Health Gao Qiang. "It might be a miracle in the international history of disaster relief work."

Gao said at a press conference on May 15 that the Ministry of Health had sent 190 medical rescue teams from 18 provinces, municipalities and autonomous regions totaling 1,755 people, and that there were rescue teams sent by governments of provinces, municipalities and autonomous regions, totaling over 1,200 people.

China has allocated 400 million yuan ($57.1 million) from the central finance to the earthquake-hit areas for medical relief, said Gao.

Out of the figure, 200 million yuan ($28.6 million) would be used for the medical treatment of the injured, and the other 200 million yuan ($28.6 million) would be used to purchase emergency medicine and equipment, said Gao.

No epidemics had been reported in the regions struck by the earthquake, he added. He said to prevent any epidemic after the earthquake, the Chinese Center for Disease Control and Prevention had sent out a team of epidemic prevention experts to Sichuan, and a total of 144 epidemic experts from other provinces and municipalities were also working in the field with local staff.

He said qualified psychologists would join the medical staff teams sent to the quake-hit regions to help survivors traumatized by losing family members, and relatives and children scared during the quake.

28.4 THE BEIJING OLYMPICS, 2008

The tragedy in Sichuan cast a shadow over the 2008 Olympics, which opened in Beijing less than three months after the earthquake. The leadup to the Games had also been tarnished by riots in Tibet, foreign protests, boycotts, and attempts to disrupt the Olympic torch run. But at the opening ceremonies on August 8, a jaw-dropping spectacle showcased a confident China to the world, presenting a curated version of the long sweep of Chinese history that spotlighted Confucius but effectively airbrushed out Mao Zedong. After the conclusion of the Games, *Beijing Review* tallied the following scorecard for China's performance in the international limelight.

Beijing has successfully delivered an Olympic Games to the world. The 2008 Summer Games were marked with distinct Chinese elements, while the rules specified in the Olympic Charter and the International Olympic Committee's (IOC) written agreement with the host city were strictly followed.

Seven years ago, when granting the hosting rights of the Games of the XXIX Olympiad to Beijing, the IOC was confident in the city, and believed that holding the Games in China would facilitate the dissemination of the Olympic spirit among its 1.3 billion people, leaving an unrivalled legacy in Olympic history.

Data about the 2008 Games suggest that the IOC made the right decision in choosing Beijing as the host.

According to the Beijing Organizing Committee for the Games of the XXIX Olympiad, 38 world records and 85 Olympic records were broken in the 2008 Games. More world records and Olympic records were broken in the Beijing Games than in the Athens or Sydney.

Numerous Olympic miracles and glorious moments were born in the 12 new Olympic venues, including the Water Cube and the Bird's Nest. In addition, 11 renovated venues and eight temporary venues in Beijing, as well as six sports arenas in the co-hosting cities, were also used for the Games.

A total of 11,468 athletes from 204 countries and regions competed in the Beijing Games. Beijing saw the largest number of female athletes competing in the history of the Games, to the relief of the IOC, which is committed to popularizing Olympic ideals and gender equality.

About 100,000 Olympic volunteers, 400,000 city volunteers, and 1 million social volunteers formed the largest volunteer team in Olympic history. Their smiles and dedication made the Olympics more beautiful.

The Beijing Olympics were one of the most watched Games in the history. More than 220 television agencies and over 25,000 journalists covered the event. The IOC site logged 5 million clicks during the entire process of the Beijing Games, whereas it logged 2.8 million clicks during the Athens Olympics.

More than 80 heads of states and governments participated in the opening ceremony of the Beijing Games. About 80 percent of the people in China and about half of the people in the United States and Europe watched the opening ceremony on television. This was a record number. Few other events have received so much attention.

Medals were awarded to 87 Olympic delegations, the largest number since the Olympics began. Afghanistan, Mauritius, Tajikistan and Togo won their first Olympic medals in history, and Bahrain, Mongolia and Panama won their first Olympic gold, while India won its first gold in an individual event. Many delegations and athletes fulfilled their Olympic goals.

Team China had a remarkable performance. When the Games concluded on August 24, they had pocketed 51 golds, 21 silvers and 28 bronzes, making exactly 100 medals in total.

The Olympic Games have also popularized sports in China's schools, and helped to promote friendship and understanding between nations.

A total of 556 model schools of Olympic education have been selected from schools across China. More than 200 middle or primary schools have established friendly ties with the Olympic committees of other countries or regions. The Olympic spirits of solidarity, friendship, peace, and fair competition have been spread to innumerous students. The scale of Olympic education is unprecedented.

More than 400 youths, including 10 disabled youngsters, from 204 Olympic committees gathered at the Beijing Olympic Youth Camp in Beijing in August. The young campers experienced Chinese culture and customs, and watched the torch relay and Olympic competitions, actively promoting friendship and peace.

28.5 CHARTER 08

On December 10, 2008, a group of dissidents published a document titled "Charter 08," a manifesto calling for political reform. Written in imitation of "Charter 77," an inspirational declaration by Czechoslovakian dissidents in 1977, the launch of Charter 08 coincided with the sixtieth anniversary of the Universal Declaration of Human Rights. The original signatories included lawyers, journalists, academics, and Liu Xiaobo, a prominent literary critic and human rights activist. Liu and others who signed the document were soon detained and tried on charges of subversion. While serving his eleven-year prison sentence, Liu Xiaobo received the 2010 Nobel Peace Prize.

The text of "Charter 08" is reproduced below in its entirety. As its provisions indicate, the manifesto boldly called for the end to one-party rule in China and the revision of the constitution to reflect the separation of powers and political freedoms. Since its publication, more than ten thousand people have signed the charter in support.

I. PREAMBLE

This year marks 100 years since China's [first] Constitution, the 60th anniversary of the promulgation of the *Universal Declaration of Human Rights*, the 30th anniversary of the birth of the Democracy Wall, and the 10th year since the Chinese government signed the *International Covenant on Civil and Political Rights*. Having experienced a prolonged period of human rights disasters and challenging and tortuous struggles, the awakening Chinese citizens are becoming increasingly aware that freedom, equality, and human rights are universal values shared by all humankind, and that democracy, republicanism, and constitutional government make up the basic institutional framework of modern politics. A "modernization" bereft of these universal values and this basic political framework is a disastrous process that deprives people of their rights, rots away their humanity, and destroys their dignity. Where is China headed in the 21st century? Will it continue with this "modernization" under authoritarian rule, or will it endorse universal values, join the mainstream civilization, and build a democratic form of government? This is an unavoidable decision.

The tremendous historic changes of the mid-19th century exposed the decay of the traditional Chinese autocratic system and set the stage for the greatest transformation China had seen in several thousand years. The Self-Strengthening Movement [1861–1895] sought improvements in China's technical capability by acquiring manufacturing techniques, scientific knowledge, and military technologies from the West; China's defeat in the first Sino-Japanese War [1894–1895] once again exposed the obsolescence of its system; the Hundred Days' Reform [1898] touched upon the area of institutional innovation, but ended in failure due to cruel suppression by the die-hard faction [at the Qing court]. The Xinhai Revolution [1911], on the surface, buried the imperial system that had lasted for more than 2,000 years and established Asia's first republic. But, because of the particular historical circumstances of internal and external troubles, the republican system of government was short lived, and autocracy made a comeback.

The failure of technical imitation and institutional renewal prompted deep reflection among our countrymen on the root cause of China's cultural sickness, and the ensuing May Fourth [1919] and New Culture Movements [1915–1921] under the banner of "science and democracy." But the course of China's political democratization was forcibly cut short due to frequent civil wars and foreign invasion. The process of a constitutional government began again after China's victory in the War of Resistance against Japan [1937–1945], but the outcome of the civil war between the Nationalists and the Communists plunged China into the abyss of modern-day totalitarianism. The "New China" established in 1949 is a "people's republic" in name, but in reality it is a "party domain." The ruling party monopolizes all the political, economic, and social resources. It has created a string of human rights disasters, such as the Anti-Rightist Campaign, the Great Leap Forward, the Cultural Revolution, June Fourth, and the suppression of unofficial religious activities and the rights defense movement, causing tens of millions of deaths, and exacting a disastrous price from both the people and the country.

The "Reform and Opening Up" of the late 20th century extricated China from the pervasive poverty and absolute totalitarianism of the Mao Zedong era, and substantially increased private wealth and the standard of living of the common people. Individual economic freedom and social privileges were partially restored, a civil society began to grow, and calls for human rights and political freedom among the people increased by the day. Those in power, while implementing economic reforms aimed at marketization and privatization, also began to shift from a position of rejecting human rights to one of gradually recognizing them. In 1997 and 1998, the Chinese government signed two important international human rights treaties. In 2004, the National People's Congress amended the Constitution to add that "[the State] respects and guarantees human rights." And this year, the government has promised to formulate and implement a "National Human Rights Action Plan." But so far, this political progress has largely remained on paper: there are laws, but there is no rule of law; there is a constitution, but no constitutional government; this is still the political reality that is obvious to all. The ruling elite continues to insist on its authoritarian grip on power, rejecting political reform. This has caused official corruption, difficulty in establishing rule of law, the absence of human rights, moral bankruptcy, social polarization, abnormal economic development, destruction of both the natural and cultural environment, no institutionalized protection of citizens' rights to freedom, property, and the pursuit of happiness, the constant accumulation of all kinds of social conflicts, and the continuous surge of resentment. In particular, the intensification of antagonism between the government and the people, and the dramatic increase in mass incidents, indicate a catastrophic loss of control in the making, suggesting that the backwardness of the current system has reached a point where change must occur.

II. OUR FUNDAMENTAL CONCEPTS

At this historical juncture that will decide the future destiny of China, it is necessary to reflect on the modernization process of the past hundred and some years and reaffirm the following concepts:

Freedom: Freedom is at the core of universal values. The rights of speech, publication, belief, assembly, association, movement, to strike, and to march and demonstrate are all the concrete expressions of freedom. Where freedom does not flourish, there is no modern civilization to speak of.

Human Rights: Human rights are not bestowed by a state; they are inherent rights enjoyed by every person. Guaranteeing human rights is both the most important objective of a government and the foundation of the legitimacy of its public authority; it is also the intrinsic requirement of the policy of "putting people first." China's successive political disasters have all been closely related to the disregard for human rights by the ruling establishment. People are the mainstay of a nation; a nation serves its people; government exists for the people.

Equality: The integrity, dignity, and freedom of every individual, regardless of social status, occupation, gender, economic circumstances, ethnicity, skin color, religion, or political belief, are equal. The principles of equality before the law for each and every person and equality in social, economic, cultural, and political rights of all citizens must be implemented.

Republicanism: Republicanism is "joint governing by all, peaceful coexistence," that is, the separation of powers for checks and balances and the balance of interests; that is, a community comprising many diverse interests, different social groups, and a plurality of cultures and faiths, seeking to peacefully handle public affairs on the basis of equal participation, fair competition, and joint discussion.

Democracy: The most fundamental meaning is that sovereignty resides in the people and the government elected by the people. Democracy has the following basic characteristics: (1) The legitimacy of political power comes from the people; the source of political power is the people. (2) Political control is exercised through choices made by the people. (3) Citizens enjoy the genuine right to vote; officials in key positions at all levels of government must be the product of elections at regular intervals. (4) Respect the decisions of the majority while protecting the basic human rights of the minority. In a word, democracy is the modern public instrument for creating a government "of the people, by the people, and for the people."

Constitutionalism: Constitutionalism is the principle of guaranteeing basic freedoms and rights of citizens as defined by the constitution through legal provisions and the rule of law, restricting and defining the boundaries of government power and conduct, and providing appropriate institutional capability to carry this out. In China, the era of imperial power is long gone, never to return; in the world at large, the authoritarian system is on the wane; citizens ought to become the true masters of their states. The fundamental way out for China lies only in dispelling the subservient notion of reliance on "enlightened rulers" and "upright officials," promoting public consciousness of rights as fundamental and participation as a duty, and putting into practice freedom, engaging in democracy, and respecting the law.

III. OUR BASIC POSITIONS

Thus, in the spirit of responsible and constructive citizens, we put forth the following specific positions regarding various aspects of state administration, citizens' rights and interests, and social development:

1. Constitutional Amendment: Based on the aforementioned values and concepts, amend the Constitution, deleting clauses in the current Constitution that are not in conformity with the principle that sovereignty resides in the people, so that the Constitution can truly become a document that guarantees human rights and allows for the exercise of public power, and become the enforceable supreme law that no individual, group, or party can violate, establishing the foundation of the legal authority for democratizing China.

2. *Separation of Powers and Checks and Balances:* Construct a modern government that separates powers and maintains checks and balances among them, that guarantees the separation of legislative, judicial, and executive powers. Establish the principle of statutory administration and responsible government to prevent excessive expansion of executive power; government should be responsible to taxpayers; establish the system of separation of powers and checks and balances between the central and local governments; the central power must be clearly defined and mandated by the Constitution, and the localities must exercise full autonomy.

3. *Legislative Democracy:* Legislative bodies at all levels should be created through direct elections; maintain the principle of fairness and justice in making law; and implement legislative democracy.

4. *Judicial Independence:* The judiciary should transcend partisanship, be free from any interference, exercise judicial independence, and guarantee judicial fairness; it should establish a constitutional court and a system to investigate violations of the Constitution, and uphold the authority of the Constitution. Abolish as soon as possible the Party's Committees of Political and Legislative Affairs at all levels that seriously endanger the country's rule of law. Prevent private use of public instruments.

5. *Public Use of Public Instruments:* Bring the armed forces under state control. Military personnel should render loyalty to the Constitution and to the country. Political party organizations should withdraw from the armed forces; raise the professional standards of the armed forces. All public employees including the police should maintain political neutrality. Abolish discrimination in hiring of public employees based on party affiliation; there should be equality in hiring regardless of party affiliation.

6. *Human Rights Guarantees:* Guarantee human rights in earnest; protect human dignity. Set up a Commission on Human Rights, responsible to the highest organ of popular will, to prevent government abuse of public authority and violations of human rights, and, especially, to guarantee the personal freedom of citizens. No one shall suffer illegal arrest, detention, subpoena, interrogation, or punishment. Abolish the Reeducation-Through-Labor system.

7. *Election of Public Officials:* Fully implement the system of democratic elections to realize equal voting rights based on "one person, one vote." Systematically and gradually implement direct elections of administrative heads at all levels. Regular elections based on free competition and citizen participation in elections for legal public office are inalienable basic human rights.

8. *Urban-Rural Equality:* Abolish the current urban-rural two-tier household registration system to realize the constitutional right of equality before the law for all citizens and guarantee the citizens' right to move freely.

9. Freedom of Association: Guarantee citizens' right to freedom of association. Change the current system of registration upon approval for community groups to a system of record-keeping. Lift the ban on political parties. Regulate party activities according to the Constitution and law; abolish the privilege of one-party monopoly on power; establish the principles of freedom of activities of political parties and fair competition for political parties; normalize and legally regulate party politics.

10. Freedom of Assembly: Freedoms to peacefully assemble, march, demonstrate, and express [opinions] are citizens' fundamental freedoms stipulated by the Constitution; they should not be subject to illegal interference and unconstitutional restrictions by the ruling party and the government.

11. Freedom of Expression: Realize the freedom of speech, freedom to publish, and academic freedom; guarantee the citizens' right to know and right to supervise [public institutions]. Enact a "News Law" and a "Publishing Law," lift the ban on reporting, repeal the "crime of inciting subversion of state power" clause in the current *Criminal Law*, and put an end to punishing speech as a crime.

12. Freedom of Religion: Guarantee freedom of religion and freedom of belief, and implement separation of religion and state so that activities involving religion and faith are not subjected to government interference. Examine and repeal administrative statutes, administrative rules, and local statutes that restrict or deprive citizens of religious freedom; ban management of religious activities by administrative legislation. Abolish the system that requires that religious groups (and including places of worship) obtain prior approval of their legal status in order to register, and replace it with a system of record-keeping that requires no scrutiny.

13. Civic Education: Abolish political education and political examinations that are heavy on ideology and serve the one-party rule. Popularize civic education based on universal values and civil rights, establish civic consciousness, and advocate civic virtues that serve society.

14. Property Protection: Establish and protect private property rights, and implement a system based on a free and open market economy; guarantee entrepreneurial freedom, and eliminate administrative monopolies; set up a Committee for the Management of State-Owned Property, responsible to the highest organ of popular will; launch reform of property rights in a legal and orderly fashion, and clarify the ownership of property rights and those responsible; launch a new land movement, advance land privatization, and guarantee in earnest the land property rights of citizens, particularly the farmers.

15. Fiscal Reform: Democratize public finances and guarantee taxpayers' rights. Set up the structure and operational mechanism of a public finance system with clearly defined authority and responsibilities, and establish a rational and effective system of decentralized financial authority among various levels of government; carry out a major reform of the tax system, so as to reduce tax rates, simplify the tax system, and equalize the tax burden. Administrative departments may not increase taxes or create new taxes at will without sanction by society obtained through a public elective process and resolution by organs of popular will. Pass property rights reform to diversify and introduce competition mechanisms into the market; lower the threshold for entry into the financial field and create conditions for the development of privately-owned financial enterprises, and fully energize the financial system.

16. *Social Security:* Establish a social security system that covers all citizens and provides them with basic security in education, medical care, care for the elderly, and employment.

17. *Environmental Protection:* Protect the ecological environment, promote sustainable development, and take responsibility for future generations and all humanity; clarify and impose the appropriate responsibilities that state and government officials at all levels must take to this end; promote participation and oversight by civil society groups in environmental protection.

18. *Federal Republic:* Take part in maintaining regional peace and development with an attitude of equality and fairness, and create an image of a responsible great power. Protect the free systems of Hong Kong and Macau. On the premise of freedom and democracy, seek a reconciliation plan for the mainland and Taiwan through equal negotiations and cooperative interaction. Wisely explore possible paths and institutional blueprints for the common prosperity of all ethnic groups, and establish the Federal Republic of China under the framework of a democratic and constitutional government.

19. *Transitional Justice:* Restore the reputation of and give state compensation to individuals, as well as their families, who suffered political persecution during past political movements; release all political prisoners and prisoners of conscience; release all people convicted for their beliefs; establish a Commission for Truth Investigation to find the truth of historical events, determine responsibility, and uphold justice; seek social reconciliation on this foundation.

IV. CONCLUSION

China, as a great nation of the world, one of the five permanent members of the United Nations Security Council, and a member of the Human Rights Council, ought to make its own contribution to peace for humankind and progress in human rights. Regrettably, however, of all the great nations of the world today, China alone still clings to an authoritarian way of life and has, as a result, created an unbroken chain of human rights disasters and social crises, held back the development of the Chinese people, and hindered the progress of human civilization. This situation must change! We cannot put off political democratization reforms any longer. Therefore, in the civic spirit of daring to take action, we are issuing *Charter 08*. We hope that all Chinese citizens who share this sense of crisis, responsibility, and mission, whether officials or common people and regardless of social background, will put aside our differences to seek common ground and come to take an active part in this citizens' movement, to promote the great transformation of Chinese society together, so that we can soon establish a free, democratic, and constitutional nation, fulfilling the aspirations and dreams that our countrymen have been pursuing tirelessly for more than a hundred years.

Bibliography and Credits

CHAPTER 1

1.1 Wen Bing, *Dingling zhulüe* [A brief account of the Chongzhen reign], in Xie Guozhen, ed. *Mingdai nongmin qiyi shiliao xuanbian* [Historical materials related to peasant uprisings of the Ming era] (Fuzhou: Fujian renmin chubanshe, 1981), pp. 202–203.

1.2 Shen Zan, *Jinshi congcan* [Fragmented pieces on recent events], in Xie Guozhen (1981), p. 204.

1.3 and 1.4 Song Yingxing, *Yeyi* [Unbridled comments] (Shanghai: Shanghai renmin chubanshe, 1976), pp. 5, 35–39.

1.5 Li Zicheng, "Jinjun Huangzhou xiwen" [Call to arms upon entering Huangzhou], in Xie Guozhen (1981), pp. 173–74.

1.6 Baoyang sheng (pseud.), *Jiashen chaoshi xiaoji* [An account of events in 1644], vol. 7, in Xie Guozhen (1981), pp. 181–83.

1.7 Gu Gongxie, *Xiaoxia xianji zhaichao* [Selections from leisurely accounts to pass the summer], in Xie Guozhen (1981), pp. 184–85.

1.8 Song Maocheng, *Jiu yue ji* [Nine flute collection] (Beijing: Zhongguo shehui kexue chubanshe, 1984), pp. 112–18.

CHAPTER 2

2.1 Jiang Liangqi, *Donghua lu* [Records of the Eastern Flower Gate] (Beijing: Zhonghua shuju, 1980), p. 7.

2.2 Zheng Tianting, comp., *Ming-Qing shi ziliao* [Materials related to the history of the Ming and Qing dynasties] (Tianjin: Tianjin renmin chubanshe, 1980), vol. 2, pp. 2–3.

2.3 Zheng (1980), pp. 3–4.

2.4 Zheng (1980), pp. 6–7.

2.5 *Qing shilu, Shizu* [Qing Veritable Records, Shizu Reign], vol. 5, Fifth Moon, Renyin Day, 1644. With thanks to Professor Andrew Hsieh for providing this document.

2.6 *Qing shilu, Shizu* [Qing Veritable Records, Shizu Reign], vol. 14, Sixth Moon, Bingyin Day, 1645. With thanks to Professor Andrew Hsieh for providing this document.

2.7 Xu Chongxi, "Jiangyin chengshou houji" [A later account of the defense of Jiangyin], in *Dongnan jishi* [Recorded events of southeastern China], comp. Zhongguo lishi yanjiushe [Academy of Chinese history] (Shanghai: Shenzhou guoguangshe, 1951), pp. 81–85.

CHAPTER 3

3.1 Jiang Liangqi, *Donghua lu* [Records of the Eastern Flower Gate] (Beijing: Zhonghua shuju, 1980), pp. 137–138.

3.2 Shi Lang, ed., Wang Duoquan, annot., *Jinghai jishi* [Records of pacification of the seas] (Fuzhou: Fujian renmin chubanshe, 1983), pp. 80–91.

3.3 Fang Bao, *Fang Bao Ji* [Complete works of Fang Bao] (Shanghai: Shanghai guji chubanshe, 1983), vol. 2, pp. 709–712.

3.4 "Valedictory Edict, 1717" from *Emperor of China: Self-Portrait of K'ang-Hsi* by Jonathan D. Spence. Copyright © 1974 by Jonathan D. Spence, copyright renewed 2002 by Jonathan D. Spence. Used by permission of The Wylie Agency LLC and Alfred A. Knopf, a division of Random House, Inc. Any third party use of this material, outside of this publication, is prohibited. Interested parties must apply directly to Random House, Inc. for permission.

CHAPTER 4

4.1 Wang Yupu, *Shengyu guangxun zhijie* [An extensive exposition of the Sacred Edict], translation from Chinese text in F. W. Baller, *The Sacred Edict* (Shanghai: Shanghai Inland Mission, 1924), pp. 20–21, 74–87, 88–93.

4.2 Baller (1924), pp. 184–211.

4.3 *Yongzheng shangyu neige* [Edicts of the Yongzheng reign issued through the Grand Secretariat], 27th day of the 4th month, the 5th year of Yongzheng.

CHAPTER 5

5.1 Wu Jingzi, *The Scholars,* trans. Yang Hsien-yi and Gladys Yang (Peking: Foreign Languages Press, 1964), pp. 65–77.

5.2 Zhongguo diyi lishi dang'anguan [First Historical Archives], Zhongguo shehui kexueyuan lishi yanjiusuo [Chinese academy of social sciences history research center], ed., *Qingdai dizu boxue xingtai* [Landlord exploitation during the Qing era] (Beijing: Renmin chubanshe, 1982), pp. 53–55.

5.3 Jiang Liangqi, *Donghua lu* [Records of the Eastern Flower Gate] (Beijing: Zhonghua shuju, 1980), vol. 1, p. 1.

5.4 *Ji Shen zhilüe* [A brief account of the execution of Heshen], in *Ming Wuzong waiji* [An unofficial account of Ming Wuzong] (Shanghai: Shenzhou guoguangshe, 1951), pp. 265–274.

5.5 *Ji Shen zhilüe* (1951), pp. 265–274.

5.6 "Neu Heo, or The Female Instructor," *The Chinese Repository* 9 (December 1840), pp. 542–545.

CHAPTER 6

6.1 *Lord Macartney's Commission from Henry Dundas, 1792* (Hartford: Trinity College Watkinson Library, typescript of manuscript copy), pp. 1–14.

6.2 and 6.3 From *An Embassy to China; Being the Journal Kept by Lord Macartney During his Embassy to the Emperor Ch'ien-Lung, 1793–1794*, ed. J.L. Cranmer-Byng, pp. 122–124 and 236–240. © J.L. Cranmer-Byng 1962. Reprinted by permission of Pearson Education Limited.

6.4 and 6.5 From *Changing China: Readings in the History of China from the Opium War to the Present*, ed. J. Mason Gentzler, pp. 23–28. Copyright © ABC-CLIO Inc, 1977. Reprinted with permission.

CHAPTER 7

7.1 John Slade, *A Narrative of the Late Proceedings and Events in China* (Canton: Canton Register Press, 1839), pp. 1–5.

7.2 Slade (1839), pp. 18–26.

7.3 Slade (1839), pp. 34–35.

7.4 Slade (1839), pp. 135–139.

7.5 Sir Frederick Whyte, *China and Foreign Powers: An Historical Review of their Relations* (London: Oxford University Press, 1928), pp. 42–48.

CHAPTER 8

8.1 Qian Yong, *Luyuan conghua* [Discursive talks from Lu garden] (Beijing, Zhonghua shuju, 1979), vol. 21, Appendix, pp. 575–578.

8.2 Liang Fa, *Quanshi liangyan* [Good words to exhort the age], in *Jindai shi ziliao* [Modern history materials] (repr. Beijing: Zhonghua shuju, 1979), vol. 39, pp. 25–32.

8.3 Joseph-Marie Callery and Melchior Yvan, *History of the Insurrection in China*, trans. John Oxenford (New York: Harper and Brothers, 1853), pp. 100–106.

8.4 Lindesay Brine, *The Taeping Rebellion in China* (London: J. Murray, 1862), pp. 371–375.

8.5 Brine (1862), pp. 386–391.

8.6 From *Changing China: Readings in the History of China from the Opium War to the Present*, ed. J. Mason Gentzler, pp. 65–67. Copyright © ABC-CLIO Inc, 1977. Reprinted with permission.

8.7 "Letter to his Younger Brothers" by Deng Guofan (tr. Janice Wickieri). First published in *Renditions* Nos. 41 & 42 (1994), pp. 135–136. Reprinted by permission of the Research Centre for Translation, The Chinese University of Hong Kong.

CHAPTER 9

9.1 Yung Wing, *My Life in China and America* (New York: Henry Holt and Company, 1909), pp. 142–153.

9.2 W. A. P. Martin, *A Cycle of Cathay, or, China, South and North, with Personal Reminiscences* (New York: Fleming H. Revell Co., 1897), pp. 301–303.

9.3 Kiyo Sue Inui, *The Unsolved Problem of the Pacific* (Tokyo: Japan Times, 1925), p. 286.

9.4 Inui (1925), pp. 333–341.

9.5 "A Discussion of Railroads (1879)" from *Strengthen the Country and Enrich the People: The Reform Writings of Ma Jianzhong (1845–1900)*, Ma Jianzhong, trans. Paul J. Bailey, Copyright © Paul Bailey 1998. Reproduced by permission of Taylor & Francis Books UK.

9.6 "A Popular Broadsheet from a Nanking Correspondent," in *The Anti-Foreign Riots in China in 1891,* ed. North-China Herald (Shanghai: North-China Herald Press, 1892), pp. 182–83.

CHAPTER 10

10.1 Sun Yat-sen, "A Letter to Li Hung-chang." Reprinted with the permission of Scribner, a Division of Simon & Schuster, Inc., from *Modern China: From Mandarin to Commissar* by Dun J. Li. Copyright © 1978 by Dun J. Li. All rights reserved.

10.2 Tientsin Press, eds., *Verbal Discussions During Peace Negotiations Between the Chinese Plenipotentiary Viceroy Li Hung-Chang and the Japanese Plenipotentiaries Count Ito and Viscount Mutsu at Shimonoseki, Japan* (Tientsin: Tientsin Press, 1895), pp. 1–16.

10.3 Zhang Zhidong, *China's Only Hope, An Appeal By Her Greatest Viceroy, Chang Chih-Tung*, trans. Samuel I. Woodbridge (Edinburgh and London: Oliphant, Anderson and Ferrier, 1901), pp. 55–62.

10.4 "The Flying Boat"; "Preserving the Written Word for the Sake of Filial Piety"; "Would That He Be Faithful . . ."; "The Ducks with the Golden Innards"; "Burying a Living Buddha"; "A Turn of Events at the Telegraph Office" (tr. Don J. Cohn). First published in *Renditions* No. 23 (Spring 1985), pp. 50, 58, 61, 62, 65, 68. Reprinted by permission of the Research Centre for Translation, The Chinese University of Hong Kong.

10.5 and 10.6 Shandong daxue lishixi, Zhongguo jindaishi jiaoyanshi [Shandong University history department, modern Chinese history teaching and research section], comp., *Shandong yihetuan diaocha ziliao xuanbian* [Selected collection of materials from an investigation of the Boxer rebellion in Shandong province] (Jinan: Jilu shushe, 1980), pp. 131–134, 66–70.

CHAPTER 11

11.1 Zou Rong, *Gemingjun* [The Revolutionary Army], translation from Chinese text in John Lust, *The Revolutionary Army, A Chinese Nationalist Tract of 1903* (The Hague: Mouton and Company, 1968), pp. 18–23.

11.2 Qui Jin, "Song of the Precious Sword." Reprinted from Wilt Idema and Beata Grant, *The Red Brush: Writing of Women of Imperial China*. Cambridge, Mass.: Harvard University Asia Center, 2004, pp. 774–775. © 2004 The President and Fellows of Harvard College. By permission of the Harvard University Asia Center.

11.3 Qui Jin, "An Address to My Two Hundred Million Women Compatriots in China." Reprinted from Wilt Idema and Beata Grant, *The Red Brush: Writing of Women of Imperial China*. Cambridge, Mass.: Harvard University Asia Center, 2004, pp. 780–782. © 2004 The President and Fellows of Harvard College. By permission of the Harvard University Asia Center

11.4 T'ung-meng Hui, "A Public Declaration." Reprinted with the permission of Scribner, a Division of Simon & Schuster, Inc., from *Modern China: From Mandarin to Commissar* by Dun J. Li. Copyright © 1978 by Dun J. Li. All rights reserved.

11.5 Anon., *Diary of the Revolution: Extracted from the Hankow Daily News* (Hankow: The Daily News, 1911), October 12, 1911 and October 14, 1911.

11.6 B. L. Putnam Weale, *The Fight for the Republic in China* (New York: Dodd, Mead, and Company, 1917), pp. 393–97.

11.7 "Selecting a Wife" by Zhu Ziqing (tr. Tao Tao Liu). First published in *Renditions* No. 38 (Autumn 1992), pp. 57–59. Reprinted by permission of the Research Centre for Translation, The Chinese University of Hong Kong.

CHAPTER 12

12.1 Yuan Shikai, "Poem to the Soldiers," *New York Times,* November 18, 1912, p. 4.

12.2 *The "People's Will,"* An Exposure of the Political Intrigues at Peking against the Republic of China (Issued by Authority of Republican Government of China, 1916), p. 20.

12.3 Wunsz King, comp., *V. K. Wellington Koo's Foreign Policy, Some Selected Documents* (Shanghai: Kelly and Walsh, 1931), pp. 87–90.

12.4 George T. B. Davis, *China's Christian Army, A Story of Marshal Feng and His Soldiers* (New York: The Christian Alliance Publishing Company, 1925), pp. 9–21.

12.5 Zhang Zongchang, "With Pleasure Rife" from *Living China: Modern Chinese Short Stories* (Reynal & Hitchcock, 1937), ed. Edgar Snow, pp. 222–225. Reprinted with permission of Lois Wheeler Snow.

12.6 Zhou Shou-juan, "We Shall Meet Again," *Bulletin of Concerned Asian Scholars*, Vol. 8, No. 1, Jan-March 1976, trans. Perry Link, pp. 15–19. Reprinted with permission of Critical Asian Studies (www.criticalasianstudies.org).

CHAPTER 13

13.1 Reprinted by permission of the publisher from *China's Response to the West: A Documentary Survey, 1839–1923*, by Ssu-yü Têng and John King Fairbank, pp. 240–245, Cambridge, Mass.: Harvard University Press, Copyright © 1954, 1979 by the President and Fellows of Harvard College. Copyright © renewed 1982 by Ssu-yü Têng and John King Fairbank.

13.2 Li Dazhao, "Bolshevism de shengli" [The victory of bolshevism], *Xin qingnian* [New Youth] 5:5 (November 15, 1918), in *Zhongguo xiandaishi ziliao huibian*

[Compilation of materials on the contemporary history of China] (Hong Kong: Wenhua ziliao gongyingshe, 1976), pp. 14–19.

13.3 Deng Chunlan, "My Plan For Women's Emancipation and My Plan for Self-Improvement," From *Women in Republican China: A Sourcebook*, trans. and ed. Hua R. Lan and Vanessa L. Fong (Armonk, NY: M.E. Sharpe, 1999), pp. 121–123. English translation copyright © 1999 by M.E. Sharpe, Inc. Reprinted with permission.

13.4 Lu Xun, "A Madman's Diary," from *Selected Stories of Lu Hsun* by Lu Hsun, translated by Yang Xianyi and Gladys Yang. Copyright © 1960. Used by permission of W. W. Norton & Company, Inc.

13.5 Lu Xun, "What Happens After Nora Leaves Home?," *Selected Works, Vol. 2*, trans. Yang Xianyi and Gladys Yang, pp. 85–92 (Beijing: Foreign Languages Press). We have made diligent efforts to contact the copyright holder to obtain permission to reprint this selection. If you have information that would help us, please write to Permissions Department, W. W. Norton & Company, Inc., 500 Fifth Avenue, New York, NY 10110.

CHAPTER 14

14.1 Guangdong geming lishi bowuguan [Guangdong revolutionary history museum], comp., *Huangpu junxiao shiliao* [Historical materials of the Whampoa Military Academy] (Guangzhou: Guangdong renmin chubanshe, 1982), pp. 44–56.

14.2 Lu Xun, "Sudden Notions," *Selected Works, Vol. 2*, trans. Yang Xianyi and Gladys Yang, pp. 178–181 (Beijing: Foreign Languages Press). We have made diligent efforts to contact the copyright holder to obtain permission to reprint this selection. If you have information that would help us, please write to Permissions Department, W. W. Norton & Company, Inc., 500 Fifth Avenue, New York, NY 10110.

14.3 Chiang Wei-Shu, "Clinical Notes," *Taiwan Literature: English Translation Series*, No. 20, Jan. 2007, translated by Peng Fengxian and Steven L. Riep, pp.125–128. Reprinted with permission of Center for Taiwan Studies.

14.4 Secretariat, the Kuomintang of China, ed., *Nationalist China* (Canton: Central Political Council of Kuomintang, Canton Branch, 1927), pp. 14–15.

14.5 and 14.6 Secretariat, the Kuomintang of China (1927), pp. 15–17, 25–26.

14.7 Soong Ching-ling, *The Struggle for New China* (Peking: Foreign Languages Press, 1952), pp. 7–11.

CHAPTER 15

15.1 Hu Shih, "Failure of Law in Nationalist China," *North-China Herald,* June 22, 1929, p. 501.

15.2 Tang Liang-li, *Suppressing Communist Banditry in China* (Shanghai: China United Press, 1932), pp. 97–98.

15.3 Japan Ministry of Foreign Affairs, *Relations of Japan with Manchuria and Mongolia* (Tokyo, 1932), Document B, pp. 126–29.

15.4 P. Ohara, *Manchoukuo, The World's Newest Nation: Facing Facts in Manchuria* (Mukden: Manchuria Daily News Press, 1932), pp. 5–6.

15.5 Department of Foreign Affairs, Manchoukuo Government, comp., *The Chief Executives' Proclamation, Organic Law of Manchoukuo, and Other Laws Governing Various Government Offices*, Series no. 2 (Hsinking, Manchuria, November, 1932), p. 1.

15.6 Marion Yang, "Control of Practicing Midwives in China," *The China Medical Journal* 44 (1930), pp. 428–431.

15.7 Y.C. James Yen, *The Ting Hsien Experiment*, pp. 7, 9–11, 16–32, 38–39. Reprinted with permission of International Institute of Rural Reconstruction.

15.8 Hsi-Huey Liang, "General von Falkenhausen's Advice to Chiang Kai-Shek, 1936" from *The Sino-German Connection, Alexander von Falkenhausen between China and Germany 1900–1941*, pp. 199–204. Reprinted with permission.

CHAPTER 16

16.1 "The Land Law 1932," Translated by Dun J. Li, *The Road to Communism: China Since 1912* (Van Nostrand Reinhold Co., 1969), pp. 143–148. We have made diligent efforts to contact the copyright holder to obtain permission to reprint this selection. If you have information that would help us, please write to Permissions Department, W. W. Norton & Company, Inc., 500 Fifth Avenue, New York, NY 10110.

16.2 Yeng Chengwu, "The Tale of the Luding Bridge, 1935," *Recalling the Long March*, eds. Bocheng Liu, Po-ch'eng Liu, pp. 88–110 (Beijing: Foreign Languages Press). We have made diligent efforts to contact the copyright holder to obtain permission to reprint this selection. If you have information that would help us, please write to Permissions Department, W. W. Norton & Company, Inc., 500 Fifth Avenue, New York, NY 10110.

16.3 Madame Chiang Kai-shek, *General Chiang Kai-shek and The Communist Crisis* (Shanghai: China Weekly Review Press, 1935), pp. 55–73.

16.4 New Life Promotion Society of Nanchang, *What Must Be Known about New Life* (Nanjing: 1935), pp. 216–220.

16.5 C. W. H. Young, *New Life For Kiangsi* (Shanghai: China Publishing Company, 1935), pp. 64–65, 104–08.

16.6 *Yi'er jiu yundong* [The December 9 Movement] *Zhongguo xiandaishi ziliao congkan* [China contemporary history materials series], (Beijing: Renmin chubanshe, 1954), pp. 44–50.

16.7 Mi Zanchen, *The Life of Yang Hucheng* (Hong Kong: Joint Publishing 1981), pp. 118–20.

16.8 From *General Chiang Kai-shek: The Account of the Fortnight in Sian When the Fate of China Hung in the Balance* by General and Madame Chiang Kai-shek, copyright 1937 by Doubleday, a division of Random House, Inc. Used by permission of Doubleday, a division of Random House, Inc. Any third party use of this material, outside of this publication, is prohibited. Interested parties must apply directly to Random House, Inc. for permission.

CHAPTER 17

17.1 Japan Foreign Federation, *Official View of The Sino-Japanese Conflict* (Tokyo: Maruzen Company, 1937), pp. 8–12.

17.2 Hirosi Saito, "The Conflict in the Far East," *World Affairs* (December 1937), pp. 3–7.

17.3 Chiang Kai-shek, *Generalissimo Chiang Speaks* (Hong Kong: The Pacific Publishing Company, 1939), pp. 73–123.

17.4 H.J. Timperley, "Bearing Witness," *Japan Advertiser*, Dec. 7, 1937. Reprinted with permission.

17.5 H.J. Timperley, "The Nanjing 'Murder Race'," *Japan Advertiser*, Dec.14, 1937. Reprinted with permission.

17.6 Feng Zikai, "Bombs in Yishan," *The Chinese Essay*, ed. David Pollard, pp. 199–205. © C. Hurst & Co. (Publishers) Ltd., 2000. Reprinted with permission of the publisher.

17.7 Wang Jingwei, "Radio Address by Mr. Wang Ching-wei, President of the Chinese Executive Yuan, June 24, 1941," *Tokyo Gazette* 5:2 (August, 1941), pp. 82–88.

17.8 Liu Shao-Chi, "Why Communists Must Undertake Self-Cultivation," *How to Be a Good Communist*, pp. 1–9, 45–47 (Beijing: Foreign Languages Press). We have made diligent efforts to contact the copyright holder to obtain permission to reprint this selection. If you have information that would help us, please write to Permissions Department, W. W. Norton & Company, Inc., 500 Fifth Avenue, New York, NY 10110.

CHAPTER 18

18.1 Wang Kang, *Wen Yiduo zhuan* [Biography of Wen Yiduo] (Hong Kong: Joint Publishing Company, 1979), pp. 434–37.

18.2 "Statement by General Marshall, January 7, 1947," *The Department of State Bulletin*, XVI no. 394 (January 19, 1947), pp. 83–85.

18.3 From Ming-min. *A Taste of Freedom Memoirs of a Formosan Independence Leader*, 1E. © 1972 Global Rights & Permissions, a part of Cengage Learning, Inc. Reproduced by permission. www.cengage.com/permissions

18.4 Mao Tse-Tung, "Order to the Army for the Country-Wide Advance (April 21, 1949)," *Selected Works of Mao Tse-Tung, Vol. IV*, pp. 387–389 (Beijing: Foreign Languages Press). We have made diligent efforts to contact the copyright holder to obtain permission to reprint this selection. If you have information that would help us, please write to Permissions Department, W. W. Norton & Company, Inc., 500 Fifth Avenue, New York, NY 10110.

18.5 Mao Tse-Tung, "Proclamation of the Chinese People's Liberation Army (April 25, 1949)," *Selected Works of Mao Tse-Tung, Vol. IV*, pp. 397–400 (Beijing: Foreign Languages Press). We have made diligent efforts to contact the copyright holder to obtain permission to reprint this selection. If you have information that would help us, please write to Permissions Department, W. W. Norton & Company, Inc., 500 Fifth Avenue, New York, NY 10110.

18.6 Mao Tse-Tung, "On the People's Democratic Dictatorship (June 30, 1949)," *Selected Works of Mao Tse-Tung, Vol. IV*, pp. 411–416, 417–419, 422–423 (Beijing: Foreign Languages Press). We have made diligent efforts to contact the copyright holder to obtain permission to reprint this selection. If you have information that would help us, please write to Permissions Department, W. W. Norton & Company, Inc., 500 Fifth Avenue, New York, NY 10110.

CHAPTER 19

19.1 "Treaty of Friendship, Alliance, and Mutual Assistance between the Union of Soviet Socialist Republics and the People's Republic of China, February 14, 1950," in *The People's Republic of China and the Law of Treaties*, trans. Hungdah Chiu (Cambridge: Harvard University Press, 1972), Appendix B, pp. 125–126.

19.2 "The Marriage Law of the People's Republic of China as Promulgated by the Central People's Government, May 1, 1950," in *Chinese Communist Society: The Family and the Village*, trans. C. K. Yang (Cambridge: MIT Press, 1972), Appendix, pp. 221–26. See also Albert P. Blaustein, *Fundamental Legal Documents of Communist China* (South Hackensack: Fred B. Rothman and Co., 1962), pp. 206–275.

19.3 Ding Ling, *The Sun Shines over the Sanggan River*, trans. Yang Xianyi and Gladys Yang, pp. 308–318 (Beijing: Foreign Languages Press). We have made diligent efforts to contact the copyright holder to obtain permission to reprint this selection. If you have information that would help us, please write to Permissions Department, W. W. Norton & Company, Inc., 500 Fifth Avenue, New York, NY 10110.

19.4 Hu Shih-tu, "My Father Is an Enemy of the People," *Hong Kong Standard,* September 24, 1950, p. 5. The Chinese text appears in *Ta Kung Pao*, September 22, 1950, pp. 1–3.

19.5 Chiang Kai-shek, *President Chiang Kai-shek's Messages: October 10,1954 February 14, 1955* (Taipei: The Fourth Department, Central Committee of the Kuomintang, 1955), pp. 1–9.

CHAPTER 20

20.1 Mao Tse-Tung, "The Chinese People Cannot Be Cowed by the Atom Bomb, (January 28, 1955)," *Selected Works of Mao Tse-Tung, Vol. IV*, pp. 152–153 (Beijing: Foreign Languages Press). We have made diligent efforts to contact the copyright holder to obtain permission to reprint this selection. If you have information that would help us, please write to Permissions Department, W. W. Norton & Company, Inc., 500 Fifth Avenue, New York, NY 10110.

20.2 Mao Tse-Tung, "U.S. Imperialism is a Paper Tiger (July 14, 1956)," *Selected Works of Mao Tse-Tung, Vol. IV*, pp. 308–311 (Beijing: Foreign Languages Press). We have made diligent efforts to contact the copyright holder to obtain permission to reprint this selection. If you have information that would help us, please write to Permissions Department, W. W. Norton & Company, Inc., 500 Fifth Avenue, New York, NY 10110.

20.3 Lu Dingyi, "Let Flowers of Many Kinds Blossom, Diverse Schools of Thought Contend," *People's China* (Beijing, 1956), pp. 3–14.

20.4 Chang Po-sheng and Huang Chen-lu, *The Hundred Flowers Campaign and the Chinese Intellectuals*, ed. Roderick MacFarquhar. Copyright © 1960 by Stevens and Sons Ltd, London. Reprinted by permission of the editor.

20.5 Deng Xiaoping, "Report on the Rectification Campaign to the Third Plenum of the Central Committee, September 23, 1957," in *Communist China 1955–1959: Policy Documents with Analysis*, eds. Robert Bowie and John K. Fairbank (Cambridge: Harvard University Press, 1962), pp. 358–359.

CHAPTER 21

21.1 Chen Boda, "Under the Banner of Comrade Mao Tse-Tung," in *Chinese Communism, Selected Documents*, eds. Dan Jacobs and Hans H. Baerwald (New York: Harper and Row, 1963), pp. 135–44. Original appeared in *Red Flag,* July 7, 1958.

21.2 Yin Tse-ming, "The Strength of the Masses Is Limitless," in Jacobs and Baerwald (1963), pp. 106–108. Original appeared in *Six Hundred Million Build Industry* (Beijing: Foreign Languages Press, 1958).

21.3 "Hold High the Red Flag of People's Communes and March On: Editorial in People's Daily, September 3, 1958" in *Communist China 1955–1959: Policy Documents with Analysis*, eds. Robert Bowie and John K. Fairbank (Cambridge: Harvard University Press, 1962), pp. 460–462.

21.4 "A Brief Biography of Li Shuangshuang" by Li Zhun (tr. J. Hood & R. Mackie). First published in *Renditions* No. 68 (Autumn 2007), pp. 52–70. Reprinted by permission of the Research Centre for Translation, The Chinese University of Hong Kong.

21.5 "Decision Approving Comrade Mao Zedong's Proposal That He Will Not Stand as Candidate of Chairman of the People's Republic of China for the Next Term of Office," in *Sixth Plenary Session of the Eighth Central Committee of the Communist Party of China*, (Beijing: Foreign Languages Press, 1958), pp. 50–51.

21.6 "Statement of the Government of the People's Republic of China on the Successful Explosion of an Atomic Bomb," *China Reconstructs* 8:12 (December 1964), pp. 4–5.

CHAPTER 22

22.1 Li Feng, "An Admirable Fool" From Hunter, *We the Chinese: Voices from China*, 1E. © 1971 Heinle/Arts & Sciences, a part of Cengage Learning, Inc. Reproduced by permission. www.cengage.com/permissions

22.2 Lin Biao, "On People's War," *Peking Review* 36 (September 3, 1965), pp. 9–30.

22.3 and 22.4 "Peking Review, August 11, 1967," repr. in Jaap Van Ginneken, *The Rise and Fall of Lin Piao* (New York: Avon Books, 1977), p. 80.

22.5 Chi Hsin, *Teng Hsiao-ping: A Political Biography* (Hong Kong: Cosmos Books, 1978), pp. 54–64.

22.6 "I Saw Chairman Mao!" From *China's Cultural Revolution, 1966–1969: Not a Dinner Party,* ed. Michael Schoenhals (Armonk, NY: M.E. Sharpe, 1996), pp. 148–149. Copyright © 1996 by M.E. Sharpe, Inc. Reprinted with permission.

22.7 "As we watched them beat him..," From *China's Cultural Revolution, 1966–1969: Not a Dinner Party,* ed. Michael Schoenhals (Armonk, NY: M.E. Sharpe, 1996), pp. 166–169. Copyright © 1996 by M.E. Sharpe, Inc. Reprinted with permission.

Chapter 23

23.1 "Joint Communiqué," *Peking Review* 9 (March 3, 1972), pp. 4–5.

23.2 "Teng Hsiao-ping's Address at the United Nations," in Chi Hsin, *Teng Hsiao-ping: A Political Biography* (Hong Kong: Cosmos Books, 1978), pp. 163–175.

23.3 From Laifong Leung, *Morning Sun: Interviews with Chinese Writers of the "Lost Generation"* (Armonk, NY: M.E. Sharpe, 1994). Copyright © 1994 by M.E. Sharpe, Inc. Reprinted with permission.

23.4 "Barefoot Doctors," *Peking Review* 16:21 (May 25, 1973), pp. 15–17, 21.

23.5 *A Barefoot Doctor's Manual: Translation of a Chinese Instruction to Certain Chinese Health Personnel* (Washington D.C: U.S. Department of Health, Education, and Welfare, National Institute of Health, 1974), pp. 35–38, 51, 77–79.

23.6 "Mourning with Deepest Grief the Passing Away of the Great Leader and Great Teacher Chairman Mao Tse-tung," *Peking Review* 3 (September 13, 1978), pp. 6–11.

Chapter 24

24.1 Deng Xiaoping, *Speeches and Writings of Deng Xiaoping* (New York: Pergamon, 1984), pp. 62–74.

24.2 "The Fifth Modernization: Democracy (December 1978)," from *The Courage to Stand Alone: Letters from Prison and Other Writings* by Wei Jingsheng translated by Kristina M. Torgeson, translation copyright © 1997 by Wei Jingsheng. Reproduced by permission of Penguin Books Ltd and Viking Penguin, a division of Penguin Group (USA) Inc.

24.3 Liu Qing, "Sad Memories and Prospects: My Appeal to the Tribunal of the People" from *Wild Lily, Prairie Fire: China's Road to Democracy, Yan'an to Tian'anmen: 1942–1989* edited by Gregor Benton and Alan Hunter. © 1995 Princeton University Press. Reprinted by permission of Princeton University Press.

24.4 He Shinguang, "Xiangchang shang," *Renmin wenxue*, Vol. 8, August 1980, pp. 18–23. We have made diligent efforts to contact the copyright holder to obtain permission to reprint this selection. If you have information that would help us, please write to Permissions Department, W. W. Norton & Company, Inc., 500 Fifth Avenue, New York, NY 10110.

Chapter 25

25.1 "Open Letter of the Central Committee of the Communist Party of China to the General Membership of the Communist Party," translated by Ai Ping. From *Chinese Sociology & Anthropology* 24, no. 3 (Spring 1992), 11–16. English-language translation copyright © 1992 by M.E. Sharpe, Inc. Reprinted with permission.

25.2 "Report on the Conditions Regarding the Work of Family Planning (March 22, 1984)," translated by Ai Ping. From *Chinese Sociology & Anthropology* 24, no. 3 (Spring 1992), 31–39. English-language translation copyright © 1992 by M.E. Sharpe, Inc. Reprinted with permission.

25.3 "'Liberation Army Daily' Examines Background to Bitter Love," BBC Summary of World Broadcasts, May 21, 1981. Reprinted by permission of BBC Worldwide Americas Inc.

25.4 Liu Binyan, "A Case of Persecution in Xi'an in Disregard of Central Instructions," *People's Daily*, August 25, 1984, repr. *BBC Summary of World Broadcasts*, September 8, 1984 (LexisNexis Academic).

25.5 "The Joint Declaration by Britain and China Defining the Future of Hong Kong," September 26, 1984.

25.6 Fang Lizhi: An Interview with Tiziano Terzani. Excerpts from "Dissent" from *Seeds of Fire: Chinese Voices of Conscience* by Geremie Barmé and John Minford. Copyright © 1988 by Geremie Barmé and John Minford. Reprinted by permission Hill and Wang, a division of Farrar, Straus and Giroux, LLC and Geremie Barmé.

25.7 and 25.8 "Fang Lizhi's Expulsion," in Barmé and Minford (1988), p. 336.

CHAPTER 26

26.1 "Bixu qizhi xianming de fandui dongluan," [We must unequivocally oppose turmoil], *Renmin Ribao* [People's daily], Overseas Edition (April 26, 1989), p. 1.

26.2 "Demonstration on April 27," *China News Agency*, np.

26.3 "Open Declaration of a Hunger Strike, May 1989," *Jiushi niandai,* June 16, 1989.

26.4 Li Peng, "Transcript of Remarks by Chinese Prime Minister Announcing Crackdown," *New York Times,* May 20, 1989, A6.

26.5 Deng Xiaoping, "Deng's June 9 Speech: 'We Faced a Rebellious Clique' and 'Dregs of Society'" from *The New York Times*, June 30, 1989. © 1989 The New York Times. All rights reserved. Used by permission and protected by the Copyright Laws of the United States. The printing, copying, redistribution, or retransmission of this Content without express written permission is prohibited.

CHAPTER 27

27.1 The Dalai Lama, excerpts from "The Nobel Peace Prize Lecture" from *The Dalai Lama, A Policy of Kindness: an Anthology of Writings By and About the Dalai Lama*, edited by Sidney Piburn. Copyright © 1990, 1993 by Sidney Piburn. Reprinted by arrangement with The Permissions Company, Inc., on behalf of Shambhala Publications Inc., Boston, MA. www.shambhala.com.

27.2 "The Wolf and the Lamb" by Wei Jingsheng, *The New York Times*, November 18, 1993, A27. Reprinted by permission of the author.

27.3 William Clinton, "Remarks by President Clinton during the Announcement of the Renewal of MFN Trade Status for China," CNN Transcript No. 406–2, May 26, 1994 (LexisNexis Academic).

27.4 Li Boning, "General Plan for Population Resettlement," From Dai Qing, *The River Dragon Has Come! The Three Gorges Dam and the Fate of China's Yangtze River and Its People*, ed. John G. Thibodeau and Philip Williams; trans. Yi Ming (Armonk, NY: M.E. Sharpe, 1998), pp. 40–50. English-language translation copyright © 1998 by M.E. Sharpe, Inc. Reprinted with permission of the publisher, Dai Qing and Probe International www.probeinternational.org.

27.5 From *Yangtze! Yangtze!*, by Dai Qing, edited by Patricia Adams and John Thibodeau. Reprinted with permission of Dai Qing and Probe International: http://journal.probeinternational.org/.

27.6 "In a Glass Darkly: An Interview with Gu Yue," From *Shades of Mao: The Posthumous Cult of the Great Leader,* ed. Geremie R. Barme (Armonk, NY: M.E. Sharpe, 1996), pp. 177–182. Copyright © 1996 by M.E. Sharpe, Inc. Reprinted with permission.

CHAPTER 28

28.1 From "China Can Say No" (Zhongguó keyi shuo bù: Lengzhànhòu shídài de zhèngzhì yu qínggan juézé) by Zhang Zangzang, Zhang Xiaobo, Song Qiang, Tang Zhengyu, Qiao Bian, and Gu Qingsheng (Beijing: Zhonghua gongshang lianhe chubanshe, 1996), pp. 242–246. Translated into English by Janet Chen. We have made diligent efforts to contact the copyright holder to obtain permission to reprint this selection. If you have information that would help us, please write to Permissions Department, W. W. Norton & Company, Inc., 500 Fifth Avenue, New York, NY 10110.

28.2 From *The Corpse Walker: Real-Life Stories, China from the Bottom Up* by Liao Yiwu, translated by Wen Huang, introduction and translation copyright © 2008 by Wen Huang. Used by permission of Pantheon Books, a division of Random House, Inc. Any third party use of this material, outside of this publication, is prohibited. Interested parties must apply directly to Random House, Inc. for permission.

28.3 Li Li, "Fortitude in Adversity," *Beijing Review* 51:21 (May 22, 2008), pp. 3–6.

28.4 Yi Jiandong, "Beijing's Olympic Scorecard," *Beijing Review* 36 (September 4, 2008), p. 20.

28.5 English translation by Human Rights in China (HRIC), an international Chinese human rights NGO based in Hong Kong and New York (http://www.hrichina .org/). This translation was first published in *China Rights Forum*, 2010, No. 1, "Freedom of Expression on Trial in China," http://www.hrichina.org/crf/article/3203. Reprinted with permission.